Department of Superintendence

NINTH YEARBOOK

Five Unifying Factors in American Education

*Studies in Pupil Promotion, Community
Relationships, Teacher Preparation,
Finance, Principles of
Articulation*

PUBLISHED BY

THE DEPARTMENT OF SUPERINTENDENCE

OF THE NATIONAL EDUCATION ASSOCIATION
OF THE UNITED STATES

1201 Sixteenth Street Northwest, Washington, D. C.

FEBRUARY, 1931

THE DEPARTMENT OF SUPERINTENDENCE

Officers, 1930-31

President, NORMAN R. CROZIER,
   Superintendent of Schools_____Dallas, Texas

First Vicepresident, FRANK CODY,
   Superintendent of Schools_____Detroit, Michigan

Second Vicepresident, DANIEL S. KEALEY,
   Superintendent of Schools_____Hoboken, New Jersey

Executive Secretary, SHERWOOD D. SHANKLAND,
   1201 Sixteenth Street Northwest_____Washington, D. C.

Executive Committee

FRANK M. UNDERWOOD, Assistant Superintendent of Schools, St. Louis, Missouri

PAUL C. STETSON, Superintendent of Schools, Indianapolis, Indiana

DAVID E. WEGLEIN, Superintendent of Schools, Baltimore, Maryland

CHARLES B. GLENN, Superintendent of Schools, Birmingham, Alabama

The Commission on the Articulation of the Units of American Education

HERBERT S. WEET, Superintendent of Schools, Rochester, New York, *Chairman*

CHARLES H. JUDD, Director, School of Education, University of Chicago, Chicago, Illinois

JESSE H. NEWLON, Professor of Education, and Director of Lincoln School, Teachers College, Columbia University, New York City

CARROLL R. REED, Superintendent of Schools, Minneapolis, Minnesota

ROBERT E. TIDWELL, Director of Extension, University of Alabama, University, Alabama

JOHN W. WITHERS, Dean, School of Education, New York University, New York City

Committee on Promotion Problems

DAVID E. WEGLEIN, Superintendent of Schools, Baltimore, Maryland, *Chairman*

HOBART M. CORNING, Superintendent of Schools, Colorado Springs, Colorado

GEORGE D. TAYLOR, Principal, Susan B. Anthony Elementary School, Rochester, New York

HERBERT S. WEET, Superintendent of Schools, Rochester, New York

[3]

Committee on the Articulation of the Schools and the Community

CARROLL R. REED, Superintendent of Schools, Minneapolis, Minnesota, *Chairman*

LOTUS D. COFFMAN, President, University of Minnesota, Minneapolis, Minnesota

CHARLES H. JUDD, Director, School of Education, University of Chicago, Chicago, Illinois

A. B. MEREDITH, Professor of Educational Administration, New York University, New York City

JUSTIN WASHBURN, County Superintendent of Schools, Rock Island, Illinois

Committee on the Relation of General to Professional Education of Teachers

JOHN W. WITHERS, Dean, School of Education, New York University, New York City, *Chairman*

JAMES R. ANGELL, President, Yale University, New Haven, Connecticut

NED H. DEARBORN, Director, Teacher Training Division, New York State Education Department, Albany, New York

BEN W. FRAZIER, Specialist in Teacher Training, U. S. Office of Education, Washington, D. C.

RAYMOND A. KENT, President, University of Louisville, Louisville, Kentucky

Committee on the Fiscal Aspects of Articulation

ROBERT E. TIDWELL, Director of Extension, University of Alabama, University, Alabama, *Chairman*

ARTHUR J. KLEIN, Professor of School Administration, Ohio State University, Columbus, Ohio

FRANK D. McELROY, President, Mankato State Teachers College, Mankato, Minnesota

JOHN K. NORTON, Director, Research Division, National Education Association, Washington, D. C.

Committee on Principles of Articulation and Functions of Units

JESSE H. NEWLON, Professor of Education, and Director of Lincoln School, Teachers College, Columbia University, New York City, *Chairman*

WINFIELD D. ARMENTROUT, Director of Instruction and Professor of Education, Colorado State Teachers College, Greeley, Colorado

WALTER D. COCKING, Professor of School Administration, George Peabody College for Teachers, Nashville, Tennessee

L. THOMAS HOPKINS, Curriculum Specialist, Lincoln School, Teachers College, Columbia University, New York City

FRED J. KELLY, Lecturer in Higher Education, University of Chicago, Chicago, Illinois

JOHN A. SEXSON, Superintendent of Schools, Pasadena, California

A. L. THRELKELD, Superintendent of Schools, Denver, Colorado

FOREWORD

WITH THIS Yearbook the Commission on the Articulation of the Units of American Education, appointed by President Randall J. Condon in April, 1926, presents its second report and completes its work.

"Let us keep our eye steadily on the whole system" was the challenge made by the Commission on the Articulation of the Units of American Education in the *Seventh Yearbook,* which was its first report. Parents and teachers were urged to look upon the child's education as a continuous forward movement, rather than as a disjointed series of unrelated accomplishments. A well-articulated school system was defined as one made up of several segments—such as elementary, secondary, and collegiate units—which are jointed similar to limbs of the human body, but which function as a coordinated whole.

An inarticulation was defined as any point within our public school system or between the school and the society which it serves at which the continuous growth, development, progress, or transition of an individual is hindered by reason of the organization, methods, materials, or practices of our schools.

To facilitate the preparation of its first report, the *Seventh Yearbook,* the Commission on the Articulation of the Units of American Education organized five committees to study problems of articulation in these five horizontal divisions of the school system: (1) elementary education, (2) secondary education, (3) professional and higher education, (4) teacher training, and (5) adult education. Each of these committees studied inarticulations occurring at the level with which it was concerned, and between this level and the ones immediately above and below.

After two years' study, organized on this horizontal basis, the Commission thought it desirable to reorganize so that certain crucial problems of inarticulation which extend vertically throughout whole school systems might be more effectively attacked.

Accordingly, the horizontal committees responsible for the preparation of the *Seventh Yearbook* were discontinued, and these five vertical committees were formed and charged with the preparation of the *Ninth Yearbook:*

    I. Promotion Problems
    II. School and Community
    III. Relation of General to Professional Education of Teachers
    IV. Finance
    V. Principles of Articulation and Functions of Units.

In this Yearbook, each of these committees reports on its specific problem as it extends throughout the entire range of American education from the kindergarten through the graduate school. An exhaustive treatment of each problem was not attempted; rather, certain phases of each were selected for study. There are many additional articulation problems to be solved. Only a beginning has been made in attacking the five treated in this Yearbook. Each report was prepared under the limitation of time and pressure of work to which all school executives are subject.

The Articulation Commission does not suggest a standardized procedure for all school systems to follow. It maintains that articulation does not mean standardization. Often standardization results in the suppression of new ideas and necessary experimentation. Such values as there are in standardization should be sought out, but its extremes carefully avoided. It is also the definite policy of the Articulation Commission that none of its conclusions be presented with finality. Both the 1929 and the 1931 Yearbooks have been drafted in this spirit.

The Commission takes this opportunity to thank the several thousand superintendents of schools, supervisors, principals, and teachers who helped by reporting the major inarticulations in their local schools and by supplying data on pupil promotion problems. An expression of appreciation is also due the 1500 summer school students who rated inarticulations as to their seriousness, to the 48 state departments of education who generously supplied data on the fiscal aspects of articulation, and to many college specialists who contributed so largely of their time and thought.

Acknowledgment is also due the Research Division of the National Education Association. The Committee on Finance is particularly indebted to William G. Carr. Margaret Alltucker Norton has been secretary of the Commission during its four years' program. To her has fallen the difficult task of preparing many inquiry blanks, summarizing and analyzing the data obtained from them, making preliminary drafts of certain chapters, and editing the entire Yearbook.

In the United States, articulation of our school units is not a problem that can be settled nationally. Each local, county, and state school system must iron out its own inarticulations. Furthermore, in a dynamic and developing system of education, no sooner is one set of articulation problems solved than another arises.

If this Yearbook stimulates local school systems to analyze their own inarticulation problems and offers some guidance in the continuous study and research necessary for their solution, it will have fulfilled its purpose.

CONTENTS

FIVE UNIFYING FACTORS IN AMERICAN EDUCATION

INTRODUCTION

THE PURPOSE of this introductory chapter is to identify some of the major issues dealt with in the five committee reports which comprise this Yearbook. The end will be attained, however, only as the points raised here show the importance of the contributions contained in each report, and so lead the reader to a careful study of the entire Yearbook. Such study is necessary to an adequate understanding of the conclusions reached by the Commission and its committees.

Report of the Committee on Pupil Promotion Problems—The crux of the problem of articulation, according to many teachers and school administrators, lies in the circumstances surrounding the promotion of pupils from grade to grade or from one administrative unit to another. Non-promotion, with consequent retardation, is an obvious break in the continuous forward movement of a pupil. The presence of many failures in a school system is necessarily a matter of grave concern. Realizing the seriousness of this crucial problem, the committee in charge has carried on a two-year study of present trends and practices in promotion, in order that its findings and recommendations might be based on existing facts. The materials presented in this report should be of great assistance to teachers and supervisors as well as to school administrators.

The report includes a tentative statement of general principles relative to pupil promotion, actual case studies indicative of promotion practices, and an extensive discussion based upon questionnaire and field studies of the most acute problems of pupil promotion. The case studies gathered from Baltimore, Colorado Springs, and Rochester offer a careful analysis of typical and concrete situations which serve as a background for later recommendations and also suggest a technic for the study of pupil promotion problems in other communities.

Two of the most vexing problems of articulation before the country, as evidenced by the comments evoked in response to the committee's questionnaire, are these: (1) How best to meet the needs of low-mentality and over-age pupils, and (2) How best to meet the needs of superior pupils. The report reveals a thoughtful awareness of the special difficulties involved, a sane viewpoint with reference to the solution of these problems, and concrete suggestions which should prove extremely helpful in actual practice. To illustrate, the report includes a description of some of the characteristic differences of bright and slow pupils, a statement of principles involved in differentiation of instruction, illustrations of differentiated units of work, and procedures from specific school systems and from higher institutions of learning for meeting the needs of individual pupils. These statements will serve to set the problem and its possible solutions clearly before teachers and administrators at all educational levels. In so doing, the committee opens the way for a conscious and determined effort to avoid the inarticulations resulting from inequalities of attainment in various mentality ranges.

Report of the Committee on the Articulation of the School and the Community—To those who have conceived of adult education as a program of education for the under-privileged administered through the usual evening school, or a program of teaching adults to read and write the English language, this report presents a new outlook. It points out that the machine age with its accompanying technological unemployment and the rapidly changing industrial order leads thousands of people to seek through education some means of preserving their adaptability, of increasing their resourcefulness, and of opening new avenues of livelihood for themselves. In addition, the industrial order has brought more leisure than mankind has ever known. Hence thousands of those engaged in what is popularly known as adult education are there not because they are looking for industrial or occupational preferment, but principally because they wish to enjoy life more fully.

Just how far shall the educational institutions of any community assume responsibility for adult education? Quite obviously not even an intelligent attempt to answer this question can be made without first ascertaining what the adult education interests and needs of a community are. This report includes not only a technic for making such a survey, but also the results obtained from applying this technic to a particular community. These are set forth in a study of "Adult Educational Activities Engaged in by Clubs, Societies, and Public and Semi-Public Institutions and Agencies in the City of Minneapolis." Those making this study were particularly interested in knowing what kind of informal educational programs are available to adults in Minneapolis when education is their avocation, rather than their vocation. It is at once apparent that such a study takes one far afield from the usual form of adult education offered in public evening schools, and necessitates consideration of the programs of recreational groups, organizations of employees in commercial establishments, women's clubs, churches, and lodges.

The activities of civic, cultural, political, and religious organizations found in every large community are not commonly regarded as related to the educational responsibility which the public schools and the colleges of the same community have to assume, nor are they articulated with the educational institutions of the community in which they exist. Nevertheless, they often represent serious, and at times misdirected, efforts toward the education of adults. However, the one thing needed to suppress many of these voluntary efforts and destroy whatever merits they have would be to standardize them through the direction of some formal educational institution. But the desirability of a cooperative relationship deserves consideration. Is it possible that a real contribution could be made by a public school system, for example, if it had on its staff an able leader who could give, upon invitation from these voluntary organizations, the kind of constructive help and direction which the organizations themselves only too often crave? The committee does not attempt to answer this question. Each local community must decide for itself upon the advisability of a cooperative relationship between its public schools and its voluntary agencies for adult education.

This report also presents detailed follow-up studies of pupils who stopped school previous to graduation; of those who entered community life from subnormal classes; of those who graduated from high school; and of adults enrolled in evening school classes. These studies are definite attempts to ascertain the extent to which various types of public schools are actually articulating with community life. The findings reported from studies made in one community are of general interest, for they at once lead the reader to question to what extent similar conditions exist in his own community. His next question is, What shall be done about it? The report presents in considerable detail the technic developed in Minneapolis, where these follow-up studies were made. This report is a definite contribution to the solution of that difficult problem—the articulation of the schools and the community.

Report of the Committee on the Relation of General to Professional Education of Teachers—In the whole range of formal educational activities in this country, it is doubtful whether there are inarticulations more disastrous and far-reaching in their results than those which exist with reference to the professional education of teachers.

The following is illustrative of one of many types of articulation problems in this field: While the principle has been established, as the result of years of experience, that laboratory opportunities for the working out of theory should be regarded as of equal importance and necessity with provisions for the most thorough and scholarly presentation of educational theory, many public school systems are unwilling to join with teacher-training institutions in offering their students adequate opportunities for practice teaching. The notion that any public school system can bring into its service fully equipped and competently trained teachers and at the same time be freed from all responsibility for the professional training of these teachers, either pre-service or in-service, is one that the Commission believes must be abandoned. The constructive solution of such problems of articulation as this deserves most careful attention.

The committee in its report briefly traces the development of teacher preparation through the period during and immediately following the Great War. It points out the need for continuing studies of teacher supply and demand. It presents a tentative statement of general principles relative to teacher education and lists problems for future study.

Since the Congress of the United States in 1930 appropriated $200,000 for a National Survey of Teacher Training which is already under way, the report of the committee on teacher preparation in this Yearbook is purposely brief, and merely points out some of the major issues involved.

Report of the Committee on the Fiscal Aspects of Articulation—That the machinery set up for meeting the cost of schools is an important factor in their articulation is the considered judgment of the Commission. A committee on the financial aspects of educational articulation was therefore charged with the function of preparing a report which would show how methods of school financing affect the development of a smooth and well-coordinated educational program, how the states are using methods of financial control as an articulating agency in their educational programs, and what methods in school finance promise most in the development of an articulated program. These are intricate and interesting problems. This section of the Yearbook represents one of the first attempts to make a nation-wide investigation of this problem in its many ramifications.

At the very outset the vital relation of school finance to the whole problem of articulation is stated in unequivocal terms. The committee points out that "the character of the machinery set up to pay for the various units which constitute a state's educational program will, in a large measure, determine what that program will be. It will not only significantly influence the development of the units found at each educational level—elementary, secondary, and higher—but will crucially affect the ability of these units to work together, to build upon the work of the preceding unit, and to add the largest possible educational increment before passing the child on to the next level."

After a preliminary overview of the general nature and scope of its problem, the report names these three principal factors through which financial coordination of educational enterprises has been secured: (1) common agencies of control, (2) state budgetary procedures involving not merely educational enterprises but all state governmental activities, and (3) informal and non-governmental cooperative arrangements. Each of these factors is discussed in a separate chapter. Concrete illustrative material showing the application of the underlying principles in each case is presented. Throughout the entire discussion runs the central theme that "the financing of education is not an isolated problem to be considered separately from the whole question of a state's economic condition or of the needs of other governmental services."

City and state school executives will be especially interested in the chapter of this report which shows the present distribution of expenditures for education. This chapter first presents the relation existing between national income and school costs. Next it shows how the total public budget is divided as between education and other governmental activities. It then carries the analysis a step further and shows how the education budgets of the several states are distributed as between elementary and secondary schools, teacher-training institutions, and other higher educational agencies. The chapter points out the effects of such special factors as private educational enterprise and the varying educational needs of the several states on this distribution of educational expenditures. Fully as important as the information thus made available are the technics and suggestions for further study which may be applied by school executives to their own local situations.

The concluding chapter of the report offers a series of underlying principles which govern the relationships between the articulation of school finance and the articulation of educational programs. First, the problem of school finance needs to be studied in terms of its wider social setting. School finance involves the problem of distributing the total social income of the nation in a way which will yield the greatest ultimate dividends in human welfare. To this end it is necessary that there be cooperation among those agencies which are responsible for governing the schools and other governmental bodies. The report, however, cautions against assuming that cooperation between education and other public services means subordination of education to other purposes. Policies which promise most in the direction of economy, educational effectiveness, and smooth articulation are policies which recognize the fundamental importance of education in a democratic commonwealth.

As a second principle, the report calls attention to the need for a comprehensive educational program which is presented and supported by the solidly unified educational forces of each state or local community. It deplores undignified competition for funds among educational institutions and interests, and suggests the presentation of a unified and coherent program of education as an essential step in securing adequate financial support at every point.

The third fundamental principle advanced is the need for individual study of methods and devices for securing the unification of educational finance. The report warns against uncritical adoption of cooperative plans which are in effect elsewhere. No single ready-made plan of cooperation will fit the needs of every state and community. The experience of other states may be highly significant, but, in the last analysis, careful study of the individual situation must be the real basis of successful financial coordination.

As its fourth basic principle, the report calls attention to the reciprocal relation between articulated school finance and articulated educational policies. It suggests the need for a clear definition of functions in education as the first and essential phase in financial articulation. It points out that the financial machinery for the support of education should reflect a carefully articulated educational program. Accidental and unrelated fragments of school fiscal legislation constitute a shaky foundation on which to erect a well-proportioned educational structure.

As its final principle, the committee suggests the need for democratic cooperation in the development of a unified financial program for education and for the state as a whole. It points out that, while undoubted value attaches to formal and governmental cooperative arrangements, there is in the last analysis no substitute for friendly understanding and mutual appreciation. "In the long run," the report concludes, "an educational system will be best articulated in its financial aspects when all educational interests cooperate under democratic leadership to evolve a unified policy of support which considers the educational needs of the state as a whole, sound economic and social theory, and intelligent allocation of funds and functions."

Report of the Committee on Principles of Articulation and Functions of Units—The formulation of guiding principles of articulation is in many ways the most difficult aspect of the work of the Articulation Commission. Two basic principles of educational philosophy are commonly accepted: (1) that the content of the curriculum must be established in accordance with the needs of society; and (2) that the educative process or method must be in harmony with child nature in continuous growth. There is no fundamental lack of harmony in American education concerning these two principles. There is, however, difference of opinion as to whether child nature or social outcome shall be the dominating and determining factor in school procedure.

In the report of the Committee on Principles of Articulation and Functions of Units, different attitudes and emphases are apparent. The members of the Commission on Articulation held varying views on the important questions discussed in this section of the report. It was agreed, however, that a report on articulation should bring forward points of view which may contain valuable suggestions for greater integration, though not at the moment representative of the thought of all members of the Commission. This section of the report, therefore, is sponsored by those committee members whose names are attached to the various chapters, rather than by the Commission as a whole.

Articulation is a matter not only of the curriculum and of methods but also of school administration. Grades and units in the school system often tend to divide the school into rigid compartments rather than to foster the idea of continuous growth. To offset this tendency, teacher cooperation, supervisory coordination, and pupil guidance must be utilized to secure regularity in the progress of every individual. The committee discusses in detail the importance of these three phases of school administration in relation to articulation, and suggests guiding principles of administration.

Coupled with its statement of principles, the committee submits the report of a questionnaire study of inarticulations existing in school systems from the kindergarten through the university. If the list seems appalling in its scope, it must be hopefully remembered that the purpose of the study was not merely to discover where the schools have failed to advance the uninterrupted progress of pupils, but to make use of such data as a point of departure for improved practice. Inarticulations ranking high as matters of frequent difficulty deserve attentive and analytical study in every school community with a view to remedial attention and sensible change.

The recommendations of the committee for removing the more serious maladjustments in the school system are indicative of the pathway to be followed in bringing about a more satisfactory situation.

These recommendations involve continuous curriculum revision, elimination of memoriter and other cramming methods of instruction, administrative procedures to secure coordinated supervision and more intensive teacher cooperation, a broader training of teachers, and a revision of traditional methods of admission to college. The recommendations with reference to college entrance requirements are a challenge to cooperative service on the part of the secondary schools and of the colleges. The committee feels that the plan of college entrance outlined in this report will be welcomed by progressive high schools and colleges throughout the country.

In recapitulation, this Yearbook considers the articulation of the units of American education as it is affected by five selected integrating factors: Pupil promotion, community relationships, teacher preparation, finance, and principles of articulation and functions of units. The entire study is unified around a central core of effort to bring educational conditions into harmony with the ideal of continuous, wholesome growth for every individual to whom the public schools of this country extend their service.

PART I
PUPIL PROMOTION PROBLEMS

CHAPTER I

PROMOTION PROBLEMS FROM THE KINDERGARTEN THROUGH THE GRADUATE SCHOOL

Introduction

A SCHOOL system should be organized and administered so as to provide for the smooth, continuous, natural progress of every pupil. Of the factors which contribute to the articulation of the administrative units of American education, none are more important than the philosophy and practice relative to pupil promotion.

If teachers, supervisors, and administrators at any particular level and at different levels in a school system can cooperatively arrive at reasonable agreement as to fundamental principles and administrative practices which should govern promotion—i. e., the advancement of a pupil from one grade to another and from one school to another—perhaps the principal factor contributing to inarticulation in public education would be removed. Part I of this Yearbook presents material recommended by the Articulation Commission for study and discussion in local school systems in working toward such agreement. This material is organized in seven sections:

I. Tentative Statement of General Principles Relative to Pupil Promotion

II. Promotion Practices as Revealed by 742 Individual Pupil Case Histories

III. Seven Promotion Problems Discussed by 555 Superintendents of Schools:

    A. What Are the Most Acute Promotion Problems in Local School Systems?
    B. What Are the Bases for Pupil Promotion?
    C. In Which Elementary Grades and Subjects Is Pupil Failure the Greatest?
    D. What Are the Best Means for Reducing Pupil Failure in Elementary and Secondary Schools?
    E. What Is the Value of Semi-Annual as Compared with Annual Promotions?
    F. Are Trial Promotions Desirable?
    G. Statements Concerning Relationships between School Units:
        1. Elementary School Relationships
        2. Junior High-School Relationships
        3. Senior High-School Relationships

IV. Status of Senior High-School Promotion Plans

V. How Supervision Can Help To Put Pupil Promotions on a More Scientific Basis

VI. How Elementary and Secondary Schools Are Meeting the Needs of Individual Pupils

VII. How Higher Institutions of Learning Are Meeting the Needs of Individual Students.

Tentative Statement of General Principles Relative to Pupil Promotion

Pupil promotion is a problem which faces every teacher and principal. In solving this problem, are there certain general principles which everyone should consider? The Committee on Promotion Problems of the Articulation Commission feels that there are such principles.

In preparing this report, this Committee, with the help of selected groups of teachers, principals, supervisors, and assistant superintendents in Baltimore and Colorado Springs, developed the following tentative statement of general principles relative to pupil promotion. It represents the composite opinion of a selected group of several hundred people.

In Colorado Springs, these general principles were submitted to seventeen people in key positions in the school system. Each person was asked to surround himself with a group of people whose opinions would be worthwhile. An average of five people met with each of the seventeen. The result was the composite opinion of 92 people.

Seventeen people in the Baltimore school system were also asked to report in writing their reactions to this tentative statement of general principles relative to pupil promotion. The reactions given in the seventeen composite reports from Colorado Springs together with the seventeen reports from Baltimore are included in the statement below. These reactions represent a number of diverse viewpoints. They are included here because, in the judgment of the Articulation Commission, they offer an excellent basis for discussion in local faculty groups.

The statement of general principles is similarly submitted as a basis for discussion and as a starting point from which local school systems may develop general principles for promoting pupils, applicable to their local situations.

Six general principles are laid down, and promotion cannot be settled on the basis of any one of them alone—the six must be taken as a whole.

A. *Promotion should be decided on the basis of the individual pupil.*

B. *Promotion should be on the basis of many factors. The final decision as to whether a particular pupil should be promoted should rest not merely on academic accomplishment, but on what will result in the greatest good to the all-around development of the individual.*

In answer to the question: Under what conditions is this principle not applicable? the following suggestions were made by individual teachers, principals, and supervisors in the cooperating school systems. Many of these suggestions are only individual opinions.

1. This principle would not apply when next year's work depends entirely upon this year's mastery of subject-matter, as in foreign language. This principle is not applicable in a school or system where the classes are based on accomplishment in subject-matter only. There are certain subject-matter requirements in a graded public school system that must be fulfilled before promotion can be given. Special and opportunity classes help to lessen the stigma of non-promotion and make possible a more flexible gradation system.

2. Promotion on this basis presupposes an administrative set-up which is sufficiently flexible to prevent the maladjustment of pupils. If administrative machinery of this type does not exist, promotion is not apt to bring the greatest good to the all-around development of the pupil and should not, therefore, be granted. When the school system is too small to have homogeneously grouped classes and opportunity rooms, this principle of promotion may be desirable but not practical.

3. This principle is not applicable when the correct placement of a particular child interferes with the progress and development of the rest of the class. The greatest good for the greatest number must be considered. When the promotion of a particular pupil may result in harm to the group, then the single pupil should be sacrificed rather than the larger number.

4. Administrative conditions, such as overcrowding, may make it difficult to carry out this principle. To illustrate, small numbers of pupils standing near the border line between promotion and non-promotion might be placed in the higher or the lower grade, depending on where they can best be accommodated.

5. Another condition under which this principle is not practical is an uncooperative corps of teachers.

A review of the above comments leads to this question: What proportion of the responsibility for failure should be allotted to the community, the school, and the teacher? And what proportion to the child?

Should not one take the complete history of each child, consider what will result in the greatest good to his all-around development, and place him in the grade where he can best advance? There are serious administrative complications, but if a school system is equipped with a variety of "stations" or grades where children can work, these complications can be reduced. Ideally, should a school be made flexible enough so that a pupil will not fail?

C. *In order that promotion procedures may be more or less uniform throughout a particular school system, a definite set of factors should be agreed upon, which each teacher will take into consideration in forming his judgment as to whether or not a particular pupil should be promoted.*

The members of the reviewing committees were asked to list the seven factors (ranking them in order of importance) which they felt each teacher should take into consideration in promoting a pupil. Table 1 on page 20 summarizes these thirty-four reports and shows that there is a decided consensus of opinion that school history (scholarship attainment or mastery of subject-matter), mental ability, present health conditions, personal characteristics (including emotional stability and character traits), unusual talents, physical history, and special disabilities, are the factors which are given major consideration in determining a pupil's promotion. Scholarship attainment or mastery of subject-matter ranks first in Table 1. Is it ranked as the most important factor in pupil promotion on the assumption that it records the outcome of intelligence, health, personal characteristics, and other factors listed in Table 1?

D. *Criteria for promotion must take into consideration the curriculum offerings of the next higher grade or unit and the flexibility of its organization, its courses of study, and its methods.*

To illustrate, before promoting a pupil from the kindergarten to the first grade, one should know what sort of first-grade curriculum is provided. Are differentiated activities and methods available for pupils of different levels of ability? If reading is to be the chief activity in a particular first grade, then it follows that reading readiness is one of the chief criteria for promotion to that particular class. Is only one standard academic procedure followed, or are adaptations made to fit needs of individual pupils?

In other words, the kindergarten teacher must consider into which one of the following typical first-grade situations she is promoting a pupil:

1. School with sufficient enrolment so that pre-primary and three differentiated sections of low-first grade are organized and provided with differentiated curriculums.

2. School with one section of low-first-grade work conducted on traditional academic lines.

3. School with one section of low-first-grade work which is made flexible due to the attitude of mind of the teacher who recognizes individual differences and makes such provision as she can for them.

4. School with no pre-primary classes and with only two sections of low-first-grade work.

5. One-room school with several grades.

6. Large school with several sections of first grade, but no curriculum differentiation.

All reports were unanimous in agreeing that "criteria for promotion must take into consideration the curriculum offerings of the next higher grade or unit and the flexibility of its organization, its courses of study, and its methods." However, twenty-five out of the thirty-four answered "Yes" to the question: Is this an unfortunate condition? In two of the nine reports where the answer was "No," it was qualified as follows:

A school system should plan an articulated program of studies. The very origin of the grading system was to care for individual differences; and grades are set up for the smooth and continuous growth of pupils.

TABLE 1.—FACTORS TO BE CONSIDERED IN PROMOTING A PUPIL, RANKED IN ORDER OF IMPORTANCE

Factors To Be Considered in Promoting a Pupil	Number Times Listed	Number Times Each Factor Was Rated						
		Rating						
		1	2	3	4	5	6	7
1. School history (scholarship attainment or mastery of subject-matter)	34	21	5	2	2	3	0	1
2. Mental ability	33	3	14	8	6	0	1	1
3. Present health conditions	29	7	4	9	5	1	3	0
4. Personal characteristics, including emotional stability and character traits	25	0	0	4	6	7	3	5
5. Unusual talents	23	0	0	2	2	8	6	5
6. Physical history	21	2	4	4	6	1	3	1
7. Special disabilities	20	0	0	3	2	2	9	4
8. Family conditions	15	0	0	0	1	2	5	7
9. Chronological age	8	1	1	3	1	1	1	0
10. Social age, maturity, or adaptability	7	1	2	0	1	1	1	1
11. Application to work or emotional reaction toward school	7	0	2	0	1	2	0	2
12. Present acceleration or retardation	5	0	1	1	1	1	0	1
13. School expectancy	4	0	0	0	1	2	1	0
14. Attendance	2	0	1	0	0	0	0	1
15. Effect on class morale	1	0	0	0	0	0	0	1

Unless the curriculum and the flexibility of the succeeding grade or unit are taken into consideration, promotion may bring maladjustment to the pupil which will result in lasting injury. Moreover, lack of consideration of these elements might tend toward an appreciable lapse in an attitude of responsibility for genuine growth. In short, ignoring the requirements and conditions of the succeeding grade might bring injury to the pupil and lower aims and standards of reasonable accomplishment. It becomes, however, an unfortunate condition when promotion is based upon these considerations to the exclusion of what constitutes the greatest good to the pupil.

E. *It is the duty of the next higher grade or unit to accept pupils who are properly promoted to it from the lower grade or unit and to adapt its work to fit the needs of these pupils.*

All thirty-four reports were unanimous in accepting this principle in theory. However, when asked to describe the conditions under which this principle was not applicable, the following comments were made in individual reports:

1. It is not applicable when the work from one grade to another is not articulated through: (1) A philosophy of education permeating the whole school system, (2) experimentally determined courses of study, (3) vertical supervision in the major subjects of the curriculum, and (4) promotional standards agreed upon by the promoting and receiving teachers. Neither is this principle applicable when an inflexible curriculum is followed and common standards are applied.

2. The tendency of those working with younger children, whom they must accept as the home sends them, is to build upon the actual conditions of the children themselves. The desire of upper-grade teachers is usually that the basis for promotion be the acquisition of the fixed amount of subject-matter and skills called for in the traditional curriculum. The solution is reached only by a mutual adjustment in the two groups—the primary group producing the achievement, while retaining its practice of educating children in modes of wholesome living; and the intermediate group continuing its aim for facts and skills but tempered with the realization that high standards in these matters cannot compensate for the want of those knowledges, habits, and point of view which serve to make an individual a wholesome contributing member of society. In other words, the above principle is not applicable when the teacher is bound by traditional group procedure and cannot adjust herself to the viewpoint of the case method.

3. When there are other classes in the school or system where the child would be happier because the work would be adapted to his mental growth and physical condition, the child should be transferred. This naturally presupposes that no teacher would promote pupils so much below minimum requirements for promotion that the receiving teacher would be compelled to give individual attention out of all proportion to the size of her class. Effective work on the part of the teacher in the next grade depends on her not having too many problem cases.

Neither should the application of this principle result in large numbers of children being promoted into the next higher grade or unit unprepared to do the work of the course of study because: (1) the preceding grade has neglected to do the work outlined for it but has devoted its time to other work, or (2) because a teacher has not provided for individual differences and endeavored to bring her weak pupils up to standard. Unless pupils are pretty well prepared to meet the requirements of the course of study outlined for the next grade, grade divisions break down and children are always "below grade." If the course as outlined cannot be accomplished it should be changed.

4. Knowing that the unit above will meet the children on their own level, the unit below may grow lax and careless. The administrator must see that each unit

is stimulated to do its best and then apply the above principle, namely, that it is the duty of the next higher grade or unit to accept pupils who are promoted to it from the lower grade or unit and to adapt its work to fit the needs of these pupils.

5. This principle is not applicable in school systems where close articulation from grade to grade does not exist. Inasmuch as the principle seems to be sound, the inarticulations should be remedied.

The greatest good to the greatest number is probably the necessary aim in deciding many school problems. But it seems clear that to give each individual the conditions that allow and assist the best development is a long step toward securing the best good of all. To realize this ideal the schools need the best possible teaching force, well adapted courses of study, adequate equipment and supplies, and intelligent and flexible administrative plans.

F. *Promotion procedures demand continuous analysis and study of cumulative pupil case history records in order that refinement of procedure may result and guesswork and conjecture be reduced to a minimum.*

The thirty-four reports unanimously agreed that such continuous analysis and study should be carried on by representative groups of teachers, principals, and supervisors within each school system.

Conditions under which pupils live and work are constantly changing. Educational procedures should be based on the changing needs of the society which the schools serve. Hence the need for continuous study of the bases and procedures of pupil promotion.

The Articulation Commission stresses the desirability of basing promotion on carefully and systematically provided pupil records.

CHAPTER II

PROMOTION PRACTICES AS REVEALED BY 742 INDIVIDUAL PUPIL CASE HISTORIES

T HE COMMITTEE on Pupil Promotion Problems developed a case history technic by which it could study promotion practices through an analysis of individual records. A case history blank was prepared upon which could be collected data concerning each pupil which a teacher should consider in determining whether an individual should be failed or promoted. The blank used in the study herewith reported is shown on pages 24-27.

The scope of the study was limited by selecting those levels in the public schools of Baltimore, Colorado Springs, and Rochester between which there is usually inarticulation through non-promotion. The following levels are dealt with:

1. From Kindergarten to First Grade
2. From First Grade to Second Grade
3. From Third Grade to Fourth Grade
4. From Sixth Grade to Seventh Grade
5. From Ninth Grade to Tenth Grade
6. From Twelfth Grade to College or Business.

The promotion practices in these three cities were then investigated by applying the case history technic to a representative sampling of pupils at these six promotion points. The Committee was aware that an investigation within such restricted limits could not produce conclusive results. However, it was planned that if the case history technic as applied within these narrow limits resulted in any significant findings, the method could then be used more widely, and more dependable conclusions could be arrived at. A second value of this technic is that it can be applied in other school systems or individual schools.

The data collected upon the case history blanks were tabulated upon sheets of the type illustrated by Table 2 on page 28. The complete picture of one high-sixth grade in Colorado Springs is presented on this tabulation sheet. If all teachers had before them as complete information in as compact a form, promotion and failure would certainly be more logically determined than occurs under the prevailing subjective "judgment of the teacher" method.

The sort of analysis which is possible by using the tabulation sheets as a step in the case study technic is presented in the discussion and tables which follow. Each case of failure is critically reviewed in the light of all the evidence.

Pupil Case History

Pupil_____
School_____
Entrance grade in this school system_____
Number of terms (½ years) in school since entering first grade_____
Amount of acceleration, provided it is one-half year or more*_____
                  (State in terms of ½ years)
Amount of retardation, measured in terms of continuous school progress, provided it is one-half year or more*_____
                  (State in terms of ½ years)

Date_____ Grade_____
Teacher_____ Entrance grade in this school_____

Grades skipped_____ Grades repeated_____
Reading readiness tests: Name of test_____ Score_____ Norm_____
   (At kindergarten level)
Kindergarten prognosis tests: Name of test_____ Score_____ Norm_____

Accomplishment in Standardized Subject Tests

	Based on What Test	Date of Test[1]	Age Equivalents Years-Months	Grade 3	4	5	6	7	8	9	10
				Age 8	9	10	11	12	13	14	15	16
I. Q.											
Percentile rank on intelligence test											
Chronological age											
			(M. A.)								
Achievement average											
Reading											
Arithmetic											
Language											
Spelling											
Handwriting											

[1] As spring, 1929; or fall, 1928.
In the space at the right, under grade and age, draw broken lines to show pupil's records, and vertical lines to represent grade standard.

* NOTE: Taking six to seven years as the standard for entering the low first grade, the normal age for any higher grade is determined by adding a half year to the standard of the preceding grade.

Local School and City Accomplishment Tests for Current School Year

(The use of this test is optional. Where standardized tests have not been given, it should probably be used. It might also be used for recording the current term grade in each subject.)

Subject	Rating on Percentile Rank in Class	Subject	Rating on Percentile Rank in Class

Physical condition:

1. Physical development: Height _____, Norm for age _____; Weight _____, Norm for age and height _____

2. Physical defects: Eyesight _____, Hearing _____, Heart _____.

NOTE: Rate the above as: Good, Fair, Poor. When items are based upon records of doctor's examination, put "D" after your notation; when based on personal judgment of teacher, put "T" after your notation; when based on records of school nurse, put "N" after your notation.

Deformities _____, Speech defects _____

3. Disease history, including nervous and mental disorders:

Disease	Approximate date	Mild	Severe

Home conditions: _____

NOTE: Rate as unfavorable, favorable, or neutral, as it affects pupil's school advancement.

Pupil Case History (*Continued*)

Personal characteristics: Social adaptability------------------------ In this rating, consider such emotional

NOTE: Rate social adaptability as normal or average, above average, or below average.

attitudes as fear, shyness, and companionability.

	None	Little	Average	Much	Unusual
Independence					
Perseverance					
Initiative					
Cooperation					
Cheerfulness					
Accuracy					

NOTE: Rating on these six characteristics is optional, except in those school systems where it is carried out as a general practice.

Foreign language difficulty: Does pupil understand, speak, and write the English language adequately for his grade?
Yes----------- No----------- Comment---

Foreign language used in the home---

School attendance for term just ending---

NOTE: Take the average daily attendance for the city as a whole as "satisfactory"; anything which is two percent or more above this average as "good"; and anything which is two percent or more below, as "poor." To illustrate, if the average daily attendance for your city is 93%, a pupil who has this average will be rated as "satisfactory"; one with an average of 95 or better, "good"; and one with an average of 91 or below, "poor."

Major extra-curriculum interest, such as: Music, Art, Athletics, Debating, etc.

Unusual talents, if any---

Marked academic disabilities, if any---

Teacher's estimate of pupil's ability, based not merely on standing in term's work but on his general knowledge of the pupil: A, B, C, D, E (circle letter which expresses the rating given). A—Very good; B—Good; C—Average; D—Poor; E—Very poor.

Disposition of case:

1. Promoted: (   )

Into what grade and classification _____

_____

_____

NOTE: This will include a brief description of flexibility of organization, of administration, and curriculum offerings of the grade and section into which the pupil is promoted. To illustrate, in the case of a kindergarten pupil: "Promoted to sub-primary class, where reading readiness will be developed"; or "Promoted to low first grade in the section of superior ability where children make rapid progress in reading"; or "Promoted to first grade, where only one section is available, and where considerable reading readiness is demanded of all pupils"; etc.

While at the transition from the junior high school to the senior high school interest centers chiefly in the passing of particular subjects, a sufficient number of subjects have to be passed before the pupil is sent on to the senior high school—except in those cases where over-age and other factors enter in which make it appear desirable to send the pupil on to the senior high school to get what he can out of it. In either case, the terms "promoted" or "not promoted" will still apply.

2. Not Promoted: (   )

If pupil failed of promotion, was it due to general weakness in practically all school work, or to failure in one or two subjects? _____ If it was failure in one or two subjects, name them _____

3. Reason why case was disposed of as it was _____

_____

_____

NOTE: Please give as much information as possible on this item.

4. Other factors, if any, in addition to those listed above, which entered into the disposition of the case in regard to promotion or non-promotion _____

_____

_____

In Table 3 below is shown the number of failures and promotions among the limited sampling of pupils at the various grade levels of the three cities. Even in these cities which for some time have been striving consistently to adjust the procedure to the needs of individuals, failure has not been eliminated entirely. The question naturally arises, are these failures justified when all facts are considered? An analysis of the failures reported will show that in some instances the failing of the child was not entirely consistent with the data presented.

Among 124 pupils studied at the kindergarten level, seven cases of failure were reported. A limited amount of objective and subjective data were furnished at this level. Of the seven who must repeat the kindergarten, four were failed because of underageness and immaturity; three of these four also rated low on the Detroit test and were rated low in attendance, social qualities, and general ability by their teacher. If these children were underage when they were admitted to the kindergarten, their failure at that level is not serious since overageness does not result. Because of this immaturity, they probably can profit by an additional year of kinder-

TABLE 3.—PROMOTIONS AND FAILURES IN THREE CITIES AS SHOWN BY INDIVIDUAL CASE STUDIES IN TYPICAL CLASS GROUPS

Promotion Level	City	Number Pupils	Number Failures	Number Promotions	Number Conditions	Not Reported	Number Subject Failures
Kindergarten to First Grade	Baltimore	34	4	30	0	0	0
	Colorado Springs	No report					
	Rochester	90	3	87	0	0	0
First Grade to Second Grade	Baltimore	No report					
	Colorado Springs	34	2	32	0	0	0
	Rochester	32	5	27	0	0	0
Third Grade to Fourth Grade	Baltimore	42	0	42	0	0	0
	Colorado Springs	30	2	28	0	0	0
	Rochester	85	2	83	0	0	0
Sixth Grade to Seventh Grade	Baltimore	46	5	41	0	0	0
	Colorado Springs	30	0	30	0	0	0
	Rochester	101	4	93	4	0	0
Ninth Grade to Tenth Grade	Baltimore	39	0	27	11	1	15
	Colorado Springs	33	0	33	0	0	0
	Rochester	77	1	74	0	2	8
Twelfth Grade to College or Business	Baltimore	35	4	31	0	0	0
	Colorado Springs	34	0	34	0	0	0
	Rochester	No report					

garten experience. The justification for the failure of two other kinder-gartners is that they were graded low by the teacher in social qualities. The seventh child who failed is a cripple—one hand and arm missing, and this condition is apparently the reason for his failure. Contradictory evidence is offered in the facts that his teacher marked him above average in social adaptability, and "C" in general ability. Seventeen other members of the class were promoted who were marked "C" or below in general ability and yet this one individual was failed. Was it because of data not supplied on the case history blank?

Two classes of first-grade pupils were studied. Of the sixty-six children in these classes seven were failures. In Colorado Springs the two failures were twin sisters with I. Q.'s of 70 and 73 with a record of very irregular attendance and failure in all school subjects.

In Rochester all of the five failures had already been retarded one-half year, and were reported as failures in reading. Three were reported "slow mentally" and two "immature," while nine other members of the class were similarly marked but given promotion. The retention of one pupil (R. P.) was probably justifiable on account of illness and poor attendance, but eight of those promoted were also reported as having poor attendance. M. P.'s attendance was satisfactory and he was equal to or better than eight of those promoted in social adaptability and personal characteristics. The teacher's estimate of this pupil's reading ability seems to have been the chief basis of promotion. Table 4 gives an analysis of the failures in this group. In reviewing this table, it should be remembered that the teacher had an all-around knowledge of the pupils, the complete details of which are not set

TABLE 4.—ANALYSIS OF FAILURES IN THE FIRST GRADE

City	Pupil	No. in Class	½ yr. Re-tard-ed	Number Who Were Promoted with Equal or Lower Rating in			Defects	Reasons Given for Failure
				Social adapt-ability	Personal charac-teristics	At-tend-ance		
Colorado Springs	F. B.	34	0	11	2	7	Speech	Failure in all subjects Irregular attendance Border-line intelligence
Colorado Springs	R. B.	34	0	11	2	7	Speech	Failure in all subjects Irregular attendance Border-line intelligence
Rochester	O. A.	32	1	12	2	17		Mentally slow Reading failure
Rochester	A. G.	32	1	12	2	27		Mentally slow Failure in reading and penmanship
Rochester	M. P.	32	1	24	8	17		Slow mentally Failure in reading and penmanship
Rochester	R. P.	32	1	12	8	8		Failure in reading Illness—immaturity
Rochester	C. S.	32	1	12	8	8		Backward Failure in reading

forth in the table. In other words, some of the factors which may have entered into the teacher's judgment in failing these pupils are not given in the report. When objective tests for attitudes and for skills supplement the tests we now have for knowledge, teachers' promotion of pupils may be more consistent with what teachers think about pupils as checked in these case histories.

At the third-grade level only four failures were reported out of 157 cases. These four failures are analyzed in Table 5. It is quite evident that in accomplishment these four children in all subjects were at or near the foot of the class. If academic achievement is to bear much weight in the determination of failure at this level, the failure of these four children would seem to be justified. However, there is no evidence as to whether or not any phases of the individuals' development other than academic performance were given consideration. In any event, promotion of any one of these four would be questionable; for, unless the school system is particularly organized to do remedial work, advancement to the next grade would not be desirable for these four children and would result in an increase in the number of problem cases in the fourth grade.

An analysis of the thirteen failures in the sixth grade is presented in Table 6. Some questionable promotion practice is observed at the sixth-grade level.

Case 1—G. A. M., I. Q. 96. Already retarded two half years. Reason for failure "weak in arithmetic." Yet eleven others graded as low or lower in arithmetic were promoted. In all subjects except history, G. A. M. rated well in comparison with other members of the class. Thirty-eight members of the class who were promoted rated as low or lower in geography. Should not this distinct leadership in geography be quite as determining a factor as his somewhat below average work in arithmetic? G. A. M. is marked low in social adaptation because he possesses "little perseverance." The teacher in whose hands rested the fate of this child should have asked whether failure because of comparative weakness in one phase of his achievement and in spite of distinct leadership in another equally important phase would tend to furnish the urge for greater perseverance. Furthermore, had

TABLE 5.—ANALYSIS OF FAILURES IN THE THIRD GRADE

Pupil	Number in Class	Number Who Were Promoted with Equal or Lower Rating in					Reasons Given for Failure
		Spelling	Geography	Arithmetic	Language	Reading	
C. M.	13	0	0	2	1	0	General weakness Poor reading
A. N.	13	1	1	1	5	0	General weakness Needs more foundation
C. F.	30	0	...	0	...	1	General weakness Prolonged absence
W. H.	30	0	...	0	...	1	Too young and immature General weakness—had been accelerated when mid-year promotions were discontinued—not able to bridge gap

TABLE 6.—ANALYSIS OF FAILURE IN TWO CLASSES AT THE SIXTH-GRADE LEVEL

Class	Pupil	Age-Grade Placement		I.Q.	Number in Grade	Number Who Were Promoted with Equal or Lower Rating in							Physical Defects	Social Adaptability	Reasons for Failure
		½ yr. accel.	½ yr. retard.			I.Q.	Spelling	Arithmetic	Language	Geography	Reading	History			
Class 1.	C. L.	0	0	105	46	31	......	11	......	2	......	20	Poor eyes	Average	Absence—good work when present
Class 1.	G. A. M.	......	2	96	46	18	......	11	......	38	......	5	Poor heart	Little perseverance	Weak in arithmetic
Class 1.	A. N.	0	0	115	46	37	......	23	......	17	......	19	None	Average	General weakness—absence
Class 1.	G. N.	......	1	100	46	29	......	26	......	7	......	5	None	Little perseverance	General weakness
Class 1.	W. S.	......	1	91	46	14	......	11	......	19	......	38	None	Little perseverance	General weakness
Class 2.	J. G.	0	0	......	31	......	0	0	2	0	0	......	Poor hearing	Average	General weakness / Not prepared
Class 2.	J. B.	......	4	......	31	......	21	0	2	2	3	......	None	Little initiative or independence	General weakness / Lacks foundation
Class 2.	F. W.	......	3	......	31	......	0	0	1	7	3	......	Poor tonsils	Little initiative or independence	General weakness / Needs to repeat
Class 2.	R. W.	0	0	......	31	......	0	0	1	15	9	......	None	Little initiative or independence	General weakness—not able to meet requirements of 7th
Class 2.	A. G.*	0	0	......	31	......	21	10	0	21	1	......	None	Average	Lang. poor; read. fair
Class 2.	G. L.*	0	0	......	31	......	6	0	4	0	9	......	None	Little cooperation	General weakness
Class 2.	D. R.*	0	0	......	31	......	15	0	16	0	9	......	Poor hearing	Little independence	General weakness / Unable to do 7th
Class 2.	M. S.*	......	1	......	31	......	15	0	16	15	21	......	None	Above average	Needs extra arithmetic / No repeating class so must repeat grade

* Conditioned, i. e., is promoted on trial, see Table 3, page 28.

adequate diagnostic and remedial measures been applied, one wonders whether this normal child (I. Q. 96) would have stood so low in his class in arithmetic.

Case 2—A. N., I. Q. 115. Reason for failure, "general weakness, absence." This child was considered generally weak, yet of those promoted 37 were equal or lower in I. Q.; 23, in arithmetic; 17, in geography; and 19, in history. General weakness is not indicated by definite accomplishment measured by objective tests. With an I. Q. of 115, a rating in social qualities of "average," and with his high rating in achievement, one wonders why this child was not promoted.

Case 3—G. N., I. Q. 100. Reason for failure, "general weakness." G. N.'s ranking among the members of the class does not indicate general weakness. Although his teacher claims he possesses but "little perseverance," he had persevered until, at the end of the sixth grade, of those promoted in a class of 46, 26 had equal or lower rating in arithmetic. Seven members of the class in geography and five in history were promoted with as low or lower ratings than his. Of those promoted, 29 out of a class of 46 had equal or lower rating in native ability as measured in terms of I. Q.

Case 4—W. S., I. Q. 91. Reason for failure, "general weakness." General weakness does not seem to be indicated by the fact that W. S. was as good as or better than 11 members of the class in arithmetic who were promoted; 19, in geography; and 38, in history.

Case 5—M. S. Reason for failure, "needs extra arithmetic." His social adaptability is rated as above average. It is natural to inquire: if extra arithmetic is so imperative a need as to cause failure when all other evidence points clearly toward promotion, why was "extra arithmetic" not given during the previous school year?

In the ninth grade three classes reported failures, all of which are subject failures. Table 7 presents an analysis of these failures. In Class 3, of which there are 39 members of average ability, ten failed in mathematics. This large percentage of failure gives rise to the question, "Was not the school to blame if so many were not successful?" In Class 4, two pupils are reported as failing in mathematics. H. S. failed to pass in mathematics although six others had scores as low or lower, and V. W. failed in mathematics although three others in the class were passed who had lower grades than V. W.'s. In Class 5, consisting of 26 pupils, six cases of failure in Latin are reported, and in this class the range of I. Q.'s would indicate that at least five of these six failures are above average in mental ability.

No failures were reported in the twelfth grade. What is the significance of this fact?

No final conclusions concerning promotion practices can be drawn from a study based upon so limited a sampling of students as was included in this preliminary study. If the technic proves of value, the study can be extended to include a sampling so general that valid conclusions could be drawn. Even from this limited study certain tentative conclusions can be drawn.

1. There is need of making further adjustments to individual differences if failure is to be completely eliminated.

2. Types of questionable practice follow:

    a. Failure of a child because of weakness in one subject when objective data show he is strong in other subjects.

    b. Failure of a child because the teacher rates him low in a given subject or subjects when objective evidence shows that the teacher's estimate is wrong. Is the explanation that the teacher's estimate is based on different criteria from the objective test data?

TABLE 7.—ANALYSIS OF CASES OF SUBJECT FAILURE AT THE NINTH-GRADE LEVEL

Class	Pupil	I.Q.	Social Adaptability	Number in Class	Subject Failed	Age-Grade Placement		Number Who Were Promoted with Equal or Lower Rating in			
						½ yr. Accel.	½ yr. Retard.	Eng.	Math.	Latin	Sci.
Class 3	C. B.		Average	39	Latin Math.		2				
Class 3	C. D.		Average	39	Latin Math.						
Class 3	W. H.		Average—Little independence Little perseverance	39	French Math. Latin	2					
Class 3	H. K.		Average	39	Math.	4					
Class 3	B. M.		Average	39	Math.	2					
Class 3	L. N.		Average	39	Math.	3					
Class 3	M. S.		Average	39	Math.	0	0				
Class 3	C. S.		Average	39	Math.	3					
Class 3	B. S.		Below average Little indep'ence	39	Eng.	0	0				
Class 3	F. S.		Average	39	Math.	2					
Class 3	M. S.		Average	39	Math.		4				
Class 4	H. S.		Below average	25	Math.	0	0	2	6	10	8
Class 4	V. W.		Above average No cooperation	25	Math.	0	0	10	3	20	21
Class 5	I. A.	114	Below average No initiative	26	Latin	0	0	8	2	0	1
Class 5	E. H.	113	Below average Little initiative	26	Latin	0	0	8	2	0	6
Class 5	V. H.	103	Average Little initiative	26	Latin	0	0	8	2	10	6
Class 5	H. M.	111	Below average Little initiative	26	Latin	0	0	0	2	2	6
Class 5	D. M.	108	Average Little initiative	26	Latin		2	8	2	2	6
Class 5	P. T.	85	Below average Little initiative	26	Latin		2	0	7	10	1

Blank spaces in all columns, except those dealing with age-grade placement, indicate that data were not supplied on pupil case histories.

   c. Failing a child because of weakness in certain subjects, but passing children in the same class who by the teacher's rating are still lower in the same subjects. Is the explanation that the teacher made promotion in terms of her estimate of the pupil's capacity to grow in the subject rather than on the basis of objective standards?

   d. Failing a pupil upon a single phase of his academic accomplishment without taking into consideration other phases of his accomplishment.

   e. Failing a pupil upon his lack of academic accomplishment without considering other factors such as social and physical development.

   f. Failing a pupil because he does not satisfy the prescribed promotional formula required by the teacher for all pupils of the class.

   g. Failing a large number of a class, for example, 33 percent—in a given subject.

   h. Failing more children in a comparatively mechanical subject like arithmetic than in the more complicated and fundamental subject—reading.

3. Evidence shows that mass instruction must be supplemented by diagnostic and remedial measures if failure is to be reduced.

4. There is evidence that teachers are so bound by traditional group procedures that they fail to consider the needs of the individual in promotion practice.

5. From the variety of practice reported, it is evident that a promotional philosophy needs to be developed which will govern procedures within a school system. Would not training in the use of the case method technic help to reduce teachers' inconsistencies in their judgment of pupils' fitness for promotion?

If the complete picture of a child is before the teacher, he will be more apt to consider all aspects of the child's development than to determine his placement upon any one or two considerations. Undoubtedly some of the failures reported in the study could have been avoided if the case method had been applied before the promotion lists were completed.

The school systems in which the study was conducted report that the case studies developed the consciousness on the part of teachers that promotion is an individual problem and that present questionable practice indicates that promotion is a problem which needs careful analysis and study.

The Articulation Commission recommends that school systems generally use the case method in the study of their pupil promotion procedures. It is the purpose of this chapter to present the basic materials and to illustrate a technic of applying this method. Aided by this procedure, teachers throughout the nation will be made more conscious of the problems involved in dealing with pupil promotions and will be enabled to clarify their thinking and improve their practice in this important phase of articulation.

CHAPTER III

SEVEN PROMOTION PROBLEMS DISCUSSED BY 555 SUPERINTENDENTS OF SCHOOLS

THIS section of the report is based on a questionnaire sent to all members of the Department of Superintendence. It included these seven questions: (1) What are the most acute promotion problems in local school systems? (2) What are the bases for pupil promotion? (3) In which elementary grades and subjects is pupil failure the greatest? (4) What are the best means for reducing pupil failure in elementary and secondary schools? (5) What is the value of semi-annual as compared with annual promotions? (6) Are trial promotions desirable? (7) Statements concerning relationships between school units. Complete replies from 555 superintendents of schools were received in time for tabulation.

A. What Are the Most Acute Promotion Problems in Local School Systems?

Do promotion problems differ in different sized school systems? Do they differ in different sections of the United States? Are certain promotion problems more acute in small school systems than in large? Are some problems common to all school systems? To secure answers to these questions, in an inquiry sent to all members of the Department of Superintendence, this question was included: What are the most acute promotion problems in your school system? Replies from 555 superintendents of schools representing all the 48 states, arranged in six population groups, are summarized below. In some instances, the exact statements of superintendents of schools are given to illustrate what they consider to be their most acute promotion problems.

Factors Involved in Most Acute Promotion Problems in Cities Under 2,500

1. Low-mentality and overage cases—handling of "slow" pupils many of whom will never earn true promotion in the common school subjects, and the school is not equipped to give them proper manual or vocational work.

Various problems connected with children of low intelligence were reported. The following are typical comments from superintendents of schools:

The subnormal child of parents who do not realize his condition—*Frederick M. Nickerson, Superintendent of Schools, Newport, Maine.*

In a school the size of ours, it is impossible to have special help classes to any extent; there is a group that needs an ungraded room yet must be carried along with the other children in situations that are beyond their experience and ability to comprehend—*Edward T. Whiting, Superintendent of Schools, Gordon, Neb.*

2. Lack of enough courses, especially finding courses, by which it is possible to meet varying needs of individual pupils.

3. Lack of objective requirements for promotion from grade to grade.

4. How to provide for the especially bright child.

5. Large drifting population, with the result that the schools get additions and lose pupils every week.

6. Poorly enforced attendance laws.

7. Lack of properly trained teachers.

8. The critical attitude teachers take toward the lower-grade teacher if pupils are not all bright.

The plain "passing of the buck" to each other, when it is no one's fault but the simple condition of the child. One superintendent of schools writes: "How can we get teachers to see that they must not measure the abilities of the pupils coming into their grades by those who are going out to the next grade?"

9. Short-term schools.

10. Lack of adequate supervision.

11. Semi-annual promotion plan.

12. Unevenness in size of classes.

13. Language handicap due to foreign parentage.

14. Sending pupils from rural districts to city high schools at the completion of the eighth grade.

15. Pressure on the part of parents to have pupils moved along rapidly.

Factors Involved in Most Acute Promotion Problems in Cities 2,500-5,000

1. Low-mentality and overage cases:

The problem of border-line cases and morons which the schools are trying to handle, due to the lack of county or state agencies to handle such problems—*McCall Aldrich, Superintendent of Schools, McGill, Nev.*

Overage pupils are usually the ones who are failing. Keeping them in the grade in which they can do the prescribed work makes them a social problem. There are no textbooks in reading or arithmetic which fit them mentally and do not seem too childish for their age. They resent childish work even if they cannot do it. Ungraded rooms merely segregate the problems. The only solution seems to be a number of special help teachers and possibly stepping away from the entire graded system—*J. E. Murphy, Superintendent of Schools, Hurley, Wis.*

Our schools are too small to offer special groupings for poorer pupils—*W. R. Dunwiddie, Superintendent of Schools, Port Washington, Wis.*

2. The superior pupil—deciding on advisability of advancing superior pupil by special promotion—what to do with the brilliant pupil who socially and physically belongs with those who progress normally.

3. Lack of flexibility or inability to adjust the curriculum to all the special or semi-special classes.

4. Difficulty in breaking away from old plans and traditions:

   a. Teachers are too much concerned with skills, facts, and knowledge.
   b. More time should be given to establishing the proper attitudes and ideals. Promotion and graduation should be on the basis of (b) as well as (a)— *F. Oral Grounds, Superintendent of Schools, St. Clair, Mich.*

5. Different standards and notions of teachers as to when a pupil should be promoted, and variation in teachers' marks. Failure to meet the teacher's notion of 75 percent or "D" or "B" or whatever the rating is. Lack of objective data in assigning teachers' marks.

6. Desire of parents to have pupils promoted whether they are prepared for it or not.

7. Persuading teachers to allow their more mature and advanced pupils to transfer to other class groups. Each teacher dislikes to lose her leaders and spend the necessary time developing other leaders.

8. Shifting population in and out of the school district due to industrial conditions.

9. Lack of parental cooperation in home study.

10. What to do with the indifferent pupil.

11. Irregular pupil attendance.

12. Pupils who fail successively in one subject.

Factors Involved in Most Acute Promotion Problems in Cities 5,000-10,000

1. Low-mentality and overage cases:

Our most acute promotion problem is to know what is best to be done with the overage boy or girl who seems unable to profit or to do satisfactorily the average classroom work. We have an opportunity class for such pupils in grades 1-4, but we do not have one for the intermediate grades above the fourth, and therefore have to allow overage pupils to remain in the fifth and sixth grades, who do not seem to profit by the regular classroom work—*Arthur W. Hale, Superintendent of Schools, Franklin, Mass.*

To retain an overgrown retarded moron in a grade with considerably younger children is to set up a moral situation fraught with many bad possibilities. To promote unprepared pupils is to have classes that cannot do the work of their grade. In a small school system of 1,250 pupils with three grade buildings, homogeneous grouping in both high school and elementary school is impossible. How can one meet all the exigencies of these conditions?—*W. T. White, Superintendent of Schools, Bonham, Texas.*

It is difficult for many teachers to appreciate the needs of the slow-moving pupils. There is always a tendency to compare them with the normal groups and to expect just as much from them—*Sheridan Linn, Superintendent of Schools, Patchogue, N. Y.*

Our most acute promotion problem is children in the first grade who show such a marked inability to read that they are retained and then because of association with children decidedly younger than they are, become social misfits and lose confidence in themselves—*Ralph I. Underhill, Superintendent of Schools, Scarsdale, N. Y.*

2. The superior pupil—how to meet his needs:

The most acute problem is getting teachers and board members to recognize the able—*John R. Moss, Superintendent of Schools, Paris, Ill.*

3. Lack of differentiated courses of study to fit the needs of pupils of different levels of ability:

The problem of handling overage dull pupils—how to secure their interest and hold them in school, how to solve their discipline problems, and how to differentiate subject-matter to fit their needs—*H. C. Fries, Supervising Principal, South Plainfield, N. J.*

4. Lack of common promotion standards:

All promotions and failures should be eliminated by devising a scheme of continuous jobs from grades 1-12 inclusive, a completion of which makes up a coherent, continuous procedure. The teacher and the pupil should not be hampered by promotions, failures, and needless repetitions—*J. F. Bemiller, Superintendent of Schools, Galion, Ohio.*

5. Parental interference:

The biggest problem that we have is to get pupils and parents to take the right attitude toward needed repetition of half grades. We are gradually solving this problem through publicity—steady, continuous publicity on the point. We are attempting to get all concerned to see that repeating a half grade is not a cause for feeling disgraced, but it is a perfectly normal thing and should be considered as an opportunity. The course is not made for everybody to complete in the same number of years, and repetition is the only way that the slower workers have of taking more time. There is no more disgrace about it than for a smaller man to take more hitches to move a load than a bigger man would for the same load. Those who do not get the work the first time over need to be retaught. The second time over the work is easier and the pupil frequently and in fact usually finds himself and begins to get joy of improved comprehension. Non-promotion is not failure. It is simply the result of natural differences between individuals. It is perfectly normal and to be expected—*R. V. Hunkins, Superintendent of Schools, Lead, S. D.*

6. Crowded conditions which make it necessary to move pupils along at times when they are poorly prepared.

7. Promotion of pupils in elementary schools who fail in only one subject.

8. How to get graduation requirements to satisfy student needs and college entrance requirements at the same time.

9. Irregular pupil attendance and shifting population.

Factors Involved in Most Acute Promotion Problems in Cities 10,000-30,000

1. Low-mentality and overage cases:

The greatest problem is with pupils who are incompetent to do the regular work generally offered. They are not poor enough to be among mental defectives, but need special attention to make even moderate progress. These are the habitual repeaters—*E. H. Burdick, Superintendent of Schools, Middletown, N. Y.*

The most difficult problem is with the child who is possibly a year or two years mentally retarded. He is not three years mentally retarded and is, therefore, not placed in special classes for the mentally handicapped. The Massachusetts pupils three years or more mentally retarded have to be placed in special classes with about fifteen in each class. Without doubt the best way to take care of a pupil who is one or two years mentally retarded and is a misfit in a regular class because of his large size is to place him in a special room where he is grouped according to his size and age, and where work is adapted to him as an individual. In other words, a plan of individualized instruction will solve this problem—*James J. Quinn, Superintendent of Schools, Winchester, Mass.*

On the high-school level it is difficult to organize courses that challenge the interest and are on the basis of accomplishment for the groups which twenty years ago were eliminated in the sixth grade, but who now reach the tenth grade in high school—*B. C. Berg, Superintendent of Schools, Newton, Iowa.*

Inadequate courses in high school for pupils with low I. Q. is a serious problem— *A. I. Tiss, Superintendent of Schools, Fort Madison, Iowa.*

It is difficult to get parents to face the problem of the difficulties and mental handicaps of their child, when naturally they want to think that their boy or girl is just as bright as any other boy or girl—*Edgar F. Down, Superintendent of Schools, Ferndale, Mich.*

2. Small building enrolments that prevent desirable grouping and adaptations :

It is difficult to provide for those who need special facilities or special attention and adjustment in the smaller schools distant from the thickly settled areas of the city where often there are only enough children entering each year to half fill a room so that each teacher has two year levels in her room—*Frederick W. Porter, Superintendent of Schools, Greenfield, Mass.*

3. Training teachers to consider pupils as individuals, taking into account native ability, home environment, and other personal factors. Training them to prevent failures by diagnosing difficulties and correcting them :

We have materially cut down failures by compiling and issuing to teachers a semester report on distribution of class marks, by organizing a system of records in which teachers and principals participate, by letters to parents, and by year-end conferences between teachers and assistant superintendent of schools, in which each failure is discussed in the light of work done with the pupil during the year, and his retardation or promotion decided upon in the light of individual and group welfare—*Margaret S. Brainerd, Assistant Superintendent of Schools, Martins Ferry, Ohio.*

4. Lack of a definition of standards:

Lack of positive assurance that the pupil will succeed in the next grade is a major problem. Failure of even the best tests to get at the real fitness of the pupil for work of advanced grade—*Charles C. Richardson, Superintendent of Schools, North Adams, Mass.*

At the present time we have committees representing every grade in our elementary system setting up minimum essentials for promotion, one committee for each grade. When these committees have presented their reports, a general committee will review these reports for the purpose of bringing about a set of minimum essentials that will show promotion from grade to grade by a series of well regulated steps—*Frank Hendry, Superintendent of Schools, Royal Oak, Mich.*

In the past, teachers have marked too much by numerals. Teachers have varying ideas about oral recitations and answers to old type examinations. We are getting away from traditional marking by giving consideration to scholastic attainments, abilities, purpose, physical soundness, and other general items that really determine the rate of speed an elementary school pupil should maintain. To promote on this new basis involves a vast amount of consultation with parents, but we believe it pays to become really co-partners with them in the interest of the children's welfare—*Fred A. Verplanck, Superintendent of Schools, Manchester, Conn.*

5. What to do with pupils of superior ability.

6. The lack of understanding of promotion standards on the part of parents.

7. Irregular attendance and unstable population.

8. What to do with the pupil who fails in one or two subjects.

9. What to do with the pupil who has no interest in school.

10. Retardation in first and second grades due to large percentage of non-English-speaking pupils.

11. Social and physiological maladjustments.

Factors Involved in Most Acute Promotion Problems in Cities 30,000-100,000

1. Low-mentality and overage cases:

Our problem is keeping pupils within their social age and at the same time giving them work adapted to their mental age—*Raymond C. Burdick, Superintendent of Schools, Watertown, N. Y.*

Our plan is to take subnormal children out of group instruction entirely and let them advance at their individual rates in special classes—*James H. Risley, Superintendent of Schools, District No. 1, Pueblo, Colo.*

Many pupils who are slow in learning cannot even with extended time and effort accomplish those standards of scholastic attainment which are set up for the grade in consideration. These pupils therefore pass up from year to year through the school system somewhat overage for the grade in which they are working, yet unable to accomplish regular standards. All teachers and school administrators must be conscious of the fact that the curriculum for these pupils must be modified to suit their needs—*Virgil E. Dickson, Assistant Superintendent, Director, Bureau of Research and Guidance, Berkeley Public Schools, Berkeley, Calif.*

2. How to provide for the very bright pupils so as to give them enough to do without promoting them beyond their physical and social maturity.

3. Some small building enrolments which prevent desirable groupings and adaptations.

Our elementary schools, consisting of kindergarten through the first six grades, range in enrolment from 100 to 600. It is extremely difficult to arrange a system of promotion on any safe and rather formal basis and make it applicable to all these different schools. We assume that we owe as much to the children in the small schools as we do to those in the larger schools. To meet such requirements in any real sense would require so expensive an organization as to make it almost prohibitive. While it is true that we take out from these schools the decidedly subnormal children and segregate them into a special school, we still have children, the so-called border-line cases, left in all schools that accentuate the difficulties in mass promotion—*Arthur Deamer, Superintendent of Schools, Cedar Rapids, Iowa.*

Our most difficult problem is the promotion of pupils based upon the homogeneous grouping plan when the buildings are small and consist of a few classes, wherein we run into one or two extremes—there are too few pupils to form a group or too many to form a group—and the number of classrooms is commensurate with the number of grades involved. In a large building, consisting of a great number of pupils, groups, and rooms, this almost insurmountable difficulty does not exist. In small schools, this real difficulty is especially objectionable in the very lowest grades, where the age of the pupil is such as to prevent transferring to other districts—*James F. Rockett, Superintendent of Schools, Woonsocket, R. I.*

4. Lack of a definition of standards:

Leading teachers to see the importance of using objective data as a basis for promotion is a big problem—*Frederick F. Martin, Superintendent of Schools, Santa Monica, Calif.*

Inability to define what graduation from each unit of the school system really means—*Frank G. Pickell, Superintendent of Schools, Montclair, N. J.*

5. How to designate that a "z" promotion is on a different basis from an "x" promotion.

6. How to reduce failures in the first grade. How to detect unreadiness for reading before pupils are admitted to first grade.

7. What to do with the pupil who fails in the same subject successively.

8. Failure of parents to understand what teacher is trying to do for pupil.

9. What should be the relative emphasis placed upon teachers' judgments and group test scores?

10. Language difficulties of pupils from foreign homes.

11. Overcrowded classrooms and too few coaching teachers.

12. Irregular pupil attendance.

13. What to do with the indifferent pupil.

Factors Involved in Most Acute Promotion Problems in Cities Over 100,000

1. Low-mentality and overage cases:

The ever-growing number of mental misfits gives us most of our problems. Our workshop classes are of great help but the problem grows—*Allen P. Keith, Superintendent of Schools, New Bedford, Mass.*

Believing that every boy and girl should have the socializing influence, the citizenship training, the occupational information, and the tryout courses of the junior high school, how are those of low ability to be handled when promoted without meeting any standard but age? How can a grade standard be maintained under such a policy? With such a lowering of the bars for the mentally weak, how are the superior pupils to be urged to extreme effort?—*John H. Kingsley, Director, Bureau of Research, Albany, N. Y.*

2. Better educational service for super-bright pupils.

3. Lack of differentiated courses of study to fit the needs of pupils of different levels of ability.

4. Lack of coordination of courses:

One difficulty is that of coordinating the differentiated courses of study so that pupils may progress from one group to another and may be assimilated in such groups with the least possible amount of readjustment—*James J. Reynolds, District Superintendent, Public School 90, Brooklyn, N. Y.*

5. Promotion from one administrative unit to another:

The problems of the first grade; the problem of the last year of the elementary school; and the problem of the last year of junior high school—*Elizabeth L.*

Woods, Director, Division of Psychology and Educational Research, City Schools, Los Angeles, Calif.

6. Variation in pupil promotion rates and standards between individual schools in the same system.

7. What should be the requirements for promotion in each grade?

Should there be minimum essentials with one hundred percent mastery of these? What are they? How much acceleration should be permitted? How much retardation should be permitted? In view of the individual differences in ability among children, how can we hold all of them to any specific requirement? Is evidence of individual growth the only requirement we should demand?—*F. M. Underwood, District Superintendent, Elementary Schools, St. Louis, Mo.*

8. Keeping standards definite yet flexible enough to care for needs of individual pupils.

9. What to do with the pupil who fails in the same subject successively.

10. Irregular attendance and unstable population.

11. Language difficulties of pupils from foreign homes.

Promotion problems common to school systems of all sizes—A careful tabulation of replies from 555 superintendents of schools, representing cities of all sizes, shows that low-mentality and overage cases result in the most acute of all promotion problems. What to do with the pupil of very superior ability is the problem which ranks second in order of difficulty.

A third problem which overlaps both of the above problems, and which is particularly acute in small school systems, is the small building enrolments which prevent desirable groupings and adaptations. To quote Supt. Potter of Greenville, Mass.:

It is difficult to provide for those who need special facilities or special attention and adjustment in the smaller schools distant from the thickly settled areas of the city where often there are only enough children entering each year to half fill a room so that each teacher has two year levels in her room.

Supt. Potter pictures the difficulties that prevail where a teacher has two grades in one room. According to the United States Office of Education, there were 153,306 one-room schoolhouses used in 1927-28.[1] Here it is even more difficult to group pupils according to ability.

However, even in large school systems where pupils are segregated into more or less homogeneous groups, promotion problems are by no means solved. The promotion problems which superintendents of schools in large cities listed as most acute were: (1) what to do with the overage pupil of low mentality; (2) what to do with the very superior pupil, and (3) lack of differentiated courses of study to fit the needs of pupils of different levels of ability.

[1] U. S. Department of the Interior, Office of Education. *Biennial Survey of Education, 1926-1928.* Bulletin, 1930, No. 16. Washington, D. C.; Government Printing Office, 1930. p. 468.

B. What Are the Bases for Pupil Promotion?

What are the bases for pupil promotion in your school system?—This question was included in the inquiry sent to all members of the Department of Superintendence. They were asked to list the bases for pupil promotion in their local school systems at these six levels: (1) From kindergarten to first grade, (2) from first grade to second grade, (3) from sixth grade to seventh grade, (4) from eighth grade to ninth grade—in school systems organized on the 8-4 plan, (5) from ninth grade to tenth grade—in school systems organized on the 6-3-3 plan, and (6) for graduation from high school.

This section summarizes the replies from over 500 superintendents of schools.

Bases for promotion from kindergarten to first grade—Statements from 505 superintendents of schools, relative to the bases on which pupils are promoted from kindergarten to first grade in their local school systems, were first divided into six population groups, and then tabulated according to frequency of mention. Careful analysis showed that the bases for pupil promotion at this level are practically the same in cities of all sizes. The 505 statements are summarized below—there is a great deal of overlapping in the classification:

Bases for Promotion from Kindergarten to First Grade

	Frequency of Mention
1. Chronological age	201
2. Teacher's judgment	159

> Judgment of teacher as to child's ability to progress with group and do the work of the first grade; judgment of teacher checked by supervisor's judgment; teacher-principal judgment; teacher's rating of development; teacher rating according to specified standard; teacher's estimate of general fitness.

3. Mental age, mental maturity	94

> Mental age of 5 years; mental age of 5½ years; mental age of 6 years; child must show on an intelligence test that he will reach the mental age of 6 before the following April in order to be admitted in September; child's mental growth in comparison with group; intelligence rating.

4. Test and examination scores	86

> Tests to determine first-grade readiness; kindergarten tests; reading readiness tests; first-grade tests; tests given by supervisors.

5. Physical maturity	57

> Physical growth and development; size; physical fitness; maturity of six-year level; normal development.

6. Social age, social maturity, social adaptability	56

> Social and group adaptations; ability to participate in an organized group; ability to cooperate in a spontaneous group; ability to adjust self to group situation; development of habits of social usage.

7. Achievement or accomplishment .... 5?

> School record; daily work; passing grade for the year; achieving specified minimum essentials in the kindergarten; completion of prescribed course of study; knowledge of colors, name, address, salute to the flag, seasons, days of the week, and months of the year; ability to count number of pupils in class, recognize and write numbers to 10, sing several rote songs, speak distinctly, memorize nursery rhymes, and use crayons, paint, clay, and other school materials; growth in power to express meanings or desires in words, in plastic materials, and in song and dramatic play; development of those skills which fit child for first grade.

8. Reading readiness 25

> Probability of being ready to learn to read; elementary recognition of words; sentence sense; interest in materials and activities leading toward study of reading, ability to read and comprehend simple words.

9. No requirements, all kindergartners are given opportunity to try first-grade work 22

10. Time spent in kindergarten............................... 19

> Completion of one year of kindergarten; number of terms in kindergarten not to exceed three.

11. Regular attendance in kindergarten...................... 13

12. Sense of responsibility.................................. 11

> Ability to assume simple responsibilities; ability to care for self and for one's possessions; personal neatness; respect for property.

13. Ability to take directions and follow simple instructions........ 10

> Must listen and give attention when someone else is speaking.

14. Oral language 7

> Power of expression; child must have growing vocabulary and be able to converse on topics he knows most about; ability to speak English.

15. School habits 7

> Reasonable development in right school habits—courtesy, neatness, respect for others; ability to conform to school standards; amenability to discipline; right attitude toward school rules and teacher's requests.

16. Interest span 6

> Interest in reading and doing things which take some time; be able to maintain sustained attention; interest span of 20 or 30 minutes.

17. Number concept.. 5

> Interest in activities and materials leading toward number study; be able to write numbers from 1 to 10.

18. Individual welfare of pupil.............................. 4

> Will pupil profit most by promotion or retention?

19. Initiative and leadership shown in kindergarten group.......... 4
20. Consideration of home conditions and environment............ 3
21. Ability to work intelligently.............................. 3

> Does child plan his work? Growing habit of working with a clear, definite purpose in mind.

22. Conclusions of psychiatrist who has tested child.............. 3
23. Growth in enjoyment of beauty........................... 1

Bases for promotion from first grade to second grade—Statements from 536 superintendents of schools, relative to the bases on which pupils are promoted from first grade to second grade in their local school systems, were first divided into six population groups and tabulated according to frequency of mention. Careful analysis showed, as in the case of promotion from kindergarten to first grade, that the bases for pupil promotion at this level are practically the same in cities of all sizes. The 536 statements are summarized below—there is a great deal of overlapping in the classification:

Bases for Promotion from First Grade to Second Grade

Frequency of
Mention

1. Reading ability.. 277

> Accomplishment in reading tests; word recognition test; comprehension test; ability to read and discuss the content of first-grade reading material; mastery of reading habits and skills according to growth level; reasonable proficiency in reading primers and several first readers; right attitude toward reading—desire to read.

2. Teacher's judgment.................................... 214

> Teacher's opinion that pupil has completed the work of first grade well enough to do second-grade work; opinion of teacher that pupil can do the work of the second grade more profitably than to repeat the first grade; judgment of teacher and principal; combined judgment of teacher, principal, and supervisor.

3. Educational achievement................................ 165

> Satisfactory accomplishment in subjects; scholarship, ccompletion of grade standards set up by state or local course of study; achievement of minimum objectives and minimum attainments in subject-matter; teacher's record of work done; an average of "D" or above; class achievement estimated by daily or weekly marks with special tests; classroom work; average of 75, determined by tests, examinations, and daily marks.

4. Arithmetical ability................................... 74

> Ability to do number work required of the second grade. Child should have a rather clear idea of number concepts—reasonable mastery of the fundamental processes in arithmetic; should be able to count to 100, do a small amount of addition, subtraction, and multiplication.

5. Standard tests.. 70

> Satisfactory achievement on standard educational tests of various kinds; test and examination scores.

6. Chronological age.. 69

Overage pupils may be promoted although below required accomplishment.

7. Ability to do second-grade work........................ 57

Ability to do the work ahead as indicated by the work already done; ability to attack new subject-matter; ability to continue to grow and develop somewhat to the degree that will be expected of him by the group to which he is going; increased power of concentration.

8. Mental age 49

Intelligence as disclosed by group and individual examinations; mental development.

9. Social development and maturity........................ 41

Social age; ability to get along in the group, to participate in social activities; right social attitudes and habits for a second-grade child.

10. Writing ability 37

Ability to write according to specified standard; ability to write all the small letters and some of the capitals, small words, and short sentences in legible fashion; muscular coordination which permits simple penmanship.

11. Length of time in grade............................... 31

No pupil retained more than two years in grade; those who are repeating grade are nearly always promoted; two years in grade automatically promotes.

12. Language ability 29

Child's ability to express himself orally so that he may be understood; speak in complete sentences; tell an interesting experience in a simple way, using correct English; write name and short sentences in correct form, using capitals and punctuation.

13. Greatest good to the individual determined on basis of case history 29

Promotion largely determined by answering the questions: In what grade or section will this pupil profit most? Will he profit more by promotion or retention? Will he profit more by being in a new situation?

14. Size and physical development......................... 26

Physical maturity, stature, and general health.

15. Effort, personal responsibility, independence, self-control....... 24

Ability to care for self and own possessions; ability to find out things for himself; self-reliance; habit of completing work assigned.

16. Spelling ability 20

Passing grade in spelling; write name and easy words from dictation; ability to spell 50 words orally and in writing.

17. School citizenship, good schoolroom habits and attitudes........ 17
18. Attendance 14
19. Ability to follow simple directions promptly.................. 7
20. Home factors 6
21. Class distribution based on normal curve—failures limited to five percent 3
22. Report from psychiatrist on doubtful cases.................. 2
23. Administrative conditions, such as size of group; sometimes promote to make room for others............................ 2
24. Perseverance 1

Bases for promotion from sixth grade to seventh grade—Statements from 555 superintendents of schools as to the bases used in their local schools for promoting pupils from sixth grade to seventh grade are summarized below:

Bases for Promotion from Sixth Grade to Seventh Grade

Frequency
of Mention

1. Mastery of minimum essentials in major subjects.............. 231

Fundamentals in arithmetic, reading, and language; mastery of minimum essentials as outlined by the course of study in major subjects: arithmetic, social studies, spelling, grammar, and reading; satisfactory accomplishment in subjects which would indicate ability to carry seventh-grade work; passing all subjects, with one or two possible conditions.

2. Teacher's judgment 205

Promotion decided by teacher; by teacher in conference with supervisor; by teacher and principal.

3. Class marks, scholarship................................. 186

Teacher's record of work done; class recitation marks; completion of course of study with a general average of 50 in all major subjects; daily record plus quarterly and semi-annual examinations.

4. Scores made on standard tests of achievement................ 148
5. Chronological age 100
6. Intelligence rating, I. Q., mental age..................... 92
7. Teacher's, principal's, supervisor's, or superintendent's monthly and term examinations.................................. 67
8. Educational age—time spent in grade..................... 57

Pupils failing for two years are promoted or transferred to the next higher grade.

9. What is best for the individual pupil...................... 51

Every child is placed where the school can help him to do the very best of which he is capable. "Will the associations and exploratory subjects of the junior high school develop the pupil into a better citizen? If so, he should be promoted, regardless of his scholarship." In some school systems, it is not a question of promotion from sixth to seventh grade, it is merely a matter of determining whether the promotion is to a fast group, an average, a slow, or a subnormal group.

10. Pupil's social development and adjustment.................   44

> The ability of pupil not only to work with groups, but to adapt himself to an increasing share of responsibility and freedom.

11. Physical development, size, and general health...............   32

> Possession of adolescent characteristics which places child apart from pre-adolescent group with which he has been associated.

12. None   15

> All sixth-grade pupils are passed on into junior high school.

13. School citizenship   12

> Shows proper attitude toward school and a desire to succeed.

14. Regularity of attendance...................................   10
15. Development of satisfactory study habits....................   10
16. Achievement based on ability...............................   8
17. Ability to interpret silent and oral reading..................   7
18. Home conditions   5
19. Effort   4
20. Pupil case history...   4
21. State examinations   4
22. Class distribution on normal curve.........................   4
23. Future educational needs..................................   3
24. County examinations   3
25. Report from psychiatrist on doubtful cases..................   2
26. Aptitude tests   1

Bases for promotion from eighth grade to ninth grade in schools organized on the 8-4 plan—Statements from 320 superintendents of schools as to the bases used in their local school systems for promoting pupils from eighth grade to ninth grade are summarized below:

Bases for Promotion from Eighth Grade to Ninth Grade

Frequency
of Mention

1. Achievement in major subject-matter fields—promotion by subject on grade of 70 or better................................   172

> Passing mark in major phases of work: mathematics, English, science, and history. Be able to do eighth-grade work well enough to take up ninth-grade work understandingly. In some school systems a pupil must receive a passing grade in all eighth-grade subjects in order to be promoted to the ninth grade. In other school systems, he is allowed one or two conditions.

2. Teacher's judgment   92

> In some cases the teacher's judgment is supplemented by that of the supervisor or the principal.

3. Standard achievement tests............................... 63
4. Record of class work—teacher's marks..................... 59
5. Chronological age 50
6. Intelligence test, mental age, I. Q....................... 49
7. State examinations 46
8. Final examinations prepared by teacher, principal, or superintendent 35
9. Best interest of the individual pupil...................... 30
10. Time spent in school—amount of retardation................ 23
11. County examinations 13
12. Social development and adaptability....................... 12
13. Health and physical development.......................... 8
14. Pupil's interest in and attitude toward school............. 7
15. Effort, power of application.............................. 5
16. Study habits 5

    Pupil's ability to study with progressively less dependence as shown by reading skills, facility of expression, problem solving, and ability to acquire information from outside sources.

17. Regularity of attendance................................. 4
18. Normal curve of distribution............................. 3
19. Pupil case history....................................... 3
20. Report from psychiatrist in doubtful cases................ 2
21. Pupil's future plans..................................... 2
22. Supervisor's examination................................. 2

Bases for promotion from ninth grade to tenth grade in schools organized on the 6-3-3 plan—Statements from 269 superintendents of schools as to the bases used in their local schools for promoting pupils from eighth grade to ninth grade are summarized below:

Bases for Promotion from Ninth Grade to Tenth Grade

Frequency
of Mention

1. Credits earned, subject-matter achievement.................. 153

    Pupils completing a requisite number of required credits of ninth-grade work are automatically passed into tenth grade. Some school systems require 4 credits, some 3¾, some 3½, and some only 3.

2. Promotion by subject—70% passing grade.................. 77
3. Teacher's judgment 47
4. Class marks, teacher's record............................ 38
5. Standard achievement tests.............................. 30
6. Teacher's examinations 29
7. Mental age, intelligence................................. 19
8. Best interests of pupil.................................. 19
9. Chronological age 18
10. Ability to do tenth-grade work.......................... 11

    Sufficient mastery of junior high-school work so that the pupil can work with some degree of efficiency in the senior high school.

11. Social maturity and adjustment...........................   9
12. Health and physical development........................   9
13. Attitude   7
14. State examinations   6
15. Time spent in school—amount of retardation...............   5
16. Future needs and interests.............................   4
17. Regularity of attendance...............................   3
18. Case history   2
19. Application or effort...................................   2
20. Habits of study and initiative...........................   2
21. Normal curve of distribution...........................   1

Bases for graduation from high school—Replies from over 500 superintendents of schools in answer to the question, What are the bases for graduation from your local high schools? were practically unanimous in saying: "Completion of a specified number of academic units." This was the only requirement listed, except in a very few instances "satisfactory moral conduct" was added. These findings agree with a recent study [1] made by the U. S. Office of Education, which shows that the total amount of credit required for high-school graduation ranges from 29 to 36 semester credits or units.[2] Thirty-two semester credits (16 units) is the median requirement, being uniform in 35 states; 30 semester credits is the standard in 10 states.

Comparison of bases for promotion at six different levels—The preceding summary of replies from over 500 superintendents of schools as to bases for promotion in their local school systems shows that the three factors which have most weight in promoting pupils from the kindergarten to the first grade are: (1) chronological age, (2) teacher's judgment, and (3) mental age; from the first grade to the second grade: (1) reading ability, (2) teacher's judgment, and (3) educational achievement; from sixth grade to seventh grade: (1) mastery of minimum essentials in major subjects, (2) teacher's judgment, and (3) class marks or scholarship; from eighth grade to ninth grade: (1) achievement in major subject fields—promotion by subject on grade of 70 or better, (2) teacher's judgment, and (3) standard achievement tests; from ninth grade to tenth grade: (1) credits, (2) school marks, and (3) teacher's judgment; and for graduation from high school, completion of a specified number of academic units.

Beyond the second grade, the acquisition of prescribed subject-matter appears to be the most important factor in current practice in deciding a pupil's promotion. In the kindergarten and in the first grade, there seems

[1] Jessen, Carl A. *Requirements for High-School Graduation.* U. S. Department of the Interior, Office of Education, Bulletin, 1928, No. 21. Washington, D. C.: Government Printing Office. 24 p.

[2] In most localities the following definition of a unit course of study, set up by the North Central Association of Colleges and Secondary Schools, is accepted:

A unit course of study in a secondary school is defined as a course covering an academic year that shall include in the aggregate not less than the equivalent of one hundred twenty 60-minute hours of classroom work—two hours of shop or laboratory work being equivalent to one hour of prepared classroom work.

to be a more definite recognition of the various phases of child growth—mental, physical, social, and emotional—and a definite policy to consider the extent to which the child can profit from the school activities that are ahead. In the higher grades, the tendency is to look backward and to measure closely the degree of success which the pupil has had in meeting a program which has been prescribed. This review of current practice as to bases for pupil promotion at six different levels raises many questions, which call for detailed study on the part of local groups. For example, is current practice consistent with the general principles relative to pupil promotion tentatively set forth in Chapter I, pages 17-22?

C. In Which Elementary Grades and Subjects Is Pupil Failure the Greatest?

In which of the first six grades in your school system do the largest number of pupils fail? In what subject do pupils in this grade fail most often? Replies to these questions were received from 493 superintendents of schools and are summarized in Table 8. This table shows that in cities of all sizes the first grade is the one in which the largest number of pupils fail. Out of 493 superintendents of schools, 344 reported that the first grade is the one in the first six where pupil failure is greatest. The subject of greatest difficulty is reading.

Chief reasons why pupils fail in reading [1]—Each of the 493 school systems was asked to report not only which one of the first six grades has the largest number of pupil failures, but also the subject of greatest difficulty

---

[1] Those interested in remedial work for pupils who are failing in reading will find helpful suggestions in the following references:

Anderson, C. J., and Merton, Elda. "Remedial Work in Reading." *Elementary School Journal* 20: 685-701; 772-91; May and June, 1920.

Anderson, C. J., and Merton, Elda. "Remedial Work in Silent Reading." *Elementary School Journal* 21: 336-48; January, 1921.

Gates, Arthur I. *The Improvement of Reading,* A Program of Diagnostic and Remedial Methods. New York: The Macmillan Company, 1927. 440 p.

Gates, Arthur I. *New Methods in Primary Reading.* New York: Bureau of Publications, Teachers College, Columbia University, 1928. 236 p.

Gist, Arthur S., and King, William A. *The Teaching and Supervision of Reading.* New York: Charles Scribner's Sons, 1927. 337 p.

Gray, Clarence Truman. *Deficiencies in Reading Ability,* Their Diagnosis and Remedies. Boston: D. C. Heath & Co., 1922. 420 p.

Gray, William S. *Remedial Cases in Reading: Their Diagnosis and Treatment.* Supplementary Educational Monographs, No. 22. Chicago: University of Chicago, 1922.

Gray, William S. *Summary of Investigations Relating to Reading.* Supplementary Educational Monographs, No. 28. Chicago: University of Chicago, 1925. 275 p.

Gray, William S. "Summary of Reading Investigations (July 1, 1924, to June 30, 1925), I-IV." *Elementary School Journal* 26: 449-59; 507-18; 574-84; 662-73; February, March, April, and May, 1926.

Gray, William S. "Summary of Reading Investigations (July 1, 1926, to June 30, 1927), I-III." *Elementary School Journal* 28: 443-59; 496-510; 587-602; February, March, and April, 1928.

in that grade and the three chief reasons for failure in that subject. The letter of transmittal sent with this inquiry asked each superintendent, insofar as it was practical, to call together those members of his staff who could furnish accurate data relative to the questions contained in the inquiry. Most of the returns stated that this was done, and these replies were based on actual facts. In some instances, where staff conferences were not held, the replies represent the superintendent's judgment.

Table 8 shows that the subjects of greatest failure in the first six grades are reading and arithmetic. The chief reasons given as to why pupils fail in reading are summarized below and are arranged according to frequency of mention by 493 superintendents of schools:

1. Inability, too young to comprehend—mental immaturity_____ 191

> The mental age of many pupils at time of entrance into first grade is less than six years.

2. Irregularity in attendance_____ 162

> This is due chiefly to illness from contagious childhood diseases, late entrance in school, bad weather, and change of schools.

Continued from preceding page:

Gray, William S., chairman. "Report of the National Committee on Reading." *Twenty-Fourth Yearbook,* National Society for the Study of Education, Part I. Bloomington, Ill.: Public School Publishing Company, 1925. 356 p.

Jacobson, P. B., and Van Dusen, E. C. "Remedial Instruction in Reading in the Ninth Grade." *School Review* 38: 142-46; February, 1930.

Jordan, A. M. *Children's Interests in Reading.* Chapel Hill, N. C.: University of North Carolina Press, 1926. 103 p.

Mingo, Jane. "A List of Materials and Books Suitable for Use in Remedial Reading." *Teachers College Record* 31: 137-47; November, 1929.

National Education Association, Department of Superintendence. "Research in Constructing the Elementary School Curriculum." *Third Yearbook.* Washington, D. C.: the Association, 1925. Chapter V, "Reading," p. 152-204.

Osburn, W. J. "Remedial Work in Reading." *Elementary English Review* 5: 122-26; 150-53; April and May, 1928.

"Silent Reading, Suggestions for Testing and for Corrective Work." *Maryland School Bulletin,* Vol. V, No. 11. Baltimore: Maryland State Department of Education, March, 1924. 88 p.

Stone, Clarence R. *Silent and Oral Reading,* A Practical Handbook of Methods Based on the Most Recent Scientific Investigations. Boston: Houghton Mifflin Company, 1926. 332 p.

Theisen, W. W. "Provisions for Individual Differences in the Teaching of Reading." *Journal of Educational Research* 2: 560-71; September, 1920.

Uhl, Willis L. *Materials of Reading: Their Selection and Organization.* New York: Silver, Burdett & Company, 1924. 386 p.

Willing, Matthew H. *Valid Diagnosis in High School Composition.* Contributions to Education, No. 230. New York: Bureau of Publications, Teachers College, Columbia University, 1926. 64 p.

Woody, Clifford. *Practices in Teaching First-Grade Reading in the Public Schools of Michigan.* Bureau of Educational Reference and Research Bulletin, No. 58. Ann Arbor: School of Education, University of Michigan, 1923. 34 p.

Zirbes, Laura. *Comparative Studies of Current Practice in Reading,* with Techniques for the Improvement of Teaching. Contributions to Education, No. 316. New York: Bureau of Publications, Teachers College, Columbia University, 1928. 229 p.

TABLE 8.—GRADE AND SUBJECT IN WHICH THE LARGEST NUMBER OF PUPILS FAIL IN THE FIRST SIX GRADES IN 493 SCHOOL SYSTEMS

Number and Size of Cities	Subject						
	Reading	Arithmetic	Language or English	Geography	History and Social Studies	Writing	All Subjects
1	2	3	4	5	6	7	8
Under 2,500 (70)							
Grade: First	25	4	4				33
Second	4						4
Third	3	1					4
Fourth	1		1	1			3
Fifth	1	11	1		1		14
Sixth		8	3		1		12
							70
2,500–5,000 (106)							
Grade: First	62	5	2			1	70
Second	1	1					2
Third	2	3	1				6
Fourth	1	9	2				12
Fifth		8	3		1		12
Sixth		3	1				4
							106
5,000–10,000 (105)							
Grade: First	64	4					68
Second	1	1					2
Third	2	2					4
Fourth	2	7					9
Fifth		9	2	1			12
Sixth	2	4	2	2			10
							105
10,000–30,000 (116)							
Grade: First	84	3	1				88
Second	3						3
Third	2	3					5
Fourth		3		3			6
Fifth	1	7		1			9
Sixth		3			2		5
							116
30,000–100,000 (63)							
Grade: First	50	2	4				56
Second							
Third	1	1					2
Fourth	1	2		1			4
Fifth							
Sixth		1					1
							63
Over 100,000 (33)							
Grade: First	29						29
Second	1						1
Third							
Fourth		2					2
Fifth							
Sixth		1					1
							33
Cities of All Sizes (493)							
Grade: First	314	18	11			1	344
Second	10	2					12
Third	10	10	1				21
Fourth	5	23	3	5			36
Fifth	2	35	6	2	2		47
Sixth	2	20	6	2	3		33
Total	343	108	27	9	5	1	493

Read above table thus: Out of 70 superintendents of schools in cities under 2,500 in population, 33 report that the grade in which the largest number of pupils fail is the first. Of these 33 superintendents who report that the greatest amount of pupil failure is in the first grade, 25 state that the subject in which pupils in this grade fail most often is reading; 4 state that it is arithmetic; and 4 others state that it is language or English. Out of the 70 superintendents reporting from cities under 2,500 in population, 4 state that the second grade is the one in which the largest number of pupils fail, and that the subject in which pupils in this grade fail most often is reading.

Similarly read the data for other grades, and for other population groups.

3. Physical and social immaturity of pupils at time of entrance____ 133
4. Language difficulty, resulting from foreign language being spoken in the home_____ 84
5. Lack of background of experience and vocabulary—lack of reading readiness_____ 82

> Often there is not enough of an activity program in which the child is allowed to develop naturally. He is forced into class routine, such as learning to read, before he is ready for it. Pre-primary classes are often necessary.

6. Lack of skill in teaching due to inexperienced and poorly trained teachers _____ 63
7. Pupil illness, poor physical condition, and physical handicaps such as defective sight and hearing, carious teeth, diseased tonsils and adenoids_____ 61
8. Too large classes—too many pupils per teacher to allow for individual help_____ 39
9. Failure of the school to diagnose individual needs and provide proper remedial measures and differentiated materials_____ 34
10. Poor home conditions such as unfavorable background and lack of cooperation with the school_____ 31
11. Inability of some first-grade children to adjust to schoolroom conditions _____ 19
12. Tendency on part of teachers to regard reading as a basal subject. Promotion from first grade is largely based on ability to read, and much emphasis is put on the mechanics of reading_____ 19
13. Difficulty in securing suitable reading materials_____ 17
14. Lack of pupil interest in school work, chiefly in reading_____ 16
15. Emotional instability on part of pupils_____ 10
16. Too rapid progress required. Pupils are crowded ahead faster than they can master the technics of reading_____ 3

Chief reasons why pupils fail in arithmetic [1]—Out of 493 superintendents of schools who reported on the subject which elementary pupils find

---

[1] These are among the references which contain helpful suggestions for those interested in remedial work for pupils who are failing in arithmetic:

"Arithmetic Goals, Suggestions for Testing and for Corrective Work." *Maryland School Bulletin,* Vol. VII, No. 3. Baltimore: Maryland State Department of Education, October, 1925. 67 p.

Brownell, William A. "Remedial Cases in Arithmetic." *Peabody Journal of Education* 7: 100-07; September, 1929. See also: Vol. VII, Nos. 3, 4, 5, and 6; 147-55; 208-17; 290-98; 362-72; November, 1929; January, 1930; March, 1930; and May, 1930, for additional articles on this subject by other writers.

Brueckner, Leo J. *Diagnostic and Remedial Teaching in Arithmetic.* Chicago: John C. Winston Co., 1930. 341 p.

Brueckner, Leo J. "A Necessary Step in the Diagnosis of Pupil Difficulties in Arithmetic." *Bulletin (Third Yearbook)* 3: 290-309; July, 1924. Washington, D. C.: Department of Elementary School Principals, National Education Association.

Buswell, Guy Thomas. "Summary of Arithmetic Investigations (1927)." *Elementary School Journal* 28: 702-09; 730-42; May, June, 1928.

most difficult, 108 named arithmetic. Each superintendent listed what, in his judgment, are the three chief reasons for failure in this subject. They are listed below according to frequency of mention.

1. Poor teaching technics_____ 39

> Poor presentation—failure on the part of the teacher to plan lessons and present them so that they appeal to the child's interest and understanding.

2. Lack of mental ability on the part of pupils_____ 29
3. Lack of interest which results in lack of application_____ 23
4. Lack of skill in fundamental operations_____ 21
5. Lack of comprehension of thought problems in arithmetic—failure of pupil to grasp number significance and number combinations and processes_____ 20
6. Standards of achievement in arithmetic are more exact and therefore more arbitrarily administered_____ 19

Buswell, Guy Thomas, and Judd, Charles H. *Summary of Educational Investigations Relating to Arithmetic.* Supplementary Educational Monographs, No. 27. Chicago: University of Chicago, 1925. 212 p.

Greene, Harry A. "A Critique of Remedial and Drill Materials in Arithmetic." *Journal of Educational Research* 21: 262-76; April, 1930.

Judd, Charles H. *Psychological Analysis of the Fundamentals of Arithmetic.* Supplementary Educational Monographs, No. 32. Chicago: University of Chicago, 1927. 121 p.

Merton, Elda L. "The Elimination of Mechanical Difficulties." *Bulletin (Second Yearbook)* 2: 395-411; July, 1923. Washington, D. C.: Department of Elementary School Principals, National Education Association.

Myers, Garry Cleveland. *The Prevention and Correction of Errors in Arithmetic.* Chicago: The Plymouth Press, 1925. 75 p.

National Committee on Mathematical Requirements. *The Reorganization of Mathematics in Secondary Education,* Final Report of the Committee. Boston: Houghton Mifflin Company, 1927. 181 p.

National Council of Teachers of Mathematics. *Curriculum Problems in Teaching Mathematics,* Second Yearbook. New York: Bureau of Publications, Teachers College, Columbia University, 1927. p. 154-72.

National Education Association, Department of Superintendence. *Research in Constructing the Elementary School Curriculum.* Third Yearbook. Washington, D. C.; Department of Superintendence, National Education Association, 1925. Chapter III, "Arithmetic," p. 35-109.

National Society for the Study of Education. *Twenty-Ninth Yearbook,* Report of the Society's Committee on Arithmetic. Bloomington, Ill.: Public School Publishing Company, 1930. 749 p.

O'Brien, F. P. "Improvement of Instruction in Arithmetic," *Bulletin of Education,* Vol. I, No. 4. Lawrence, Kan.: University of Kansas, October, 1927. 42 p.

Osburn, Worth James. *Corrective Arithmetic.* 2v. New York: Houghton Mifflin Company. (v. 1, 1924, 182 p. v. 2, 1929, 279 p.)

Reeve, William D. *A Diagnostic Study of the Teaching Problems in High-School Mathematics.* Boston: Ginn and Company, 1926. 117 p.

Young, J. W. A. *The Teaching of Mathematics in the Elementary and the Secondary School.* New York: Longmans, Green & Company, 1924. 451 p.

7. Difficulty of subject and lack of differentiation of materials to fit pupils of different levels of ability_____ 15
8. Pupil's inability to read arithmetic problems understandingly____ 14
9. Irregular pupil attendance_____ 13
10. Nature of arithmetic such that it requires judgment and reasoning power, rather than memorization_____ 13
11. Failure of the school to diagnose individual needs and provide proper remedial measures_____ 12
12. Lack of emotional stability on the part of pupils_____ 11
13. Poor home conditions, such as unfavorable background and lack of cooperation with the school_____ 9
14. Poor arithmetic textbooks_____ 7
15. Insufficient purposeful drill_____ 5
16. Language difficulty due to foreign parentage_____ 4

In which of the first six grades in your school system do next to the largest number of pupils fail? In what subject do pupils in this grade fail most often?—The replies to these questions from 428 superintendents of schools are summarized in Table 9, which shows that the grade in which next to the largest number of pupils fail is the second. However, there is no such unanimity of opinion expressed here as there was in Table 8. The 428 superintendents of schools reporting differ widely as to the grade in which next to the largest number of pupils fail—at least 50 vote for each one of the first six grades. The subject in which next to the largest number of pupils fail is arithmetic. When the first grade is omitted from consideration, arithmetic is the subject in which failure is greatest, according to superintendents of schools.

D. What Are the Best Means for Reducing Pupil Failure in Elementary and Secondary Schools?

Means for reducing pupil failure which ordinarily lie within the reach of the classroom teacher—The following means are ranked in order of frequency of mention by 555 superintendents of schools. They are a summary of replies from superintendents of schools to this question: From your experience, what are the six best means for reducing pupil failure, which ordinarily lie within the reach of the classroom teacher? For example, diagnosing reading difficulties of individual pupils.

Means by Which Teachers May Reduce Pupil Failure
(Reported by 555 superintendents of schools)

1. Using achievement and diagnostic tests followed up by special help and remedial work—test for deficiencies and diagnose pupil difficulties in each subject _____ 374[1]

---

[1] The numbers in this column are the numbers of times each of these means was suggested by 555 superintendents of schools when asked to list from their experience the six best means for reducing pupil failure, which ordinarily lie within the reach of the classroom teacher.

TABLE 9.—GRADE AND SUBJECT IN WHICH NEXT TO THE LARGEST NUMBER OF PUPILS FAIL IN THE FIRST SIX GRADES IN 428 SCHOOL SYSTEMS

Number and Size of Cities	Subject					
	Arithmetic	Reading	Language or English	Geography	History and Social Studies	All Subjects
1	2	3	4	5	6	7
Under 2,500 (55)						
Grade: First...........	1	2				3
Second..........		9	1			10
Third..........	4	3				7
Fourth.........	6	1		3		10
Fifth..........	7	2	3			12
Sixth..........	10	1	1		1	13
						55
2,500–5,000 (85)						
Grade: First..........	3	5	2			10
Second..........		13	1			14
Third..........	4	5			1	10
Fourth.........	9	1	2			12
Fifth..........	6	4		1	1	12
Sixth..........	16	4	5	2		27
						85
5,000–10,000 (91)						
Grade: First..........	1	11	1			13
Second..........		18				18
Third..........	3	5	1			9
Fourth.........	9	5	2		2	18
Fifth..........	7	1	3	2	1	14
Sixth..........	12	1	3	1	2	19
						91
10,000–30,000 (107)						
Grade: First..........	4	10	1			15
Second..........	2	20	1			23
Third..........	7	5				12
Fourth.........	17	2	1	1		21
Fifth..........	13	5	1	4		23
Sixth..........	8	2	2		1	13
						107
30,000–100,000 (57)						
Grade: First..........	2	2	1			5
Second..........	1	13				14
Third..........	7	3				10
Fourth.........	5		1			6
Fifth..........	7	5	1	2		15
Sixth..........	5	1	1			7
						57
Over 100,000 (33)						
Grade: First..........	2	2				4
Second..........	3	13				16
Third..........	1	1				2
Fourth.........	3					3
Fifth..........	2		1	1		4
Sixth..........	2		2			4
						33
Cities of All Sizes (428)						
Grade: First..........	13	32	5			50
Second..........	6	86	3			95
Third..........	26	22	1		1	50
Fourth.........	49	9	6	4	2	70
Fifth..........	42	17	9	10	2	80
Sixth..........	53	9	14	3	4	83
Total................	189	175	38	17	9	428

Read the above table thus: Out of 55 superintendents of schools in cities under 2,500 in population, 3 report that the grade in which next to the largest number of pupils fail is the first.   Of these, one reports that the subject in this grade in which most pupils fail is arithmetic.   Two other superintendents of schools report that it is reading.

Out of these 55 superintendents, 10 report that the grade in which next to the largest number of pupils fail is the second.   Of these 10, 9 report that the subject in the second grade in which pupils fail most often is reading; one reports that it is language.

Similarly read the data for other grades and for other population groups.

2. Giving individual attention to pupil needs and interests_____ 300

   Teachers sufficiently interested to learn to know pupils as individuals, to show sympathetic understanding, and to give individual help during class periods and in personal conferences.

3. Grouping according to ability, providing differentiated courses of study, and applying teaching methods suitable to each ability level _____ 199

4. Keeping work within the grasp of the pupil_____ 175

   Study individual needs and then formulate units of instruction in the light of them; give pupils of low ability simple assignments; develop units of work that will tax the powers of superior pupils—reorganize the course of study.

5. Learning about pupil's home conditions and securing cooperation of parents _____ 170

   Visit parents of absentees and of children whose work is unsatisfactory; have knowledge of pupil's home and an understanding of home difficulties and personal ambitions; hold conferences with parents after special reports are made to them; strive to secure a fine cooperation with the home in developing a satisfactory attitude on the part of the child.

6. Diagnosing reading difficulties of individual pupils and giving remedial treatment _____ 157

   Improving reading ability of every pupil beginning in the first grade; encouraging good reading habits; reading with attention to details; training pupils to comprehend what they read; putting more emphasis on rapid silent reading; providing more easy reading that the child may give his attention to the content and meaning of the story, rather than to the words, and thus form the habit of thinking while he reads; introducing wide range of recreatory reading to arouse new interests; and securing careful attention to and feeling of responsibility for vocabulary building in content subjects.

7. Creating an esprit de corps _____ 153

   Maintaining high morale; developing enthusiasm for subject by teacher; arouse sufficient interest in each subject to carry the pupil over the necessary mechanics of the subject; encouraging close concentration through securing the interest and effort of the child in successfully completing the work required; judicious use of praise rather than reprimand; sufficient freedom in work to satisfy the interests of children and to use those interests to motivate the school activities; capitalize success in certain lines as a motive for achievement of attainable immediate goals in others; and appeal to pride and ambition of pupil.

8. Improving teaching methods _____ 119

   Give more thought to the preparation of the daily lesson plan; make liberal use of teaching plans and devices; vary method of attack; use project method; develop socialized recitation; create a problem situation as a technic of lesson assignment; use laboratory type of class procedure; differentiate methods for slow pupils; and adjust manner of thinking to the thought capacity of the child.

9. Providing thorough, purposeful, and motivated drill for accuracy _____ 106

> See that the class and the individual student have drill exercises suited to their needs; give more time and attention to a few subjects; drill for thought getting; teach all subjects with the idea of mastery of minimum requirements in mind.

10. Teaching pupils how to study and how to organize their work_ 96

> Develop good study habits; teach children what mastery means through right study habits in school; develop general aids for studying and methods of attack which apply to particular subjects such as spelling, social studies, and geometry. Supervised study—make recitation a helping period instead of a hearing period.

11. Improving health of children _____ 91

> Have health inspection each morning; refer cases of illness to doctor or nurse; see that physical handicaps are diagnosed and corrected; emphasize necessity of health habits; give attention to physical comfort in classrooms—adjustable seats, proper lighting, correct temperature, and fresh air.

12. Giving individual instruction _____ 84

> Individual instruction particularly in tool subjects; and, according to one superintendent of schools, "At determined points of difficulty, keeping a record of these points encountered, and laying special emphasis on them during the following year."

13. Securing better school attendance_____ 50

> Make effort to reduce absence; careful check up of all pupil absences; parents promptly notified of child's absence; more attention to pupil's work after absence.

14. Improving one's professional training while in service _____ 40

> Through summer school attendance, extension courses, and professional reading, secure better professional equipment.

15. Applying flexible promotion .standards _____ 32

> Develop a democratic promotion scheme, for example: Base promotion on pupil's attainment as compared with his ability; provide extra promotion for superior pupils, put less stress on arbitrary grade standards and more stress on individual growth.

16. Arranging periods for special help for pupils _____ 31
17. Having pupils keep their individual records of achievement __ 27

> Individual and class graphs of achievement kept by pupils under supervision of teachers serve as a means of encouragement and stimulus.

18. Working for a definite aim—specific objectives_____ 26

> More definite objectives on the part of both teacher and pupils; definite standards of attainment should be set up, so that pupils may realize the full year's requirements. One superintendent of schools recommends daily, weekly, and monthly objectives.

19. Taking special care in making lesson assignments clear _____ 22

20. Providing a working atmosphere in the classroom—this will include suitable teaching equipment, supplies, and supplementary reading _____ 22

21. Dividing large classes into small groups_____ 20

> If large classes are necessary, there can be smaller groups arranged within each class.

22. Providing expert guidance for pupils _____ 20

> This will include proper direction in choice of subject-matter.

23. Developing a child-centered activity program, arranging for greater pupil participation _____ 18

> In this program the teacher's chief interest is in developing pupil's abilities, rather than in teaching subjects.

24. Seeing that practical textbooks suited to the pupil's interest and vocabulary are provided _____ 15

25. Giving immediate attention to low grades _____ 13

> Diagnosing difficulties at time when best results for improvement can be brought about. Checking on all failures at the end of each report period and not waiting until the end of the term.
>
> One superintendent of schools reports that each teacher in his school system makes a weekly report to his principal, indicating names of pupils who are failing to do standard work, what he thinks are the reasons for each pupil's failure, together with a statement of what steps he has taken or proposes to take to help the pupil remedy his failure.
>
> Another superintendent of schools reports that all his teachers make mid-semester reports on pupil failures to their principals, who notify the parents of the pupils concerned.

26. Developing self-confidence in pupils and encouraging them to assume responsibility for their own success _____ 12

27. Requiring home study _____ 11

> Suggesting proper methods of home study through bulletins to parents; getting parents to take more interest in having pupils do home reading. In extreme cases, require home study and daily report plan.

28. Promoting rivalry between classes _____ 10

29. Suggesting vacation school to potential failures _____ 9

30. Holding pupils back who are unprepared _____ 9

> Hold pupils back in primary grades unless sure they are really ready for promotion; hold back all pupils who are on the border line of failure.

31. Assuming a definite responsibility for pupil failures_____ 9

32. Using visual aids _____ 8

33. Integrating subject-matter and correlating subjects _____ 6

34. Using brighter pupils to help the slower ones _____ 6

35. Giving pupils share in setting up aims _____ 6

> See that each child is given a task, a plan, and freedom of his own choosing.

36. Tutoring outside of school _____ 6
37. Helping pupils to eliminate speech defects or language difficulties 5
38. Giving slow pupils more time _____ 4
39. Making trial promotions _____ 4
40. Developing proper system of marking _____ 4
41. Referring difficult cases to psychiatrist for clinical treatment __ 4
42. Making work as concrete as possible _____ 4
43. Teaching pupils to reason _____ 3

> Start reasoning process to functioning earlier—Stop the memorizing plan to understand things.

44. Applying knowledge of laws of learning _____ 3
45. Holding pupils responsible for work assigned _____ 3
46. Administering preliminary tests, before pupil elects subject ___ 2
47. Assuming scientific attitude in solving difficulties of pupils ____ 1
48. Bringing into play the influence of class opinion in controlling the individual pupil _____ 1
49. Finding something that each child can do fairly well and using that as his medium of expression through difficulties _____ 1
50. Enriching vocabulary of foreign child _____ 1

Means for reducing pupil failure which involve a change in educational policy and administrative reorganization—As in the preceding section, the following means are ranked in order of frequency of mention by 555 superintendents of schools. The following pages summarize replies to this question: From your experience, what are the six best means for reducing pupil failure, which involve a change in educational policy and administrative reorganization? For example, homogeneous grouping and differentiation of courses of study.

Means for Reducing Pupil Failure through Changes in Educational Policy and Administrative Reorganization
(Reported by 555 superintendents of schools)

1. Organizing homogeneous grouping _____ 243

> Division into groups according to ability (the bases for classification should include other factors than intelligence), with flexible regulations which will permit transfer when achievement or lack of achievement justifies.

2. Differentiation of curriculums and courses of study to fit pupils of different levels of ability _____ 94

> Better organized and graded courses of study which more nearly meet present-day life needs and are adjusted to the needs of children. Rich and flexible curriculum adapted to all types of children. Minimum and maximum requirements in quantity as well as quality of work for each grade level. Reorganization of material to provide greater inherent interest.

3. Applying rational promotional practices _____ 94

> Remove artificial barriers for promotion; promote child at any time during the term when his rate of growth and development shows that he is ready; promote child on basis of what is best for him individually; keep each pupil doing the best he can rather than establish a common hurdle for all; develop policy of promotion in which "failure" is not a means for stimulation to better work, but a result of poor adaptation.

4. Providing special classes _____ 88

> Special classes for children physically handicapped; low I. Q.; backward or atypical; new entrants; exceptionally bright; with special talents; overage; maladjusted; with foreign language difficulty; weak in a particular subject; and with a special vocational interest.

5. Employing better teachers _____ 84

> Selection of higher-powered teachers who are more experienced and better trained, and through inservice training keeping them up to a high grade of efficiency.

6. Using standardized tests _____ 80

> A definite testing program, including mental tests, accomplishment tests, diagnostic tests, and prognostic tests.

7. Adapting the schools to meet individual needs of pupils _____ 78

> Provision for individual differences, including individual attention and in some cases individual instruction.

8. Reducing size of classes _____ 74

> Smaller classes with provision for individual contacts between pupil and teacher.
> One superintendent of schools suggested increasing the number of pupils per teacher in some subjects and reducing the number in other subjects; another suggested smaller groups in beginning first grade; another, smaller classes for those of limited ability; and many asked for a general reduction in pupil-teacher load.

9. Developing a consistent program of child guidance or counseling 58

> An adequate plan of school counseling—educational, health, social, and vocational guidance—in both the junior and senior high schools under the direction in each building of one or more specially trained school counselors.

10. Providing helping or coaching teacher _____ 53

> Assignment of extra teachers to each school to instruct slow children individually or in groups. Special teachers well trained and fitted temperamentally.

11. Providing an accurate supervisory program _____ 49

> Definite intelligent supervision, which improves teachers in service, encourages study of pupils, and results in creative teaching. More unified supervision, including research, diagnosis, and follow up.

12. Securing better motivation through project teaching, enriched materials, and pupil activity programs _____ 46

13. Carrying out a vigorous health program _____ 42

Health program designed to discover and remedy, as far as possible, physical conditions which interfere with school progress—better physical environment, health service which will exclude pupils with contagious diseases including colds, physical examination of all pupils, corrective physical training, and health courses designed to develop good health habits and proper attitudes and ideals toward health.

14. Providing better equipment _____ 34

Buildings, equipment, and materials of instruction suitable to program of studies and varied needs of pupils, adequate library and laboratory facilities, and teaching aids.

15. Introducing departmental instruction _____ 28

Some superintendents of schools urged that departmental work be introduced as low as the third grade, others that it be introduced in grades 4-6, and some did not want it until the sixth grade or above.

16. Administering a well-balanced program of extra-curriculum activities _____ 28

Increase pupil's interests through music, art, dramatics, and athletics; provide adequate supervision of extra-curriculum activities.

17. Organizing the schools on supervised study plan _____ 26
18. Establishing closer contacts with parents _____ 24
19. Introducing new methods of organization and teaching _____ 21
20. Employing visiting teachers _____ 20
21. Lengthening the school day or the school year _____ 19

A longer school day which permits the inclusion of many worthwhile and interesting activities; a school day long enough to complete all work in classrooms, thus eliminating home work; longer school term.

22. Admitting pupils to first grade only when they are mature enough to do first-grade work _____ 18

Admission to first grade only to those apparently ready to progress, regardless of age, but with sub-primary provisions for those not ready.

23. Setting up definite educational aims _____ 17

While some superintendents of schools argued for a clear-cut definition of objectives expressed in measurable terms, others urged that there be less concern over mastery of skills and technics and more emphasis put on attitudes and ideals in learning.

24. Revising marking system _____ 17

Insistence that teachers have a clear notion of what rating or marking really means; marking and report system which emphasizes citizenship qualities; requiring different standards of pupils of different levels of ability—several superintendents of schools eliminate grades on report cards, giving instead a statement as to whether or not the pupil's work is satisfactory, i. e., whether he is doing his best.

25. Improving faculty meetings and faculty relationships _____ . 17

Less formalism in faculty relationships—securing the understanding and cooperation of teachers through committee work and study of common problems; regular teachers' meetings for organized study of pupils' needs, prevention of pupil failures, and discussion of individual cases.

26. Offering more elective subjects _____ 15
27. Providing parallel curriculums _____ 14
28. Enforcing attendance laws more strictly _____ 14
29. Supplying more carefully selected textbooks _____ 13
30. Providing summer classes _____ 11
31. Organizing larger administrative units, consolidation of small schools _____ 11
32. Making child growth and development the chief objective of education _____ 10
33. Maintaining a better system of records, less dependence on memory, careful cumulative records _____ 9
34. Encouraging teachers to pursue professional courses while in service, which will react on the work of the classroom _____ 9
35. Requiring fewer subjects, providing a lighter course of study __ 9
36. Improving conditions for the teaching personnel _____ 9

Better salary schedules, partial salary during sabbatical leave, adequate retirement system, and financial recognition of professional growth.

37. Publication of school bulletins or use of some other definite method of enlightening the teaching corps regarding definite policies or methods _____ 7
38. Providing psychological clinic for study and treatment of maladjusted pupils _____ 7
39. Building up a better morale among the whole teaching body ___ 5
40. Analyzing causes of pupil failure throughout the school system 5
41. Exercising great care in placing pupils _____ 5

Careful placement of late entrants and out-of-town entrants; right placement in early grades; grade placement on basis of social and physical, as well as mental, development.

42. Revising present time allotments in local courses of study _____ 5
43. Introducing "home-room" organization in junior and senior high school _____ 3
44. Supplying aids for visual instruction _____ 3
45. Carrying out cycle organization where teacher stays with the same group for several years _____ 2
46. Separating the sexes in certain branches or throughout the secondary school period _____ 2
47. Insisting on more home study _____ 2
48. Organizing a demonstration school _____ 2
49. Bringing about a closer articulation of the various administrative units _____ 1

E. What Is the Value of Semi-Annual as Compared with Annual Promotions?

On what promotion bases are elementary schools organized?—Table 10 shows that in cities under 10,000 in population the great majority of schools promote pupils annually. In cities of 10,000-30,000, promotion practice is about equally divided between the annual and the semi-annual plans. In cities 30,000-100,000, 75 percent of the 68 school systems answering this question follow the semi-annual promotion plan—as compared with 25 percent that promote pupils annually. In cities over 100,000, the ratio is approximately 5 to 1 in favor of semi-annual promotions.

It is interesting to note that out of 555 school systems reporting, within the past ten years 51 have changed from semi-annual to annual promotions; and 68 have changed from annual to semi-annual. Of the 41 school systems contemplating a change in promotion plans at the present time, 26, or 63 percent, are planning to change from the semi-annual to the annual; 10, or 25 percent, from the annual to the semi-annual; and 5, or 12 percent, are planning to promote pupils at any time during the year—three of these are somewhat in favor of quarterly promotions.

Among the reasons given by those school systems which are contemplating a change from semi-annual to annual promotions are these:

1. Much time is lost in semi-annual reorganization.

2. Just as teachers begin to understand the nature and needs of their pupils they are transferred and each teacher has a new and strange group.

3. Covering the same subject-matter twice a year is deadening to teachers.

TABLE 10.—PROMOTION BASES ON WHICH ELEMENTARY SCHOOLS ARE ORGANIZED IN CITIES OF SIX POPULATION GROUPS

Size of City	Present Promotion Plan				Change Has Been Made in Past Ten Years		Is a Change from Present Practice Contemplated?			
	Semi-annual	Annual	Blank	Total number re-port-ing	From semi-annual to annual	From annual to semi-annual	Yes	From annual to semi-annual	From semi-annual to annual	To any time during the year
Under 2,500...	11	66	7	84	9	7	2	0	2	0
2,500–5,000...	26	81	8	115	16	16	7	5	2	0
5,000–10,000...	45	68	6	119	13	21	12	3	7	2
10,000–30,000...	59	62	4	125	10	16	10	1	8	1[1]
30,000–100,000.	51	17	2	70	2	7	6	0	4	2[1]
Over 100,000...	33	6	3	42	1[2]	1	4	1	3	0
Total	225	300	30	555	51	68	41	10	26	5

[1] Several school systems which reported that they planned to promote pupils at any time during the school year stated that they leaned toward the quarterly promotion plan.

[2] Richmond, Va., has changed from semi-annual to annual promotions in one or two of its schools, according to Miss Charlotte Staokley, Supervisor, Primary Grades.

Read the above table as follows: Out of 84 school systems in cities under 2,500 population, 11 have semi-annual promotions, 66 have annual promotions, and 7 did not report on this point. Within the past ten years, 9 of these 84 school systems have changed from semi-annual to annual promotions; and 7 have changed from annual to semi-annual promotions. At the present time 2 of these 84 school systems are contemplating changing from the semi-annual to the annual. Similarly read data from school systems in cities of the other five population groups.

4. Frequently midyear classes are too small. This is especially true in the junior and senior high schools in small school systems.

5. When half-year grades are small due to the semi-annual promotion plan, a teacher often has to handle two groups as 2A and 3B. Annual promotions permit of improved teaching through homogeneous grouping, for then each teacher has only one group or grade.

6. The semi-annual promotion scheme is very expensive because half-year classes in the junior and senior high school are small, making necessary the employment of too many teachers.

7. With ability grouping and trial promotions, the old reason of saving time by semi-annual promotions loses its force.

8. Semi-annual promotions retard further refinement in homogeneous grouping; the range in mental or achievement age in regular grades includes all pupils in the midyear groups.

9. Many parents do not like to start pupils in the primary department in midyear. Others do not like to have pupils enter high school in midyear.

10. The idea that semi-annual promotions will gain time for the pupil is largely imaginary. Many high-school pupils who graduate in the middle of the year continue in high school to the end of the year, for they cannot enter many colleges until the following September.

One superintendent of schools in a city of over 100,000 in population, which now has the semi-annual plan of pupil promotion, writes as follows:

Excessive retardation and elimination have grown out of the assumption that there are grade standards. To insure continuous progress we are considering a unit plan of work that will make unnecessary needless repetition. Progress should be continuous, and minor reorganizations and reclassifications can be made as seems desirable; major adjustments will be made once a year. These major adjustments will be equivalent to promotions, but there will be no assumption that all pupils have attained the same standard of achievement.

Among the reasons given by school systems which are contemplating a change from annual to semi-annual promotions are these:

1. If pupils may enter in midyear, they do not need to enter when too young as often happens, neither will they lose a half year or more of time.

2. Semi-annual promotions give greater flexibility and more chance to adjust the curriculum and organization of the school to the needs of the individual child.

3. Semi-annual promotion is fair to the pupil. The capable can be advanced more easily; the slow or unsatisfactory pupil does not get set back so far as to utterly discourage him. Pupils who fail lose only a half year instead of a whole year.

While only 5 out of the 555 school systems reporting are contemplating a change in promotion plans whereby pupils may be promoted at any time during the school year, the following comments made by their superintendents of schools show what strong convictions they hold:

Why talk about annual or semi-annual promotions? Neither name means a thing. It is what is done with the boys and girls that counts. Promotion should be continuous hour by hour. The less often pupils change teachers the better, because the better a teacher knows all sides of a pupil's personality the more profitably can she guide him. It might be well for the primary teacher to stay with the same group three years, and the intermediate teacher the same.

Neither annual promotions nor semi-annual promotions seem to satisfy. Although we have midyear promotions, we promote a considerable number of elementary pupils about each quarter. We find that, when achievement and intelligence tests are given, a large percentage of elementary pupils have surpassed in achievement other members of their group and that a regrouping is necessary. These tests are usually given about November and April; and we have, therefore, almost adopted a quarterly system of promotion. I believe promotions should be based on individual accomplishments and that all traditional grouping should be unmercifully smashed.

There is no real need for two special promotion periods with the usual disruption of school. We will promote at any time when the pupil is prepared. We would like to forget the idea of "promotion." If pupils are properly classified the school's training should be gradual, continued progress from the kindergarten through the high school.

Any promotion either annual or semi-annual emphasizes in the minds of pupils, parents, and even teachers that promotion is something that takes place at periodic intervals, instead of being a gradual day-by-day satisfactory progress of the pupils in all phases of the school program.

We want to consider a scheme of promotion which will look after individual differences of children more carefully and will, at the same time, hold to the social age of the child. We wish to eliminate retardation.

To what extent are special cases promoted at any time during the school year?—To secure information on this point, the following question was included in the inquiry sent to superintendents of schools: While the majority of your elementary pupil promotions occur either annually or semi-annually, is it your policy to promote a considerable number of special cases at any time during the school year?

Table 11 summarizes the replies to this question from 504 superintendents of schools.

TABLE 11.—EXTENT TO WHICH SPECIAL ELEMENTARY SCHOOL PROMOTIONS ARE MADE IN CITIES OF SIX POPULATION GROUPS

| Size of City | Promotion at Any Time During School Year | | | | Blank | Total |
| | Yes | | No | | | |
	Number	Percent of Those Replying	Number	Percent of Those Replying		
Under 2,500............	40	52	37	48	7	84
2,500–5,000............	55	51	53	49	11	119
5,000–10,000...........	49	48	53	52	13	115
10,000–30,000..........	63	56	50	44	12	125
30,000–100,000.........	40	60	27	40	3	70
Over 100,000...........	22	59	15	41	5	42
Total...............	269	53	235	47	51	555

Table 11 shows that 269, or 53 percent, of the 504 school systems reporting promote a considerable number of special cases at any time during the school year. In cities of over 10,000 in population, from 56 to 60 percent of the school systems reporting follow this practice. In addition, many of the other 235 school systems reporting stated that they promoted a few special cases at any time during the school year.

Advantages and Disadvantages of Semi-Annual Promotions

What are the chief advantages of the semi-annual promotion plan?— The inquiry sent to superintendents of schools asked not only for information as to whether the annual or semi-annual promotion plan was followed, but also included this question: What, in your judgment, are the chief advantages and disadvantages of the promotion plan followed at present in your school system?

This section summarizes the replies from 225 superintendents of school systems where the semi-annual promotion plan is followed. The arguments in favor of semi-annual promotions are arranged in order of frequency of mention:

1. Semi-annual promotions make it unnecessary for pupils to repeat entire year's work, if they fail either on account of non-attendance, lack of application, or inability. A pupil frequently needs to repeat a part of the work of a grade, when it would not be wise for him to repeat the work of an entire year. Summer, or vacation, schools are of more use when they can make up a half year for pupils rather than attempt a whole year.

2. Semi-annual promotions result in a more flexible school organization— they make frequent adjustments possible.

3. Semi-annual promotions make it easier to accelerate those of superior ability. Double and trial promotions can be more easily made. Frequently a pupil can do three terms' work in two, or he can skip a half year with less loss.

4. With semi-annual promotions the cost of operating the schools is less. If it is necessary to have a pupil repeat his work, it is more economical to have the repetition restricted to a half year.

5. Semi-annual promotions result in more frequent evaluation of the achievements of pupils. They force a careful evaluation of pupil status twice instead of once a year—in fact, they compel frequent judgment of pupils by teachers.

According to one superintendent of schools:

Pupils as well as teachers work better and are held to a higher standard of achievement by the semi-annual promotion because of the shorter period, and the kind of inventory that comes at the end of the term. There is always something challenging in a new start—in the chance to correct mistakes and to try out new schemes, and even in the change of "scenery" that comes from new classes and new teachers.

6. Semi-annual promotions make it easier to accommodate the transient school population which enters by transfer from other school systems, especially from those systems where the semi-annual promotion plan is followed. They also enable pupils forced to be out of school temporarily to return with minimum loss of credit and time.

7. Where ability grouping is not practiced, semi-annual promotions usually provide fewer extremes in ability and achievement than do annual promotions. They tend to keep pupils of more nearly the same social age together.

8. The goal of promotion is more immediate where promotions are made semi-annually. Pupils are stimulated to greater effort since there is an accounting twice during the year, and their goals are more real to them than when they are nine or ten months in the future.

9. Semi-annual promotions result in less discouragement for pupils. They obviate the condition where a pupil relaxes effort early in the year when he knows he is going to fail, as is frequently the case in annual promotions.

10. Semi-annual promotions reduce the amount of retardation in a school system. [1]

11. Semi-annual promotions permit midyear entrance. Some pupils gain a half year by entering at the middle of the year. Entrance into the kindergarten is not delayed for six months or more. Hence children are nearer the same social age when they enter.

12. Semi-annual promotions result in more teacher contacts. A pupil has a shorter time with a poor teacher. Or if he doesn't get on well with a particular teacher, he has a chance to change at the end of a half year. One superintendent of schools writes, "Twenty weeks is long enough for any pupil to be under a poor teacher."

13. Semi-annual promotions call for a definite curriculum for each half year. The result is that the curriculum is better fitted to the pupil. Basic curriculum units short enough not to become wearisome to teacher and pupil have to be provided.

14. Parents do not object so seriously if pupils are retained an extra half year in a grade as they do when they are retained a full year.

15. Semi-annual promotions provide for administrative relief in the shifting of pupils and teachers if necessary.

16. Semi-annual promotions help to hold pupils in school longer.

17. With semi-annual promotions, each teacher becomes more of a specialist in his half-year's work.

18. Semi-annual promotions distribute the enrolment load over the school year. As a result, in a large school system, according to one superintendent of schools, fewer teachers are required.

What are the chief disadvantages of the semi-annual promotion plan? [2]— Each of the 225 superintendents whose schools are organized on the semi-annual promotion plan were asked to list the disadvantages, as well as the advantages, of semi-annual promotions. In the following paragraphs the disadvantages are listed according to frequency of mention.

1. In small school systems, semi-annual promotions bring too many small sections into both the elementary school and the high school at the beginning of the second semester.

Small sections require classrooms and cost as much to teach as large sections. Where some sections are large and others small, there is an unequal distribution of teachers' time to pupil groups.

---

[1] For objective data on this point see: Greene, Harry A. "The Effects of Annual and Semi-Annual Promotions as Revealed by Pupil Progress." *American School Board Journal*, 78: 67, 86, and 89; May, 1929.
[2] See also: "Are Semi-Annual Promotions Desirable?" *Journal of Education*, 111: 387-88, 471-73, and 499-500; April 7, April 28, and May 5, 1930.

In very small elementary schools, semi-annual promotions result in a lack of efficiency through the necessity of the teacher having to teach two or more grades in a single classroom.

Small high schools face the difficulty of grouping pupils so as to give the proper elections at the proper time.

2. Semi-annual promotions require too frequent exchange of teachers; as a result a teacher does not have time to get well acquainted with his pupils.

Often a teacher-pupil contact is broken at a critical time. A teacher may be working for certain standards which can only be attained by a program extending over a longer period than a half year.

Semi-annual promotions do not enable a teacher to check pupil progress throughout the year following diagnosis of the situation in September followed by a remedial program. They also interrupt the operation of large units of work.

3. Homogeneous groupings are more difficult to arrange when pupils are promoted semi-annually. In many small school systems, semi-annual promotions prevent homogeneous groupings.

4. Semi-annual promotions often result in loss of time in reorganization of classes at the beginning of each term. Furthermore, new situations may result in loss of time for pupils. Too often a child has just adjusted himself to a situation when he is taken away from that and put into another which also requires a period of adjustment.

5. Semi-annual promotions multiply the work of organization and involve a great deal of administrative work.

6. With semi-annual promotions, a larger teaching force is required because classes are smaller.

7. Semi-annual promotions increase the amount of clerical work.

8. Pupils graduating from a school in midyear are at a disadvantage when they immediately enter another school. The school receiving them is usually not so well prepared to take them at midyear as in September.

9. High-school promotion in midyear without having midyear graduation requires students to finish in $3\frac{1}{2}$ or $4\frac{1}{2}$ years, or in four years without graduation exercises.

In some high schools, many midyear graduates who expect to enter college in the fall merely mark time as post-graduates from January to June.

10. Semi-annual promotions make schedule and program-making more complex.

11. With semi-annual promotions, some teachers tend to withhold promotion in border-line cases because such pupils "will lose only half a year."

12. With semi-annual promotions, some parents over-stress rate of progress of pupils through the grades; others worry about children entering school at mid-term.

13. With semi-annual promotions, work is more likely to become stale for teachers. When teaching the same half year's work over and over again, unprogressive teachers get in a deep rut.

14. Semi-annual promotions encourage a teacher to think in terms of grade levels rather than pupil growth.

15. Testing and promotion expenses are doubled with semi-annual promotions.

Advantages and Disadvantages of Annual Promotions

What are the advantages of the annual promotion plan?—The preceding section summarized the advantages and disadvantages of semi-annual promotions cited by 225 superintendents of school systems where promotions are made semi-annually. This section summarizes the arguments for and against annual promotions which were made by 300 superintendents of school systems where promotions are made annually.

The advantages of the annual promotion plan, arranged in order of frequency of mention, are these:

1. Annual promotions are easier to administer, particularly in small school systems. A number of superintendents of small school systems wrote that annual promotion is the only plan feasible in small schools.

2. When pupils are promoted annually, a teacher has the same pupils throughout the whole year.

3. Annual promotions eliminate the necessity of having two or more half-year grades in each room in small elementary schools. One section per teacher permits of more individual work and better supervised study. He learns to know them well—their capacities and their inclinations—and he can more effectively adapt himself and the work to their needs. He has a longer time and better opportunity to work out problems after he has diagnosed them.

To quote one superintendent of schools: "One year is short enough time in which to understand, teach, and promote pupils."

4. With annual promotions there is no loss of time due to period of re-organization at midyear.

5. Annual promotions lower expenses, particularly in small schools.

6. Annual promotions do away with the small midyear classes.

7. The annual promotion plan does not narrow too greatly the scope of the materials of instruction which the teacher uses. Subject-matter can be organized and developed in larger units.

8. With annual promotions there is less disruption in the high school at the end of the fall semester, since there are no entering students. This applies particularly to the small high school. Several superintendents of schools stated that when midyear pupils did come into a small high school, they often found it difficult to make out satisfactory schedules. Some try to graduate in three and one-half years, which is undesirable in many cases.

9. Annual promotions make possible homogeneous grouping in small school systems.

10. Homogeneous grouping gives all the essential flexibility claimed for semi-annual promotions.

According to one superintendent of a large city school system:

With ungraded classes, opportunity schools, open-air schools, differentiated curriculums, and homogeneous grouping, pupils can be and are moved from school to school or group to group whenever advisable, thus allowing the school to give maximum service individually, rather than reorganize classes wholesale twice a year.

11. Annual promotions are in accord with practice in most of the school systems of certain states. Hence pupils transferring from one school system to another usually fit into assigned places.

12. With annual promotions a smaller teaching force is required, particularly in small school systems.

13. The annual promotion plan makes it possible to run the school plant more economically, for fewer rooms are required.

14. With annual promotions there are no mid-term high-school gradu·ates who usually have to wait until September to enter college.

15. Annual promotions conform with custom of the community.

One superintendent of a small school system writes: "Semi-annual promotions would be confusing to parents, teachers, and pupils."

16. Annual promotions offer more opportunity for emphasis on "the child" rather than on a set course of study.

17. Annual promotions give time in the summer vacation to make a very careful reorganization of the schools.

One superintendent of a large school system writes:

Each year we gather extensive data on every pupil. These data are used as a basis for classification and guidance. The assembling of these data would be practically impossible if we should attempt a semi-annual reorganization of our schools.

18. With annual promotions parents are more apt to learn to know their children's teachers.

What are the disadvantages of the annual promotion plan?—Superintendents of 300 school systems where pupil promotion is on the annual basis were asked to list the chief disadvantages of this plan of promotion. The following summary lists, in order of frequency of mention, the disadvantages of annual promotions:

1. There is a loss of a whole year instead of a half year in case of non-promotion.

For unavoidable reasons a pupil sometimes fails, and as a result he must spend two full years in the same grade, if the annual promotion plan is strictly adhered to. In the same way, a semester's absence means a whole year lost. Unfortunately, pupils failing are required to repeat a whole year's work, part of which they may be already thoroughly familiar with. In some cases, teachers would rather promote a pupil than cause him to lose a whole year—even though he is very weak in certain phases of the work.

2. Annual promotions have a tendency to retard the superior pupil. It is harder to skip a whole year than a half year. When annual promotions are strictly followed out, bright pupils must mark time with the dull and average pupils.

3. Annual promotions are not flexible enough for the welfare of individual pupils. They pre-determine the time pupils must spend in school, regardless of their ability.

The semi-annual plan provides an easier means for retaining a pupil a half year or for giving him an opportunity to advance more rapidly.

4. Pupils entering from systems which have semi-annual promotions are in an unfortunate position, since under the annual promotion plan classes begin basic courses only once a year. As a result, students moving into a system having annual promotions often lose a half year.

5. Annual promotions sometimes reduce length of school attendance. When a pupil in one of the upper grades fails, there is often a tendency for him to drop out of school if he is required to repeat a whole year's work. He loses interest in graduation.

6. Annual promotions increase the amount of pupil retardation.

7. Annual promotions raise per capita cost, for when a pupil fails he repeats a whole year instead of a half year.

8. Annual promotions prevent beginners entering at mid-term.

To quote one superintendent of schools:

In our system pupils are allowed to enter in September if they are six years old on or before the following January first. Thus we get many who are too young; and we still keep out a large number who are six years old in January and February.

9. Annual promotions make program making in the high school very difficult, since pupils who fail at the end of the first semester have few opportunities to take up other subjects.

10. Annual promotions do not give a chance for a change of teachers for a pupil whose temperament needs a certain type of teacher. If a teacher is poor, pupils lose more in a year than in a half year with him.

When special means are provided for caring for individual differences, are semi-annual promotions necessary?—To secure the opinion of superintendents of schools on this point, the following request was included in the inquiry sent to superintendents of schools:

Comment on the following statement: According to some school administrators, the plan of semi-annual promotions was adopted in order to make the machinery more flexible. Now when special classes, homogeneous grouping, parallel curriculums, and differentiated courses of study are provided, semi-annual promotions are not necessary. In fact, they may make the organization and administration of these differentiated programs very difficult.

Comments made by 97 out of the 112 superintendents of schools in cities over 30,000 in population who replied are summarized below:

According to 54 of the 97 superintendents, in spite of innovations, most school systems still need more flexibility; semi-annual promotions contribute to this end.

One superintendent of schools writes: "I have not found it wise to dispense with semi-annual promotions even though we provide all these additional school aids."

According to another superintendent:

With the present plan of pupils entering at the age of six, with as yet imperfect attendance machinery, much absence due to sickness, inadequate provision for all problem cases, and pupils needing special classes, it appears that the organization of the school is aided by semi-annual promotions and that instruction can be more effectively planned.

Forty-three out of these 97 superintendents of schools reported that the statement is correct in the case of large school systems, where it is practical to have homogeneous grouping, special classes, and parallel curriculums. In other words, they hold that semi-annual promotions are rendered less important as individual differences and individual advancement are recognized. However, several superintendents while approving this plan in theory make this comment:

Comparatively few school systems have more than a superficial homogeneous grouping, very few have parallel curriculums, hence midyear promotions still serve a valuable purpose in many schools.

F. Are Trial Promotions Desirable?

Table 12 shows that in the judgment of 381, or 76 percent, of 500 superintendents of schools answering this question, trial promotions are desirable.

TABLE 12.—DESIRABILITY OF TRIAL PROMOTIONS—SUMMARY OF JUDGMENTS OF 555 SUPERINTENDENTS OF SCHOOLS

Size of City	Are Trial Promotions Desirable?					
	Yes		No		Blank	Total
	Number	Percent of Those Replying	Number	Percent of Those Replying		
Under 2,500............	53	68	25	32	6	84
2,500–5,000............	83	81	19	19	13	115
5,000–10,000...........	78	74	28	26	13	119
10,000–30,000..........	91	80	24	20	10	125
30,000–100,000.........	51	80	12	20	7	70
Over 100,000...........	25	70	11	30	6	42
Total...............	381	76	119	24	55	555

This does not mean that trial promotions are a panacea in preventing failure. Neither does it mean that every pupil should be promoted to the next standard grade. Trial promotions depend on circumstances. They are desirable in the case of a pupil who is in most respects ready and able to profit by the program of the next unit, but who has not met the more specific requirements for promotion due to absence on account of illness, accident, or change of system.

Each case has to be handled individually. The individual is the determining factor. Hence one superintendent of schools writes:

Trial promotions are, or are not, desirable, depending on the following conditions:

1. The pupil's attitude or temperament.
2. The mental and chronological age of the pupil.
3. The ability of the teacher in the next grade to care for individual differences.

Some pupils are disheartened and lose ambition when not promoted. Giving them a trial usually inspires them to greater effort. On the other hand, trial promotion may impress some pupils with the idea that they can achieve advancement without effort or mental growth. Each case should be considered from all angles and parents taken into confidence. Then the decision should rest where the child will do the best for himself.

Some superintendents of schools feel that trial promotions are desirable if the practice is not used by the teacher as a means of evading responsibility in failing pupils who should be failed.

Many superintendents emphasize the point that all trial promotions should be carefully followed up and in many cases given individual help.

To quote one superintendent:

With the use of an individual instructor who gives special attention to the conditionally promoted pupils for the first twelve weeks, we have been able to hold approximately 90 percent of the pupils in the grades to which they were conditionally promoted.

Some emphasize the need of being specific as to the length of the trial period. They feel that the "trial" must be brought to a definite conclusion to be kept effective. Others feel that if the curriculum, method of instruction, and classification of pupils are based upon the adjustments necessary to meet individual differences, and the instructional service and other factors necessary for satisfactory progress of the pupil have been provided, pupils should be able to progress from unit to unit without the doubtful expediency of trial promotions. It is better to advance pupils through the school at different "levels" using a "standard" not as a "barrier" against advance or a hurdle to be surmounted, but rather as a measure of the accomplishment reached by the individual pupil. He goes on but at whatever level he is able to reach.

The following paragraphs summarize the desirable and undesirable features of trial promotions as seen by 500 superintendents of schools. Some statements are contradictory. This doubtless is the result of differences in philosophies, attitudes, and procedures of different superintendents of schools.

Why trial promotions are desirable—According to 381 superintendents of schools, trial promotions are desirable for these reasons:

1. The stimulus of "making good" is a means of changing a pupil's attitude and promoting purposeful learning.

The following statements on this point from three superintendents of schools are typical:

A pupil whose general attitude and grades seem to warrant a trial promotion is put upon his mettle to succeed. Careless and lazy habits are often corrected. New associates may create a higher standard of citizenship and eliminate many discipline problems.

We have promoted on the basis of trial promotions for several years past. In most cases we have found that the trial is a spur to the best efforts of the pupils to make good; and it is a challenge to the teacher to supply the missing links in preparation. Many such pupils have become honor students in high school because the work was more interesting to them than the work in the elementary school, and because the pupils were given to realize that they had to overcome a handicap. In these cases, the challenge was accepted by the pupils. We have recognized this fact also: Pupils get the most out of a grade the first time over it. Rarely has there been enough interest to warrant the repetition. Too often failing students leave school rather than repeat. We feel that it is better to carry a slow pupil on minimum assignments rather than discourage him completely.

Trial promotions are desirable because many pupils promoted on trial do the work of the following year successfully. If trial promotions were not granted, these pupils would become discouraged and lose time. If trial promotions are made, it should be with the distinct understanding that if the pupil so promoted fails in his work, he will voluntarily go back to repeat his grade.

2. Trial promotions are generally successful, particularly when they are followed up. It is the lack of personal touch that frequently ruins trial promotions. Trial promotions with a follow-up remedial program usually result in a pupil's success.[1]

3. Promotion is often a matter of question with the teacher. A trial may be necessary to determine whether a student can do the advanced work. Trial promotion overcomes, in some degree, the possibility of error in judging a child's development.

According to one superintendent of schools:

Trial promotions are advisable in many instances, because they give a check on the pupil's ability and the teacher's judgment. Sometimes a pupil is held back through no fault of his own, because a teacher has failed to discover the cause for his special disability.

Another superintendent of schools writes:

Too often teachers do not feel that the failure problem is their problem, but only that of their pupils. Trial promotion puts the matter of pupil success squarely up to the teacher: If the plan is to succeed, the teachers must find out the pupils' difficulties and work definitely for their elimination.

4. Trial promotion eliminates the depression of failure. The pupil feels that he is being given an opportunity.

5. Trial promotion offers encouragement, and places responsibility on the pupil.

---

[1] The following studies also point out that in the majority of cases trial promotions are successful:

"Probationary Promotion in Ohio." *Elementary School Journal,* 25: 723-25; June, 1925.

"Trial Promotions." *Elementary School Journal,* 27: 162-64; November, 1926.

"Trial Promotion." *Elementary School Journal,* 29: 564-66; April, 1929.

Klene, Vivian, and Branson, Ernest P. "Trial Promotion Versus Failure." *Educational Research Bulletin* 8: 6-11. Los Angeles: Los Angeles City Schools, January, 1929.

McKinney, H. T. *Promotion of Pupils, A Problem in Educational Administration.* Doctor's Thesis. Urbana, Ill.: University of Illinois; 1928. 180 p. ms.

Records 13,500 pupils advanced on the basis of 100 percent advancement for six weeks' probation. This method of advancing pupils showed a saving of about three out of every four repeaters.

6. Old material is not interesting. New material is. Children gain very little by mere repetition of the same material. "Half-sucked oranges are not appealing to their appetites."

According to one superintendent, personnel studies usually show that pupils repeating a subject the second time get by on a passing grade. Often exposure to new materials does as much for the mastery of an old subject as does repetition.

7. Sometimes a "personality clash" may occur between teacher and pupil —a trial promotion is often the solution. A different teacher many times overcomes the prior teacher's trouble and inspires a pupil to do what he has never done before.

8. Trial promotion permits adaptation of school work to needs and capacities of individuals who vary widely from the average.

Pupils who show exceptional ability should not be kept going in lock-step fashion.

9. Trial promotions generally keep a pupil with his age group. Each group holds certain interests in common. A trial promotion appeals to a pupil's pride to go on with his mates.

10. Trial promotions are more satisfactory to parents. They usually enlist the parents' help and create a better attitude toward the school.

11. In schools run on the yearly promotion plan there is too much loss to the pupil and too great an added expense to the community not to practice trial promotions.

12. Trial promotions give a pupil entering from another school system a chance to work in the grade where he thinks he belongs.

13. Trial promotions serve to check the value of such outside instruction as summer school and private tutoring.

14. Trial promotions tend to keep in school pupils who would otherwise become discouraged and drop out.

Why trial promotions are undesirable—One hundred nineteen out of 500 superintendents of schools feel that trial promotions are undesirable for these reasons:

1. The effect on a pupil is likely to be demoralizing if the trial fails and the pupil is returned to his former grade.

One superintendent of schools writes:

Demotion often gives a pupil a sense of inferiority and of failure which will have a detrimental effect upon his whole life.

2. With proper diagnostic testing and competent remedial instruction, trial promotions are unnecessary.

This is the viewpoint of one superintendent of schools:

If the evidence of five (or ten) months is not sufficient to justify promotions, an additional month is not going to furnish it. The teacher who has worked with the pupil for a year should know whether or not he would benefit most by advancement to the next grade or by repetition of the work. He should not pass that problem on to the next teacher.

3. Pupils promoted on trial usually fail and have to be demoted. They are not able to keep up with work in the advanced grade and become discouraged.

4. Some children take advantage of the plan and take chances on getting a trial promotion when they might earn a regular promotion.

One superintendent of schools writes:

Standards must be maintained so that pupils will learn to work, as they will be required to do when they leave school.

Another superintendent of schools writes:

Trial promotions are based on future accomplishment rather than upon past accomplishment. If a pupil has been given the proper conditions under which he may work and has received the proper care and encouragement throughout his school year, he must give an account of himself on the basis of past performance. Pupils must realize that the school has to take inventories as well as do business firms. Occasionally there may be situations that would make trial promotions desirable. It would depend upon the individual case, but as a general rule it would be detrimental inasmuch as many pupils will merely lower their standard of accomplishment in order to secure a possible trial promotion, rather than a regular promotion.

5. Pupils promoted on trial have a feeling of inferiority which handicaps them.

According to one superintendent of schools:

A trial promotion implies a doubt relative to the good standing of the pupil in the previous grade; thus handicapped, too large a load is placed on the mind of the child. He is under a nervous strain in trying to make the grade and avoid failure.

6. Trial promotions tempt teachers to find reasons for promoting everyone. They make it easy for teachers to avoid responsibility.

7. Children promoted on trial usually remain, even though their work is not satisfactory. There is seldom sufficient follow-up; and the conditional status is overlooked and the pupil becomes a problem later.

8. Parents fail to consider the significance of trial promotions.

According to one superintendent of schools:

Often if a pupil does not succeed, the responsibility is placed where it does not belong as far as the parents are concerned.

9. The child promoted on trial will do just enough work to keep from being put back.

One superintendent of schools writes:

In most cases the pupil tries for a month and then assumes that he is "safe."

10. Teachers in the next grade are reluctant about demoting pupils promoted on trial.

11. Trial promotions set a wrong example to those who have met the requirements.

12. Trial promotions are undesirable unless arrangements are perfected to take care of children who enter with a handicap.

G. Statements Concerning Relationships Between School Units
Elementary School Relationships

Since promotion policies are largely determined by what superintendents of schools consider to be more or less ideal conditions in each administrative unit, the following question was included in an inquiry sent to members of the Department of Superintendence:

Which of the following statements, concerning a six-grade elementary school, comes nearest to describing this institution as you believe it should exist ideally? Check the statement which you prefer.

a. The elementary school is an institution which takes children of varying physical and intellectual capacities who are approximately six years of age, and for six years offers them the educational opportunities which seem best suited to their needs. They get what they can, and when they are approximately twelve years of age they are promoted to the junior high school. If they have shown themselves to be above average in ability they may even be promoted at an earlier age _____ ( )

b. The elementary school is an institution which takes children of varying physical and intellectual capacities who are approximately six years of age, and requires them to reach certain minimum standards of educational accomplishment before they are promoted to the junior high school. Unless they are of average ability or above, this may involve seven, eight, or more years of attendance in the elementary school; and promotion to junior high school at the age of thirteen, fourteen, or older_____ ( )

Remarks _____

Table 13 summarizes the replies from 555 superintendents of schools which were received in time for tabulation.

TABLE 13.—SUPERINTENDENTS' CHOICE OF STATEMENTS DESCRIBING AN IDEAL SIX-GRADE ELEMENTARY SCHOOL

Size of City	Number of Superintendents Expressing Choice for						Total Number Replying
	Statement (a)		Statement (b)		Neither		
	Number	Percent	Number	Percent	Number	Percent	
Over 100,000........	24	57	9	21	9	21	42
30,000–100,000.....	47	67	17	24	6	9	70
10,000– 30,000.....	79	63	37	30	9	7	125
5,000– 10,000.....	52	44	49	41	18	15	119
2,500– 5,000.....	68	59	37	32	10	9	115
Under 2,500........	54	64	21	25	9	11	84
Total.............	324	58	170	31	61	11	555

Read above table thus: Out of 42 superintendents of schools in cities over 100,000 in population, 24, or 57 percent, prefer statement (a); 9, or 21 percent, prefer statement (b); and 9, or 21 percent, prefer neither statement, but express a choice for a combination of the two.

According to Table 13, 324 out of 555 superintendents of schools, or 58 percent, hold that an ideal six-grade elementary school is one which takes children of varying physical and intellectual capacities who are approximately six years of age, and for six years offers them the educational opportunities which seem best suited to their needs. They get what they can, and when they are approximately twelve years of age they are promoted to the junior high school. If they have shown themselves to be above average in ability they may even be promoted at an earlier age.

Among the remarks made by superintendents of schools who prefer this type of elementary school, were the following:

Progression from year to year in the grades, junior high school, and senior high school should depend upon starting pupils in the first grade at a mental age of six years, rather than a chronological age of six years—*James F. Rockett, Superintendent of Schools, Woonsocket, R. I.*

While promotion must always carry with it the idea of achievement, achievement must be made possible to children of varying physical and intellectual capacities—*Leon J. Deming, Superintendent of Schools, Oyster Bay, N. Y.*

Physiological development moves forward regardless, to a great extent, of mental development. Discipline problems frequently result from overgrown pupils. Nothing can be gained by having the land plowed over again and again if the plow goes no deeper. Education is deep thinking and the shallow mind becomes no deeper. Why not let it spread?—*W. H. Ward, Superintendent of Schools, Walterboro, S. C.*

A "slow" pupil should not be retarded more than two years out of his social group. I would apply the same rule to the gifted child and would accelerate only if an enriched course could not be provided from year to year—*Margaret Brainerd, Assistant Superintendent of Schools, Martins Ferry, Ohio.*

Ideally no child should fail, each should advance as he can; but in school, as out of school, progress is largely a comparison with others—*John S. Alan, Superintendent of Schools, Salem, Ohio.*

Statement "a" is as it should be; "b" is what is done in practice—*H. W. Dodd, Superintendent of Schools, Allentown, Pa.*

The majority of problem cases in our elementary schools today are the overage pupils who are compelled to mark time with children who are younger socially and physically. Our overage problem would be greatly increased if statement "b" were to be considered ideal—*Charles D. Dawson, Assistant Superintendent of Schools, Grand Rapids, Mich.*

Standards must be somewhat flexible. There should be minimum requirements for those who have no ability to reach them. It should always be possible to promote a pupil when this action is the best solution of his own peculiar problem—*R. H. Erwine, Assistant Superintendent of Schools, Akron, Ohio.*

The statement under "b" seems to us to describe a condition which would be quite intolerable to our community—*Virgil E. Dickson, Assistant Superintendent of Schools, Berkeley, Calif.*

One hundred seventy, or 31 percent, of the 555 superintendents of schools reporting would require pupils to reach certain minimum standards of educational accomplishment before they are promoted to the junior high school, even though this may involve seven, eight, or more years of attendance in the elementary school and promotion to junior high school at the age of thirteen, fourteen, or older.

Among the remarks made by superintendents of schools who prefer this type of six-year elementary school were the following:

I have checked "b" because it represents average conditions. I think "a" is the better plan if schools could be financed so as to equip classrooms and train teachers to carry it out—*J. W. Carrington, Superintendent of Schools, Cairo, Ill.*

This statement is preferred, with the proviso that pupils more than two years overage go into differentiated classes—*William H. Eddy, Deputy Superintendent of Schools, Providence, R. I.*

Promotion standards should be flexible enough to permit exceptions where individual traits in pupils may seem to warrent them. Some slow pupils will profit from repetition. However, there is no value in repetition, unless it actually leads to greater mastery. Repetition is justified for important material if greater mastery comes out of it as it usually does—*R. V. Hunkins, Superintendent of Schools, Lead, S. D.*

There are just as many reasons for expecting some pupils to take longer than six years to complete the first six grades as to expect some pupils to do it in less time. In most cases, such pupils will receive more benefits from school if they remain longer in the elementary school—*M. A. Steiner, Supervising Principal, Ingram, Pittsburgh, Pa.*

I believe that a minimum standard of requirements is very essential to the best possible effort on the part of both teachers and pupils. Responsibility is a much used word but little practiced. It is an important stone in the structure of progress. We should all be held responsible for a reasonable task—*F. W. Wallace, Superintendent of Schools, Poultney, Vt.*

For purposes of organization, administration, and maintenance of a system of standards, a minimum level of achievement seems necessary—*Wilbur S. Young, Superintendent of Schools, Springfield, Tenn.*

I sympathize with secondary school teachers who receive pupils *en masse* under "a" conditions—*Roland Chatterton, Union Superintendent of Schools, Portsmouth, R. I.*

If the whole school program could be reorganized, and if we could abolish the credit system in high school, and if we could really have the help and the means to offer each elementary school child what he most needs, then "a" would be right. But as high school and college now stand, "b" is best—*N. F. Hutchinson, Superintendent of Town Schools, Salem, Ind.*

The above statements indicate that many of the respondents were thinking in terms of present practice, rather than in terms of ideal practice where in each grade work is differentiated to fit pupils of varying levels of ability and to enlist the whole-hearted interest of all pupils. Under more ideal conditions failure and retardation would be reduced, for, while a pupil might not be promoted to the section of the next grade where the highest level of accomplishment is expected, he could be promoted to that section where accomplishment commensurate with his ability is expected.

Sixty-one, or 11 percent, of 555 superintendents of schools reporting did not vote for either statement "a" or "b"; 39 of these left the question blank; and 22 made comments showing that they were not satisfied with either statement. These were the remarks made by three superintendents of schools, who voted for a "sane" combination of statements "a" and "b":

For children of average ability or above "b" is correct. For children definitely below average there should be a modified curriculum which enables them to complete the six grades of the elementary school in not more than eight years and in not less than seven—*Carleton Washburne, Superintendent of Schools, Winnetka, Ill.*

Neither of the statements describes an ideal six-year elementary school. Statement "a" should include the point that pupils below average in ability, who put forth excellent effort and who have records of good conduct and attendance, may be promoted on trial to see what the broader curriculum of the junior school may awaken in their slower minds—*Herbert W. Lull, Superintendent of Schools, Newport, R. I.*

A composite of "a" and "b" is better. In the ideal elementary school, the normal child is required to reach standard goals before being promoted to junior high school. Provision is made for acceleration and for retention of pupils, so long as moderate efficiency in the tool subjects is advisable. And there is special provision for placement of pupils in the junior high school under the plan of adjustment of problem cases—*H. Ambrose Perrin, Superintendent of Schools, Joliet, Ill.*

A review of the foregoing vote and comments, concerning the issues raised by the two statements on page 79 relative to an elementary school, suggests that the majority of school superintendents favor statement "a"; and that a considerable percentage of the minority voting for "b" are sympathetic with the viewpoint expressed in "a," providing existing practical difficulties can be overcome. The small percentage voting for neither "a" nor "b" suggests a third plan which is preferred to either of the other two.

Junior High-School Relationships

Since a public school administrator's philosophy relative to what constitutes an ideal junior high school more or less influences his decision as to when a pupil should be promoted to junior high school, the following question was included in an inquiry sent to members of the Department of Superintendence:

Which of the following statements, concerning a junior high school (grades 7, 8, and 9), comes nearest to describing this institution as you believe it should exist ideally? Check the statement which you prefer.

a. The junior high school receives pupils from the elementary school who are approximately twelve years of age, and who have spent approximately six years in the elementary school, and offers them the educational opportunities which their capacities and accomplishments at the time of entering the junior high school seem to justify _____ ( )

b. The junior high school admits only those pupils who have successfully achieved certain minimum accomplishments in the elementary school. In fact, pupils should not be admitted to this institution until these accomplishments have been achieved, even though this may require, in many cases, that seven, eight, or more years be spent in the elementary school. This means that some pupils will be thirteen or fourteen years of age, or even older, before entering the junior high school _____ ( )

Remarks _____

Table 14 summarizes the replies from 555 superintendents of schools.

According to Table 14, 348 out of 555 superintendents of schools, or 63 percent, hold that an ideal junior high school, grades 7-9, is one which receives pupils from the elementary school who are approximately twelve years of age, and who have spent approximately six years in the elementary school, and offers them the educational opportunities which their capacities and accomplishments at the time of entering the junior high school seem to justify.

Among the remarks made by superintendents of schools who prefer this type of school were the following:

Except in rare cases, it is better for the junior high school to take care of the pupils who are older than those of the elementary level. A better social situation and better stimulation result—*F. H. Barbee, Superintendent of Schools, St. Joseph, Mo.*

The schools should conform to the children—*Leon O. Smith, Assistant Superintendent of Schools, Omaha, Neb.*

A somewhat flexible policy is needed here, although there should be definite educational requirements for those who have the ability but lack the will to do—*R. H. Erwine, Assistant Superintendent of Schools, Akron, Ohio.*

I subscribe to the above theory while realizing that much work will have to be done to determine what educational opportunities are appropriate to the varying capacities of junior high-school pupils admitted—*Bessie Bacon Goodrich, Assistant Superintendent of Schools, Des Moines, Iowa.*

This statement is approximately correct for children who are decidedly below average in ability and whose curriculum has had to be modified for them, so that they could reach the junior high school by the age of twelve or thirteen years; "b" is correct for the majority of children, but only under very rare conditions would a child be over thirteen years old on entering the junior high school—*Carleton Washburne, Superintendent of Schools, Winnetka, Ill.*

As the high schools are now organized, "b" must prevail. The whole scheme should be changed. The credit system and the graduation system should be abolished. Then the elementary and secondary school programs should be determined by needs of the pupils, and should be coordinated with a sensible program of guidance—*N. F. Hutchinson, Superintendent of Town Schools, Salem, Ind.*

This is an ideal situation, but administratively impossible beyond a certain point in this state, because the children must pass regents' examinations in order to be promoted—*Ralph I. Underhill, Superintendent of Schools, Scarsdale, N. Y.*

The junior high school is an institution which should provide a wide range of exploratory possibilities. It should also offer many activities and opportunities for social development. Children may be somewhat weak in the accomplishment of the first six grades and yet may receive a great deal of value from the junior high school ideally organized—*R. S. Hicks, Superintendent of Schools, Casper, Wyo.*

This is my ideal, but I realize that schools and teachers' standards must be reorganized to bring it about—*John S. Alan, Superintendent of Schools, Salem, Ohio.*

One hundred thirty-eight, or 25 percent, of the 555 superintendents of schools reporting would have the junior high school admit only those pupils who have successfully achieved certain minimum accomplishments in the elementary school. In fact, they feel that pupils should not be admitted to this institution until these accomplishments have been achieved, even though this may require, in many cases, that seven, eight, or more years be spent in the elementary school and that some pupils will be thirteen or fourteen years of age or even older before entering the junior high school.

TABLE 14.—SUPERINTENDENTS' CHOICE OF STATEMENTS DESCRIBING AN IDEAL JUNIOR HIGH SCHOOL

Size of City	Number of Superintendents Expressing Choice for						Total Number Replying
	Statement (a)		Statement (b)		Neither		
	Number	Percent	Number	Percent	Number	Percent	
Over 100,000........	27	64	5	12	10	24	42
30,000–100,000......	56	80	9	13	5	7	70
10,000– 30,000......	84	67	31	25	10	8	125
5,000– 10,000......	63	53	41	34	15	13	119
2,500– 5,000......	61	53	34	30	20	17	115
Under 2,500........	57	68	18	21	9	11	84
Total............	348	63	138	25	69	12	555

Among the remarks made by superintendents of schools who prefer this type of junior high school were the following:

Regardless of chronological age, a mental age of twelve years is essential to success in the junior high school—*F. L. Smith, Superintendent of Schools, Lancaster, N. Y.*

I would not recommend the holding of any pupil more than two years in any grade. If they are not able to get the work in that time, they are not able to get it at all; and so I would let them go on to the next grade and get what they can— *F. W. Wallace, Superintendent of Schools, Poultney, Vt.*

Proficiency in reading, spelling, language, and simple fundamental arithmetic should be pre-requisite to junior high school, regardless of pupil's age—*Roland Chatterton, Union Superintendent of Schools, Portsmouth, R. I.*

Provision can be made in the junior high school for a group of pupils overage in the elementary schools; but they should not be expected to do the regular junior high-school work. They should have work on the level of their needs and accomplishments—*Ballard D. Remy, Superintendent of Schools, Longmeadow, Mass.*

One of the objects of the junior high school is to permit of such a differentiation of the course of study as to permit pupils of greatly varying abilities to carry the work. Yet I believe they should be held for the achievement of certain accomplishments—*J. B. McManus, Superintendent of Schools, La Salle, Ill.*

A review of the above statements shows that the respondents were thinking of pupils of varying degrees of dullness. Some who thought of the very dull child could not think of him in a junior high school. Some thought of him in a special class in the junior high school; others thought of him attempting the standard curriculum. Many thought in terms of current practice, rather than in terms of ideal practice, where work in each grade is differentiated to fit pupils of varying levels of ability and to enlist the whole-hearted interest of all pupils.

The statement of one superintendent follows:

The first sentence of "b" comes pretty close to expressing a phase of our philosophy at Bronxville. I should follow this with the following statement: "Through a system of administration and the use of self-instruction materials which enable each child to advance at his own rate in each subject, independently of every child in the group, sufficient economy of time is achieved so that even pupils of relatively inferior capacity are enabled to complete the minimum requirements in approximately six years. A rich activity program provides socializing experiences which aim to develop a social maturity qualifying the student to enter the seventh grade at approximately the same time. A combination of slow social development and retarded accomplishment would be considered enough to delay advancement into junior high school by a year and possibly two years."—*Willard W. Beatty, Superintendent of Schools, Bronxville, N. Y.*

Out of 69, or 12 percent, of the 555 superintendents who voted for neither statement "a" nor "b," 54 left this question blank, and 15 stated that they were not satisfied with either plan.

Senior High-School Relationships

The preceding sections present a summary of opinions of 555 city superintendents of schools as to what constitutes an ideal elementary school and an ideal junior high school. To secure their views relative to the senior high school, this question was put to them:

Which of the following statements, concerning the senior high school (grades 10, 11, and 12), comes nearest to describing this institution as you believe it should exist ideally? Check the statement which you prefer.

a. The senior high school receives pupils from the junior high school who are approximately fifteen years of age, and who have spent approximately six years in the elementary school and three years in the junior high school. The senior high school offers them the educational opportunities which their capacities and accomplishments at the time of entrance seem to justify _____ ( )

b. The senior high school admits only those pupils who have successfully achieved certain minimum accomplishments in the junior high school. In fact, pupils should not be admitted to this institution until these accomplishments have been achieved, even though this may require, in many cases, that four or more years be spent in the junior high school. This means that some pupils will be considerably overage when entering the senior high school _____ ( )

Remarks _____

Table 15 summarizes the replies from 555 superintendents of schools which were received in time for tabulation.

TABLE 15.—SUPERINTENDENTS' CHOICE OF STATEMENTS DESCRIBING AN IDEAL SENIOR HIGH SCHOOL

| Size of City | Number of Superintendents Expressing Choice for | | | | | | Total Number Replying |
| | Statement (a) | | Statement (b) | | Neither | | |
	Number	Percent	Number	Percent	Number	Percent	
Over 100,000........	20	48	11	26	11	26	42
30,000–100,000......	50	71	15	21	5	7	70
10,000– 30,000......	76	61	30	24	19	15	125
5,000– 10,000......	57	48	44	37	18	15	119
2,500– 5,000......	58	50	37	32	20	17	115
Under 2,500........	51	61	22	26	11	13	84
Totals...........	312	56	159	29	84	15	555

According to Table 15, 312 out of 555 superintendents of schools, or 56 percent, hold that an ideal senior high school, grades 10-12, is one which receives pupils from the junior high school who are approximately fifteen years of age, and who have spent approximately six years in the elementary school and three years in the junior high school; and the senior high school offers them the educational opportunities which their capacities and accomplishments at the time of entrance seem to justify.

Among the remarks made by superintendents of schools who prefer this type of senior high school were the following:

Our junior and senior high schools more nearly meet "b," but we are working toward "a."—*A. H. Naylor, Superintendent of Schools, Port Jervis, N. Y.*

If the junior high school is to be a democratic institution, the senior high school must also follow—*Francis V. Grant, Superintendent of Schools, Williamstown, Mass.*

Courses and subjects should be offered which will enable all interested to profit by attendance and work—*J. J. Schafer, Superintendent of Schools, Midland, Mich.*

One could never satisfy present associations of secondary schools and colleges or college entrance requirements by adhering to the ideal situation described in statement "a"—*A. F. Cook, Superintendent of Schools, Hinsdale, Ill.*

The elementary schools and junior high schools accept the ideal expressed in statement "a" quite naturally and freely. It is more difficult to secure this acceptance from senior high-school principals and teachers. The senior high-school personnel seem to adhere more tenaciously to traditional standards of academic achievement. Their attitude is, in part, due to the pressure of college entrance requirements—*C. R. Reed, Superintendent of Schools, Minneapolis, Minn.*

One hundred fifty-nine, or 29 percent, of the 555 superintendents of schools reporting checked statement "b," indicating that they considered an ideal senior high school one which admits only those pupils who have successfully achieved certain minimum accomplishments in the junior high school. In fact, pupils should not be admitted to this institution until these accomplishments have been achieved, even though this may require, in many cases, that four or more years be spent in the junior high school and that some pupils will be considerably overage when entering the senior high school.

Among the remarks made by superintendents of schools who hold the above viewpoint were the following:

The large mortality in the senior high school comes from students who do not have the mental ability to do the work. They would be better off in some technical school—*D. E. Batcheller, Superintendent of Schools, North Tonawanda, N. Y.*

Pupils who have achieved certain minimum accomplishments should be guided into other fields of endeavor than the senior high school—*R. S. Hicks, Superintendent of Schools, Casper, Wyo.*

There must be some place along the road where low ability pupils reach their level. Cost prevents an idealistic program. At present the end of the junior high school seems the best place to stop—*C. Ray Gates, Superintendent of Schools, Grand Island, Neb.*

Of the 84, or 15 percent, of the 555 superintendents of schools reporting who did not check either statement "a" or "b" as ideal, 66 left the question blank; i. e., they made no reply. However, 18 stated specifically that they preferred an intermediate statement. The following is a more or less typical reply:

The senior high school should offer widely differing courses to meet widely differing needs, and should accept pupils of widely differing abilities. On the other hand, for the majority of pupils certain definite standards should be attained. It should be only in very exceptional cases that a pupil would be more than fifteen years of age on entering the senior high school—*Carleton Washburne, Superintendent of Schools, Winnetka, Ill.*

A review of the above statements shows that some superintendents of schools think of the senior high school as an institution with a heterogeneous student body drawn from every group in the community with corresponding diversity of background, capacity, and future prospect, for whom differentiated courses of study as well as varied curriculums are provided—in which varying rates of progress are made.

Other superintendents of schools think of the senior high school as an institution with a more or less homogeneous student body chosen from the average and superior ability groups in the junior high school where each pupil has achieved certain minimum standards of accomplishment in specified subject-matter.

CHAPTER IV

STATUS OF SENIOR HIGH-SCHOOL PROMOTION PLANS

SINCE plans for the promotion of high-school pupils, marks and marking systems, and provisions for individual differences in secondary schools will be treated extensively in the National Survey of Secondary Education,[1] the Articulation Commission has made no attempt to duplicate this study. These topics, however, are so vitally connected with the problem of articulation that at least some mention should be made of them here, awaiting the time when the complete report of the National Survey of Secondary Education is issued. Hence there is presented below a summary of one of the most comprehensive studies [2] of senior high-school promotion plans now available, made by John Francis Montague. Two of the primary purposes of his study were: (1) to collect, organize, and interpret significant data relative to present practices in secondary schools as to classification of pupils, special provision for individual differences through instruction, bases for promotion, and method of promotion; and (2) to evaluate promotion plans on the basis of number of teachers required, failures, courses dropped, and pupils leaving school.

In this study, the term "promotion plan" was used as a general term to apply to all those provisions in school organization which propose to minimize the problems resulting from group instruction for pupils of varying interests, aptitudes, and capacities. Such provisions, according to the investigator, may be roughly grouped under these four heads: (1) Bases for classification; (2) special provisions for individual differences in instructional procedure; (3) bases for promotion; and (4) general method of promotion. Previous studies have been made to determine the various types of organization employed by high schools, the kind of pupils eliminated and the kind of pupils retained, and the extent to which pupils fail. The studies pertaining to school organization are somewhat extensive in nature, while those dealing with specific phases such as failures and eliminations are confined to a small number of schools. This is one of the first attempts made to analyze specific types of plans in terms of failure, courses dropped, and elimination.

Method of attack—The total number of schools included in this study represents approximately one-third of all the cities in the United States having a population of more than 2,500. The total number of schools

---

[1] For a brief description of the scope of this survey see pages 111-114.

[2] Montague, John Francis, *Status of Senior High-School Promotion Plans.* Ph. D. Thesis. Columbia, Mo.: Graduate School, University of Missouri, 1926.

Public school administrators will also find this reference of interest:

Broady, Knute O. *School Provisions for Individual Differences:* Policies and Data Necessary. Contributions to Education, No. 395. New York: Bureau of Publications, Teachers College, Columbia University, 1930. 101 p.

supplying full information on failures, courses dropped, and pupils leaving school represents about one-eighth of the cities of the same group.

The inquiry, sent to superintendents of schools in all cities reporting a population of 2,500 or more, included such questions as might be grouped under the following major heads: (1) What is your plan of organization in regard to classification of pupils? (2) What special provisions are made for individual differences in instruction? (3) What is now used as the basis for promotion? and (4) What is the general method of promoting?

For purposes of comparison, schools were divided into six classes on a basis of enrolment. High schools reporting an enrolment of 100 or less were designated as Class "A" schools, 101 to 200 as Class "B" schools, 201 to 300 as Class "C" schools, 301 to 500 as Class "D" schools, 501 to 1000 as Class "E" schools, and 1001 or more as Class "F" schools. Eight hundred thirty-eight inquiry blanks were returned; 334 from high schools representing 42 states and the District of Columbia gave complete information and were selected for study of failures, courses dropped, and pupils leaving school. The distribution according to classes of schools was as follows:

NUMBER OF REPLIES DISTRIBUTED ACCORDING TO CLASSES OF SCHOOLS

Replies	Classes of Schools, Based on Enrolment						Totals
	A 100 or Less	B 101–200	C 201–300	D 301–500	E 501–1000	F 1001 or More	
By classes of schools...	30	135	158	185	191	139	838
Selected for elimination study.............	17	62	73	68	78	36	334

A. Current Practices in Promotion [1]

1. Bases for Classification:

By bases for classification is meant those measurements and devices employed in sectioning pupils for the purpose of class instruction. In view of the many factors enumerated in the reports from the field, they were classified under these six heads: (1) school marks or previous school records; (2) curriculum selected; (3) I. Q. as the important factor; (4) ability groups classified on basis of intelligence, achievement, and teachers' judgment; (5) other combinations—of such factors as school marks, intelligence, achievement, chronological age, and social age; and (6) no plan.

Who is responsible for directing pupils in their choice of courses and curriculums?—Replies from 838 high schools show that in 261 schools the principal is responsible. This is particularly true in the smaller high schools. In 114 high schools pupils are advised by faculty committees. Twenty-eight high schools report official counselors; 37, deans; and one,

---

[1] The forthcoming report of the National Survey of Secondary Education will present extensive data on many of the points included in this section.

a visiting teacher, who does the major portion of the work. Reports show that a large number of high schools consult with parents of pupils in the selection of courses and curriculums to be pursued.

How are pupils classified in those subjects having more than one section?—Table 16 shows that of the 838 high schools reporting, a total of 167 representing all classes of schools have no definite plan for classifying pupils; and that an additional 125 merely classify on the basis of curriculum selected.

TABLE 16.—NUMBER OF HIGH SCHOOLS, IN ALL CLASSES, DISTRIBUTED ACCORDING TO BASES FOR CLASSIFICATION OF PUPILS

Bases for Classification	Classes of Schools, Based on Enrolment						Totals
	A 100 or Less	B 101–200	C 201–300	D 301–500	E 501–1000	F 1001 or More	
School marks.........	10	28	34	34	39	39	184
Curriculum selected....	2	25	27	17	29	25	125
I. Q. as important factor...............	1	15	22	43	46	23	150
Ability groups........	3	5	13	7	9	13	50
Other combinations....	8	19	40	52	27	16	162
No plan.............	6	43	22	32	41	23	167
Totals............	30	135	158	185	191	139	838
Percentage no plan....	20.0	31.9	13.9	17.3	21.5	16.5	19.9

Read Table 16 as follows: School marks are used as a basis for classification in 10 Class A schools, in which the enrolment is 100 or less; in 28 Class B schools, in which the enrolment is 101–200; in 34 Class C schools, in which the enrolment is 201–300; in 34 Class D schools, in which the enrolment is 301–500; in 39 Class E schools, in which the enrolment is 501–1000; and in 39 Class F schools, in which the enrolment is 1001 or more.

The practice in classification varies for the different classes of schools, but no one plan is applicable to any one class of schools.

What curriculums are provided by secondary schools with different sized enrolments?[1]—Table 17 on page 90 shows that in the 838 high schools reporting, college preparatory curriculums are offered most frequently by high schools of all sizes; a general curriculum stands first in the three classes of schools having the smallest enrolment; and a commercial curriculum is offered in all high schools having an enrolment of 501 to 1000. The total number of curriculums in 30 high schools having an enrolment of 100 or less was 70, which makes an average of two and one-third curriculums per school. The average number of curriculums increases with the size of the school. Another important fact revealed by Table 17 is the large number of commercial, teacher-training, vocational, and manual arts curriculums reported.

Are certain pupils limited to a particular curriculum?—The practice of limiting pupils of superior ability to academic or college preparatory curriculums was reported by only nine out of 838 high schools; on the other hand, 105 of these schools, or approximately 12½ percent, limit pupils of

[1] See also: National Education Association, Department of Superintendence. *The Development of the High-School Curriculum.* Sixth Yearbook. Washington, D. C.: Department of Superintendence, National Education Association, 1928. Chapter III, "Curriculums Found in American Secondary Schools," p. 59-82.

low ability to a special type of curriculum. In the list of curriculums provided for pupils of very low ability, the vocational curriculum stands first and is followed by manual arts and general curriculums, respectively. Some 220 other schools including all classes said that pupils were advised as to the types of curriculums they should pursue, but they were not limited to any specific curriculum.

Is enrolment in certain subjects limited to particular pupils?—Ninety-seven out of 838 high schools, with all-sized enrolment, limit certain subjects to pupils of superior ability. From the replies received, it would appear that advanced mathematics is considered the most difficult subject for high-school pupils, with the modern languages ranking second.

Twenty-one high schools limit pupils of very low ability to specific subjects after they have been directed into a certain curriculum. Bookkeeping and manual training are the specific subjects to which such pupils are limited.

TABLE 17.—NUMBER AND TYPES OF CURRICULUMS REPORTED BY EACH CLASS OF HIGH SCHOOLS

Types of Curriculums Provided	Classes of Schools, Based on Enrolment						Totals
	A 100 or Less	B 101–200	C 201–300	D 301–500	E 501–1000	F 1001 or More	
General.............	24	127	141	167	172	129	760
College preparatory....	23	110	137	174	183	138	765
Commercial..........	12	89	121	153	191	129	695
Manual arts.........	4	25	52	79	119	68	347
Vocational...........	3	22	44	67	92	48	276
Teacher-training......	2	13	31	46	38	20	150
Household arts........	1	6	12	14	12	19	64
Scientific.............	1	5	6	8	19	11	50
Classical.............	0	2	1	4	11	3	21
Music...............	0	1	0	4	20	12	37
Technical............	0	0	0	2	2	6	10
Elective.............	0	0	0	0	1	2	3
Total number of curriculums.........	70	400	545	718	860	585	3,178
Number of schools.....	30	135	158	185	191	139	838
Average number of curriculums per school..	2.33	2.96	3.45	3.88	4.50	4.21	3.79

Read Table 17 as follows: Of the thirty Class A schools, 24 have a general curriculum, 23 a college preparatory curriculum, etc.

How many extra subjects are high-school pupils of superior ability permitted to carry?—Table 18 shows that 795 out of 838 schools, or about 95 percent, permit superior pupils to carry additional subjects. Of the number permitting additional subjects, 198 schools, or more than 20 percent of the total number of replies, permit pupils to carry two extra subjects; and five schools, three or more subjects.

2. Special Provisions for Individual Differences through Instruction:

According to the replies received, these are among the special plans of an instructional character which take individual differences of pupils into account after they have been classified: (1) coaching classes; (2) conference periods for slow and failing pupils; (3) North Denver plan, which singles out the bright pupils for special work and greater individual assistance; (4) Batavia plan, with large classes for directed study; (5) supervised study; (6) minimum and maximum courses, differentiated to meet the needs of individual pupils; (7) extra subjects; and (8) Dalton or contract plan.

TABLE 18.—NUMBER OF EXTRA SUBJECTS PERMITTED PUPILS OF SUPERIOR ABILITY IN EACH CLASS OF HIGH SCHOOLS

Number of Additional Subjects Permitted	Classes of Schools, Based on Enrolment						Totals
	A 100 or Less	B 101–200	C 201–300	D 301–500	E 501–1000	F 1001 or More	
One subject...........	17	81	111	141	143	99	592
Two subjects.........	9	42	38	39	40	30	198
Three or more subjects.	1	2	0	1	0	1	5
None................	2	7	6	3	3	3	24
No reply.............	1	3	3	1	5	6	19
Totals.............	30	135	158	185	191	139	838

Read Table 18 as follows: Seventeen Class A schools permit pupils to carry one extra subject; nine permit two extra subjects; one, three or more; two do not permit pupils to carry extra subjects; and one made no reply; etc.

Table 19 shows that coaching classes is by far the most common of all plans for taking care of individual differences in instruction in all classes of schools.

TABLE 19.—NUMBER OF HIGH SCHOOLS, IN ALL CLASSES, DISTRIBUTED ACCORDING TO SPECIAL PROVISIONS FOR INDIVIDUAL DIFFERENCES

Special Provisions for Individual Differences	Classes of Schools, Based on Enrolment						Totals
	A 100 or less	B 101–200	C 201–300	D 301–500	E 501–1000	F 1001 or more	
Coaching classes.......	7	30	37	55	25	48	202
Conference periods.....	0	15	16	14	18	8	71
North Denver Plan....	0	3	0	3	8	12	26
Batavia Plan..........	0	12	19	12	15	11	69
Supervised study......	3	10	9	11	13	4	50
Minimum and maximum courses........	0	3	0	0	4	5	12
Extra subjects........	1	2	14	12	12	7	48
Dalton Plan..........	2	0	0	1	3	0	6
No plan..............	17	60	63	77	93	44	354
Totals.............	30	135	158	185	191	139	838
Percentage no plan...	56.7	44.4	39.9	41.6	48.7	31.7	42.2

Read Table 19 as follows: Coaching classes are used as a means of taking care of individual differences in instruction by 7 class A schools; 30 Class B schools; 37 class C schools; 55 class D schools; 25 class E schools; and 48 class F schools; making a total of 202 schools; etc.

3. Bases for Promotion:

What measurements and administrative plans do secondary schools use in determining pupil readiness for more advanced work?—Answers from 838 high schools to the question, "Upon what did you base your promotions?" are summarized in Table 20 under four major heads: (1) school marks, (2) final examinations, (3) daily records and final examinations, and (4) other combinations, i. e., on some combination of such items as school marks, daily records, final examinations, achievement test scores, semester attendance, and points earned.

Table 20 shows that 556 high schools use "other combinations" as a basis for promotion, while daily records and final examinations rank second and school marks third.

TABLE 20.—NUMBER OF HIGH SCHOOLS, IN ALL CLASSES, DISTRIBUTED ACCORDING TO BASES FOR PROMOTION

Bases for Promotion	Classes of Schools, Based on Enrolment						Totals
	A 100 or less	B 101-200	C 201-300	D 301-500	E 501-1000	F 1001 or more	
School marks.........	3	16	18	18	36	22	113
Final examination.....	2	5	3	15	2	0	27
Daily records and examinations.........	3	29	30	31	26	20	139
Other combinations....	22	85	107	121	126	95	556
Not replying..........	0	0	0	0	1	2	3
Totals..............	30	135	158	185	191	139	838

Read Table 20 as follows: School marks are used as a basis for promotion by 3 class A schools; 16 class B schools; 18 class C schools; 18 class D schools; 36 class E schools; and 22 class F schools, making a total of 113 schools, etc.

What do secondary schools take as the unit group in assigning school marks?—Since approximately 60 percent of all high schools replying make use of the normal curve as a check on the assignment of school marks by teachers, the size of the unit group, or the number of actual pupil scores to which the curve is applied, is important. Table 21 shows that the most common practice is to take each class or section, which places the responsibility of marking upon the individual teacher. Table 21 shows that the number of schools using each class, each subject, and all pupils under the instruction of each teacher as the unit group makes a total of more than 80 percent of all schools replying and represents the most common practice in all classes of schools.

TABLE 21.—UNIT GROUPS FOR THE ASSIGNMENT OF SCHOOL MARKS, REPORTED BY EACH CLASS OF HIGH SCHOOLS

Unit Groups	Classes of Schools, Based on Enrolment						Totals
	A 100 or less	B 101-200	C 201-300	D 301-500	E 501-1000	F 1001 or more	
Each class...........	11	39	62	68	78	49	307
Each subject.........	11	53	49	52	41	36	242
Each curriculum.......	0	1	1	1	0	2	5
Each grade..........	3	14	6	10	7	9	49
Pupils of each teacher..	1	16	23	37	42	23	142
Entire school.........	1	1	1	5	7	2	17
No reply.............	3	11	16	12	16	18	76
Totals..............	30	135	158	185	191	139	838

Read Table 21 as follows: Eleven class A schools assign school marks on a class basis; 11 consider all pupils in a given subject; 3, each grade, etc.

4. General Method of Promotion:

Time of promotion—Table 22 shows that 410 schools out of 838, or approximately one-half of the total number replying, promote annually. A small number of schools stated that they promoted from section to section at any time but retained the annual or semi-annual plan for regular promotions.

Annual and semi-annual promotions are found in all sizes or classes of schools; but annual promotions are used most frequently in schools with an enrolment of less than 500. Table 22 shows that schools having an enrolment of less than 500 pupils are distinctly in favor of annual promotions, while those reporting a larger enrolment favor midyear promotions. It appears that the size of the school is a very important factor in the matter of time of promotion.

TABLE 22.—NUMBER OF HIGH SCHOOLS, IN ALL CLASSES, DISTRIBUTED ACCORDING TO TIME OF PROMOTION

| Time of Promotion | Classes of Schools, Based on Enrolment | | | | | | Totals |
	A 100 or less	B 101-200	C 201-300	D 301-500	E 501-1000	F 1001 or more	
Annually............	26	97	106	102	66	13	410
Semi-annually........	4	38	52	83	125	126	428
Totals.............	30	135	158	185	191	139	838
Percentage:							
Annual............	86.7	71.9	67.1	55.1	34.6	9.4	48.9
Semi-annual........	13.3	28.1	32.9	44.9	65.4	90.6	51.1

Read Table 22 as follows: Annual promotions are given in 26 class A schools, 97 class B schools, 106 class C schools, 102 class D schools, 66 class E schools, and 13 class F schools, making a total of 410, etc.

Do secondary schools promote by constant section, by points, or by subjects?—Table 23 shows that present practice is distinctly in favor of promotion by subject. The difficulty of administering the point system from the standpoint of records has tended to make this plan unpopular, according to statements of high-school principals. According to Table 23, only 19 schools, or about two and one-half percent of the total number of schools replying, use a point system. Twenty-nine schools, or less than four per-

TABLE 23.—GENERAL METHOD OF PROMOTION IN EACH CLASS OF HIGH SCHOOLS

| Method of Promotion | Classes of Schools, Based on Enrolment | | | | | | Totals |
	A 100 or less	B 101-200	C 201-300	D 301-500	E 501-1000	F 1001 or more	
Constant section......	1	9	8	5	2	4	29
By points............	0	3	4	7	2	3	19
By subjects..........	28	119	143	171	180	128	769
No reply............	1	4	3	2	7	4	21
Totals.............	30	135	158	185	191	139	838

Read Table 23 as follows: Promotion by "constant section" is used in 1 class A school; 9 class B schools; 8 class C schools; 5 class D schools; 2 class E schools; and 4 class F schools, making a total of 29, etc.

cent of the total number, report that they are following the old plan of promoting by constant sections. It should be added, however, that schools promoting by constant sections include all but three of the schools providing minimum and maximum courses as shown in Table 19 on page 91.

To what extent do secondary schools make provision for double promotions?—Out of 838 schools reporting, only 104 provide for skipping or making double promotions. (See Table 24.) Only two plans were given to illustrate this type of procedure, namely: (1) by tutoring and special examination for credit in the work skipped, and (2) by extra-session schools and examination. The total number of pupils receiving double or extra promotions in these schools was approximately 600, making an average of about six pupils per school. This tabulation does not include those schools placing pupils into ability groups in which the bright pupils or fast sections are permitted to complete their course in three or three and one-half years; nor does it include those making special provision for slow pupils to make up failed or conditioned work.

TABLE 24.—PROVISIONS FOR SKIPPING OR MAKING DOUBLE PROMOTIONS IN EACH CLASS OF HIGH SCHOOLS

Provisions for Skipping a Semester	Classes of Schools, Based on Enrolment						Totals
	A 100 or less	B 101-200	C 201-300	D 301-500	E 501-1000	F 1001 or more	
Tutor and examination.	1	18	12	4	13	12	60
Extra-session school and examination.....	3	2	12	15	7	5	44
Totals..............	4	20	24	19	20	17	104

Read Table 24 as follows: One school in class A permits pupils to skip a semester or make up back work by doing work with a tutor and submitting to an examination; 18 class B schools follow the same practice, etc.

Are superior pupils permitted to finish high school in a shorter time?— The fact that a large number of schools are providing extra sessions, "coaching classes," and "conference periods" for pupils in regular attendance indicates that there is a tendency to speed up the time for completing the high-

TABLE 25.—NUMBER OF HIGH SCHOOLS PERMITTING SUPERIOR PUPILS TO FINISH IN LESS TIME THAN AVERAGE OR SLOW PUPILS

Four-Year Course	Classes of Schools, Based on Enrolment						Totals
	A 100 or less	B 101-200	C 201-300	D 301-500	E 501-1000	F 1001 or more	
Finish in less time.....	11	73	84	125	138	114	545
Require full time......	15	61	63	48	37	15	239
No reply.............	4	1	11	12	16	10	54
Totals..............	30	135	158	185	191	139	838

Read Table 25 as follows: Superior pupils are permitted to finish the course in less time than the average or slow pupils in 11 class A schools, 73 class B schools, 84 class C schools, 125 class D schools, 138 class E schools, and 114 class F schools, making a total of 545, etc.

school course. Table 25 shows that 545 high schools, or approximately 65 percent of all schools replying, are now permitting superior pupils to finish the course in less time than the average or slow pupils. Another interesting fact is the dropping off of the number of high schools requiring full time for completing the course as the size of the enrolment increases to more than 300, or the class D schools.

What provisions are made for removing conditions?—By far the most common practice is to promote pupils on the condition that they make good in the advanced work. This is done without further training or special examination in all classes of schools, but to a greater extent by those schools enrolling less than 1000 pupils. Table 26 shows that a total of 566 high schools, out of 838, promote pupils on the various conditions listed. Three hundred sixty-five schools including all classes remove conditional marks if pupils make good in the advanced work; and 32 additional schools require those pupils to do at least average work in the advanced class. Forty-eight schools require pupils to attend summer school and pass a special examination in order to remove the condition. Nine schools promote pupils regularly if they do not fail in more than one subject; and 46 others say pupils are promoted if failure was due to the examination alone.

Obviously, the old practice of placing an additional burden on slow and failing pupils by requiring them to make up back work during the next semester is passing. Only 66 schools, or about twelve percent of the schools promoting on conditions, follow this plan. A fair test of this practice would be the percentage of conditioned pupils who make good their promotion. Of the 566 schools granting conditional promotions, 407 reported more than 60 percent making good; 107 schools of this group say that more than 80 percent make good. The remainder of the schools gave a smaller percentage of pupils making good their promotion, ranging from 10 to 58 percent.

TABLE 26.—PROVISIONS FOR REMOVING CONDITIONS IN EACH CLASS OF HIGH SCHOOLS

Promoted on Condition	Classes of Schools, Based on Enrolment						Totals
	A 100 or less	B 101-200	C 201-300	D 301-500	E 501-1000	F 1001 or more	
Make good in advanced work..............	11	77	85	71	76	45	365
Summer school and examination..........	5	3	7	19	7	7	48
Failed in one subject...	3	0	0	3	1	2	9
Do average advanced work..............	1	2	0	4	18	7	32
Failed examination only.	0	3	1	16	21	5	46
Make it up in next semester............	0	13	12	13	4	24	66
Totals..............	20	98	105	126	127	90	566

Read Table 26 as follows: Eleven schools in class A remove conditional marks if pupils make good in the advanced work; 77 schools in class B follow the same practice; 85 schools in class C; 71 schools in class D; 76 schools in class E; and 45 schools in class F; making a total of 365, etc.

Under what conditions are pupils required to repeat subjects?—In opposition to the apparent leniency in granting conditions, it is found that certain specific subject requirements for graduation are held to rather closely. Table 27 shows that out of 838 schools reporting, 760, or more than 90 percent, are making pupils repeat those subjects failed that are required for graduation. Another group of 14 schools require pupils to repeat the subject if they fail the final examination. Teachers' judgments of pupil needs are also a factor, as shown by the 31 schools grouped under "profit more by repeating" and "not able to do advanced work."

TABLE 27.—REQUIREMENTS CONDITIONING REPETITION OF SUBJECTS IN EACH CLASS OF HIGH SCHOOLS

Required to Repeat Subjects	Classes of Schools, Based on Enrolment						Totals
	A 100 or Less	B 101–200	C 201–300	D 301–500	E 501–1000	F 1001 or More	
Failed a required subject................	28	121	147	151	178	135	760
Failed final examination................	0	3	2	4	5	0	14
Profit more by repeating................	0	3	0	4	3	0	10
Not able to do advanced work........	0	0	3	16	0	2	21
No reply.............	2	8	6	10	5	2	33
Totals............	30	135	158	185	191	139	838

Read Table 27 as follows: Twenty-eight schools in class A require pupils to repeat a subject when they fail in it, if it is a required subject; 121 class B schools, 147 class C schools, 151 class D schools, 178 class E schools, and 135 class F schools follow the same practice, making a total of 760, etc.

Under what conditions are high-school pupils required to repeat an entire grade?—Table 28 shows a great variety of practice. The significant fact here is that a number of schools require pupils to repeat the grade if they fail in one, two, or three subjects. No doubt, the schools requiring pupils to repeat the entire grade after failing one or two subjects based their decisions upon required subjects.

TABLE 28.—REQUIREMENTS CONDITIONING REPETITION OF GRADES IN EACH CLASS OF HIGH SCHOOLS

Required to Repeat Grade	Classes of Schools, Based on Enrolment						Totals
	A 100 or Less	B 101–200	C 201–300	D 301–500	E 501–1000	F 1001 or More	
Failed in one subject..	3	1	0	2	3	0	9
Failed in two subjects..	6	13	8	4	4	2	37
Failed in three subjects.	4	18	0	11	9	3	45
Failed in all subjects..	8	61	52	66	73	57	317
Not able to do advanced work........	0	0	26	0	57	0	83
No grade repeaters....	6	31	59	91	42	68	297
No reply.............	3	11	13	11	3	9	50
Totals............	30	135	158	185	191	139	838

Read Table 28 as follows: Three schools in class A require pupils to repeat the entire grade when they fail in one subject; one class B school, two class D schools, and three class E schools follow the same practice, making a total of nine, etc.

Another important item in Table 28 is the large number of schools reporting no grade repeaters in each of the six classes of schools.

What consideration is being given to overage pupils in promotion?—Table 29 shows that only 330 schools, out of 838, give them any special consideration. The most common practice in all classes of schools is to promote them on a lower requirement. This plan is followed by 187 schools, while 105 promote them into slow sections of the advanced work. Twenty-four schools promote pupils after two years in the grade; and 14 promote them if they attend summer school.

TABLE 29.—SPECIAL CONSIDERATION GIVEN OVERAGE PUPILS IN PROMOTION IN EACH CLASS OF HIGH SCHOOLS

Consideration for Overage Pupils	Classes of Schools, Based on Enrolment						Totals
	A 100 or Less	B 101–200	C 201–300	D 301–500	E 501–1000	F 1001 or More	
Promoted into slow group..............	2	26	9	23	27	18	105
Second year in grade..	4	13	0	1	4	2	24
Lower requirement....	8	28	61	33	39	18	187
Summer school........	0	2	0	0	12	0	14
Totals............	14	69	70	57	82	38	330

Read Table 29 as follows: Two schools in class A give special consideration to overage pupils by promoting them into slow groups; 26 class B schools, 9 class C schools, 23 class D schools, 27 class E schools, and 18 class F schools follow the same practice, making a total of 105, etc.

B. Relation of Classification Plans to Failures, Courses Dropped, and Extent to Which Pupils Leave School

This particular phase of the study involved a complete report on average number of pupils per teacher, pupils leaving school, failures, and courses dropped for 334 representative high schools enrolling 199,130 pupils.[1] This information was obtained from the records for the last semester of the school year 1924-25. For those schools promoting annually, the report applies to the entire year; for those promoting semi-annually, for the second semester only.

As previously stated, promotion plans must be evaluated from the point of view of the four major divisions in the plans for adjusting the organization to care for individual differences of pupils; namely, (1) bases for classification; (2) special provision for individual differences through instruction; (3) bases for promotion; and (4) time of promotion. This section is given over to an evaluation of promotion plans from the standpoint of classification. The remaining divisions are dealt with, in a similar way, in subsequent sections.

Of the 334 high schools studied, 63 classify pupils on the basis of "school marks;" 44 according to "curriculum selected;" 68 according to "intelligence; 20 classify into "ability groups;" 85 use "other combinations;" and

[1] Out of 838 inquiry blanks returned, 334 gave complete information on average number of pupils per teacher, pupils leaving school, failures, and courses dropped.

54 have no definite plan. Statistics from all these 334 schools show that schools using "other combinations," "curriculum selected," and "intelligence groups" show the smallest percentages of pupils leaving school. A study of student failures also shows that those schools using "other combinations" as a means of pupil classification have the smallest percentage of failures. The percentage of pupils dropping one, two, and three or more subjects is practically the same for the schools using each of the bases for classification. Schools having no definite plan for classifying pupils have a larger percentage of pupils dropping courses.

Schools reporting improved classification plans have slightly more teachers than schools reporting no definite plan for classifying pupils.

C. Relation of Special Provisions for Individual Differences in Instruction to Failures, Courses Dropped, and Extent to Which Pupils Leave School

Of 334 secondary schools studied, 128 schools, or more than 38 percent, report "no plan" for taking care of individual differences through instruction; 73 schools use "coaching classes;" 26 use "conference periods;" 11 use the "North Denver Plan;" 38 use the "Batavia Plan;" 27 use "supervised study;" 7 use "minimum and maximum courses;" and 24 use "extra subjects."

The groups of schools using "conference periods," the "North Denver Plan," and the "Batavia Plan" report a smaller percentage of pupils dropping out of school during the semester than any of the other plans. Schools using "conference periods" and the "Batavia Plan" show a small percentage of elimination and a comparatively small percentage of failures in one, two, and three or more subjects.

Statistics show that promotion plans making provision for individual differences in instruction which aim at individual assistance rather than group assistance are most effective.

The evidence secured from this study relative to retardation and elimination accompanying the specific types of plans shows that the administration of the plan is quite as important as the plan itself and in many cases more important.

Promotion plans providing for individual differences in instruction in high schools require only a few more teachers than schools making no such provisions.

D. Relation of Bases for Promotion to Failures, Courses Dropped, and Extent to Which Pupils Leave School

Of the 334 secondary schools reporting in this study, 222 schools, or approximately 66 percent, used "other combinations" as a basis for promotion. Only four schools promote pupils on the basis of final examinations alone; and the enrolment in these four schools is only 1,101 pupils. Fifty schools use "school marks" as a basis for promotion; and 58 promote on a basis of "daily records and final examinations." It is evident that "other combinations" represents the most commonly used basis for promotion in this group of schools. Schools using this basis for promotion had the smallest amount of retardation and elimination in classes A, C, and E. However, the percentage of pupils, in each grade, in all classes of schools, leaving school, distributed according to bases for promotion, did not vary greatly.

Schools basing promotion upon final examinations alone are the most inefficient of all from the standpoint of retardation and elimination.

No single factor is popular or efficient as a basis for promotion.

E. Relation of Time of Promotion to Failures, Courses Dropped, and Extent to Which Pupils Leave School

Some school administrators are still attributing much of the retardation and elimination in the high school to inadequate provisions for safeguarding the welfare of pupils in the matter of promotion from the standpoint of time. It is argued that midyear promotion is not practicable for small schools in that it requires too many teachers, and that schools employing annual promotions do not provide sufficient opportunities for gaining time and may actually tend to mechanize the whole administrative plan. This section of the report shows the amount of retardation and elimination accompanying administrative plans providing for annual and semi-annual promotions. However, it must be kept in mind that the data reported by schools granting midyear promotions are for the second semester only.

Out of the 334 secondary schools studied, 192 promote annually and 142 promote semi-annually. The average number of pupils per teacher was 20.6 for the group of schools promoting annually and 23.9 for the group of schools promoting semi-annually. This may lead to an erroneous conclusion unless it is remembered that the group promoting annually is made up largely of high schools with small enrolments and consequently it has a smaller average number of pupils per teacher.

From the data at hand, the investigator concludes:

The number of teachers required to operate a school is not necessarily increased by midyear promotions. This statement applies to all classes of schools.

The 142 schools promoting semi-annually eliminated 7.6 percent of all pupils enrolled during the semester; while the group of schools promoting annually eliminated 7.9 percent of all pupils enrolled during the same period.

Schools promoting semi-annually have a smaller percentage of pupils dropping courses than the group promoting annually. This is not only true for the total percentage of pupils dropping courses, but it is also true for each of the grades. Schools promoting annually, however, report a smaller percentage of pupils dropping three or more subjects.

A distribution of data on failures, courses dropped, and pupils leaving school, according to time of promotion, shows that the schools promoting semi-annually are more effective in retaining pupils in school. The percentage of pupils failing is slightly greater for the group of schools promoting semi-annually than for the group promoting annually. Just the opposite is true in regard to the percentage of pupils dropping courses.

F. Conclusions and Problems for Further Study

According to the investigator, these are among the conclusions which may be safely drawn from the detailed data which he presents in the complete study:

1. Promotion plans are administrative devices which propose to minimize the problems resulting from mass instruction for pupils of widely different capacities, interests, aptitudes, and experiences.

2. Schools employing an improved classification plan require slightly more teachers than schools making only a chance grouping of pupils.

3. Improved classification plans are accompanied by a smaller percentage of retardation and elimination than mere chance groupings.

4. Promotion plans providing for individual differences of pupils through instruction require only slightly more teachers than schools making no such provisions.

5. Instructional plans which aim at individual assistance rather than group assistance are more effective in retaining pupils in school and keeping them moving forward regularly through the grades.

6. The wide variation in the percentage of retardation and elimination found in schools employing specific types of instructional plans indicates that the administration of the plan is quite as important as the plan itself, if not more important.

7. Midyear promotions do not necessarily increase the number of teachers required to operate the school.

8. In all classes of schools, elimination is only slightly greater (less than one percent) for schools promoting annually than for those promoting semi-annually.

9. Finally, the effectiveness of promotion plans, as that of all school organization, in retaining pupils in school and keeping them moving forward regularly through the grades, resolves itself into a problem of proper administration of the plan used.

The investigator listed the following topics for further study. They are an outgrowth of his investigation:

1. Do specific types of promotion plans in high schools tend to increase or decrease achievement in subject-matter? For example, do they raise or lower the standard of attainment of those who graduate?

2. Do certain specific promotion plans in high school tend to increase or decrease the efficiency of pupils in higher institutions?

3. Do promotion plans provide for inferior, average, and superior pupils equally well? For example, is it possible that certain promotion plans are retaining more of the superior pupils and eliminating more of the low ability pupils than some other plans?

4. What promotion plans require the better trained teachers from the standpoint of efficient administration?

5. What plan, or plans, place the heavier load upon teachers? It is evident from the data reported in this study that the plan does not necessarily greatly increase the number of teachers.

CHAPTER V

HOW SUPERVISION CAN HELP TO PUT PUPIL PROMO-
TIONS ON A BETTER ARTICULATED BASIS

SINCE one of the primary functions of supervision is to coordinate and integrate the more or less separate elements of an educational program into a functioning whole, the Committee on Pupil Promotion Problems felt that supervisors should be given an opportunity to tell in this Yearbook how supervision can help to put pupil promotions on a better articulated basis.

A small selected group of supervisors were mailed special inquiries, which included these questions:

1. Do you find that different standards of promotion and different conceptions of the purposes of promotion exist in different schools in your city? Yes_____ No____. Do different standards often exist in the same school? Yes____ No____
If they do, what means have you found to be most successful in bringing about a greater unity of purpose and the wider application of acceptable principles relative to pupil promotion, with a view to remedying the situation?
2. In what ways can adequate supervision bring about better articulation of the units of American education?

Replies from 55 supervisors, representing 25 states and all branches of supervisory service,[1] constitute the basis of this chapter.

What means do supervisors find most successful in bringing about a wider application of acceptable principles relative to pupil promotion?— Of the group of 55 selected supervisors who were questioned, 96 percent report that they find different standards of promotion and different conceptions of the purposes of promotion existing not only in different schools in the same school system, but also in the same school.

In answer to the question: "What means have you found to be most successful in bringing about a greater unity of purpose and the wider application of acceptable principles relative to pupil promotion, with a view to remedying the situation?" these supervisors reported the use of the following means. They are arranged according to frequency of mention.

1. Use of standardized tests to supplement teacher judgment, followed up with remedial work where needed.

To illustrate, one supervisor of elementary grades writes as follows:

Teachers are trained in the use of tests and also in how to use the results for daily improvement of instruction. Following a city-wide testing program, in which

---

[1] These included four supervisors of kindergarten and primary education, six primary supervisors, eighteen elementary supervisors, nine grade supervisors, one general supervisor, five supervising principals, seven county supervisors, two rural supervisors, one state supervisor of elementary grades, one supervising director of instruction, and one assistant superintendent of schools.

all the teachers took part, individual profile cards for each pupil and class record sheets were made out by each teacher for her own class. The class record sheet contained a list of all the pupils, and opposite each name the pupil's M. A., C. A., I. Q., subject age, teacher's rating (made before the tests were given), and the section assignment. The teachers, principals, and supervisors planned together the bases for promotion, and for special attention for bright and dull pupils. In the case of special pupils, these factors were taken into consideration: health, age, home environment, probability of staying in school, and ability to progress in the next grade. Ability groups were formed based on the results. The whole project was a great factor in influencing the judgment of a large number of local teachers. They found that their rating was not always correct, even upon re-testing to check. The individual profile cards served as an incentive to both teachers and pupils. The failure list was reduced by one-half, and the achievement results greatly increased, as shown by later tests.

2. Group teachers' meetings, grade meetings, departmental meetings, and building meetings dealing specifically with standards of promotion, factors that should be considered in making promotions, and means of deciding individual cases.

3. Discussion of individual cases with teachers concerned, and solution of problems by application of acceptable principles.

4. Study of pupils through individual case histories—presentation of evidence of the wide range of abilities and backgrounds among pupils. In the light of these wide ranges, discuss how far the same accomplishment can be expected of all pupils.

5. Cooperative course-of-study building—setting up of minimum, average, and maximum requirements as well as provision for individual differences. Teaching subject-matter out of the lives of children, their interests and activities.

Informal testing on course of study, with results, compiled for school system and by school buildings, and discussed in individual buildings with supervisor.

6. Attention to age-grade conditions. Conferences for a discussion of the results of retardation. Discussion of the effects of non-promotion on the emotional life of the child.

7. Critical evaluation of subject-matter requirements in connection with "high spots" of failure.

8. Carefully planned intervisitations require every teacher to be familiar with the work of grade preceding as well as following his own grade.

Occasionally shifting assignments of teacher so that he has experience in the grades below as well as with the grade above his regular work.
Have each teacher visit a well-prepared class in the grade just above his own and observe its work.

9. A collection of definite evidences of the need for studying the situation of pupil promotion and failure.

According to one supervisor, "oftentimes teachers, principals, and supervisors have no very clear idea of the extent of pupil failure, and amount of retardation."

These remedies were suggested by three supervisors:

a. Analyze promotion reports to diagnose difficulties and to determine remedial measures for the child, the class, the school, and the system.

b. Follow up pupils from year to year to see if standards are high enough to insure future success.

c. Study records of pupils' progress to determine which teachers seem to have standards out of harmony with group analysis of reasons.

10. Development of a common conception of grading.

Secure greater uniformity in marking through conferences in which there is a discussion of "What Our School Grades Mean." This helps in getting a more general conception of what the grades given to pupils should indicate.

11. Exhibits in supervisor's office of school work acceptable in various buildings showing the wide range.

12. Teacher participation in defining objectives and goals for each stage of advancement, and in studying and experimenting in classroom activities and teaching suggestions for reaching the goals defined for each grade.

13. Study on the part of the school psychologist of pupils who have been unsuccessful in their work—also a study of those who are recommended for making an additional grade.

14. The positive provision for problem cases without interference with regular classroom procedure.

15. Visitation by supervisor to determine class progress in cases of new or weak teachers.

One supervisor writes: "This is largely done by principals, but the supervisor's time is so used in inverse proportion to the principal's ability."

16. Rectifying mistakes—reclassification of pupils wrongly placed tends to make teachers conscious of their errors and to improve future judgments.

17. Discussion of educational guidance in group meetings.

18. Group meetings in which topics such as the following are discussed:

a. Minimum requirements for each unit
b. Physical, mental, and social characteristics of pupils at different grade levels
c. Individual differences and how to meet them
d. Habit formation
e. Home cooperation—how to secure it
f. Development, interpretation, and use of pupil's cumulative case history.

In what ways can adequate supervision bring about better articulation of the units of American education?—This question was also put to the selected group of 55 supervisors. Their responses showed that many of them were awake to the problems of inarticulation and that, in their judgment, the first requisite to a solution was an honest recognition of these problems and a determination on the part of both teachers and supervisors to correct them. The definite relation of supervision to articulation was expressed by supervisors in statements such as these:

It is a primary function of supervision to coordinate, integrate, and weld together the separate elements of an educational program into a functioning whole.

Upon supervision rests the responsibility of keeping the teacher alert to the fact that each administrative unit is only a part of a unified school system. Supervisors must think and plan in terms of the whole education of the child, rather than in terms of certain subject-matter outlines to be covered in certain grades.

Adequate supervision implies a definitely organized program: (1) within each unit of the school system, and (2) between the different units of the system. Supervisors should have a broad view of the entire field of education, hence they should think in terms of the whole rather than a segment.

These are among the ways and means by which supervisors themselves suggest that adequate supervision can bring about better articulation of the units of American education:

1. By developing a better and clearer understanding of the educational philosophy which is to govern the whole process of education rather than a series of philosophies governing each administrative unit.

A philosophy of better articulation is also needed and a desire for it in the hearts and minds of all those directly concerned with the education of children.

2. By definitely planning a program for the whole school system from the kindergarten through the highest grade, in order to avoid breaks and overlapping.

There should be a clear understanding of the proper relationship of each administrative unit to the other, and no gaps in between. There is need for a clearer and more careful definition of education throughout the school system as a whole, and of carefully pointing out the definite contribution each unit must make to the whole. This necessitates adequate training in supervision on the part of the superintendent of schools, as well as on the part of supervisors and principals. All those concerned with supervisory activities need as part of their training a basic educational philosophy, a general conception of an entire school system from kindergarten through grade twelve at least, a knowledge of child growth and behavior, and training in diagnosing and remedying learning difficulties. A supervisor so trained is able to show a teacher of a particular grade by definite tests what children have done in a preceding grade and what is required of them in the succeeding grade.

3. By organizing programs of coordinated supervision.

Plans for supervision should be a coordinated program, not one in which each supervisor works alone in his special field or department. One supervisor describes the present situation as follows:

The work of departmental supervisors is, in most school systems, a group of separate unrelated units; whereas they should be so closely in touch with one another that the work of each supervisor would be an integral part of the whole school program as presented to the child.

This coordination could be attained by providing a head supervisor, trained for such work, who could unite the group. An assistant superintendent has sometimes been selected for this work, but too often his training has been inadequate to meet a situation where a "working" knowledge of music, art, primary and grammar school methods of teaching, and high-school and college requirements was needed.

Another supervisor writes:

The superintendent in his capacity as a supervisor should organize and direct group meetings in which all supervisors and directors of instruction would get together frequently to discuss policies and means of working them out in such a way that the entire school system may be thought of as a whole and not as a collection of different departments. By bringing together officers from different units to discuss articulation problems, a common understanding would be developed.

4. By working toward a unification of the work between the various parts of the school system, i. e., kindergarten and primary, elementary and junior high school, and junior and senior high school—such unification to be brought about by all-supervisory conferences and intervisitation of teachers and principals in the units immediately above and below them.

5. By developing courses of study representing cooperative efforts of teachers and principals from different units. These should unify the work and at the same time provide for individual differences.

A curriculum based on the needs, interests, and abilities of particular children in a particular setting will do much to insure maximum growth for the children concerned.

Committees of teachers and principals from elementary school, junior high school, and senior high school working together develop courses, so that each unit prepares for the next higher unit.

6. By seeing that a cumulative case record is sent with each pupil when he goes to the next higher grade or unit.

This provides that every teacher each year knows something of his pupil's ability, achievements, characteristics, and physical condition. In addition to seeing that these case records are kept and passed on from unit to unit, the supervisor frequently aids in their interpretation.

7. By demanding better trained teachers.

According to one supervisor, "as long as we have the traditional type of supervisors whose chief emphasis is on isolated units of subject-matter, we will have the traditional school program with the day's work broken up into kaleidoscopic fragments."

Another supervisor writes:

Teacher training should be better and more comprehensive. For example, kindergarten teachers should at least be trained for primary work; better still, they should have some acquaintance with the aims, purposes, and methods of the whole elementary school. High-school teachers should not feel it beneath their dignity to know the work of the grades. In other words, teachers should be trained so that they see in a more comprehensive way the whole process of education.

8. By providing teachers with in-service study classes based on principles, theories, and objectives common to the various units and their differences in objectives, purposes and procedures.

9. By collecting evidences of poor articulation.

This can be done by conferences, tests of various kinds, by a detailed survey of the field, by charting and graphing results. After the causes of poor articulation had been decided upon, a plan of attack could be outlined and remedial measures applied. To be effective, these would have to be worked out in a cooperative way.

The judgments of teachers, the opinions of administrators, the findings of scientific investigations, and other sources of help should be sought.

10. By using a supervisory technic based upon a single set of principles agreed upon by the entire local supervisory group.

11. By developing with teachers an overview of the entire school program—in group conferences discussing the problem of continuity of work from the skills side as well as from the child's point of view.

Teachers should entertain clearer ideas of what articulation means and of its desirability as a goal. The problems of articulation that usually concern classroom teachers most are problems of promoting, grouping, individual instruction, and recording and reporting each pupil's continuous development. In order that teachers may govern their practice in these matters by the larger considerations they need supervisory help.

12. By giving to each teacher for comparison a report of all classes in the school system on the same units of work as taught in his class.

Educational measurements scientifically used and the results intelligently applied will show a child's growth at various levels.

13. By encouraging less rigid classification, brought about by a rigid grading system.

This includes variation in assignment and requirement. For the capable group, the course of study may be enriched and thoroughly mastered. Less exacting standards and a simplified course of study may be arranged for the slow pupil.

14. By arranging (a) exchange of classroom visits between the various units and (b) exchange of teachers between the various units.

The above 14 recommendations summarize the best judgments of 55 selected supervisors as to how adequate supervision can bring about better articulation of the units of American education.

CHAPTER VI

HOW ELEMENTARY AND SECONDARY SCHOOLS ARE MEETING THE NEEDS OF INDIVIDUAL PUPILS

W HAT TO do with the dull pupil" and "how to provide for the bright pupil" are the two most acute promotion problems in American schools according to 555 superintendents.[1]
The problem of what to do with the dull pupil is revealed in practically every school survey through data which show that:

1. In chronological age there is a decided overage or retarded situation.

2. In mental age a large percentage of children are below normal, many of them so much so that satisfactory school progress, according to standard rate of progress, is impossible.

3. In school age, notwithstanding the actual retardation, the pupils are so far behind their grade classification in school accomplishment that they cannot do satisfactory work in the so-called thought, reasoning, and interpretation subjects.

These facts have led school administrators to realize that many of the present courses of study, standards of attainment, and requirements for promotion do not meet the needs of dull pupils. In the elementary schools, they have sought to remedy the situation by: (1) eliminating material from the content of courses of study, setting up minimum essentials, differentiating units of instruction, and substituting different units for pupils of different levels of ability; (2) increasing the time allowed for the completion of the elementary curriculum; (3) in some cases, lowering the standard required for promotion; (4) providing special administrative helps such as homogeneous grouping with opportunity rooms and adjustment classes; and (5) by special teaching methods.

All of these plans for (1) differentiation through administration, and (2) differentiation through instruction, call for a careful analysis of the characteristic learning differences between dull and bright pupils. Many child psychologists, classroom teachers, and school administrators are not yet ready completely to define these differences. Some more or less definite conclusions have been reached, however, relative to the characteristic differences of dull and bright pupils and general principles which should be observed for differentiation through administration and instruction.

The following tentative statements were prepared by a committee of the city schools of Baltimore, representing all types of teaching, supervisory, and administrative positions.

---

[1] See pages 35-42 of this Yearbook.

A. Characteristic Differences of Dull and Bright Pupils

Though there are many shadings in between, this brief outline throws into relief only the sharply contrasting characteristics of dull and bright children which have been observed in Baltimore and are largely corroborated by a number of specialists, who have written on this subject.[1]

DULL	BRIGHT
Inability to coordinate two or more mental functions	Ability to coordinate any number of functions
Difficulty in assimilation	Ease of assimilation
Learning through detailed, simple material	Ability to generalize, pick up clues from less concrete materials
Short attention span	Sustained attention
Slow reaction time	Quick reaction time
Restricted curiosity and limited initiative	Intellectual curiosity and initiative
Limited imagination	High imagination
Personal viewpoint	Broadminded, impersonal attitude toward problems
Dependence on criticism and approval of others	Self-criticism; intellectual approval highly satisfying
Lack of appreciation of intellectual humor	Sense of humor
Trouble with language symbols	Keen language ability
Narrow interests	Versatility and vitality of interests
Slow reading habits	Rapid reading habits
Dependence on others to show application of previously learned experiences	Sensitivity to application of knowledge
Inadequate memory for abstractions	Logical and accurate memory
Observation without generalization	Close observation
Immediate recall	Delayed recall
Judgment on inadequate data	Ability to reason without going through concrete experiences; suspended judgment until necessary data are in
Better performance through repetition without much attention to principles	Better performance through understanding principles
Emotional bias in action	Rationalized feelings
Insensitivity to intellectual and aesthetic elements in a situation, unless pointed out by others	Sensitivity to intellectual and aesthetic elements in a situation

---

[1] See:

Adams, Fay, and Brown, Walker. *Teaching the Bright Pupil.* New York: Henry Holt and Company, 1930. 249 p.

B. General Principles of Differentiation[1]

The basic aim of American education is equality of opportunity. But individual differences among pupils make the realization of this aim difficult, since variation in both content and method must, to effect it, exhibit variation as great as is the variation among human beings. The facts of individual differences require the adaptation of the curriculum to the talents and limitations of each pupil.

Hence the first principle of differentiation is this:

1. To enable each pupil simultaneously to satisfy the needs of himself and of others, it is necessary to explore the capacities, interests, and previous accomplishments of every pupil.

Nature of individual differences—Psychology and biology teach that no two human beings are alike. They differ both in amount of any trait and in kinds of traits. They differ still more in combinations of traits. Even in the case of twins some variation appears. Furthermore, in human beings variation is continuous from the least of any trait in question to the most—there are no gaps. Schemes of classifying school children into groups, such as X, Y, and Z, are but artificial practical devices. Variation within these groups exists and must be respected. Furthermore, while variation in a single trait is very great—variation in a total personality comprised of a large number of traits can and does by infinite combinations result in an infinite number of personalities. Each human being is unique as the result of heredity and environment.

---

[1] In preparing this statement, the Baltimore committee drew not only on the teaching experience of its individual members, but also upon many writers in the field, particularly on: Thorndike, E. L., and Gates, A. I. *Elementary Principles of Education,* Chapters X and XIV. New York: The Macmillan Company, 1929.

Continued from page 108:

Baker, Harry J. *Characteristic Differences in Bright and Dull Pupils.* Bloomington, Ill.: Public School Publishing Company, 1927. 118 p.

Baker, Harry J. "Educational Research and Statistics." *School and Society* 21: 570-72; May 9, 1925.

An address on "X, Y, and Z Pupils in the Detroit Public Schools," presented before Section Q of the American Association for the Advancement of Science, Washington, D. C., December 31, 1924.

Baldwin, Bird T. "Methods of Selecting Superior or Gifted Children." *Twenty-Third Yearbook,* Part I, p. 37. National Society for the Study of Education. Bloomington, Ill.: Public School Publishing Company, 1924.

Carroll, Herbert Allen. *Generalization of Bright and Dull Children,* A Comparative Study with Special Reference to Spelling. Contributions to Education, No. 439. New York: Bureau of Publications, Teachers College, Columbia University, 1930. 54 p.

Coy, Genevieve Lenore. *The Interests, Abilities and Achievements of a Special Class for Gifted Children.* Contributions to Education, No. 131. New York: Bureau of Publications, Teachers College, Columbia University, 1923. 194 p.

Goddard, Henry Herbert. *School Training of Gifted Children.* Yonkers-on-Hudson: World Book Company, 1928. 226 p.

Hence these are the second and third principles of differentiation:

2. Both in content and in method the range provided to meet the needs of all pupils must be extended to meet the great range of human talent which the schools now care for. It is the duty of the school to furnish such an environment as will bring about the optimum development of each individual.

3. In content and in method the fact that variation is continuous must be recognized and insofar as is possible provided for.

Amount of variation—The difference in weight of 3200 six-year-olds has been found to range from 36 to 54 pounds. In height the range for the same group was from 40 to 48 inches. In Pintner-Cunningham intelligence scores, 3600 six-year-olds were found to range from a score of 2 to a score of 56. It is estimated that the most gifted child will in comparison with the least gifted of the same age do over six times as much in the same time or do the same amount with less than a sixth as many errors. It is also held that the best pupil can do from 2 to 5 times as much

Continued from page 109:

Hilleboe, Guy L. *Finding and Teaching Atypical Children.* Contributions to Education, No. 423. New York: Bureau of Publications, Teachers College, Columbia University, 1930. 177 p.

Hollingworth, Leta S. *Gifted Children, Their Nature and Nurture.* New York: The Macmillan Company, 1924. 339 p.

Hollingworth, Leta S. *Psychology of Subnormal Children.* New York: The Macmillan Company, 1920. 288 p.

Inskeep, Annie Dolman. *Teaching Dull and Retarded Children.* New York: The Macmillan Company, 1926. 455 p.

Jensen, Dortha Williams. "The Gifted Child, I, Educational Concepts and Practices; II, Present School Provision for the Gifted Child." *Journal of Educational Research* 15: 34-45, January, 1927; 126-33, February, 1927.

Lamson, Edna E. *A Study of Young Gifted Children in Senior High School.* Contributions to Education, No. 424. New York: Bureau of Publications, Teachers College, Columbia University, 1930. 117 p.

National Education Association, Research Division. "Vitalizing the High-School Curriculum," *Research Bulletin* 7: 182-92; September, 1929. Washington, D. C.: the Association.

National Society for the Study of Education. *The Nineteenth Yearbook,* Part II, Classroom Problems in the Education of Gifted Children. Bloomington, Ill.: Public School Publishing Company, 1920. 126 p.

National Society for the Study of Education. *The Twenty-Third Yearbook,* Part I, The Education of Gifted Children. Bloomington, Ill.: Public School Publishing Company, 1924. 444 p.

Stedman, Lulu M. *Education of Gifted Children.* Yonkers-on-Hudson: World Book Company, 1924.

Terman, Lewis M., and others. *Mental and Physical Traits of a Thousand Gifted Children,* Genetic Studies of Genius, Vol. I. Stanford University, Calif.: Stanford University Press, 1926.

Whipple, Helen D. *Making Citizens of the Mentally Limited.* Bloomington, Ill.: Public School Publishing Company, 1927. 374 p.

Woodrow, Herbert H. *Brightness and Dullness in Children.* Philadelphia: J. B. Lippincott Company, 1919. (Lippincott's Educational Guides, ed. by Wm. F. Russell.)

in a given time as the poorest pupil, even where schools are supposedly graded well and where pupils are reclassified every six months.[1]

Individuals also grow at different rates and reach different levels of maturity. Individual differences in ability to learn those school functions which require the management of general and abstract ideas, for example, show a constant increase from year to year until the maximum development has been reached. Some are never able to learn more than the simplest forms of manual activities. A few exceed the general intelligence of their generation. Individual differences, then, demand a longitudinal as well as a horizontal specialization.

Hence this fourth principle of differentiation:

4. Different rates of progress and different lines of study are both required to fit differences in capacity and to harmonize with the different vocational, recreational, social, civic, and other duties which will characterize adult life.

Kinds of variations—While the gross amount of variation between individuals of a given age or grade is greater than has generally been recognized by schools, the kinds or varieties of personalities are infinite. The school has placed great stress on "norms." The pressure on unification has been so great that we are accused of being a nation of Babbitts. The average has probably been too much glorified. It has a tendency toward mediocrity. The schools should make greater efforts to discover and develop high points in every pupil, rather than to level them down and to lose them in general averages. Fortunately, the work of the world is also of great variety. The school has too far neglected these facts—concentrating on a comparatively narrow range of academic courses.

Hence the fifth and sixth principles of differentiation are these:

5. In the general appraisal of the work of individual pupils, there should be greater emphasis given to the development of individual talents of pupils —less averaging down, and more cultivation given to whatever even slightly useful traits a pupil may have in the hope that these may be developed into a contribution to society and to the individual himself.

6. There is need for greater recognition of the less academic activities of school.

C. Differentiation through Administration and Instruction— Present Practices

As part of the National Survey of Secondary Education now under way the following request was made of all secondary school principals in the United States in May, 1930:

[1] See: Thorndike, E. L., and Gates, A. I. *Elementary Principles of Education.* New York: The Macmillan Company, 1929. 335 p.

Will you kindly indicate on the following checking list what your school is doing to provide for the individual differences of pupils?

Note: Check (x) items in use in your school; double check (xx) items which have proved unusually successful.

1. Problem method
2. Project curriculum
3. Credit for projects or studies carried outside of school hours
4. Variation in number of subjects a pupil may carry
5. Promotions more frequently than each semester
6. Advisory program for pupil guidance
7. Educational guidance through exploratory courses
8. Vocational guidance through exploratory courses
9. Special coaching of slow pupils
10. Special coaching to enable capable pupils to "skip" a grade or half grade
11. Special classes for students who have failed

12. Oportunity rooms for slow pupils
13. Opportunity rooms for gifted pupils
14. Adjustment classes or rooms
15. Remedial classes or rooms
16. Restoration classes
17. Scientific study of problem cases
18. Psychological studies
19. Differentiated assignments to pupils in same class section
20. Long-unit assignments
21. Homogeneous or ability grouping
22. Winnetka technique
23. Individualized instruction
24. Contract plan
25. Laboratory plan of instruction
26. Dalton plan
27. Modified Dalton plan
28. Morrison plan
29. Other (name it) _____

Table 30 shows the extent to which each of the above devices for meeting the individual differences among secondary school pupils is used and whether or not it is proving unusually successful.

The National Survey of Secondary Education will include not only a comprehensive follow-up study of all those provisions listed in Table 30, which according to high-school principals are proving unusually successful, but also a review of one hundred Master's and Doctor's theses dealing with provisions for individual differences. The following paragraphs show the broad scope of this survey.

The National Survey of Secondary Education—Through a special Congressional appropriation of $225,000, a study of the organization, administration, and work of secondary schools and their articulation with elementary and higher education is under way. During the year 1929-30, $50,000 was available; $100,000 is available for the year 1930-31; and $75,000, in addition to any unexpended balances from the earlier years, during the year 1931-32.

In general, it is not the purpose of this national survey merely to add another statistical or purely descriptive account of secondary schools to such accounts as are now available. Rather it is the purpose of this survey to select and analyze typical practices and conspicuous innovations with a view to giving the public and school officers the information necessary, first, to a complete understanding of the significant trends of American secondary education, and, second, to an understanding of methods of evaluating local undertakings.

William John Cooper, Commissioner of Education, is director of the survey. Leonard V. Koos is the associate director in charge of the staff and direction of the numerous projects of the survey. Carl A. Jessen, chief specialist in secondary education of the Office of Education, is serving as coordinating officer for the survey.

Sections of the survey have been assigned to the following specialists in secondary education:

1. Junior high-school reorganization—Francis T. Spaulding, Harvard University, and O. I. Frederick, University of Michigan
2. Horizontal organization of secondary education and the secondary school population—Grayson N. Kefauver, Teachers College, Columbia University; Victor H. Noll, University of Minnesota, and Elwood Drake, Columbia University
3. Special problems in reorganization—William M. Proctor and Scovel S. Mayo, Stanford University
4. Selected secondary schools in smaller communities and rural areas—Emery N. Ferriss, Cornell University
5. Characteristics of small high schools—Walter H. Gaumnitz, Office of Education
6. District organization and administrative and supervisory staffs—Fred Engelhardt, University of Minnesota
7. Legal and other regulatory provisions of secondary education—Ward W. Keesecker, Office of Education
8. Guidance and the extra-curriculum—William C. Reavis and G. E. Van Dyke, University of Chicago
9. Provisions for individual differences and related matters—Roy O. Billett, Ohio State University

TABLE 30.—PROVISIONS FOR INDIVIDUAL DIFFERENCES IN 8,594 SECONDARY SCHOOLS [1]

Items	In Use	Used with Unusual Success
1 Problem method	3,772	444
2. Project curriculum	1,928	365
3. Credit for projects or studies carried outside of school hours	3,012	439
4. Variation in number of subjects a pupil may carry	5,633	795
5. Promotions more frequently than each semester	583	103
6. Advisory program for pupil guidance	3,064	540
7. Educational guidance through exploratory courses	1,707	193
8. Vocational guidance through exploratory courses	1,725	186
9. Special coaching of slow pupils	4,318	781
10. Special coaching to enable capable pupils to "skip" a grade or half grade	612	114
11. Special classes for students who have failed	2,262	350
12. Opportunity rooms for slow pupils	774	172
13. Opportunity rooms for gifted pupils	253	69
14. Adjustment classes or rooms	489	55
15. Remedial classes or rooms	503	90
16. Restoration classes	167	24
17. Scientific study of problem cases	1,197	146
18. Psychological studies	1,007	70
19. Differentiated assignments to pupils in same class section	3,259	788
20. Long-unit assignments	1,963	349
21. Homogeneous or ability grouping	2,019	721
22. Winnetka technique	105	14
23. Individualized instruction	1,836	309
24. Contract plan	1,828	465
25. Laboratory plan of instruction	2,288	323
26. Dalton plan	147	15
27. Modified Dalton plan	434	52
28. Morrison plan	562	175
29. Other		101

[1] Advance data supplied by courtesy of those directing the National Survey of Secondary Education.

10. Selection and appointment of teachers—Walter S. Deffenbaugh, Office of Education, and William H. Zeigel, University of Missouri
11. School publicity—Belmont Farley, Division of Publications, National Education Association
12. The curriculum—Arthur K. Loomis, Director, Curriculum Department, Denver Public Schools, and Edwin S. Lide, University of Chicago
13. Interscholastic contests—P. Roy Brammell, University of Washington
14. Articulation of high schools and higher institutions—P. Roy Brammell.

These assignments do not comprehend the full scope of the survey, as work on certain projects will be undertaken later during the current fiscal year.

Three additional major areas of contact with problems of articulation will be included in the National Survey of Secondary Education. The first deals with horizontal articulation and is a study of the relationship of general and special types of education on the secondary level. It will include these nine analyses and comparisons:

1. Prevalence and distribution of different types of provisions for secondary education.
2. Comparisons of programs offered in different types of secondary schools.
3. Effectiveness of specialized training offered under different types of organization.
4. Considerations other than outcomes of teaching affecting the organizations of secondary education.
5. Provisions and need for horizontal articulation of units of secondary education.
6. Special types of education on the secondary school level.
7. Occupations that may be entered from the secondary school level of training.
8. Provisions for guidance under different types of organization of secondary schools.
9. Articulation of secondary schools with community developed under different types of organization.

A second phase of the articulation problem will be attacked by the National Survey of Secondary Education in the section on junior high-school reorganization. This section will include a study of articulation within specific units of secondary education.

The survey will also include a study of promising innovations in the articulation of high schools and colleges—brought about by recent modifications of procedures in the colleges and other higher institutions in admitting freshmen and making adjustments for them after admission.

Since this survey will present such extensive data relative to differentiation through administration, only two brief illustrations of current practice are cited here. They are more or less typical of procedures in use in many of our more progressive public school systems. One lists the administrative devices for meeting the needs of pupils of different levels of ability in use in a city of over 800,000 population. The other shows the results of an attempt to reduce failure and consequent overageness in a city slightly over 30,000 in population. These two examples are followed by: (1) a statement relative to the decrease in retardation reported by New York City; (2) a brief presentation of arguments for and against homogeneous grouping; and (3) illustrations of course-of-study material differentiated to fit pupils of different levels of ability.

D. Differentiation through Administration in the Baltimore City Schools [1]

Among the administrative measures which are carried out on a city-wide basis to facilitate the differentiation of content and method for bright and dull pupils, the most fundamental is the classification of pupils according to ability range as indicated by mental, chronological, and achievement ages, and tastes and aptitudes as indicated by electives; second is the administrative machinery for listing and purchasing materials which aid differentiation in content and method; third is the adaptation of courses of study to provide for enrichment for the bright and simplified content for the dull; and fourth, such other administrative measures as diagnostic testing and remedial instruction, acceleration and slower than normal progress, preventive classes, and trial promotions which save a large percentage of failure among the average and dull groups.

Classification of pupils in the Baltimore city schools—It is interesting to note how pupils' achievement, reflecting as it does an interplay of intelligence, personality traits, interests, health conditions, and learning habits, becomes an increasingly important criterion for classification as the pupils progress through the grades. In the first grade, mental tests furnish the first criterion for classification. This is adjusted when necessary after teachers have had six weeks' contact with the children.

At the primary level, the judgment of the teacher concerned is the most direct agency in making these changes in classification. Since the judgments of individual teachers often vary widely, and since individual children make different manifestations of themselves with different teachers, a definite procedure is set up whereby several estimates of a child's ability contribute to his reclassification. This includes retesting, a conference of the principal and the present teacher with previous teachers, with the child himself, and with his parents. The primary supervisor, too, can often throw light on the subject from her wider knowledge of children and classroom conditions.

At the beginning of the 4-B grade, a third intelligence test is given. In the fourth, fifth, and sixth grades, the factor receiving greatest weight in classification is classroom achievement. In these grades, as in the primary, the strongest pupils save another half year, thus completing the six elementary grades in five years. Pupils who lag behind and seem unable to accomplish the work of any grade in the normal time are usually sent to review summer school to make up their deficiencies. A few who are extremely poor in their work are obliged to repeat the work of the grade. Throughout the first six grades, pupils who give indications of subnormality are reported to the division of special education. They are then tested by a school psychiatrist and if need be are transferred to subnormal classes.

Pupils entering the Baltimore junior high schools are classified according to all available information concerning their school history, including

---

[1] Prepared by a committee of the Baltimore city schools representing all types of administrative and supervisory positions.

the teacher ratings, achievement tests, and mental and chronological ages sent up from elementary schools. Separation by choice of curriculum is made when pupils enter 8-B. Here again classification within each curriculum takes place.

At the senior high-school level, as far as possible, every school is organized on the principle of homogeneous ability grouping. In the tenth grade, the grouping is on the basis of data supplied by the junior high schools. Two or three weeks after the opening of school, or immediately after the close of the first quarter, academic groups are given an objective test in some or all of their subjects. On the basis of the returns, a redistribution is made within each subject. It therefore often happens that a pupil will be in an "X" group in one subject, and in a "Y" or "Z" group in another. The twelfth-grade college preparatory group is divided into two classes organized on an ability—or rather achievement—basis. A very definite difference in the administration of these two classes is maintained. All commercial classes are similarly grouped.

These five special adjustments are also frequently carried out by Baltimore principals to facilitate differentiation: (1) Individual pupil program-making in elementary schools, which permits a pupil to get additional help in the subjects in which he is weak; (2) allowing children to continue with the same teacher for at least a year (To illustrate, at the end of two and a half years, when the accelerated third-grade children enter the fourth grade, they remain with their same teacher, who then carries on with the class the first half year of fourth-grade work); (3) classification to provide remedial group rather than individual instruction (The bases used are intelligence and accomplishment in reading and arithmetic and yield groups as follows: (a) pupils above in all three, (b) pupils below in all, (c) pupils below in reading, and (d) pupils below in arithmetic only); (4) formation of special classes of inferior 7-B pupils for whom detailed case histories are furnished teachers and on which they base their teaching content and methods of instruction; and (5) arrangement of schedule so that ability groups of the same subject and grade run parallel. This allows for redistribution by subject, to suit ability clues in each subject, without disruption of the rest of the class group.

Differentiation through selection of instructional materials—An important administrative measure affecting the differentiation of content and methods for bright and dull pupils is the machinery set up for selecting and purchasing instructional materials. In Baltimore, the following plan is used. The supervisory staff is obliged to keep informed concerning all types of instructional materials. Several of the supervisors have a "Teachers Service Bureau" which includes samples of all available materials in the field supervised. These samples are circulated among the teachers who make a study of how the use of the materials will satisfy general and specific objectives and the characteristics of the children they teach. From this study, titles of materials are recommended for listing on the annual requisition list. A limited quantity of the material is then bought. After a careful trial of it under test-controlled teaching conditions, the material is kept in the grade for which it was first recommended, regraded in the light of objective data, shifted from the list if found inadequate. This continuous study of equipment increases the sensitivity of both supervisors and teachers to the varying needs and interests of pupils.

Provisions for acceleration of bright pupils in the Baltimore city schools— In certain schools a program of acceleration for children of superior ability results in a gain of one half year in the primary grades and another half year in the intermediate grades.

In the demonstration school which the city of Baltimore provides in the buildings of Johns Hopkins University during the summer term, provision is made in all grades from the 2-B through the ninth for pupils of superior ability to gain a half year in their classification by taking the work of the summer school in its eight weeks' term.

Certain junior high schools provide for acceleration of gifted pupils to the extent of a half or a whole year. In the senior high schools of Baltimore, acceleration of bright pupils is achieved in three ways:

1. By providing a special curriculum which enables bright pupils to complete five years of work in four and to enter colleges with sophomore standing.

2. By permitting bright pupils to take five major subjects instead of four each year and thus complete four years of high-school work in three or three and a half years.

3. By permitting bright pupils to take advance work in summer school and thus secure advance standing in the regular session. This also enables such pupils to complete four years of high school in less than four years.

Provisions for dull pupils in the Baltimore city schools—Subnormal classes care for the mentally handicapped and opportunity classes make it possible to segregate those retarded for other reasons. In the largest elementary schools, special coaching teachers help pupils make up their deficiencies in particular topics. To illustrate, a coaching teacher may have 3-B arithmetic from 9:00 to 9:30. Her class may consist of three children from a 3-B class who were absent when a particular topic was explained; five children from two 4-B classes; four from more than one 4-A class; one from a 5-B; and one from a 6-B. In no instance does such a group exceed fifteen in number. From 9:30 to 10:00, this teacher may have a similar group doing 3-A arithmetic. From 10:00 to 10:30, a group from different classes may be having intensive word drill on a 2-A level of reading ability. And thus her day proceeds.

In certain junior high schools, entering pupils whose case histories show low accomplishment and ability are placed in special classes where the regular work is presented, but at a much slower rate, so that one year's work is completed in three semesters.

In addition to the academic, commercial, and technical curriculums offered in the junior high school, a fourth curriculum is recommended for backward pupils who cannot satisfactorily do the work of the junior high

school. This curriculum will be based on (1) a reduction in the amount of
subject-matter, (2) practically all content organized in short simple units,
(3) a sympathetic, helpful attitude on the part of the teacher toward the
pupil, and (4) individual rates of progress.

Provision for dull pupils in the senior high school is made by:

1. Permitting such pupils, with the approval of the principal, to carry
fewer subjects per year than called for in a given curriculum.

2. Encouraging such pupils to go to summer school and make up failures
in regular session.

Under the Rules of the School Board, a pupil is ordinarily not allowed
more than six years to complete the four-year high-school course. In order
that this rule may not work a hardship on pupils whose effort is good but
who are mentally handicapped, effort is made to transfer them to a vocational school where work is better adapted to them.

E. The Results of an Attempt To Reduce Failure and Consequent Overageness in Colorado Springs

The claim is frequently made that the amount of failure and consequent
retardation can be reduced by making the school system more flexible and
building the organization around the needs of individuals. A report is
made herewith of the effect upon the amount of failure and overageness in
the schools of Colorado Springs by the introduction of ability grouping, differentiated courses of study to meet the needs of individuals and groups, and
particular care of the needs of individuals within the groups. This study
gives rather concrete evidence that the amount of failure and overageness
was reduced by these administrative plans.

For the purposes of this study, 4,852 elementary and junior high-school
students were considered. The amount of overageness for the year 1924
was compared with that of the year 1929. Nineteen twenty-four was selected
because the data of grade placement were readily available for that year
and because up to that time no general effort had been made to adjust the
schools to the needs of individuals. The year 1929 was selected because
grade placement data for that year would show the effect of two years'
work upon the reorganized basis. Beginning with the summer of 1927, a
definite attempt was made to adjust the schools to the needs of individuals
by grouping all children according to ability, by providing differential
courses, and by allowing the greatest freedom for individuals regardless of
group placement.

Table 31 sets forth the conditions of under-ageness, at-ageness, and overageness for grades 1 to 9 inclusive for the years 1924 and 1929. The
amount of overageness in the elementary grades in 1929 was only 41 percent
of that in 1924. In the junior high-school grades, the reduction was not so
great, but there the amount of overageness in the latter year was only 53
percent of that in the earlier year. While the amount of overageness was
reduced after two years of the reorganized plan, there still remained in the
elementary schools in 1929, as Table 31 shows, 13 percent of overageness.

TABLE 31.—PERCENT OF PUPILS UNDER AGE, AT AGE, AND OVER AGE, COLORADO SPRINGS, 1924 AND 1929

Grade	Percent Under Age		Percent At Age		Percent Over Age	
	1924	1929	1924	1929	1924	1929
1......................	1.1	.17	85.2	97.1	13.7	3.0
2......................	4.8	2.0	71.3	88.1	23.9	9.7
3......................	5.8	1.9	61.6	83.6	32.6	14.4
4......................	10.5	10.9	58.3	74.9	31.2	14.2
5......................	5.9	12.1	49.3	66.6	44.8	21.2
6......................	4.6	16.4	49.8	66.0	45.6	17.6
7......................	9.3	16.1	46.5	58.6	44.2	25.3
8......................	6.8	21.8	50.9	57.0	42.3	21.2
9......................	13.1	18.8	53.3	61.9	33.6	19.3
Total elementary.........	5.4	7.1	63.2	79.9	31.4	13.0
Total junior high school...	9.7	18.9	50.1	59.5	40.2	21.2
Grand total.............	6.7	11.05	59.2	72.8	34.1	16.1

An analysis of all of the elementary children who in 1929 were more than half a year overage is reported in Table 32. It was found that there were 218 cases in the elementary schools of overageness in excess of half a year. Of these 218, 73 were overage at the time of their entrance into the Colorado Springs schools previous to September, 1928; 33 were overage at the time of their entrance in September, 1928; and 52 were overage at the time they entered the Colorado Springs schools in September, 1929. Of the 218 cases of overageness then, 158 were inherited from other school systems. This is a condition which will continually exist in Colorado Springs by reason of the fact that there is a very large shifting population. Table 32 further shows that of the 218, 49 had failed one year in the Colorado Springs schools previous to the reorganization of the schools upon the ability grouping plan, and one had failed two years before the students were reclassified. Of the 218, only 10 had become overage through failure during the two years that the schools were reorganized.

TABLE 32.—OVERAGE PUPILS—MORE THAN ONE-HALF YEAR —COLORADO SPRINGS, 1929

Grade	Overage at Entrance before September, 1928	Overage at Entrance 1928-29	Overage at Entrance 1929-30	Failure One Year before Classification	Failure Two Years before Classification	Failure One Year since Classification	Total
1......	....	....	1	....	....	2	3
2......	....	5	10	....	....	1	16
3......	18	6	9	5	....	2	40
4......	16	5	9	11	....	2	43
5......	22	7	16	16	....	1	62
6......	17	10	7	17	1	2	54
Totals..	73	33	52	49	1	10	218

In the A (Slow) Group—125 Overage
In the B (Average) Group—93 Overage
In the C (Fast) Group—0 Overage
Of 218 overage children in the elementary grades, 158, or 72.5 percent, were overage when they entered the Colorado Springs schools; 50, or 22.9 percent, were failed a year or more before classification was begun; and 10, or 4.6 percent, were failed since they were classified.

It is interesting to compare the ranges of ages by grades for the years 1924 and 1929. Table 33 shows this comparison and it will be observed that in Grades 1 to 5 inclusive the width of the age range was decidedly decreased but that in Grades 6 to 9 inclusive the width of the range was somewhat greater in 1929 than in 1924. This is explained by the fact that many children, who in 1924 were in the lower grades and who were greatly overage for those grades, by 1929 had been advanced to the upper elementary grades, but that they had not yet been advanced sufficiently to cause them to be at-age for their grade. The extreme cases of overageness then are found in the grades 6, 7, 8, and 9 at the present time.

TABLE 33.—RANGE OF AGES BY GRADES, COLORADO SPRINGS, 1924 AND 1929

Grade	Age Range in Years and Months		Width of Age Range in Years and Months	
	1924	1929	1924	1929
1.	4–9 to 10–2	5–8 to 8–8	5– 5	3– 0
2.	5–9 to 13–8	6–3 to 11–2	7–11	4–11
3.	6–9 to 12–8	6–9 to 12–2	5–11	5– 5
4.	6–9 to 15–2	7–3 to 13–2	8– 5	5–11
5.	7–9 to 16–8	8–9 to 15–7	8–11	6–10
6.	9–9 to 16–2	8–9 to 15–7	6– 5	6–10
7.	9–9 to 18–6	9–9 to 19–2	8– 9	9– 5
8.	11–3 to 18–2	11–3 to 18–2	6–11	6–11
9.	12–2 to 18–2	11–9 to 18–7	6– 0	6–10

Table 34 shows a comparison of median chronological ages by grades for the year 1929 as compared with the year 1924. It is significant that the median chronological ages in 1929 in all grades are perceptibly less than those in 1924.

TABLE 34.—MEDIAN CHRONOLOGICAL AGES BY GRADES, COLORADO SPRINGS, 1924 AND 1929

Grade	Median Age		Grade	Median Age	
	1924	1929		1924	1929
1.	6– 5	6– 3	6.	12– 0	11– 4
2.	7– 8	7– 3	7.	13– 1	12– 6
3.	8–10	8– 3	8.	14– 0	13– 4
4.	9– 7	9– 4	9.	14–10	14– 4
5.	11– 1	10– 5			

F. Decrease in Retardation in New York City

Supt. William J. O'Shea of New York City, in a recent report,[1] shows that there has been a steady increase since 1922 in the number and percentage of elementary school pupils making rapid or normal progress in their school work, and a constant decrease in the percentage and number of those "left back."

[1] O'Shea, William J. *Thirty-First Annual Report of the Superintendent of Schools.* New York: Board of Education, City of New York, 1929. p. 559-66.

For the city as a whole, Dr. O'Shea finds that 340,520 pupils, or 51 percent, of the total register in September, 1928, are making normal progress, while 15 percent are accelerated, and 34 percent are retarded. This is the first time that more than 50 percent of the students are in the normal-age group.

The report shows that, while retardation is a problem of considerable importance in all school districts, it is a much greater problem in some districts than in others. Some of the districts having the greatest amount of retardation are districts which are known to have many pupils of low mentality, but in other cases other factors seem to be operating.

According to Dr. O'Shea, the reduction in the number of pupils making slow progress has been steady since the compilation of the first statistics. In September, 1922, 43.01 percent of the pupils in elementary schools were making slow progress. In September, 1928, this percentage was reduced to 34 percent of the register. The reduction has been accomplished by gradual stages, and there is reason to anticipate further reductions.

It seems evident that failure as one of the most serious phases of the problem of articulation can be reduced to a minimum if school authorities will recognize that promotion is an individual and not a group problem and if an organization is set up which makes possible the treatment of individual differences among children.

G. Arguments For and Against Homogeneous Grouping

The preceding section shows the results of reduction in overageness in one school system where homogeneous grouping is carefully administered, where courses of study are differentiated to meet the needs of individuals and groups, and where particular care is given the wants of individuals within groups. Are the results of homogeneous grouping equally successful in all school systems?

The following section pools the experience of 500 superintendents of schools in cities of all sizes. The data were secured through an inquiry blank sent to all members of the Department of Superintendence which included these two questions:

1. From your experience, what are the chief arguments in favor of sectioning classes into homogeneous groups?

2. From your experience, what are the chief arguments against sectioning classes into homogeneous groups?

The frequency with which advantages of homogeneous grouping are mentioned far exceeds that of the disadvantages. In evaluating these replies one should remember that while each superintendent of schools answered out of his own experience—no two had had the same experience. Some superintendents of schools have given homogeneous grouping a trial, while others have not. Some have used far more scientific bases for classification than others. Some have administered the plan far more judiciously than others.

Some have kept the way open for pupils to move from one ability group to another. Some have provided differentiated materials and special teaching methods adapted to each group. Some have definitely recognized the special need for individual consideration within each group. Some have recognized the factor of specificity, namely that a group may be more or less equal in ability in one subject but differ widely in ability in another subject, others have not recognized this factor. Some have carefully seen to it that classification brought no embarrassment to any pupil. Some have found their communities in sympathy with homogeneous grouping. And some have had staffs trained to administer homogeneous grouping adequately.

All these and other conditions undoubtedly influenced the replies of the 500 superintendents of schools, who were asked to speak from their own experience. These facts must be kept in mind in evaluating the following statements.

From your experience, what are the chief arguments in favor of sectioning classes into homogeneous groups?—In response to this question, 500 superintendents of schools wrote at considerable length. Their replies are summarized below.

Arguments in Favor of Homogeneous Grouping

(Offered by 500 superintendents of schools)

Frequency of
mention

1. Homogeneous grouping makes differentiation of curriculums easier. There is better opportunity for differentiation of courses of study without resorting to individual instruction. It takes care of the assignment problem 195

2. Slow learners in separate groups are not discouraged by the superiority of others, but compete on more equal terms and develop their own leaders. Grouped together pupils feel freer to admit their slowness and to ask the questions necessary to their better understanding. They do not feel awkward or timid through being conscious of the brighter and faster pupils 173

According to one superintendent of schools, homogeneous grouping gives a teacher a better opportunity to know his pupils. In mixed classes the brighter pupils are apt to usurp too much attention.

3. Homogeneous grouping places pupils in competition with others of fairly equal ability. It sets a pace that is a real challenge and a standard that is attainable 153

4. Children having more than average ability tend to form habits of idleness, inattention, and mental laziness if compelled to mark time in classes made up of average and below average pupils. When superior pupils are grouped together activities and discussions are on a higher plane. Greater opportunity is offered for more oral expression that others can follow 152

5. Homogeneous grouping enables the teacher to adapt methods of teaching to meet the needs of varying groups. He does not have to interest all in a presentation fitted only for a few. He can make a much more effective division of the time allotted to development, drill, and application. He is allowed more latitude in experimentation............. 115

6. Homogeneous grouping facilitates the work of the teacher. It is easier to teach a more nearly homogeneous group. The faster groups can be made larger and the slower groups smaller, so that the latter may receive more individual attention. Since the range in the ability of the group as a whole is so much less the teacher sees more clearly the needs of each individual 113

7. Competition is keener, pupils are more likely to work up to their capacities—better work results 100

8. Homogeneous grouping adds to the happiness of children. The sting of inferiority and failure is removed. Each child is happy achieving in his group and experiencing the joy of success........................ 82

9. Homogeneous grouping lessens pupil failure and discouragement and reduces the amount of retardation. The slow pupil is not constantly compared with the bright child 53

10. By limiting the range of variation within a group, more time can be given to the individual pupil. Individual instruction is made easier, special interests can be emphasized, and special aptitudes and abilities developed 34

11. Leaders are developed in all groups. Every homogeneous group, so-called, lacks enough in homogeneity to furnish leaders for the slower portion of the group, without the danger of the leaders getting so far ahead that they cease to function as such................................ 31

One superintendent writes: Homogeneous grouping encourages pupils to do their best and tends to develop latent initiative, originality, and leadership. Even in the low groups, the skilful teacher is able to develop leaders—pupils who can size up the situation, devise the proper line of action, and lead or direct their fellow pupils in the solution of problems within their grasp.

12. Homogeneous grouping reduces the number of disciplinary problems, by giving pupils work suited to their abilities and a chance to succeed among their equals 28

13. Homogeneous grouping usually provides groups which are more congenial socially. It associates together those who may best profit from cooperation and competition.. 28

14. Homogeneous grouping makes for more flexible promotion. It permits adjustment of standards of achievement to varying levels of ability with the result that more just standards of rating and promotion usually obtain 25

15. Homogeneous grouping prevents the development of an inferiority complex on the part of the dull.................................... 19

16. Homogeneous grouping prevents the development of a superiority complex on the part of the bright. It is possible that a better attitude toward his own ability may result if a pupil is matched with his peers.. 11

17. There is opportunity for better teacher preparation. Teachers may specialize in teaching the group in which they are most interested.. 6

18. The teacher with the so-called "best" group works harder because he knows that more is expected of his pupils........................ 5

19. Homogenous grouping prevents low standards from dominating the whole group 2

20. A greater retention of pupils results from homogenous grouping.. 1

From your experience, what are the chief arguments against sectioning classes into homogeneous groups?—In response to this question, 500 superintendents of schools also wrote at considerable length. Their replies are summarized below.

Arguments Against Homogeneous Grouping

(Offered by 500 superintendents of schools)

Frequency of
mention

1. With homogeneous grouping, the slower groups lose the stimulus and
the contributions of the brighter pupils............................   150

According to several superintendents of schools this argument is not
valid for these reasons: (1) Even when pupils are grouped homogeneously there is still a sufficient range of ability within each group so that
the more capable pupils set standards for the less aggressive who need
to have their pride awakened to work up to capacity; and (2) The power
gained by a certain few of the lower groups who become leaders in their
groups fully takes the place of anything they might gain if they were in
classes in which brighter pupils are leaders.

2. Pupils put in the lower ability groups sometimes develop a sense
of failure and inferiority...................................   99

3. Pupils put in the higher ability groups are apt to develop a superiority complex. It may cause bright pupils to under-evaluate the worth of
qualities other than intellect, and thus promote intellectual snobbishness.
It prevents brighter children from learning tolerance for those with
less intellectual ability   75

One superintendent of schools writes that the argument that homogeneous grouping creates inferiority and superiority complexes appears to
be based on the assumption that the old grading system did not create
any such complexes. This assumption is unsound; for it does not take
any pupil long to discover whether or not he is the best or poorest in
his class. The pupil classifies himself even if the school does not.

4. Homogeneous grouping is undemocratic and tends to create class
distinctions in the minds of some pupils. Through it there is danger of
developing an intellectual caste.................................   68

5. The adjustment of teachers to the various groups is difficult, particularly the lower groups. Some teachers object to teaching the dullest
group. Relatively few teachers can handle this group competently..   64

According to one superintendent of schools, homogeneous grouping
has a tendency to take away the element of variety in teaching that the
teacher enjoys in the heterogeneous group.

Another superintendent writes as follows: Some old-fashioned teachers
cannot be dynamited out of their ruts of thinking of definite subject-
matter goals, rather than the growth of all their pupils. Some of our
very best teachers of yesterday are in this group.

6. With homogeneous grouping, there are no outstanding leaders to
inspire the slower groups. The slow child may become discouraged and
even slower   63

7. It is very difficult to divide pupils into truly homogeneous groups,
for a group that is more or less homogeneous in one subject may be
heterogeneous in another. To illustrate, a group that has more or less the
same ability and test scores in arithmetic may differ widely in ability
and test scores in geography[1]   56

8. A certain stigma is often attached to the lower groups, and they
are referred to as "dumb-bells"   55

9. Homogeneous grouping is sometimes misunderstood and resented
by parents   44

---

[1] For a further discussion of this point see: McGaughy, J. R., "Homogeneous Grouping,"
Childhood Education, Vol. VI, No. 7, pp. 291-96.

10. Few teachers succeed in adequately differentiating the materials of instruction. They do not know how to handle the differences in groups, especially for the upper and lower thirds........................... 40

One superintendent of schools writes: We have found only one real difficulty with homogeneous grouping. Textbooks and courses of study are in large measure prescribed for us. The result is we have to drag slow pupils over too much ground, and we don't have enough for the faster groups to do. Homogeneous grouping is ineffective unless each course of study provides for differentiation. Different methods of teaching are also necessary.

Another superintendent points out that knowledge of desirable variations between methods of instruction for different levels of ability is frequently not made available.

11. Homogeneous grouping complicates school administration, makes the mechanics of promotion and sectioning more difficult, and requires closer scheduling 31

12. Homogeneous grouping is impossible or difficult except in schools of considerable size. If tried in small schools, it makes too many groups, which necessitates the preparation of too much work by the teacher 25

13. There is a tendency for teachers to be complacent with low achievement in low groups. Some teachers of "Z" sections do not feel the need of putting extra effort into their work, since they feel that little can be expected of these dull groups 23

14. Grouping on an ability basis frequently results in pupils with poor social background being all grouped together, whereas citizenship improves by association with higher type pupils...................... 17

Several superintendents, on the other hand, argue quite the opposite and state that one of the disadvantages of ability grouping is that social groups are broken up.

One superintendent states that social adjustments are not serious because the general mixing of pupils from all classes in the home-room, clubs, and playground will overcome any injury that may come from grouping according to scholastic ability. It is common to life that individuals of somewhat uniform intellectual ability tend to associate with and enjoy each other. Hence this arrangement in school is in harmony with life.

15. There is a tendency for teachers to view grouping as a substitute for individualization rather than as a device for increasing its efficiency. Teachers tend to deal with a class as if all the pupils in it were equally bright or equally dull in all subjects, instead of studying individual differences—the result is that the individual is submerged .. 14

16. The average, or above average pupil, loses the opportunity of helping the dull child. 10

17. It is difficult to maintain a right attitude on the part of the pupil toward the grouping, particularly in the slow sections. Homogeneous grouping, if not properly handled, causes jealousy and resentment_____ 8

One superintendent of schools writes: After eight years of experience, I am frank to say that I believe that this is not a legitimate argument. At first some pupils disliked to be placed in the slower moving groups, for it may have appeared to be somewhat of a disgrace inflicted upon them. But that is now considered an advantage, as all are working to full capacity.

18. Homogeneous groups, whether based on ability or achievement, are only relative. There is much overlapping of ability, intelligence, and achievement in most so-called homogeneous groups 7

19. The poor group accomplishes little because the teacher "knows"
they can't do much. Fixed attitudes with respect to intelligence are
developed by teachers in dealing with pupils grouped homogeneously—
usually to the disadvantage of the low ability groups   6

20. Some pupils will deliberately do poor work so as to rate low in
tests in order to get into slow groups, as less work is required of
them there   5

21. Discipline cases usually collect in the low division   5

22. Homogeneous grouping offers no advantage to a school with an
activity program and a correlated curriculum. It is only advantageous
when a formal curriculum is followed. Unit methods within the class
have obviated to a large extent the necessity of homogeneous grouping ..   2

H. Differentiation Through Instruction

Practically all school administrators are agreed that homogeneous grouping is of little value unless courses of study and teaching methods are
differentiated to fit the abilities of the various groups and allowance is also
made for a wide range of abilities and interests within each group.

In a preceding section, the Baltimore city school system was cited as
one of many systems where some differentiation is achieved through administration. That illustration would be incomplete unless it were supplemented by statements showing how differentiation is further achieved
through instruction. Hence, there is included below a brief description of
how differentiated materials are planned and four illustrations, supplied by
teachers of that city concerning the reactions of dull and of bright pupils
to such carefully planned units. The procedure described and the units
included are merely illustrative. Each school system will develop its own
technic for differentiation and prepare units of work suited to the particular
needs of its classes.

*How differentiated courses of study are developed in the Baltimore
public schools*[1]—In furthering a program of differentiation it has been
necessary for teachers in conference with local supervisors and through
experimentation under test-controlled conditions to:

1. Decide on the goals of each unit that are attainable and desirable for
bright pupils and those for dull pupils.

2. Examine all available instructional materials to find the books through
which bright pupils may be led to discover for themselves the basic understandings in the units; and to select the books having an easy vocabulary
and simple organization through which the dull pupils may work under
teacher supervision on short, simple, and definite units.

3. Determine what can be carried on by the bright pupils with the aid
only of good mimeographed or printed assignments, what will need to be
presented by the teacher or interpreted by her in conference with the pupils,
and what flexible arrangements can be made for the teacher's supervision of
individual pupils at work rather than for her "hearing of lessons."

---

[1] This procedure was followed in developing *Geography in the Junior High Schools*, Baltimore Public Schools, Baltimore, Md., 1926; also in *English in Secondary Schools*, in preparation. Sections of this bulletin are now available in mimeographed form.

4. Write units covering several days' or weeks' work so that, as far as possible, the bright pupils will get their study-aids through silent reading, will have constant reminders of the central theme of the unit, will learn through reasoning rather than through rote memory, will use libraries freely, and will have ample opportunities for individual reports and open forum discussions.

Write short units for dull pupils so that assignments will be simple and direct. The teacher will demonstrate the procedure of work to be followed, and will have the pupils try out the directions under her supervision before permitting them to study independently. With dull pupils, emphasis is always placed on developing efficient habits rather than reasoning about procedures.

5. Select or make self-corrective, self-administered practice materials which bright pupils can use when they *recognize* their need for drill on any phase of the unit.

The dull pupils are constantly checked by the teacher herself, and are given frequent supplementary, easy written and oral repetitions and reviews so that mastery will be the final outcome.

6. Select or make practice tests useful to bright pupils in self-checking as they progress over certain sub-units in the larger unit. Dull pupils may be checked orally or in writing by the teacher or by pupils who show mastery of the sub-unit.

7. Study the bright pupils as they work so as to help them diagnose their needs and safeguard them from superficiality or inaccuracies in their processes of thinking.

Study the dull pupils so as to aid them with specific directions and encouragement at each small step of progress they make.

8. Create a new situation which will test the brighter pupils' mastery of the skills and understanding, and will, under teacher direction, encourage the dull to "review."

9. Evaluate the unit for its teachability and its intrinsic values to each type of pupil.

10. Require of bright pupils and of dull pupils the application in the next unit of any skill mastered in this.

Differentiation through individualized instruction—The movement toward individualization of instruction in the Baltimore city schools has arisen from scientific study and from a philosophy of education which states its outcomes for secondary school pupils as: (a) A wide range of interests with the discovery of some dominating interest, and (b) the capacity for self-dependent intellectual life, both of which imply self-control and the acquisition of a range of methods of thinking and of study which remove the pupil from constant dependence on the teacher. Attention has been shifted from specific technics of teaching to the functional application of technics as the learning needs require. Self-corrective drills, discussions for appreciation, interpretative thinking, directed study, excursions, library activities, and visual aids are introduced where relevant in the learning process. This deepening of the meaning of method has been accompanied by the teacher's gathering objective evidence of pupil growth in knowledge, skills, and attitudes, including evidence of immediate pupil needs as well as those adult needs which can be reasonably expected to be of value to the maturing pupil. The creative and scientific thinking of teachers working out these units has done more than any other single factor to make teachers conscious of differences of pupils. It has aided them also in adapting their assignments in length and depth to the varying abilities and interests of their pupils, and has given them objective data, as they observe their pupils at work, on the relative difficulty of the instructional materials available to the pupils.

So carefully has this work been carried out in the junior high geography department that the teachers know exactly which assignments are the hurdles for the dull group and which for that gradually shading off from average to bright pupils.

Five years of careful experimentation under test-controlled situations has shown the futility of giving dull pupils contracts or guide sheets covering several weeks' work with "interest pockets" and assignments that carry their own motivation to the average and bright pupils. The dull pupils need specific directions and assignments following the organization of the simplest textbook available. The motivation and supervision of study have to be given constantly by the teacher. Self-teaching material is relatively ineffective for dull pupils. The average pupils can add ideas and utilize the organization of several books and other sorts of instructional material. The bright pupils can and have set up individual projects, growing out of the written clues in the contract. Each contract adds new challenges to reflective thinking, more mature reading skills, and larger opportunities for individual initiative in written expression.

The four detailed reports which follow show the reactions of dull and of bright pupils to carefully differentiated units of work.

1. A Unit for 4B in the Geography and History of Egypt Showing Differentiation for Bright and Dull Pupils

The data used in this report resulted from the study of Egypt in five experimental 4B classes. Two of these classes were predominantly bright groups, while the remaining three were largely made up of dull pupils. These five classes were also representative of varying types of communities extending from poor crowded industrial neighborhoods to prosperous and cultured residential sections. Differentiation was made in recognition of the characteristic differences of the pupils as listed on page 108 of this Yearbook.

Differentiation in Content

Dull Children

Only the simplest content was selected under each of the following topics:

The life of the early Egyptians—their settlement in the Nile and Tigris-Euphrates valley, their work as farmers, their beliefs.

The growth of Egypt into a strong nation.

How we learned about the early people.

How the things the early people did help us today.

The effect of hot sun and little rainfall upon the water supply, vegetation, lives of the people, and means of travel.

The importance of the Nile to Egypt and the work which it makes possible.

Life in Egypt today—the big cities of Cairo and Alexandria.

The study of Babylonia, ordinarily used in conjunction with Egypt, was omitted in these dull classes, the work with Egypt being considered sufficient to give an understanding of these early people. In one of the classes, however, slight contact with Babylonian life was gained through the use of this content for regular reading lessons.

Most of this study was a carefully directed process of development, the teacher guiding the pupils in their work.

Bright Children

In addition to the content listed in the opposite column, the bright pupils included in their study such related topics as:

Egyptian writing materials and records. Ways in which ancient Egypt carried water.

Irrigation, the work of the Egyptian Pharaoh Menes.

Social life of the Egyptians and Babylonians.

Egyptian religion.

Study of an oasis as a temporary habitation for desert people and for passing caravans.

Desert hospitality, beliefs, and customs.

Trade relations between the desert people and the surrounding countries of Egypt, Babylonia, India, Arabia, and Phoenicia.

A comparison of the deltas and flood plains of the Mississippi and Nile Rivers.

A study of Egyptian weaving and tapestry, pottery and glass blowing.

Special places of interest in modern Cairo and Alexandria.

Much of this content was carried on through independent investigation and extensive reading.

Differentiation in Types of Problems

Simple, direct problems were employed with the dull pupils. Examples:

Why is the camel used on the desert?

Why do the nomads wear the kind of clothing they do in such a warm place?

Large, inclusive problems were used by the bright children. Examples:

How does the climate force the desert dwellers to wander?

How does the oasis change the life of the wandering tribes?

Differentiation in Activities

Activities involving simple manipulative and dramatic experiences, rather narrow in scope, and requiring short periods of time for their accomplishment, were utilized with the dull group.

The bright children utilized the simpler and shorter activities as separate parts of a more complex and larger unit.

Differentiation in Activities (Continued)

Dull Children

The concrete nature of these activities served to stimulate and maintain the pupils' interest, to increase their actual learning, and to provide opportunities for the recognition of special aptitudes of pupils. Individual pupils were given responsibility within the activity for phases of the work for which they had special aptitude. The constant guidance and encouragement of the teacher accompanied these activities. Typical illustrations of the sort of activities employed in these three dull classes follow:

Making collections of Egyptian pictures.

Planning and making a visit to the Art Museum to see Egyptian exhibits and to see and hear an illustrated lecture on Egypt.

Making pottery such as desert dwellers or Egyptians use.

Making posters of scenes of Egyptian life.

Working out a desert scene on the sand table, showing the Nile river and sailboats.

Dramatizing scenes from desert and Egyptian life, such as Caravan Travel.

The accomplishment of these activities involved coordination with other subjects of the curriculum and this coordination, in turn, provided further opportunities for such repeated contact with the subject-matter of the unit that the needed drill was gained. These coordinations, likewise, were simple, direct, and concrete, requiring little time for their accomplishment. Illustrations of such coordinations follow:

Bright Children

Many of the activities of the more gifted pupils radiated from the central group activity into numerous avenues of associated interests which extended throughout the whole unit of study, and which resulted in many original and completed projects.

Examples of these activities are listed below:

The making of a classbook containing stories and colored illustrations of desert and Egyptian life.

The building of a Current Events Chart with Egyptian news items.

The development of an original play entitled, "A Trip to Egypt."

The making of several wall hangings illustrating Egyptian industries and life on the desert; such as, glass blowing, pottery making, farming, and the passing of a caravan.

The making of a library reference chart. Both of these bright classes had access to very good school libraries.

Research work and reports on such topics as desert beliefs and customs, Egyptian irrigation, the pyramids, obelisks, and sphinxes.

Some individual activities

An Egyptian picture book (a collection of pictures, with short introductory sentences beneath each picture).

Drawings and weavings of Egyptian designs.

A book of colored drawings.

Research work and reports on the lotus flower, papyrus, uses of the palm tree, Menes, the Egyptian Pharaoh.

Because of the versatility of interest of the superior children, their activities led to subject coordinations which were greater in number, broader in scope, and richer in content than those used in the dull group.

Dull Children (Continued)

Constructive English

Telling and writing imaginative stories on simple topics in connection with the study of desert and Egyptian life.

Writing the dialogue for the dramatizations of desert and Egyptian life.

Writing invitations to other classes to see dramatizations.

Writing business letters in order to arrange for the trip to the museum and to acknowledge courtesies extended the class.

Writing cooperative group compositions for class booklets.

Reading and Literature

Reading stories of desert and Egyptian life.

Reading Bible stories, as The Story of Joseph.

Reading stories and poems of desert animals, as How the Camel Got His Hump, The Plaint of the Camel.

Spelling

Learning to spell new words, learned in connection with the unit, such as, delta, irrigation, source, upstream, downstream, rapid, dam, etc.

Arithmetic

Solving problems in connection with the cost of the trip to the museum.

Music

Using, for appreciation, such records as, Dance of the Arabs, Nutcracker Suite; and Morning and Ahitra's Dance from the Peer Gynt Suite.

Bright Children (Continued)

Constructive English

Giving oral reports of research work done in the library. Example: The description of the Pyramids.

Writing summaries of the day's history lesson. Example: Early Trade Routes, Desert Travel, etc.

Organizing compositions on Egyptian topics into a summary paragraph for the classbook. Example: Each child of the class wrote a composition on the industries of the Egyptians. In a second lesson a class paragraph was developed from these compositions.

Writing notices for the play.

Developing and writing an original three act play, "A Trip to Egypt."

Technical English

The punctuation needs of the classbook gave rise to lessons on the period, the capital, the apostrophe, the hyphen, and the use of commas in series.

Reading and Literature

Collecting and reading stories of Egyptian life from outside sources and introducing these stories to the rest of the class.

Listing all Egyptian books and stories in the school library. A committee of children reviewed this material before listing it. Six thirty-five-minute library periods were required for this work by one of the bright classes. The children of the class read the books listed on the chart.

Spelling

The history summaries and the classbook created needs in spelling, such as Nile, Tigris, industries, Pharaoh, tombs, pottery, cataract, strait, horizon, zenith. In addition, the words used with the dull group were learned.

Arithmetic

Measuring scenery, subtracting dates, reading and writing numbers.

Music

Same as listed for the dull children plus the following additional music:

2 records—Ballet Egyptian (No. 1 and No. 2) Serial No. 538-D—Luigini.

2 records—Ballet Egyptian (No. 3 and No. 4) Serial No. 539-D—Luigini.

Differentiation in Materials

Dull Children	Bright Children

Books

Each of the three classes reported the use of 3 or more textbooks in the study of this unit, supplemented by the use of from 9 to 14 reference books. This afforded the pupils the opportunity of meeting the same information in varying situations and this repetition made the necessary provision for drill and for materials adapted to the individual differences of the pupils.

The two bright classes used all the geography, history, and reading textbooks available for the grade. In addition, they gathered many supplementary books. From the school library and outside sources, they collected all kinds of reference material, books, encyclopedias, magazines, and newspaper clippings. Altogether 8 different textbooks and 27 various reference books were used.

Visual Materials

Extensive use was made of visual materials. These dull pupils were thus afforded another concrete source from which knowledge was gained. The visual materials included lantern slides and stereographs; pictures from books, magazines, and newspapers; actual articles from Egypt. Through these visual aids the pupils had direct and vivid opportunities for gaining information about the work of the Egyptians, the remains of ancient Egyptian civilization, and features of modern-day Egypt.

The bright children, because of their keen observation and power to deal with abstract facts, used the visual material listed in the opposite column more as a means to seek further knowledge than to make concrete facts that they already knew. Example: A picture of a pyramid under construction, showing slaves, overseers, and rulers, etc., led them to seek knowledge on the government and social customs of Egypt.

Work Materials

Information and ideas were made concrete, also, through the translation of facts that had been gathered through reading and illustrative material into models and representations. References to the activities before mentioned will indicate that these dull pupils made pottery, models of the pyramid and sphinx, Egyptian sailboats, costumes, scenery, and posters. Thus through the media of clay, wood, crayons, and paints, abstract ideas were made real.

The various work materials included in the activities of the bright children were used to shape creative ideas, to build up relationships, or to summarize previous knowledge. For example: The industries of Egypt were illustrated in color on a wall picture, in collections of painted clay models, in exhibits of soap carvings, and in different designs of weaving.

2. Art Expression—Reactions from Bright and Dull Pupils

At the Guilford School in Baltimore, art expression takes place in work periods of a free type. The children, regardless of individual differences, are exposed to all types of materials and are given the same experiences as a basis for their art work. They are free to select any art medium they wish, and the activities performed are of the children's own choosing.

Differentiation in the art curriculum is made by the children themselves, the dull choosing activities at their level of ability and the bright selecting more complex activities at their level. The differentiation in method comes about as the teachers endeavor to help each child grow according to his own capacity.

For the purposes of this study, twelve teachers were asked to fill out questionnaires describing the children's work. Each teacher answered four for the bright group and four for the dull group, making a summary of the work of ninety-six children, ranging from the kindergarten through the sixth grade.

The following tables show the conclusions drawn as to the variations in reactions of bright and dull children.

a. The Child's Choice of Materials

	Bright	Dull
With suggestions from class or teacher	10	36
Without suggestions from class or teacher	38	12

Types	Bright	Dull	Types	Bright	Dull
Paints	41	29	Cardboard	4	0
Clay	28	23	Linoleum	3	0
Crayons	27	20	Blocks	2	0
Paper	23	19	Plasticene	2	0
Wood	16	22	Paste	2	0
Textiles	14	11	Oilcloth	1	0
Scissors	7	6	Soap	1	0
Chalk	5	2			

It is readily seen that most bright children select their materials without suggestion, while most of the dull must have help. The bright children need a greater variety and quantity of materials to satisfy their needs. The dull children's choices are fewer. With the exception of wood, the rank in choice of materials seems to be the same for both dull and bright, the differentiation lying in the greater variety of materials used by the bright group.

b. The Child's Choice of Activities

	Bright	Dull
With suggestion from class or teacher	12	38
Without suggestion from class or teacher	36	10
Simple activity	19	40
Complex activity	29	8

Types	Bright	Dull	Types	Bright	Dull
Houses	12	5	Birdhouses	3	2
Boats	11	4	Rugs	3	1
Animals	8	7	Vases	3	1
Airplanes	6	3	Costumes	2	2
Fruits	6	1	Trees	2	2
Friezes (in oil)	4	1	Portraits	2	1
Dolls	3	4	Busts	2	0
Household utensils	3	3			

Thirty-seven other activities were made individually by the bright children, and 18 other activities were made by the dull ones. These were interests in connection with units of work such as a wigwam in the study of Indian life and the Parthenon in relief in connection with Greek life.

The bright and dull seem to like best the same activities, but while the dull are content to make just one thing, the bright make many more and more varied things in a given time.

c. The Child's Method of Procedure

	Bright	Dull
Long interest span	42	19
Short interest span	6	29
Tenacity of purpose	44	19
Flitting	4	29
Cooperation	43	20
Lack of cooperation	5	28
Self-control	45	27
Lack of self-control	3	21
Satisfied with work	8	35
Felt need for improvement	40	13
One interest	9	21
Varied interests	39	27
Use of art principles:		
Great	29	13
Little	19	35
Conscious	25	5
Unconscious	23	43

d. The Child's Finished Product

	Bright	Dull
Creative	35	10
Imitative	13	38
Realistic	32	42
Impressionistic	16	6
Good technic	33	10
Lack of technic	15	38

e. The Teacher's Method of Procedure for:

Bright	Dull
Little stimulation was needed to have the bright children start work.	Great stimulation was needed to have the slow children start their work.
The teachers gave little help in the choice of materials and in the selection of activities.	The teachers gave a great deal of help in the choice of materials and the selection of activities.

e. The Teacher's Method of Procedure for:

Bright (Continued)

Much encouragement was given because of the over-critical attitude of the bright children toward their own work. These children's standards were so very high that they became discouraged over their inability to reach them.

Where the children were content to imitate, an effort was made to have them want to create; also to work from the realistic to the impressionistic and abstract where more imagination could be brought into play.

Some help in the handling of tools was necessary.

Help in technic was given when asked for by the children.

The children were taken to the Art Museum for lectures, observation, and work.

Dull (Continued)

With the young children, much encouragement was given to keep up a good attitude toward art. With the older children, an effort was made to raise the standards where the children were too satisfied with their work.

When the children constantly used the same medium and made the same type things, a variety of stimuli were placed about to encourage other types of art expression.

At times some of the slowest children had to be allowed to work purely by imitation of some other child or teacher.

Plenty of help was given with technic. These children's experiences were enlarged by many excursions.

Training in careful observation was given.

Every opportunity was seized to praise the children who had confidence.

The teachers were careful to make little comparison of other children's work in the dull group.

As a finale of the work of the year, an exhibition was held. Two art supervisors surveyed the work of the school, and pictures and art objects were selected to be placed on view. One hundred forty-five pieces were shown. The following table shows the intelligence rating of the children whose work was in the exhibit.

Intelligence	Number of children
X	52
Y+	21
Y	32
Y—	24
Z	16

3. A Critical Study of an Arithmetic Lesson in Two 5B Classes

In adjoining classrooms of the Montebello School are two 5B classes largely similar in environmental factors but differing widely in native ability and academic achievement. One class has a median I. Q. of 124, a median score (in February, 1930) on the Stanford Reasoning Test in arithmetic of 68, and a median score on the Stanford Computation Test of 63. The other class has a median I. Q. of 86, a median score (in February, 1930) on the Stanford Reasoning Test in arithmetic of 60, and a median score on the Stanford Computation Test of 60.

The following report shows the provisions which teachers of these classes are making for adjustment to differing pupil abilities in an introductory lesson on subtraction of fractions with unlike denominators. Before reports of the lesson as taught in both classes are presented, it is well to note the basic understandings and steps of difficulty involved in the subtraction of fractions of unlike denominators. Three skills are essential:

1. The ability to change fractions to a common denominator
2. The ability to subtract fractions of like denominator
3. The ability to reduce fractions to lowest terms.

Moreover, this phase of subtraction of fractions may be analyzed into the following degrees of difficulty:

1. Examples including related fractions, one given denominator the common denominator, no reduction. Example: 3/4 — 1/8
2. Examples including related fractions, one given denominator the common denominator, reduction. Example: 2/3 — 1/6
3. Examples including related fractions, one given denominator the common denominator, remainder zero. Example: 3/6 — 1/2
4. Examples including unrelated fractions, common denominator the product of the given denominators, no reduction. Example: 3/4 — 2/3
5. Examples including unrelated fractions, common denominator the product of the given denominators, reduction. Example: 4/5 — 2/4
6. Examples including related fractions, lowest common denominator to be found, no reduction. Example: 5/8 — 1/12
7. Examples including related fractions, lowest common denominator to be found, reduction. Example: 4/6 — 4/9

Detailed reports of both lessons follow exactly as they took place on the same day in the two classrooms. In conclusion, points of differentiation are summarized.

Introductory Lesson on the Subtraction of Fractions with Unlike Denominators—Dull 5B Class

Preliminary drill—In response to the teacher's query, the pupils decided that reduction of fractions to lowest terms was proving most troublesome to them. Accordingly, the first ten minutes of the period were devoted to the four following types of drill, each type lasting for a few moments only but serving to focus and maintain interest and to make correct responses automatic.

1. Drill with flash cards. Fifteen cards bearing fractions to be reduced to lowest terms were used. Individual pupils were called on for rapid oral reduction of these fractions. The cards were then distributed to various pupils who stationed themselves about the room, while fifteen other children received cards with fractions which were the reduced form of those on the first set of cards. The children then matched their cards to the correct unreduced fraction, and the accuracy of the pairing was checked by each group of partners and by teacher and class.

2. Ladder drill, with a fraction to be reduced on each
rung. Many children were called upon to climb the
ladder through quick oral reduction of this series of fractions. Some difficulty was evidenced with 3/6 and 2/6,
and these fractions were noted immediately upon the
board by the teacher and given special drill.
3. Crossing a stream drill, each rock being a fraction
needing reduction. Again this was a short drill and many
pupils participated. The simplicity of the fractions will
be noticed.

| 2/8 |
| 5/10 |
| 3/9 |
| 3/6 |
| 4/8 |
| 2/6 |

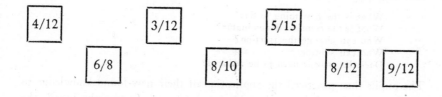

4. Written drill in which all children took part simultaneously. The
fifteen fractions listed below were dictated by the teacher, and the pupils
reduced them to lowest terms and checked their accuracy.

2/6, 3/6, 3/9, 4/8, 2/8, 5/10, 4/12, 3/12, 6/8, 4/10, 4/16, 5/15,
8/10, 9/12, 8/12.

This last drill included all of the fractions which had been used in the
other three types of practice, so that pupils thus met these very simple
problems of reduction in two or more drill settings. Another point worthy
of note is the fact that while the three earlier drills used many children in
an individual oral response, this last drill included every child in a written
activity.

Drill on finding the common denominator—Because ability to find a
common denominator is involved in the subtraction of fractions with unlike
denominators, a drill was provided in this skill. A group of twelve related
fractions, such as /2, /4; /12, /3, was used, first for oral response by individual pupils, then as a written exercise by all pupils. Accuracy in this
written drill was also checked.

Additional practice was afforded by a series of questions requiring finding the common denominator which had been worked by the children
before school. These two types of drill upon common denominator served
to recall in fresh relationship an older, previously-taught skill which the
new step was going to require.

Introduction of the New Topic

Step 1—Learning to subtract related fractions, one given denominator the common denominator, no reduction—The teacher introduced this difficulty through direct teaching, using for the step of initial learning the four examples:

$$\begin{array}{cccc} 3/4 & 1/2 & 3/4 & 5/9 \\ 1/8 & 1/4 & 3/8 & 1/3 \\ \hline \end{array}$$

Although in each case children did the work, bit by bit, the teacher guided their thinking with pointed questions, using these same questions for all four examples:

> What is the first thing to do?
> What is the common denominator?
> Who can change the fraction?
> Who can subtract?
> Does the answer need to be reduced?

The pupils then practiced the application of their new-found knowledge to the four questions below, all children working—a few at the board, the rest at their seats. Each question was checked before the next was given. Three children added and this point was corrected.

$$\begin{array}{cccc} 11/12 & 4/5 & 3/4 & 2/3 \\ 5/6 & 1/10 & 2/12 & 1/9 \\ \hline \end{array}$$

Step 2—Learning to subtract related fractions, one given denominator the common denominator, reduction—This step of difficulty was introduced through the question, $2/3 - 1/6$. A pupil did the work without help and reduced the answer without hesitation, a fact which the teacher was quick to commend. Individual children then worked three more examples of this type without the necessity for any direct teaching by the teacher. All of the pupils, either at the blackboard or at their seats, worked five more questions of this type, each one being checked with the class as it was finished.

$$\begin{array}{ccccc} 5/6 & 5/6 & 2/3 & 3/4 & 11/12 \\ 1/3 & 1/2 & 5/12 & 1/12 & 2/3 \\ \hline \end{array}$$

Step 3—Learning to subtract related fractions, one denominator the common denominator, remainder zero—The procedure in this step of the lesson was similar to that used in the earlier stages of difficulty. The teacher guided the work, presenting two examples at the board.

$$\begin{array}{cc} 3/6 & 5/10 \\ 1/2 & 1/2 \\ \hline \end{array}$$

Individual pupils worked three examples orally with the teacher recording, and then worked four more independently at their desks or on the blackboard.

4/8	4/12	3/9	1/4
1/2	1/3	1/3	4/16

The last example, it will be noted, makes use of the fraction with the larger denominator as the quantity to be subtracted, a different situation from the earlier examples, and therefore a gauge of real comprehension of this step. Pupils experienced no difficulties in this work.

Meanwhile, three boys who had found the steps of subtraction with reduction troublesome were given five additional problems of that sort so that they might receive the needed extra drill.

Final check upon learning—As a means of measuring the learning which had resulted and the points, if any, at which further teaching or drill was needed, all pupils were given the six-example test which appears below. It will be noted that the first and second questions test comprehension of the first step of difficulty, the third and fourth involve the second step (reduction of the answer), while the fifth and sixth have a zero remainder. This care in having the difficulties appear in the same order as that in which they were learned is a thoughtful adjustment to the limitations of slow pupils in this early stage of the application of new learning.

5/8	2/3	6/8	6/10	10/15	3/4
1/4	1/12	1/2	1/5	2/3	6/8

The results of this test were as follows:

6 questions correct—27 pupils
5 questions correct— 8 pupils (5 of the 8 had difficulty with reduction of 4/10)
4 questions correct— 2 pupils (these 2 did not finish)

A study of these results reveals the fact that, since a majority of the pupils had all examples correct, no further direct teaching was necessary with these three steps of difficulty. More drill, however, must be given if responses are to become automatic, since ten pupils made at least one error. This condition is also an evidence that the teacher did not spend undue time upon the development and drill of these steps. Reduction of 4/10 to lowest terms needs further stress.

Introductory Lesson on the Subtraction of Fractions with
Unlike Denominators—Bright 5B Class

Preliminary Drill—Drill on Reduction to Lowest Terms:

1. Easy reductions:

A quick oral drill in which individual pupils reduced fractions was the first phase of drill given by the teacher. The material for this drill was drawn from a mixed list of 36 easy and difficult fractions which appeared in the form of a blocked chart upon the blackboard. Such easy reductions as the following were first selected from this chart: 2/6, 2/8, 6/12, 4/10, 5/10, 4/6, 12/24, 3/6, and 3/9. No difficulties were encountered in these easy reductions as contrasted with the dull children's trouble with 3/6, 2/6, and 4/10.

2. Difficult reductions:

The quick oral drill was extended to include other, much more difficult reductions, such as 9/12, 14/36, 12/20, 4/30, 6/28, 14/16, and 8/20. A second trial had to be given the following fractions: 9/12, 4/30, 14/16, and 6/28. A third trial was given 6/28, and the teacher analyzed the difficulty with the pupils.

Additional difficult reductions were given as a written drill, all pupils participating simultaneously at their seats or at the blackboards. In this case the teacher dictated the fractions to be reduced. Examples of these fractions were: 10/24, 10/25, 9/36, 12/15, 12/18, 24/36, 9/24, 21/30. Errors were made in 24/36 and 9/24. Those children who made errors recorded the fraction and its correct reduction in their drill notebooks.

Introduction of the new topic—The new phase of subtraction, i. e., the subtraction of fractions with unlike denominators, was introduced through having the children discover how a series of examples on the blackboard differed from their previous work. These examples were:

| 3/4 | 1/2 | 2/3 | 7/10 | 3/6 | 5/10 | 3/4 | 1/2 | 4/5 | 2/3 |
| 1/8 | 1/4 | 1/6 | 1/5 | 1/2 | 1/2 | 2/3 | 1/3 | 2/4 | 4/8 |

They readily perceived this difference. The teacher followed with this question, "Who will take the first example and tell me what to do?" The need for finding a common denominator was given immediately by a pupil, and the work completed independently by another child. The next example was similarly worked without guidance by the teacher.

The teacher next asked the children if they could find any difference in the third example of the series. After a rapid solution of the example, a pupil volunteered the fact that the answer must be reduced to lowest terms. The fourth example was worked without further discussion or any difficulty.

Without any guidance from the teacher, and with great eagerness to discover its new aspect, the pupils worked the fifth problem which introduced the third step of difficulty, the zero remainder. The teacher's only contribution in the way of explanation at this point was in regard to the writing of the answer 0/6 as 0. A second example of a zero remainder was worked with ease by the pupils.

In response to the question, "Would you like to find out what the next step is?" the pupils worked the seventh example involving unrelated fractions and discovered for themselves the way in which it differed from the preceding examples. Further application was given through the eighth example.

Finally, the ninth and tenth examples were worked with ease and with a similar quickness in discovering the new point of difference. It will be noted that all of these steps of introduction were characterized by pupil activity and leadership, the teacher doing no direct teaching.

At the completion of this step of progressive and fairly rapid response to these five steps of difficulty in the subtraction of fractions, the teacher asked if there was anyone who felt he could not do them all. The pupils were eager to prove their comprehension. Accordingly, drill was given in the following questions, all of which were worked by pupils in notebooks or at blackboards.

11/12	4/5	3/4	5/9	5/6	4/5	1/3	3/5	2/4
5/6	1/10	3/8	1/3	1/3	2/10	8/24	1/2	2/7

The difficulty of these questions as compared with those used in the dull group, especially in the matter of common denominator and reduction of fractions, is apparent. The wisdom of the teacher in including such difficult reductions in the early drill was evident in this connection. Little trouble was experienced with any except 2/4 — 2/7 which received class attention.

Final check upon learning—The test which followed was given the class at the close of the lesson. It will be noted that the first six examples are identical with those used by the teacher who taught the slow 5B group. The second part of the test introduced a new topic—subtraction of mixed numbers. This was deliberately included to discover the extent to which these bright pupils could apply knowledge to a new situation.

Part 1:	5/8	2/3	6/8	6/10	10/15	3/4	6/7	2/3	2/6	6/9
	1/4	1/12	1/2	1/5	2/3	6/8	2/3	5/8	1/5	1/2

Part 2:	3 3/4	4 4/5	2 5/8	6 3/4	7 2/3
	2/4	1/5	1/4	1/8	1 1/2

The results were as follows:

Part 1: 10 examples correct—22 pupils   Part 2: 5 examples correct—32 pupils
          9 examples correct—11 pupils   4 examples correct— 7 pupils
          8 examples correct— 4 pupils   3 examples correct— 1 pupil
          7 examples correct— 5 pupils   2 examples correct— 1 pupil
                                                    1 example correct— 1 pupil

It is evident that pupils in this bright 5B class understood the new work of the period, since 22 of the 42 had all examples correct and 15 more had only one or two errors. Ability to apply this knowledge to a new situation is also apparent in the fact that 32 made no error in the work with mixed numbers to which they had had no previous introduction. Further drill is undoubtedly needed if accuracy of response is to be established.

Summary of Points of Differentiation Exhibited in These Lessons

Differentiation in content—Although each of these lessons was a forty-minute period of work on the same topic, marked differences are apparent in the scope and difficulty of the content. Dull pupils worked with three steps of difficulty only, while bright pupils grasped five steps and applied them to a new situation in which they had had no directed learning—the subtraction of mixed numbers. Many more examples of application were used with the dull group than were necessary in the bright class. Comparison of the fractions used in the two groups reveals equally distinct differentiation in the difficulty of the material. Especially was this true in the reduction aspect of the work, as reference to the detailed reports of these lessons will show.

These differences were conscious adjustments to the slow reactions of dull pupils, their limited responses to stimuli, their need for repeated experiences of a similar nature; as compared with the multiplicity of associations which bright individuals make quickly and independently to a variety of stimuli, their power of sustained attention, and their ability to generalize and to apply knowledge to new situations.

Differentiation in method: 1. Differences in preliminary drill—The fact that dull pupils are slow and limited in their reactions to specific stimuli and that they must therefore be given wide opportunities for drill was recognized in the provision of four types of drill on a single phase of the work— the reduction of fractions. Fractions were presented singly, on flash cards or on the board, so that pupils met only one difficulty at a time. This was in contrast to the drill provided the bright pupils, where 36 fractions arranged in a chart confronted them and they had to concentrate on a single item within a total group. Definite adjustment to the emotional nature and short span of attention of dull children and the consequent need for appeal to their interests was made through the provision of such short attractive drills as climbing a ladder and crossing Herring Run (a neighborhood stream known to all of them as a picnic site). The single, complicated drill used with the bright pupils, with no element included for the purpose of stimulating their interest beyond the intellectual appeal of the work, stands out in contrast.

Another difference is apparent in the inclusion of a drill on finding the common denominator for dull pupils as compared with the absence of any such review of old knowledge for bright pupils. This differentiation constitutes a recognition of the power of bright pupils to see, within a new situation, the possibility of application of knowledge and skills which have been previously learned. This power of analysis and transfer is not characteristic of the dull pupil, and it was therefore necessary to marshal all the needed and previously-acquired skills into relationship to the new learning.

2. Differences in introduction of new content—Perhaps the most marked contrast between the two lessons is to be found in the method of presentation of new content. In the dull class each step of difficulty was introduced through direct teaching. Illustration of the new work was given with several examples, and the children were provided an opportunity for immediate practice with similar problems until success in this phase was achieved. Their need for learning through constant practice with specific details and their dependence upon guidance and encouragement in a new undertaking were thus met. On the other hand, the bright pupils met five steps of difficulty progressively, without requiring any direct teaching or guiding explanation and with ability to discover and name the new steps of the work. Not until all types of subtraction of fractions had been encountered was there opportunity for extensive application of these facts. This is striking evidence of the bright pupil's intellectual curiosity, his power of sustained attention,

and ease of assimilation. The independent, self-initiated work of these children, with evidences of joy in the accomplishment in this mental work, differs widely from the closely-directed activity of the dull pupils in which each bit of success was so carefully capitalized through the immediate approval of the teacher and the provision of work within their power of achievement.

Differentiation in measurement of pupil growth—With the dull group, the teacher was contented to check, through simple examples, the actual content which had been presented in the lesson. This immediate check served to give the pupils a feeling of successful accomplishment, and the results indicated to the teacher their state of preparedness for further work. On the other hand, the members of the bright class not only had through the final test an opportunity to measure their achievement, but were also given a chance to try their ability in a new line of work. Again there was recognition of the gifted child's intellectual curiosity and his ability to reason and to transfer, as compared with the dull pupil's need for encouragement and his dependence upon direction in his learning.

4. Differentiation in Secondary School English Courses

A careful plan of differentiation according to aptitudes and tastes has been set up in the elective curriculums in the secondary schools of Baltimore. Within each of these curriculums there is some differentiation in subjects according to brightness and dullness of pupils. The glaring need, however, is for differentiation in content and method in the subject which forms the core of all curriculums, i. e., English.

The characteristic learning differences between dull and bright pupils[1] suggest the following obvious differentiations experimentally tested in the Baltimore secondary schools.

Content in Literature

Dull	Bright
Reading by pupils of easy contemporary fiction and biography; factual material in newspapers and magazines. Very simple units short in time duration and depth of comparative analysis, grouped around such psychological needs of adolescents as—adventure, sports, dramatization, making something, mystery.	Classics (college entrance requirements) greatly enriched with collateral reading, grouped around such intellectual and creative interests as literary types (short story, biography, poetry), literary themes (the sea, the growth of democracy), literary technics (short story writing, newspaper editorials, verse-making). For example: "Building Pictures with Words," "What Poets Write About," "Writing a Letter That Will Be Answered," "People Worth Knowing," "The Pirate in Literature and in Life."
Presentation of the "classics" through movies, dramatization by bright pupils, or oral reading by the teacher of sections of high interest.	

[1] See page 108 of this Yearbook.

Content in Expression

Dull	Bright
Such functional grammar as will help to eliminate gross errors from oral and written English needed in the following:	The same as for the dull heightened in effectiveness and correctness of the English
Conversation, recounting personal experiences	
Writing friendly letters	
Writing business letters and forms, including reports of accidents, write-ups for trade journals, etc.	Creative expression in poetry and prose
Recording telephone message	
Sales talking needed in buying and selling	
Writing memo for shopping, directions to maid, etc.	
Listening and asking questions	
Preparing a brief talk, resolutions, making a motion, and addressing chair, needed in such fraternal and civic organizations as may attract them	Spelling of all words needed
	Skill in use of dictionary for verification of the spelling of new words
Spelling of 4,000 commonest words	

Method of Teaching

Story telling and reading aloud by teacher	Silent reading with oral discussion
	Constructive projects originated by pupils
Silent reading of easy material after the teacher has developed strong interest in the material	Independent research in library
Dramatization, especially pantomime and prepared oral reading by the "better" pupils	Comparison of several authors' treatment of the same theme, same type, etc.
Reading and discussion of material with rather obvious plot development and simple characterization, strong element of poetic justice, completed rather than "broken ending" of the kind that suggests the characters "live on perhaps happily or unhappily after the book ends"	Analysis of creative technics author used to secure dominant impression attained through first reading
	Consciousness of the magic of words
	Experimentation in writing on same theme, type of literature, etc.
Introduction to very simple criticism of books, plays, and movies such as appears in daily newspapers	Development of rules of grammar and principles of writing before drill
Writing with real motive and under teacher guidance	Use of self-corrective practice material to gain mastery of technical English
Drill on correct forms without rules	Self-appraisal, using standards set up with or without teacher aid

A Selected List of Courses of Study Providing for Differentiation of Material To Meet Differences in Pupil Abilities

Table 35 has been prepared for those who are especially interested in seeing how other school systems are differentiating their course-of-study ma-

TABLE 35.—THIRTY-FOUR COURSE-OF-STUDY BULLETINS PROVIDING FOR DIFFERENTIATION OF MATERIAL TO MEET DIFFERENCES IN PUPIL ABILITIES [1]

School System Issuing Bulletin	Title of Course-of-Study Bulletin	Year of Publication	Number of Pages
	Courses for Special Classes		
Denver, Colo........	Differentiation of Curriculum for Slow-Learning Children.	1928	38
Detroit, Mich.......	Course of Study for Specia lClasses..............	1926	97
Detroit, Mich.......	Promotion Standards for X, Y, Z Groups, Grades 1–6.	1926	162
Hamtramck, Mich...	Course of Study for Special Classes.............	1928	*
Los Angeles, Calif....	Manual for Development Schools and Rooms......	1924	149
Minneapolis, Minn...	Suggested Course of Study for Retarded Children..	1924	*
Oakland, Calif.......	Bulletin on C-Courses in Grades 9–12...........	1926	*
Oakland, Calif.......	Handbook of Suggestions for Use in Atypical Classes.	1923	39
San Francisco, Calif..	Course of Study for Atypical Classes............	1926	68
South Bend, Ind.....	Courses of Study for Girls' Prevocational School..	1928	*
Springfield, Mass....	Course of Study for Auxiliary Classes...........	1929	75
Trenton, N. J........	Course of Study, Special Classes...............	1924	64
Wisconsin (State)....	A Course of Study for Classes for Mentally Handicapped Children in the Public Schools of Wisconsin.		233
	Arithmetic		
Chicago, Ill.........	Tentative Course of Study in Arithmetic, Grades 1–6.	1927	252
Cleveland, Ohio.....	Tentative Course of Study in Arithmetic, Kgn.–Gr. 4.	1927	102
Denver, Colo........	Courses of Study in Arithmetic and Reading for the Slow-Learning, Monograph 29, Grades 1–6.	1930	209
Oswego, N. Y. (State Normal School).	Tentative Outline for Special Class of Subnormal Children.		23
	Art		
Detroit, Mich.......	Course of Study in Art Education, Grades 1–8....	1925	410
	English		
Chicago, Ill.........	Tentative Course of Study in English, Gr. 7B.....	1927	69
Los Angeles, Calif....	English for Z Pupils..........................	1923	187
	General		
Los Angeles, Calif....	Course of Study for Third and Fourth Grades.....	1924	348
Los Angeles, Calif....	Course of Study for Fifth and Sixth Grades.......	1924	330
	Geography		
Cleveland, Ohio.....	Course of Study in Geography, Grades 3–4, 1929–30.	1929	74
Cleveland, Ohio.....	Course of Study in Geography, Grades 5–6, 1929–30.	1929	136
	Language		
Cleveland, Ohio.....	Tentative Course of Study in Spoken and Written English, Grades 3–6, 1927–28.	1927	193
Detroit, Mich.......	Course of Study in English, Grades 1–6..........	1925	426
Texas (State).......	A Course in English for Non-English Speaking Pupils, Grades 1–3.	1930	126
	Literature		
Detroit, Mich.......	Literature Methods and Materials for Slow-Learning Groups, Grades 1–8.	1930	136
	Mathematics		
Cleveland, Ohio.....	Tentative Course of Study in Mathematics, Grades 7–9, 1928–29.	1928	204
Long Beach, Calif....	Mathematics for "Z" Groups, Grades 7–8........	1929	145
Schenectady, N. Y...	Course of Study Presenting General Mathematics Objectives for Intermediate Schools, Grades 7–9.	1928	32
	Reading		
Denver, Colo........	Courses of Study in Arithmetic and Reading for the Slow-Learning, Monograph 29, Grades 1–6.	1930	209
Rochester, N. Y.....	Standards and Achievements in Reading, Grades 1–6.		117
	Science		
Detroit, Mich.......	Course in Nature Study, Grades 1–2.............	1927	224

* Mimeographed material of less than 100 pages.
[1] This list of courses was secured through the cooperation of the Curriculum Laboratory of Teachers College, Columbia University.

terials to fit pupils of different levels of ability. It lists 34 course-of-study bulletins. These have been selected as types to illustrate the various methods employed by different school systems to provide for differentiation of material which will meet differences in pupil abilities.

While many school systems do not have bulletins setting forth special courses of study for pupils of different levels of ability, their regular courses outline minimum essentials, optional materials, and supplemental opportunities. Others outline minimum requirements, medium assignments, and maximum assignments. In some cases it is mainly a matter of difference of emphasis. A common means of designating which materials in the course are to be covered by the different ability groups is to double star those topics which constitute the minimum basis for advancement. These are required of the slowest group.

The average group covers these and additional materials indicated by a single star. Those of superior ability not only discuss the given topics more fully, but also use a larger amount of supplementary material. In such cases, the adjustment of the course is more or less a problem of application for each individual teacher.

The following excerpts taken from recent course-of-study bulletins are more or less typical of the suggestions given to teachers for the adaptation of materials to pupils of different levels of ability.

The subject committees have set up a definite organization of specific objectives, suggested activities, suggested procedure, and desirable outcomes, both direct and indirect, as a means of developing the scope of each particular subject. More specific objectives have been set up in most cases than can be attained. The content is to be construed in all cases as suggestive. This provides for selection and adaptation of subject-matter to the needs of individual pupils—*Senior Mathematics for the High School, Curriculum Bulletin No. 24, St. Louis, Mo., 1926, p. 11.*

It has proved inadequate in the Trinidad public schools to give the pupils in the upper groups merely *more* work and those in the lower groups *less* work. It is quite apparent that the need is for *different* work, retaining as far as possible the fundamentals for the various grades. . . . Our efforts for next year and in succeeding years will be devoted mainly to differentiating the work to meet the needs of the various levels of ability which are peculiar to the Trinidad public school system—*Foreword to Tentative Course of Study, Trinidad, Colo., 1928.*

If possible, a teacher should keep and use "master cards" and "personality cards" for individual students. A master card contains all the possible information that the teacher tactfully is able to obtain about the student's home environment, habits, interests, ambitions, and previous record. A personality card records the estimate of traits of character of each pupil, compiled from personality tests, the records of teachers and the administration officers. A case record file should be kept. This would include the master card, personality card, and all other evidence that might make for an understanding of the student's abilities and interests, such as good or poor compositions, outlines, maps, charts, and graphs; accounts of voluntary projects; evidence of exceptional social efficiency or its lack; and evidence of worthy use of leisure or its lack—*General Foreword to Course of Study in Social Science for Senior High School, Rochester, N. Y., September, 1929, p. 22.*

In some of the schools, it may be possible to adapt the regular courses to the slow groups, but in other schools, there are certain types of pupils that should be given entirely different training. To meet the especial need of these pupils, a separate course has been planned for the ninth and tenth years—*English, High School, Grades IX-XII, Curriculum Bulletin No. 209, San Francisco, Calif., 1928, p. 17.*

CHAPTER VII

HOW HIGHER INSTITUTIONS OF LEARNING ARE MEETING THE NEEDS OF INDIVIDUAL STUDENTS

PROMOTION problems, in their larger aspects, extend throughout the college, university, and graduate school, as well as throughout the elementary and secondary schools. This section presents data showing how nine higher institutions of learning are meeting the needs of individual students. While some of this work is still on an experimental basis, it is full of suggestions for all college and university administrators, as well as secondary school principals and superintendents of schools.

No attempt has been made to present a comprehensive survey of personnel problems at the higher education level. The material here presented is merely illustrative of what a few selected institutions are doing. It is more or less typical of the personnel work carried on in many higher institutions of learning.

A. How Individual Students' Needs Are Met at Yale University [1]

The Yale University Department of Personnel Study was established in 1927 by gift of Charles H. Ludington to centralize procedure in matters of personnel and placement and to conduct research in these fields.

The department assists students in planning their courses of study, in which function it aims to supplement the work of Freshman Counselors. Cumulative records of each student's classroom work and extra-curriculum activities have been established as a basis for personnel conferences.

The department also aids undergraduates in their choice of careers, by collecting information about business and professional occupations and making it available to students and counselors. Interviews are arranged for seniors with representatives of business firms and with deans of schools for graduate or professional study.

Student records—According to the 1929 Report of the Director of the Department of Personnel Study and Bureau of Appointments, the central cumulative undergraduate record system, initiated at entrance of the Class of 1931 and continued for subsequent classes, is proving of value both to this office and to other departments of the university.

The data for the personnel office records are obtained from a number of different offices, each of which is interested in some particular phase of the student's history rather than in the student himself as an individual. The personnel office record, combining as it does the most important facts about

---

[1] Based on letters to the Research Division, National Education Association, from Albert Beecher Crawford, Director, Department of Personnel Study, and Percy T. Walden, Dean of Freshmen, Yale University, and bulletins issued by the Department of Personnel Study and Bureau of Appointments, Yale University.

the student's family, school, and other pre-matriculation history, followed by a cumulative record of his classroom work, extra-curriculum activities, self-supporting employment, and such additional information as may be pertinent to individual cases (furnished by the Department of Health, the D_ans' Offices, Board of Admissions), forms the only readily available and complete picture of the individual as a whole. The information thus available also facilitates the study of various personnel problems referred to the department for analysis.

Personnel research—Research problems vary from year to year; however, the following, studied during the year 1929, are more or less typical:

> Continuation of an analysis of various criteria of selection used in admission to the Yale School of Law; and development of a Legal Aptitude Test.
> Validation of Law School examination questions.
> Investigation of relation between age at entrance and grades in Freshman Year. This showed that age at entrance is, to a marked degree, inversely related to academic success.
> Continuation of an analysis in behalf of the Sheffield Scientific School of factors affecting their enrolment.
> Analysis of Freshman Year grades.
> Continued investigations into the prediction of scholastic potentiality, through statistical combination of various pre-matriculation academic criteria into a single index, predictive of individual grades in the Freshman Year. As the technic of this method is improved through careful analysis and comparison of actual with predicted results, its prospective usefulness becomes increasingly more apparent.
> Experiments in the determination of students' educational aptitudes. A battery of seven tests, intended to measure students' relative aptitudes for one or another general type of study, was given to an experimental group of 130 members of the Class of 1933, in their Freshman Year. The list included Strong's Analysis of Occupational Interests, and tests of scientific, mathematical, literary, and verbal facility, a test of attitudes, and one of facility in dealing with spatial relations.
> The department has for some time been collecting data concerning business and professional occupations of particular interest to college students. In this connection a special investigation has been initiated into the occupational histories, since graduation, of members of the Yale Class of 1926. This project will be taken up in more detail by the Yale Graduate Placement Bureau. It contemplates analysis of the possible relationships between both scholastic and extra-curriculum achievements in college on the one hand and subsequent progress in business or the professions on the other, the relative supply and demand for college graduates in different fields, and comparison of individuals' relative achievements in their respective occupations and of their opinions and advice thereon.

Affiliation of the Department of Personnel Study with the Institute of Human Relations should enable the department to obtain extremely helpful and specialized guidance as to the feasibility of its personnel research work and the best methods of carrying it out.

"The Freshman Year" at Yale—All undergraduates, whether they are to be candidates for an Arts, Science, or Engineering degree, are enrolled during their first year in one class under a separate faculty and dean. The or-

ganization of the Faculty of Freshman Year is similar to that of other undergraduate faculties and the duties and responsibilities of the Dean are those which generally appertain to that office.

Freshman Week at Yale—First-year students are required to begin their residence in New Haven a few days ahead of the rest of the university in order that they may have ample opportunity to discuss their choice of courses with their advisers and thus avoid, as far as possible, mistakes which might seriously handicap their future work. By reporting early they also have time to become familiar with their new surroundings and to receive preliminary instruction in regard to the various activities of life at Yale.

The session begins with a registration meeting on Wednesday morning, which is followed by conferences with counselors and two assemblies. The class is addressed by the President of the University, the Dean of Freshmen, the Chief Counselor, a selected member of the faculty who speaks on curriculum, and by representatives of various departments of the university and organizations with which the students are concerned.

The Counselor System at Yale—It has been said by an eminent member of the Yale faculty that no instructor can afford to omit his counseling because of the help which accrues to his teaching. Counselor service is entirely voluntary. Each year between 60 and 65 instructors offer to act in this capacity. This number adequately cares for a class of 850 students.

In September, the Counselor Committee meets to assign counselors to the freshmen, all of whom have then been admitted. There is one unalterable rule in this connection and that is that the counselor shall be one of the student's instructors. The assignment is made after a careful consideration of the temperamental peculiarities, needs, and intellectual interests of each student, as indicated on blanks filled out by the students themselves and by preparatory school headmasters. Before the meeting for the organization of the class, copies of this information are sent to each counselor so that when his counselees report to him he can have some picture of the persons with whom he has to deal.

The first contact between counselor and student is during Freshman Week, as mentioned above. In the course of the year, copies of his counselees' grades are sent to each counselor and if a student "comes up for action" for scholastic deficiency or disciplinary reason, the counselor is asked to give the Rules Committee personal information on the case and to meet with that body as a voting member. In the spring every freshman registers his final decision as to the degree for which he will be a candidate. In coming to this decision he is placed in touch by his counselor with authorities, such as the Department of Personnel Study, who can best advise him as to his choice of future work.

Aside from all this, the relation between counselor and counselee is purely informal and the nature of the contacts is left to the judgment of the counselor.

After ten years' experience, it is felt that the counselors are an invaluable aid in the difficult task of handling first-year students.

B. The Junior Area at Ohio State University [1]

Writing recently in the *Journal of Higher Education,* George W. Rightmire, President, Ohio State University, summed up the need of closer articulation between the state university and the high schools of the state as follows:

> In state universities many students enter at the bottom but comparatively few go over the top. The great exodus is below the junior year, most of it is in the freshman year. This is due to several causes, some beyond university control: ill health, poverty, domestic conditions, wanderlust, chronic weariness, micaw-berism—for these the university can do little. But there are many defections not traceable to these causes, cases in which the university's obligation is perhaps insufficiently appreciated or inadequately met or perchance neglected.[2]

The following paragraphs describe the Junior Area at Ohio State University.

The Pre-College Guidance Program of the State of Ohio

A basic principle of the administration of the work of the Junior Area at Ohio State University is that guidance properly begins in the secondary schools. The law of the state requires that the university accept applicants for admission who have graduated from first-grade high schools. However, the ability to graduate from high school does not guarantee success in college. Recently a committee of the North Central Association reported the results of a study of freshman mortality and found that one freshman in every four fails in one or more subjects during or at the end of his first term in residence. At state universities the percentage of freshmen failing in one or more subjects during their first semester is 33.9.[3] Some consider this an indictment of the high schools, others an indictment of the colleges and universities.

In the spring of 1929 the Junior Council of Ohio State University, recognizing the seriousness of the freshman failure problem, published and sent to all high-school principals of the state of Ohio a thirty-five page booklet entitled *A Suggested Program of Pre-College Guidance for High Schools.* The booklet, designed to assist high-school principals and counselors in their talks with students about their readiness for college work, discussed such factors as these in their relationship to college success: intelligence test score, high-school grades, size of the high school from which a student enters, age, sex, time devoted to study, self-support in college, and extra-curriculum activities. Factual data were presented so that in their counseling with students high-school advisers might talk with statistical authority. Charts were presented to demonstrate, for example, that 73.4

---

[1] Prepared by W. H. Cowley, Bureau of Educational Research, Ohio State University, Columbus, Ohio.
[2] Rightmire, George W. "The Floundering Freshman." *Journal of Higher Education,* Vol. I, No. 4; April, 1930. p. 185.
[3] Maxwell, C. R. "A Report on College Freshmen for the First Semester of 1928-29," *The North Central Association Quarterly,* Vol. IV, No. 4; March, 1930. p. 484-596. See Table XIV, p. 591.

percent of the students rating in the highest decile in the Ohio College Association intelligence test do at least one year of satisfactory work at the university, while only 47.9 percent of median decile students succeed during the same period, and only 20 percent of those in the lowest decile. All the other factors listed were similarly discussed with statistical data, and the booklet closed proposing a tentative high-school counseling program. In January, 1930, the State Department of Education called a state school guidance conference to discuss the development of a coordinated state-wide guidance program. From that meeting has developed a coordinated plan sponsored jointly by the high schools of the state through the State Department of Education, the Ohio College Association, and the State University. The details of the program have not as yet been completely worked out. The plan is, in fact, still in the blue print stage, although the foundations have been laid.

It is proposed that the scholastic aptitude of all high-school students in the state be determined by an extensive testing program to be carried out through all four years of the high-school course. Already the intelligence test program is under way. Early in November, 1929, 30,000 seniors in the high schools of the state took the intelligence test of the Ohio College Association under the direction of Dr. H. A. Toops of the Ohio State University faculty, research director for the association. These test results are now available for high-school principals and advisers in their counseling with students. Next year the intelligence test will be given again, and it is hoped that other tests may also be given at other times during the year not only to seniors but to all high-school students. These other tests will be subject-matter tests similar to the placement tests being developed by numerous colleges and universities. By the time students reach their senior year the principals and their guidance assistants will have at their disposal a mass of objective data which will give them a more or less accurate idea of the ability of any particular student to make good in college.

These data, it is proposed, will do more than predict college success. They will be available for the guidance of the student whether or not he plans upon a college course. Efforts are also under way to develop more and better occupational information for the use of high-school pupils who do not plan to go to college.

Freshman Week at Ohio State University—Since the fall of 1927, Freshman Week exercises have been conducted at Ohio State University for nearly 3,000 entering freshmen. That the program has found a permanent place in the life of the university is attested to by the results of an evaluation made by a faculty committee in the fall of 1929.[1]

[1] See: *Report of the Freshman Week Council and the Evaluation Committee.* Columbus, Ohio: Ohio State University, 1929. p. 63.
Those particularly interested in Freshman Week as it is conducted in many institutions should see:
Knode, Jay C. *Orienting the Student in College,* with Special Reference to Freshman Week. Contributions to Education, No. 415. New York: Bureau of Publications, Teachers College, Columbia University, 1930. 140 p.

The program of the week during the three years of its existence—
slightly modified each succeeding year—has included some 24 events, eleven
of which have been administrative and the remainder social and informa-
tive. The administrative events included six tests—intelligence, science
and mathematics, foreign language, English, chemistry, and social sciences—
a physical examination, measurement for military uniforms, and a talk by
the R. O. T. C. commandant for the men, registration with the Dean of
Women for the women, and try-outs for the musical organizations for the
several hundred freshmen interested in musical activities.

After this program had been carried out for three years, an Evaluation
Committee was appointed by the President of the university to answer two
questions about Freshman Week:

1. Does the university community consider Freshman Week important and valuable enough to be continued?

2. If question number one be answered in the affirmative, should the organization of Freshman Week be amended as a result of this evaluation?

To answer these questions a large portion of the freshman participants
filled out an extensive questionnaire, as did members of the faculty, parents,
upperclassmen, and administrative officers. Returns showed that 88 percent of the freshmen, 87 percent of the upperclassmen, and 98 percent of
the student leaders, i. e., upperclassmen who helped with the program,
were in favor of Freshman Week.

Several criticisms of the program were offered together with suggestions
for improvement. In the light of these, each of the 24 events of Freshman
Week was studied. The changes suggested were in general of minor importance—with one exception. The committee urged that more importance
be given to the interview between each freshman and some member of
the faculty. Freshmen coming to the university direct from high school,
and in many cases away from home for the first time, found the faculty
interview the one event of the program which helped them most to become
oriented to their new environment.

The organization plan of the Ohio Freshman Week calls for a division
of the 3,000 freshmen into 100 sections of 30 students each. In charge
of each section is a faculty member assisted by an upperclassman. These
two leaders share the responsibility of directing their section through the
program, but in every case the faculty leader does the interviewing, giving
each student about half an hour sometime during the week. In these interviews the most important values of Freshman Week have been achieved.
To their faculty leaders students bring their problems. These range
from questions about registration and living quarters to fraternity membership and choice of vocation. As thoroughly as possible the faculty leader
seeks to go over the entire orientation problem of the student that he may
begin his work at the university under the best of circumstances. At the
end of each interview the faculty leader makes a report which becomes part
of the student's permanent personnel record in the office of his junior dean.

Next year these interviews will be so scheduled that all freshmen will have an opportunity to talk with faculty members in their own college. Faculty leaders will be able under the new plan to perform more effectively since no longer will engineers be talking to arts men, agriculturists to students planning business careers, or education students to specialists in optics, veterinary medicine, accounting, or nursing.

Instead of a faculty and a student leader, the committee has proposed that there be two faculty leaders and that each be responsible for interviewing but 15 instead of 30 students. This change will make it possible for each faculty leader to give much more attention to each student.

The 1930 program, modified in the light of the suggestions from the Evaluation Committee, included these events:

Administrative:

1. Physical examination: both men and women
2. Measurement for military uniform: men
3. Registration with Dean of Women: women
4. Intelligence test
5. Chemistry placement test
6. English placement test
7. Musical try-outs

Orientational:

1. Faculty interview
2. Assembly: Address by the President
3. Illustrated talk on the history of the university
4. Tour of the campus
5. Tour of the library
6. Talk on extra-curriculum activities: to be given by a few experts several times rather than by student leaders whose effectiveness proved uneven last year
7. Talk by the Senior Dean of each college on the functions of his college
8. Talk by the Junior Dean of each college on Student Adjustment
9. Half a dozen social and recreational events: the YM-YW Mixer, YWCA Tea, church receptions, intra-mural recreational athletics, a visit to the stadium to see the football team in practice, an evening given over to a student stunt night managed by upperclassmen
10. A conference for parents at which the junior area program will be described that parents may be informed of the university program.

The Junior Dean Program at Ohio State University—The seven colleges at Ohio State University which admit freshmen are Agriculture, Arts, Commerce and Administration, Education, Engineering, Pharmacy, and Veterinary Medicine. Of these, two admit from thirty to sixty freshmen, and the other five divide among them the remaining twenty-six or twenty-seven hundred incoming students. In the small colleges it is no serious burden for the dean to know all his students and to keep actively interested in the progress of each. In the larger colleges this is impossible, hence five junior deans were appointed two years ago, one each in the Colleges of Agriculture, Arts, Commerce and Administration, Education, and Engineering. These junior deans work to counteract impersonal mechanistic tendencies. Their interests are confined to the junior area: to the freshman and sophomore years. Their responsibilities are these:

1. To assist freshmen and sophomores in their personal adjustments to the university. This involves helping with methods of study, helping individuals with employment problems to find work, discussing vocational ambitions, directing students with physical ailments to the Medical Service, discovering and sending to the Psychological Clinic students suffering from emotional maladjustment, working out problems of student-instructor incompatibility, and in general helping each student to the maximum degree of personal adjustment to the university.

2. To advise with students concerning the academic regulations of the faculty in the junior area, keeping in mind that the rules are to be administered flexibly to provide for individual differences.

3. To represent the university in its contacts with parents of junior area students and to increase as widely as possible such contacts.

4. To encourage and assist in the development of programs of pre-college guidance seeking to encourage able students to come to the university, to discourage poorly equipped students, and to help articulate such programs with the guidance plans of the university.

5. To cooperate with the other personnel agencies of the university.

6. To represent the university in its public relations having to do with the junior area.

7. To cooperate with the Senior Dean and department heads in their efforts to develop improved curriculums.

8. To cooperate with instructional departments in their efforts to improve instruction in the junior area.

9. To encourage and to assist in the development of special individual and group programs for gifted students.

10. To encourage and to assist in the development of individual and group programs for poor students.

These ten functions divide into two groups. The first six concern themselves with extra-instructional or personnel functions. The remaining four have to do with molding the instruction in the junior area following the principles of individual differences.

Junior Area Personnel Activities at Ohio State University

At state universities where restricted enrolments are not possible, personnel units are especially important. In 1895, 696 students were registered at Ohio State University. Today there are almost 11,000 in residence during the year and another 5,000 during the summer. Obviously the administrative organization that sufficed for 1895 cannot be expected to run smoothly today, nor can the President and the deans know their students as they did formerly. At Ohio State University the personnel program on the junior level is directed by the junior deans working with a group of other personnel officers. The personnel functions of both the junior deans and these staff personnel officers are briefly reviewed below.

The personnel functions of junior deans—The personnel duties of the junior deans focus upon individual adjustment. The junior deans make it their business to know students and to permit no extraneous personal considerations to interfere with the primary job of instruction. No student can work up to capacity until he has made the environmental and social adjustments that are involved in leaving home, in joining a new community, and in meeting large numbers of unfamiliar people. This adjustment process is not simple. It requires expert thought and continuous attention.

The staff personnel officers—In their work the junior deans cooperate with eight or ten staff personnel officers who are not attached to any particular college but who serve the entire university; that is, these staff personnel people cooperate with all the junior deans and the secretaries of the colleges who are the personnel officers on the senior level. If the personnel work of the university might be described in military terms, the junior dean is the chief line personnel officer on the junior level, with instructors doing their less specialized share also as line personnel workers. Supplementing the work of the line personnel people are the staff personnel officers who function for all the colleges and report directly to the President—with one or two exceptions—rather than to a dean. These staff officers include the Dean of Men, the Dean of Women, the University Examiner, the Director of the Student Medical Service, the Director of the Psychological Clinic, the Managers of the Ohio Union (men's clubhouse), the Pomerene Hall (women's clubhouse), the Director of the Remedial Clinic, the secretaries of the Y. M. C. A. and the Y. W. C. A., the Director of Dormitories, and several others.

Three of these staff officers are particularly interested in freshmen: the Dean of Women, the Dean of Men, and the University Examiner.

In describing her work, the dean of women writes:[1]

Our first responsibility is to discover the potentially undeveloped and the potentially maldeveloped. Our second responsibility is to invent education for the undeveloped and re-education for the maldeveloped. Our third challenge, which is really a sub-head of the second, is to develop an intelligent and discriminating attitude of self-orientation upon the part of each undergraduate woman with which she may learn to define the desirable characteristics of a college woman and individually work toward these ideals.

The dean of men does a correspondingly important work for the men students in supervising their housing arrangements and extra-curriculum activities.

The university examiner makes a large contribution to the personal adjustments of the students who pass through his office. He is in a position to discuss career objectives, to keep in touch with the work of the high schools of the state and their articulation with the programs of the university, to interpret for students state requirements for professional education, and especially to talk with transfers about their adjustment to the university and to the work of the particular college in which they are enrolled.

Instructional Developments in the Junior Area at Ohio State University

Instructional development is quite as important as personnel development. At Ohio State University much thought is being given to freshman instruction. For example, freshmen studying chemistry are not shunted off for instruction by graduate assistants, but are taught by specialists in the field

---

[1] Gaw, Esther Allen. "Social Education." *Journal of Higher Education* 1:24; January, 1930.

who give special attention to the development of the freshman course. Among the special devices for helping freshmen in their work are the following:

The interview sections—Every instructor is a personnel worker. Some instructors, however, assume their personnel responsibilities naturally, others find themselves too absorbed in their scholarship to take much interest in their students as individuals and they merely become a name or number in the instructor's classbook. Against this tendency the junior deans have set up the interview section program. Every quarter each junior dean arranges with a group of instructors in his college to interview every student in his sections at least once during the quarter. Informally and unacademically student and teacher visit, talk over the student's work, the general implications of the course content, and anything else that may occur to either of them as important to be talked about. In this fashion the instructor becomes acquainted personally with all his students, learns of their difficulties, sets them straight individually, and gauges his teaching as he discovers the difficulties of his students. During this present year over 100 interview sections have been conducted with freshman students. Recently the junior deans devoted one of their weekly meetings to an evaluation of the work of the interview sections. For the meeting data had been collected probing into the opinions about the plan of both students and instructors. The returns were so cordial that the interview section experiment will be continued next year with the hope that in time the practice will permeate the entire instructional staff and be a regular part of the responsibility of every instructor.

Elementary instructional supervision—Another instructional device in which the junior deans are interested, although for which they are not administratively responsible, is the supervision of elementary courses. In every department giving elementary instruction a supervisor directs all beginning courses. In every case the supervisor is a full professor who directs the teaching of the instructors who teach freshmen and sophomores. These supervisors are organized as a group, meet once a month, discuss their common problems, and in general keep actively interested in improving the quality of elementary instruction. No spectacular improvements in method have yet been promoted by these supervisors, but as the group becomes older in organization very likely significant developments will issue from their conferences.

Placement examinations—Two placement tests are used at Ohio State University. The Chemistry Department uses one, the English Department the other. Last year during Freshman Week other tests were given to selected groups for experimental purposes, and it may be that soon other departments will perfect tests which they will use in sectioning students by ability.

Remedial work for probation students—A well organized program under the direction of a member of the psychology department aids students who find themselves in scholastic difficulty. This work is of two sorts. In the fall quarter students whose records suggest the possibility that they will go on probation are assigned to a course which is designed to increase their skill in reading, in setting to work to master an assignment, in budgeting their time, and in acquiring some of the basic skills that are needed in English and mathematics and other elementary courses. Over a period of years the faculty member in charge of this course has been experimenting with methods of measuring the previous preparation of college freshmen, and in this course for danger-line students the findings are put to work to save students from disaster.

This pre-probation course is scheduled for the fall quarter, and then during the winter quarter a course is set up for those students who have failed to keep up during the fall. These freshmen are automatically assigned to the probation course by their junior deans, and they are required to take it as a regular part of their schedule. A personal interview is held with each student and his difficulties are gone into in great detail. When needed, help is also secured from the Student Medical Service and from the Psychological Clinic.

Meanwhile, the corrective classroom work in study habits, time budgeting, work organization, and the like continues regularly. Throughout the course few of the usual classroom methods are employed. Instead individual work is stressed. Each student is diagnosed as an individual and set to work on his special course of remediation.

Special instructional developments in elementary courses—While the remedial work goes on, effort is also made to prevent students from needing remediation. Attention is given to improving the methods of instructing elementary courses. In several departments important experiments are under way. For example, in both botany and zoology, the functional approach is made rather than the morphological. To illustrate, in botany, instead of presenting a complete logical review of plant structure, pertinent questions are raised concerning the functioning of plants. A typical problem has to do with the food-getting activities of plants. This question is raised in class discussion, and answers suggested by the class are deftly experimented with to produce experimental answers. And so with all the content of the course: all subject-matter is presented as problems, and the data of the course are worked out experimentally with the active participation of the class.

Since the emphasis in these elementary science courses is upon function, the student is given expert drawings and he is required to work with these rather than to use up an excessive amount of time in drawing specimens.

In the zoology department teaching methods are similar to those in the department of botany. A flexible lecture-demonstration-laboratory technic is employed. Questions are raised and experimentally answered. Throughout the problem-solving, humanized point of view prevails.

In zoology courses, to determine where emphasis in teaching should be placed, a pre-test is given all elementary students at the beginning of the course. In this department, an individual workroom has been established to which students are sent to work out problems with which they are having difficulty or upon which the especially gifted may want to do more advanced work than that being done by the average student. This workroom is open several hours a day, six days a week, and at all hours an instructor is on hand to help set up experiments, to answer questions, and in general to help students solve their problems.

Objective examinations—Tests are needed not merely to measure information, but also to measure the more complex factors involved in the learning process. At Ohio State University effort is made to establish devices to measure such abilities as these: (1) Ability to master descriptive facts; (2) ability to read and think technical terminology; (3) ability to draw inferences from facts; (4) ability to test hypotheses; and (5) ability to apply principles.

Conclusion—Much still remains to be undertaken in many directions, but results of the program thus far are encouraging. During the fall quarter of 1929, the percentage of deficient students throughout the university dropped eight percent, and during the winter quarter of 1930, the deficiencies dropped two percent more. The large state university has been condemned for its mass production methods, its impersonality, its inadequate educational technics. The Ohio State University program described above is a concentrated effort to demonstrate that there is no reason why a state university should not offer its students all the advantages of a small institution plus the many advantages of a large university.

C. How Freshman Needs Are Met at the University of Buffalo [1]

Preliminary course on "How To Study" for freshmen entering college— During the summer, the University of Buffalo offers a three weeks' course in the technics of study for all entering freshmen who have not done well in high school but who wish to take a college course.

The first summer it was required only of those from the lowest two-fifths of their high-school graduating class, but now it is required also of those from the middle fifth of the smaller high schools of the state, even if these applicants have received high scores in intelligence tests.

What effect has this preliminary course had on the enrolment in college? Before the course was instigated, about 20 percent of the entering freshmen came from the lower sections of their high-school classes, and would now be required to take the course. The percentage has steadily decreased, so that in 1929 only 12 percent of the incoming freshmen were from the lower scholastic division. This is probably due partly to the fee charged for those taking the course, partly to the strenuous nature of the course, and partly to the general attitude of the registrar's office tending to discourage these "poor risks" from attempting a college course.

[1] This report is based on a letter from Edward S. Jones, Director of Personnel Research, University of Buffalo, to the Research Division, National Education Association, and the following articles:

Jones, Edward S. "Testing and Training the Inferior or Doubtful Freshman." *The Personnel Journal*, Vol. VI, No. 3; October 1927.

Jones, Edward S. "The Preliminary Course on 'How to Study' for Freshmen Entering College." *School and Society* 29: 702-5; June 1, 1929.

The students who have taken this course are unanimous in the opinion that it is the most arduous toil that has ever been required of them as students. From nine o'clock until four-thirty they have to apply themselves to lectures, drills, or examinations. And there is a good deal of home-work in addition.

On the basis of unsigned reports from students at the end of the course and from comments given later to the personnel office, those responsible for the course have classified its various aspects in the approximate order of their value from the student's point of view:

1. Practice in taking notes from lectures stands out as the most valuable drill.

Twelve lectures, an hour in length, are delivered; eight of these are on the various technics of study by those administering the course, and four are by other speakers on more general topics. At the end of each lecture, all the notes are collected, carefully graded, and marked; and the next day each student is interviewed on this basis, usually by the person delivering the lecture. The notes are all discussed with each student, as to their logic, their completeness, their accuracy, and their form. All are urged to adopt the outline method in order to avoid danger of becoming mere recorders. By a fairly objective device for scoring notes, it is possible to show marked improvement in note-taking over the three weeks' period. Many of these students have never taken notes before, and only a few have given attention to the effectiveness of their notes.

2. Next in value come the drills in writing English themes, followed by individual conferences with expert college instructors in this subject. These themes are usually written under pressure of time, before the instructor, and are then read aloud to the student later, with particular attention given to correct sentences and to clarity. A certain level of spelling ability is required, based on outside home drill by the student himself.

3. The content of the lectures is considered next in importance by these students. The most frequently mentioned as valuable are the lectures on note-taking, purpose, habits, memory, reading, and attentiveness. Comments have been made to the effect that such lectures give them new insights, concrete suggestions to try out in their studying. As one man put it, it made studying for the first time "something to get excited about."

4. For drills in rapid reading, long newspaper clippings or other selections are passed to each student at least once a day, and record is made of the time required for reading these by each student. The comprehension, or ability to answer questions on the printed matter, is also checked, so that the mere skimming over of pages without understanding can be detected.

5. For training in assimilating the content of books, required assignments are given from two or three books on study, and additional assignments from which selection is optional are suggested. For example, one year, those intending to study medicine were advised to read and report on *Arrowsmith* by Sinclair Lewis.

6. Problems in mathematics are also of value to those planning for a mathematics or a science major. There is a partial review of the main concepts of intermediate algebra, but particular stress is placed on the methods of solving and checking simple problems.

7. To acquire practice in using library reference books, a number of assignments are given to look up information in twenty miscellaneous common reference books. Various dictionaries, encyclopedias, and almanacs are discussed, and finally the students are examined as to their ability to trace the best source of information for a number of unfamiliar subjects.

8. Oral ten-minute reports are required on outside reading. The form and the content of what is discussed are both critically examined later.

9. Experiments are tried out in memorizing lists of foreign words. One year, there were demonstrations, rather than drills, in the use of a set of cards for building up vocabularies.

10. A good deal of time is spent on drill in taking notes from difficult and abstract mimeographed excerpts from textbooks.

Taken altogether, the results of this preliminary course justify its continuation as a regular procedure. During the years 1926-29, the proportion of individuals surviving the freshman year with an average of C or better was doubled; that is, increased from 25 percent to 50 percent of the total number. And the number of those who failed entirely and dropped out of college was reduced from about 40 percent to 15 percent.

Those who had taken the "How To Study" course were compared, subject for subject, with the other students admitted who were not from the upper two-fifths of the better high schools.

The conclusions from this comparison are:

1. The "how to study" group seems to average as high as those from the middle fifth of the larger high schools and the upper two-fifths of the smaller schools of the state.

2. There is a decided tendency for the "how to study" group to benefit particularly in those courses which are drill subjects. That is, they are relatively better in foreign languages, mathematics, and English composition.

In answer to the question, If there are to be low or doubtful students admitted to college, and if a "how to study" course is available, should this be given in the summer before the college opens, or during the fall term, in addition to the regular college work?—those in charge of this course at the University of Buffalo are inclined to favor the first plan. The student is not so apt to taste failure and give up. Then, too, a student who is doing poor work in any class is a retarding influence, interfering with the normal progress of the class.

The comment is frequently made that it should not be the business of a college to teach study habits and rapid reading, that these should be handled by the grammar school and the high school. The practice followed at the University of Buffalo is to take the time of the students before they enter college, on a pre-collegiate basis entirely, with extra tuition. This is apparently superior to the current procedure in certain other higher institutions of learning of allowing many such students who are sadly defective in these respects to enter college.

Office of Personnel Research, University of Buffalo—To administer to the needs of the individual student, the Office of Personnel Research was organized at the University of Buffalo as a separate staff office directly under the Chancellor.

Chief emphasis has been put on two activities: (1) research investigations of occupations available for college students, and studies of entering students and their methods of study; (2) extensive interviews with all students regarding occupations, results of aptitude and achievement tests given upon entrance, and interests, with a view to considering each student's fitness for one or more occupations, and the schedule of courses desirable for each individual. The amount of work for each student, and the type of course, are regulated to some extent at the time of these interviews.

D. How Freshman Needs Are Met at Oberlin [1]

What is done before the prospective student arrives—Previous to the student's coming to Oberlin, he is mailed a copy of the *Students' Handbook,* which includes information of special interest to freshman students and is edited by the director of personnel service.

Actual detailed selection of courses for the freshman year is made by correspondence during the summer; of course, some changes in schedule are made after the student reaches Oberlin in September. These changes are discussed with the student by the assistant academic dean.

Freshman Week—The freshman classes both of the College of Arts and Sciences and of the Conservatory of Music begin their work at Oberlin College a few days earlier than do the other classes. The purposes of this preliminary period, called Freshman Week, are the following:

1. To help the new freshman man and woman bridge the gap between high school and college with a minimum of difficulty.
2. To acquaint the student with his new living conditions.
3. To acquaint him with Oberlin College.
4. To complete certain routine procedure previous to the beginning of regular classroom work.
5. To help freshmen become acquainted with one another unhampered by the distracting presence of a large body of older students.
6. To offer the opportunity of meeting some members of the college staff and faculty.

During Freshman Week, students are given individual physical examinations by the doctors of the departments of physical education. There are administered also the scholastic aptitude tests which later are of some value

[1] This statement is based on a letter from J. Anthony Humphreys, Director of Personnel Service, Oberlin College, to the Research Division, National Education Association, under date of February 26, 1930, together with excerpts from *Students' Handbook, Oberlin College, 1929-1930.*

in advising with students concerning their educational and vocational plans. In addition to completing the process of formal registration—securing of final class schedule and paying of term bills—the freshmen, by means of lectures by members of the faculty, are instructed concerning the following necessary topics: use of the library, efficient budgeting and use of time and money, academic regulations, social customs and regulations, and care of personal health.

Each afternoon there is opportunity for outdoor games, for walks to points of interest, and for getting acquainted with other freshmen. Evening affords time for informal dances, sponsored by the college, and for class sings.

Freshman Week affords opportunity also for electing temporary class officers.

Faculty advisers and deans—At present, Oberlin does not have a special group of advisers for freshmen selected from the teaching faculty. There is ample opportunity, however, for individual interviewing and counseling by the assistant dean of the college, the deans of men and women, and the director of personnel service. Although the deans have specialized tasks to perform, and therefore in their contacts with students must necessarily take care of certain aspects of college life, yet their interest is definitely in students as individual men and women. The deans become acquainted with the students as rapidly as possible and render friendly assistance.

The dean and assistant dean of the College of Arts and Sciences and the director of the Conservatory of Music are primarily concerned with the student's scholastic success. The deans of men and women of the College of Arts and Sciences and the Conservatory of Music have contact with students particularly in connection with the following situations: living conditions, financial problems, including student aid and loans, scholarship to a certain extent, college regulations, management of student organizations and social affairs, certain matters of personal interest to the student.

The assistant dean of the college acts as general adviser to all freshmen and to all new students during their first year. At stated intervals, he interviews freshmen who are not making satisfactory academic progress. Near the close of the first year and before the preliminary registration period in May, students apply for assignment to general advisers. During the registration period, a thorough-going conference is held with the adviser concerning the choice of courses for the following year and the general plan for the remaining years of the course. It is necessary to secure the signature of the general adviser before the registration can be considered complete. At the end of the second year, a student chooses his major work. The head of the major department then becomes major adviser and approves all courses elected in the major.

Special help given freshman women—Each year a group of upperclass women in the College of Arts and Sciences and in the Conservatory of Music is carefully chosen to act as counselors to freshman women. This activity is under the supervision of the deans of women. There is also a group of Y. W. C. A. "Big Sisters" to whom freshman women are assigned. Naturally, the functioning of these student counselors varies a great deal. The deans of women require the attendance of freshman women once a week during the first semester at a series of talks for the purpose of orienting the women to college life in general.

Department of Personnel Service—This department recognizes that students differ in background, ambitions, abilities, interests, and personal situations, and that they need individual help. It is responsible for coordinating those activities of Oberlin College which have as their objective assisting the individual student through his own efforts to develop himself, or herself, "to the limit of his capacity for growth, and to help him to apply his powers, so developed, most effectively to the work of the world."

Ample opportunity is given to freshman men and women to have individual interviews with the director of personnel service during the first few weeks of the first semester. These conversations, initiated by the students, serve to make the director personally acquainted with the students, to reveal points at which early help may be needed, and to fill evident gaps in the information on file in the department of personnel service.

The director of personnel service in his report for 1928-29 states:

According to the present conception, the following are direct responsibilities of the department of personnel service:

1. To coordinate student personnel activities within Oberlin College.
2. To expand and improve personnel activities in the entire institution.
3. To collect all kinds of information concerning all students that may be of value in assisting students to help themselves.
4. To transmit information, either in whole or in part, to members of the staff or faculty who may be concerned or who can render special assistance to an individual student.
5. To discover individual students who may want or need help, to diagnose the situation in a preliminary manner, and to refer the student to the person best qualified to handle the situation.
6. To act as a personnel counselor, within limits, to many students.
7. To carry the primary responsibility for helping a student who is in a strained or abnormal mental or nervous condition.
8. To gather vocational information of value to college students, to make it easily accessible to them, and to counsel with students concerning their vocational plans and problems.
9. To teach the elective course known as "Vocational Information."
10. To assist the student to secure employment: (a) during term time (campus employment); (b) during summer vacations; (c) after graduation.
11. To initiate research, both within and without the department, which will increase the effectiveness of the personnel idea and methods for the institution as a whole.

How the department of personnel service cooperates with other departments—The department of personnel service cannot handle all the details of situations, but must secure the cooperation of other officers and members of the faculty. For example, students with speech defects are referred to two faculty members in the department of psychology. In case a student needs expert psychiatric attention, a qualified doctor in Cleveland is called in.

The department of chemistry discusses methods of study in chemistry with new students in that department. The director of the department of personnel service is hoping to make a definite arrangement whereby students needing instruction in methods of study may secure it.

Instructors are furnished with digest of admissions data—The department of personnel service furnishes· to each instructor of freshmen, soon after the opening of the first semester of the academic year, a digest of admissions data for each freshman. The purpose of these digests is to introduce the new freshman to all his instructors in a more personal way than has been possible in the past. The following data are included in the digests: name, class, home address; date and place of birth; antecedents, race; parents' occupations; religious affiliation; ranking in high school and number in class; high school attended and date of graduation; extra-curriculum activities in high school; vocational experiences; vocational preferences at present; interests, hobbies, or preferred amusements; amount of probable self-support; and special notes.

E. How Freshman Needs Are Met at the University of Minnesota [1]

Purpose of Freshman Week—The University of Minnesota turns over its facilities to the service of the freshmen for this initiatory week. It attempts to organize and systematize what every freshman would have to do for himself, so that the three thousand or more prospective students can matriculate and become adjusted to the new ways of doings things with fewer disappointments and jams. An attempt is made to put through with machine-like precision what the freshmen would necessarily have to do for themselves. A Direction Hour which all freshmen are required to attend begins the program for Freshman Week.

Registration—Registration for freshmen is in two stages. The first is registration for Freshman Week. The second, included as one of the Freshman Week exercises, is registration for the work of the fall quarter. Before any student may register for Freshman Week, he must take the English and College Ability Tests. These tests may be taken at certain local high schools or examination centers during the preceding year, or they may be taken at the University of Minnesota two days preceding Freshman Week. The College Ability Test must be taken before Freshman Week in order that the results can be used in arranging a fitting study program for the student.

On presenting a certificate showing the completion of the English and College Ability Tests, each freshman receives a card to be filled out which carries complete instructions for the remaining steps in the preliminary registration process. The programs and tours of Freshman Week, which in many cases are optional, are systematized by means of a coupon book

---

[1] Based on a letter from Anne Dudley Blitz, Dean of Women, University of Minnesota, to the Research Division, National Education Association, under date of March 4, 1930, and on a University of Minnesota Bulletin entitled "Freshman Week, Sept. 25-28, 1929."

arrangement. The student is directed to present the coupon book at each exercise. The proper coupon is detached by the assistants at the door and serves as a record of the student's attendance.

The student who has not definitely decided upon the profession or life work for which he wishes to prepare is given "unassigned" classification. This places him under the direction of the Committee on Vocational Guidance which renders special assistance in such cases. He has the advice of a member of this committee in arranging his schedule for the fall quarter and until such time as he selects the course of study he wishes to follow.

The Vocational Guidance Committee consists of ten members: the vocational counselor for women, two representatives from the School of Business Administration, and one representative from each of the following: Department of Agriculture; Division of Home Economics; College of Education; Division of Forestry; College of Science, Literature, and the Arts; College of Engineering and Architecture; and the School of Chemistry.

Freshman examinations and lectures—A physical examination is required of every freshman. All attend a lecture on "What Is a University Library?" and a lecture on "How Do We Study?" All pre-legal students attend a lecture on "Law" by the dean of the Law School. All pre-dental students attend a lecture on "Dentistry" by the dean of the College of Dentistry. All pre-medical students attend a lecture on "Medicine" by the dean of the School of Medicine. All pre-business students attend a lecture on "Business" by the dean of the School of Business Administration.

These lectures give information and advice on the training for the various professions. They are intended primarily for the students who register for the respective courses, but any freshman who is interested is urged to attend.

Library inspection—Tours through the library are made under the direction of the university librarian, or one of his assistants, who gives the freshmen instruction on the facilities of the library and the opportunities it offers. The students are shown the reading, reference, and periodical rooms, and told how to use the card catalog and how to obtain books.

Program of study—The program of study is made out by the student in conference with a faculty adviser from the college which he desires to enter.

Each college of the university provides faculty advisers who assist in arranging study schedules and all matters pertaining to registration. By consulting his faculty adviser, a student gains information necessary to insure that his course selections are in harmony with his educational plans and purposes. The names and campus addresses of the faculty advisers of each college are listed in the *Freshman Handbook*.

The Committee of Faculty Counselors functions throughout the year and aims to assist the individual student to make the best possible adjustment to the opportunities available within and without the university, and to foster a friendly relationship between individual members of the faculty and students desiring such contact.

According to the *Freshman Handbook,* students should feel free to consult members of the committee in regard to curriculum matters, methods of study, living conditions, associations and habits, interests, extra-curriculum activities, health, and any and all matters which affect the student's work. Some of the faculty members serving on this committee devote as much as half time to this work.

Campus tours—For the purpose of acquainting new students with the campus, its buildings, its landscape, its athletic as well as academic facilities, tours are arranged which cover the grounds of the university. Student guides conduct the parties and endeavor to make the tours interesting and profitable.

The educational program is supplemented by a number of entertainments given by the Student Committee. This committee is active during the summer. Student representatives are appointed throughout the state to give information to all prospective freshmen in their communities. During Freshman Week, the Student Committee cooperates with the faculty advisers in making the freshman feel at home by helping him in every way possible. The Student Committee arranges entertainment for the freshmen to dovetail with the program arranged by the faculty committee.

The Deans and Faculty Counselor Committee—At the University of Minnesota there are no freshman deans in the strict sense of the term. The assistant to the dean of student affairs has the freshmen under his surveillance, and the freshman girls are under the general supervision of the dean of women.

In a letter concerning his work with freshman men, the assistant dean of student affairs writes:[1]

Late in the summer, I send out a letter to all freshman men previous to their registration at the University of Minnesota. This letter outlines some of the problems which may face them at the time of their registration and in the first few months of college. I invite them to come to my office, as early as possible, for the purpose of getting acquainted and solving any difficulties that may face them at that time. From then on, most of my contacts are through the medium of personal conferences and meetings with various freshman groups. Some of these groups, through which I make the most valuable contacts, are the pledge groups of fraternities and the freshman football team. I keep a record of each man interviewed, stating his problem and disposition of the case, working with the faculty counselors, staff of the Y. M. C. A., and other guidance agencies.

The Faculty Counselor Committee consists of seventeen members chosen from the various departments and includes the director of the Minneapolis Women's Occupational Bureau. A letter is sent to every freshman telling him of the opportunity of receiving advice from the faculty counselors. Besides this, a vocational interest test is given to all freshmen by the psychology department. All other interest tests are recommended by the advisers and given under the direction of the psychology department. Students who have no specific vocational interest are advised to register for an

---

[1] Letter from Otis C. McCreery, Assistant Dean of Student Affairs, University of Minnesota, to the Research Division, National Education Association, under date of April 1, 1930.

orientation course open only to freshmen. Maladjusted students are advised to register for a course entitled "How To Study" offered by the psychology department.

Helps to good study habits—Eight pages of the *Freshman Handbook* set forth principles of effective study prepared by the psychology department. These six principles are discussed in language which appeals to and is easily understood by incoming students:

1. *A definite motive is necessary*—A first essential for effective study is a "will to learn," an intense desire to broaden and deepen knowledge to become expert in one or more fields.

2. *Plan the work of each day*—It is very unfortunate that the phrase "plan your day" suggests slavery to routine, whereas experience of busy people indicates that planning not only favors better work, but permits the enjoyment of more leisure time. . . . During your first quarter, particularly, you will be obliged to select from a multitude of demands upon your time those deserving attention.

3. *Skilful reading habits are essential*—Improvement in speed and comprehension occurs with practice. Devote some time each day to practicing reading against time and guard against too much activity of the vocal organs.

4. *Develop problem-solving attitudes in study*—The reading method neither favors critical attitudes nor the comparison of ideas and facts, and is less valuable than the method of recitation. The method of recitation, requiring us to ask questions, favors active attitudes and a critical examination of the subject. . . . When preparing a textbook assignment, form the habit of using the table of contents to obtain, in the shortest time, a general idea of the subject. Following this, if problems or questions are given at the end of chapters, study them to cultivate a critical attitude and to anticipate some of the important points in the assignment.

5. *Good notes are an aid in learning*—Lectures, if they are to be mastered, require a record of the main points in your notebook.

6. *Form the habit of distributed study*—The attempt to master an assignment at a single sitting is often disastrous. You are likely to get lost in details, to suffer from fatigue, and to form the uneconomical attitude of studying merely to pass examinations.

How the President of the University of Minnesota aids incoming students—A greeting to the members of the incoming class from the president of the university is included in the *Freshman Handbook*. On Thursday of Freshman Week all freshmen assemble on the plaza before the Northrop Memorial Auditorium to hear an address of welcome by President Coffman. Representatives of the Board of Regents, the faculty, and upperclassmen are also there to greet the new students.

Every Tuesday morning at 8:30 throughout the first quarter, President Coffman meets all the freshmen in a freshman assembly, talks to them about matters of vital importance, and discusses problems that confront them as students.

University of Minnesota student record card—This card is made up of three sections: (1) personal history information, (2) college record section, and (3) records of tests and scholarship. It is a four-page cardboard folder, size 9 x 12 inches.

F. How Individual Student Needs Are Met at Columbia College [1]
A Brief Account of Personnel Work

The student body is divided into groups, according to the intentions of the students for their life-occupation, as follows: (1) Architecture; (2) Business; (3) Dentistry; (4) Engineering; (5) Journalism; (6) Law; (7) Medicine; (8) Theology; and (9) those not coming under the previous headings.

To facilitate administration and to aid in giving advice, the Dean of Columbia College has organized a group of seven members of the staff who are designated as assistants to the dean, and are assigned as advisers to these sections.

It is to one of these that the student ordinarily goes for counsel as to program, degree requirements, and whatever personal matters he may see fit to discuss. Group meetings are held at which prominent men of the particular profession discuss with the students specific material of particular interest to them. Every reasonable effort is made to acquaint the undergraduate with the profession he proposes to enter. Advisers have their teaching schedules reduced, so as to have time for personal attention to each case. Students are encouraged to make the most of the facilities offered in this regard.

The most important feature of this personnel work is the fact that the dean is directly accessible without restriction to every student of the College at normal periods during the day. He not only welcomes such contacts, but insists upon the opportunity for them, and this naturally takes a great deal of his time.

All available information about students is centralized through the advisers and other administrative officers in the dean's office, where it becomes available to interested members of the staff. Since the success of this system depends on keeping the confidence of the student, the dean naturally discriminates in giving information as the factors in the case warrant. The Offices of Admission, of the Medical Officer, of the Secretary of Appointments, and of religious organizations contribute to the adviser in the case of each student material, the aggregate of which is a fairly life-like word-picture of the undergraduate.

A photograph is taken of the student as part of the routine of his initial registration, and copies forwarded to the dean, the appropriate adviser, the registrar, the bursar, and the Director of the Bureau of Appointments, where they are affixed to his permanent card record in each office.

Under the direction of Ben D. Wood, professor of collegiate educational research, a large card-folder is kept for each student.

Thus in the case of each student, his academic career, interests, and activities, as well as special accomplishments, and factors in his life are recorded on a "time-projection" basis over a period of years. This card for purposes

[1] Based on *Report of the Dean of Columbia College for 1929*, Bulletin of Information, Columbia University, October 12, 1929, and additional material supplied by H. E. Hawkes, Dean of Columbia College, Columbia University, to the Research Division, National Education Association, in March, 1930.

of ready reference is kept up to date by a specialist in the dean's office. The use of this card as a folder permits of filing complete memoranda and reports which are important in the case of the student. At each registration the student makes a report on his present health and financial condition and any unusual happening that may have occurred in the previous period.

Each adviser has in his office a file in which he keeps individual records of the students' grades, interviews and advice given, memoranda of disciplinary actions, and hours used in outside work and commuting.

The Office of Admissions obtains a great deal of valuable material by the time the student registers as an undergraduate. Nearly all applicants have a personal interview with some representative of that office, and a memorandum is made of the essential points of this interview. Certain other important material appears on the personal application, the principal's recommendation, and the school record. Before the student is finally admitted, he must present certain forms having to do with his health. Part of the admission procedure involves taking a psychological examination or mental test, the results of which constitute, in the majority of cases, reliable indices of the student's capacity to do college work. Knowledge of the mental test result, of the preparatory school and health records, of extra-curriculum activity record, and of the student's available time (in case he commutes, or does part-time work for his support), as well as of the particular conditions for study in his case, enables the adviser to help him arrange a schedule which is suitable to his needs and general welfare. The essential points of all this material are gathered in the dean's office.

The activities of freshmen are limited in scope, in order that they may put the proper emphasis on academic work, and everything is done to make them appreciate this.

In order to acclimate the freshman to his new surroundings, compulsory lectures are prescribed once a week, for which no degree credit is given. These are called "orientation" lectures, and the material taken up has to do with the history and traditions of Columbia College, methods of study, the position of the College in the University, its inter-relationship with the professional schools, the advantages of being located in the City of New York, the use of the library and of books, and the proper place of extra-curriculum activities in the life of the student.

A feature of the fall term is the so-called "round-up" which comes immediately after the mid-term marks have been reported. All freshmen whose work has not been completely satisfactory are considered by members of the faculty concerned, at this meeting. Here it is that the advantages of this system of personnel record appear prominently, for each man is discussed freely and with a good deal of frankness. His picture and a record of his marks are thrown on the screen, as he is more easily recognized and discussed with this aid.

The secretary of appointments is in close touch with the dean and the advisers, and keeps them posted as to the information available in his office, having to do with the students. Everyone who obtains a position has a report sent to the dean who forwards it in turn to the proper adviser. This report gives the time used in the work, the firm or person employing the student, and a general idea of the salary obtained. Problems of vocational fitness or professional adaptability are made the subject of careful study in which the department of psychology collaborates.

The advisers to student religious organizations are active in making students at home in their new surroundings. Often the freshmen are organized into groups meeting bi-weekly, and their contacts with the faculty developed in an informal manner.

Freshman Week is a regular part of the pre-registration period for first-year men. During this time, placement examinations are given, and the freshmen are introduced in a group to the college administrative officers, to some of the academic work done in the university, to undergraduate leaders, and to the campus in general.

Placement tests—In his 1929 Report, the Dean of Columbia College makes this statement relative to placement tests:

In September, 1928, each student in the entering class at Columbia College was asked to take placement tests in the modern language which he presented for admission, in English, and in such sciences as he proposed to continue in college. He was also advised to apply for an achievement test in any subject in which he felt sufficient confidence in his ability and training to justify a trial. As a result of these tests it turned out that 48.6 percent of the incoming class showed competency to enter upon some phase of college work in advance of the point indicated by the entrance record. In all, 1115 semester hours, aggregating 37 student years of college work, were anticipated in this way. Four students anticipated 20 or more semester hours by means of these tests. A few students were demoted as a result of the tests, and were asked to take courses lower than the ones indicated by the entrance records. Such courses were taken without college credit unless the student maintained a very high record in the course to which he was demoted. In such a case it seemed fair to the student to assume that there was a reasonable doubt as to whether he ought to have been put back into a lower course without credit. . . .

The success of the policy of advancing students as described rests upon the quality of the work that the students actually did in the courses to which they were promoted. Throughout the year the work of these students was observed, and at no time did trouble seem to be developing. In the early weeks of the winter session a few of the promoted boys expressed the fear that they were beyond their depth, but they were urged to fight it out and in every case the student found himself completely before the middle of the year. After the final examinations in May, 1929, a careful study of the accomplishment of the promoted students was made. It turned out that of all the students who carried the course to which they were promoted only one individual received a failure, and one other received a mark of D. All of the rest not only passed, but the average of their work was distinctly above that of the class as a whole. . . .

One year's experiment is not enough to afford final conclusions. But unless all signs fail, a device is here in process of development which will go farther toward stimulating the superior student to his best effort at the most critical period of his college course than anything that has come to my attention. Half of the incoming class were saved from taking some work that was too easy for them, and instead were placed where they had something to bite on. And they bit very vigorously. To save this group of our ablest students from the tendency to develop habits of loafing and from the boredom that comes from marking time in too elementary a class is certainly a contribution to the problem of the gifted student. This is one of the promising fruits of the new curriculum.

The new curriculum in Columbia College—The new curriculum recognizes the fact that there are these three types of students in Columbia College: (1) the student who is definitely looking forward to a professional school; (2) the student who by temperament and ambition is a scholar and who wants to specialize in some field of scholarly interest; and (3) the ordinary citizen whose intellectual development is not obtained through research, but who wishes a good education.

According to the Dean, in the new curriculum at Columbia College, the pre-professional programs are constructed so as to enable the student to find out whether his professional ambition is really suited to his tastes and abilities, and to capitalize this ambition in affording an adequate motivation for a serious and sound preparation for his life work.

The new curriculum is also adapted to the needs of the person of scholarly temperament. However, it does not assume that the only kind of education that is worth anything is gained through intensive application to a narrow field of learning. The urge toward scholarship that the new curriculum provides finds its origin in two sources, according to the Dean of Columbia College. One is inside the student and the other is outside him. The survey courses, like the course in Contemporary Civilization, serve as a powerful stimulus to more extended work in the direction indicated by the course. The curriculum of the first two years contains a sufficient number of survey courses to justify the statement that the freshman and sophomore years are exploratory and are intended to awaken the student to intellectual ambitions consistent with his talents. By the end of the sophomore year, the student has had an opportunity to gain an introduction to any field which his taste or ambition or plan for life work may indicate, and is ready for the more advanced work built on the work of the first two years.

The urge that comes from outside the student is in the form of the requirement that each student shall obtain 60 so-called maturity credits before receiving his degree. Maturity credit accompanies courses which are normally built upon sophomore work. Courses bearing maturity credit, then, imply two years of college residence, and an appropriate amount of specific preparation for the course in question. The number of maturity credits which a course carries is equal to the number of points toward the degree assigned to the course. If a student must acquire 60 maturity credits during his junior and senior years, he must take practically all of his work in advanced courses. A careful study of the nature of the so-called sequences of study taken under the old curriculum convinced the Committee on the Curriculum that, with the Columbia College student body as it is, any requirement of a specific subject of concentration beyond that implied by the requirement of 60 maturity credits was unnecessary. As a consequence, the type of student described above as the citizen-to-be who wants a good education can get it in the manner just described, provided he has adequate ability, preparation, and willingness to work.

For the allurement of the young scholar, each department either has or will organize facilities for study reaching as far out toward the unknown as is practicable. These more advanced courses will usually be given in the seminar style, and can be assigned point value appropriate to the intensity with which the student goes to work.

For the youthful scholar, the courses of the Graduate School are open, either as lecture courses or as supervised study under proper guidance. According to the Dean of Columbia College, the new curriculum bids fair to accommodate itself almost automatically to the ideals of the College in the University. The student body is divided into "pass" and "honor" students —not by an organization of an honors college or group, but by the intellectual stimulation of the first two years of college followed by a broad and flexible opportunity for the student of scholarly interests to select his specialty unhampered by rules or petty limitations.

Survey courses at Columbia College—Contemporary Civilization is a two-year course. The emphasis during the first year is upon the nature of man as a psychological entity and as a social unit, followed by a survey of the features of the civilization developed in Europe and America most significant for an understanding of the social order of the present day. In the second year of the course, economic and governmental questions are considered, in order that the student may be brought to a knowledge of the kind of world he lives in, an understanding of the major problems of our modern civilization, and an appreciation of the various ways in which men have attempted and are attempting to meet them.

Each of the natural and physical sciences has organized an elementary course, meeting three times a week, with a minimum of laboratory work, intended for students whose major interest may lie in other fields but who wish to gain an introduction to the science in question. In the departments of botany and geology, this course not only serves as a survey of the subject for the person who does not plan to pursue further studies in that field, but as an introduction to more advanced work in the department as well. In physics, the first half of the survey course prepares the student for further departmental work; while in chemistry and in zoology, the survey course does not automatically prepare the student to enter more advanced courses.

A course on the Historical Bases of English Literature is offered chiefly for sophomores in collaboration by the departments of history and English. It is the conviction of both of these departments that this course will afford not only the basis for an intelligent appreciation of the life and the literature of the period considered, but will give a solid foundation for scholarly work in both fields.

In the same spirit, the introductory course in the department of philosophy, which normally comes in the junior year, is a comprehensive course in the history of philosophy rather than a detailed study of one author or period.

G. How Purdue University Meets the Needs of Individual Students[1]

Orientation period for freshmen—Purdue University has a plan whereby all freshmen are given special instruction and assistance. Through the orientation period, each student is enabled to make a better start with his work and to adjust himself more effectively to the new conditions of university life. Four days previous to the opening of the fall term, freshmen meet for lectures on important university regulations and customs, to become acquainted with the university campus and buildings, and to have an opportunity to know members of the faculty. During this time also, each student is given the following tests for the purpose of enabling the university to advise him regarding his educational program: chemistry aptitude test, English tests, home economics placement tests, mathematics training test, and physical and psychological examinations. The results of orientation tests enable the university to know better how to classify students and consequently to help them.

Personnel Service, Schools of Engineering, Purdue University

Purpose of the personnel service—To develop the personality, as well as the mind, the body, and the character of the student, is the chief purpose of the Personnel Service of the Schools of Engineering at Purdue University, according to the director of personnel. He reports that it is difficult for the student to see himself as others see him. He does not often know what others find objectionable about him and yet, without a knowledge of his objectionable characteristics, he may be greatly handicapped. The personnel service endeavors to give to the student his true picture and to assist him to develop himself.

The major duties of the personnel service are: (1) Personality Development—to assist the students in the improvement of their personalities. (2) Occupational Information—to assist in the vocational guidance of students by giving them occupational information. (3) Placement—to assist in the placement of senior students in proper employment after graduation, and to help juniors and underclassmen to secure summer work. (4) Records—to keep up-to-date personnel records of all engineering students. (5) Assistance to Graduates—to assist engineering graduates of the university in employment and other personnel matters.

The student's development during his four years at the university is studied in its four phases—mind, physique, character, and personality.

Personality development—Before the freshman arrives at Purdue, information concerning him, his family, his high-school record, and his practical experience is obtained, with a self-rating of his personality, and five references. A personality rating blank, as shown on page 175, is sent to each of those five references to be used by the personnel director and others to assist the student in making, from the start, his adjustment to college.

---

[1] Based on the following leaflets supplied to the Research Division, National Education Association, by J. E. Walters, Director of Personnel, Schools of Engineering, Purdue University, Lafayette, Ind.: *Bulletin of Purdue University,* Vol. 29, No. 16, July, 1929; and Information Concerning the Personnel Service.

In the middle of the first year, personnel blanks are filled out by each freshman on which he gives the names of ten additional persons, five teachers and five students, who are qualified to rate him on the traits of his personality. The personality rating scale presented on the opposite page is sent to each of the references given by the student.

With each rating blank sent to the fifteen references is a letter asking for ratings of the student's personality in comparison with men of similar age, educational preparation, and environment. As soon as the ratings are received by the personnel office, they are compiled, averaged, and recorded on the student's personnel record.

If in the freshman year the average of the ratings of all of the characteristics places the student in the lowest quarter of his class, he is interviewed by the director of personnel, and methods of improvement are pointed out and his progress is followed up.

This procedure is repeated in the junior year. As soon as the ratings from the junior references reach the personnel office, a careful study is made of them, and the opinions are again averaged. If the characteristics are not improved, the student is invited for another conference and follow-up program. He is urged to take advantage of the opportunity to improve during his senior year.

Occupational information—Descriptive literature of hundreds of industrial concerns, special publications, lectures, and conferences are used to help the student to become familiar with the trends of engineering as they affect the technically trained engineer. This occupational information is of value to the students in guiding themselves vocationally. An endeavor is made to harmonize the student's vocational preference and his fitness. He obtains a synthesis of his fitness and preference (1) by reading about engineering and the careers of successful engineers and others; (2) by conferences with successful engineers about their profession and duties; and (3) by "try-outs" of actual work in engineering or related work.

Employment—The employment work of the personnel service embraces assistance to seniors in securing proper employment after graduation and the placing of undergraduates in suitable occupations during their summers.

Records—Each student's personnel record contains a composite of his personality ratings, his scholastic record, his health ratings, and all other useful personnel information concerning him. This is kept up to date for use by the various offices on the campus and by industrial concerns. Copies of the personnel records are furnished periodically to the heads and staffs of the Engineering Schools to assist them in making better adjustments of the students.

After graduation when sufficient time has elapsed to show the caliber of work which the young alumnus will do, a progress report, a personality rating scale, is sent to each graduate. He is asked to take it to his employer for a rating of his personality and for a discussion about his work, his progress, and how he can improve. The employer's rating is sent to the personnel office.

PERSONALITY RATING SCALE—PURDUE UNIVERSITY

1. ADDRESS AND MANNER: Remarks—	Repellent	Bearable	Makes fair impression	Likable	Very pleasant
2. ATTITUDE: Remarks—	Uninterested	Willing to be interested	Tries to be interested	Attentively interested	Enthusiastically interested
3. CHARACTER: Remarks—	Dishonest	Open to temptation	Fairly reliable	Generally trustworthy	Absolutely trustworthy
4. COOPERATIVE ABILITY: Remarks—	Obstructive to others	Frequently cannot work with others	Cooperates moderately	Can work with others	Goes out of his way to assist others
5. DISPOSITION: Remarks—	Grouchy or surly	Temperamentally bad natured	Fairly good natured	Generally pleasing	Very pleasing, cheerful, and well liked
6. INDUSTRIOUSNESS: Remarks—	Lazy	Does enough to get by	Fairly good worker	Persistent on assigned work	Hard worker, does extra work
7. INITIATIVE: Remarks—	Must be told	Depends greatly on others	Moderately aggressive	Develops assigned field of work	Self starter on original work
8. JUDGMENT: Remarks—	Has poor sense of values	Jumps at conclusions too quickly	Tries to reason things out	Has common sense	Has unusually sound judgment
9. LEADERSHIP: Remarks—	Is a follower	Leads others with difficulty	Influences others fairly well	Can organize and direct others	Precedes, and leads others well
10. NATIVE CAPACITY: Remarks—	Dull, learns after many repetitions	Learns on repetition	Learns fairly quickly	Bright, grasps ideas on statement	Very bright, anticipates new ideas

What are his particularly strong points? ----

What are his particular weaknesses? ----

H. How Freshman Needs Are Met at the University of Michigan[1]

Application for admission, a detailed blank—The application for admission to first-year work at the University of Michigan consists of three parts. Part I is a general information blank to be filled out by the applicant in his own handwriting. It calls for a considerable amount of information relative to the interests, ideals, and past experiences of the candidate. The applicant may, if he so desires, confer with the principal before filling out the blank, but it is not the desire of the university that the principal correct, criticize, or modify the facts, language, spelling, or arrangement of the applicant's replies to the questions. Part II is a personal qualifications blank to be filled out by the high-school principal or by a teacher to be designated by the principal. Such factors as intellectual capacity, originality, evenness of disposition, leadership, popularity, health, industry in studies, and vigor in games are rated on a six-point scale. Additional information supplementary to Part II is obtained in border-line cases. Such information is obtained on a special personal rating blank similar to the one adopted by the American Council on Education, calling for illustrations of conduct which are consistent with the personality of the student. These illustrations are obtained from four of the teachers in the senior year of the high school, all of whom have had the individual student in class. Part III is a detailed statement of scholarship standing and certificate of recommendation to be filled out by the principal after the applicant has completed all requirements for high-school graduation.

Parts I and II were prepared by a committee of the University of Michigan in cooperation with a committee of the Department of High-School Principals of the Michigan Education Association. In preparing these parts (according to a statement printed on the application blank) the committees had the following general aims in view: (1) To prepare a blank that would stimulate prospective students to think carefully about their college plans; (2) to include questions that would acquaint parents and teachers with some of the problems and difficulties that confront students in transition from high school to college; and (3) to secure as far in advance as possible such information as will enable the university officials to counsel and advise with students how best to anticipate some of the problems and difficulties of a university course; at the same time helping the principals to impress upon their students the sincere desire of the University of Michigan to aid well-prepared, serious-minded, ambitious, and responsible high-school graduates in making their plans for college work.

Information given prospective freshmen—A pamphlet has been prepared in accordance with recommendations received from committees of the University of Michigan and of the Department of High-School Principals of the Michigan Education Association, who have met jointly to consider matters of admission to the University of Michigan from the high schools.

[1] Based on letters from Alice C. Lloyd, Dean of Women, and Philip E. Bursley, Counselor to New Students, University of Michigan, Ann Arbor, Mich., to the Research Division, National Education Association, and bulletins and other printed material used in carrying out the activities of the first week of college.

The purpose of the committees in sanctioning such a leaflet is to facilitate the process of admission with advantage to the student, the high-school principal, and the university admissions officers. An attempt has been made to compile in the pamphlet material which is of value and interest to applicants wishing to enter the university directly from the high or preparatory school.

Orientation Period

Faculty advisers—When each prospective freshman's application for admission is approved, he is mailed an Orientation Period program and directions for registration, a permit to register, and a group schedule card. This card indicates the number of the group to which he has been assigned for the Orientation Period, his adviser's name and office number, and the schedule for the week of the particular group to which he belongs. The incoming student reports to his adviser as the first step in registration. Groups are also created for students transferring from other colleges and universities. These groups are entirely separate from any freshman organization. The students are advised by members of the faculty appointed in the same manner as those provided for the freshmen, but the program is much simpler than that planned for the student intending to spend at least four years at Michigan.

In general, twenty freshmen are assigned to each faculty adviser. Advisers are given opportunity to enlist the aid of an upperclassman, this assistant to be used wherever necessary by the adviser to check attendance and to take messages. The student helpers are in no case, however, allowed to give advice to entering freshmen in regard to the election of courses. This information, according to the "Directions for Advisers," should be given out solely by the adviser or the proper faculty member. Application forms, which contain the student's high-school record and other personal data, are regarded as strictly confidential by the adviser, and he alone has access to what they contain. Under no condition are the blanks given into the hands either of the freshman or the student assistant.

In 1929-30, 107 members of the faculty served as student advisers. Students are assigned to advisers according to their pre-professional interests as reported on their application blanks. Advisers function intensively during the Orientation Period and somewhat less consistently and conscientiously during the rest of the semester. The freshman keeps the same adviser during the entire year, and at the opening of the second semester he is required to obtain the approval of his adviser in the matter of his choice of courses pursued.

Freshman deans are not a part of the administrative organization at the University of Michigan; neither are special large orientation courses and individual guidance programs provided. Hence special care is taken to make the Orientation Period function in as constructive and helpful a way as possible.

Pre-professional conferences—During the first day of the Orientation Period, the dean of each of the following departments: Law, medicine, dentistry, pharmacy, business administration, education, physical education, forestry and conservation, general science, and engineering, meets and addresses groups of students interested in his particular field as a profession. He also holds informal conferences with students.

On the first evening of the Orientation Period, the first general assembly of the year is held. The President of the University delivers the principal address, and the Dean of Women, the Dean of Students, and the Chairman of Orientation Period make brief addresses of welcome.

Group inspection trips and conferences on "how to study"—Generally each pre-professional group, as law, medicine, forestry, makes a tour of inspection of the campus, and a trip through the library. Conferences on "How To Study" are held at the end of the second week.

Examinations for placement—For the purpose of guiding and directing the physical activities of students, particularly to restrain them from undertaking work for which they are physically unfit and to prevent the entrance and spread of contagious diseases, a physical and medical examination is required of each student before he is fully admitted to the university. This examination is conducted under the direction of the University Health Service. A medical examination is required of all women students each year as preliminary to physical education activity. As a result of this examination each student is classified for activity according to condition as follows: Class I, unlimited activity; Class II, slightly modified activity; Class III, light activity; Class IV, corrective work; and Class V, a program of hygiene and special activity under medical supervision.

These four examinations are given all freshmen during the Orientation Period: (1) English content examination, (2) rhetoric examination (except engineers), (3) scholastic aptitude test, and (4) mathematics content examination. These examinations are a part of the university's general program in which it seeks to be of more service to each individual student. The scores made on these examinations by each student form a part of his permanent record. They are not used to determine any qualifications for admission. They have proved very useful, however, in helping students to select their future courses and to plan their daily work. To illustrate, in the examination in rhetoric, each student chooses one topic from a list of approved subjects and writes an essay upon it. The papers are corrected by the rhetoric staff for logical planning, coherence, unity, and mechanics of composition. The results of this examination, together with the results of the content examination in English, are used to place the student in ability groups.

I. How Individual Student Needs Are Met at Smith College [1]

The Personnel Office of Smith College was established in 1925 in the belief that there is need of someone in the college who will "deal with data supplied by many teachers and functionaries and focus them for the benefit of the individual student." In the beginning, the work was experimental,

---

[1] This report is based on data furnished the Research Division of the National Education Association by Mabelle B. Blake, Personnel Director, Smith College, under date of November 20, 1930.

and the first year was spent in studying the particular needs of Smith College in an effort to establish a form of organization best fitted to meet these needs.

Personnel work at Smith College is defined as that which helps the student to make satisfactory progress in her educational and vocational careers. The educational career is made a means of helping students to discover their interests and aptitudes—which is the first step towards self-discovery, self-mastery, and contribution to the community.

The objectives of the personnel work of Smith College are:

To study the present status of the individual student from the point of view of contributory causes which have made her what she is, and to give her the assistance necessary for removing obstacles which interfere with progress. This entails:

> An analysis of her present status
> An estimate of her abilities and disabilities in the light of her accomplishment
> A study of her personality as evidenced in her academic and social behavior and which has been conditioned by her environment
> The discovery of her occupational interests and aptitudes and the suggestion of opportunities which she may reasonably follow
> The motivation necessary for planning her courses purposefully and connectedly.

The Personnel Office is responsible to the President. Its staff consists of the director, the associate director, the vocational secretary, and three office secretaries. The work of a part-time psychiatrist is also an integral part of the personnel program.

Tests and interviews—Each entrant is required to take the Scholastic Aptitude Test and a Smith College Intelligence Examination. The scores made in at least one of these tests are available before the first interview is held with the student.

The results of interviews to date show that the difficulties with which students are most often concerned are these:

Academic:
  Poor preparation
  Difficulty in changing from secondary school to college
  Absent from school for a year or more
  Lack of knowing best methods of study
  Selection of courses without definite purpose

Social:
  Difficulty in mingling with groups
  Improper balance of social interests with academic
  Slow adaptation to college

Personal:
  Lack of confidence in ability
  In college against desire
  Physical handicap beyond control
  Family worries
  Lack of emotional balance

Vocational:
  Lack of knowledge of opportunities open to college graduates
  Inability to choose courses in view of future interests

Special help in technic of study—The majority of freshmen do not know the best methods of study. Many show a deplorable lack of tool subjects— reading, English composition, and grammar. The most obvious difficulty to achievement is the lack of a schedule of the proper distribution of time for work as well as leisure. To meet these difficulties each freshman is given a pamphlet on How To Study. Some are sent to the Psychology Department for special help in improving reading habits. Some are referred to the Committee on Special Assistance in Written English. Special help is given in the planning of time schedules, the proper method of taking notes, the value of review, and the importance of seeing the relationships of subjects. The greatest emphasis has been placed upon the importance of getting the right attitude toward study; a real interest for the sake of creativeness, mental stimulus, and development.

The Vocational Division—The aim is to help all students, by a sytematic study, to gain knowledge about the various opportunities open to college women, to secure up-to-date information about occupations for the vocational files, to help seniors and alumnae to secure positions, and to develop new resources for establishing cooperation of employers.

Student records at Smith College—An accumulative record is kept in a folder for each student who comes to the Personnel Office for consultation. This record includes these fourteen pages:

Page 1	Contains the significant factors pertaining to home environment, personal characteristics, and self-help, as well as a space for additional factors.
Page 2	Contains the health record (physical and mental) and results of psychological tests.
Pages 3, 4, 5, 6	Include the academic record for the four years, as well as faculty ratings.
Page 7	Includes social relationships of the student, including the report of the Head of House and extra-curriculum activities.
Page 8	Contains the ratings of associates and students.
Pages 9, 10	Contain student's own interpretations.
Pages 11, 12	Contain the guidance given, including both educational and vocational.
Pages 13, 14	Include summaries of previous record.

After this record, which pertains to the four years in college, there follows a record of the student as an alumna, with references from the Faculty and Head of House, as well as employment records after the student has been in the field for a year or longer.

After interviews are given, the factors which are significant to an understanding of the student are recorded and all subsequent data are added. These records are confidential and seen only by those who are helping to get a complete picture of the student for purposes of advisement. All correspondence or any other information pertaining to the student is included in the folder.

PART II

THE ARTICULATION OF THE SCHOOLS AND THE COMMUNITY

CHAPTER VIII

INTRODUCTION—ADULT EDUCATION, THE HOPE OF A RAPIDLY CHANGING CIVILIZATION

THE SECTIONS of this report are briefly outlined as follows:

Introduction

I. Post-School Adjustment of Pupils:
   A. Those Who Stopped School Previous to Graduation
   B. Those Who Graduated from High School
   C. Those Who Entered Community Life from Subnormal Classes
II. A Study of Adults Enrolled in Evening School Classes
III. Adult Educational Activities Engaged in by Clubs, Societies, and Other Agencies:
   A. In a Community (Minneapolis)
   B. In a State (Minnesota, Exclusive of Minneapolis)

Introduction

In considering the relation of education to the needs of the community as a whole, attention must be given to two kinds of needs—common and unique.

The common needs are those which all communities have, while the unique needs are those which are of interest to, and bear a direct relation to, the development and welfare of given communities. From the very beginning it has been assumed that the "common schools" of this country would supply training in those things which are essential to the discharge of one's daily duties and to the proper maintenance of his daily contacts. Common intercourse required common knowledge.

There has been a tendency also in many sections of the country and in many communities to provide education of a highly local character. It has been presumed that an agricultural community should emphasize agriculture; a mining community, mining; a manufacturing community, manufacturing. When one looks over the programs designed to satisfy the needs of given communities, he finds that for the most part they emphasize immediate goals, while the fundamentals, or what might properly be called the core of the entire program of education, coincides in essence with that which communities in general require. It is true that an effort has been made, and is still being made in many communities, to provide vocational training of special and direct interest to those communities. Shops are established and installed, and students are taught the things they need to know for the practice of various trades. Education thus furnishes a shortcut for the old apprenticeship system. This has meant great economy so far as the trades themselves are concerned, and it has increased their output.

The problem of providing, through education, those things which are essential for the stability of our social institutions, and at the same time of providing those things which contribute to material progress, constitutes a perennial dilemma for the educational leaders. Now we are living in what is generally admitted to be a great industrial era. Attempts on a vast scale are being made to increase productivity, to increase buying power of the consuming public. Business sits on the throne. It takes toll of every human institution. It takes heavy toll of education. Education responds quickly to the spirit of the times, and the spirit of the times is the spirit of commerce and business.

At the same time it should be remembered that commerce and business are not static. They, too, are subject to change. Not long since, most of the industries of this country were handicraft industries. With the coming of machines, social and industrial maladjustments began to display themselves. Every time there is a breakdown in the social order, it turns to some general public institution for relief. Usually, it turns to education. When the old apprenticeship system of teaching of trades began to fail, the schools took on manual training. When the artisan trades began to disappear in the face of new machines, the schools began to introduce vocational training of all kinds. This vocational training was introduced, not for the purpose of teaching students obsolete trades, but for the purpose of teaching them new trades, thus opening to them new avenues of employment and promotion.

Vocational training in the beginning was designed to provide special skills for the practice of specific trades or occupations. Gradually this point of view shifted. It was found that, even though students were trained for specific lines of work, permanency of employment could not be assured them. New machines were constantly being invented and introduced; and with the coming of every new machine, a certain number of persons were thrown out of employment no matter how skillful they may have been in the practice of their trade. It was discovered, too, that the training of students for specific trades closed the avenues of promotion for them. It fitted them for industrial niches. It tended to make of them industrial slaves. And while this may have been agreeable to some, inevitably there came a reaction from the workers themselves. They rebelled against the fastening of an industrial proletariat upon the country. They rebelled against the restrictions which were thus being placed upon the exercise of one's inherent human rights; that is, the privilege and opportunity of advancement.

Today vocational training is clothed with a new philosophy. It emphasizes the relations between employer and employee. It studies the history, the operation, the probable outcome of industrial revolution in all of its forms. It touches the meaning as well as the forms of operation and administration of many trades. It lays a background of information and philosophy calculated to make of the individual a more competent citizen, a more intelligent worker. In other words, instead of attempting to restrict him to narrow channels and to the confinements of limited vocational areas, it is making every effort to preserve his initiative and increase his resourcefulness and adaptability. It recognizes, furthermore, that vocational training is something which should not be confined to youth, but that it is equally necessary for men and women well advanced in life, who, due to the processes of the shifting industrial world, are being caught in its network. So that from the standpoint of the industrial sanctions and the pressures of the times, vocational and adult education have the same social justification.

Through invention and science more material progress has been made in the last thirty years than was made during the preceding three hundred. The coming of the machine has added greatly to the power of man. Today every man has the equivalent of approximately seventy-five mechanical slaves working for him, while in 1870 he had only about three such slaves.

There is really nothing new in this process of mechanization except that it has been speeded up. While mechanization does create new jobs, at the same time it retires persons from jobs in other lines. The machine is increasingly building up a surplus of labor and deficit of employment.

The physical machine displaces hand labor; the business machine, or the great organizations of capital or talent, which is the counterpart of the physical machine, displaces brains. We have group medicine, great corporations of lawyers, chain stores, a group or chain banking system, and so on through a long list, in each of which a few of the bigger and better jobs at the top and center are filled by extraordinary men, but the tendency is distinctly to lower the type of minor executives, repress their initiative, curb their authority, and convert them from leaders to cautious placeholders. A youth today, whenever he goes out for employment in the business world, is likely to secure a job that has all of the work already mapped out for him. He is not expected to make mistakes and to profit by them. He is expected to do his work largely as he is told to do it. He, and all of his kind, are in danger of developing a routine type of mind. The fact of the matter is that business may be more interested in dividends than it is in personality. Efficiency is the modern god before whom we bow in order that dividends may be paid.

Even in agriculture we find that 800,000 persons have left the farms in the last ten years to work in the factories and cities. The rural population is steadily decreasing. The city and industrial population is steadily increasing. It may be claimed, and with justice, that initiative and individuality, those qualities which have made America, are as desirable today as ever. It may also be claimed that there are as many opportunities for them to be displayed today as ever, but the hard fact nevertheless remains that with standardization, mass production, long-term and indefinite apprenticeship of a routine character, a permanent and perhaps increasing problem of unemployment, and the difficulty of men past forty-five years of age to secure employment when displaced by industry, there are increasing thousands of persons in America who are anxiously and diligently searching, through education, for some means of preserving their adaptability, of increasing their resourcefulness, and of opening new avenues of livelihood for themselves. Many persons look upon education—secondary education, vocational education, college education—as a possible means of salvation from the industrial order. This, no doubt, is one of the reasons why so many persons, and especially adults, are seeking some means of continuing their education.

The movement for adult education, however, cannot be attributed solely or entirely to a desire for emancipation from the industrial order. The industrial order has brought more leisure than mankind has ever known. Men work fewer days per month and fewer hours per day than ever before, and it seems fair to assume that in the future they will work still fewer hours and still fewer days per week and per month. Millions of persons are trying to find ways of satisfying their cravings during their leisure hours. The thousand and one organizations now in existence are evidences that like-minded groups are seeking ways of improving themselves and the social order.

At the same time, education has been gathering more momentum. There has been a lengthening of the school year, a lengthening of the school day, an enrichment of the curriculum, improvement in the qualifications of teachers. The program offered students in the schools is far more comprehensive and richer than it has ever been. Public confidence in the worth of the schools has increased from year to year, so that, as man has acquired new leisure due to mechanized industry and to the organization of capital and talent, he has had on the other hand the stimulating effects that have come from American education, the most powerful of all of the social forces of American life. It is difficult for him to avoid continuing his intellectual pursuits; he has been taught those things that constitute the intellectual and social background for the interpretation of existing conditions. He has been made to realize that failure to continue to read, to study, and to grow means stagnation. At the same time that these two powerful and imperious forces have been at work, newspapers, magazines, books, moving pictures, radio, television, as well as the automobile have widened the scope of human interests and enlarged the individual's intellectual horizon. Formerly one knew only his neighbors and information was spread from mouth to mouth. Now one's neighbors may reside in distant parts of the country, or even in remote parts of the world.

Of course, the most fundamental excuse for learning is that it enables us to enjoy life more fully. Thousands of those engaged in what is popularly known as adult education are there not because they are looking for industrial or occupational preferment, but principally because they wish to enjoy life more fully. The time is past when the knowledge gleaned through formal education is sufficient. Today the man who closes his ears to new information for a single year, whether he be a farmer, or a doctor, or a mechanic, becomes sadly old-fashioned.

If men wish to, they can use their increased leisure to become slaves, or they can use their extra time for their improvement and social advancement. It is a fact that there are more persons interested in art with no thought of becoming artists, in music with no thought of becoming public performers, in sports with no thought of becoming athletes, in religion, social service, public welfare, education, with no thought of becoming great leaders in these fields; not only more so far as actual numbers are concerned but more proportionately than ever before. It is a fact also that men generally exercise more independence of thought and are less docile in following political leaders than ever before. In other words, there is less followership and more leadership on the part of the common people because of the agencies for mass education, for public discussion, for travel, that now exist.

It is not too much to say that in this situation lies the only hope of democracy; for, after all, democracy is a process of continuous education. With the world becoming narrower, communication swifter, the whole world possible auditors, the possibilities of adult education almost exceed the limits of one's imagination. Education in school and out, formal and informal, specific and general, available for all the people, thus becomes a necessity.

It is through the processes of adult education that many of our most difficult problems will be solved, problems of capital and labor, questions relating to the tariff, agricultural problems, the conservation of our natural resources, the cure of human disease, the prolongation of human life, instruction in art, music, literature, the development of a cosmopolitan type of mind. These may be, indeed many think they will be, the ultimate outcome of the demand for adult education.

Thus we see that the forces that are responsible for the movements for vocational and adult education are exactly the same as those that are responsible for the development and expansion of public education generally. All education ultimately has the same social sanctions. Individual features and aspects of it may spring up out of a new matrix here and there because some special group or need is not being met or satisfied, but the existing system of education by a close analysis always reveals that the new type of education bears close kinship to the old in fundamental matters. As society grows more complex, its problems more numerous and more difficult, more education rather than less will be required by the people. The strength of a democratic people depends upon the level of trained intelligence maintained among them. The success of an industrial era depends upon the intelligence and skill of the workers. And both of these mean more vocational and more adult education.

The problem of articulating the schools with the community is one of cooperative interaction of school and community. It is just as necessary that the community make adjustments to assist education as it is that education adjust itself to fit the community. Both the school and the community should be interested in educational adjustments which will fit the school to the needs of all types of students. School and community should be equally interested in providing for the needs of adults who are in search of some means of increasing their resourcefulness in earning a livelihood or who desire leisure-time training which will enrich life.

Consideration of school and community interest in securing better educational and social adjustment for its members suggests the following questions:

With what comparative success do pupils emerging at the different educational levels fit into the occupational life of the community?

Do modern industrial trends point to the need for greater stress in schools upon the study of industrial problems and occupational orientation rather than upon the teaching of specific vocational skills?

To what extent do pupils of the lower intelligence levels become self-supporting and law-abiding members of society?

Is there a tendency for pupils emerging at certain educational levels to leave school with attitudes that are socially and industrially undesirable?

Whom do the public evening schools serve and what is the quality of the academic work of those who attend these schools?

What is the extent and nature of the educational work carried on by clubs, societies, public and semi-public institutions in the city of Minneapolis and in the state of Minnesota?

The above questions and others are considered in the studies which form the major portion of this section of the Yearbook.

The departments of attendance, administrative research, and school counseling in Minneapolis have made a careful check of the facts concerning school leaving during the past five years. The average number on roll for the last five years has been 77,903. The potential school-leaving group can best be estimated by the number of children in the sixteen-year-old age group. According to the United States census in 1930, the number of sixteen-year-olds in Minneapolis would be 6,550. The average number of sixteen-year-olds for the past five years would be 6,255. The average total of withdrawals per year of all ages for the past five years has been 14,780. This number includes all those who have ceased school attendance because of graduation or other causes. After making a careful check of these withdrawals to separate those which represent permanent school leaving from those which are caused by entrance into private schools or removal from the city or death, the average number of withdrawals that are actually school leaving amount to 6,268 per year. This approximates the sixteen-year-old group.

On the basis of the records which are available in Minneapolis the post-school adjustments of pupils have been studied in three different groups: (1) those who left school previous to graduation, during the junior high-school period; (2) those who have graduated from high school; and (3) those who have entered community life from the subnormal classes. The educational opportunities available for adults have been surveyed by examining (1) Minneapolis evening schools; (2) educational programs of secular and church organizations of Minneapolis; and (3) opportunities for adult education offered throughout the state of Minnesota.

CHAPTER IX

POST-SCHOOL ADJUSTMENTS OF DROP-OUTS AND GRADUATES FROM THE MINNEAPOLIS PUBLIC SCHOOLS

A. School Records and Post-School Adjustments of Pupils Who Withdrew from the Minneapolis Schools in the Junior High-School Grades, 1924-1929

PURPOSE—The purpose of this study was (1) to get a picture of pupils who withdraw from school at the junior high-school level in regard to intelligence, overageness, scholarship, reasons for withdrawal, and social and economic background; and (2) to determine how these people have adjusted vocationally by studying the jobs held, wages received, and unemployment reported.

Method—This study was limited to pupils who had withdrawn from the seventh, eighth, and ninth grades and from the vocational schools of Minneapolis during the years 1924 to 1929. All the pupils studied had been out of school from one to six years, long enough to have made adjustments and some progress vocationally. It was further restricted to those who had withdrawn as over compulsory age, 16 years of age, presumably to go to work. Those who withdrew to leave the city, to transfer to private schools, or on account of illness were not included.

With these criteria set up, cases were selected by random sampling. The Attendance Department has in its dead file a card for each pupil who has withdrawn from the Minneapolis schools for any reason. This file consists of 113 drawers. From each drawer were pulled the first 13 cards which were found to satisfy the conditions set up. After some eliminations due to clerical errors, this gave a total of 1355 cases. This was 16 percent of the pupils over 16 years of age who withdrew from the junior high-school grades and from the vocational schools during the years 1924-1929. For these 1355 pupils data available on the school records were tabulated and analyzed. Four hundred fifteen of these pupils were then located and interviewed in their homes by school counselors, visiting teachers, and attendance officers. Information regarding their home life, their reasons for leaving school, and their jobs was entered on schedules.

Analysis of Data

Sex and birthplace—These 1355 pupils were distributed by sex as follows:

	Number	Percent
Boys	749	55.25
Girls	606	44.72

The preponderance of boys over girls reflects the general tendency for more boys than girls to withdraw from the junior high-school grades.[1] Foreign birth is not an important factor causing withdrawal. Of the children in Minneapolis between 15 and 19 years of age, 8.31 percent were foreign born,[2] but of the withdrawals studied only 7.23 percent were foreign born.

Age at withdrawal—The Minnesota Compulsory Education Law makes it impossible for children to withdraw from school until they are 16 unless work permits are secured. The law forbids the giving of work permits to children under 16 unless they have finished the eighth grade; and the policy in Minneapolis has been to give work permits to children under 16 who have finished the eighth grade only in cases of definite economic need. Consequently, only 81 of the 1355 cases reported were of children under 16.[3]

The age of these pupils at the time they withdrew from school was as follows:

Age	Percent
Under 16 yrs.	5.98
16 yrs.—16 yrs., 5 mos.	67.31
16 yrs., 6 mos.—16 yrs., 11 mos.	12.18
17 yrs.—17 yrs., 5 mos.	8.04
17 yrs., 6 mos.—17 yrs., 11 mos.	2.95
18 yrs. or over	3.54

Over two-thirds of them left school as soon as the law permitted. Apparently it was not interest but compulsion which kept them in school.

Grade at time of withdrawal—The distribution of pupils by grades at the time they withdrew was as follows:

Grade	Percent	Grade	Percent
7B	3.76	9B	20.00
7A	6.49	9A	20.15
8B	9.67	Vocational	19.85
8A	20.07		

Almost one-fifth of these pupils left school before entering the 8A grade. An equal percent left in each of the other grades and while attending vocational schools. It was the sixteenth birthday rather than grade which determined the time of withdrawal, and any method of reducing withdrawals will have to consider pupils as they approach this age no matter what grade they are in.

Overageness—A normal child will be in the 10A grade at the time he reaches his sixteenth birthday, according to the Strayer-Engelhardt age-grade norms. Therefore in a city having a compulsory education law such as Minneapolis has, all junior high-school withdrawals will be retarded. The retardation of this group in terms of the Strayer-Engelhardt age-grade norms was as follows:

[1] During the school year 1928-1929, 680 boys and 403 girls withdrew from the junior high-school grades, and 222 boys and 357 girls withdrew from the vocational schools, in Minneapolis.
[2] Department of Commerce, Bureau of the Census. *Fourteenth Census of the United States,* 1920, Vol. III, p. 508. Washington, D. C.: Government Printing Office, 1922.
[3] An average of 79 work permits a year were issued during the years 1924-1929.

Retardation	Percent	Retardation	Percent
½ year	1.01	3 years	11.14
1 year	18.23	3½ years	7.37
1½ years	21.09	4 years	1.66
2 years	23.39	4½ years	.92
2½ years	15.19		

The largest group, 23.39 percent, were two years retarded. About 10 percent were retarded three and one-half years or more.

Further evidence of lack of success is seen by the fact that all except 17.6 percent of these pupils had repeated one or more grades since entering the Minneapolis school system. About 20 percent of the pupils had failed their grades five times or more.

Marks received at school—For each pupil for whom school marks could be obtained (1115 pupils), all the marks reported for the junior high-school grades and during attendance at vocational schools were averaged. For purposes of averaging, an A was given a value of four, B three, C two, D one, and F zero. The score was therefore the total points divided by the number of marks recorded. The percentage of pupils having specified scores was as follows:

Score		Percentage
3.00-4.00	(B, B+ & A)	1.26
2.00-2.99	(C, C+)	21.08
1.00-1.99	(D, D+)	62.15
00- .99	(D—, F)	15.51

The percentage getting B or A grade is negligible, the percentage getting C is far below normal, the bulk of the pupils had received grades of D or less.

Results of intelligence tests, Terman and Haggerty group tests, were available for only 404 of the 1355 cases and they were recorded in terms of ability grouping rather than in intelligence quotients. The distribution, however, is similar to that for school marks. Less than 1 percent were in the A group, 5 percent in the B group, 35 percent in the C group, 26 percent in the D group, and 33 percent in the F group.

Thus we get a picture of these withdrawals as a discouraged, unsuccessful group, getting low marks in school, failing grades frequently, being very much overage, and lacking ability to master the work set for them to do. They escape from school as soon as the law permits.

Age of those pupils followed up by interviews—The group of 415 persons more intensively studied was similar to the group described above as to sex, withdrawal school, age and grade at time of withdrawal, school marks, and ability grouping. At the time they were interviewed they ranged in age from 16 years to 24 years. Only three pupils were 16 years old, 21 percent were 17, 25 percent were 18, 25 percent were 19, and 16 percent were 20. About 11 percent were over 20 years old. They had been out of school from nine months to over five years. Only six had been out less than a year. About one-fourth had been out of school each of one, two, and three years. The rest had been out four years or more.

Home conditions—The Sims Socio-Economic Score Card was selected as the best simple measure of home background available. It was made a part of the schedule filled out by the interviewer.[1] This score card consists of 23 questions which can be answered by yes or no regarding culture in the home as shown by number of books and magazines in the home, education of parents, and organizations belonged to; economic status as shown by the size of house, where vacations are spent, number of automobiles owned, and occupation of father. In order to obtain norms for a typical Minneapolis junior high-school group, the same score card was filled out by 1213 9A pupils in eight schools which were selected by several school administrators as representing different socio-economic levels of the city. For the withdrawal group home conditions were measured after the pupils had been working from one to five years. The probabilities are that when they became wage earners, the socio-economic conditions in their families became better if anything, and that had family conditions been rated at the time of withdrawal, the median for this group would have been lower. Although there are pupils in both groups who come from all types of homes as measured by this score card, the withdrawal pupils group along the lower range of the possible scores as compared with the ninth-grade pupils. This is seen in the following summary of scores received by both groups:

	Withdrawals	Ninth-Grade Pupils
Range of Score	0-31	2-36
Q1	8.51	14.48
Median	12.04	19.04
Q3	15.49	23.54

The median for the withdrawal group was seven points lower than for the ninth-grade pupils. Only 13 withdrawals got a score above the third quartile score of the ninth-grade pupils; of these, nine had gone back to school, either day or evening school, for further instruction. When the scores of the withdrawals from each school were compared with those of the ninth-grade pupils of the same school, the median of the withdrawals was five points or more lower in each school. Evidently, then, poorer socio-economic background than that of the group with whom they were associated at school characterizes the junior high-school withdrawals.

Examination was made of certain items on the score card which would show cultural standards. Seventy-three percent of the withdrawal group had parents with less than a high-school education as compared with 41.3 percent of the ninth-grade pupils. Only 1.5 percent of the withdrawals had parents both of whom went to college as against 9 percent of the ninth-grade pupils. A similar difference in the percentage of pupils of each type having a specified number of books in their homes is seen in the following summary:

---

[1] For a copy of this score card see: Sims, Verner Martin. *The Measurement of Socio-Economic Status.* Bloomington, Illinois: Public School Publishing Company, 1928. 33 p. Or: Hartshorne, Hugh, and May, Mark A. *Studies in Deceit*, Book One. New York: The Macmillan Company, 1928. p. 194-98.

Books in Home	Withdrawals	Ninth-Grade Pupils	Books in Home	Withdrawals	Ninth-Grade Pupils
None	13.98%	3.71%	126-500	5.54%	24.32%
1-25	45.30	26.63	501 or more	1.93	4.62
26-125	33.25	40.07	Not Stated		.66

The reading material was extremely meager, less than 25 books per home, in about 60 percent of the homes from which the withdrawals came as against 30 percent of the homes of the ninth-grade pupils. A comparison of number of magazines which the families have regularly in their homes showed the same trend: none in 47.47 percent of the homes of the withdrawals, none in 11.71 percent of the homes of the ninth-grade pupils.

Economic status of a family is to some extent indicated by the occupation of the father. The difference in the two groups, in terms of percent, was as follows:

Occupations of Fathers	Withdrawals	Ninth-Grade Pupils
Professional men and higher executives..	.48%	14.67%
Commercial service and business proprietors	5.78	23.00
Artisan proprietors	15.66	27.29
Skilled laborers	42.41	21.68
Unskilled laborers	19.76	11.46
Not Stated	15.90	1.90

On the whole the low socio-economic standards at home as well as inability and failure to achieve at school characterize this group of withdrawals.

Reasons for leaving school—These 415 persons were asked to examine a check list of twenty-two reasons why people leave school and check the three reasons that fitted their cases best. It was not expected that such a procedure would give objective data about why these people left school, but rather that it would give an indication of the mental and emotional reactions of these people to the combination of circumstances which caused them to leave school. The reasons checked were classified into six groups. They were distributed as follows:

	Percent
School difficulties	37.56
Wanted to earn money	20.30
Had to work to help family..................................	16.67
Other family difficulties	6.57
Wanted to learn a trade....................................	4.81
Other reasons	14.08

School difficulties included being overage, not getting along with the teacher and principal, being uninterested in school, and disliking school. Reasons of this sort were given most frequently, as one would expect after studying the school records of these young people. The large percent who gave as their reason the need or desire to earn money was also to be expected from the evidence of low economic background as evidenced by the Sims socio-economic scores. In fact, the reasons given for leaving school were just what one would look for from the group described. They add to our picture of these withdrawals as pupils who dislike school and are unsuccessful there, and who leave at the first opportunity, lured away by a promise of a job, by the prospect of more spending money, or by the pressure of inadequate funds at home. In many cases leaving school results from combination of factors in which lack of success in school and desire to earn money both loom large. This situation was expressed by one mother who said, "Yes, Frank is seventeen and he is going to finish high school, he gets good marks and just loves school. But Willie hated school and he was only in the eighth grade and with my husband laid off and doctor's bills, we thought he might as well go to work as soon as he was sixteen."

Further schooling—Although opportunities to take courses at evening school are available and the courses are inexpensive, three-fourths of these withdrawals had not taken more school work. Of the 104 who did get further schooling, 32 had attended a day school such as a commercial college, parochial school, or trade school. Sixty-eight had enrolled in evening school, but 38 had dropped out before completing a semester's work. Evidently then we cannot assume that these pupils are going on to evening school to finish their education. Formal education is finished for them when they withdraw from the junior high-school grades.

Unemployment—At the time they were interviewed 83 persons, or 20 percent, were unemployed. This may be an unusually high percentage, due to the business depression during the spring months of 1930. Of the boys, 23.59 percent were unemployed as compared with 15.54 percent of the girls. The unemployment reported for these withdrawals was less by 10.5 percent than that reported for pupils from special classes for retarded pupils who were followed during the same months, 30.6 percent of whom were found to be unemployed.[1] It was, however, more by 12 percent than that reported for high-school graduates of 1929 followed during the same months, 8.42 percent of whom were found to be unemployed.[2] Apparently those emerging from the lower school levels find it more difficult to get and to keep jobs. Whether this is because of lack of the skills taught in school or because of lack of the intellectual ability and home background which enable some children to stay on in school while others withdraw is a question requiring further research.

Within the limits of the withdrawal group, unemployment was greater among those getting the lower marks in school. Over 26 percent of those having less than a D average were unemployed. This dropped to 22 percent of those having a D average, and 10 percent of those having a C average. It was 14 percent for those having a B average, but this is probably influenced by the small number of cases; only seven pupils had a B average.

The total amount of unemployment since leaving school was tabulated from the intervals of unemployment reported by pupils between their jobs. This did not include occasional days of being "laid off" while holding jobs, but only the longer intervals between the giving up of one job and

---

[1] A Study of Post-School Adjustments of Boys and Girls of Special Classes for Retarded Children in the Minneapolis Public Schools. See pages 205-10 of this Yearbook.
[2] Occupational Distribution of Pupils Who Graduated from Minneapolis High Schools in 1929. See pages 200-04 of this Yearbook.

getting another. The percentage of pupils reporting having been un-employed a specified number of months since leaving school was as follows:

	Percent
No Unemployment	32.77
Up to 3 months	23.86
3 to 7 months	16.87
7 to 12 months	12.52
More than 12 months	6.75
Not Stated	7.23

Minneapolis has no continuation school law and these young people, most of them of high-school age, are without supervision by public authorities during their periods of unemployment. It would have been profitable to go into the question of the morals of these withdrawals by finding out how many had been before the courts, but time prevented.

Shifting from job to job—Only jobs were reported that had been held for a month or longer, except for the present job, which was reported, even though the person had been working less than a month. The amount of shifting is therefore less than in other studies of similar groups that count all jobs held, even though the person worked only a day or two. The number of jobs reported varies from one to ten. One-fourth of the pupils reported having held only one job, one-fourth reported having held two jobs. and slightly less than one-fourth reported having had three jobs. Only five percent reported having held more than five jobs.

Almost one-third of the girls as compared with one-fifth of the boys had held only one job. Less than 3 percent of the girls, as compared with about 10 percent of the boys, reported more than five jobs. Girls do far less shifting from job to job than boys, and they reported less unemployment. One hundred twenty pupils, or 28.92 percent, held their first jobs less than three months. Almost one-half stayed on their first job six months or longer, over one-third stayed a year or longer, and 7.41 percent held the same job for three years or longer. Shifting from job to job does not seem to be a very serious problem for most of this group.

Persons interested in problems of vocational education will want to know whether, when these pupils shift from one employer to another, they pursue the same type of work or shift to a different type. The jobs held were classi-fied into eleven types and analysis made of the different types of work each person had done. For example, if a pupil had done factory work consist-ently, even though he had worked for three different employers, he was said to have done one type of work; but if he had been an errand boy, a factory worker, and a shipping clerk, he was said to have tried three types of work. Classified this way, these pupils range in percent as follows:

	Boys	Girls		Boys	Girls
One type	32.88%	50.78%	Four types	8.56%	3.11%
Two types	31.53	33.16	Five types	2.25	.....
Three types	23.87	12.95	Six types	.90	.....

One-half of the girls as compared with one-third of the boys had done only one kind of work, and only six of the girls as compared with twenty-six of the boys had tried four or more types of work. Two boys reported having tried six different types of work. One of these, in the two and a half years since leaving school, had been a packer in a factory, an auto mechanic's helper, a harvest hand, a shipping clerk, a truck loader in a warehouse, and a laborer for a creosote company. At the time he was interviewed he was a waiter and cook in a sandwich shop.

Jobs held—Table 36 contains an analysis in terms of percent of the first positions held by these boys and girls after leaving school and of the positions they held at the time they were interviewed:

TABLE 36.—COMPARISON OF THE PERCENTS OF THE FIRST AND LAST JOBS OF 415 JUNIOR HIGH-SCHOOL DROP-OUTS, CLASSIFIED ACCORDING TO ELEVEN TYPES OF WORK

Type of Work	Percent of 222 Boys		Percent of 193 Girls	
	First Job	Last Job	First Job	Last Job
Factory Work	18.47	20.27	25.39	34.20
Skilled Trades and Helpers in Skilled Trades	18.47	27.48	7.25	3.63
Selling	7.21	7.21	15.03	15.03
Store Clerical Work	7.21	13.51	7.77	7.77
Office Work	1.35	5.86	11.92	17.10
Errands and Messengers	24.77	8.11	1.55	....
Transportation	7.21	8.11	....	....
Telephone and Telegraph	....	....	4.14	2.59
Domestic and Personal	1.35	2.25	19.69	14.51
Agriculture	6.31	2.70	....	....
Miscellaneous	5.86	4.05	2.59	1.04
Not Stated	1.80	.45	4.66	4.15

Read this table as follows: Of 222 boys who dropped out of Minneapolis junior high schools and went to work, 18.47 percent did factory work on their first jobs; when interviewed some time later, 20.27 percent were doing factory work. Of 193 girls who dropped out of Minneapolis junior high schools, 25.39 percent found their first jobs in factories; and 34.20 percent found their last jobs there. Similarly, read the data relative to skilled trades and helpers in skilled trades and the other nine types of work.

Factory work gave employment to a larger percent of these young people at the time they were interviewed than did any other type of work. One-fifth of the boys and over one-third of the girls were doing this work.[1] There was a definite tendency especially among the girls to settle into this type of work as they got older. No specific jobs in factories gave employment to large numbers of these young people. Almost as many different jobs were reported as there were people reporting. The following are a few of the tasks included: packing candy, folding and inspecting knit goods, labeling bottles, operating such machines as a drill press, a knitting machine, an air brush, and a planer. These people worked in knitting factories, sash and door factories, upholstering establishments, plants manufacturing greeting cards, and plants where foods were being manufactured. None worked in the flour mills.

Under skilled trades and learners in skilled trades were included all those doing work requiring definite skill and those doing work in which

---

[1] Only 3.13 percent of the Minneapolis high-school graduates of the class of 1929 were found to be working in factories a year after they graduated.

they might be expected to pick up a trade or a part of a trade, even though there was no formal apprenticeship. Such jobs as the following were included: electric repair worker, jeweler's helper, window decorator's helper, beauty parlor workers, upholsterers, linoleum layer's apprentice, dressmakers, printers, and automobile garage workers. Of the boys, 18.47 percent reported such work as their first job and 27.48 percent reported such work as their last job. It was indeed encouraging to find so many boys of the type that had not learned readily in school doing work in which there was real training value. The negligible number of girls found in the skilled trades is no doubt because there are so few trades in Minneapolis in which women can find employment.

Only 7 percent of the boys and 15 percent of the girls were engaged as salespeople. The girls were employed mostly in the basement and aisle counters of department stores and in the five and ten-cent stores. Many of the boys were clerks in grocery stores. Store clerical work was the last employment reported by 14 percent of the boys and 8 percent of the girls. This included non-selling jobs, such as cashiering, stock room work, shipping room work, and bundling. The older boys frequently reported working as shipping clerks or stock room clerks. It was somewhat surprising that such a small percentage of these young people were engaged in selling.

Office positions included office boys, file clerks, information clerks, mail clerks, multigraphers, calculating machine operators, and a very few typists and stenographers. In spite of their rather limited school training, almost 12 percent of the girls obtained work in offices when they left school, and at the time of this survey 17.10 percent were doing such work. It should be noted that Minneapolis employs a very large number of office workers, and that office positions were obtained by 73 percent of the girls who graduated from high school in 1929 and who took jobs. The high-school graduates were for the most part typists and stenographers. The junior high-school girls were for the most part doing clerical work of a more routine nature. A bit of evidence as to the influence of schooling on this type of employment is seen in the fact that all but two of the girls whose first jobs were in offices were in the ninth grade or attending Girls' Vocational School at the time they withdrew from school.

Only three boys left the junior high-school grades to take positions in offices, but at the time of the survey about 6 percent reported such work. Most of these were office boys.

About one-fourth of the boys left school to work as errand boys and messengers, but when the last jobs were analyzed only 8.11 percent were doing this work. The largest number were employed by Western Union and Postal Telegraph. A boy who does such work usually stays less than a year and then changes to something more suitable for an older fellow. The boys who started as messengers were found in factory work, office work, in stores, or in the trades.

Only two boys were working for the railroads; the others classified as employed in transportation were truck drivers, helpers on trucks, and chauffeurs. The very small number of girls employed by the telephone and

telegraph companies indicates that these concerns set up educational qualifications for which these girls could not qualify.

Domestic and personal service included such workers as housemaids,
nursemaids, cooks, waitresses, and bus boys. Almost one-fifth of the girls left
school to take such positions, but the percentage decreased noticeably when
the last jobs were analyzed. Of the 38 girls who took such jobs when they
left school only seven were still doing it at the time of the survey. Ten had
gone into the factories, seven had secured positions in stores and offices, and
twelve were no longer employed.

As might be expected, only a few city boys took jobs on farms when they
left school. The decrease in the percentage reporting this as their present
job may be due in part to the fact that this survey was made in the early
spring months before there was a demand for farm labor.

Time required to learn the jobs held—Each person was asked to estimate
how long it would take a new worker to learn the job he was doing. Judgments of this cannot be considered very reliable, but they indicate roughly
the amount of training necessary for the work from the employee's point
of view. The percentage of people estimating specified periods as necessary
to learn their first and last jobs is given below:

	First Job	Last Job
Less than 1 day	46.48%	39.92%
More than 1 day, less than 1 wk.	26.20	31.69
More than 1 wk., less than 1 mo.	10.14	9.05
More than 1 mo., less than 3 mos.	6.20	7.41
More than 3 mos., less than 5 mos.	4.23	4.12
More than 5 mos.	6.76	7.82

Apparently about three-fourths of these people left school to take positions
requiring so little in the way of specific skills that they could be learned in
less than one week. Even when these people had been out of school from
one to five years, almost three-fourths of them were doing work that a new
worker could learn in less than a week. In the skilled trades, a training
period of three months or over was reported by one-half of these workers.
For all other types of work, including office work, the majority of the
workers said their jobs could be learned in less than a week.

Because of the very limited amount of skill required and because of the
great variety of jobs held by these young workers, definite training in school
which is trade preparatory seems out of the question. Possibly these young
people could be prepared more adequately in school to meet other problems
arising from their industrial life, namely, how to apply for positions, how to
utilize periods of unemployment, how to handle their earnings, an understanding of safety and labor laws, and a wholesome respect for the types of
work that so many of them will eventually do.

Wages received—To some extent the success of these young people in
the community can be gauged by their ability to earn. The minimum wage
in Minnesota for boys under 21 and for girls under 18 is $12.00 a week,
with provision for a learner's wage as low as $7.68. The median salary for
boys on their first jobs was $13.54 a week, and almost 10 percent of the

boys got $20.00 or more a week on their first jobs. At the time of the survey the median wage for the boys had increased to $18.16. This was about $4.00 more than the median reported for pupils from special classes and $2.00 more than that reported by high-school graduates a year after they left school. Moreover, 35 percent of the boys were earning over $20.00 a week. The median salary for girls on their first jobs was only $10.78, and it had increased to only $11.78 when the last salaries were analyzed. There was, however, more variation in the final wages reported and a larger percentage at the higher wage levels. It should be remembered that salaries for girls are usually lower than those received by boys and that girls advance in salary much more slowly. In general salary returns show this group of junior high-school boys to be far more successful in earning a living than they were in getting on at school.

Conclusions

Pupils who withdraw from school in the junior high-school grades are on the whole a discouraged, unsuccessful, overage group who fail grades frequently, get low marks when they pass, and lack ability to do the tasks set before them. They escape from school as soon as the law permits. Only a very limited number of them enroll later for evening school work.

Although there are among them pupils from all kinds of homes, they typically come from homes with decidedly lower socio-economic standards than those typical of the ninth-grade pupils in their communities. Their homes are lacking in books and magazines, their parents have little education, and their fathers for the most part belong to the laboring groups rather than to the professional or commercial groups.

They leave school for a combination of reasons usually including a dislike for school accounted for by their lack of success there and a desire to earn money due to limited incomes in their homes.

For the most part they take jobs in factories, stores and offices. The work they do is so varied and it can be learned so quickly that vocational training before leaving school is impractical.

Although one-fourth of the boys get into trades, specific trade training for this group is also impractical because so few of the boys are absorbed into any one trade and because the trades are splitting up into specialties which require little training.

These young people are far more successful in industry than in school. They tend to stay by their jobs a fairly long time, they get wages which compare favorably with those of other young people of their ages, and their wages increase with experience and age.

The unemployment reported among them is greater than among high-school graduates, and more among the boys than among the girls. The long and frequent periods of unemployment during which time they are undirected by any agency indicates a serious economic waste and a moral hazard.

B. Occupational Distribution of Pupils Who Graduated from Minneapolis High Schools in 1929

Purpose—This study was undertaken to determine:

1. What proportion of Minneapolis high-school graduates go on to school or college, what schools they go to, and what courses they take.

2. What proportion go to work, what kinds of work they secure, and what wages they receive.

3. How closely these students carry out the plans regarding work and further schooling which they made before graduation.

Method—The Minneapolis Public School Placement Department has on file a personnel card for each high-school graduate made out by the school counselor showing the pupil's high-school record and his plans at the time of graduation. The Placement Department keeps data regarding placement after graduation on these cards. Using these cards as a starting point, the placement counselors followed all the high-school graduates of the classes of January and June, 1929, by means of letters, telephone calls, and personal interviews. This was done between January and June, 1930, about a year after graduation. Each student was asked whether or not he was attending school, if so where and what course; or whether he was working, if so where, what work he was doing, what salary he was receiving, when he obtained his position, and how he obtained his position. Returns were received from 87.8 percent of the group of 2908 people studied. Their present location is indicated in Table 37.

TABLE 37.—PRESENT LOCATION OF MINNEAPOLIS HIGH-SCHOOL GRADUATES, CLASSES OF JANUARY AND JUNE, 1929

Present Location	Percent		
	Boys	Girls	Total
At School or College	32.01	29.27	30.50
At Work	45.23	44.90	45.05
Unemployed	6.42	10.07	8.42
At Home	.08	1.63	.93
Miscellaneous	2.06	2.44	2.27
Married		1.06	.58
Not Located	14.20	10.63	12.24

Analysis of data—Only 30.5 percent of these young people had entered college or other types of schools. This percentage might be increased slightly if this group were followed again a year later, for a considerable number stay out to work a year before going on to school. However, this gain would perhaps be offset by the number of students who enter college but withdraw during their freshman year. A smaller proportion of the 1929 graduating classes went on to school than of the 1926 graduates who were followed with a similar study in 1927. The decrease was 7 percent for the boys and 2 percent for the girls. Following the War, the number who entered college increased very rapidly, but it may be that the peak has been reached and that there is now a downward trend. However, this condition may be a temporary one due in part to the business depression. Subsequent follow-up studies will be needed to give more evidence regarding this trend.

Forty-five percent of the graduates stepped from high school into some kind of remunerative occupation. If we include the number of persons who were seeking work at the time of this survey, over half of these 1929 high-school graduates left school to join the ranks of wage-earners. The proportion of girls going to work was practically the same as for boys. A comparison of this class with the 1926 class shows a 7 percent increase in the number who went to work.

The percent of unemployment reported was 8.42 percent. In spite of the business depression, the total percentage of unemployment for this 1929 class was practically the same as for the 1926 class. It is noteworthy that the unemployment reported was far less than for groups of students with less school training. Twenty percent of a group of Minneapolis pupils who withdrew during the junior high-school grades were unemployed, and 30 percent of the Minneapolis pupils who had attended special classes for retarded children were unemployed.

The "at home" group was with one exception girls who were caring for the family or assisting in the household tasks. How completely some occupation outside her father's home is the accepted thing for a girl is indicated by the meagre 1.63 percent of girls listed as "at home."

Schools and colleges entered—The girls in the high-school graduating classes outnumbered the boys, and a larger number of girls than boys went on to college. However, the percentage of boy graduates who enrolled for further schooling was higher than for girls. This may be because a large number of girls are definitely prepared for a vocation in the high-school commercial departments. Perhaps it indicates that families consider higher education more essential for the boys than for the girls. See Table 38.

TABLE 38.—HIGHER INSTITUTIONS OF LEARNING ENTERED BY MINNEAPOLIS HIGH-SCHOOL GRADUATES OF 1929

Higher Institutions	Boys		Girls		Total	
	Number	Percent	Number	Percent	Number	Percent
University of Minnesota.........	328	78.28	308	65.81	636	71.70
Other Colleges or Universities...	65	15.51	54	11.54	119	13.42
Other Schools:	26	6.21	106	22.65	132	14.88
Teachers Colleges............	4		41		45	
Nurses' Training Schools......	0		21		21	
Business Colleges............	4		33		37	
Trade Schools...............	10		3		13	
Music and Art Schools........	8		7		15	
High-School Post Graduate...	0		1		1	
Total Number in Higher Institutions....................	419	100.00	468	100.00	887	100.00

Since the University of Minnesota is located in Minneapolis, it was not surprising that the largest number of those going on to school, 71.7 percent, entered that institution. Still it would no doubt surprise a góod many high-school teachers to find that of the whole group of graduates only one boy out of four and one girl out of five entered the university. Even if there were added to this group the 119 who entered all other colleges and universities, only one-fourth of those who graduated went on to school. Teaching high-school subjects with the group who are going on to college primarily in mind, as so many instructors do, is giving far too much consideration to one-fourth of the pupils—a fraction which would be greatly reduced if one included the large number of pupils who attend high school but who do not stay to graduate.

Only 26, or 6.21 percent, of the boys who went on to school, as against 106, or 22.65 percent, of the girls, attended institutions other than colleges and universities. Business colleges, nurses' training courses, and teachers colleges enrolled most of these girls. Only 10 boys enrolled in schools for trade training.

The proportion of pupils going on to school varies considerably in the different high schools, depending no doubt upon the social and economic conditions in the neighborhoods from which pupils in different high schools come. Table 39 shows that the percentage going on to school ranges from 57 percent in high school A to 16 percent in high school H. Preparation for college entrance needs to be a chief concern in school A, but preparation for entering immediately upon employment needs to be the chief concern of school H. Therefore uniformity in high-school programs of study, in content of courses, and in objectives seems undesirable in a city like Minneapolis. The best interests of the community can be served by modifying procedures in each school to conform with the probable post-school adjustments of its pupils.

TABLE 39.—PERCENT OF 1929 GRADUATES FROM EACH MINNEAPOLIS HIGH SCHOOL WHO WENT ON TO SCHOOL

High School	Entered College	Entered Other Schools	Total Percent Who Went on to School
A.	52.8	4.4	57.2
B.	46.5	3.9	50.4
C.	29.9	3.6	33.5
D.	23.8	6.2	30.0
E.	16.7	7.5	24.2
F.	18.5	4.7	23.2
G.	16.1	4.8	20.9
H.	12.9	3.1	16.0

Those who went to work—Office work of various kinds gave employment to one-third of the boys and to about three-fourths of the girls. For the boys this meant such positions as office boy, mail clerk, billing clerk, and other kinds of clerical work. Only 19 boys had positions as typists or stenographers and only two as bookkeepers, though some others were operating calculating machines. Of the 526 girls doing office work, 314 were listed as stenographers or typists. Other positions held by girls were file clerks, comptometer operators, and general office workers who usually do some typing and stenography. Table 40 shows the positions held by these graduates.

TABLE 40.—POSITIONS HELD BY MINNEAPOLIS HIGH-SCHOOL GRADUATES OF 1929 WHO WENT TO WORK FOLLOWING GRADUATION

Types of Positions Held	Boys		Girls		Total	
	Number	Percent	Number	Percent	Number	Percent
Office Work........................	194	32.77	526	73.	720	54.96
Selling in Stores or Elsewhere.......	67	11.32	42	5.84	109	8.32
Clerical Work in Stores...........	67	11.32	10	1.39	77	5.88
Errands and Messengers...........	64	10.81	17	2.37	81	6.18
Skilled Trades and Helpers in Skilled Trades........................	85	14.35	19	2.65	104	7.94
Factory Work....................	24	4.05	17	2.37	41	3.13
Telephone and Telegraph..........			34	4.74	34	2.60
Professional (Actors, Musicians, Artists, Etc.)...................	10	1.68	10	1.39	20	1.53
Domestic and Personal Service......	5	.84	13	1.81	18	1.37
Miscellaneous...................	48	8.12	1	.14	49	3.74
Not Stated.....................	28	4.73	29	4.04	57	4.35
Number Holding Positions.........	592	100.00	718	100.00	1310	100.00

Eleven percent of the boys and 5.84 percent of the girls were employed as salespeople in grocery stores, department stores, hardware stores, or elsewhere. In addition to this, there were 11.32 percent of the boys and 1.39 percent of the girls doing clerical work in stores. These boys were for the most part shipping clerks. The girls were doing bundling, cashiering, and stockroom work. A surprisingly small number of girls were found working in the stores either as saleswomen or on these clerical jobs.

The boys who took positions in offices and stores (listed as office work, selling, and store clerical work) numbered 328. This was exactly the same number that entered the University of Minnesota. Much attention is paid in the high schools to preparing the latter group for college entrance, but comparatively little attention is given to preparing this other group for entering the business world. The commercial courses as offered in Minneapolis fit the needs of girls preparing for stenographic, typing, and bookkeeping positions, but few boys enroll for these courses and no courses are offered in the use of calculating machines, in salesmanship, or in advertising. Possibly valuable additions to the program of studies could be made if an analysis were undertaken of the office positions accepted by these boys, with special emphasis upon the general qualifications and specific skills required.

Only 3 percent of the high-school graduates were found employed in factories, but 25 percent of the junior high-school withdrawals were doing this work when interviewed.

Eighty-five of the boys, or 14.35 percent of those who went to work, were employed in jobs which were classified as skilled trades or helpers in skilled trades. Twenty of these were doing some kind of electrical work, such as battery work, repairing or installing telephones, testing meters, and radio service work. Sixteen were doing drafting; 15 were in machine shop work; 8 in automotive work; and 7 in printing.

Salaries—The median salary received by boys after they had been out of school approximately one year was $14.08. For girls it was $13.40. Only five girls were receiving over $24.00 a week, while salaries of $24.00 and up were reported by 39 boys. The girls' salaries tend to group between $12.00 and $16.00 a week; the boys report a wider range. Beginning salaries for high-school graduates are higher than for pupils who withdraw at lower levels.

Vocational plans at time of graduation—Whether or not a high-school education is fitting young people most effectively for community living depends somewhat upon the extent to which these young people carry out the plans they had in mind at the time they chose their high-school courses. A comparison was made of plans made by these pupils before graduation as reported to the school counselor with the actual situation in which they were found a year later. Of the 1070 pupils who planned to enter school or college by the September following their graduation, 744 or almost 70 percent carried out their plans as made. Of 181 who planned to go to work for a year or more and enter college later, 136 were at work and 19 at school, or a total of 155, 85.63 percent, were doing what they planned to do insofar as their plans could be checked within a year after graduation. Of 963 who planned to go to work, 758, or 78.71 percent, carried out their plans. Analysis of the positions these people took as compared with the occupations they planned to get into would show far less agreement, for these inexperienced beginners usually must take the positions that are open. Later those who are persistent and determined may get located in lines of work which they had selected.

Conclusions

Less than one-third of these high-school graduates went on to school anywhere and only one-fourth of the graduates entered college. The proportion entering college varies so greatly in the different high schools as to justify a decided lack of uniformity in the high schools as to the program of studies, content and objectives of the courses offered.

Over one-half of the high-school graduates left school to seek immediate remunerative employment. Unemployment was less frequent and beginning salaries were higher than for those pupils who withdrew at lower school levels.

Office work was the type of position secured by a large proportion of both the boys and girls who graduated and went to work. The girls are definitely prepared in high school for office positions, but the boys receive little specific training for office work.

About three-fourths of the pupils studied carried out their more general vocational and educational plans as stated before leaving high school, an indication that pupils can be prepared in high school for more or less specific post-school adjustments.

C. A Study of Post-School Adjustments of Boys and Girls of Special Classes for Retarded Children in the Minneapolis Public Schools

The problem and its history—The purpose of this study was threefold: first, to gather information concerning adjustments made both in industry and in society by boys and girls who have attended the special classes for retarded children in the Minneapolis public schools; second, to determine from the results what modifications of the curriculum are necessary; and third, to inaugurate a procedure for accumulating data concerning social adjustments of the special class group.

Since 1912, when special classes were first organized in Minneapolis, "follow-up" work has been done only by those teachers who were particularly interested in their pupils, with the exception of a survey made by the Director of Special Classes.[1] Until the fall of 1929 no further detailed, organized work in this direction was done. At that time a committee appointed by the Director of Special Education undertook the present investigation. The committee was composed of the two mental examiners and the visiting teacher for the Department of Special Education. Contributions were made by the teachers of special classes and the personnel of the Placement Bureau of the Board of Education.

Procedure—Registration cards of all children who had left school from the special classes constituted the "Dead File." The file, containing 1573 cards, was the point of departure for the study. After segregating all cards marked "Left City," "Parochial Schools," "Returned to Grades," "Institutions," "Unknown," and "Deceased," there remained 806 cards on which intensive work centered. These were checked first by teachers, then with the census department files, and finally with the City Directory. One hundred sixty letters were sent to former pupils, of which 47 were returned by the Post Office Department. These were then added to the list marked "Unknown."

Calls were made on 611 boys and girls, 337 were interviewed and the desired information obtained. Final distribution of the cards in the dead file may be seen at a glance in Table 41.

TABLE 41.—CLASSIFICATION OF 1573 CASES FORMERLY IN SPECIAL CLASSES IN THE MINNEAPOLIS PUBLIC SCHOOLS

Classification	Boys		Girls		Boys and Girls	
	Number	Percent	Number	Percent	Number	Percent
Deceased........................	10	.9	4	.9	14	.9
Left City......................	264	23.3	92	20.7	356	22.7
Returned to Grades or Transferred to Parochial Schools............	160	14.3	68	15.3	228	14.5
Excluded......................	41	3.6	34	7.6	75	4.9
Left Special Class for Institutions..	59	5.2	35	7.9	94	5.5
Unknown	344	30.4	125	28.2	469	29.9
Interviewed...................	252	22.3	85	19.4	337	21.6
Totals.......................	1130	100.0	443	100.0	1573	100.0

[1] Bryne, May E. "After School Careers of Children Leaving Special Classes in Minneapolis," *Ungraded*, Vol. X, No. 4; January, 1925.

Out of the total number it has been possible to account for all but 469 pupils or 29.9 percent of all the cases.

Mental ability—The range of I. Q. for the 1573 cases was from 40-85, with but three cases below 50 and ten above 80. The largest number of cases fell in the 60-69 group.

Employment—By April 1, 1930, 337, or 21.6 percent, of the cases had been interviewed. Of this number 175 boys and 59 girls had jobs of some kind at the time they were interviewed. This figure, considering all factors, compares somewhat better than one would expect with the results of the Minneapolis study made of boys and girls who have dropped out of junior high schools, in that 80 percent of that group were employed as compared with 70 percent in this special class group.[1] However, the types of work done and wages earned are not comparable. The percentage of employed at this time is much higher than in the previous study.[2] At that time 33 1/3 percent of the group (162) were employed. Even though the employment situation in Minneapolis during the months in which the investigation was made seemed to be very unstable, the fact remains that 70 percent of these boys and girls had secured work. Among the 59 girls employed were counted the 16 who are married and maintaining their own households. Two percent of the boys were in the army and navy and one boy was a student at the Federal Art School.

Table 42 gives a detailed list of the various tasks being done by these 234 employed girls and boys who at one time had been in special classes in the Minneapolis public schools.

TABLE 42a.—TYPES OF WORK IN WHICH 59 FORMER SPECIAL CLASS GIRLS ARE ENGAGED

Domestic		Packing, Labeling (Factory)		Stores and Shops	
Waitress	3			Salesgirl	1
Clearing tables	1			Clerking	3
Cafeteria	4	Pastes labels	2	Wraps packages	1
Taking care of chil-		Packs toast	1	Check in clothes	1
dren	5	Packs candy	1	Stock girl	1
House work	2	Packs flour	1		—
Married	16	Packs butter	1		7
	—	Wraps cakes	1	*Miscellaneous*	
	31	Wraps packages	1	Practical nursing	1
Machines		Testing cans	1	Farm help	1
Gloves	1	Inspecting films	1	Sewing cushions	2
Box	1	Making rubber hose	1	Laundry	1
Rugs	1			Filing	1
	—			Sewing tassels on furn.	1
	3		11		—
					7
				Grand total	59

---

[1] See: "A Study of School Records and Post-School Adjustments of Pupils Who Withdrew from the Minneapolis Schools in Junior High-School Grades, 1924-1929," pages 189-99 of this Yearbook.

[2] Bryne, May E. "After School Careers of Children Leaving Special Classes in Minneapolis." *Ungraded*, Vol. X, No. 4; January, 1925.

TABLE 42b.—TYPES OF WORK IN WHICH 175 FORMER SPECIAL CLASS BOYS ARE ENGAGED

Automobiles
Oil station helper 3
Putting tires on rims . 1
Garage repairman ... 1
——
5

Bakeries
Puts biscuits in oven . 1
Icing rolls 1
Makes cakes 1
——
3

Building and Related Work
Sash and door making 3
Cement work 1
Making card tables . 1
Tinner's helper 1
Glazing windows ... 1
Plumber's helper 1
Carpenter 1
Carpenter's helper ... 3
Learning millwright . 1
Crating 1
Sets up staves for kegs 1
Nailing boxes together 2
——
17

Delivery
Delivering mail (office) 1
Telegraph messenger 1
Errand boy 3
——
5

Domestics (Restaurants and Personal Service)
Cook 1
Page boy 1
Bus boy 3
Janitor 1
——
6

Electrical
Assembler 1
Dipping battery plates 1
Making thermostats .. 1
Spot welder 1

Electrical (continued)
Polisher 1
Bench foreman 1
Making batteries 1
——
7

Furniture
Springing furniture .. 7
Upholstering 4
Furniture finisher 1
Cushion maker 1
Padding cushions 1
——
14

Iron or Foundry Work
Learning moulders
  trade 1
Helps making core ... 1
Grinder 3
Riveting 1
Cuts sheet iron 1
Making holes 1
Foundry helper 3
——
11

Machines
Printing and type 4
Metalware 1
Lumber 1
Knitting 1
Tending machine ... 7
——
14

Painting
Painting beds 1
Street car floors 1
Boxcars 1
Furniture 1
Machines 1
Interior decoration .. 4
——
9

Railroad Shops
Helper 2
Picks up scraps 1
Sweeps 2
Roundhouse worker . 1

Railroad Shops (cont.)
Repairing cars 1
Firing 2
Icing cars 1
——
10

Stores
Handy man 2
Meat cutter 1
Delivering 8
Shipping room 3
Marking goods 1
Selling (clerking) ... 6
Stockman 2
——
23

Miscellaneous
Handyman or helper . 9
Farm work 5
Oiler 1
Clerical 1
Trimming brooms ... 1
Making boxes (paper) 2
Sells papers 1
Shoveling 2
Shining shoes 1
Deck hand 1
Digging 1
Shoe repairing 1
Shoe cutter 1
Pressing 1
Freight handler 1
Peddling 1
Odd jobs 1
Glove factory 2
Stamp and stencil
  maker 1
——
34

Trucks (Hauling)
Driving truck 11
Loading 2
Hauling 4
——
17

Grand total 175

A study of this table reveals the fact that most of the boys' occupations are routine mechanical, unskilled, and semi-skilled types of labor. This is what is normally to be expected of boys of the level of intelligence contributing to special class personnel. Very few found work on farms, in offices, or in domestic service.

The work of girls is mostly domestic and personal service. In the Minneapolis public schools there are two special classes for girls where training for cafeteria and lunch room work is being given, which may have influenced the results to some extent. Counting 16 who are married, we find 31, or over half the cases, so employed. The second largest group of girls have factory jobs, packing and labeling. The third largest group are helpers in stores and some are salesgirls.

In the same way the type of training given the special class boys in wood working shops, to some degree, may have influenced the figures, in that 17 were found in the building and related work.

Some are working in furniture factories, although up to the present time no upholstering or actual making of furniture (with the exception of reed furniture making) has been taught in the special classes. Here again the use of tools and shop experience have, no doubt, been of value.

The distribution of weekly wages for boys ranged from board and room to nearly $40; for girls from board and room to $20. The median wage for boys is $15 a week; for girls, $10. See Table 43.

Sixteen girls working for board and room include those who are married. Although the 16 receive no definite wage, they are considered as employed. Three boys working for board and room are employed on farms.

TABLE 43.—RANGE OF WAGES RECEIVED BY 234 BOYS AND GIRLS FROM SPECIAL CLASSES

	Board and Room	$3.00 to $4.99	$5.00 to $9.99	$10.00 to $14.99	$15.00 to $19.99	$20.00 to $24.99	$25.00 to $29.99	$30.00 to $34.99	$35.00 to $39.99	Wages Un-known	Total
Boys.......	3	1	6	37	61	22	13	4	2	26	175
Girls.......	Married 16	4	7	19	9	......	......	......	......	4	59
Total......	19	5	13	56	70	22	13	4	2	30	234

A study of the relation between the length of time since leaving special class and the time on the present job, shows that the greatest number have been out of school from one to two years, and most of them have held jobs less than seven months. This may indicate that boys do not get jobs immediately upon leaving school, but that some time is required for them to work into steady positions. The United States Department of Labor considers a job held over three months as permanent employment. One hundred forty-two (81 percent) of employed boys held steady jobs at the time of the interview.

Most of the girls interviewed have been out of school one to two years. Seventy-eight percent of the total number employed have permanent jobs other than homemaking, and 13 girls have been working less than four months.

A study was also made of the relationship between the length of time out of special class and the total time employed. This study included both employed and unemployed boys, for the reason that many boys who were unemployed at the time of the interview had been holding steady jobs, but, because of slack employment, were out of work for the winter. The minimum wage law in Minnesota requiring employers to pay the wage set by law may have some effect on the employment of boys under 21, as employers hiring boys under that age are subject to wage investigation by the Industrial Commission. It is impossible to judge from the data in the present study what effect this situation may have upon special class boys. All but 52 of the boys have been employed more than six months since leaving special class. Out of that number, 22 had not been out of special class less than two years, indicating again that work is not available or steady immediately upon leaving school. The figures indicate, however, that on the whole most of the boys have not been out of employment for very long periods of time since withdrawal from special class.

It is interesting to note that there is a higher proportion of girls who have never worked than there is of boys. This, of course, is mainly due to the fact that frequently in large families girls are kept at home to help the mother, and in some cases the family, recognizing the girl's handicap, have kept the lives of these girls sheltered.

The minimum wage law applies to girls up to 18 years, and it is apt to have more effect on the employment of girls than that of boys, because girls over 18 are as capable as those under that age and can work for any price without subjecting the employer to a wage investigation. There are 17 girls who have been employed less than seven months, and ten of this number have been out of special class less than two years. The girls, as well as the boys, seem to require time to find employment when they leave school.

A study of living conditions was made. It was found that most special class boys and girls live at home with their parents, either paying a definite amount for board and room or giving the parents their entire wage. The average amount of board paid is $5 a week. The maximum is $15 a week. Very few are boarding away from home. Only a small number, comparatively, are supported by their parents while they are employed. Thirteen boys and 16 girls are married and maintaining their own homes. It was found that special class boys and girls are at least partially, if not entirely, self-supporting.

Court records of pupils formerly in special classes for retarded children— Much has been written about the extremely large percent of delinquents who belong in the subnormal group. As more data are gathered in this field, it is encouraging to find first in one city, then in another, that a large percentage of the subnormal group has no record of delinquency.[1] This study brings further facts to prove that all mentally defective school children do not become delinquents during their school life or immediately following it. Less than one-fifth of the total group which were located had any record of court appearance; and of this number, 3.8 percent had minor

---

[1] Healy, William, and Bromer, A. F. *Delinquents and Criminals, Their Making and Unmaking.* New York: The Macmillan Company, 1926. p. 149.

court records. A minor court record in the Juvenile Court of Minneapolis does not entail an adjudication, but is only an informal hearing before the chief probation officer. Sixteen percent of the group appeared in Juvenile Court and were put on probation or sent to a county or state institution. The percentage of girls having court records is much lower than that of boys. The recidivists are found almost entirely among the boys. One-half of the boys with court records appeared more than once.

Types of recreation indulged in by special class children—The figures here again are not conclusive, as this information was very vague and difficult to obtain. Few of them could give definite information at to what they did for recreation, and most of them had so little money to spend that they felt their recreation was limited. For boys, shows, dances, motoring, and outdoor sports seem to be the most popular types. Very few are in church activities, and very few take advantage of the recreational facilities of neighborhood houses and park board centers. The only general conclusion that could be drawn from the investigation of recreation is that special class boys and girls, lacking resources within themselves for providing recreation, either have very little or confine it to the type that can be bought. The results indicate the need of further and more intensive research.

Summary and Conclusions

Special class pupils who have been out of school for some time are difficult to locate.

A definite system of follow-up for at least two years after they leave special class would be valuable.

The employment situation for this group is somewhat better than was expected by the investigators. Seventy percent of the former special class boys and girls were employed at the time of the interview, as compared with 80 percent of the junior high-school group who had dropped out of school. In 1922, only $33\frac{1}{3}$ percent of the former special class cases studied were employed.

It seems to take about two years for pupils of this group to find themselves and secure anything like a steady job. Considering a job held over three months as permanent employment, we find that 142, or 81 percent, of the employed boys held steady jobs at the time of the interview. The girls' group was too small a number from which to draw definite conclusions, but 78 percent of the total number employed have permanent jobs other than homemaking.

The median wage for boys is $15 weekly and for girls $10. They tend to remain at that wage level irrespective of age, indicating little or no chance for promotion.

The type of employment is routine mechanical, unskilled, and semiskilled.

The majority of the group live at home and are at least partially self-supporting, but are unable to save money.

A comparison of the results of this study with those of similar studies does not show an abnormal amount of anti-social conduct in this group.

References to Additional Follow-Up Studies

Those who are particularly interested in the post-school adjustments of pupils will want to review some of the following references to follow-up studies made in many different cities:

"After High School, What?" Department of Research and Guidance, Providence, R. I. *Providence Public School Bulletin* 3: 2-5; March, 1928.

Arnold, Frank J. *A Comparative Study of the Educational Results of a Cooperative Commercial Group and a Noncooperative Commercial Group in Secondary Education.* Master's Thesis. New York: New York University, 1928.

Carpenter, Mary S. *A Study of the Occupations of 207 Subnormal Girls After Leaving School.* University of Michigan, School of Education, Vocational Education Department, Special Studies No. 2. Ann Arbor: School of Education, University of Michigan, 1925.

Cowen, P. A. "How They Make a Living." *New York State Education* 17: 807-09; May, 1930. (Rochester, N. Y.)

Crockett, A. C., and Clow, Jennie M. *Occupations of Junior Workers in Detroit.* Ann Arbor: Vocational Education Department, University of Michigan, 1923.

Davis, P. L., and Evans, J. E. "Investigating the Alumni of a High School." *School Executives Magazine* 49: 223-25; January, 1930.

Evans, Owen D. *Educational Opportunities for Young Workers.* New York: The Macmillan Company, 1926. 380 p.

Fleming, R. D. "A Human Survey." *New York State Education* 17: 301-03; December, 1929.

"Follow-Up Studies." *Providence Public School Bulletin* 4: 3-20; May, 1929.

"Follow-Up Study of High School Graduates." *Vocational Guidance Magazine* 6: 349-50; May, 1928.

Foster, F. K. "Study of Elimination in a Boys' Technical-Vocational High School." *School Review* 36: 58-66; January, 1928.

Foye, H. B. "After School, What?" *Vocational Guidance Magazine* 7: 169-71, 173; January, 1929.

Griscom, Anna B. *The Working Children of Philadelphia: A Survey of the Work and Working Conditions of 3300 Continuation-School Children.* The White-Williams Foundation cooperating with the Junior Employment Service. Board of Education, Philadelphia, Bulletin Series No. 3, 1924.

Hayes, Mary H. S. *Opportunities for Vocational Training in New York City.* The Vocational Service for Juniors, 122 East 25th St., New York City. September, 1930.

Hisey, Walter Edwin. *A Twelve-Year Follow-Up Study of the Educational and Vocational Interests of High-School Students.* Master's Thesis. Bloomington, Ind.: University of Indiana, 1928. 50 p.

Hollingworth, Leta S. "After High School, What?" *Parents' Magazine* 4: 20-21; June, 1929.

Holt, F. O. "Expectation of College Attendance among High-School Seniors in Wisconsin." *School Review* 37: 642-43; November, 1929.

Hutchings, Raymond R. *Comparison of the January, 1925, and the June, 1925, Graduating Classes of the Junior High School, as Shown by the Records Made in the Senior High School.* Santa Barbara City Schools, Santa Barbara, Calif. June 15, 1928. Hectographed, 7 p.

Iowa. Bureau of Labor. *Special Investigation of Children in Industry Attending Part-Time School.* Bulletin No. 17. The Bureau, 1926.

Katenkamp, Chester H. "A Study of the Commercial Graduates of Forest Park High School." *Baltimore Bulletin of Education* 8: 13-15; September-October, 1929. Baltimore, Md.

Lee, E. A. "Counseling the Non-University High-School Pupil." *Industrial Arts Magazine* 19: 48-51; February, 1930.

Leech, B. R. "Analytic Study of the Graduates of the Harvard, Nebraska, High School." *Educational Research Record* 2: 127-39; February, 1930.

McClure, Helen M., and Woodside, Margaret G. *A Study of Five Hundred Employed Pupils*. Pittsburgh Public Schools, Department of Vocational Guidance, Pittsburgh, Pa. 14 p. October 1, 1925.

Mueller, Alfred D. *A Vocational and Socio-Educational Survey of Graduates and Non-Graduates of Small High Schools of New England*. Doctor's Thesis. New Haven: Yale University. State Normal School, Worcester, Mass. (In preparation for publication.) 1927.

National Industrial Conference Board. *The Employment of Young Persons in the United States*. New York: The Board, 1925.

Nuding, Jeremiah Albert. *Geographical and Occupational Distribution of the Graduates of Frankton, Ind., High School*. Master's Thesis, June, 1927. Bloomington, Ind.: Indiana University. 67 p. (Unpublished.)

"Occupational Distribution of Denver High-School Graduates." *Monthly Labor Review* 29: 1412-13; December, 1929.

"Occupational Survey of Cardozo High School, Washington, D. C." *School Life* 15: 31; October, 1929.

"Occupational Survey of Commercial Graduates, Drop-Outs, and Evening School Pupils, Pittsburgh High Schools." *Curriculum Study and Educational Research Bulletin* 4: 163-82; March, 1930. Pittsburgh: Public Schools.

Olsen, J. C., and Smith, G. B. L. "Scholarship and Employment Record of Evening Students." *Journal of Chemical Education* 6: 931-42; May, 1929.

Ormsbee, Hazel G. *The Young Employed Girl*. The Woman's Press, 1928.

Palmer, Emily G. *Pupils Who Leave School*. Part-Time Education Series, No. 17; Division of Vocational Education Bulletin, No. 24. Berkeley, Calif.: University of California, January, 1930. 142 p.

Palmer, Emily G., and Noall, Irvin S. *The Part-Time School and the Problem Child*. Part-Time Education Series, No. 14; Division of Vocational Education Bulletin, No. 18. Berkeley, Calif.: University of California, April, 1926.

Prunty, Merle C. "A Study of the Graduates of the Class of 1925 of the High School of Tulsa, Oklahoma." (Abstract of unpublished master's thesis.) *Bulletin of the Department of Secondary-School Principals of the National Education Association*, No. 24, p. 135-39; January, 1929.

Rutledge, R. E. *Follow-Up Report of High School Graduates*. Oakland, Calif.: Bureau of Curriculum Development, Research and Guidance; June, 1928. Mimeographed, 11 p.

Rutledge, R. E. *Follow-Up Report of High School Graduates*. Class of June, 1927. Oakland, Calif.: Bureau of Curriculum Development, Research and Guidance; December, 1927. Mimeographed, 6 p.

Schmid, Calvin F. *Special Investigation of the Part-Time School and Junior Worker in the City of Seattle*. Bulletin, No. 4, Trade and Industrial Series, No. 2. Olympia, Wash.: Washington State Board of Vocational Education, 1929.

Schmidt, Hans W. "Study of the Vocational Trends among High School Students." *Industrial Arts Magazine* 15: 307-09; September, 1926.

Segel, David. *Occupations for High School Graduates Based upon a Study of the Class Graduating at Polytechnic High School in 1924*. Long Beach, Calif.: Department of Research, Public Schools, 1930. 8 p.

Shannon, J. R. "Post-School Careers of High-School Leaders and High-School Scholars." *School Review* 37: 656-65; November, 1929.

Stine, J. Ray. *Comparative Study of the Intelligence, Work Experiences, Social Status of Part-Time Public School Students Indicative of the Part-Time Problem in Ohio*. Columbus, Ohio: Ohio State University, Department of Vocational Education. 1927. 84 p.

Thorndike, E. L., and Symonds, P. M. "Occupations of High-School Graduates and Non-Graduates." *School Review* 30: 443-51; June, 1922.

Woodbury, H. S. *The Working Children of Boston*. Bureau Publication, No. 89. Washington, D. C.: Children's Bureau, U. S. Department of Labor. 1922.

Yust, W. F. "After Graduation." *Wilson Bulletin* 4: 455; May, 1930. New York: Wilson Co.

CHAPTER X

A STUDY OF MINNEAPOLIS PUBLIC EVENING SCHOOL PUPILS

Part I—What Are the Characteristics of Evening School Pupils?

A PARTIAL answer to the above question for the city of Minneapolis makes up one section of this report. An attempt was made to secure an answer in the belief that evening schools, to be of greater service, need detailed information concerning the people they serve.

Sources of data—A questionnaire was prepared to secure information from evening school pupils concerning their age, race, nationality, sex, certain family conditions, day-school history, reasons for discontinuing day school, history of extension schooling, reasons for attending evening school, how evening school was heard about, and employment history. This questionnaire was presented to the evening school pupils of the Minneapolis commercial school, the academic high school, and the ten English schools, of which one was high-school preparatory, and the remaining nine English schools for the foreign-born. To insure complete and accurate data, pupils were taken in reasonably small groups in order that a trained corps of assistants could go among them and give individual help when needed. The records of the academic high school were used to supplement data secured from the questionnaire. Only the most significant results are included in this report as space does not permit a more complete discussion.

Evening schools in Minneapolis—The Minneapolis Public School Extension Division operates, as a part of its program, ten evening English schools enrolling approximately 875 pupils each semester, a commercial school enrolling approximately 1,140 each semester, and an academic high school enrolling approximately 640. The pupils attend three evenings a week. For the most part, the English schools give work to fit the needs of the foreign-born pupils who wish to learn the English language, and to native-born pupils who have less than a six-grade education. Some pupils, however, are given a preparatory course which fits them to do high-school work. The evening commercial school offers some courses that are especially designed to meet the needs of adults. Thirty-one courses are offered in all. The evening academic high school offers the following fifty courses: ten in English; four each in French, German, Latin, and Spanish; seven in mathematics; eight in science; and nine in social science.

Characteristics of Evening School Pupils

Age—Table 44 on page 214 indicates that more than half of the commercial school and academic evening high-school pupils are under 23 years of age. The range of ages is from 16 to over 40. Less than one-third of those attending English evening schools are under 23 years of age and twenty-five percent of this group are over 40 years of age.

TABLE 44.—PERCENT OF EVENING SCHOOL PUPILS OF SEVEN AGE GROUPS IN FOUR DIFFERENT TYPES OF SCHOOLS IN MINNEAPOLIS

Type of School	Percent at Each Age Level							Number Cases Upon Which Percent Is Based
	16–18	19–20	21–22	23–24	25–29	30–39	Over 40	
English Schools[1] (Average of 9 Schools)	6	11	12	9	18	19	25	318
High-School Preparatory	22	7	12	8	27	20	4	108
Commercial School	22	21	16	11	17	10	3	794
Academic High School	33	21	11	8	9	13	5	457

[1] For pupils wishing to learn the English language.

Read this table as follows: Of 318 evening school pupils attending schools in Minneapolis specially designed for teaching English to foreigners, 6 percent are between 16–18 years of age; and 11 percent are between 19–20 years of age. Similarly read data for other age levels and for other types of schools.

Previous education—Although a wide age range is to be expected among evening school pupils, a certain uniformity in amount of previous education might be expected, especially for those evening school pupils at the elementary level. An analysis of their level of day-school education is presented in Table 45. Thirteen percent of English evening school pupils have had high-school work. This situation is accounted for by the fact that many

TABLE 45.—AMOUNT OF DAY SCHOOL EDUCATION OF 1,593 MINNEAPOLIS EVENING SCHOOL PUPILS

Type of School	Percent of Each Evening School's Pupils Who Have Reached Each Level of Day School Education											Number of Cases
	Less than 8th grade	Grad- uate 8th grade	1 yr. h. s.	2 yr. h. s.	3 yr. h. s.	4 yr. h. s. not grad.	H. S. grad.	Some col- lege work	1, 2, 3, 4 yr. grad. col- lege	Col- lege de- gree		
English Schools[1] (Average of 9 Schools)	67	20	5	4	2	0	2	0	0	0		280
High-School Preparatory	40	26	9	10	3	0	12	0	0	0		107
Commercial School	2	13	10	10	10	1	44	7	3	0		746
Academic High School	3	17	11	14	17	14	20	3	0	1		460

[1] For pupils wishing to learn the English language.

Read table thus: Of 280 evening school pupils attending English schools, 67 percent have had less than an eighth grade education in day school; 20 percent are eighth grade graduates; 5 percent have had one year of high school, etc.

foreign-born pupils who are learning English have had the equivalent oi high-school training in their native countries. Although Table 45 shows that 67 percent have had less than an eighth-grade education, no doubt many of them have completed the elementary school which may be fewer years in length in their native country.

Apparently the majority of commercial school pupils are not attending for the purpose of getting high-school credit since 54 percent of them are high-school graduates or better; the same is true of 24 percent of the academic evening high-school pupils.

Wages—Table 46 gives the percent of pupils falling at each of several wage levels in the four types of schools. The median weekly wage of 1,363 cases included in this study is less than $20. Only a small percentage of these pupils received more than $35 a week. The most interesting point seems to be that the median weekly wage of pupils of all four types of schools is about the same. However, the median salary of pupils in the commercial school is less than the median wage in the academic group. This is probably due to the fact that 80 percent of the commercial group are women.

TABLE 46.—WEEKLY WAGE LEVEL OF 1,363 EVENING SCHOOL PUPILS IN MINNEAPOLIS

Type of School	Percent at Each Wage Level												Number of Cases
	$75-99	$51-74	$46-50	$41-45	$36-40	$31-35	$26-30	$21-25	$16-20	$10-15	Under $10	Median	
English Schools[1] (Average of 9 Schools) .	0	0	1	3	2	4	13	17	23	22	16	$18.60	227
High-School Preparatory...............	0	2	0	2	5	3	8	23	20	33	4	$19.30	99
Commercial School...	0	1	1	2	2	3	7	15	33	32	4	$17.80	642
Academic High School	1	1	1	2	4	6	9	18	24	28	6	$19.30	395

[1] For pupils wishing to learn the English language.

Read table thus: Of 227 evening school pupils attending English schools, 0 percent receive wages of $75-99 or $51-74 weekly; and 1 percent receive a weekly wage of $46-50. Similarly read data for other wage levels; and for pupils attending other types of evening schools.

Sex—In general, differences in findings throughout this report on the basis of sex are negligible. This does not hold true with the wage factor, however, in two noteworthy instances. The men attending the commercial evening school average about $10 a week higher in wage than do the women. In the English schools there is a group receiving less than $10 per week, and this group contains a greater proportion of women. A study of the occupations of English school pupils reveals the fact that 220 out of 284 women, 77 percent, are either housewives or domestic employees. If they are domestic employees, their wages may be less than $10 per week, but they are receiving maintenance in addition to this wage.

In the English schools 58 percent are men and 42 percent are women; in the evening academic high school the sexes are about equally divided; but in the evening commercial school, 80 percent of the student body are women. See Table 47.

TABLE 47.—PROPORTION OF MEN AND WOMEN IN EVENING SCHOOLS IN MINNEAPOLIS

Type of School	Percent of Each Sex		Number of Cases on Which Percents Are Based
	Men	Women	
English Schools[1] (Average of 9 Schools).......	58	42	320
High-School Preparatory..................	67	33	108
Commercial School.......................	20	80	794
Academic High School....................	54	46	460

[1] For pupils wishing to learn the English language.

Reasons for discontinuing day school—As a means of determining which reasons for leaving day school operate to the greatest extent, a list of possible causes was placed in the questionnaire, and students were asked to check in order of importance the ones which applied to them.

A summary of their replies in Table 48 shows that the largest percentage of those taking evening high school work in Minneapolis were forced to discontinue their day school education because of "lack of funds or support." This included such factors as poor health, illness in the family, and the necessity of helping support the family.

It may be seen in Table 48 that "insufficient desire" played an important role in determining withdrawal from day school by English school pupils, while "lack of funds" and "preferred to earn money" were the most important considerations of pupils now enrolled in the academic evening high school and the commercial evening school.

TABLE 48.—REASONS GIVEN BY 1615 EVENING SCHOOL PUPILS FOR DISCONTINUING DAY SCHOOL

Type of School	Percent for Each Reason						Number Cases
	Insufficient desire	Conditions not encouraging	Preferred to earn money	Social	Lack of funds or support	Married	
English Schools[1] (Average of 9 Schools)..........	43	9	35	1	12	0	362
High-School Preparatory.	34	14	21	2	29	0	104
Commercial School......	20	6	34	2	37	1	759
Academic High School...	16	13	33	3	34	1	390

[1] For pupils wishing to learn the English language.

Part II—What Is the Quality of Evening High-School Pupils' Work

Even though it is granted that evening high-school pupils have the desire and the need for further education, some question what they accomplish. This section presents, briefly, the results of a comprehensive study of the achievement of pupils attending the academic evening high school in Minneapolis.

The Minneapolis academic evening high school—The academic evening high school operates very similarly to the academic day high school. It has the same half-year courses with the usual two semesters. The total number of class hours per semester is somewhat different, however, being 108 hours as compared with 180 hours in day school. The teachers are chosen, for the most part, from the best of the day school force. There are, however, some distinct and typical differences between the day and the evening high schools that have bearing on academic accomplishment.

Differences between evening and day pupils—Differences which seem to favor the achievement of evening pupils are:

1. Greater maturity
2. An experience and background which go with post-school endeavor
3. Greater earnestness and desire to learn on the part of many who are continuing their school work because of a definite need.

Differences which seem to favor the day students are:

1. Somewhat higher average intelligence
2. More time in which to study
3. Not attending classes after a day of work
4. Five class hours per subject per week instead of the three of evening school pupils.

Sources of data for this study—To secure data bearing on the evening school achievement versus day school achievement, batteries of objective tests were selected or were prepared which would be reliable instruments for measuring the measurable results of instruction. In many instances, several tests were used in one course. Achievement was worked out on a basis of status at the end of a semester and, in some instances, on the amount of growth made during the semester. In as many courses as possible the day school classes used as "controls" or "comparative groups" were taught by the same teacher who taught the corresponding courses in evening school. In addition, data relative to intelligence quotients were secured for both day and evening school classes.

The achievement of evening school pupils—Data were obtained from both day and evening pupils in the following classes: Two in general science, two in chemistry, two in geometry, two in algebra, three in civics, one in physics, two in American history, one in economics, and eleven in

English. Table 49 presents the results in English classes only as they are quite typical of results in other classes. Seven tests were given to both day and evening classes. Table 49 shows that more evening classes scored higher in English than did day classes.

TABLE 49.—EVENING CLASSES IN ENGLISH SCORING HIGHER OR LOWER THAN DAY CLASSES ON OBJECTIVE TESTS

Evening School Class in	Same Teacher Day and Evening	Median Outcome of Each Test Used (H indicates the evening class median to be higher than the day class median; L indicates that the evening class median is lower)								
		Number of Tests							Total	
		1	2	3	4	5	6	7	Higher	Lower
Eng. 12A Gr..	Yes	H	L	H	L	L	L	H	3	4
Eng. 12A Gr..	Yes	L	H	H	L	L	H	H	4	3
Eng. 12A Gr..	Yes	H	H	H	H	H	L	H	6	1
Eng. 12B Gr..	Yes	L	H	L	L	L	L	......	1	5
Eng. 12B Gr..	Yes	H	L	L	L	L	L	L	1	6
Eng. 11B Gr..	Yes	H	H	H	L	H	L	......	4	2
Eng. 10A Gr..	Yes	H	L	H	H	H	......	H	5	1
Eng. 10A Gr..	Yes	H	H	H	H	H	......	L	5	1
Number of Higher........		6	5	6	3	4	1	4	29	....
Number of Lower........		2	3	2	5	4	5	2	....	23

Nineteen tests were given in classes other than English, and in only four instances did an evening school median fail to exceed the median of the day school comparative class.

In 63 of the comparisons made between evening and day classes, the pupils were measured both at the beginning and at the end of the semester, which made it possible to determine the number of score points of growth each pupil made during the semester. In 73 percent of these 63 comparisons, the evening classes exceeded the median performances of the day classes. In some cases, however, the teacher element was not controlled. A different teacher taught the evening classes than taught day classes, which makes some of the results of doubtful value. The results indicate quite conclusively, however, that evening school pupils do achieve as much as do day pupils. And there is some evidence to show that they achieve even more than do day pupils.

CHAPTER XI

A STUDY OF ORGANIZED INFORMAL ADULT EDUCATION ACTIVITIES IN MINNEAPOLIS

Part I—Procedure

WHAT kind of informal educational program confronts the adult in Minneapolis when education becomes his avocation rather than his vocation? What are his opportunities for keeping step with an ever-changing civilization? To secure answers to such questions as these, the Minneapolis Council for Adult Education made this survey.

Certain kinds of organizations, such as recreational groups, lodges, and organizations of employees in commercial establishments; and unorganized bodies of people, such as radio listeners and library readers, were excluded. The types surveyed are secular organizations [1] including clubs and societies, and public and semi-public institutions and agencies not organized for profit; and church organizations.

This roster of organizations was prepared by combining the lists obtained from several sources, such as the Business and Municipal Branch of the Public Library, American and foreign language papers, the classified section of the telephone directory, social agencies, the Minneapolis Church Federation, administrative headquarters of parent organizations, and club calendars. This roster, although not complete, is a well-rounded record of organized clubs of adults within the city.

The survey was begun by sending a questionnaire, Form 1, to all organizations in the city of Minneapolis, asking for information on major and minor objectives, affiliation, size and range of membership, and occupational constituency of members. See page 229.

As the questionnaires came back, the organizations indicating "education" as either a major or a minor objective were sent a second questionnaire, Form 3, requesting information relative to the purpose of the educational program, the methods and means of instruction, financial sources and costs, cooperation received or given to other adult education movements, membership, attendance, and time and place of meetings. A copy of Form 3 is included on pages 230-33.

---

[1] *Secular organization* denotes an organization having no affiliation with any church, mission, or denomination; *church organization* denotes any society affiliated with a church, a mission, or a denomination, or an interdenominational organization.

The number of organizations responding to these questionnaires, both Forms 1 and 3, are as follows:

	Secular	Church
A. Number of organizations contacted on Form 1..............	653	695
B. Number responding with usable answers to Form 1 on first and follow-up contacts	544	370
C. Number indicating "education" as a major or a minor objective	464	246
D. Number of educational organizations responding with usable answers to Form 3 on first and follow-up contacts..........	314	150

Although it was impossible to obtain a complete roster of organizations for the survey and to get responses from all those contacted, the list for study is large enough to be a fair sampling of the clubs and societies in Minneapolis. The data received from the individual organizations were checked and discussed by the staff workers through contact with all organizations where data appeared to be unreliable or incomplete. Daily conferences were held by the staff during the first part of the study to insure uniformity of interpretation.

In order to condense the report and simplify the data, both secular and church organizations are classified according to major interests and not as individual units. The church organizations are grouped according to the denominations of their respective churches. The secular are grouped according to the divisions listed below.

1. Civic:
    Clubs for the study of civic problems and the promotion of governmental efficiency; e.g., Taxpayers' Association; Commonwealth Club
2. Cultural:
    Clubs which aim to give opportunity for intellectual growth and cultural development; e.g., Shakespeare Club; Minneapolis Society of Fine Arts; Apollo Club
3. Ethical:
    Clubs to promote moral conduct; e.g., Woman's Christian Temperance Union
4. Occupational:
    Clubs composed of people of like vocation; e.g., Housewives' League
5. Patriotic:
    Organizations to promote interest in national cultures and history—American or other; also to preserve memorials of the past; e.g., American Legion; Daughters of the American Revolution; Minneapolis Zionist District
6. Political:
    Clubs for the study of political and governmental questions; e.g., League of Women Voters; partisan political clubs
7. Professional:
    Clubs to promote cooperation among those engaged in business or professional work; e.g., Minneapolis Teachers' League; Engineers' Club
8. Religious:
    Clubs for the study of religious subjects but not affiliated with a church; e.g., Bible Study Club
9. Social:
    Clubs with programs designed primarily for social fellowship and enjoyment; e.g., Woman's Auxiliary, Hennepin County Medical Association; Enterprise Social Club

10. Community and Social Service:
    a. Agencies organized to give service to the community (usually sharers in the Community Fund) ; e.g., Hennepin County Tuberculosis Association; Minneapolis Urban League; Family Welfare Association
    b. Groups organized to give special service, usually neighborhood; e.g., The Concordia Society of the Swedish Hospital; Parents and Teachers Associations
    c. Institutions organized to give service to the community (usually sharers in the Community Fund) ; e.g., settlement houses and homes of refuge.

Table 50 gives the number of organizations in the secular division which received and returned Forms 1 and 3.

TABLE 50.—QUESTIONNAIRE RESPONSES FROM SECULAR ORGANIZATIONS IN MINNEAPOLIS, CLASSIFIED ACCORDING TO MAJOR INTEREST

Interest Groups	Number Responding to Form 1	Number Reporting Education as an Objective	Number Responding to Form 3[1]
Civic	16	14	6
Cultural	110	110	103
Ethical	19	18	18
Occupational	23	19	4
Patriotic	85	69	56
Political	14	14	13
Professional	28	26	16
Religious	4	3	2
Social	29	20	16
Social and Community Service:			
a. Agencies	26	25	20
b. Groups	170	132	48
c. Institutions	20	14	12
Grand Total	544	464	314

[1] Form 3 was sent only to those organizations which reported education on Form 1 as an objective.

It will be noted that there are a greater number of groups organized for community and social service than for any other purpose. The next largest division is the cultural. This is followed closely by the patriotic groups.

Table 50 shows a total of 544 secular organizations responding to the first questionnaire; 464 of these organizations reported education as a major or minor objective; 314 of the 464 organizations filled in the detailed questionnaire.

Listings of church organizations were secured from pastors by the use of Form 2a. See page 234. These organizations were contacted by means of

Forms 1 and 3 in the same manner as the secular organizations. The summary of the number of responses received from church organizations is given in Table 51.

TABLE 51.—QUESTIONNAIRE RESPONSES FROM CHURCH ORGANIZATIONS, CLASSIFIED ACCORDING TO DENOMINATIONS

Denomination	Number Churches Contacted	Number Responding to Form 2a[1]	Number Groups Contacted, Form 1	Number Groups Responding to Form 1	Number Groups Reporting Education as Objective	Number Groups Responding to Form 3[2]
Adventist, Seventh Day...	3	1	0	0	0	0
African M. E., Baptist Episcopal, M. E. (Negro)	17	6	34	16	6	6
Baptist.................	26	18	66	36	32	18
Catholic:						
A. Liberal.............	1	1	3	3	1	1
B. Orthodox..........	6	6	19	8	4	3
C. Roman.............	27	11	41	26	10	8
Christian Science.........	7	3	0	0	0	0
Congregational..........	19	14	46	26	17	10
Disciples...............	7	4	14	10	6	4
Episcopal..............	16	9	45	25	13	6
Evangelical.............	5	3	11	1	1	1
Evangelical Free.........	6	2	1	1	1	1
Evangelical Swedish Mission Covenant.........	6	3	13	2	2	1
Interdenominational......	1	1	2	0	0	0
Jewish.................	11	9	21	13	6	1
Latter Day Saints........	1	1	3	2	2	2
Lutheran...............	88	40	175	77	48	32
Methodist Episcopal......	28	17	105	67	54	36
Missions...............	14	5	5	3	3	0
Presbyterian...........	20	13	67	37	27	11
Salvation Army..........	1	1	0	0	0	0
Spiritualist.............	5	2	2	0	0	0
Swedenborgian..........	1	1	0	0	0	0
Unitarian..............	1	1	4	4	4	4
Universalist............	2	2	9	6	5	5
Miscellaneous...........	18	9	9	7	4	0
Total.............	337	183	695	370	246	150

[1] Form 2a was sent to pastors in order to obtain listings of church organizations.
[2] Form 3 was sent only to those organizations reporting "education" as an objective on Form 1.

Table 51 shows, for example, that in the church list there are 88 Lutheran churches, of which 40 submitted lists of their affiliated organizations numbering 175. These 175 organizations were sent Form 1; 77 responses were received. Of these, 48 gave "education" as a major or minor objective; 32 responded to Form 3.

Tables 50 and 51 show 544 secular organizations and 370 church organizations, or a total of 914 groups responding to Form 1. Of these 914 organizations 710, or 78 percent, reported education as an objective. This high percentage of educationally-interested organizations seems to indicate a major interest upon the part of our adult population to continue education as an avocation.

Part II

Part II is a resume of information obtained on Form 3 which was sent to organizations listing "education" as a major or a minor objective. The number of responses to this questionnaire are recorded in Tables 50 and 51 in Part I of this study.

A. Subjects Studied, Type of Program, Methods and Means of Instruction

The subjects studied by the secular organizations were classified into 24 subject groups as shown in Table 52.

TABLE 52.—DISTRIBUTION OF SUBJECTS STUDIED BY SECULAR GROUPS (BY PERCENT)

Subject	Percent Studying Subject	Subject	Percent Studying Subject
1. Child welfare, parenthood, related educational problems..	8	12. Politics....................	.3
2. Civic and community life problems, civics, citizenship......	9.5	13. Art, literature, drama, music, etc.........................	15
3. Business, commerce, etc.......	1	14. Nationalistic cultures, patriotism......................	13
4. Education problems: teachers' methods, professional studies.	2	15. Sociology, psychology, economics, etc.....................	2
5. Character building, prohibition, purity...................	6	16. Vocations..................	.4
6. English for foreign-born, French, etc................	1	17. English, parliamentary law, public speaking............	2
7. Health.....................	1	18. Bible, religion (not affiliated with a church).............	1
8. Peace, international affairs, world friendship...........	8	19. Lip-reading, Braille..........	.3
9. Legislation, political science....	3	20. Nature study...............	.3
10. History, travel, etc...........	6	21. Current events.............	5.5
11. Homemaking, home life, home crafts, etc................	5	22. Social service..............	.5
		23. Science...................	.2
		24. Miscellaneous..............	9

Art, literature, drama, and music were the subjects of study reported most frequently by all the organizations (15 percent). "Nationalistic cultures" was reported next in frequency (13 percent). Then came subjects having to do with political and civic problems, listed as civic and community life problems; peace and international affairs; child welfare; and next subjects having to do with character building, history and travel, current events, and home making.

A broad range of subject-matter was reported by groups of organizations with the same predominant interest. The organizations classified as cultural reported studying subjects in 16 of the 24 subject groups listed; the agencies interested in community and social service studied subjects in 18 of the 24 subject fields listed. On the whole, these organizations are characterized by the diversified programs offered, and by a tendency of clubs to show the most interest in various cultural subjects and in problems having to do with civic and political problems.

The methods of instruction enumerated in Table 53 fall into many combinations. Most of those organizations which report the regular use of discussion also report the use of either a speaker or a paper. Tables showing the relationships between these methods of instruction are not included in this Yearbook; it is enough to state that discussion is almost always linked with either a speaker or a paper. There exist, however, many organizations that feel that discussion should not accompany either of these methods, as such procedure is a discourtesy to the instructor.

A study of the organizations which use but one method of instruction shows that only three groups use discussion alone, while thirty-five base their entire instructional program on lectures. Those organizations which study textbooks, reference books, or journals almost always accompany this study with two or more activities. The most common methods used are lecture, discussion, and report.

TABLE 53.—PERCENT OF SECULAR ORGANIZATIONS USING DIFFERENT KINDS OF INSTRUCTION REGULARLY

Type	Total Number of Organizations	Total Number of Regular Activities	Percent Using							
			Speaker	Discussion	Papers and Reports	Circulars	Text, Reference Book, Journal	Performance, Demonstration, Recital	Other Means	No Report
Civic................	6	9	34	11	11	11	11	......	......	22
Cultural.............	103	243	7	25	37	1	23	4	2	1
Ethical..............	18	56	4	32	34	......	30	......	......	......
Occupational.........	4	6	33	17	17	......	17	16	......	......
Patriotic............	56	157	22	8	23	7	9	18	12	1
Political............	13	50	4	24	24	16	20	12	......	......
Professional.........	16	24	38	17	17	......	8	4	8	8
Religious............	2	4	50	25	25	......	......	......	......	......
Social...............	16	30	20	23	33	6	12	6	......	......
Community and Social Service:										
a. Agencies.........	20	49	24	12	12	12	20	12	6	2
b. Groups..........	48	78	39	13	12	8	5	6	3	14
c. Institutions......	12	28	32	25	......	7	11	25	......	......
Total[1]...........	314	734	17	20	25	5	17	9	4	3

[1] 314 organizations reported 734 activities used regularly. Of these 734 kinds of instruction, 17 percent were speakers.

The church organizations reporting education as a major objective and responding to questionnaire Form 3 were classified into five groups according to educational interest. These groups were: religious, social service, academic studies in the social field, academic studies in the cultural field, and miscellaneous studies. Naturally, a large number were engaged in studies pertaining to religion; yet this group was less than half of the total number of church organizations. About one-fourth of the total number of organizations were engaged in social service studies, with a somewhat smaller proportion interested in academic studies, either in the social field or in the cultural field.

The methods and means of instruction used by the church and secular organizations are much alike.

In very few church organizations is there any remuneration paid to a leader, while in secular organizations a large percentage of the instructors receive either a fee or expenses.

B. Economic Status of Those Participating in Adult Education

This study would not be complete without revealing something of the economic status of people who take advantage of adult education activities. As a rule, the previous training of these people varies in direct relation to the kinds of occupations they profess. It is, therefore, important to know whether the adult education programs are taking care of only those who are already highly trained, such as the professional people, or whether they are appealing to the slightly trained, such as the skilled and unskilled laboring people.

The material on occupational constituency was taken from Form 1. The occupations reported were so great in number that it became necessary to group them according to level. The levels which were arbitrarily selected are listed at the top of Table 54 on page 226 and are placed in relative positions for the convenience of interpretation.

Many organizations which are composed of persons in several or all occupational levels have been classified under "heterogeneous." Housewives have been put into a separate group, because the occupation of housewife includes performances at all levels and so cannot accurately be classified within any one of the other levels.

The most significant feature of Table 54 is that the members of very few adult education organizations belong to the skilled or unskilled labor levels. No doubt some of the men in these labor levels are taking work at trade institutions, such as Dunwoody Institute; but other than this there is little educational opportunity for them. Adults of the labor levels, as a group, are probably less able to organize, finance, and study conditions for themselves than the persons on other levels, and therefore should receive added encouragement and assistance in studying governmental, economic, social, and parenthood problems. Unless the city accepts a responsibility for doing much more in adult education than is being done at present, it can hope for little progress from the present situation in the conduct of municipal and community affairs.

If the "heterogeneous" and the "housewives" groups are eliminated from the table, it will be found that nearly all of the adult education work is engaged in by persons on professional or business levels. The situation becomes more serious when it is remembered that the majority of organizations in Minneapolis are educational to some extent; it would seem, therefore, that while there are opportunities, they are not fairly distributed throughout the occupational groups.

Assuming that the number of adult education opportunities for people in the labor levels is no better provided for in a large majority of other cities than in Minneapolis, it is clear that a problem of vital significance presents itself to every community throughout the United States.

TABLE 54.—ECONOMIC STATUS OF PARTICIPANTS IN ADULT EDUCATION AS SHOWN BY OCCUPATIONAL LEVELS (BY PERCENT)

Type of Organization	Total Number of Organizations	Professional Level	Large Manager Level	Small Manager Level		Skilled Labor Level		Labor Level	Heterogeneous Level		
		Professional (Mixed)	Executive	Business (Mixed)	Clerical	Public Service	Trades	Labor	Hetero-geneous	Housewives	Students
Civic	16	30	....	33	....	......	....	......	30	7	....
Cultural	110	14	....	12	9	......	....	......	18	46	1
Ethical	19	......	....	46	....	......	....	......	8	46	....
Occupational	23	33	3	33	....	8	6	3	3	11	....
Patriotic	85	3	....	13	....	......	....	......	61	23	....
Political	14	......	....	......	....	......	....	......	100	....	....
Professional	28	76	....	15	3	......	3	......	3	....	....
Religious	4	......	....	......	....	......	....	......	50	50	....
Social	29	10	3	7	....	......	....	......	37	43	....
Community and Social Service:											
a. Agencies	26	17	....	12	....	13	....	......	43	13	2
b. Groups	170	37	....	1	....	1	....	......	45	16	....
c. Institutions	20	......	....	......	8	......	....	......	84	....	8
Total	544	24	1	11	2	2	1	1	33	24	1

Read table thus: Of the membership in the 16 civic organizations studied, whose major objective is education, 30 percent are on the professional level; 33 percent are on the small manager level; 30 percent are on the heterogeneous level; and 7 percent are housewives.

C. Adult Education Activities Carried On by Public and Endowed Organizations in Minneapolis

It was the aim of this survey to deal primarily with the informal education in organizations rather than with the formal education in schools and institutions. In order to present a complete picture of the adult education movement in Minneapolis, it is necessary to give a brief summary of school work. However, nothing is reported on schools and institutions except subject offerings. All other factors will be left for future consideration.

Although the institutions included in this study are limited in number, they are the largest and most important offering extension work. See Table 55.

TABLE 55.—ADULT EDUCATION ACTIVITIES CARRIED ON IN MINNEAPOLIS BY PUBLIC AND ENDOWED ORGANIZATIONS AND SCHOOLS

[D—Day; N—Night; S—Summer]

Activities	Extension Division, Public Schools	Public Library	Minneapolis School of Arts	Dunwoody Institute	American Institute of Banking	Y. M. C. A.	Y. W. C. A.	Minnesota College	Talmud Torah School
I. Class Instruction:									
Academic High-School subjects.	N					N	DN	....	....
Commercial subjects..........	N					N	DN	DN	....
Advanced business............					N	N		DN	....
English for the foreign-born and native illiterate..............	DN					N	N		
Fine arts....................	N			DN		N			
Home arts and maintenance...	DN					N	DN		
National cultures.............									N
Naturalization—civics........	DNS					N			
Religion.....................						DN	DN		
Vocational subjects...........	DN			DNS	N	N	N	DN	
II. Club Activities...............	DN					DN	DN		
III. Individual Instruction:									
English.....................	D					N			
Home arts and maintenance...	D								
Naturalization—civics........	D					N			
IV. Lectures....................		DN	N				DN	DN	
V. Readers' Service.............		DNS							

Summary—Among the essential findings of this survey are these:

1. Education is the avocation of hundreds of adults in the city of Minneapolis as shown by the fact that 464 secular organizations and 246 church organizations—or 78 percent of the total number of organizations contacted—reported "education" as an objective.

2. These organizations tend to concentrate on subjects of a cultural nature and subjects having to do with civic and political problems. A broad range of subjects is reported by clubs organized primarily to study specific problems.

3. The personnel of the informal education groups is drawn chiefly from the professional and managerial occupational groups, with a notable lack of members from the unskilled labor group. It is evident that the laboring man is not pursuing education through groups of the type reported here. If the laboring man is improving his educational status, it is through some other channel, perhaps through the public evening schools.

Problems deserving further study—In the course of this survey many problems such as these arose which are worthy of study:

1. Thousands of adults are banding together in clubs and organizations of various types to carry on education as an avocation. The informal nature of these organizations suggests that desire for social contact, as well as interest in education, forms a part of the urge to affiliate with such groups. If the members of these clubs were asked to give their reasons for belonging, such as reported in this study, to what extent would their purposes be social and to what extent educational?

2. This survey excludes educational enterprises operated for profit. Every large community contains many privately and commercially operated schools offering day, evening, and correspondence courses. A roster of such schools will include many ethical, worth-while organizations, but it will also include too many of the "shyster" type. These are sometimes characterized by excessive fees, by contracts regarding payments which bind the students but not the schools, by extensive advertising that is misleading, by the acceptance of students unfitted by educational background and by ability for the courses offered, and by ineffective teaching. Creditable extension and evening schools carried on through state, city, or endowed organizations have not the financial backing to advertise extensively, and thus to compete with organizations operated for money-making purposes. It would be worth while to discover to what extent adults, in their zeal for more education, are being exploited by schools of the type described, and to study methods which might be employed for controlling such schools.

———

The forms used in collecting data in the foregoing study of organized informal adult education activities in Minneapolis are presented in the following six pages.

ADULT EDUCATION SURVEY
Minneapolis Council for Adult Education
Inventory of Minneapolis Organizations—Form 1

A. NAME OF ORGANIZATION ....

B. ADDRESS................................. TELEPHONE...........

C. OFFICERS
   1. President .... Address .... Tel. ....
   2. Secretary .... Address .... Tel. ....

D. YEAR ORGANIZED...............................

E. MAJOR AND MINOR OBJECTIVES
   (The objective of an organization is the purpose for which the organization is functioning. It need not be related to the objective of the parent or affiliated organization; e. g., a club affiliated with a church may have a purely social objective.)
   Check (Major x, Minor ∨):

   Fraternal .... Political ....Educational ....
   Philanthropic ..... Civic ....Physical Training....
   Social Service...... Economic ....Social ....
   Religious .... Commercial ....Other ....

F. MEMBERSHIP
   1. Number (Include all members, both active and associate)...............
   2. Sex (Check) Men................ Women................
   3. Constituency (For example, doctors, carpenters, bricklayers, bank employees, business women, housewives, mixed, etc.)

....

   4. Distribution (Check)

   Neighborhood ....City-wide ....:County ....

   District ....

G. PARENT AND AFFILIATED ORGANIZATIONS
   (Name below in the appropriate space the parent and any other organization with which your organization is affiliated or of which it is a part.)

City .... County ....
District .... State ....
National .... International ....
Church ....

Date................. Reported by.........................

             Address............ Telephone.........

ADULT EDUCATION SURVEY

Minneapolis Council for Adult Education

Report on Organizations Which Have an Educational Objective—Form 3

NAME OF ORGANIZATION_____

ADDRESS_____TELEPHONE_____

Person Reporting_____Address_____Telephone_____
           (name)   (office)

I. INSTRUCTIONAL PROGRAM

A. Purpose

1. Definition

(State **explicitly** the purpose for which the **educational program** in your organization is functioning. If the educational purpose is stated in your by-laws, prospectus, etc., please quote, or attach a marked copy.)

_____

_____

_____

_____

2. Classification

(Please check in squares below, the purpose that characterizes or is most applicable to your educational program. Under items checked, write any descriptive comment that will make them clear.)

a. To provide for general broadening.

(In this group should be included all educational programs which are undertaken for avocational non-practical purposes.)

☐ (1) Enrichment in a specific field (i.e., the program is limited to one field of study; such as music, The Thursday Musical; art, The Sketch Club; nature, The Audubon Society; etc.)
State specifically_____
Comments_____

☐ (2) Broadening in varied fields (i.e., the subject under consideration varies from time to time or from meeting to meeting)
State specifically_____
Comments_____

☐ b. To develop skill in an occupation or other specific endeavor, such as homemaking, training for civic duties, etc.
State specifically_____
Comments_____

☐ c. To foster a point of view or specific program (e.g., certain political clubs, religious associations, etc.)
State specifically_____
Comments_____

☐ d. Other_____
Explain_____

B. Method by which group is instructed

(Check in proper space below)

	Used regularly	Used frequently	Used occasionally
1. Lecture			
2. Reading papers or giving reports			
3. Discussion			
4. Performance, recital, etc.			
5. Demonstration			
6. Laboratory (e.g., field trips, practice of any kind)			
7.			
8.			

C. Instructional means

	Used regularly	Used frequently	Used occasionally
1. Speakers			
2. Papers and reports			
3. Circulars, posters, illustrative materials (e.g., in health campaigns, etc.)			
4. Textbooks			
5. Reference books			
6. Newspapers, journals, and magazines			
7. Radio			
8. Phonograph			
9. Movies, slides, etc.			
10.			
11.			

D. Instructors and leaders

	Always	Usually	Occasionally
1. Source			
a. Members of own group			
b. From without the membership			
(1) Local (city)			
(2) Outside of city			
c.			
2. Remuneration			
a. Salary or special fee			
b. Serve without pay			
(1) Expenses allowed (e.g., transportation, meals, etc.)			
(2) No expense			

ADULT EDUCATION SURVEY
Minneapolis Council for Adult Education
Report on Organizations Which Have an Educational Objective—Form 3 (Cont.)

	Always	Usually	Occasionally
3. Qualifications			
a. Expert (professional)____			
b. Layman_____			
c. _____			
4. Other comments_____			

II. FINANCIAL SOURCES

(This should include only the financing of the **educational** program.)

A. Fees and dues_____   H. Commercial projects_____
B. Tuition_____   I. No expense involved_____
C. Contribution_____   J. Others_____
D. Collection_____
E. Subscription_____   K. Endowment_____
F. Sale of tickets_____
G. Special sales (e.g., bazaars, etc.)   (State how and by whom endowed)

III. COOPERATION WITH OTHER ORGANIZATIONS TO PROMOTE ADULT EDUCATION

	Provided by organ- ization	Accepted from other organ- ization	To or from what organ- ization	To what extent
A. Financial assistance____				
B. Talent_____				
C. Place of meetings_____				
D. Materials or equipment__				
E. Other means_____				
_____				
_____				
_____				

IV. MEMBERSHIP

(This does not necessarily include **all** members of your organization; only those who participate in your **educational** program should be included.)

A. **Qualifications for admission**
   (State any qualification for admission to educational privileges, such as religion, vocation, age, sex, education, etc.)

B. **Limit of membership**
(For example, one member from each profession; maximum limit at 50, etc.)

_____

C. **Number**

(Define what membership means)

1. Active_____
2. Associate_____
3. Affiliated_____
4. Reserve_____
5. Honorary_____
6. Other_____

D. **Attendance**

1. Numbers
(As close an approximation as possible will be satisfactory.)

Number attending regularly_____
Number attending occasionally_____
Average attendance per meeting_____

2. Devices for holding attendance; e.g., course completion, attendance certificates, fines, etc.

_____
_____

E. **Trend of membership fluctuation over last two years**
1. One hundred per cent or more increase_____
2. A substantial increase_____   4. A considerable decrease_____
3. Approximately the same_____   5. Fifty per cent or more decrease

V. MEETINGS

A. **Place** (check)
☐ 1. Homes

(State definitely; e.g., Wesley
M. E. Church, Labor Lyceum,
Summer Branch Library, etc.)

☐ 2. School_____
☐ 3. Church_____
☐ 4. Clubhouse, hall, or association building
☐ 5. Library_____
☐ 6. Neighborhood house_____
☐ 7. Commercial establishment_____
☐ 8. No regular place_____
☐ 9. Other_____

B. **Frequency of meetings**_____
C. **Hour of meeting**_____
D. **Length of meeting**_____
E. **Type** (luncheon, dinner, etc.)_____
F. **Meetings open to members only**_____
G. **Meetings open to limited groups of outsiders**_____
H. **Meetings open to the public**_____

ADULT EDUCATION SURVEY

Minneapolis Council for Adult Education

Inventory of Religious Organizations—Form 2a

NAME OF CHURCH ....

ADDRESS .... TELEPHONE...............

PASTOR ....

ADDRESS .... TELEPHONE...............

DENOMINATION.................... NATIONALITY...................

APPROXIMATE MEMBERSHIP........................

TOTAL NUMBER OF ASSOCIATIONS AND CLUBS.......................

Please give information for each organization connected with your church, as indicated below:

NAME OF ORGANIZATION..

President or Secretary.......................................

Address............................... Telephone............

NAME OF ORGANIZATION..

President or Secretary.......................................

Address............................... Telephone............

NAME OF ORGANIZATION..

President or Secretary.......................................

Address............................... Telephone............

NAME OF ORGANIZATION..

President or Secretary.......................................

Address............................... Telephone............

Date..................... Reported by.......................

Address............. Telephone.......

CHAPTER XII

A SURVEY OF ADULT EDUCATION ACTIVITIES IN THE STATE OF MINNESOTA

THIS survey covers the entire state of Minnesota, with the exception of the city of Minneapolis. The information relative to St. Paul and Duluth was obtained by making personal calls upon the persons in charge of the adult education agencies. The university activities were studied through an analysis of student records and annual reports from various departments and personal interviews with the deans of the various colleges.

The activities throughout the state were studied by the questionnaire method. First, a questionnaire was sent to all the public school superintendents asking for a report upon the activities sponsored by the schools and a list of the names of clubs, firms, and other agencies engaged in adult education. Nearly all the school superintendents responded to this request. As soon as these reports were received, other blanks requesting information were sent to the various agencies found in the rural communities.

The adult education activities divide themselves into seven types as follows:

1. Educational activities with farmers
2. Educational activities having cultural and liberalizing aims
3. Educational activities within the trades and industries
4. Education for commercial or business occupations
5. Education for the professions
6. Education for home membership and health
7. Miscellaneous educational agencies.

1. Educational Activities with Farmers

The agencies which are engaged in instructing Minnesota farmers are: (1) University of Minnesota, (2) county farm agents, (3) evening schools for farmers, (4) private utilities and industrials, (5) farm periodicals, and (6) farmers' union.

Table 56 on page 236 shows the services rendered by the Agricultural Extension Division of the University. The data concern six different activities.

According to 1925 statistics, which are the latest available, there are 188,231 farms in Minnesota. Using the farm as a unit enables one to obtain the facts that there are .25 club members per farm, .2 visits per farm, .6 telephone calls per farm, and .8 of the farms were represented by a person calling on the county agent at his office.

Of the 87 counties in Minnesota, 63 are served by county agents and 24 are not. The 24 which do not have county agents contain 27.4 percent of all the farms in the state.

TABLE 56.—SIX SERVICES, AGRICULTURAL EXTENSION DIVISION, UNIVERSITY OF MINNESOTA

Service	Number Workers	Counties Served	Number People Reached	Type Person Reached
County Agricultural Agent	66	63	47,000 club members	Rural men and women
State—County Agent Supervisor	4	....	39,548 farm visits 107,461 telephone calls 157,020 office calls 37,209 Club 4H members	Farmers Farmers Farmers
Rural—County Home Dem. Agent	10	10	9,814 enrolled in projects 85 percent completing	Farm women
City Home Dem. Agent	3	3	....	City women
Home Dem. Spec......	8	54	45,256 reached in all	City and farm women
Agri. Subj. Matter Spec.	19	63	52,081 total attendance at project meetings 58,391 total attendance at general meetings	Farmers
4H Club Work........	7 state workers 66 co. agents 35 local co. leaders	85	16,225 boys 20,984 girls Completing: 12,741 boys 16, 567 girls	Farm boys and girls 10-24 years old
Radio Publications....	25 hrs., 100 periods University staff	....	148,910 news letters 500,000 bulletins	Mostly farmers
Community Service....	....	....	Programs sent to 1,000 clubs.	....

Agricultural subject-matter experts talked to 110,472 persons. These obviously were not 110,472 different persons, as many attended more than one meeting. Five hundred thousand bulletins and 148,910 news letters were distributed. The University of Minnesota has 19 agricultural subject-matter specialists. This work is done in conjunction with other workers in the field, particularly the county agents.

A check-up on the new practices adopted by farmers revealed a total of 107,193 having been adopted. These practices consist of testing seed, treating seed for diseases, culling cows and chickens, and modifying household practices.

The following table shows the enrolment for university short courses for farmers:

TABLE 57.—ATTENDANCE IN UNIVERSITY OF MINNESOTA SHORT COURSES[1] FOR FARMERS IN 1928-1929

Activity	Total	Livestock Feeding	Dairying	Poultry	Farmers' and Home-makers' Week	Horti-cultural	Fur Farming
Short Courses...	2,363	....	116	73	1,902	166	106
Livestock Days.	1,200	1,200	(4 livestock days are held each year)				

Where a minimum of seven farmers respond to the opportunity to establish classes, a high-school teacher of agriculture organizes a class for farmers in dairying, farm management, soils, horticulture, poultry, or some other

[1] Attendance of short courses is definitely on the increase. Five times as many people attended these courses in 1928-29 as in 1909-10.

farm subject. In 1929 there were 33 such classes with an enrolment of 1,627. The ratio of men to women was 6.4 to 1.

In addition to the university representatives and the county agent working with the farmer to educate him, one must consider the less systematic work of private industrials. The work of these agencies is motivated by pecuniary gain arising from the prosperity of the farmer. This does not minimize the educational value of these efforts.

By means of full-time staffs of specialists, the railroads, the farm implement companies, and the feed companies make many contacts with the farmer. Bulletins and pamphlets reach many farmers through the energy and initiative of private companies. Table 58 shows the educational contacts made with Minnesota farmers in 1929 by private industrial agencies.

TABLE 58.—EDUCATIONAL AND INSTRUCTIONAL CONTACTS MADE WITH MINNESOTA FARMERS IN 1929 BY PRIVATE INDUSTRIAL AGENCIES [1]

Agencies	Personnel	Number of Pamphlets, Bulletins, and Folders Distributed	Monthly Publication	Livestock Placed in Minnesota	Number of Exhibit Trains	Number of Adult Farmers Visiting Exhibit Trains	Number Attending Special Days, Tractor Schools, Moving Pictures, and General Meetings
4 Railroads in Minn.	12[2]	45,000	....	Sheep— 12,920 on 374 farms Cattle— 1,695 on 380 farms[3]	7	175,000	....
Farm Implement Co.	Dealers and special men	50,000[4]	240,000 subscribers	....	....	....	216,150
N. W. Crop Improvement Assn.	Grain dealers and one full-time man (4,500 members)	500,000 (6 news stories to 1,000 newspapers 6-12 radio talks)	....				....
Minn. Crop Improvement Assn.	897 members	....	....	....	....	....	Annual Convention, Certify Seed
Livestock Breeders Assn.	....	....	....			....	Conduct Annual Meeting, and Encourage Fairs

[1] One will hardly agitate a polemical response by holding that the educational and instructional value of their work is not vitiated by their ulterior aim which is profit. Railroad and implement companies probably (they frankly admit this) operate on the basis that their prosperity depends in part at least on the prosperity of the farmer.
[2] Some of these work in other states part of the time.
[3] This is financed through the Agricultural Credit Corporation. The value of these sheep and cattle totals $308,223.27.
[4] Estimated.

The farm magazines are another source of education for the farmer.
The circulation of farm magazines in Minnesota is classified in Table 59.
The average number of magazines per farm in Minnesota is three and one-
third.

TABLE 59.—CIRCULATION OF FARM MAGAZINES IN MINNE-SOTA, CLASSIFIED ACCORDING TO SUBJECT-MATTER

Type	Circulation
Poultry...	23,947
Horticulture...	1,524
Livestock (hogs)...	8,048
Dairying...	33,775
General..	487,686
Magazine for Farmer's Wife...	71,908
Total...	626,888

The Farm Bureau, Farmers' Union, and State Horticultural Society
have 45,000 members, and their activities are shown in Table 60.

TABLE 60.—MEMBERSHIPS AND YEARLY ACTIVITIES OF FARM BUREAU, FARMERS' UNION, AND MINNESOTA STATE HORTICULTURAL SOCIETY

Organization	Member-ship	Publica-tions for Members	Personnel	Distribu-tion of Plants	Replies to Inquiries	Circulating Library Service
Farm Bureau[1].........	35,000	1 weekly 1 monthly	5 speakers addressed 375,000	....	....	....
Farmers' Union[2].......	6,000	....	....	....	....	....
State Horticultural Society	4,000	1 monthly	....	9,000	750	75-100 par-ticipating
Conference for Prevention of Rust	....	An organization working in all of Northwest. Distributes 500,000 pieces of literature and sponsors local programs.				
Total...........	45,000					

[1] Cooperates closely with county agent movement.
[2] Three hundred attended a convention and 5,000 a flower show.

2. Educational Activities Having Cultural and Liberalizing Aims

The agencies in this field cover a great variety of varied interests. The
level of instruction ranges from the most elementary to the most advanced,
from the most informal to strictly formal.

The Minnesota State Historical Society does considerable work in disseminating information relating to Minnesota history. This society is
composed of 1500 members, and was created by law shortly after Minnesota became a state. It maintains a large historical library and a museum
open to the public. In 1929 from thirty to forty thousand people visited the
museum.

Sixteen county historical societies are affiliated with the state society and cooperate with it and are helped by it in promoting interest in Minnesota and local history. These local societies hold monthly meetings, gather information about local history, and perform other activities which are designed to preserve for future generations the history of Minnesota.

Work in adult education done by colleges is given below in tabular form.

Activity	Teachers Colleges	Endowed Colleges
Summer school attended by persons employed during the remainder of the year	5	4
Part-time classes for employed persons	3	..
Evening classes for employed persons	3	1
Correspondence classes	..	1
Radio broadcasts	1	3
Short courses	..	1
Chorus work with the public	3	4
Community drama service	1	1
Open forum discussion attended by the public	1	..
Lecture series open to the public	4	8
Alumni meetings having definite educational objectives	1	2
Speakers who appear before the public with educational lectures	4	5
Library service open to the public	1	5
Specific request for information answered	4	3

Several agencies within the state are active in furnishing music education to the adult. Chorus groups, bands, and orchestras are assisting in this work, both in cities and in rural communities. Table 61 reports the groups active in adult music education.

TABLE 61.—INFORMAL GROUPS ACTIVE IN ADULT MUSIC EDUCATION IN MINNESOTA

Type	Number of Groups Reporting	Number of Persons Reached	Rural People in Group	Urban People in Group	Number of Leaders
Male choruses	25	469	286	183	23
Bands and orchestras	14	364	310	54	15
Mixed choruses	13	655	543	112	14

An extensive program of activities designed to educate the adult in a cultural and liberalizing way is carried on by various federated and independent clubs. Among these are local study clubs, the Association of University Women, Parent and Teacher Association, and the Federated Women's Clubs. The Minnesota Parent and Teacher Association circulates a monthly magazine, holds a yearly convention, and distributes literature to local associations. At present there are 500 local associations in the state. The membership is 36,633.

3. Educational Activities within the Trades and Industries

Within the trades and industries several agencies are furnishing instruction for the adult. The activities of the various agencies in this field are given in Table 62.

TABLE 62.—AGENCIES ENGAGED IN ADULT EDUCATION IN TRADES AND INDUSTRIES IN MINNESOTA

Agency	Number Reporting	Enrolment	Ages From—To	Activities
Evening Classes, Public Schools	9	308	16–52	Formal instruction in electricity, machine shop, auto mechanics, woodworking
Packing Plants........	1	Not given	All ages	Formal instruction in merchandising, packing house operation, foremanship, mathematics, by the company specialists
Radio Schools........	1	16	25–35	Formal instruction in practical radio service. A 30-day course given by two structors two evenings per week
Railroads, Mining Co., Steel Co.	11	Exact figures not given	....	Safety and first aid school for all employees. Quite informal
Good Will Industries...	2	1001 per year, 150 at any one time	All ages	Shop training of unfortunate persons in various semi-skilled trades
Aviation Schools......	2	30 by one school	Av. 25	Formal instruction in aviation ground work. Flying for private pilot
Beauty Schools.......	1	50	20–30	Formal instruction in hairdressing and cosmetology
Commercial Art School.	1	50	19–25	Formal instruction in commercial art and advertising
Popular Music Schools.	1	93	20–30	Formal instruction in popular music. Vocational objective mainly
Organizations for the Blind	2	25	All ages	Instruction in Braille, weaving, and basketry
Schools for Physically Handicapped	2	25	All ages	Instruction in toy-making, leather work, and wrought-iron work
Correspondence Schools	6 (All except one are sub-offices of main office in the East)	No exact records are available	....	Correspondence work in steam engineering
Division of Rehabilitation	....	130	18–55	Places disabled persons for training in various schools and shops
University of Minnesota[1]	....	....	....	....
Y. M. C. A..........	1	10	20–30	Offers a course in show card writing

[1] See discussion of General Extension Division.

In the field of trades and industries several magazines are active in disseminating educational material among the persons engaged in these occupations. Information relative to these periodicals is given in Table 63.

TABLE 63.—NUMBER AND CIRCULATION OF TRADE AND INDUSTRIAL MAGAZINES IN MINNESOTA

Type	Number of Magazines Reported	Circulation
Barbering and Hairdressing	3	1,295
Contracting	15	6,235
Transportation	13	3,130
Manufacturing	31	3,805
Laundry	3	263
Plumbing	3	631
Painting	2	251
Metal Working	11	696
Mining	2	609
Miscellaneous	7	2,683
Steam Engineering	1	1,670
Typographical	1	1,153
Total	92	22,421

In an evaluation of the educational opportunities provided for the adult in the field of trades and industries, it is necessary to keep in mind that in general the entrant upon one of these occupations is trained through a period of apprenticeship. This system of education has not been studied, as it classifies definitely as full-time and not as part-time training organized on the basis of giving additional opportunity for self-improvement to the employed adult.

Even though the apprenticeship training is kept in mind, the extent of the provisions for adult education in this field is not impressive. Only 1,738 adults are reported as participating in these activities. Even if the agencies that failed to report the number of persons reached are considered, the sum total of learners will be but a very small fraction of the total population belonging to this class of employed.

If the activities of the various agencies discussed in this chapter are viewed in the light of the opportunities they offer the worker for preparing himself for a change of vocation, as is so often required today in the field of industry due to changes in methods of production, the situation is far from promising. In the first place, it is quite impossible for the person living in a community away from a population center to continue temporarily in his old occupation while he prepares himself in a new occupation in anticipation of a move to the city. In view of the enormous influx of rural men and women to the city which has taken place during the last decade, it would seem that much suffering and waste of human resources could be avoided if the person moving to the city could be trained in a city occupation before he leaves his old environment.

Provisions which prepare workers for making occupational shifts in the cities are somewhat better but are far from adequate. The Good Will

Industries is organized rather definitely on the idea of helping the unfortunate and the occupational misfits make necessary readjustments on the lower occupational levels. The organizations for the blind and the handicapped aim at doing the same for those incapacitated through accident or disease.

As none of the trade schools offer any great opportunities for readjustment and the industries offer nothing in this respect, it can be said that the adult education agencies operating at present are not adequate for the training of persons who must find new types of employment.

4. Education for Commercial or Business Occupations

Within the field of the insurance business eight agencies or companies reported having classes for the salesmen employed by the specific firm. The eight agencies reporting state that 348 employees participate in the instruction offered. Seven of the companies report holding weekly or semi-monthly meetings at which the various phases of insurance salesmanship are discussed.

Among the agencies engaged in disseminating information about correct sales methods is the Twin City Sales Association. The association is reported as being "made up of salesmen who are trying to better themselves through study and seeing how real hard sales are being made." The work is done through meetings with educational programs and the study of salesmanship. The total membership is 1800, while the average attendance at the weekly meetings is about 150. Attendance at these meetings is entirely voluntary, which possibly explains the low percentage of attendance at each meeting. That many of the members follow salesmanship as a sideline is indicated by the fact that 1000 members are reported as being skilled tradesmen and 400 as being laborers.

Considerable educational work is done by the banks in the state. The banks are united into the Minnesota Bankers' Association, which has at present a membership of 954. The association is mainly concerned with informal educational activities, such as issuing bulletins on banking to the members and the holding of an annual convention which is attended by 1000 persons. The association sponsors the educational work done by the local chapters of the American Institute of Banking. The work of this institute is in the nature of formal instruction and class work in banking, commercial law, economics, negotiable instruments, public speaking, and accounting. The instructors are usually men from among the experienced bankers. Sometimes college professors are engaged to give the work.

Within the group of business concerns engaged in direct selling, several types of adult training are found. A typewriter agency reports that all the salesmen are called in on Saturday morning for a conference on sales methods and other problems pertaining to selling. In addition, each salesman receives from the home office weekly letters on salesmanship in selling the specific product of the company. Another company selling office machines gives its new salesmen a few weeks of training in the field under an experienced man and then sends them to the home office of the company for training in selling, operating, and servicing the machines. Later each salesman receives daily letters relating to new developments within the field covered by the company.

Considerable informal educational activity is carried on by the various trade associations. These trade associations represent practically every branch of business endeavor. There are between thirty and forty state trade associations and local units in the larger cities of nearly all the state groups. In turn the state associations are usually affiliated with the specific national organization.

Only ten of these trade associations responded to the request for information regarding the activities sponsored. The activities reported by these ten are all informal in nature, such as annual conventions, periodic meetings with educational programs, informational service through monthly or weekly bulletins and publication of an association paper.

A total of five weekly and seventeen monthly publications devoted to the dissemination of news and information relating to the business world are published in Minnesota. The total circulation of these publications as reported in Ayer's Directory is 74,410. A total of 159 publications of this type are reported as having a circulation of 59,416 in Minnesota. The bases for these figures are the Standard Rate and Data Service, 1929, and reports direct from the magazine publishers. Table 64 shows the classification of these magazines.

TABLE 64.—NUMBER AND CIRCULATION OF MAGAZINES RELATED TO BUSINESS

Type of Magazine	Number of Magazines	Circulation
Advertising	8	1,493
Amusements	3	1,342
Automotive Business	15	10,902
Aviation	6	3,314
Banking	7	1,132
Building Supplies	11	6,689
Bakery	3	711
Cleaning	2	295
Business Management	9	7,770
Retailing and Sales	49	15,489
Miscellaneous	11	3,752
Machinery	5	1,445
Petroleum and Oil	9	1,481
Hotels and Restaurants	5	945
Dairy Products	7	683
Insurance	5	1,234
Printing	4	739
Total	159	59,416

In Table 65 at the top of page 244 is given a summary of activities providing education for commercial or business occupations.

TABLE 65.—TYPES OF ADULT EDUCATION AGENCIES IN THE FIELD OF BUSINESS IN MINNESOTA

Type of Agency	Number Reporting	Number Participating	Activities
Insurance Co............	8	348 employees............	Instruction in insurance selling
Twin City Sales Assn.....	1	1800 members—150 per meeting	General meetings, instruction in salesmanship
Bankers Assn..........	1	954 members—1000 attend convention	Bulletin service, convention
Am. Institute of Banking.	....		Formal class work in banking
Department stores.......	3	All clerks..............	System training, salesmanship, etc.
Direct selling agencies....	3	All salesmen.............	Formal instruction in salesmanship; informal bulletin and letter service
Wholesale Co..........	1	....	....
Merchants Associations...	10	8650 members—6000 others receive bulletin service	Annual convention, bulletin, service information, service store, planning service, and merchants institutes
University of Minnesota..	....	1085 attend institutes; 100 attend small town conference (See University Extension for course work)	Institutes, conferences, information service. Formal course work
Publications.............	159	59,416 subscribers........	....

5. Education for the Professions

Comparatively few agencies in Minnesota are engaged in offering opportunities for professional improvement to the members of the professions. The University of Minnesota is the most active agency in this field.

Other activities in which the professional person takes part are membership in his respective association, attendance at the annual convention and a few local meetings, and reading of professional journals. Table 66 lists these activities.

TABLE 66.—ADULT EDUCATION ACTIVITIES OF PROFESSIONAL ASSOCIATIONS IN MINNESOTA [1]

Name of Association	Membership	Publications	Convention Attendance	Other Activities
Dental Assn.........	1,400	....	2,000	District and local meetings
Pharmaceutical Assn...	....	....	1,000	....
State Bar Assn.......	1,567	Minn. Law Review, edited and published by U. of M.	....	....
Minn. Educ. Assn.....	15,000	M. E. A. Journal to all members	5,000	Divisional meetings.
Nat. Educ. Assn.......	7,500 (Minn.)	N. E. A. publications to all members	....	....
Minn. Med. Assn......	2,052	Minnesota Medicine...	1,000	Local meetings, information service.
Minn. State Veterinary Assn.	240	....	....	Meet twice annually for clinics and lectures
Minn. Public Health Assn.	....	Everybody's Health...	....	Conducted six tuberculosis institutes for physicians.

[1] In addition to the above professional organizations, there are the Minnesota Nurses Association, the Dental Hygienist Association, and the Dental Assistants Association.

In addition to the agencies active in offering educational opportunities to the teaching profession mentioned in Table 66, the state department of education and the colleges of the state make provision for educating teachers. Five of the teachers colleges and four endowed colleges offer summer school for persons working during the remainder of the year. The state department of education conducts annually two-day county teachers' institutes for the eight thousand rural school teachers. Attendance is compulsory. Within the state department of education, a board of eight members selects certain books which are recommended to the rural school teachers for their professional reading.

Several law schools offer evening work to persons employed during the day. Only one of these schools is located outside of Minneapolis. In this school, formal instruction in law is given by judges and practicing attorneys of the city. At present two hundred men and four women are enrolled in this school. It is reported that about fifty percent of the persons entering the school drop out before or by the end of the first year of attendance, and the other fifty percent complete the course. This school charges a tuition fee for students.

The Minnesota State Medical Society sponsors the following activities:

The society publishes *Minnesota Medicine,* which goes to 2052 members.

It cooperates with the University of Minnesota in giving short courses for medical men.

It conducts an annual meeting to which the best medical men in the state and country bring the results of their latest experience and research.

It furnishes the members with prompt and confidential information on any subject relating to the practice of medicine through the Consultation Bureau.

It sends weekly health stories to 250 rural newspapers.

It maintains for the use of physicians and the public a file of information on quack cures and fake practitioners.

It gives weekly health talks over the radio.

It conducts various health tours throughout the state.

The number of professional journals entering the state of Minnesota is shown in Table 67.

TABLE 67.—NUMBER AND CIRCULATION OF PROFESSIONAL JOURNALS IN MINNESOTA

Type of Journal	Number of Journals	Total Circulation
Medicine	8	9,293
Dentistry	6	9,396
Pharmacy	3	2,814
Law	2	1,890 for one
Court Reporting	3	Not given
Nursing	4	1,253
Education	33	25,587
Engineering	12	2,108
Scientific	17	1,925

Although the agencies working with the professional groups are not numerous, there is found a certain atmosphere of intense application connected with the activities which are sponsored.

6. Education for Home Membership and Health

The activities relating to home membership and health are so closely related that they are discussed under one heading. Some of the local chapters of the Red Cross give free instruction to adults as well as to children in first aid, life saving, hygiene, and home nursing. The records are kept in such a way that it is impossible to separate adults from children. However, one chapter reported that 150 women were taking the courses in hygiene and home nursing.

One of the Y. W. C. A. units offers during the winter formal courses in sewing and food preparation. About 50 women attend these classes, for which a tuition fee is charged.

Seventeen public schools give part-time home economics instruction to 1457 housewives ranging in age from 18 to 60. Sewing, cooking, and budget making are taught in these classes.

Practically all the larger department stores offer from time to time short periods of instruction to the public in sewing, knitting, and cooking. One daily newspaper gave a course in cooking. These agencies do not have records of the number of women reached. The object of giving this work is to stimulate the trade of the store. Generally the women are required to buy the material to be used in the store offering the instruction.

The Minnesota State Department of Health has been so handicapped because of lack of funds during recent years that it has been forced to curtail its adult education activities to a great extent. The main educational activity conducted by it is that done by the Division of Child Hygiene, which has its office on the University campus. This division offers through the General Extension Division a free course in hygiene of infancy and maternity to residents of Minnesota. In 1929, 1008 women were enrolled for the course. All, however, did not complete it during the year. The same course is given in classes by four public health nurses employed by the division. The number attending these classes as well as some given by the 130 field nurses is not available. However, considerable numbers are reached by these field workers.

The Minnesota Public Health Association is active in teaching health to the general public and in supporting agencies promoting health. The association was originally organized for the purpose of combating tuberculosis. In addition to its original program, it today sponsors many other health activities. The association is composed of individuals, medical and lay, from various parts of the state. The activities are presented in outline form below:

I. Health Activities with Incidental Adult Education Features:
    A. Public Health Nursing Service:
        1. 1834 home visits
           a. 12 tuberculosis surveys made
        2. 1343 persons examined at chest clinics with incidental health instruction
        3. 17,823 school children inspected in school health surveys

B. Clinics:
    1. 1591 others given chest examinations
    2. 4517 children examined at infants' clinics
    3. 228 persons examined at orthopedic clinics
    4. 304 persons examined at eye, ear, nose and throat clinics
    5. 584 persons examined at general health clinics
C. School Health Program.

II. Educational Activities Reaching the Adult Direct:
    A. 16,096 health posters distributed
    B. 50,017 free health pamphlets distributed
    C. 16,379 health pamphlets sold
    D. 9 health films circulated among adults
    E. 195,000 copies of *Everybody's Health* (a layman's health journal)
    F. 30 exhibits at fairs
    G. 26 lectures given on health on various occasions (2546 persons attended these lectures on health)
    H. 20 or more talks on health over radio
    I. 6 tuberculosis institutes for physicians at the sanatoria in the state
    J. Sends a packet of health education material to each rural teacher in the state.

It will be noted that with the exception of the physicians' institutes, all the activities of the Minnesota Public Health Association are of an informal nature.

Classes in physical education for adults, such as swimming, golf, and fencing, are conducted by the public schools in evening classes, the Y. M. C. A., the Y. W. C. A., and other agencies.

The activities of the University of Minnesota in the field of home-making and health show that the University is a very important factor in this type of work.

Although there is in some cases a lack of intensiveness in the instructional methods used by some of the agencies in this field, the persons reporting cited various unmeasurable and subjective indications showing that the work is effective in modifying human behavior from a health and personal relationship standpoint.

7. Miscellaneous Educational Agencies

The State Department of Conservation in Minnesota does considerable educational work in preserving and reestablishing vanishing wild life.

The Division of Game and Fish publishes a monthly *Fins, Feathers, and Fur*, with a circulation of 14,000. The articles contained in it relate to the various phases of animal, bird, and water life. The staff members answer from 300 to 500 inquiries about birds and animals each year. One speaker from the division gives on an average two illustrated lectures per week before audiences ranging in size from 100 to 300 persons. The division makes exhibits at about 30 different fairs each year.

The Minnesota Division of Forestry performs work very similar to that of the Division of Game and Fish. The staff members give radio talks and lectures. These lectures are attended by about 15,000 persons annually.

The division also makes exhibits at fairs and conventions. It is estimated that about 450,000 persons visited these exhibits last year.

An activity somewhat related to the Americanization movement is the educational work done at the state prison under the direction of the superintendent of the Stillwater schools. In the evening after work, some of the prisoners are permitted to attend classes taught by certain better educated prisoners.

Within the state, the libraries are rendering valuable service to the adult public. The following libraries are doing various kinds of educational work:

125 Public libraries   1 State Traveling Library
 11 County libraries   1 J. J. Hill Reference Library
 19 High-school libraries   5 College libraries
  1 State Historical Society Library   1 University of Minnesota Library

Among the activities sponsored by 43 of the public libraries are these:

29 conduct loan service through the mails.
38 give advice to readers as to desirable reading programs.
27 give out reading lists.
40 answer verbally requests for information on specific topics.
24 answer requests for information by correspondence.
 4 give special aid by developing club programs.
 1 conducts a Missionary Reading Circle and a Child Welfare Class.
 1 sponsors all Americanization work of a city of 6000 population.
 2 send circulating sets of books to the hospitals.
 1 sends circulating sets to the factories.
 4 publish a reading list in the local paper.
 2 have a truck giving service to outlying districts.
29 offer library facilities to more than one community through loan service.

The activities reported indicate that the libraries are doing a great deal toward aiding adults in obtaining information. The type of reading done by the adult patrons of these libraries is indicated by the circulation of the various classes of books. Some of the libraries do not keep records of the various classes, but others do. The information at hand is reported in Table 68.

TABLE 68.—NUMBER OF LIBRARY BOOKS READ BY ADULTS IN MINNESOTA

Class of Books	Number of Libraries Reporting	Total Circu- lation	Class of Books	Number of Libraries Reporting	Total Circu- lation
History...............	19	15,622	Drama...............	8	2,203
Science...............	19	18,856	Literature Appreciation.	16	25,909
Biography...........	20	22,632	Religion.............	17	2,999
Travel...............	20	19,374	Geography...........	4	4,237
Sociology...........	18	42,884	Art.................	13	8,164
Psychology..........	13	3,251	Music...............	10	4,849
Education...........	6	1,407	Agriculture..........	4	1,052
Philosophy..........	11	3,273	Engineering..........	4	179
Home Economics......	7	2,176	Hygiene.............	5	399
Economics...........	7	1,873	Useful Arts (Includes Agriculture, English, Hygiene, Home Economics).............	6	6,955
Child Welfare........	6	418			

The large number of books of a liberalizing nature as contrasted to the small number belonging to the "useful arts" is worthy of note. In the library, the adult is at liberty to choose and select according to his own inclination and felt need. His selections in these cases indicate a demand for cultural and liberalizing material.

To give an impression as to the influence of the press, the various newspapers and magazines published in Minnesota with their circulations as given by the Ayer's Directory have been classified in Table 69. Nearly every

TABLE 69.—NUMBER AND CIRCULATION OF PERIODICALS PUBLISHED IN MINNESOTA

Type	Number	Circulation	Type	Number	Circulation
Collegiate.............	17	37,410	Professional and Scientific.................	17	91,542
Fraternal.............	10	122,525	Labor.................	5	14,500 [1]
Religious and Philanthropic.............	13	100,698	Travel and Sport......	5	84,595
Rural Newspapers.....	458	439,475	Very Light Fiction.....	6	559,350
Business and Industry..	27	110,635	Health...............	2	35,000
Agriculture..........	18	1,980,985	Miscellaneous.........	47	444,201
			Dailies...............	40	835,097

[1] Circulation of two labor periodicals.

rural weekly has one or more pages devoted to educational material relating to the various problems of interest to the readers. The same is true of the professional, agricultural, and other journals. The large circulation of very light fiction published in Minnesota should be noted.

The number and circulation of more or less general magazines given by the Standard Rate and Data Service as having a circulation in Minnesota show that the two leading groups are the Women's Journals and the more or less general magazines as *World's Work, Outlook,* and *Independent.*

Summary

This extensive survey of adult education activities in the state of Minnesota reveals several trends worthy of further consideration, two of which are:

1. The agricultural group is offered more extensive and better organized programs for occupational improvement than is the trades and industries group. Table 56 lists the number of well-organized services reaching thousands of farmers, while Table 62 lists only a limited number of educational agencies reaching a few hundred members of the trades and industries group. This advantage of the agricultural group extends into the field of occupational magazines. Table 59 shows a total circulation of 626,888 farm magazines, while Table 63 shows a total circulation of 22,421 trade and industrial magazines, and of this limited circulation 75 percent are for the employer and only 25 percent for the employee.

The section of this chapter treating informal adult education in the city of Minneapolis shows quite clearly that the trades and labor groups are not served by informal education such as is furnished by clubs and societies. This corroborates the findings of this particular survey. There are undoubtedly a number of reasons which account for the greater educational opportunity afforded the farmer, but the fact that he is securing superior service, as compared to those in the trades and industries, is worthy of some thought and attention.

2. While a numerical count of agencies and organizations which are offering opportunities for educational improvement or which are disseminating educational information undoubtedly gives a rough index of the interest in adult education, it gives no information as to the efficacy of the various agencies. Modern improvements in communication have made the dissemination of information relatively simple. We are constantly surrounded by radio speakers, advertisers, representatives of industrial concerns, and others who are ready to inform us. What desirable changes are wrought by our numerous adult educational contacts? What improvements in farming have been brought about by county agents, radio addresses on farm topics, or by 4H clubs?

PART III

THE RELATION OF GENERAL TO PROFESSIONAL
EDUCATION OF TEACHERS

CHAPTER XIII

THE RELATION OF GENERAL TO PROFESSIONAL EDUCATION OF TEACHERS

Introductory Statement

COMPREHENSIVELY considered, the problem dealt with in this chapter would include the education of teachers at all levels and of every type of service from the pre-school and the kindergarten to and including the university. However, since the present study was undertaken especially for the Department of Superintendence, the report submitted will confine itself to the consideration of the professional education of teachers for the public elementary and secondary schools, touching upon other phases only insofar as they influence the education of teachers in these two fields.

During and immediately following the Great War, three glaring weaknesses of our educational system became clearly evident. First, not enough teachers were available, even at the low standards for certification then in force, to staff the schools. The shortage of teachers was not confined to the elementary schools, but was present also in the high schools and colleges. Secondly, existing standards of certification were altogether too low to guarantee the selection of competent teachers; and thirdly, the salaries paid were wholly inadequate to attract to the profession persons of requisite native ability and professional equipment.

Hence, during the past ten or twelve years, attention and effort have been largely concentrated on the problem of teacher recruiting, the raising of standards of certification, and the increasing of salaries. This problem has been intensified at the high-school and college levels by the rapidly increasing enrolment in these institutions—enrolment in both the high schools and colleges having more than doubled during the past ten years.

As a result of the effort put forth, salaries have been increased, standards generally have been raised, and the problem of recruiting teachers in accordance with the standards for certification and appointment at present in force has been solved so that the difficulty is no longer one of meeting an annual shortage of teachers but of preventing a surplus beyond present and prospective needs. This problem of over-production on the basis of present standards of certification is already a crucial one in some localities, especially at the high-school level.

The need for a national survey of teacher demand and supply and some of the difficulties involved in making such a survey are discussed below.

Teacher Demand and Supply

The need for a national survey—Facts as to teacher demand and supply in the United States are so incomplete that only one definite conclusion can be drawn from them, namely, We need more facts. Fortunately, two studies to obtain facts on a nation-wide basis as to teacher demand and supply are now under way. One study is under the direction of the Committee on Economic Status of the Teacher of the National Education Association. The members of the committee are: B. R. Buckingham, Chairman; Florence Barnard, W. W. Coxe, E. C. Hartwell, J. R. McGaughy, and Frederick L. Whitney. Facts on the status of teacher demand and supply in 1929-30 have been obtained by this committee from over 40 state departments of education. It is expected that the published report will stimulate both state and local school officials to more extensive and intensive surveys of teacher personnel problems.[1]

A second source of nation-wide facts on teacher demand and supply will be the National Survey of Teacher Training. The U. S. Office of Education is proceeding "to make a study of the qualifications of teachers in the public schools, the supply of available teachers, the facilities available and needed for teacher training, including courses of study and methods of teaching," as authorized by the recent Congress with an appropriation of $200,000. William John Cooper, Commissioner of Education, is director of the survey. Edward S. Evenden is associate director. The board of consultants includes: William C. Bagley, W. W. Charters, George W. Frasier, William S. Gray, M. E. Haggerty, Henry W. Holmes, John A. H. Keith, William W. Kemp, W. P. Morgan, Shelton Phelps, and D. B. Waldo. In addition to the above advisers, a number of specialists will work out the details of the survey. The first problem of the survey is to obtain a comprehensive picture of the training, work, and personal qualifications of American teachers. Data are to be obtained from 1,000,000 questionnaires sent to teachers through the offices of local and state school officials. It is estimated that the inquiry will require three years to be completed.[2]

The U. S. Office of Education and the Committee of the National Education Association are working in close cooperation in the study on teacher demand and supply.

Common evidence on teacher demand and supply—What is the status of teacher demand [3] and supply [4] in the elementary and secondary schools of

---

[1] The appointment of this committee was authorized at the Seattle meeting of the National Education Association in 1927. Its first report will probably be available in printed form shortly before the summer meeting of the Association in June, 1931.

[2] A full statement as to the Teacher Training Survey will be found in the *Journal of the National Education Association*, December, 1930. p. 309.

[3] Demand for a given year is usually defined as the number of newly appointed teachers to care for replacements and extensions in teaching positions. Dr. B. R. Buckingham adds to this definition the number of vacancies and positions filled by temporary substitutes. Definitions in the investigations up to date do not vary widely from the first sentence above.

[4] Annual supply is commonly defined as the number of graduates of accredited teacher-training courses plus those persons certificated for the first time on the basis of examinations in place of professional preparation. Other additions to a given state's supply are those teachers entering from other states, and those returning to teaching after an absence of a year or more.

the United States? The present answers to this question are incomplete and conflicting. Let us examine some of the common sources of the conclusions that a teacher surplus exists.

1. Applications in the offices of superintendents of schools—A few city superintendents have been quoted recently as saying that they have hundreds of applicants for whom no vacancies exist. Such evidence of a surplus in a given state is inconclusive because (a) a number of these same applicants are holding positions in other cities, (b) many applicants have asked for positions in several cities, (c) a number of applicants refuse to leave the vicinity of the large city although positions exist in smaller communities of the state, and (4) much of the clustering of an "apparent" over-supply around the large cities of the United States is simply a part of the general movement of rural teachers to better paid urban positions. At the present time, New York is overwhelmed with an estimated over-supply of 4,000 teachers.[1] How many of these have refused to accept positions in up-state New York? How many of these really belong to the supply of New Jersey, Pennsylvania, Connecticut, and other nearby states? Perhaps the problem is one of distribution of teacher personnel, not of over-supply.

2. Applications in commercial placement bureaus—The reports of an over-supply of teachers in commercial placement bureaus must be discounted somewhat because of the many duplications. Teachers often have their records on file at several placement offices and fail to report back when employment is obtained.

3. Applications in placement bureaus of teacher-training institutions— The same points apply here as were presented in (2) above. In addition, training schools have to contend with two types of unemployed students: (a) Those with peculiar types of training for which no real demand exists, and (b) those who refuse to leave the vicinity of the training school. Both types are really not a part of the supply [2] because they cannot or will not put themselves "in the market."

4. Number of applications for a particularly attractive position—A state superintendent in the Far West recently reported that there were over 200 applications for a particular principalship in his state. This rush for a single position may indicate only an alertness on the part of placement bureaus. Furthermore, the major portion of the applications in the above case were from persons in other states. In other words, a surplus in one state may flow over and disturb the teacher demand and supply equilibrium in another state.

5. Number of persons granted teaching certificates—Sometimes the number of licenses issued in a given year by certification agencies is compared

---

[1] Based on statements of school officials as reported in the *New York Times* during the spring of 1930.

[2] See the definition of supply given on opposite page. In economics the supply is "that part of the commodity offered on the market," not the total amount of the commodity in existence.

with the annual demand. Such comparisons are apt to be misleading because of (a) extensive changes in certification laws, and (b) the large demand for state certificates by outsiders. An example of the first condition is the "up-grading" of many teachers in Indiana and Illinois during the past few years. The imposition of higher professional standards has required many persons in service to exchange their old licenses for new certificates. A report of total certificates, therefore, includes many renewals, who are really not a part of the new supply.

Examples of factor (b) above are the states of California, Colorado, and Arizona. These states issue certificates to many outsiders who want to go West for health and climatic reasons. Obviously, such persons are not always a part of a particular state's available supply. Certainly, the total number of certificates cannot be compared directly with the annual demand.

6. *Number of persons completing teacher training*—Often the number of graduates of teachers colleges in a state is taken as the annual supply of new teachers. At the present time, this number is probably the best single index of supply. Yet the number of graduates is not entirely exact, because of the number who drop out for such reasons as marriage, death, placement in private school teaching positions, removal to other states, and continuance of professional study. Table 70, from Myers' study[1] in Ohio, partially supports this point.

TABLE 70.—NUMBER OF TEACHERS TRAINED IN OHIO
IN 1925-26

Type of Training Agency	Number Trained	Number Known to Be Teaching in Ohio Public Schools	Probable Number Teaching in Ohio Public Schools
1	2	3	4
State institutions	1,309	792	1,026
Municipal universities	172	153	153
City normal schools	207	136	136
Denominational and endowed colleges	1,697	878	973
Catholic colleges and normal schools	182	3	3
Private kindergarten schools	143	84	84
Private commercial colleges	104	53	62
Private special schools	57	27	27
Total	3,871	2,126	2,464

Does research indicate that there are inarticulations between teacher demand and supply in various states?—Since nation-wide data do not exist, it is necessary to cite several state studies to indicate the inarticulation between the demand of the public schools for teachers and the supply from teacher-training institutions. The purpose of this section is not to prove that either a surplus or a shortage of teachers exists. Such proof awaits the collection of more extensive and more exact data. It may be added, however, that several studies show *a surplus of persons with licenses to teach,*

[1] Myers, Alonzo F. *A Teacher Training Program for Ohio.* Contributions to Education, No. 266. New York: Bureau of Publications, Teachers College, Columbia University, 1927. p. 63-65.

although there is *a widespread shortage of teachers with adequate professional preparation.*

Buckingham's pioneer study in Ohio in 1923-24 shows a shortage of teachers. These data are given as Table 71. It should be noted that Buckingham includes an estimate of 775 vacancies among the demand. On the supply side the study did not include persons who were prepared for teaching in other than accredited teacher-training colleges.

TABLE 71.—RELATION BETWEEN TEACHER DEMAND AND SUPPLY IN OHIO IN 1923-24 [1]

Demand and Supply	Number	Total
Demand:		
Total number of new teachers appointed............................	5,593	
Estimated number of vacancies....................................	775	
Total..	....	6,368
Supply:		
Graduates (1923) who taught in Ohio.............................	2,987	
New teachers trained in other states..............................	772	
Non-graduates having one year of training.........................	1,100	
Total...	....	4,859
Excess of the demand over the supply.............................	....	1,509

[1] Buckingham, B. R. *Supply and Demand in Teacher Training.* Bureau of Educational Research Monographs, No. 4. Columbus, Ohio: Ohio State University, March 15, 1926. p. 48–49.

Other inarticulations between teacher demand and supply include (1) the distribution of teachers between rural and urban school systems, (2) the competition between private and public training schools, and (3) the irregular distribution of persons preparing to teach the various high-school subjects. These points may be brought out by quoting from Buckingham's findings as follows:

1. A shortage of trained teachers existed for positions in one-room rural, graded elementary, junior high, and senior high schools.

2. Over one-half of the new appointees in the junior high school and approximately one-fifth of the new high-school appointees in 1923-24 were drawn from other parts of the school system. The question is raised as to whether these schools should be allowed to fill their needs at the expense of other branches of the service.

3. The supply of kindergarten teachers who were graduates of private institutions was sufficient to supply the entire needs of the state.

4. Among subject teachers the supply of those who majored in chemistry, English, French, German, sociology, and Spanish greatly exceeded the demand. The opposite was true with respect to commercial subjects, drawing, manual training, physical training, and especially general science, geography, and physiology.

5. Little was being done in the way of educational guidance for students in training, and information which would make possible the right type of guidance was lacking.

Peik's recent study [1] in North Dakota shows how prolific teacher-training agencies can produce an over-supply. An adaptation of his data is shown in Table 72.

TABLE 72.—TEACHER DEMAND AND SUPPLY IN NORTH DAKOTA IN 1929-30

Type of Position	Number of Positions	Need for New Teachers	Graduates of Teacher-Training Institutions	Surplus of Teachers
1	2	3	4	5
Rural elementary...............	4,361	978		
Graded elementary..............	2,603	334	1,918	606
High schools...................	1,570	273	551	278
Total..................	8,534	1,585	2,469	884

A quotation from Peik's recommendations will illustrate a few of the inarticulations between demand and supply in North Dakota. Once again the point must be made that these facts cannot be generalized to apply to all states of the United States. Conclusions on this point await further research. We are safe in saying that similar inarticulations do exist in many states. Peik recommends:

1. Careful state financial administration of schools because the rurality of the state in general will necessitate a relatively higher per pupil cost to obtain educational opportunities for its children to approach or equal those of more densely populated states. This policy should extend to the administration of teacher-training institutions.

2. An annual factual self-survey of all state teacher-training institutions, with the use of more carefully prepared, detailed, uniform reports than hitherto furnished by each institution to the Board of Administration. The compiled reports to furnish the basis for policies of expansion or retrenchment after careful study and discussion in a conference of all institutional heads and the Board of Administration. Types of records are suggested.

3. A state supervised, integrated program of teacher training which coordinates the program of each institution with the others to fit the demands and needs of the entire state system of public schools without overproduction and unnecessary duplication. The aim is to build a program of high quality at minimum cost under state supervision which will advance as rapidly as possible the present standards to the needs indicated.

4. A more intensive program of professional training for rural teachers of open country schools on the part of normal schools and teachers colleges.

5. Modification of the certification law to fall in line with integrated state program of teacher training is recommended.

Urgency of the Problem and Complicating Factors

If a great oversupply of teachers does exist, the outcome is likely to take one of three possible directions. First, through the sharp competition of the large and increasing surplus of candidates for the available positions, a general lowering of salaries will result, together with an increasing temptation to political interference with the appointment of teachers and a corre-

---

[1] Peik, W. E. *The Training of Teachers in North Dakota.* Unpublished study made for the North Dakota State Board of Administration. 1930. 58 p. mimeo.

sponding depression of the spirit and morale of the teaching profession and of the desirability and personal fitness of those who enter it.

The second possibility would be the immediate recognition, by the agencies now engaged in the preparation of teachers, of the present situation and the crisis to education in general and to the teaching profession in particular, which it involves, and the necessity of decreasing by properly directed joint effort the present rate of teacher production, especially for secondary schools.

The third possibility, and for every reason a supremely desirable one, is that, first, of providing and maintaining salaries and other conditions at a level that will continually attract into teaching, in competition with other available occupations, the most desirable type of people on the score of native ability, personal fitness, and professional equipment; and secondly, of raising and keeping the standards of professional preparation and personal fitness at such a level as will guarantee the selection and availability of such a number of those who are best qualified as will not be too much in excess of the actual need.

Evidently the best solution of the problem would involve a satisfactory combination of the second and third of these possibilities.

Complicating factors—While the problem is concerned with the preparation of teachers both prior to their appointment and while engaged in service, it is especially complicated at the pre-service stage by a number of conditions which must be considered:

First among these may be mentioned the absence of any well-defined and generally accepted educational policy. Programs of education, organization of effort, the nature of the work to be done, the character and quality of the service needed, and the best equipment of those who are to render that service, all should depend upon a well-defined conception of the place and function of the public school among the other fundamental agencies and interests of modern life. The fact that we have no generally accepted philosophy of public education complicates the problem of teacher preparation. Not only must we inquire what knowledge is of most worth for children of our schools to have, but also what outcomes other than knowledge are supremely worth while in their education and what kind of teacher preparation is best suited to guarantee these results.

A second complicating factor is the changing nature and content of the accepted fields of experience from which the materials of education are chiefly drawn and the relative importance of these materials in relation to the activities and purposes of life. How shall such materials be selected and taught, and how shall teachers be prepared to teach them properly? New discoveries of science are constantly being made and strenuous effort put forth to make each new discovery minister in some way to ever-changing and increasing needs and desires. The prevailing philosophy of life at any time is determined by the values which people recognize and appreciate. These values grow out of the active experiences of life which are determined by the conditions under which people live. These conditions are constantly changing. The practical philosophy of life by which the conduct and appreciations of people are governed cannot under these circumstances remain fixed. Twenty-five percent of the occupations in which men and women are now engaged were wholly unknown thirty years ago. Conclusions of science taught to freshmen in high school or college as valid and true may have to be considerably revised before these students graduate and enter into occupations in which such conclusions are supposed to be applied.

How, then, shall proportionate emphasis upon general and professional education of a high-school teacher, for example, be announced in any authoritative way when the place and function of the high school must necessarily undergo continued revision with varying emphasis upon what is taught? Old subjects of instruction suffer decline and pass out, new subjects are introduced, and other receive a new emphasis. Methods of learning once chiefly cared for outside must now be provided for to a large extent inside the schools. The question then turns not simply upon the amount of general education but upon the kind of general education the teacher should have in order to render the needed service. What place should the teacher be prepared to occupy, not only in the schools, but as a worthy and valued member in the life of the community? What should be his equipment in knowledge, technical skill, general culture, personal characteristics, and his philosophy of life and education? In what ways should this equipment vary with change of school level and type of occupation for which the teacher is being prepared on account of changing conditions and the need of progressive adaptation of the work of the schools to the changing requirements? Continuous change and modification in the work of the schools calls for corresponding readjustment of our conceptions and practices in the education of teachers. What may be considered satisfactory at one time in one community or under one set of conditions cannot necessarily be so regarded for another. The problem must be continuously studied, relative emphasis changed, readjustments made, and the foundation and disposition for continuous growth and improvement of the teacher in service established. The general and subordinate problems of teacher education may be defined and the principles in accordance with which their solution may be progressively sought can be stated, but the notion of finding any particular solution that is always and everywhere applicable should be abandoned as unnecessary and undesirable. Such a notion tends to promote a fixed point of view and procedure in the education of teachers for a service that under existing conditions should be constantly changing and adaptable.

A third complicating factor is found in the agencies that are relied upon for the education of teachers. It is practically useless to set up a program for the professional education of teachers indicating what relation should hold between the general and professional factors in such education without taking into account the character and relation of these agencies, since they must be relied on to make any such program effective. The established psychology of these agencies and its effect cannot be overlooked. The nature, accepted function, present attitude, developing tendencies, and relative influence of these agencies must be studied to determine the extent to which they can and should be relied upon to assist in setting up a satisfactory program of teacher education and to cooperate without unnecessary waste of energy or duplication of effort in carrying such a program into effect. The agencies that should be considered are both direct and indirect.

Direct agencies—Of the direct agencies there are three general sorts: (a) those which are concerned with the certification of teachers for the public schools and the determination of standards for this purpose, (b) those which are engaged in the pre-service education of teachers, and (c) those which are responsible for the growth and improvement of teachers in service. Let us consider these in this order.

(a) One of the greatest difficulties in carrying into effect a satisfactory program of teacher education in many states at present is the number and variety of the agencies authorized to certificate teachers and the diversity of standards actually employed for this purpose. There is the greatest confusion, both in theory and practice, as to what these standards should be. In some states, a hundred or more different agencies are authorized to certificate teachers. In such states, anything approximating uniformity of standards is out of the question and those who are authorized to grant certificates are often wholly incompetent to determine what standard requirements should be. Local prejudice or political influence of one sort or another is often the deciding factor. Under these conditions the agencies engaged in the pre-service education of teachers, no matter how worthy or how well prepared their graduates may be, have no assurance that the schools will be permitted to use their services, for there is no certainty that those who are best prepared will be certificated and appointed.

A nation-wide study of present practices in teacher certification is needed to determine the nature of these practices, the directions in which they are changing, the improvements that are being made in the definition of standards, and the relative emphasis that is being placed on general and professional elements in the certification of teachers both for the elementary schools and for the high schools. The study should summarize the information available and discover the additional facts necessary for a full statement of what is now done, and point the way to the needed improvement of present practices, and more effective cooperation of certificating agencies with the institutions engaged in the education of teachers.

(b) The institutions whose effective cooperation is required in the pre-service education of teachers for the public schools are chiefly the public normal schools and teachers colleges, both state and municipal; colleges of education in state universities, and privately endowed colleges of arts and science. That normal schools and teachers colleges should contribute to the solution of problems of teacher preparation goes without saying. This is their supreme and only function. They have been created and are supported by the state for this purpose. The contribution of arts colleges must also be studied to determine their desirable place and part in the whole program of teacher education. To an extent often little understood or appreciated even by themselves, many of these colleges are primarily institutions engaged in the preparation of teachers. Their resources and energies as a matter of fact are chiefly devoted to this work.

In a study made by the Research Division of the National Education Association for this Committee and reported in the 1929 Yearbook of the Department of Superintendence, it was found that for the five-year period from 1923 to 1927 inclusive, 199 arts colleges, representing 38 states and the District of Columbia, graduated 83,472 with baccalaureate degrees and that 37,896, or 45 percent, of these went into teaching the first year after their graduation. A number of these colleges reported that 100 percent of their graduates during that period went into teaching, and 30 of the list sent more than 80 percent of their graduates into this work.

A study of professional curriculums for the pre-service education of teachers for different levels and types of teaching service in the public schools is needed. The direction in which the best present opinion and practice of the profession are moving in the construction and administration of such curriculums should be pointed out.

An up-to-date study is needed of what is actually being done in the way of the education of teachers, making generally available any new tendencies that may be in evidence with regard to the relation of cultural and technical aspects in such education. This study should reveal many new tendencies that may be in evidence with regard to the relative emphasis upon cultural and technical subjects in these new curriculums.

(c) The problem of every institution which prepares teachers should be twofold: first, that of providing the best preparation possible for its students; and second, the adjustment of its graduates to teaching.

Practice facilities in most institutions are at best somewhat artificial, and students rarely experience true classroom conditions until they are actually placed as teachers. The wide variety of situations in the field also makes it difficult to prepare students for successful teaching. Furthermore, all teachers, regardless of how complete their pre-service preparation may have been, need continued stimulus to professional growth. More help should be given to experienced teachers in making adjustments to new positions and in meeting the demands of continually changing educational programs. That teachers themselves feel the need of in-service preparation is evidenced by the fact that in a total of 649 summer schools in 1930, 273,494 teachers, or 29 percent of the teaching body of the United States, were enrolled in courses in education.

Careful study is needed to determine what differentiation is needed between types of courses offered for the initial preparation of prospective teachers and those offered for the advanced and "continuation" training of teachers who have had experience.

The in-service courses offered by any local institution should be planned through conferences with local school authorities—superintendent, supervisors, and principals. At present, "the consumer's viewpoint" is too often not fully taken into account in planning the field services of a teachers college.[1] These services might also be extended to include such helps as research projects, regional conferences, educational clinics, circulation of selected bibliographies and professional books, and assistance to local course-of-study committees.

Intensive research is needed relative to the range of in-service opportunities provided and to determine the most efficient organization and administration of programs offered.

Indirect agencies—One does not go very far in his study of the work of arts colleges and teachers colleges in the preparation of teachers until he discovers that consideration must also be given to the contributions of graduate schools of education and graduate schools of arts and science, for both of these are indirectly involved in determining the relative emphasis actually placed upon general and professional education in the preparation of teachers for the elementary and secondary schools. It is in institutions of both of these types that the teachers of arts colleges, normal schools, and teachers colleges are prepared for their work. It is interesting to note the extent to which the energies of the graduate schools of arts and science in American universities are being devoted to the education of teachers. As reported by R. L. Kelly in an article on "Educating the Educators" in the Bulletin of the Association of American Colleges,[2] from 60 to 80 percent of the Ph.D. graduates of American universities are going into college teaching as a career.

A fourth factor complicating the problem is the presence and outworking of two ideals of education and the inevitable influence of these ideals on the preparation of teachers. Both of these ideals are important. How to integrate their presence and influence in a satisfactory program for the preparation of teachers is a vital question. The first ideal emphasizes scholarship, learning and culture, pure science, and knowledge chiefly for its own sake. This ideal in its historical evolution is academic in method and selective in character and purpose. The second ideal grew out of the essential principles of democracy as these were understood and practiced in the early development of the American nation. It therefore naturally found its first expression at the level of elementary education. It is the ideal of universal education, not merely for the benefit of any individual or class of individuals, but for the protection and safety of the state as a whole and its efficient functioning as a democratic society. It therefore places emphasis not primarily upon knowledge and culture for their own sake, but upon these in the sense and to the extent that they minister to a richer and fuller life of the people collectively and individually. In this ideal, knowledge, culture, and scholarship are treated as means to desirable ends and not as ends in themselves.

---

[1] There are notable exceptions. For example, see the report in the November and December, 1929, issues of *The Elementary School Journal* of how the Massachusetts State Normal School at Westfield plans conferences to meet the needs of its recent graduates.
[2] Kelly, Robert Lincoln, "Educating the Educators." *Association of American Colleges Bulletin* 15:342-79; November, 1929.

The first ideal gave us originally our colleges and universities, and the second our public schools. The first began at the top of our educational system and moved downward, and the second at the bottom and moved upward.

The influence of these two ideals upon the development of education in general and upon the education of teachers in particular is well illustrated in the educational system of Pennsylvania. In that state the first ideal took precedence historically over the second. Pennsylvania had colleges and universities to the number of twenty or more in full operation before the public school system of the state was established. It had colleges and universities before 1800, but it did not get its public school system until 1834.

In the establishment of secondary education in Pennsylvania, the original motive was the discovery and preparation of students for satisfactory work in college. Colleges were therefore first to extend their influence, and consequently their ideal of academic scholarship, into the field of secondary education. The teachers of secondary schools were trained for their work in the colleges with emphasis naturally upon scholarship of the type in which the colleges at the time were especially interested. Under this ideal and the influence of the college spirit, these teachers naturally introduced into the secondary schools the objectives of the colleges, their general point of view, and their methods of work. The colleges originally had little or no interest in the preparation of teachers for the elementary schools. For this purpose the state had to establish its own agencies.

The first real confusion in the outworking of these ideals occurred where the elementary schools were joined to the high schools. And the confusion grew out of the effort to extend the democratic ideal upward to include secondary education. Both Philadelphia and Pittsburgh had for many years a superintendent of elementary schools and also a director of high schools, and in both cities the director of high schools dictated to the superintendent of schools the conditions under which graduates of the elementary schools could be admitted to the high schools. The resulting problem of integration has only recently been worked out in these two cities and in each of them this has been brought about largely by the influence of the democratic ideal in its extension upward, and in part by the introduction of the junior high school as an integrating agency.

The confusion as to the place and relative importance of these two ideals, however, still exists in greater or less degree in many high schools of Pennsylvania and in other states. It constitutes a fundamental problem of present-day secondary education. The one ideal emphasizes the function of selective education and regards the high school as chiefly an institution for the selection and preparation of young people for higher learning in colleges and universities, and the other emphasizes universal education and regards the high school as an institution whose primary purpose is that of preparing adolescent boys and girls with different interests and abilities for the part which they are to play in life, whatever that part may prove to be.

The professional education of teachers as a distinct undertaking and the establishment of agencies and of curriculums for this purpose began at the level of elementary education. When the democratic ideal pushed its way into secondary education and public high schools were established, the state did not at the time extend its program of teacher training upward to prepare teachers for these schools, but called upon the colleges for this service. The colleges responded to the call and up until a year or so ago the state relied almost wholly upon these agencies for its supply of high-school teachers. Consequently the teachers who had been employed in the public high schools as well as those employed in the private preparatory schools have been inclined to emphasize subject-matter and the education of a selected group preparing for college rather than the educational needs of all the students admitted to the high schools, regardless of whether they were going to college or not.

As the democratic ideal became more and more prominent in the recognized functions of the public high schools and in the determination of their general policy and programs of study, the inadequacy and unsuitability of this unmodified type of teacher preparation have become increasingly apparent. Nevertheless Pennsylvania has, practically up to the present time, relied almost wholly upon the colleges of the state for its supply of high-school teachers. These institutions are now practically supplying this need, and the indications are that the supply from this source alone will exceed the demand in the immediate future, if present certification standards remain unchanged. Meanwhile thirteen state normal schools have been converted into state teachers colleges offering four-year curriculums. and also authorized to prepare teachers for the high schools. A surprisingly large percentage of the students now enrolling in these institutions intend to become high-school teachers and have no intention, apparently, of teaching in the elementary schools.

It is clear, therefore, that under present conditions Pennsylvania is definitely headed toward an available supply of high-school teachers greatly and increasingly in excess of the demand, and consequently the problem of articulating the agencies and adjusting the conditions in the preparation of secondary teachers for the state is one of real and immediate importance. It is not easy to say what its solution will be. Many difficult questions will have to be answered. For example: Is the professional education of high-school teachers that is being furnished by the arts colleges unsatisfactory? If it is, what is wrong with it? Can it be made satisfactory? If it can be, should the state continue to rely upon these institutions to prepare its public high-school teachers? Is the unsatisfactory service of these institutions such as to justify the state in ultimately taking over entirely the professional education of all teachers for the public schools? Is the situation one that calls for the increased expenditure of public funds that this would require? What, in fact, are the essential requirements in the professional education of teachers for the high schools, and what is the proper relation of professional to academic or cultural education? Is the right solution of this problem one that can best be worked out by a shared responsibility and distribution of function and of effort between the teachers colleges and professional schools of education and colleges devoted to academic and cultural education? If so, how should such distribution be made? What kind of cooperation should be followed? How can misplaced and wasted energy be avoided? Those who are responsible for Pennsylvania's program of teacher education must face the necessity of giving immediate and serious attention to the solution of this problem.

As already indicated, Pennsylvania does not stand alone in this matter. What is true there is either true now or rapidly coming to be true in many states. To some extent this problem must be dealt with in practically every state where four-year state teachers colleges have been established and where graduates of arts colleges are also being certificated for service in the high schools.

A fifth complicating factor is involved in certain institutional prejudices and points of view. Largely owing to the presence of the two ideals of education already pointed out and their influence on the historical development of American colleges and normal schools, certain conditions have resulted which make it difficult and at the same time highly desirable that arts colleges and teachers colleges should cooperate more closely than they have hitherto done in working out a satisfactory program of teacher education for public schools.

Teachers colleges have only recently and rather suddenly been transformed from two-year normal schools, charged with the preparation of elementary school teachers, into four-year institutions authorized to grant baccalaureate degrees—and some of them master's degrees—and to educate teachers for high schools. These degrees have been long years in existence; they have developed in the colleges and universities and have gained a certain prestige which the colleges naturally wish to maintain with lustre undimmed. Moreover, normal schools suddenly converted into teachers colleges are apt to be thought of as still only normal schools and therefore academically unworthy of being admitted to a full standing among colleges.

On the other hand, these converted institutions show a tendency to demonstrate their own worthiness of such standing and to show that their baccalaureate degree is not in reality inferior to that of the arts colleges. They endeavor to do this by pointing to their faculties and comparing them with the faculties of the arts colleges as to the degrees they hold, especially the percentage of Ph.D. degrees. In doing this the natural, not to say inevitable, outcome is a strong tendency to emphasize in these teachers college degrees that which is prominent in the arts college degrees with which they are compared; namely, the amount, quality, and kind of academic scholarship which they represent. This tendency, wherever it exists, is away from the claim by which the coming of teachers colleges into the field of preparing high-school teachers has been justified and toward the very thing which they have opposed as inefficient preparation for high-school teaching on the part of the arts college graduate; namely, an over-emphasis upon academic scholarship to the neglect of teaching ability. This tends to befog the issue as to what really constitutes the best professional education of high-school teachers.

The situation thus brought about is confusing and unfortunate for another very important reason. It centers attention of the teachers colleges too much upon the problem of educating teachers for high schools and diverts an undue portion of their energy toward solution of that .problem to the corresponding neglect of the large elementary school field, where there is no controversy and where the responsibility of teachers colleges for the education of elementary teachers is practically unchallenged.

The elementary school field is therefore in grave danger of not receiving the sort of teacher preparation that it needs. Moreover, the tendency referred to misses the essential meaning of the problem and fails to concentrate energy and effort at the point where they are needed; that is to say, not upon mere academic respectability but upon the proper determination of what really constitutes most effective professional education, how to go about providing it, and what study should be made to answer objectively and by truly scientific methods the subordinate questions as well as the main issues at stake. Attention is centered too much in this way upon the mere fact of a degree, without proper consideration of what the degree in any case really means, and what its value is in deciding the fitness to teach of the person who holds it.

Functions of Teacher Education

A program of teacher education has six main functions. These may be briefly described as follows:

The first function of a program of teacher education is to provide a reasonable mastery of the subject taught and of subject-matter related to it. The demands upon a teacher in any field require a broad and deep reservoir of knowledge which may serve not only his regular daily needs as a classroom teacher, but which may be used as an emergency supply of information and understanding. Parallelism, comparison, and contrasts are effective in their proper time and place in teaching. Hence the need for a reasonable mastery of related subject-matter in addition to scholarship in a given field of knowledge.

The second function of teacher education is to assist each prospective teacher in the formulation of a definite philosophy of education. This is the practical application of a philosophy of life to a special field of service. Human beings are guided by some standards of conduct, even though unconsciously. He who knows his purposes, outlines a plan of action, and executes a program of daily conduct in terms of his plan and purposes, achieves his goal. Education as the fundamental basis of social progress must have just this kind of leadership. And the followership must have an intelligent appreciation of the purposes, plans, and programs advocated by the leaders. Hence the importance of a definite philosophy of life and of its application to the field of education.

The third function of teacher education is to provide a thorough understanding of child nature. The teacher must understand the physical, mental, and emotional aspects of child development if stimulation, encouragement, and guidance are to be effective in child growth.

The fourth function of teacher education is development of powers of evaluation. Knowing subject-matter and child nature, and possessing a working philosophy of life, the teacher then faces the obligation of selection. What subject-matter will function now or later? How can it be organized most usefully? What methods will be most effective? When shall the child be introduced to particular subject-matter? To what extent shall repetition occur? How shall curriculum materials be coordinated and integrated? Curriculum construction and methods of teaching are not routine matters. They demand a deep and extensive education such as will develop powers of evaluation.

The fifth function of teacher education is training in professional ethics. This phase of education is based on ideals of conduct with respect to working relationships among members of the profession. To illustrate, rumor has it that a certain position will be vacant soon. What should the anxious and ambitious aspirant for that position do in this case? Unfortunately, home education, active participation in community affairs, or observation of professional workers in other fields does not always enable the prospective teacher to decide wisely in such a case. The responsibility of providing instruction of this kind lies in programs of teacher education. Just as there are ethical standards in other professions and ideals of conduct for the everyday world, there must be an ethical code for the profession of teaching. It must be founded on ideals, consciously formulated, and on habits of action grounded in reflection and practice.

The sixth function of teacher preparation is education for life outside the classroom. The five points mentioned above relate to the vocational interests of teachers. There are, however, many obligations that make their demands in the non-vocational or avocational life of teachers. Social life in the home, community problems, economic, political, and social questions that reach beyond neighborhood or local community boundaries, all of these call for wide information and a well-balanced sense of personal responsibility. Education for teaching that neglects these demands falls far short of the mark. Professional education and non-vocational education have mutual values for the purposes of each. But these purposes will be realized more effectively if programs of teacher education set up one group of studies directed primarily to the ends of one, and another group to the ends of the other. Furthermore, the teacher who establishes himself as a valuable member of society, apart from his profession, commands a degree of respect and confidence that inevitably wins lay support for organized education. His work as a teacher, therefore, becomes increasingly effective as he merits the badge of worthy community membership.

The foregoing statement of the functions of teacher education presupposes a program of continuous education for teachers irrespective of the length of pre-service training. Knowledge which makes it possible for the teacher to do a better job of teaching is increasing so rapidly that systematic attempts to keep abreast of the times are essential to the professional life of the alert teacher. On the side of the teacher's non-vocational education, the development of intellectual interests, the extension of boundaries of knowledge, and the increase in the understanding of the world in which we live have no end. Hence the need for a program of in-service teacher education that is continuous and coordinate with the pre-service program.

Principles Underlying Solution of Problems Relating to the General and Professional Education of Teachers

The Committee offers no formula for the solution of the many problems that arise out of the relation of professional to general education in the preparation of teachers. Instead, it presents the following twelve general principles which underlie their solution.

1. *Problems must be solved in the light of a total education program for teachers.* Total education should be conceived as professional and non-professional or avocational. Professional education should consist of (a) a reasonable mastery of subject-matter to be used and of related knowledge, (b) a comprehensive understanding of modern life and its relation or application to educational procedures, (c) the acceptance, in terms of habitual usage, of a body of professional ethics, (d) skill in methods and in the use of special devices, and (e) a thorough knowledge of child nature. These five points are not mutually exclusive and are intended mainly to clarify the definition of professional education.

Non-professional or avocational education should be concerned primarily with worthy community membership. It will consist of the development of (a) intellectual interests, (b) aesthetic appreciations, (c) high ideals of conduct, (d) habits of effective thinking, and (e) habits of active sharing in community responsibility. These outcomes are also to be sought in professional education. There is an advantage, however, in making a separate classification of education designed with primary emphasis on preparation for life outside the school requirements—even though each type of education overlaps the other and is of immense value to the other.

2. *A program of total education should lead to constant observation of changing life and its bearing on education.* Conditions and trends in modern civilization will serve as guides to an immediately practical program of education. This point need not run counter to idealism, especially if the progress of civilization is conceived as a gradual and long-term evolution of practice. Change is inevitable, and schools as social agencies must meet the new conditions and needs of society. The acceptance of this principle presupposes the ability to understand life and, what is perhaps more important and more difficult, the wisdom to apply this understanding to educational program-making and administration.

3. *Professional education should lead the teacher to an appreciation of the child as an integral part of society.* To educate the child for the present or for his future life is a futile distinction. Both are necessary. Competent foreign students of American education have made the observation that our teachers seem to think of the child as a thing apart from society, something that must be molded or fashioned in such a way that he may be fitted into some pattern of society at the end of his formal education. This practice, if general, is deplorable. Teachers must visualize human society as a whole and each child as an important unit of the whole.

4. *Professional education should produce inspired leaders as well as skilled technicians.* The imponderables of personal influence made effective through high ideals, advanced intellectual achievement, and exemplary conduct give substance to inspirational leadership. This leadership may be subtle; it may operate inconspicuously; but it constitutes the essence of art in teaching. Science and art must go hand in hand. In our commendable eagerness to develop a science of education, the importance of the present immeasurable aspects of teaching must not be disregarded.

5. *A program of total education for teachers must recognize the inescapable demand for continuous growth.* No program of preliminary education can be even temporarily satisfactory. Developments in the science of education, to say nothing of changing conditions of civilization, make continuous education imperative. Standards related to the preliminary or pre-service education of teachers constitute an immediate, practical problem, but along with this pressing question attention must be centered more than ever before on the problems of in-service education. If the functions of a program of teacher education stated elsewhere in this report are sound, and if the principle of continuous growth is accepted, in-service education of teachers is equally important with pre-service preparation. In-service education is not only an extension of education but it is often a re-education. This is consistent with the concept and fact of change. In-service education should develop unity and progress, and pre-service education attempts to embody them. There should be unity between the two, and each should include some professional and non-professional study.

6. *A program of teacher education must recognize differing needs of teachers as well as individual needs of pupils.* Teachers differ in mental ability, in social ability, in health, and in outlook on life. Economic conditions and environment as well as native capacity have made teachers heterogeneous in their composition. Hence, attention must be given in a practical way to individual teacher needs. Intellectually, emotionally, physically, socially, teachers must be educated according to their needs. The outcome should not be a standardized product, rather the result of observing this principle in the education of teachers should be a maximum development of each along all possible and desirable lines.

7. *Selection of the most competent is of prime importance in the development of a program of teacher education.* Many contend, convincingly, that selective admission of students for teacher-training schools and colleges is the most important single factor or problem in the organization and ad-

ministration of a program of teacher preparation. It is at least one of the most important problems, and demands study both of the qualities desirable for effective teaching and of methods for detecting and measuring these qualities.

8. *Teacher education should lead to a recognition of the true importance of each of the various phases of school service.* The term "level of service" unfortunately implies to some that the second grade is more important than the first, and that the high school is more important than the elementary school. Salaries, promotion standards, certification requirements, and social and professional recognition for teachers, in many cases, strengthen or confirm this implication. Any unit of the school system is comparable to a link in a chain. It is important to the whole, and its importance must not be discounted.

9. *Economy of effort, time, and money is important in planning and administering a program of teacher education.* Next steps must take into account all existing agencies for teacher preparation. Useless duplication of programs is unwarranted. Private and public institutions engaged in the education of teachers must coordinate their efforts harmoniously. The demands of a "total education" program are so many and varied that extravagance and waste must be eliminated. To cite a few examples: Prospective teachers who are incompetent should not be admitted to the profession; two or more departments should not be maintained in a given state if one supplies a sufficiently large number of adequately prepared teachers for the needs of that field; only essential courses should be offered and only essentials should be included in these courses.

10. *The preparation of faculties engaged in the education of teachers is a matter of great importance.* Members of such faculties should be "master teachers." Their scholarship, technical skill, professional ideals, and personal qualities should be of the highest rank. These qualities, and others, will depend upon formal education, practical school experience, and natural abilities. Each faculty member should be chosen for his special fitness for a given field of service. While these ideals hold for all teachers, the strategic position of schools and colleges for preparing teachers demands most careful attention to the selection of their faculties. Some hold that teachers should be prepared to meet the present requirements of public schools, others that teachers should be prepared to effect the needed changes in public education. A well-chosen faculty, ever alert to professional demands, will meet both of these ideals.

11. *The function of the state in the general direction of teacher education is of great importance.* The state, after cooperative research and unification of resources have become matters of reality, should assume administrative responsibility for teacher education through certification regulations, financial support, and educational leadership. The state's relationship to different types of agencies may vary considerably in degree and kind, but it can never vanish. The solution of teacher education problems will rest with states (or regions at the most) and not with the nation as a whole. National ideals may be formulated but the ability of states or regions to realize these

ideals will necessitate individual state or regional effort. The unequal distribution of wealth alone would require this. State responsibility for education has long been commonly accepted as having Constitutional sanction. Teacher education then, as a leading part of the total state program of education, is a state function.

12. *The public school should be recognized as an important but not the only social agency for education.* The family, the church, the community, and even industry and agriculture may contribute to the advancement of civilization in an educational way. There is grave danger of exaggerating the importance of the public school to the point of forgetting that it was organized to serve society. When public education assumes that society is obligated to maintain it without any accounting of stewardship, then dissolution is inevitable. Other social agencies, history clearly indicates, have faced the same danger. Some have escaped the danger and continued as useful servants of society. Others have been less fortunate and have seen their influence wane in proportion to their blindness. Even though the position is taken that public education is the most important agency for the improvement of society, it cannot lose sight of its primary purpose nor of the educational importance of other social agencies. In fact, a coordinated program of education by all such agencies of society is an ideal that will receive an increasing amount of serious attention as time passes and new conditions of changing civilization require it.

Problems To Be Solved and Questions for Study

These are some of the questions that need investigation. They are typical of the kinds that arise when the problem of the relation of professional to general education in the preparation of teachers is analyzed.

1. What types of schools exist for teacher education?

State teachers colleges and normal schools constitute a large group organized for the sole purpose of preparing teachers for the public schools. There are many other types of schools, however, whose graduates enter the teaching profession: city training schools, municipal colleges and universities, high-school training classes, county normal schools, privately supported colleges and universities, and special schools. The latter usually represent some specialized field such as commerce, music, art, or physical education. To what extent is each type of teacher education agency important in American educational systems in terms of the numbers of graduates admitted to the profession?

2. In connection with each type of teacher education institution, thoroughgoing investigation should be made in connection with the following points:

    a. Admission requirements
    b. Graduation requirements
    c. Faculty preparation
    d. Curriculums
    e. Practice facilities
    f. Library facilities

g. Growth of enrolment in relation to field demands for teaching service

h. Capacity of schools in connection with enrolment and in relation to field needs for the various forms of teaching service

The investigations should be conducted beyond the point of finding out prevailing practices. The most important studies would be experimental in nature, attempting to find out what standards should prevail. Comparisons should be made among the various types of schools in relation to various topics studied.

3. What factors are involved in the in-service education of teachers?

Various forms of teacher education have been planned and carried out by school superintendents. For example, supervision, faculty meetings, group conferences, curriculum revision, attendance at local, state, and national meetings, leaves of absence for study or travel, summer school study, correspondence study, readings and discussions, and extension courses. The latter method has been by far the most popular. States should be made to see which methods are the most popular and which can be effectively organized in unified programs. The relation of teacher's health, salary, length of school year, and service load should be studied. They are in many cases important conditioning factors in a program of in-service education.

4. What are the trends and conditions of modern life that influence programs of public education?

The criticism is frequently made that the school program lags behind the conditions of modern society. A constant check on trends and conditions is imperative if the school program is to be kept up to date. Practically all agree that change is one of the most significant aspects of our present civilization. If schools are to serve society, the school program must be observant of the changes in modern life and readily adaptable to the demands of society.

5. How can a state coordinate the various agencies of teacher education?

If investigations related to the first question of this list are made, it will be found that in nearly all states a variety of teacher education agencies exist. The state departments of education are becoming increasingly important in the supervision and administration of teacher education. These departments have naturally exercised their greatest influence over the state supported institutions. State certification of teachers is, however, a method of supervision that can be a strong controlling force in the teacher education work of any institution. Study should be made of the way in which certification can be wisely used in this connection. Is the certification of teachers a parallel responsibility of the state education department with the supervision and administration of teacher education programs? If so, how can the relationship be developed properly in a unified administration of both fields?

6. What part does teacher certification have in the development of a state education program?

Many states have recognized the importance of studying in a careful manner the number of teachers in each field of service, the number of additional positions in each field of service, and the number of new teachers needed each year. If information of this kind is used in connection with an adequate knowledge of sources of supply, the problem of certification standards will have a firm basis for solution. As pointed out in (5), certification standards properly formulated will have a profound effect on the teacher education programs of every institution engaged in the work.

7. What effect will the character and organization of a state education department have on a program of teacher education?

Does the appointment of a state commissioner of education by a state board of education, or his appointment by the governor, or his election by popular vote, tend to have any bearing on the size and quality of the education department under his direction? Assuming that the state education department is a highly professionalized group, will the internal organization of the department have any influence on the state program of teacher education? There are a sufficient variety and number of practices throughout the country to provide opportunity for analysis of problems of this nature.

8. What relative emphasis should be placed on professional and general education of teachers?

In this question it is assumed that professional education will include all types of preparation for the vocational aspects of teaching, and that general education has reference to that type of preparation which has for its primary purpose the education of teachers outside their vocational applications. Many questions arise in connection with this point. How much of the various kinds of professional education should be given preliminary to a teacher's regular appointment? How much general education should be given? How much of each should be given as a part of the in-service education of teachers? What values should be stressed in the organization and provision of professional education? of general education? What is required or can be expected of a teacher as a member of society?

9. To what extent should we rely upon public support of teacher education? on private support?

In many states, public schools have depended on liberal arts colleges for their supply of high-school teachers. These institutions are mainly supported by private endowment. Many times colleges and universities conduct special curriculums in such fields as music, art, health and physical education, and commercial education. When the work done by these institutions is accepted from the standpoint of state standards, should the state attempt to develop a program of teacher education whereby the cost would be borne entirely by the state? Should a state attempt to transfer the entire functions of teacher education to state supported institutions?

PART IV

THE FISCAL ASPECTS OF ARTICULATION

CHAPTER XIV

STATEMENT OF THE PROBLEM

A<small>N EDUCATIONAL</small> system is well articulated when its various parts work together to offer the fullest educational opportunity to the children, youths, and adults who come under its influence. There are a series of factors which may affect favorably or adversely the degree of coherence which a school system may possess. This section of the Yearbook is concerned with one of the more important of these. It deals with the relation of school finance to the general problem of articulation.

The character of the machinery set up to pay for the various units which constitute a state's educational program will in a large measure determine what that program will be. It will not only significantly influence the development of the units found at each educational level—elementary, secondary, and higher—but will crucially affect the ability of these units to work together, to build upon the work of the preceding unit, and to add the largest possible educational increment before passing the child on to the next level.

Numerous illustrations of fortuitous schemes for the financing of education exist in the nation today. Many of them are rooted in obsolete educational conceptions of past generations, or are the outgrowth of piecemeal and more or less accidental educational legislation. These schemes for the financing of education nevertheless fundamentally influence the trends of educational development. In some cases their effect is in a direction opposite from that which the public of today might desire and which an intelligent educational policy might dictate. Many of the educational in-articulations, that is, the failures of the schools to work together with maximum benefit, dealt with in this Yearbook, are the fruit of poorly planned systems of educational finance. Before these inarticulations can be remedied, the inarticulations in the financial machinery which lie lack of them must be removed.

This section presents certain principles and practices of school financing which promise most in the promotion of effective educational articulation. Before considering these in detail, it is well to have in mind a series of factors which contribute to the complexity of the problem.

A wide variety of educational units and institutions is involved—At the lower level is the elementary school, preceded in many communities by the kindergarten and in some instances by the nursery class. Elementary education is cared for in a school varying considerably in different communities as to the number of grades encompassed. Secondary education is in many communities taken care of by the four-year high school. In other places, the junior high school and the junior college precede and follow various modifications of the traditional four-year unit. On the higher level are the state colleges and universities offering liberal and professional education and exhibiting a variety of organization. The normal schools and teachers colleges constitute one of a series of institutions offering professional or technical training and having to do with the education of special groups. Various forms of adult education carry on the work beyond the regular period of formal schooling and complete the broad outlines of the picture.

The specialization of educational activities enters into the situation— Education, like all phases of our life, is marked by growing specialization. Types of educational work unheard of a few generations ago, but now firmly established and generally accepted as desirable, must be financed. This tendency is inevitable if education is to meet the demands of an increasingly complex civilization. It frequently brings with it, however, a specialization of group interest and a lack of a broad understanding of the relationships which are essential to the building of a coordinated system of education.

A series of governmental units are concerned—Both the Federal and state political units contribute to the support of education at every level as do a series of local units such as the county, the town, the township, and the various regular and special school districts. This is a reflection of the fact that education has national as well as state and local aspects. The nation as a whole is affected if incoherence rather than coherence marks our policy for financing education. The welfare of the nation depends upon the maintenance in all regions, whatever may be the local ability to support education, of opportunities for schooling sufficient to insure certain minimum standards of social and political effectiveness. The increasing ease and frequency with which students and workers move from one state to another make it impossible to consider educational financing from the standpoint of individual states or localities alone. The problem also has a national aspect because the collection of the facts and the conduct of surveys essential as a basis for the intelligent development of the various state educational programs cannot be accomplished effectively or economically except upon a national scale.

Although these national interests are important and probably will be of increasing concern in the future, the state with its subdivisions constitutes the basic governmental and geographic unit, and is the dominant factor in the financing of education in the United States. The major emphasis of the subsequent material affecting fiscal articulation and education will therefore be upon the state aspects of this problem.

Private educational effort is involved—A wide variety of private agencies, with social, religious, and commercial purposes, participate in education.[1] Some offer education which parallels rather closely the work of the public schools. Others are supplementary in the scope of their offerings. The expenditures of these schools are derived from the total social income. Their support constitutes a part of the total problem of educational finance.

School financing is a phase of the problem of paying for all governmental undertakings—A study of fiscal articulation as it relates to the various

---

[1] See pages 317-18 in Chapter XVIII.

units and levels of education is essentially an attempt to discover the proportion of public expenditures needed to serve best the social needs of the nation and its various political units when the financing of education is attacked as a properly articulated or single problem. No doubt this proportion is variable, changing with economic and social evolution. Its proper determination involves the consideration not only of educational needs, but of all activities conducted at public expense.

The multiplicity of forms of school organization, the specialization of educational activities, the wide variety of governmental units concerned with school finance, the parallel educational activities of public and private agencies, the fact that education is but one of a series of enterprises carried on at governmental expense; these factors all combine to make financial articulation in the field of education a complicated and difficult problem.

Conflicts among educational units—The educational picture as it concerns its fiscal aspects reveals in many states a series of conflicts between the various units and levels. Conflicts exist between the higher institutions and the elementary-secondary level, between teachers colleges and universities, between state colleges and state universities, and between various subject-matter fields. In such an environment an articulated plan for the financing of education can hardly be expected. When each of the numerous units and interests constituting an educational system clamors for its own development, for a larger share in the social income without reference to, or in antagonism to, the claims of other educational factors and with little reference to the system as a whole, an articulated plan of school finance is not likely to result. Fratricidal strife among leaders of various educational levels and institutions is a poor basis upon which to attempt financial articulation. Such a procedure in the financing of education is viewed with regret by the friends, and with impatience by the antagonists, of education. Starvation for all phases of education, rather than coordinated and efficient expenditure, is likely to be the result of such a chaotic policy.

Prerequisites to the articulation of school finance—A coordinated policy for the financing of education is the reflection of a coherent educational program. Chaos will characterize the method of financing education in a state if each phase of its educational program is considered as a separate problem unrelated to the rest of the program. Coherence and articulation in the financing of education can be achieved only when the financial demands of each phase of an educational system are considered not only from the viewpoint of the particular phase concerned, but also in relation to the other elements constituting the whole system. If such consideration is to be secured, educational leaders must not only appreciate the importance of the single phase of education with which they are immediately concerned, but must have a broad and sympathetic understanding of other phases of a state education program. Understanding and cooperation among educational leaders are prerequisite to the establishment of a well-rounded educational system in a state and to the development of an articulated plan for the financing of this system.

When coherence is achieved within the educational system, it is then possible to articulate this system with other governmental activities. Whatever the justification for the present allotment of public money as between education and other public activities, education will have no conclusive argument for receiving a larger proportion, or indeed for receiving what it now does, unless it undertakes to finance its various elements and levels upon a basis of cooperation and broad understanding.

What has the form of organization of the state agencies of educational control contributed to fiscal articulation? What is the relation of state budget systems to the problem? What is the function of informal conferences and voluntary associations in the attack on this problem? What is the present distribution of expenditures for education? What are some of the special financial factors affecting articulation? What conclusions and recommendations may be drawn from a consideration of these topics? The remaining chapters of this part of the Yearbook will deal with the foregoing questions.

CHAPTER XV

FISCAL ARTICULATION THROUGH THE ORGANIZATION OF THE AGENCIES OF EDUCATIONAL CONTROL

I F THE educational system of a state were so simple and so small that a single organization encompassed all its elements and controlled every aspect of its work, the problem of unified financial management would be greatly simplified. But this is not the case. The state programs of education include a great variety of units—elementary and secondary schools, state universities, land grant colleges, junior colleges, teachers colleges and normal schools, professional schools, and technical institutions, and separate institutions devoted to women, to negroes, and to specific vocations. Units are determined upon bases of educational level, sex, race, vocation, and even upon grounds of abstract educational theory, and our system of public education has developed in such a way as to favor a separate governing body for each such unit. Under these conditions, fiscal articulation of education through the agencies of immediate control becomes exceedingly difficult.

Coordination of educational finance may be brought about in three principal ways: through common agencies of control, through state budgeting, and through informal methods and agencies. This chapter deals with the first of these, reserving for succeeding chapters the other two methods.

Purpose of financial coordination—Before presenting the experience of the states in using common boards of control for two or more educational units, certain limitations of the problem must be made. It should be noted at the outset that financial coordination is seldom the sole or even the dominant factor in determining the consolidation of governing bodies for educational units. Articulation of educational programs is usually the purpose that is given most prominence in discussion of proposed consolidations of control, although economy is frequently the basis of appeal to legislators and an argument that has force with the public. Nevertheless, common control of all or of a number of units tends to make financial plans for the support of education reflect a carefully articulated educational program. In the discussion that follows in this chapter, therefore, it is assumed that centralized control of the educational program carries with it some degree of authority and ability to coordinate the financial program.

State and local relationships—Attention has already been called in Chapter XIV to the fact that while the state is the primary unit in fiscal articulation of the state systems of education, the method and extent of state control over this phase of education are conditioned by the powers and financial responsibilities of local educational agencies and by the educational policies of the Federal government.[1] In order to place in correct perspective the relationship of the state's central public school office to the other units of control over state-supported education, it is desirable to discuss briefly the relationships of local and Federal educational control to that of the state department of education.

In spite of constitutional mandates which vested responsibility for education in the state, our educational history began with local control of the educational program and local school support. The relation of local units to the state government during the early stages of educational development was generally merely that arising from state legislation that permitted or required local political units to provide a minimum amount of schooling. Gradually, however, through prescription of standards as to plant, qualifications of teachers, and instructional programs, and through state financial measures of support for local schools, the state has centralized in its own educational office a constantly increasing amount of influence over local units. The extent of such centralization varies greatly from state to state but it is still true that the district, township, town, and county units of school management remain the principal agencies of administration. It would perhaps be accurate to describe the state's activity as that of advisory supervision rather than control. Subsequent discussion, therefore, which treats the state department of education [2] as an agency of fiscal control for public education does so only in the sense that whereas these offices quite frequently hold the balance of power, they seldom exercise actual administrative control over local schools.[3]

Federal and state relations—The outstanding example of the influence of Federal educational policy upon state fiscal control of public school education is the Federal subsidization of vocational education. This program, administered by the Federal Board for Vocational Education, provides for joint Federal and state support under a plan by which the Federal grant is matched, dollar for dollar, by the state or its subdivision. Several types of relationship to the state's chief educational office are possible under the terms of the Federal Vocational Education Law. First, the state and the state department of education may have no real financial connection with the program, fiscal responsibility for matching Federal funds for the purposes of vocational education being left to local school units. This is the case in two states, Iowa and Utah.

Second, the state may designate the state department of education as its agent in relations with the Federal Board for Vocational Education and

[1] See page 278 in Chapter XIV.

[2] Throughout this discussion reference will be made to the State Department of Education although the body ultimately responsible may be the State Board of Education.

[3] State high schools, such as the agricultural high schools of Minnesota and the state junior colleges of Arkansas which include high-school units, are only apparently exceptions to this statement. These institutions are supported by state rather than local funds and are not controlled by local bodies. Usually some form of independent governing body other than the state board of education intervenes between the state and the individual school. Thus in Minnesota the Board of Regents of the University is the governing body for the State Agricultural High School. In Arkansas each junior college has its own governing board that is responsible for the management and financing of the institutions.

may appropriate funds to be expended by this board. In this case it is apparent that the state's control of its educational program is retained. However, the desire to secure Federal aid may tend to distort the state's fiscal program in support of education. The state may thus provide money to match the Federal grant, although the state's resources might be expended more advantageously upon other phases of public education.

As a third possibility, the state may create a separate board for vocational education to act as its agent in relations with the Federal Board for Vocational Education and may appropriate money to be expended by this board to match the Federal subsidies. In instances of this kind the state's central control over both the program and the financing of education tends to become a dual control. If in addition the state provides, as does Wisconsin, for the creation of local boards for vocational education there result, in effect, two parallel and separate public educational systems within the state, one dealing with certain phases and types of vocational training and the other dealing with the remaining aspects of education.

The preceding description of certain local and Federal limitations upon the powers and responsibilities of the state department of education as an agency of fiscal control over the state's educational program must be kept in mind in the discussion that follows. This discussion assumes, under the limitations indicated, that the state's chief public school office is an agency of control comparable to the board of regents of a university. In fact, this assumption is subject to large exceptions; it is justified, however, by the large powers exercised by the central state school office in many states either by law, by professional leadership, or both.

Articulation through common governing bodies—Under the limitations and definitions noted, this chapter examines the extent and nature of the articulation of public educational agencies through provision for common governing bodies responsible for two or more of these units. Diversity of practice and the number of units involved make difficult the presentation of this material. However, it is possible to distinguish degrees of coordination through concentration of control over different types of units. The method of presentation will group the facts so as to consider first the states that have made practically no use of this method of articulating fiscal management; next, states which use common governing boards to a limited degree; and finally, those that show a high degree of centralization of educational boards. For purposes of illustration, typical methods and forms of common control will be described in some detail. This illustrative material should not distract attention from the main purpose of the discussion, which is to present the methods adopted to secure articulation of the financing of the various levels and types of state educational activities through the provision of a common board to govern two or more educational units.

Complete decentralization—The greatest decentralization of control exists in those states in which each unit or element of the educational system has its own governing body individually responsible for financing the unit that it controls and authorized to approach the legislature or other state fiscal authority directly and independently for funds. Such complete decentralization, although it may, of course, be materially reduced by the operation of informal cooperative agreements,[1] exists in 13 states: Arizona, Arkansas, Delaware, Illinois, Kentucky, Missouri,[2] North Carolina, Ohio, Pennsylvania, South Carolina, Utah, Washington, and Wyoming. Table 73 lists each institution in these states that has its own independent governing body charged with financial and general responsibility for the management of the institution. In no instance does the state support any other educational institutions.[3] None of these states has adopted the device of bringing two or more of its educational agencies under the control of a cannon governing board in order to secure fiscal articulation.[4]

---

[1] See Chapter XVII, pages 310-14.
[2] For a description of informal coordination in Missouri, see Chapter XVII, page 311.
[3] Penal, correctional, and charitable institutions, and schools for the deaf and blind are not considered in this discussion.
[4] The School of Mines in Missouri is part of the University of Missouri and is governed by the Board of the University although it is located approximately 150 miles from Columbia. A branch of the Utah Agricultural College is maintained in the southern part of the state under the control of the Board of the Agricultural College.

TABLE 73.—STATES IN WHICH EACH EDUCATIONAL INSTITUTION HAS AN INDEPENDENT GOVERNING BODY

State	Institution
Arizona	1. State Department of Education[1] 2. University of Arizona—Tucson 3. Northern Arizona State Teachers College—Flagstaff 4. Tempe State Teachers College
Arkansas	1. State Department of Education 2. University of Arkansas—Fayetteville 3. Arkansas State Teachers College—Conway 4. Henderson State Teachers College—Arkadelphia 5. Agricultural, Mechanical and Normal School[2]—Pine Bluff 6. State Junior College—Jonesboro 7. State Junior College—Magnolia 8. State Junior College—Monticello 9. State Junior College—Russellville
Delaware	1. State Department of Education 2. University of Delaware—Newark 3. State College for Colored Students[2]—Dover
Illinois	1. State Department of Education 2. University of Illinois—Urbana 3. Southern Illinois State Normal University—Carbondale 4. Eastern Illinois State Teachers College—Charleston 5. Northern Illinois State Teachers College—De Kalb 6. Western Illinois State Teachers College—Macomb 7. Illinois State Normal University—Normal
Kentucky	1. State Department of Education 2. University of Kentucky—Lexington 3. Western Kentucky State Teachers College—Bowling Green 4. Morehead State Teachers College 5. Murray State Teachers College 6. Eastern Kentucky State Teachers College—Richmond 7. Kentucky State Industrial College for Colored Persons[2]—Frankfort 8. West Kentucky Industrial College for Colored Persons—Paducah

[1] Throughout this discussion reference will be made to the State Department of Education although the body ultimately responsible may be the State Board of Education.
[2] Negro land grant college.

TABLE 73.—STATES IN WHICH EACH EDUCATIONAL INSTITUTION HAS AN INDEPENDENT GOVERNING BODY (Continued)

State	Institution
Missouri	1. State Department of Education 2. University of Missouri—Columbia 3. Southeast Missouri State Teachers College—Cape Girardeau 4. Northeast Missouri State Teachers College—Kirksville 5. Northwest Missouri State Teachers College—Maryville 6. Southwest Missouri State Teachers College—Springfield 7. Central Missouri State Teachers College—Warrensburg 8. Lincoln University[1]—Jefferson City
North Carolina	1. State Department of Education 2. Western Carolina Teachers College—Cullowhee 3. State Normal School[2]—Elizabeth City 4. State Normal School[2]—Fayetteville 5. East Carolina Teachers College—Greenville 6. Winston-Salem Teachers College[2] 7. University of North Carolina—Chapel Hill 8. State College of Agriculture and Engineering—Raleigh 9. North Carolina College for Women—Greensboro 10. North Carolina College for Negroes[2]—Durham 11. Appalachian State Normal School—Boone 12. Agricultural and Technical College[1]—Greensboro 13. Cherokee Indian Normal School—Pembroke
Ohio	1. State Department of Education 2. Ohio State University—Columbus 3. Miami University—Oxford 4. Ohio University—Athens 5. Kent State College 6. Bowling Green State College 7. Normal and Industrial Department, Wilberforce University[2]—Wilberforce
Pennsylvania	1. State Department of Education 2. Pennsylvania State College—State College 3. State Teachers College—Bloomsburg 4. State Teachers College—East Stroudsburg 5. State Teachers College—Edinboro 6. State Teachers College—Indiana 7. State Teachers College—Kutztown 8. State Teachers College—Lock Haven 9. State Teachers College—Mansfield 10. State Teachers College—Millersville 11. State Teachers College—Shippenburg 12. State Teachers College—Slippery Rock 13. State Teachers College—West Chester 14. State Teachers College—California 15. State Teachers College—Clarion 16. Cheyney Training School for Teachers[2]
South Carolina	1. State Department of Education 2. University of South Carolina—Columbia 3. Clemson Agricultural College—Clemson College 4. The Citadel—Charleston 5. State Agricultural and Mechanical College[1]—Orangeburg
Utah	1. State Department of Education 2. University of Utah—Salt Lake City 3. Utah Agricultural College—Logan
Washington	1. State Department of Education 2. State Normal School—Bellingham 3. State Normal School—Cheney 4. State Normal School—Ellensburg 5. University of Washington—Seattle 6. Washington State College—Pullman
Wyoming	1. State Department of Education 2. University of Wyoming—Laramie

[1] Negro land grant college.
[2] Colored.

This multiplicity of financial control is sometimes further complicated by the substantial subsidies granted by the state to private institutions. In Pennsylvania, for instance, substantial subsidies are granted to three privately controlled universities (Temple University, the University of Pennsylvania, and the University of Pittsburgh) and to three schools of medicine (Jefferson, Hahnemann, and Women's Medical Colleges).[1] An interesting practice in this respect is found in Maryland, where a system of state grants to privately controlled higher institutions in return for free scholarships to certain graduates of the public high schools is in effect.

The Pennsylvania plan of independent boards for each unit of the state educational system is modified, so far as institutions for preparing teachers are concerned, by the fact that, although there is a local board of trustees appointed by the governor for each institution, the several budgets are submitted separately through the state department of education to the state budget secretary. The appropriation for maintenance of the teacher-training institutions is made in a lump sum to be used as may be directed by the state superintendent. A similar lump sum appropriation is made for capital outlays. Chart I summarizes the general budgetary plan of Pennsylvania with reference to education in general and higher education in particular.

Delaware affords an interesting example of a small state in which educational coordination is secured largely through legislative enactment without provision for the joint government of two or more of the state's agencies of education. The public schools are supported almost wholly by state legislative appropriations, very little money for this purpose being raised locally. The University of Delaware at Newark grew out of a private college chartered by the legislature in 1833. It was designated by the legislature as the beneficiary under the Morrill Act about 1870. It was operated under combined state and private ownership until 1913 when it was taken over entirely by the state. The present method of control, effected in 1921, consists of a board of 32 trustees, of whom four—the governor of the state, the president of the university, the master of the state grange, and the president of the state board of education—are members ex-officiis.[2] The University of Delaware is the state university, the state land grant college, and the state institution for the professional preparation of white teachers. An itemized budget is submitted by the university trustees to the state auditor separately from the budget for public schools submitted by the State Board of Education and from the budget for the colored normal school.[3] Legislative control over the state budget for the elementary and secondary schools is secured, first, by fixing the amount of the appropriation; and second, by

[1] See Townsend, Arthur P., budget secretary. *The Budget of the Commonwealth of Pennsylvania for 1929-31.* Submitted to the General Assembly by John S. Fisher, governor. See also, "Comparative Amounts Approved for Education for Bienniums of 1927 and 1929." *Pennsylvania School Journal* 77: 598; June, 1929.
[2] University of Delaware, *Annual Catalogue, 1926-1927*, p. 9, 15.
[3] Delaware, *State Budget Submitted to the General Assembly.* Robert P. Robinson, governor. January, 1929. p. 87-90.

CHART I

Fiscal Aspects of Educational Articulation in Pennsylvania

(Arrows indicate direction of budget estimates)

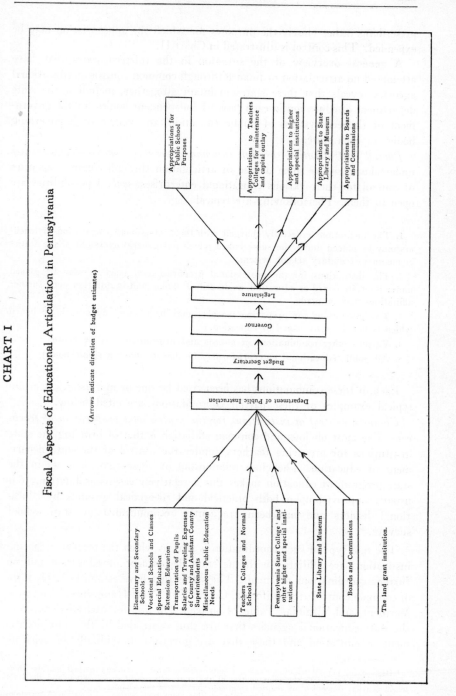

The land grant institution.

prescribing rather closely the purposes for which the appropriation may be expended. This control is illustrated in Chart II.

A general overview of the situation in the thirteen states that have attempted no articulation of finance through common control of educational agencies reveals that these states maintain altogether, including the state department of education in each case, 91 independent bodies for the government of thirteen systems of public education, an average of 7 governing bodies in each state.

Partial centralization through common governing boards—When states undertake to secure some degree of articulation through common agencies of control for their various educational enterprises, several possibilities are open to them. The following are typical:

1. The institutions especially charged with the professional preparation of teachers may be placed under the same board which has general oversight of the state's elementary-secondary school system.

2. The institutions for the professional preparation of teachers may be placed under the state board of education, as described above, and in addition some further affiliations may be made.

3. The institutions for preparing teachers may be placed under a single board which is not the state board of education.

4. Various other combinations of boards and institutions may be made.

5. All public educational enterprises may be placed under a single board.

Each of these combinations has been tried by one or more states. Certain typical examples of these partial consolidations are cited below.

Common control of institutions for the professional preparation of teachers—The most obvious and common affiliation is that of bringing the state institutions for preparing teachers[1] under the control of the state department of education. The close relationship of these two elements in the state program of education makes this a relatively easy consolidation. It is usually approved upon both practical and theoretical grounds by educational leaders and has been frequently recommended by state school surveys.[2]

The first type of such coordination is that in which the teacher-preparing institutions are affiliated with the state department of education but no further coordinations are made. The states that have established this form of common control are California, Connecticut, New Hampshire, Tennessee, Vermont, and Virginia. Table 74 on page 290 lists for each of these states the state educational agencies that are thus controlled by the state department of education and those that are governed individually by separate

---

[1] High-school normal training classes, county normal schools, and city normal schools which are ordinarily subject to the joint control of the state department of education and the local school districts concerned are omitted from consideration in this chapter.

[2] For a summary of opinion and evidence on this point see: National Education Association, Research Division. "A Self-Survey Plan for State School Systems." *Research Bulletin* 8: 109-10; May, 1930. Washington, D. C.: the Association.

CHART II

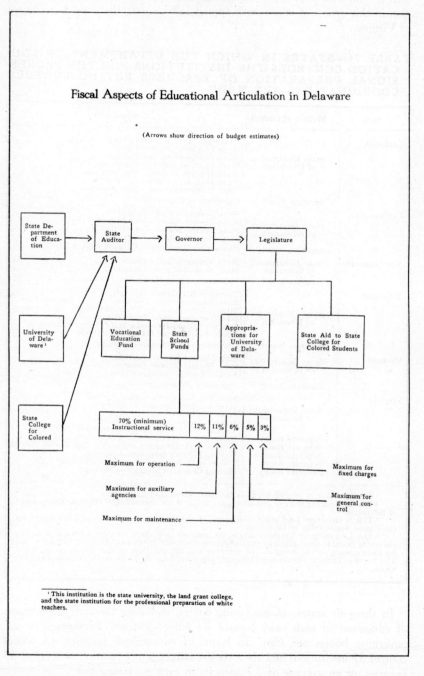

Fiscal Aspects of Educational Articulation in Delaware

(Arrows show direction of budget estimates)

[1] This institution is the state university, the land grant college, and the state institution for the professional preparation of white teachers.

boards; and Chart III shows the typical fiscal aspects of educational articulation in this group of states with special reference to the state government of Virginia.

TABLE 74.—STATES IN WHICH THE DEPARTMENT OF EDUCATION CONTROLS THE INSTITUTIONS FOR THE PROFESSIONAL PREPARATION OF TEACHERS BUT NO FURTHER COORDINATIONS ARE MADE

State	Method of Control	Institution
California	State Department of Education	Humboldt State Teachers College—Arcata State Teachers College—Chico State Teachers College—Fresno State Teachers College—San Diego State Teachers College—San Francisco State Teachers College—San Jose State Teachers College—Santa Barbara
	Separate Board	University of California[1]
Connecticut	State Department of Education	State Normal School—Danbury State Normal School—New Britain State Normal School—New Haven State Normal School—Willimantic
	Separate Board	Connecticut Agricultural College[2]—Storrs
New Hampshire	State Department of Education	State Normal School—Keene State Normal School—Plymouth
	Separate Board	University of New Hampshire—Durham
Tennessee	State Department of Education	Tennessee Polytechnic Institute—Cookeville East Tennessee State Teachers College—Johnson City Middle Tennessee State Teachers College—Murfreesboro West Tennessee State Teachers College—Normal Agricultural and Industrial State College[3]—Nashville Austin Peay Normal School—Clarksville
	Separate Board	University of Tennessee—Knoxville
Vermont	State Department of Education	State Normal School—Castleton State Normal School—Johnson Normal Course—Lyndon Center
	Separate Board	University of Vermont[4]—Burlington
Virginia	State Department of Education	State Teachers College—East Radford State Teachers College—Farmville State Teachers College—Fredericksburg State Teachers College—Harrisonburg Virginia Normal and Industrial Institute[3]—Ettrick
	Separate Board	University of Virginia—Charlottesville
	Separate Board	Virginia Agricultural and Mechanical College—Blacksburg
	Separate Board	Virginia Military Institute—Lexington
	Separate Board	College of William and Mary—Williamsburg
	Separate Board	Medical College of Virginia—Richmond

[1] Common control over divisions at Berkeley, Davis, and Los Angeles.
[2] Teacher-training work in this land grant college is also controlled by the State Department of Education.
[3] This is the negro land grant college but is classified as a teacher-training institution by the United States Office of Education.
[4] The University of Vermont should be regarded as a state institution inasmuch as the governing board is constituted by the legislature selecting 9 members and the board itself 9, and by the presence on the board of the governor and the president of the university *ex-officiis*. The Teacher-Training Course here is directly supported by state funds, and is under state supervision.

In these six states, 16 governing bodies, including the state department of education in each case, control six school systems, an average of 2.7 governing bodies per state. In terms of educational agencies, 16 bodies control 37 institutions and six state departments of education, a total of 43 agencies, or an average of 2.7 agencies to each governing body.

CHART III

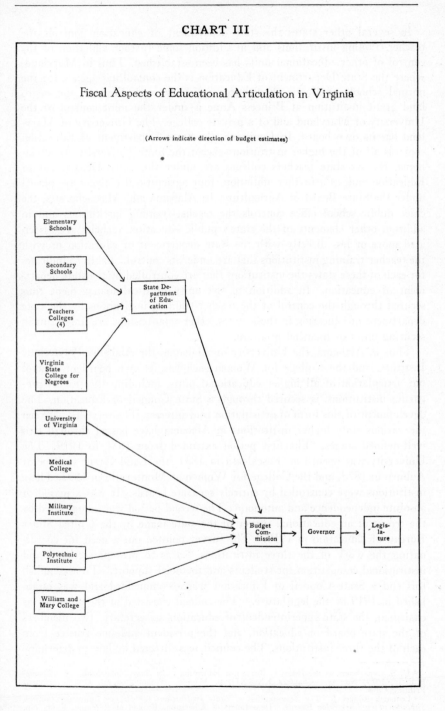

Fiscal Aspects of Educational Articulation in Virginia

(Arrows indicate direction of budget estimates)

Elementary Schools

Secondary Schools

Teachers Colleges (4)

Virginia State College for Negroes

University of Virginia

Medical College

Military Institute

Polytechnic Institute

William and Mary College

State Department of Education

Budget Commission

Governor

Legislature

In several other states the state department of education controls the teacher-training institutions and in addition some further affiliation of the control of other educational units has been established. Thus in Maryland, where the State Department of Education is the controlling agency for the normal schools at Bowie, Frostburg, Salisbury, and Towson, the negro land grant institution at Princess Anne is under the joint control of the University of Maryland and of a private college. The University of Maryland has its own board. In Louisiana, the State Department of Education controls all of the higher institutions except the State University. In Oklahoma, the six state teachers colleges are under the State Department of Education and, as a further affiliation, four agricultural colleges are placed under the State Board of Agriculture. In Alabama and Massachusetts, the chief public school office controls the teacher-training institutions and in addition other elements of the state's public education agencies are associated more or less directly with the state department of education or with the teacher-training institutions that are under its control. Table 75 indicates for each of these states the institutions that are controlled by the state department of education. In addition to the unity of fiscal management thus secured through the control of the teacher-training institutions by the state department of education in these states, other relationships are important in securing unity of financial program.

Thus in Alabama, the University of Alabama, the Alabama Polytechnic Institute, and the College for Women each has its own board of control but articulation of all higher educational units, including the teacher-preparing institutions, is secured through a State Council of Education. The development of this form of articulation is of interest. The relations between the various state higher institutions in Alabama have passed through two well-defined stages. The first period extended from 1831 to 1919. The University was opened at Tuscaloosa in 1831, the Land Grant College at Auburn in 1873, and the College for Women at Montevallo in 1897. These institutions were controlled by entirely separate boards. It was a period of absolute independence and autonomy. The second period was inaugurated by the report of an educational survey of the state made by the United States Bureau of Education in 1919.[1] The survey pointed out a need for coordinating the work of the three institutions "so as to prevent sectional and institutional competition for students and financial support." To accomplish this end a State Council of Education was recommended and was established in 1919 by the legislature.[2] The council consisted of the governor as chairman, the state superintendent of education as secretary, two members of the state board of education, and the president and one trustee from each of the three institutions. The council was directed by law to determine

---

[1] U. S. Department of the Interior, Bureau of Education. *An Educational Study of Alabama,* Bulletin, 1919, No. 41. Chapters XX-XXII, p. 383-486. Washington, D. C.: Government Printing Office.

[2] Leonard, Robert J. *The Coordination of State Institutions for Higher Education through Supplementary Curricular Boards.* Department of Education, Bureau of Research, Study No. 13. Chapter III. Berkeley, Calif.: University of California, 1923. 188 p.

TABLE 75.—STATES IN WHICH INSTITUTIONS FOR THE PRO-
FESSIONAL PREPARATION OF TEACHERS ARE CONTROLLED
BY THE STATE DEPARTMENT OF EDUCATION AND CERTAIN
OTHER AFFILIATIONS ARE MADE

State	Method of Control	Institution
Alabama	State Department of Education	State Normal School—Daphne State Teachers College—Florence State Teachers College—Jacksonville State Teachers College—Livingston State Teachers College[1]—Montgomery State Agricultural and Mechanical Institute[2]—Normal State Teachers College—Troy
	Separate boards with provision for coordination through the State Council of Education	University of Alabama—University Alabama Polytechnic Institute—Auburn Alabama College for Women—Montevallo
Louisiana	State Department of Education	Louisiana State Normal College—Natchitoches Southern University and Agricultural and Mechanical College[2]—Scotlandville Southwestern Louisiana Institute—Lafayette Louisiana Polytechnic Institute—Ruston Southeastern Louisiana College—Hammond Negro Normal and Industrial Institute—Grambling
	Separate Board	Louisiana State University—Baton Rouge
Maryland	State Department of Education	State Normal School[1]—Bowie State Normal School—Frostburg State Normal School—Salisbury State Normal School—Towson
	University Board of Regents	University of Maryland—College Park
	University Board of Regents jointly with a private board	Princess Anne Academy[1]
Massachusetts	State Department of Education	State Normal School—Bridgewater State Normal School—Fitchburg State Normal School—Framingham State Normal School—Hyannis State Normal School—Lowell State Normal School—North Adams State Normal School—Salem State Normal School—Westfield State Normal School—Worcester Massachusetts School of Art—Boston
	Separate board submitting budget estimates through the State Superintendent	Massachusetts Agricultural College—Amherst
Oklahoma	State Department of Education	Central State Teachers College—Edmond East Central State Teachers College—Ada Northeastern State Teachers College—Tahlequah Northwestern State Teachers College—Alva Southeastern State Teachers College—Durant Southwestern State Teachers College—Weatherford
	State Board of Agriculture	Cameron State School of Agriculture[3]—Lawton Connors State School of Agriculture[3]—Warner Oklahoma Agricultural and Mechanical College—Stillwater Panhandle Agricultural and Mechanical College—Goodwell
	Separate Board	Colored Agricultural and Normal University[2]—Langston
	Separate Board	Eastern Oklahoma College[3]—Wilburton
	Separate Board	Murray State School[3]—Tishomingo
	Separate Board	Northeastern Oklahoma Junior College[3]—Miami
	Separate Board	Oklahoma College for Women—Chickasha
	Separate Board	University of Oklahoma—Norman
	Separate Board	University Preparatory School and Junior College[3]—Tonkawa

[1] Colored.
[2] The negro land grant college, but classified by the United States Office of Education as a teacher-training institution.
[3] Junior College.

the educational needs of the state and to allocate types of work to each of the institutions. The statute was indefinite in describing how the decisions of the council were to be enforced. Two advisory boards—one lay and one professional—were also provided to assist the council in its work. This second period may be described as a period of supplementary and advisory state control.[1] In Massachusetts, the State Agricultural College submits estimates and legislative requests through the office of the State Superintendent of Public Instruction, who supervises the public educational system and controls the teacher-training institutions also.

For these five states—Alabama, Louisiana, Maryland,[2] Massachusetts, and Oklahoma—it is approximately correct to say that 20 governing bodies control the five state educational systems, an average of four to each state, and that these 20 bodies control 56 educational agencies, including the elementary-secondary schools in each case, an average of 2.8 agencies to each controlling body.

Table 74 on page 290 and Table 75 on page 293 together show that in eleven states the principle of unified state control over both public schools and teacher-training institutions is recognized rather fully, without, however, applying the principle of fiscal control by the state department of education to any large extent to other units in the states' educational systems. It should be added that the discussion of this chapter hinges upon fiscal control and coordination. It is recognized that other methods of control may be effectively used to correlate state programs of education.[3] Furthermore, the unity of control over the state agencies that prepare teachers for service in the public schools of these eleven states seldom extends to cover the departments of education in the state universities and other higher institutions. In only one state, Connecticut, so far as data available indicate, does the State Department of Education exercise even approximate fiscal control over the teacher-training department of the State University and Land Grant College. In all other cases discussed up to this point, these important phases of teacher-preparing activity appear to be removed from the sphere of influence of the state department of education as far as direct fiscal coordination is concerned.

In a number of states the department of education does not exercise direct fiscal control over the teacher-preparing institutions, but these institutions have been united under a single board upon which the chief state school officer is represented or over which he exercises an indirect fiscal influence. Thus in Colorado, Indiana, Maine, Michigan, Minnesota, Nebraska, Texas, and Wisconsin (all of which have more than one institution for the professional preparation of teachers), a single board controls all of these institutions within the state. Table 76 shows for each of these states the institutions that are thus united under a single board responsible for the

---

[1] Abercrombie, John W. "A State Education Program." *Proceedings, 1929.* Vol. 67. Washington, D. C.: National Education Association, 1929. p. 264-70.
[2] A Commission on Higher Education is now investigating the state's financial policy as it affects the State University and state-aided colleges. This commission will report to the 1931 Session of the Maryland Legislature.
[3] For a summary of these methods as they apply to the preparation of teachers, see: McConnell, J. M. "Judicious Control of Teacher-Training by State Departments of Education." *Proceedings, 1927.* Vol. 65. Washington, D. C.: National Education Association, 1927. p. 944-9.

TABLE 76.—STATES HAVING SEVERAL INSTITUTIONS FOR THE PROFESSIONAL PREPARATION OF TEACHERS WHICH ARE CONTROLLED BY A SINGLE BOARD (NOT, HOWEVER, THE STATE BOARD OF EDUCATION)

State	Type of Control	Institution
Colorado	Single Board	Adams State Teachers College—Alamosa Colorado State Teachers College—Greeley Western State Teachers College—Gunnison
	Separate Board	Colorado Agricultural College—Fort Collins
	Separate Board	Colorado School of Mines—Golden
	Separate Board	State Junior College—Grand Junction
	Separate Board	State Junior College—Trinidad
	Separate Board	University of Colorado—Boulder
Indiana	Single Board	Ball State Teachers College—Muncie Indiana State Teachers College—Terre Haute
	Separate Board	Indiana University—Bloomington
	Separate Board	Purdue University—Lafayette
Maine	Single Board	Aroostook State Normal School—Presque Isle Eastern State Normal School—Castine Madawaska Training School—Fort Kent State Normal School—Farmington State Normal School—Gorham Washington State Normal School—Machias
	Separate Board	University of Maine—Orono
Michigan	Single Board	Central State Teachers College—Mount Pleasant Michigan State Normal College—Ypsilanti Northern State Teachers College—Marquette Western State Teachers College—Kalamazoo
	Separate Board	Michigan College of Mining and Technology—Houghton
	Separate Board	Michigan State College—East Lansing
	Separate Board	University of Michigan—Ann Arbor
Minnesota	Single Board	State Teachers College—Bemidji State Teachers College—Duluth State Teachers College—Mankato State Teachers College—Moorhead State Teachers College—Saint Cloud State Teachers College—Winona
	Separate Board	University of Minnesota—Minneapolis
Nebraska	Single Board	Nebraska State Normal College—Chadron Nebraska State Teachers College—Kearney Nebraska State Teachers College—Peru Nebraska State Teachers College—Wayne
	Separate Board	University of Nebraska—Lincoln
Texas	Single Board	Austin State Teachers College—Nacogdoches East Texas State Teachers College—Commerce North Texas State Teachers College—Denton Sam Houston State Teachers College—Huntsville Southwest Texas State Teachers College—San Marcos Sul Ross State Teachers College—Alpine West Texas State Teachers College—Canyon
	Single Board	Prairie View State College[1] Texas Agricultural and Mechanical College—College Station
	Separate Board	College of Industrial Arts—Denton
	Separate Board	Texas College of Arts and Industries—Kingsville
	Separate Board	Texas Technological College—Lubbock
	Separate Board	University of Texas—Austin
Wisconsin	Single Board	Central State Teachers College—Stevens Point State Teachers College—Eau Claire State Teachers College—La Crosse State Teachers College—Milwaukee State Teachers College—Oshkosh State Teachers College—Platteville State Teachers College—River Falls State Teachers College—Superior State Teachers College—Whitewater
	Separate Board	Stout Institute—Menomonie
	Separate Board	University of Wisconsin—Madison

[1] Colored.

normal schools and teachers colleges and also the nature of the control over the other educational agencies of the state.

The method of fiscal procedure in the case of the teacher-training institutions thus brought under the common control of a board other than the state department of education may be illustrated by Minnesota. That state has six state teachers colleges all controlled by the State Teachers College Board. This board is required to report to the Commission of Administration and Finance, four months before the meeting of the Legislature, a detailed budget for each of the teachers colleges, with reasons for any increases that may be asked. The commission combines these budgets and, with such amendments as it may make, presents them to the Governor, who transmits them to the Legislature with his recommendation for their approval. The budget is handled before the Legislature by a designated committee of the board, and no lobbying whatever is done by the individual institutions in behalf of their own appropriation.

Detailed examination shows that this group of eight states employs 36 bodies of control for 70 institutions, counting the elementary-secondary schools in each state as one institution. This represents an average of 4.5 bodies of control for each state and an average of 1.9 agencies under the control of each such body.

Miscellaneous units of control—There are eleven states in which the methods of coordinating educational institutions are so varied as to render further classification of little value. In all of these, centralization of control over the institutions for preparing teachers is not a prominent characteristic. In this group affiliations may include teacher-preparing institutions but in no case is the state department of education brought into unity with the group by means of common control. Most of these affiliations are found in only one state.

Thus, in Georgia, the State Department of Education has no direct connection with the higher institutions, but all of the state colleges and higher schools are associated with the University. Owing to a provision in the State Constitution which limits state support to the University of Georgia, all public higher institutions are called branches of the state university. Their connection with the University is maintained by making the University Board a body interlocking with the separate boards of each of the state institutions. Each institutional board is represented upon the University Board and, theoretically at any rate, the University Board is superior to the separate boards. The inter-relationships involved are described in the following quotation:

By an act of the General Assembly, approved August 23, 1889, the government of the University is vested in a Board of Trustees, appointed by the Governor for a term of eight years, and confirmed by the Senate. The Board consists of one member from each Congressional District of the State, four from the State at large, and three from the city of Athens, four additional members, elected by the Alumni Society of the University of Georgia, under the provisions of the Act of 1925, and the following ex-officio members: The Governor of Georgia, the Chairman of the Board of Trustees of the North Georgia Agricultural College, the Chairman of the Board of Directors of the Georgia State College for Women, the President of the Commissioners of the Industrial College for Colored Youths, the Chairman of the Board of Trustees of the College of Agriculture, the Chairman of the Board of Trustees of the Georgia State Teachers' College, the President of the Board of Directors of the Medical College, the President of the Board of Trustees of the Georgia State Woman's College, the President of the Board of Trustees of Bowdon State Normal College, the Chairman of the Board of Trustees of the South Georgia Agricultural and Mechanical College, and the State Superintendent of Schools.[1]

In addition, the local board for the State College of Agriculture includes three members of the University Board of Trustees appointed by the chairman of the latter.[2] This cumbersome device for avoiding the letter of the constitution functions from the fiscal standpoint by reason of the fact that the University business officer is the chief business officer of the entire group of institutions. However, this does not prevent independent institutional approach to the legislature for funds.

In Iowa all the public higher institutions, the separate State University, the Land Grant College, and the Teachers College, are controlled fiscally and otherwise by the State Board of Education which, however, is a body entirely distinct from the State Department of Public Instruction and has no connection with the public schools. In Kansas a similar board known as the State Board of Regents is the governing body for the separate State University, the Land Grant College, and the three state teachers colleges. In Nevada there is in fact but one public higher institution, the State University, but the State Normal School is regarded as a distinct unit and the university and normal school are controlled by a single Board of Regents that is not associated with the State Department of Education. In South Dakota the Board of Regents controls the separate State University, the Land Grant College, the School of Mines, and the four teacher-training institutions. In New Mexico a single board controls the University and the Agricultural and Mechanical College but each of the two teacher-training institutions has its own board. Mississippi has a similar plan under which the State University, the Land Grant College, the College for Women, and the Alcorn Agricultural and Mechanical College are under a single board. At the same time, each of the two state teachers colleges has a controlling board of its own.

In Oregon and North Dakota the separate State University, the Land Grant College, and the state normal schools are all under one board which has no connection with the State Department of Public Instruction. The development of this form of centralized control in Oregon is of interest since the Oregon Board of Higher Education may be regarded as the most recent example of a form of control that is attempted through a single board for all higher institutions. Until 1929 the State University at Eugene and the State Land Grant College at Corvallis were controlled by separate boards. From 1885 to 1929 an interlocking membership on the two boards

---

[1] University of Georgia, *Announcements, 1928-1929*, Bulletin, Vol. 28, No. 6; April, 1928. p. 11.
[2] For additional information concerning the functions and support of the higher institutions of Georgia, see: Georgia Department of Education, *Fifty-Sixth and Fifty-Seventh Annual Reports, 1927-1928*, p. 94-146.

was secured by making the members of the State Board of Education *ex-officiis* members of the institutional boards. Another coordinating factor operative from 1909 to 1925 was the Board of Higher Curricula consisting of five members appointed by the Governor with the confirmation of the Senate. The function of the board appears to have been exclusively curricular and its effect on fiscal articulation was only incidental.[1] In 1929 a Board of Higher Education was created which has full power to reorganize the work of the higher institutions and eliminate unnecessary duplications.[2]

Before inaugurating this program the board was required to make a complete survey of state-supported higher education in Oregon. A salaried executive secretary has been appointed and maintains his office in the state Capitol. All relationships between the State Legislature and its committees and the institutions must be carried on through the Board of Higher Education. Advertising and publicity for the higher institutions must be approved by, and carry the name of, the Board of Higher Education. The board has full power in the preparation of a budget and in the allocation of funds among the institutions. The former separate millage taxes will be combined, thus constituting a single state tax of twenty-four cents per $100.00 for higher education, subject to distribution by the Board of Higher Education.

The history of the fiscal and administrative control of higher education in Oregon is a steady movement towards centralization. Exclusive private responsibility was succeeded in turn by state and private joint control, state control and support under separate boards, experimental attempts at partial consolidation, and finally a sweeping reorganization and absolute centralization of all higher education in the state.[3] The plan now in force centralizes higher education but leaves no coordinating agency between the teacher-training activities of these institutions and the public schools.

West Virginia and New Jersey represent a mixture of various principles of control. New Jersey has created a State Board of Regents for Higher Education responsible for all publicly supported higher education. This board exercises control, therefore, over the state-supported elements of Rutgers University which contains the Land Grant College and the State Woman's College and which is governed by a private Board of Trustees with a large state *ex-officio* membership. The State Board of Regents also exercises fiscal control over the state teacher-preparing institutions which, however, are directly controlled by the State Board of Education. In West Virginia the State Department of Education exercises educational control over the eight institutions for the preparation of teachers and the West Virginia State College (negro land grant college), but fiscal supervision is exercised over

[1] Leonard, Robert J. *The Coordination of State Institutions for Higher Education through Supplementary Curricular Boards.* Department of Education, Bureau of Research, Study No. 13. Berkeley, California: University of California, 1923. Chapter IV, p. 83-132.
[2] Onthank, Karl W. "Oregon Consolidates Government of Higher Educational Institutions." *School and Society* 30: 375-78; September 14, 1929.
Chambers M. M. "State Administration of Education." *Journal of Higher Education* 1: 203-07; April, 1930.
[3] See: Almack, John C. "History of the Oregon Normal Schools." *Quarterly of the Oregon Historical Society* 21: 102 ff. (Entire issue, March, 1920).

these institutions by the State Board of Control. The State University has its own governing board, but its fiscal relations with the state are also through the State Board of Control.

The situations in New Jersey and West Virginia represent a stage of development in the direction of centralized state control of all the state's educational agencies without removing immediate fiscal and general control from separate boards.

The most significant single characteristic of this group of states—Georgia, Iowa, Kansas, Mississippi, Nevada, North Dakota, Oregon, South Dakota, New Mexico, West Virginia, and New Jersey—is dependence upon affiliated control of higher institutions without extending the powers of the governing bodies to the public schools and without bringing the state department of education into the relationship in its capacity of supervisor of public school standards and development.

Centralized control through common boards—Four states, Florida, Idaho, Montana, and New York, have developed in quite different fashion centralized control of all their public educational agencies. In Florida the State Board of Control, strictly a governing body for the higher educational institutions and not a state budget agency, exercises the functions of institutional trusteeship for the University of Florida, the Woman's College, and the Land Grant College for Negroes, which are the only state higher institutions in the state. The board is subject to the supervision of the State Department of Education which of course exercises supervision over the public schools. The State Board of Control presents the state educational budget to the State Budget Commission. The Board of Control for higher institutions is free to appear before the Budget Commission.

Idaho, Montana, and New York represent a still more complete centralization of authority. In Montana a single board supervises the public schools, the two teacher-training institutions, the University, the School of Mines, and the Agricultural College, thus providing for unity of fiscal program for the entire system of state education. In Idaho the State Department of Education controls the normal schools, the University of Idaho, and the branch Junior College of the University at Pocatello. Articulation of all the elements of the state educational system is secured through the State Commissioner of Education, an officer who in this state exercises general supervision over all state education agents, including the State Superintendent of Public Instruction.

In New York the State Board of Regents as head of the Education Department exercises, subject to the provisions of the Education Law, general supervision over the public schools and in varying degrees supervises the teacher-training institutions, the State Colleges of Agriculture, Home Economics, and Veterinary Science at Cornell University, the State College of Forestry at Syracuse, the State Agricultural Experiment Station at Geneva, the State School of Clay Working and Ceramics at Alfred University, the State Merchant Marine Academy, and the six state schools of agriculture.

The details of certain aspects of the fiscal management of the New York system are of interest.

The general management and supervision of all public education is vested in the Education Department headed by the Board of Regents of the University of the State of New York whose chief administrative officer is the Commissioner of Education. Budget requests are prepared initially by the heads of the several state educational institutions and filed with the Commissioner of Education. These requests are reviewed and recommendations are made thereon to the Commissioner of Education by appropriate officers of the Department including the Assistant Commissioner for Finance who is the Department's coordinator in budgetary matters. Similarly the budget estimates for the Department *per se,* exclusive of institutional estimates but including all state aid funds for public schools, are developed by the Commissioner's authorized representatives in these matters. Later, both the institutional and central departmental estimates are presented together with the Commissioner's recommendations to the Regents Committee on Finance and Administration. Final departmental review and approval are exercised by the Regents Committee on Finance and Administration, subject to Board ratification. At this point, the budget requests become the official estimates of the Education Department. Opportunities for special conference and hearing are afforded institution heads and departmental division heads. In this manner there are provided close financial coordination and articulation of the state's educational interests in their entirety.

Departmental estimates are then transmitted to the State Director of the Budget, an appointee of the Governor. Hearings are held before the Governor and the Director of the Budget, in the presence and with the participation of the Chairman of the Senate Finance Committee and the Chairman of the Assembly Ways and Means Committee. At the executive hearing the Department is represented by the Commissioner, usually accompanied by the Deputy Commissioner, the Assistant Commissioner for Finance, the Director of Teacher Training, and other appropriate officers, depending upon the particular affairs at hand. Subsequent to these hearings the Governor presents his executive budget to the Legislature. The Legislature may not alter the executive budget except to strike out or reduce items therein, but it may add items stated separately and distinctly from the original items, each to refer to a single object or purpose.

Summary—This chapter has passed in review a series of state[1] educational programs which vary all the way from complete decentralization to complete centralization in a single board. In this process certain typical

[1] The territories of the United States are not included in the various groupings and discussions of state school systems as presented in this report. For comparative purposes a brief statement concerning the financial administration of education in the territories is given here. In *Alaska* public schools are supported from Federal, territorial, and local sources. Federal funds, amounting to approximately $50,000 per year, are spent in schools in the sparsely settled and outlying communities. In addition, the Federal government participates in the education of the native population and in the support of higher education. The territorial funds are distributed to incorporated cities and incorporated school districts. Territorial funds are also available for the

methods of securing fiscal control stand out, but it can surely be said that the differences among state organizations are far more numerous than their similarities. Indeed, it is impossible to find two states where the elements of the educational program are identical, and the classification of the states into the certain general types inevitably involves a statement of a wide variety of special cases and exceptions.

What conclusions can be extracted from this varied body of facts? It must be said at the outset that it is not the intention of the Commission to single out any particular device for coordinating the finance of state educational programs. The data presented do indicate with perfect clearness that the states have been compelled to seek a method for the fiscal articulation of their educational systems. In this search they have followed many different paths. Some have gone far toward the goal; others have barely started on their journey.

The facts presented, when inserted against their historical background, also indicate that the whole question of fiscal articulation as it applies to education is in a state of flux. No one is wise enough to foretell with assurance what the final outcome is to be. It is certain that the next few years will witness much experimentation in this field. In view of these facts, the welfare of the schools demands that educators approach the problems of coordination which have arisen, and which will arise in increasing numbers in the future, in an open and cooperative frame of mind. It is especially important in seeking the answer to the problem of financial articulation that the experience of other states be capitalized. No state has found the one and only solution to the problem, but the pooling of the experience of all states may in time point out the solution rather clearly. The material presented in this chapter is a first comprehensive attempt to bring together the experience of the states in attacking this problem through common boards.

(Continued from page 300) education and transportation of non-resident pupils. The local elected boards levy school taxes which amount to about one-fourth of the total public school expenditures. *Hawaii* has a regular American public school system including elementary, junior high, senior high, and special schools, a normal school, and a university. All public schools in the territory, except the university, which is under a Board of Regents, are administered by a Department of Public Instruction under a superintendent appointed by the Governor and confirmed by the Territorial Senate. Funds for public education are raised by direct territorial taxes, based on the biennial appropriations of the Legislature. No Federal funds are received except the usual aid for vocational education under the Smith-Hughes and similar acts. The public schools of the *Canal Zone* are financed as a single unit. Practically all funds are derived from local taxation, less than three percent of the total receipts being derived from the Federal government. In the *District of Columbia* the public school system, which comprises kindergartens, special schools, elementary and secondary schools, and teachers colleges, is supported jointly by the proceeds of local taxation and Congressional appropriations, the latter source contributing about one-fourth of the total. Public schools in the *Philippine Islands* are supported by insular, provincial, and municipal taxation, the former contributing about two-thirds of the total cost of elementary and secondary education and practically all of the funds for the University of the Philippines. Financial administration of education in *Porto Rico* is similar to that of the Philippine Islands. Funds for the public schools are raised by the insular government and the municipalities, the former contributing about three-fifths of the total cost of elementary and secondary education and practically all of the funds for the University of Porto Rico. The Federal government participates financially in the support of higher education.

CHAPTER XVI

FISCAL ARTICULATION THROUGH THE OPERATION OF STATE BUDGET SYSTEMS

THE FINANCING of education is not an isolated problem to be considered separately from the whole question of a state's economic condition or of the needs of other governmental services. The cost of education represents but a fraction of the governmental costs of the United States. In 1928, the total tax bill, Federal, state, and local, was something over nine and a quarter billion dollars, or about one-tenth of the national income. Education costs are approximately three billions. The problem of school support is, therefore, one-fourth of the country's fiscal problems, or if the consideration is limited to state and local taxation, school support is forty percent of the fiscal problem. It follows that the requirements of the schools need to be considered in relationship to the needs of other fundamental governmental activities.

This chapter describes briefly typical agencies and methods that the states have devised to articulate all the elements of public expenditure. The list of state fiscal obligations is a long one. Debts must be paid. Roads must be built and maintained. Governmental offices must be supported. The public health must be guarded by a whole series of inspectorial and regulatory services. The people must be afforded police protection. The courts must function. The physically and mentally handicapped must be given care. Education must be made as universal and as effective as possible if the people are to live happily and productively in their social and economic relationships. How to determine what proportion of the total income shall be devoted to each of these purposes, how to distribute equitably the funds that are made available among the many functions that must be performed, how to insure economical fiscal management of specific units of activity to which money is assigned—these are questions that are not easily solved. They demand the thought and the aid of educational leaders.

Development and significance of public budgeting—Reduced to its simplest terms, a budget is "a plan of expenditures for a definite period based on a careful estimate of needs and resources, together with definite proposals for financing these expenditures." [1] A public budget, therefore, is not a mere matter of accounting. Balance sheets and audits are merely tools of budget development; the budget itself anticipates future needs on the basis of past experience. It may thus become the fiscal expression of the highest type of statesmanship, making possible the maximum public welfare for the minimum of expenditure. [2]

---

[1] Fox, Leonard P. *Pennsylvania's Appropriation Methods and Budget Systems in the States.* Harrisburg: Pennsylvania State Chamber of Commerce, 1922.

[2] "Budgets are not merely affairs of arithmetic, but in a thousand ways go to the root of the prosperity of individuals, the relations of classes, the strength of kingdoms."—*William Ewart Gladstone.* For further analysis of the significance of budgeting consult: Buck, A. E. *Public Budgeting.* New York: Harper & Brothers, 1929. Chapter I.

Chaotic conditions of public financial management prior to 1910 combined with the steadily increasing demands for improved and extended public services provided the soil out of which grew a nation-wide movement for public budgeting. The establishment of the New York Bureau of Municipal Research in 1906 and the report of the United States Commission on Economy and Efficiency in 1912 pointed the way, and experimental legislation in California and Wisconsin showed how the budget could function in state governments. [1] Every state in the Union has now enacted laws governing its public budget, but most of these laws are recent. Only three of the present state budgetary laws were enacted prior to 1919, and over half of the present laws have been enacted since 1922.[2] These laws vary widely in both their theoretical wording and practical operation. All of them, however, may be classified, in terms of the agency responsible for preparing the budget, under three principal groups with several subheadings: [3]

I. Executive control (32 states) [4]
   A. By the governor
   B. By the governor's appointee
II. Multiple budget control (15 states)
   A. By two or more state officials
   B. By one or more state officials and members of the legislature
   C. By state officials and electors
III. Legislative budget control (1 state)

In the United States as a whole the executive budget is predominant, although in the South the practice is about evenly divided between types I and II.

In order to show in some detail how the various methods of state budgetary control operate, a typical state has been selected to illustrate each of the six types of control listed. The budgetary procedures of these six states will be described with special reference to the education budget.

Type I-A. Executive control by the governor—Maryland illustrates this method of integrating school support with the financial program of other state services and agencies. The original budget system of Maryland was incorporated in the state constitution in 1916. The present system was inaugurated in 1924. For the purpose of making up his budget the governor is empowered to require itemized estimates of needs and statements of expenditures from all state departments and institutions. The actual work of gathering and compiling these estimates is delegated by the governor to a state budget officer appointed by him. This budget officer is a full-time employee of the state who gives special attention to budgetary problems just previous to the legislative sessions. After consultations and hear-

---

[1] For a brief history of state budget legislation see: Buck, A. E., *op. cit.*, p. 10-24.
[2] Irvin, Oscar William. *State Budget Control of State Institutions of Higher Education.* Contributions to Education, No. 271. New York: Bureau of Publications, Teachers College, Columbia University, 1928. p. 1.
[3] Classification adapted from O. W. Irvin, *op. cit.*, p. 12-13. A. E. Buck (*op. cit.* p. 284-9) presents a somewhat different classification of budget-making authorities.
[4] Hawaii and the Philippine Islands also operate on the executive budget plan.

ings with the boards and departments concerned, the governor may make whatever adjustments seem advisable. These adjustments are made with full knowledge of the present and probable future financial status of the general treasury derived from a report submitted to the governor by the state comptroller. Soon after the convening of the legislature, the governor submits the biennial state budget to it. This budget includes money required for the schools and for all other general state governmental undertakings. Even after the budget is submitted to the legislature, the governor may amend it by submitting a supplementary budget. Hearings on the budget are held by the finance committees of both houses of the legislature. The governor may be present at these hearings. The legislature may reduce or strike out any item in the governor's budget, but it may not increase any item. When passed by the legislature, the budget bill becomes law without further action by the governor.

Chart IV shows graphically the relationships involved in Maryland budget procedure as far as education is concerned.

Type I-B. Executive control by the governor's appointee or appointees— Illinois adopted a budget law in 1917. This law was slightly modified in 1923. Illinois uses the director of finance, a gubernatorial appointee, as its budget officer. The department of public instruction and the various state institutions and departments submit estimates to him on or before October 15 of each even-numbered year; that is, just before the convening of the legislature. The director of finance is empowered to require detailed fiscal reports from all state institutions and departments. He may visit institutions, hold hearings, and investigate records. After the state budget is so prepared by this officer, the governor has the option of making additional changes in it. He then incorporates it in his message to the legislature soon after it convenes. The finance committees of both houses of the legislature next consider the budget and may hold further hearings on it. The legislature itself may amend the budget in any way whatever and may, in case of the governor's opposition, pass the amended budget over his veto by a two-thirds vote of both houses.[1]

Type II-A. Multiple control by several state officials—West Virginia is one of the six states in which a group of elected state officials is responsible for the budget. This group of officials is called the Board of Public Works and consists of seven members: the governor, the secretary of state, the auditor, the treasurer, the attorney-general, the state superintendent of schools, and the commissioner of agriculture. Institutions and boards submit estimates of their needs biennially to this board. These needs are compared with the state's future income as estimated by the auditor. The board submits its proposed budget to the legislature in two parts, one for each of the ensuing fiscal years. The Board of Public Works may amend its budget estimates in any way even after the budget has been submitted to the legislature. The legislature may not increase any item in the budget bill,

---

[1] For a description of the internal administration of the Illinois Department of Finance, see: Buck, A. E. *Public Budgeting*. New York: Harper & Brothers, 1929. p. 292-3.

CHART IV

Fiscal Aspects of Educational Articulation in Maryland

(Arrows show direction of budget estimates)

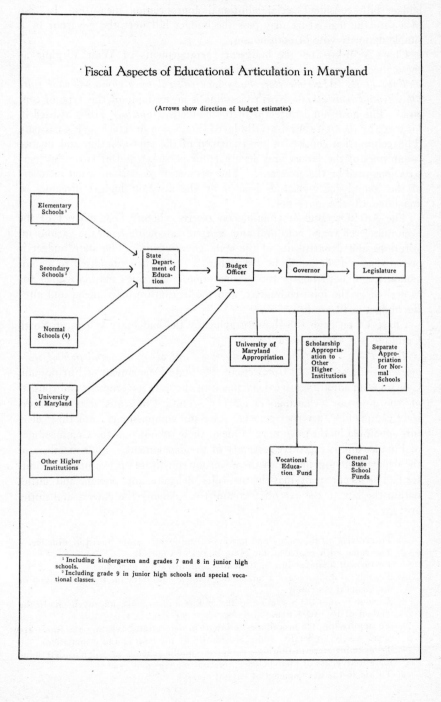

[1] Including kindergarten and grades 7 and 8 in junior high schools.

[2] Including grade 9 in junior high schools and special vocational classes.

although it may decrease any item and it may also, after the passage of the budget bill, consider special additional appropriation measures. In case of a veto the legislature may pass the budget bill over the governor by a simple majority vote of both houses.

Chart V illustrates the budgetary arrangements of West Virginia as these affect educational appropriations.

Type II-B. Multiple state budgetary control by a commission of state officials and legislators—North Carolina is an example of this type of control. The governor is director of the budget, *ex-officio*. He is assisted in his work by the State Advisory Budget Commission of which he is chairman. This commission consists of the chairmen of the appropriation and finance committees of the House and Senate (four persons) and of two other persons appointed by the governor. There is a staff of assistants, not members of the commission, which is headed by the assistant budget director, an appointee of the governor.

The Advisory Budget Commission receives, before September 1 of the even-numbered years, both oral and written statements from the various institutions and departments of the state government. The state budget is prepared and made public by December 1. It is then submitted to a joint committee of both houses for consideration. Hearings may be called for as desired by the joint committee, and the legislature may amend and alter the budget as it sees fit.

Chart VI on page 308 shows graphically the budgetary system of North Carolina as it applies to education.

Type II-C. Multiple state budgetary control by a commission of state officials and electors—In Connecticut, the State Department of Finance and Control is an administrative department of the state government and consists of: the governor (chairman *ex-officio*), secretary of state, state treasurer, state comptroller, attorney-general, state tax commissioner, and three electors appointed by the governor. One of these is known as the Commissioner of Finance and is executive secretary of the department. Four members of the department together with the governor constitute an executive committee. The department may by its rules delegate any powers and duties within the law to the executive committee. Among the powers and duties are:

1. To exercise all the rights and powers of the former State Board of Finance.
2. The same with regard to the State Board of Control.
3. To furnish financial information for administrative purposes.
4. To publish and prepare a financial statement and data for the information of the General Assembly.
5. To inquire into the operation of the budget and to make improvements in the method of its prepartion.
6. To inquire into the procedures followed in determining whether the funds are spent wisely, judicially, and economically by the boards and commissions.
7. To examine state institutions, except the public schools, in order to determine the effectiveness of their policies, internal management, etc.
8. To aid in the development of capital outlays.

CHART V

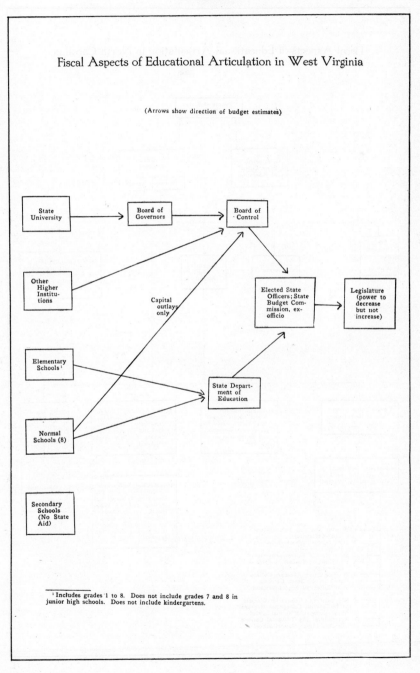

Fiscal Aspects of Educational Articulation in West Virginia

(Arrows show direction of budget estimates)

[1] Includes grades 1 to 8. Does not include grades 7 and 8 in junior high schools. Does not include kindergartens.

CHART VI

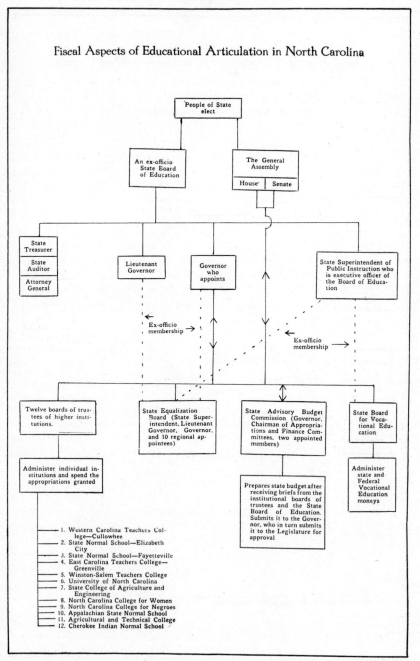

Fiscal Aspects of Educational Articulation in North Carolina

9. To establish means for caring for the physical property and to devise forms of operating reports and to require such reports from various administrative units that may be determined.

10. To amend the budget after it is submitted to the Legislature with the consent of the Legislature's Joint Standing Committee on Appropriations.

Type III.   Legislative control of the state budget—Arkansas is now the only representative of this type.   The Arkansas budget is prepared by a joint committee of the House and Senate especially constituted for this purpose.   The state auditor's office acts as a kind of staff agency for bringing the budget estimates together for the use of this committee.[1]

Summary—The preceding discussion of state budgetary systems is devoted largely to the mechanics of procedure and organization.   The charts emphasize the relation of educational units in the state system to the general plan of budgetary control.   While the purpose of this chapter is descriptive rather than critical, it should be noted that the effectiveness of the articulation of state expenditures secured through budgeting is conditioned by many factors in addition to the form of the agency set up.   Most important among these other factors are the personal interests, the limitations of knowledge, and the individual relationships of the men who prepare and execute the budget.   A successful state budgetary system calls for more than mere administrative machinery.   Trained men of wide social vision and implicit honesty who can contribute in a professional way to the development of fiscal policies are required.

What can the educational forces of a state contribute to the success of a budget program?   First, the necessity for proper budgeting of state resources can be recognized.   To urge the necessity for a coordinated state fiscal program need not lessen in the slightest degree a schoolman's devotion to the particular public enterprise in which he is engaged.   All public officials must cooperate if a state budget law is to succeed.   Not all budget laws are perfect, and it sometimes happens that in their operation such laws permit discrimination against education or otherwise handicap the professional work of school executives.   When such situations arise, it is well for school people actively to seek improvement in the law rather than to set themselves permanently outside the realm of cooperative financing.   School officials should also encourage, both in the educational units which they control and in their wider public relationships, the development of a balanced program of public expenditures.   This is equivalent to saying that educators need a sufficient grasp of the entire fiscal problem in their states so that they may view school support in proper perspective and as a phase, albeit an important phase, of the total fiscal question.   No attitude on the part of educators can do more harm to the cause of education than one of indifference and ignorance in regard to state obligations that are not directly educational.

[1] For description and brief critical discussion of the Arkansas budget control, see: Buck, A. E. *Public Budgeting.*   New York: Harper & Brothers, 1929.   p. 289.

CHAPTER XVII

FISCAL ARTICULATION OF EDUCATIONAL UNITS THROUGH INFORMAL AND NON-GOVERNMENTAL AGENCIES

THE COORDINATION of a state's program for the financing of public education may be brought about in three different ways. Under the first method, two or more educational units or institutions may be brought under common control and their financial affairs placed in the hands of a single common board. A second method is to assign the coordination of all state expenditures including those for education to a state budgeting agency. A third major type of financial articulation may be secured through the operation of informal conferences and non-governmental organizations. These three methods are not mutually exclusive. In fact, they are frequently used in combination in such a way as to supplement each other. The first method, coordination through the organization of common agencies of control, was discussed and illustrated in Chapter XV. The second method, coordination through a state budgeting agency, was discussed in Chapter XVI. The present chapter completes this survey of coordination methods by a brief discussion of informal conferences and organizations which have for their general purpose the articulation of finance in a state school system.

Importance of informal methods—The methods of coordination which are now to be presented differ fundamentally from the common boards and budgeting requirements discussed in preceding chapters. The essential characteristic of all the methods which have been discussed heretofore is that they are mandatory under the law. The methods now under consideration are merely voluntary and arise from a recognition by several agencies of mutual interests and of need for cooperative financial planning. While the importance of legal requirements for fiscal articulation is fully recognized, it should be noted that the mere creation by law of coordinating machinery is not in itself sufficient to solve the problem of fiscal articulation. However perfect this machinery may be, it cannot operate successfully unless there is back of it the human element of willingness to see the problem of educational finance as a whole. The most skillfully designed coordinating machinery will break down and become ineffective if it is operated by those with narrow or selfish viewpoints. Although the spirit of friendly cooperation may not appear on the statute books, it is nevertheless essential to the satisfactory solution of articulation problems. The spirit in which the laws described in the preceding chapters are carried out is far more important than the details of their wording.

Although informal coordinative agencies are important, an adequate description of them is a difficult task. The values with which such informal contacts deal are so intangible, and the results which arise from them may be so far removed in point of time from the original impetus, that it is extremely difficult to point to definite illustrations of fiscal coordination which have been secured by these informal agencies. Furthermore, since these agencies are extra-legal, they are not mentioned in the commonly used sources of information concerning state school systems, nor do they frequently find their way into other published documents. Consequently any treatment of these agencies is certain to be incomplete and fragmentary.

Types of informal methods—Certain major groups of agencies, however, can be identified clearly enough for the present purpose. These may be listed as follows:

1. Conferences of state or institutional officials
2. Councils sponsored chiefly by state education associations
3. Conventions and informal agreements
4. Lay organizations.

Each of these types of coordinating agencies will be briefly illustrated.

Conferences of state or institutional officials—This type may be illustrated by the association of presidents and business managers of state higher institutions in Colorado and by the conference of state educational institutions and the state superintendent of public instruction in Missouri. The former association is entirely informal. Its most important work is to develop a common legislative program before each session of the state legislature. An attempt is made to reach an agreement concerning appropriations to be requested by each institution. This association is now in its fifth year.[1]

In Missouri, each of the teacher-training institutions is governed by a separate board. This decentralized plan is somewhat modified by the voluntary creation of a conference of state educational institutions. The contribution of this conference in the decade since its organization has been estimated as follows:

1. It has promoted understanding and good will among the teachers colleges. Unwholesome rivalry has ceased to exist. As an illustration of the harmony that exists, one needs only to cite the fact that the needs of all the teachers colleges were presented to the appropriations committee of the Fifty-Third General Assembly in 1925 at a single hearing by a member of the board of regents of one of the schools.

2. It has developed mutual respect and trust on the part of the university on the one hand and the teachers college on the other. Credit is accepted hour for hour by the university and all of the teachers colleges.

3. Uniformity of administrative practice has been effected.

4. Multiplicity of courses has been discouraged.[2]

The work of state education associations—The contributions of state education associations in coordinating the finance program in their respective states have been of first importance. There is such an association in every state, and in nearly every case this association is constantly striving to become an integrating agency for all education, at least for all public education,

[1] For a description of the Colorado plan, see: Frasier, George Willard. "Experiments in Teachers College Administration; VII, An Adventure in Cooperation." *Educational Administration and Supervision* 14: 134-8; February, 1929.

[2] Hill, C. M. *A Decade of Progress in Teacher Training.* Contributions to Education, No. 233. New York: Bureau of Publications, Teachers College, Columbia University, 1927. 219 p.

within the state. For instance, in Alabama, a plan known as the "Unified Educational Program" was inaugurated in 1927. Under the leadership of the governor and the state superintendent of education, the legislative committee of the state education association prepared a single appropriation bill which reflected the needs of all phases of the state educational system from kindergarten to the higher institutions.[1] This bill was approved by the State Council of Education and submitted as an administrative measure. It was given practically unanimous approval by the legislature in 1927. This program does not change the status of the State Council of Education discussed in Chapter XV.

In West Virginia, an informal council of education has been organized under the general auspices of the state education association. An attempt has been made to represent every educational interest in the state in the personnel of this council. There are representatives of each of the major state institutions, of the various levels and units of education from kindergarten to university, of negro schools, of vocational education, and of other special groups. The council meets at various times, but its most important work is accomplished prior to the biennial sessions of the legislature. Similar organizations have been developed in other states.

Conventions and informal agreements—Still another type of informal coordination results from the wide variety of educational conferences which are held on local, state, regional, and national bases. These do not ordinarily have as their chief purpose the development of a program of educational articulation, but they contribute significantly to these programs nevertheless. It is impossible for a group of educators to come together in a county teachers' institute, in a state educational association, in a regional accreditive association, or in the annual meetings of the National Education Association without obtaining a broader view of the educational horizon. Contact with the problems faced by other units and institutions in the educational system, however incidental such contact may be, is bound to result in a steadily growing appreciation of the work being done and a greater willingness to envision the whole task of education as a single unit. In this sense, financial articulation is advanced every time a group of educational workers assembles.

The "service areas" of the state teacher-training institutions in Pennsylvania illustrate a type of informal agreement which may be reached by a group of educators and which leads to better financial articulation of a school system. In Pennsylvania, a separate board of trustees is provided for each unit in the state educational system. The separatism thus created is modified by the assignment of a "service area" to each institution. Each institution has a definite section of the state in which to work, and every section of the state is included in one, and only one, of these service areas.[2]

Lay organizations—The non-professional groups which directly or indirectly affect the formulation and execution of school finance programs are so

[1] Abercrombie, John W. "A State Education Program." *Proceedings, 1929.* Vol. 67. Washington, D. C.: National Education Association, 1929. p. 264-70.
    Alabama State Department of Education. (R. E. Tidwell, State Superintendent) *Annual Report,* 1928. Montgomery, Ala.
[2] For a map of the state showing the boundaries of these areas, see the joint advertisement of their summer sessions in: *Pennsylvania School Journal,* Vol. 78, back cover; May, 1930.

numerous and so varied in type that their total effect is particularly difficult
to summarize and evaluate. Alumni associations, taxpayers' organizations,
boards of trade, parent-teacher associations, civic clubs, service clubs, and
other groups influence the formulation of educational and financial policies
which may affect the articulation of the school system. Whether this effect
will be favorable or adverse depends largely on the attitude of the leaders
and on other special local conditions. Thus, an association of the alumni
of a particular higher institution may, through poor leadership and a selfish
viewpoint, overemphasize the financial needs of their own institution at the
expense of the proper development of other educational units. On the other
hand, a group of alumni representing several institutions may pool their
efforts in order to secure a program of coordinated financing for the educational needs of the entire state. Such a policy is contemplated in Virginia,
where an association of the alumni of the five state higher institutions is being
developed. Boards of trade in cities and towns at which state institutions
are located may demand financial support for their home institutions which
would distort the broader financial policy of the state, or may demand that
the state establish in their communities educational institutions which have
little reason for existence. Taxpayers' associations may, on the one hand, so
impede the collection of adequate school revenues that an articulated school
system is impossible, or they may champion a modern and coordinated system of public finance which will materially assist articulation. In short, lay
groups cannot be arbitrarily classified into those which aid and those which
impede articulation.

When the opposing effects are balanced, it is probably correct to assume
that the influence of organized lay groups on the articulation of education
is decidedly helpful. However, the educator and the layman are likely to
react quite differently to the same inarticulation in school finance. The layman deplores waste of public money which arises from such a condition, but
he is not likely to extend his analysis to include a consideration of the other
effects of the situation on the child. The educator, on the other hand, while
he is anxious to conserve public resources at every point, is more likely to
inquire concerning any given failure of coordination what the effect of this
failure is upon the education of the child. The layman thinks largely in
terms of wasted financial resources. The professional worker thinks first
in terms of wasted human resources. Both of these points of view are important, and a broad survey of the entire program of financing education
must be accommodated to both of them. It is only natural that the interest of lay groups should generally be centered chiefly on economies in public expenditures rather than on securing a coordinated school system. For
this very reason, however, plans prepared by laymen for the coordination of
education may need to be modified so as to place the primary emphasis where
it belongs; namely, on the provision of a method for paying for education
which will give every child full opportunity for smooth progress through the
school system.

Summarizing the field of unofficial efforts to secure the coordination of school finance, the Commission feels that the possibilities of such cooperation are more likely to be underestimated than overestimated. After all, the human element is fundamental and especially so in a series of problems so complicated as those presented in articulating a school system. In providing a coordinated program for school finance, there is no substitute for a cooperative point of view. The best plans of boards and budgets are likely to fall short of their full contribution unless these rather intangible personal values are also present.

Informal provisions for coordination may in some states be the first practical and desirable steps toward creating needed official agencies of educational articulation and of providing the contacts among educational leaders out of which may evolve the understanding basic to actual articulation. In other instances, informal agencies for coordination may make less necessary the creation of centralized boards with their possible limitation upon individual institutional autonomy and initiative. The Commission recommends, to those states which have made the least progress on the road toward coordinated educational financing, the advantages of informal, non-governmental bodies of articulation as a means to at least a partial solution of their difficulties.

CHAPTER XVIII

PRESENT DISTRIBUTION OF EXPENDITURES FOR EDUCATION

THE THREE preceding chapters have described certain existing practices for securing the articulation of educational expenditures. It is the purpose of this chapter to present a series of facts in regard to actual amounts and distributions of public expenditures both as between education and other state activities and also as among the various units of the educational work supported by the state. This presentation does not assume that these amounts and distributions are ideal or that a correct distribution can be determined upon the basis of these figures alone. Indeed, the Committee warns readers that judgments of specific local situations upon the basis of general practice or of averages of practice are, in regard to financial relationships, as unreliable and to be condemned as heartily as is any adoption of mediocrity as a standard of attainment. Rather, the correction of state and local inarticulations of educational and other expenditures should be based upon careful study in each state. The beginning of such a study is the determination of conditions now existing. The financial data presented by this chapter are merely intended as the first step in such investigation and as an indication of a technic that may be applied in greater detail to specific local situations.

If more complete data on school finance had been available, this preliminary study of the distribution of school expenditures might have been carried further. A comprehensive national survey of policies and practices in school finance is needed. Such an investigation should be undertaken by the United States Office of Education as soon as funds can be made available. It would encourage adequate support for public education without extravagance and would do much to encourage both the financial and the educational articulation of our state school systems.

Distribution of educational need—The first step in any consideration of the distribution of educational expenditures is to determine, at least in broad outline, the extent and nature of the educational need. A crude but nevertheless useful measure of need is the number of children of school age.[1] According to the 1920 census, in the United States as a whole 16.69 percent of the population is of elementary school age (6 to 13 years), 9.12 percent is of secondary school age (14 to 18 years), and 6.93 percent is of college age (19 to 22 years). If all persons between 6 and 22 years of age, inclusive, were in schools of some kind, such enrolment would amount to

---

[1] The use of this crude measure of educational need in this chapter does not imply that the Commission fails to recognize the desirability of the more accurate measures of educational need which some states are now developing.

practically one-third of the total population. The data on this distribution are presented by states in Table 77.

TABLE 77.—ELEMENTARY, SECONDARY, AND HIGHER EDUCATIONAL LOADS OF THE STATES, BASED ON 1920 CENSUS

State	Total Population	Population, Ages 6-13 Inclusive		Population, Ages 14-18 Inclusive		Population, Ages 19-22 Inclusive	
		Number	Per-cent	Number	Per-cent	Number	Per-cent
1	2	3	4	5	6	7	8
United States[1]...	105,710,620	17,645,108	16.69	9,645,887	9.12	7,321,028	6.93
Alabama.......	2,348,174	494,701	21.07	258,924	11.03	173,191	7.38
Arizona........	334,162	56,494	16.91	28,632	8.57	24,559	7.35
Arkansas.......	1,752,204	359,867	20.54	194,737	11.11	123,799	7.07
California......	3,426,861	434,444	12.68	239,947	7.00	210,539	6.14
Colorado.......	939,629	148,460	15.80	80,129	8.53	61,557	6.55
Connecticut....	1,380,631	208,642	15.11	108,626	7.87	87,316	6.32
Delaware.......	223,003	33,085	14.84	18,670	8.37	15,292	6.86
Florida........	968,470	174,694	18.04	94,502	9.76	69,471	7.17
Georgia........	2,895,832	598,265	20.66	321,586	11.11	224,961	7.77
Idaho..........	431,866	78,680	18.22	39,856	9.23	28,332	6.56
Illinois........	6,485,280	992,830	15.31	547,443	8.44	431,667	6.66
Indiana........	2,930,390	446,597	15.24	258,626	8.83	194,384	6.63
Iowa..........	2,404,021	374,203	15.57	217,489	9.05	167,843	6.98
Kansas........	1,769,257	293,396	16.58	165,133	9.33	124,833	7.06
Kentucky......	2,416,630	446,591	18.48	244,710	10.13	171,406	7.09
Louisiana......	1,798,509	354,548	19.71	196,458	10.92	138,728	7.71
Maine.........	768,014	113,687	14.80	64,956	8.46	48,897	6.37
Maryland......	1,449,661	226,148	15.60	132,110	9.11	105,765	7.30
Massachusetts..	3,852,356	557,466	14.47	303,595	7.88	249,715	6.48
Michigan.......	3,668,412	554,472	15.11	298,977	8.15	241,186	6.57
Minnesota......	2,387,125	385,673	16.16	222,156	9.31	171,989	7.20
Mississippi.....	1,790,618	376,590	21.03	206,851	11.55	133,338	7.45
Missouri.......	3,404,055	539,690	15.85	313,948	9.22	231,898	6.81
Montana.......	548,889	89,409	16.29	43,437	7.91	31,084	5.66
Nebraska.......	1,296,372	218,803	16.88	120,642	9.31	92,543	7.14
Nevada........	77,407	9,985	12.90	5,014	6.48	4,300	5.56
New Hampshire.	443,083	63,125	14.25	35,510	8.01	28,024	6.32
New Jersey.....	3,155,900	492,759	15.61	258,902	8.20	207,118	6.56
New Mexico....	360,350	69,777	19.36	35,727	9.91	25,991	7.21
New York......	10,385,227	1,504,964	14.49	820,878	7.90	697,659	6.72
North Carolina..	2,559,123	534,974	20.90	282,947	11.06	192,412	7.52
North Dakota...	646,872	129,302	19.99	63,789	9.86	44,346	6.86
Ohio..........	5,759,394	845,756	14.68	467,524	8.12	385,019	6.69
Oklahoma......	2,028,283	408,961	20.16	217,512	10.72	149,506	7.37
Oregon........	783,389	114,273	14.59	63,367	8.09	49,605	6.33
Pennsylvania...	8,720,017	1,438,689	16.50	759,579	8.71	569,346	6.53
Rhode Island...	604,397	90,220	14.93	51,584	8.53	40,966	6.78
South Carolina..	1,683,724	364,827	21.67	194,914	11.58	133,276	7.92
South Dakota...	636,547	112,872	17.73	60,599	9.52	45,751	7.19
Tennessee......	2,337,885	450,265	19.26	248,507	10.63	169,796	7.26
Texas.........	4,663,228	894,623	19.18	499,354	10.71	372,262	7.98
Utah..........	449,396	86,370	19.22	45,138	10.04	31,440	7.00
Vermont.......	352,428	52,958	15.03	30,196	8.57	21,567	6.12
Virginia........	2,309,187	440,516	19.08	240,977	10.44	174,329	7.55
Washington.....	1,356,621	197,668	14.57	107,237	7.90	86,156	6.35
West Virginia...	1,463,701	278,177	19.01	145,718	9.96	105,475	7.21
Wisconsin......	2,632,067	428,258	16.27	242,775	9.22	181,748	6.91
Wyoming......	194,402	30,755	15.82	14,907	7.67	12,856	6.61

[1] United States totals include figures for the District of Columbia.
Figures of columns 2, 3, 5, and 7 from Bureau of Census, Department of Commerce.

It should be noted that the educational loads of individual states vary from the national average. California and Nevada have the lowest elementary school load; Alabama, Mississippi, and South Carolina, the highest. The proportionate responsibility for secondary education also falls lightly on California and Nevada, while the heaviest load again is borne by such southern states as Alabama, Arkansas, Georgia, Mississippi, and the Carolinas. At the college level the western states of Montana and Nevada have the least proportionate responsibility, while such states as Georgia, Virginia, Texas, the Carolinas, and Louisiana have the heaviest proportion of the population of college age. With some exceptions, therefore, it would appear that the bi-racial South has a larger educational responsibility than the thinly populated West, other geographic areas occupying an intermediate position.

Special factors affecting educational need—Such data as these reveal the difficulties of attempting to indicate with any considerable degree of exactness the relative proportions of the school income which should be devoted to elementary, secondary, and higher education, respectively. While it is true that as a rule the states with a heavy educational load at one age-group level also have a heavy load at other levels, yet there are enough exceptions to make dangerous the arbitrary application of standards of relative expenditures. Again, when considering what proportion of the total income of a state is needed for educational purposes, it is obvious that data such as are presented in Table 77 must be taken into account. It follows that such facts as are given in Table 77 should be carefully interpreted in the light of special local or state factors affecting the total educational problem. These special conditions include the social character of the population, the income and wealth of the community, the sparsity of population, and the degree to which private enterprise participates in education.

Non-public educational enterprise—The last-named factor; namely, the extent of non-public educational enterprise, is of sufficient importance to justify brief discussion at this point. Table 78 on page 318 compares, by states, the enrolment in private and parochial elementary and secondary schools in 1927-28 with the educational load as measured by the number of persons 6 to 18 years of age in 1920. Two limitations to the accuracy of this table must be remembered. First, the population 6 to 18 years of age has probably increased in all states, though not in equal proportions, since 1920. The percent which non-public school enrolment is of total school population as given is therefore somewhat inflated. The size of this error is not known for any given state; for the country as a whole, it probably amounts to about ten percent. A second source of inaccuracy arises from the fact that many children are sent out of the state where they reside to attend private schools in other states. This factor doubtless considerably affects the situation in a state with many private schools.

Having in mind these limitations of the data, we may conclude from Table 78 that in the United States as a whole non-public schools enroll about nine percent of the total educational load at sub-collegiate levels. Figures for states vary enormously. The enrolment in non-public schools in such states as Massachusetts, New Hampshire, and Rhode Island is approximately one-fourth of the population ages 6 to 18, while in such states as Georgia, Nevada, South Carolina, and Tennessee these schools enroll less than one percent.

TABLE 78.—POPULATION OF SCHOOL AGE IN 1920 AND NON-PUBLIC SCHOOL ENROLMENT IN 1927-28

State	Population, Ages 6 to 18, in 1920	Enrolment in Non-Public Elementary and Secondary Schools in 1927-28	Percent Enrolment in Non-Public Schools Is of Population 6 to 18
1	2	3	4
United States[1]........	27,290,995	2,576,157	9.44
Alabama..............	753,625	17,826	2.37
Arizona..............	85,126	4,196	4.93
Arkansas.............	554,604	6,855	1.24
California............	674,391	57,221	8.48
Colorado.............	228,589	12,719	5.56
Connecticut..........	317,268	56,011	17.65
Delaware............	51,755	7,189	13.89
Florida..............	269,196	6,606	2.45
Georgia..............	919,851	7,730	.84
Idaho...............	118,536	2,952	2.49
Illinois..............	1,540,273	270,819	17.58
Indiana.............	705,223	67,899	9.63
Iowa................	591,692	47,371	8.01
Kansas..............	458,529	39,350	8.58
Kentucky............	691,301	37,542	5.43
Louisiana............	551,006	42,776	7.76
Maine...............	178,643	26,351	14.75
Maryland............	358,258	43,164	12.05
Massachusetts........	861,061	201,336	23.38
Michigan............	853,449	134,324	15.74
Minnesota...........	607,829	60,033	9.88
Mississippi...........	583,441	9,047	1.55
Missouri.............	853,638	70,029	8.20
Montana............	132,846	9,692	7.30
Nebraska............	339,445	24,847	7.32
Nevada..............	14,999	....	....
New Hampshire.......	98,635	26,568	26.94
New Jersey..........	751,661	127,395	16.95
New Mexico..........	105,504	8,296	7.86
New York............	2,325,842	381,325	16.40
North Carolina.......	817,921	9,091	1.11
North Dakota........	193,091	8,528	4.42
Ohio................	1,313,280	171,063	13.03
Oklahoma...........	626,473	6,746	1.08
Oregon..............	177,640	10,599	5.97
Pennsylvania.........	2,198,268	300,602	13.67
Rhode Island.........	141,804	32,648	23.02
South Carolina.......	559,741	3,449	.62
South Dakota........	173,471	10,558	6.09
Tennessee............	698,772	6,609	.95
Texas...............	1,393,977	42,068	3.02
Utah................	131,508	4,808	3.66
Vermont.............	83,154	8,544	10.27
Virginia.............	681,493	8,439	1.25
Washington..........	304,905	20,703	6.79
West Virginia........	423,895	8,336	1.97
Wisconsin...........	671,033	104,323	15.55
Wyoming............	45,662	796	1.74

[1] United States totals include figures for the District of Columbia.

In spite of this and other complicating factors, a state like Mississippi, where forty percent of the total population is potentially of school age, will certainly need to spend porportionately more for the education of its children than such a state as Nevada, which has less than twenty-five percent of its population included in the ages 6 to 22. The variations in educational load are further accentuated by a number of other factors, of which the following are important:

1. States with the highest percent of persons 6 to 22 years of age probably have also a high percentage of children under 6 years. While these children do not require ordinary school facilities, they are consumers of income.

2. The necessary accompaniment of a high percent of persons of school age and of pre-school age is a low percent of persons in the income-producing ages.

3. Those states where the educational burden is heaviest follow a policy of race-segregation in their schools. This policy, of course, involves the additional expense incident to a dual system of education.

4. The relative ability of the states to support education [1] varies significantly. These differences in ability, in general, accentuate the problem resulting from a disproportionate educational load.

Such considerations as these serve to reinforce the point that neither the fixing of proportionate expenditures for school and for public purposes nor the establishment of standards for the relative proportions of school support which ought to be allotted to elementary schools, secondary schools, teacher-training institutions and other higher institutions is possible on a national basis. Such decisions call for local and state-wide investigations of educational needs and financial resources.

School costs and total tax collections—A study of needs and resources may be a first step, but it is not the only step, in a state or local investigation of the financial aspects of educational articulation. The second step would probably be the determination of the existing relationship between school costs and other governmental costs. In the United States as a whole, school costs represent 40.18 percent of all state and local tax collections, and 26.36 percent of all Federal, state, and local tax collections. The variations from these national averages in certain states are shown in Table 79 on pages 320-21. Columns 6 and 7 of Table 79 show respectively the percent school costs are of state and local tax collections and of Federal, state, and local tax collections. Certain conclusions of interest may be drawn from a study of these columns.

First, the variations between the extreme states are great. The percent in Column 6 for New Mexico is more than half as much again as the average percent for the United States, while at the other extreme is Massachusetts with approximately three-fourths of the national average.

Second, states of the sparsely settled Rocky Mountain area spend a high percent of their total tax collections for schools. At the opposite extreme are found eastern and southern states. Such conditions, however, must be conservatively interpreted. A state may be compelled, because of sparse and

---

[1] National Education Association, Research Division. "The Ability of the States To Support Education." *Research Bulletin* Vol. IV, Nos. 1 and 2; January and March, 1926. Washington, D. C.: the Association.

TABLE 79.—SCHOOL COSTS AND OTHER GOVERNMENTAL COSTS, 1928 [1]

State	Cost of Public Education—Elementary, Secondary, and Higher—in 1928	Tax Collections, 1928			Percent School Costs Are of Tax Collections of		Rank in Column 6	Rank in Column 7
		Federal Government	State Government	Local Government	State and Local Government	Federal, State, and Local Government		
1	2	3	4	5	6	7	8	9
United States[2]	$2,448,633,561	$3,194,000,000	$1,465,000,000	$4,629,845,000	40.18	26.36	....	....
Alabama	24,540,666	19,930,560	20,782,406	31,317,000	47.10	34.07	12	17
Arizona	10,171,145	3,928,620	7,958,997	15,393,000	43.56	37.28	17	13
Arkansas	15,946,309	12,935,700	16,148,788	22,080,000	41.71	31.17	25	23
California	158,169,068	150,948,440	81,420,202	304,999,000	40.93	29.43	28	27
Colorado	28,855,704	16,225,520	13,379,693	44,002,000	50.29	39.20	7	8
Connecticut	35,181,656	41,873,340	27,977,484	64,751,000	37.94	26.14	37	37
Delaware	4,098,671	21,112,340	7,341,298	5,096,000	32.95	12.22	46	48
Florida	33,500,859	28,618,240	20,795,290	78,202,000	33.84	26.25	43	36
Georgia	21,156,251	28,043,320	20,766,116	39,809,000	34.93	23.87	42	43
Idaho	12,595,605	3,545,340	4,845,766	19,523,000	51.69	45.12	5	4
Illinois	157,559,178	244,788,160	70,524,724	307,691,000	41.66	25.29	26	42
Indiana	80,067,480	47,494,780	33,013,333	124,569,000	50.81	39.04	6	9
Iowa	61,446,373	22,549,640	29,570,654	98,985,000	47.80	40.66	11	6
Kansas	49,331,743	26,765,720	19,776,417	79,858,000	49.51	39.03	8	10
Kentucky	27,591,933	34,495,200	25,026,965	44,384,000	39.75	26.55	33	34
Louisiana	25,185,418	22,389,940	22,026,503	47,203,000	36.38	27.49	40	29
Maine	12,620,133	11,690,040	13,851,838	23,658,000	33.65	25.65	44	41
Maryland	27,279,981	37,114,280	16,727,408	52,005,000	39.69	25.77	34	39
Massachusetts	86,547,480	119,806,940	45,120,632	233,969,000	31.01	21.70	48	44
Michigan	127,686,391	186,210,200	78,642,774	232,092,000	41.09	25.69	27	40
Minnesota	60,239,295	38,839,040	42,968,390	109,125,000	39.61	31.55	35	21
Mississippi	22,928,806	10,859,600	10,818,460	46,229,000	40.19	33.77	32	18
Missouri	58,309,634	78,061,360	34,057,036	102,488,000	42.70	27.17	21	31
Montana	14,857,064	6,100,540	6,163,345	24,424,000	48.57	40.50	10	7
Nebraska	31,827,517	11,849,740	17,132,224	56,153,000	43.43	37.39	18	12

TABLE 79.—SCHOOL COSTS AND OTHER GOVERNMENTAL COSTS, 1928 (Continued)

State	Cost of Public Education—Elementary, Secondary, and Higher—in 1928	Tax Collections, 1928			Percent School Costs Are of Tax Collections of		Rank in Column 6	Rank in Column 7
		Federal Government	State Government	Local Government	State and Local Government	Federal, State, and Local Government		
1	2	3	4	5	6	7	8	9
Nevada	2,976,810	1,117,900	2,048,545	4,913,000	42.76	36.85	20	14
New Hampshire	8,600,068	5,908,900	7,312,706	18,262,000	33.63	27.32	45	30
New Jersey	110,166,133	117,730,840	74,874,418	226,333,000	36.57	26.30	39	35
New Mexico	7,288,192	2,555,200	3,313,920	7,408,000	67.98	54.89	1	1
New York	312,246,466	769,306,840	207,738,753	745,605,000	32.75	18.13	47	46
North Carolina	47,047,191	227,764,140	32,152,468	63,732,000	49.07	14.54	9	47
North Dakota	18,641,250	3,705,040	7,806,965	27,335,000	52.96	47.92	3	2
Ohio	152,899,048	163,756,380	35,401,087	297,522,000	45.93	30.79	13	24
Oklahoma	36,507,624	30,470,760	22,005,032	68,715,000	40.24	30.13	31	25
Oregon	24,272,132	9,901,400	18,615,619	44,843,000	38.25	33.09	36	20
Pennsylvania	188,023,939	279,506,940	120,599,628	328,016,000	41.91	25.82	24	38
Rhode Island	13,528,763	17,279,540	9,650,028	23,675,000	40.60	26.73	30	33
South Carolina	19,512,899	12,169,140	16,179,615	27,255,000	44.92	35.09	14	15
South Dakota	17,561,217	3,896,680	10,467,248	31,153,000	42.19	38.58	23	11
Tennessee	26,906,480	28,394,660	19,084,848	43,787,000	42.80	29.48	19	26
Texas	78,684,784	69,820,840	58,282,919	122,037,000	43.64	31.46	16	22
Utah	12,222,188	5,972,780	8,483,791	14,723,000	52.67	41.89	4	5
Vermont	6,018,651	3,800,860	6,511,243	10,307,000	35.79	29.19	41	28
Virginia	30,821,350	91,348,400	31,092,151	44,383,000	40.84	18.48	29	45
Washington	38,774,376	19,291,760	29,873,241	61,804,000	42.29	34.94	22	16
West Virginia	30,132,107	22,900,980	18,705,303	49,097,000	44.44	33.22	15	19
Wisconsin	59,077,788	59,216,760	34,781,426	124,387,000	37.12	27.05	38	32
Wyoming	7,089,619	3,162,060	3,182,303	9,241,000	57.79	45.95	2	3

[1] Source of data:
Column 2, U. S. Department of the Interior, Office of Education.
Columns 3 and 5, *Cost of Government in the United States in 1927-28*, National Industrial Conference Board, pages 66, 77, and 84.
Column 4, *Financial Statistics of States, 1928*. U. S. Department of Commerce, Bureau of the Census. (Advance figures.)
[2] United States totals include figures for the District of Columbia.

scattered population, to spend large sums of money and yet purchase relatively small amounts of schooling. It has been estimated that in states with an average of one child or less per square mile, 40 percent of the total cost of education is due to the sparseness of the population; that this percent grows slowly less as the density of population increases; and that the effect of sparseness of population is reduced to zero in states where the average number of children per square mile is 17 and over.[1] Thus a state with a concentrated population may, on the other hand, be able to offer good educational opportunities at relatively less cost. Sparsity of population is only one of many factors which operate to increase or decrease the total amounts required to operate public schools within a given state. Furthermore, a state which has an elaborate and expensive road-building program or public health service, or which engages on a large scale in other state or local government activities will, other things being equal, spend a lower percent of its total taxes for schools than a state in which governmental services other than education are undertaken infrequently and only on a small scale.

Finally, the figures in Table 79 point once more to the need for state investigations of the financial relationships between education and the other activities of government. State legislatures and educational survey commissions as well as individual citizens and taxpayers frequently raise the question, What percent of our total government expenditures should we allot to schools? The ordinary method used to answer such questions is to assemble data to show that while "we" spend only 38 percent of our taxes for schools, city A or state B spends 51 percent. Therefore, we must increase our relative expenditures for education or be disgraced. Those who oppose an increase in taxes, especially an increase in school taxes, promptly assemble data which show that city C or state D spends less than 38 percent of its taxes for schools. Pie-shaped charts now begin to make their appearance showing a meager or a generous "cut" for education, according to the point of view of the issuing agencies. In the end, the appropriations made or the taxes levied for educational purposes are too frequently controlled by extraneous and accidental circumstances. Plainly, the answer to the question should not be sought by comparative methods alone. While comparative and national data have a certain value, a financial program which will coordinate education with other public services must go beyond such general data and utilize the findings which result from careful objective study of local conditions.

School costs at various levels—The problem of fiscal coordination is only half solved when financial relationships between schools and other public interests have been determined. There yet remains the problem of distributing funds for public school purposes among the elementary and secondary schools, teacher-training institutions,[2] and other higher educational agen-

[1] Staffelbach, Elmer H. "The Relationship of School Population Density to Educational Unit-Costs in the States." *Educational Administration and Supervision* 14: 73-85; February, 1928.
[2] Throughout this chapter, unless otherwise stated, "teacher-training institution" means a separate institution conducted specifically for the professional preparation of public school teachers. It does not include departments of education in universities and colleges.

cies. This problem is, even in its simplest terms, a difficult one, and it is further complicated by the diversity of sources drawn upon for public school revenues. The Federal government, the state governments, various intermediate units such as cities, counties, and towns, and the local school districts, all contribute to the support of public education at its various levels. Furthermore, these units do not contribute uniformly or proportionately to all educational levels. Nor is the situation at all clarified by the great diversity of state and local administrative machinery for the control of school finance. Once again the need for considering local conditions and the consequent limitations of general and purely statistical data must be asserted. There are, however, certain useful types of data which will be presented at this point. These are presented not as solutions but rather as indications of the type of investigations which may supply basic data for policy-forming in the financing of a state or local school system.

Before analyzing in turn the Federal, state, and local contributions to education, it is necessary to note that many public educational institutions receive significant sums of money also from private sources. These are chiefly in the form of gifts and tuition payments. The former have been directed very largely to the education of the negro race and to the institutions of higher learning.[1] The latter, tuition charges, are now confined, in public schools, almost exclusively to higher education. Tuition payments are an increasingly important source of revenue for both public and private higher education. They amounted in 1928 to $126,940,315. Tuition payments were eleven percent of the total revenue receipts of publicly controlled universities and colleges, and thirty-four percent of the total revenue of privately supported colleges and universities.[2]

School income from Federal sources—From Federal sources $42,239,210 was provided for the support of schools in the school year 1927-28.[3] The distribution of this sum among the various educational levels is shown in Table 80 on pages 324-25. It will be noted that, broadly speaking, the greatest proportionate Federal participation in elementary-secondary education is to be found in those states in which the permanent school fund, based on Federal grants, is an important source of school revenue. In the New England states, which received practically no Federal land grants for elementary-secondary schools, an opposite condition prevails, nearly all the Federal income for schools being devoted to higher education. Table 80 as a whole also indicates that substantial sums of money are involved in the

---

[1] Cubberley, Ellwood P. *State School Administration.* Boston: Houghton Mifflin Company, 1927. Chapter 28.

Sears, J. B. *Philanthropy in the History of American Higher Education.* U. S. Department of the Interior, Bureau of Education, Bulletin, 1922, No. 26. Washington, D. C.: Government Printing Office.

[2] U. S. Department of the Interior, Office of Education. *Statistics of Universities, Colleges and Professional Schools 1927-1928.* Bulletin, 1929, No. 38. Washington, D. C.: Government Printing Office. p. 34.

Greenleaf, Walter J. "Fiscal Support of Colleges." *Journal of Higher Education* 1: 255-60; May, 1930.

[3] This does not include the support of schools in the territories or in the District of Columbia. It does include the income from state school funds and lands *based on grants of land or money made to the state* by the Federal government.

TABLE 80.—FEDERAL INCOME FOR PUBLIC EDUCATION, 1927-28 [1]

State	For Elementary and Secondary Schools	For Teacher-Training Institutions[2]	For Higher Education Other Than Teacher Training	Percent of Total Federal Income for Public Education Spent for			Rank in Column 5
				Elementary and Secondary Schools	Teacher Training	Higher Education Other Than Teacher Training	
1	2	3	4	5	6	7	8
United States	$27,907,441	$197,420	$14,134,349	66.07	.47	33.46	......
Alabama	118,850		397,978	23.00		77.00	42
Arizona	324,939		207,858	60.99		39.01	22
Arkansas	182,580	1,712	294,320	38.28	.16	61.72	32
California	800,077		306,922	72.16		27.68	15
Colorado	832,759		214,332	79.53		20.47	7
Connecticut	85,502		154,791	35.58		64.42	33
Delaware	19,300		151,072	11.33		88.67	48
Florida	338,149		232,195	59.29		40.71	24
Georgia	157,000	3,019	326,474	32.27	.62	67.11	36
Idaho	681,468		276,612	71.13		28.87	16
Illinois	1,489,015		396,997	78.95		21.05	9
Indiana	1,250,743	2,774	355,471	77.74	.17	22.09	10
Iowa	607,033		365,303	62.43		37.57	21
Kansas	605,858	12,015	286,803	66.97	1.33	31.70	18
Kentucky	127,605		340,843	27.24		72.76	39
Louisiana	317,405		278,266	53.29		46.71	27
Maine	27,228		188,366	12.63		87.37	45
Maryland	73,245		221,672	24.84		75.16	41
Massachusetts	215,078	36,594	164,410	51.69	8.80	39.51	28
Michigan	571,082		383,527	59.82		40.18	23
Minnesota	2,327,922		436,146	84.22		15.78	3
Mississippi	187,363		346,972	35.06		64.94	34
Missouri	1,912,507		383,402	83.30		16.70	4
Montana	1,203,518	35,370	247,820	80.95	2.38	16.67	5
Nebraska	954,245		292,850	76.52		23.48	11

TABLE 80.—FEDERAL INCOME FOR PUBLIC EDUCATION, 1927-28 (Continued)

State	For Elementary and Secondary Schools	For Teacher-Training Institutions[2]	For Higher Education Other Than Teacher Training	Percent of Total Federal Income for Public Education Spent for			Rank in Column 5
				Elementary and Secondary Schools	Teacher Training	Higher Education Other Than Teacher Training	
1	2	3	4	5	6	7	8
Nevada............	190,193	......	158,541	54.54	......	45.46	26
New Hampshire.....	21,467	7,167	152,620	11.84	3.96	84.20	47
New Jersey........	162,388	......	214,603	43.07	......	56.93	30
New Mexico........	1,002,281	......	167,312	85.69	......	14.31	1
New York..........	564,687	64,902	376,605	56.12	6.45	37.43	25
North Carolina....	159,539	......	363,501	30.50	......	69.50	38
North Dakota......	1,123,607	10,000	343,175	76.08	.68	23.24	12
Ohio..............	928,673	......	339,436	73.23	......	26.77	14
Oklahoma..........	1,883,959	......	484,923	79.53	......	20.47	8
Oregon............	446,236	......	193,761	69.72	......	30.28	17
Pennsylvania......	425,671	......	514,355	45.28	......	54.72	29
Rhode Island......	38,044	......	133,371	20.97	......	73.52	44
South Carolina....	129,467	10,000	368,560	26.00	5.51	74.00	40
South Dakota......	1,533,197	......	278,991	84.60	......	15.40	2
Tennessee.........	290,563	......	388,427	42.80	......	57.20	31
Texas.............	254,057	3,000	501,463	33.49	.40	66.11	35
Utah..............	424,675	......	210,769	66.83	......	33.17	19
Vermont...........	24,551	10,267	168,966	12.05	5.04	82.91	46
Virginia..........	154,903	......	349,160	30.73	......	69.27	37
Washington........	1,129,201	......	367,074	75.47	......	24.53	13
West Virginia.....	75,907	600	267,024	22.10	.17	77.73	43
Wisconsin.........	572,917	......	297,377	65.83	......	34.17	20
Wyoming...........	960,767	......	242,933	79.82	......	20.18	6

[1] Data furnished through the land grant college survey.

[2] Teacher-training statistics in this chapter refer only to institutions above the secondary level whose chief or only function is the preparation of teachers. State and city normal schools and teachers colleges are included. Schools of education in state universities, and normal departments administered as parts of high schools are not included. The separation of teacher-training statistics in this table and elsewhere, from those for other higher institutions is done merely as a matter of interest and convenience. The separation does not imply that teacher training is not a phase of higher education.

Federal contributions to education. It follows, therefore, that the extent and influence of this factor should be carefully considered in making local investigations of financial articulation.

School income from state sources—State contributions to education must also be considered. The various states differ greatly both in the relative parts which they play in school finance, and in the way in which they divide their state school moneys among the various aspects of education. Certain significant facts concerning the states' participation in school support are brought out in Table 81 on pages 328-29. This table shows the total income from state sources for public education and the proportion of this income which is devoted respectively to the elementary-secondary school system and to teacher training and other higher education.

New York, Pennsylvania, and New Jersey lead in the proportion of state income devoted to elementary-secondary schools. Delaware, with practically a single state system of public school finance, is also in this group. At the opposite extreme, devoting most of their state school income to the support of higher education, are the states of Kansas and Colorado, which have practically no state funds for the lower schools. The states which devote the smallest fraction of total state school aid to higher education are chiefly those without state controlled and supported universities.

School income from local sources—State and Federal sources of support for education provide only a minor part of the total school costs. The largest share of school costs is borne by units of lesser extent—chiefly the city, the county, the town, and the school district. The distribution of these local expenditures is displayed in Table 82 on pages 330-31. The outstanding fact shown by Table 82 is that local funds are almost exclusively directed to elementary and secondary schools. In the United States as a whole, less than one percent of the local school revenue is devoted to teacher-training and other higher institutions of learning. In eleven states, no local support is given to higher institutions. The chief higher institutions to which public local support is directed are junior colleges and municipal universities.

School income from Federal, state, and local sources—When we bring together certain of the statistics contained in Tables 80, 81, and 82, the relative parts now played by Federal, state, and local contributions become clear. This has been done in Table 83 on page 331. Table 83 shows that the state is the chief source of income both for teacher-training institutions and for other public higher education. The second source of income for these two groups of institutions is, in both cases, the institutional sources such as fees, tuitions, and sales. The least important contributory units for teacher training and for other higher education are the local districts and the counties. The local districts are more important than the counties in higher education, and less important in teacher training. What they fail to do for higher education, the local districts more than compensate for in support of elementary-secondary schools. At this level, the local units lead easily, with the state in second place, Federal contributions being of the least importance. In a sentence, Federal, state, county, local, and institutional sources contribute to every one of the units and levels of education, but the state leads in the support of teacher training and other higher education; the local districts, in the support of elementary-secondary education.

Turning from national to state-wide statistics on the distribution of school revenues, as presented in Table 84 on pages 332-33; these conclusions can be drawn:

1. The elementary-secondary school system constitutes by far the major proportion of the burden of financial support for public education. Higher education comes next, and teacher training last. In no state do the teacher-training and other higher institutions together absorb more than a fifth of the total income for public education of all kinds.

2. The Eastern states spend a large proportion of their total school budget for public elementary and secondary schools.

3. The six states which spend the greatest proportion of their school income for higher education are southern or border states. These six states are evenly divided as far as centralization of the fiscal control of higher education is concerned. Virginia, Arkansas, and North Carolina are rather decentralized; Delaware, Mississippi, and South Carolina are more centralized. There is nothing in these data to indicate, therefore, that either centralized or decentralized fiscal control of higher education results *per se* in giving a more generous share of the total school income to higher education.

4. The states which show relatively high amounts spent for teacher training (Kentucky, North Dakota, Oklahoma, and Wisconsin) are not geographically related. Nor do they exhibit any uniformity as to type of fiscal control. In one of these states, teacher training is controlled by the state board of education; in two, by boards specially created for the purpose; and in one, by a local board of trustees for each institution.

5. The same diversification of methods of control appears among the half dozen states which spend the lowest percent of their total school income for teacher training—New York, Ohio, Oregon, Montana, Indiana, and California.[1] These, too, are geographically scattered. Four of them have centralized and two of them have decentralized fiscal control of teacher training. Again it must be concluded that neither centralization nor decentralization *per se* insures a relatively high financial support for teacher training.

Elementary and secondary school costs—In all of the foregoing material, elementary and secondary education have been considered as a single unit. It would be highly desirable to segregate costs for these two levels of school organization. Unfortunately, however, such a segregation for the nation as a whole or even for a major proportion of the nation's schools is not at present available. The United States Office of Education has collected from fourteen states statistics on school expenditures separated into elementary and secondary costs. These statistics, together with certain derived

---

[1] Not including the states which maintain no separate teacher-training institutions.

TABLE 81.—STATE INCOME FOR PUBLIC EDUCATION, 1927-28 [1]

State	For Elementary and Secondary Schools	For Teacher-Training Institutions	For Higher Education Other than Teacher Training	Percent of Total State Income for Public Education Spent for			Rank in Column 5	Rank in Column 7
				Elementary and Secondary Schools	Teacher Training	Higher Education Other than Teacher Training		
1	2	3	4	5	6	7	8	9
United States	$343,453,929	$40,480,944	$109,455,850	69.61	8.21	22.18	......	......
Alabama	8,182,458	449,683	1,520,499	80.59	4.43	14.98	6	39
Arizona	1,764,356	463,619	674,433	60.79	15.97	23.24	27	30
Arkansas	3,673,593	140,720	765,956	80.21	3.07	16.72	8	37
California	24,531,367	1,937,871	8,432,441	70.29	5.55	24.16	17	26
Colorado	503,198	648,156	1,759,785	17.29	22.26	60.45	47	2
Connecticut	1,106,723	766,151	600,240	44.75	30.98	24.27	38	25
Delaware	3,608,377	....	581,524	86.12	......	13.88	4	40
Florida	2,263,917	....	2,098,658	51.89	......	48.11	30	9
Georgia	5,176,564	377,459	1,561,525	72.75	5.30	21.95	13	32
Idaho	332,910	431,044	807,838	21.18	27.42	51.40	44	6
Illinois	9,710,593	2,297,140	5,833,412	54.43	12.87	32.70	29	19
Indiana	1,836,483	867,774	3,689,682	28.72	13.57	57.71	43	3
Iowa	4,661,248	618,500	5,552,028	43.03	5.71	51.26	40	7
Kansas	521,833	1,038,020	3,062,860	11.29	22.45	66.26	48	1
Kentucky	5,838,799	1,711,795	1,379,450	65.38	19.17	15.45	24	38
Louisiana	5,600,951	433,017	1,632,731	73.05	5.65	21.30	12	33
Maine	3,658,048	270,000	567,664	81.37	6.00	12.63	5	42
Maryland	3,855,384	739,874	716,741	72.58	13.93	13.49	15	41
Massachusetts	11,735,413	1,705,875	1,178,779	80.27	11.67	8.06	7	45
Michigan	22,303,648	2,974,661	7,839,706	67.35	8.98	23.67	22	28
Minnesota	9,630,292	903,532	4,713,231	63.16	5.93	30.91	25	20
Mississippi	5,577,527	292,839	2,608,984	65.78	3.45	30.77	23	21
Missouri	3,224,893	1,243,495	1,897,732	50.66	19.53	29.81	32	22
Montana	889,033	133,335	950,987	45.05	6.76	48.19	37	8
Nebraska	2,042,397	759,000	2,133,197	41.39	15.38	43.23	41	13

TABLE 81.—STATE INCOME FOR PUBLIC EDUCATION, 1927-28 (Continued)

State	For Elementary and Secondary Schools	For Teacher-Training Institutions	For Higher Education Other than Teacher Training	Percent of Total State Income for Public Education Spent for			Rank in Column 5	Rank in Column 7
				Elementary and Secondary Schools	Teacher Training	Higher Education Other than Teacher Training		
1	2	3	4	5	6	7	8	9
Nevada	374,566	....	115,075	76.50	......	23.50	11	29
New Hampshire	926,665	212,500	657,184	51.59	11.83	36.58	31	17
New Jersey	21,490,242	1,797,797	1,457,719	86.84	7.27	5.89	3	46
New Mexico	766,580	176,750	397,570	57.17	13.18	29.65	28	23
New York	72,547,885	2,140,715	2,382,491	94.13	2.78	3.09	1	48
North Carolina	4,151,290	819,858	3,303,615	50.17	9.91	39.92	33	14
North Dakota	1,015,540	535,466	1,342,088	35.10	18.51	46.39	42	10
Ohio	6,360,408	1,248,133	6,254,654	45.88	9.00	45.12	36	12
Oklahoma	1,024,550	1,491,000	3,210,300	17.89	26.04	56.07	46	5
Oregon	2,759,093	224,523	2,579,742	49.59	4.04	46.37	34	11
Pennsylvania	29,873,342	2,704,652	1,519,417	87.61	7.93	4.46	2	47
Rhode Island	1,130,106	369,750	151,966	68.42	22.38	9.20	20	44
South Carolina	3,456,519	....	2,178,282	61.34	......	38.66	26	15
South Dakota	388,500	517,842	1,224,785	18.23	24.30	57.47	45	4
Tennessee	5,811,830	1,003,000	1,753,684	67.83	11.71	20.46	21	34
Texas	21,171,222	922,079	5,542,792	76.61	3.34	20.05	10	36
Utah	3,542,517	....	905,848	79.64	......	20.36	9	35
Vermont	863,867	210,000	139,803	71.17	17.30	11.53	16	43
Virginia	5,869,610	531,686	2,003,130	69.84	6.33	23.83	18	27
Washington	8,482,478	936,947	2,848,990	69.14	7.64	23.22	19	31
West Virginia	2,471,710	845,700	1,924,080	47.16	16.13	36.71	35	16
Wisconsin	5,488,487	2,588,986	4,531,546	43.53	20.53	35.94	39	18
Wyoming	1,256,917	....	472,006	72.70	......	27.30	14	24

[1] Data furnished through the land grant college survey.

TABLE 82.—INCOME FROM LOCAL AND COUNTY SOURCES FOR PUBLIC EDUCATION, 1927-28 [1]

State	For Elementary and Secondary Schools	For Teacher-Training Institutions	For Higher Education Other Than Teacher Training	Percent of Total Income from Local and County Sources Going to			Rank in Column 5
				Elementary and Secondary Schools	Teacher Training	Higher Education Other Than Teacher Training	
1	2	3	4	5	6	7	8
United States	$1,620,189,060	$145,905	$10,895,974	99.32	.01	.67	.....
Alabama	8,609,342			100.00			6
Arizona	7,724,086		66,510	99.15		.85	37
Arkansas	7,250,412		190,722	97.44		2.56	48
California	96,331,920		1,247,258	97.72		2.28	47
Colorado	20,449,432		53,791	99.74		.26	23
Connecticut	29,372,148			100.00			6
Delaware	536,376			100.00			6
Florida	16,739,341		136,749	99.19		.81	36
Georgia	10,914,328		64,380	99.41		.59	29
Idaho	8,780,751			100.00			6
Illinois	119,786,659		107,197	99.91		.09	18
Indiana	73,782,924	3,000	104,910	99.85	.01	.14	19
Iowa	45,149,588		22,169	99.95		.05	15
Kansas	36,167,850		203,276	99.44		.56	28
Kentucky	14,404,894		117,753	99.19		.81	35
Louisiana	13,382,792		144,004	98.94		1.06	39
Maine	7,485,583			100.00			6
Maryland	16,432,782	5,000		99.97	.03		13
Massachusetts	78,887,156			100.00			6
Michigan	74,850,087		881,506	98.84		1.16	40
Minnesota	40,245,944		176,477	99.56		.44	24
Mississippi	11,723,884		145,117	98.78		1.22	42
Missouri	35,911,744		413,269	98.86		1.14	41
Montana	11,152,252		9,533	99.91		.09	17
Nebraska	26,383,903		9,000	99.97		.03	14
Nevada	1,590,984		31,869	98.04		1.96	45
New Hampshire	6,274,321			100.00			6
New Jersey	71,274,944		157,136	99.78		.22	21
New Mexico	3,868,280	37,225	33,254	98.21	.95	.84	44
New York	194,113,754		4,255,020	97.85		2.15	46

North Carolina	28,116,287		180,596		99.36	.64	32
North Dakota	13,137,862		33,842		99.74	.26	22
Ohio	122,019,936		977,582		99.21	.79	34
Oklahoma	27,986,197		184,302		99.35	.65	33
Oregon	17,237,872		86,479		99.50	.50	27
Pennsylvania	133,028,448	13,200		.01	99.99		12
Rhode Island	13,144,497				100.00		6
South Carolina	9,580,958		59,710		99.38	.62	30
South Dakota	14,414,691				100.00		6
Tennessee	16,046,406	20,000	129,268	.12	99.08	.80	38
Texas	29,712,500		375,366		98.75	1.25	43
Utah	6,758,462		3,725		99.94	.06	16
Vermont	3,968,660				100.00		6
Virginia	14,761,430		92,306		99.38	.62	31
Washington	18,914,064		91,552		99.52	.48	25
West Virginia	22,067,422		110,348		99.50	.50	26
Wisconsin	36,133,761	67,480		.19	99.81		20
Wyoming	3,581,146				100.00		6

[1] Data furnished through the land grant college survey.

TABLE 83.—FEDERAL, STATE, AND LOCAL INCOME OF CERTAIN INSTITUTIONS, 1927-28 [1]

Institution or Level of Instruction	Income from					Chief Source of Income	Least Important Source of Income
	Federal Sources	State Sources	County Sources	Local Sources	Miscellaneous and Institutional Sources[2]		
1	2	3	4	5	6	7	8
Land grant colleges	$13,704,802	$71,423,615	$3,432,938	$3,530	$30,297,069	State	Local
Teacher-training institutions	197,420	40,480,944	137,905	8,000	6,014,358	State	Local
Other public higher education	429,547	38,032,235	271,087	7,188,419	22,085,630	State	County
Elementary and secondary schools	27,907,441	343,453,929	209,193,576	1,410,995,484	70,624,603	Local	Federal

[1] Data furnished through the land grant college survey.
[2] Includes chiefly tuition and gifts for current expenses. Excludes departmental and athletic earnings, gifts for endowments, and sale of lands.

TABLE 84.—SUMMARY OF ALL INCOME FOR PUBLIC EDUCATION, 1927-28 [1]

State	Amounts Spent for			Percent of School Income Spent for			Rank in Column 5	Rank in Column 6	Rank in Column 7
	Elementary and Secondary Schools	Teacher Training	Public Higher Education Other than Teacher Training	Elementary and Secondary Schools	Teacher Training	Public Higher Education Other than Teacher Training			
1	2	3	4	5	6	7	8	9	10
United States	$2,062,175,033	$46,838,627	$186,868,872	89.82	2.04	8.14	......	......	......
Alabama	18,734,634	885,283	2,921,502	83.11	3.93	12.96	42	10	11
Arizona	9,855,884	478,440	1,093,581	86.24	4.19	9.57	25	5	28
Arkansas	11,707,109	239,010	2,175,210	82.90	1.69	15.41	44	32	5
California	121,663,364	1,939,583	12,837,569	89.17	1.42	9.41	10	37	30
Colorado	26,116,312	825,609	2,561,567	88.52	2.80	8.68	16	19	33
Connecticut	31,326,250	766,151	1,146,848	94.25	2.30	3.45	5	24	45
Delaware	4,244,865	......	899,213	82.52	......	17.48	47	......	2
Florida	19,438,132	......	2,718,991	87.73	......	12.27	21	......	16
Georgia	17,488,775	449,863	2,988,476	83.57	2.15	14.28	38	26	8
Idaho	10,842,004	493,208	1,147,911	86.85	3.95	9.20	23	8	32
Illinois	144,852,267	2,629,793	7,353,284	93.55	1.70	4.75	7	31	42
Indiana	76,870,150	1,147,883	6,328,450	91.14	1.36	7.50	9	38	41
Iowa	52,064,972	924,606	8,418,586	84.79	1.50	13.71	32	36	10
Kansas	37,414,118	1,601,476	4,570,727	85.84	3.67	10.49	27	11	24
Kentucky	21,542,307	2,155,387	2,038,733	83.70	8.38	7.92	36	1	38
Louisiana	20,745,878	464,272	2,295,329	88.26	1.98	9.76	18	28	27
Maine	11,170,859	279,000	1,081,820	89.14	2.23	8.63	11	25	34
Maryland	20,884,124	753,737	1,905,372	88.71	3.20	8.09	14	17	37
Massachusetts	90,837,647	1,742,469	4,152,681	93.91	1.80	4.29	6	30	44
Michigan	104,737,817	3,157,269	14,727,027	85.42	2.57	12.01	30	21	18

TABLE 84.—SUMMARY OF ALL INCOME FOR PUBLIC EDUCATION, 1927-28 (Continued)

State	Amounts Spent for			Percent of School Income Spent for			Rank in Column 5	Rank in Column 6	Rank in Column 7
	Elementary and Secondary Schools	Teacher Training	Public Higher Education Other than Teacher Training	Elementary and Secondary Schools	Teacher Training	Public Higher Education Other than Teacher Training			
1	2	3	4	5	6	7	8	9	10
Minnesota	55,155,043	970,791	7,584,229	86.57	1.52	11.91	24	35	20
Mississippi	18,329,325	357,350	3,440,219	82.84	1.61	15.55	45	33	4
Missouri	41,049,144	1,670,210	3,563,714	88.69	3.61	7.70	15	12	39
Montana	13,669,702	203,838	1,463,262	89.13	1.33	9.54	12	39	29
Nebraska	30,715,289	845,499	2,921,955	89.08	2.45	8.47	13	22	35
Nevada	2,317,121	......	383,830	85.79	......	14.21	28	......	9
New Hampshire	7,387,578	282,183	1,131,833	83.93	3.21	12.86	34	16	13
New Jersey	94,665,619	1,913,032	3,145,267	94.93	1.92	3.15	3	29	46
New Mexico	5,899,876	278,748	906,432	83.27	3.94	12.79	41	9	14
New York	270,183,519	2,205,617	12,449,927	94.85	.78	4.37	4	42	43
North Carolina	34,041,548	964,298	6,038,830	82.94	2.35	14.71	43	23	6
North Dakota	15,343,163	758,226	1,885,155	85.30	4.22	10.48	31	4	25
Ohio	132,963,850	1,412,406	10,910,300	91.52	.97	7.51	8	41	40
Oklahoma	31,312,124	1,762,995	4,352,608	83.66	4.71	11.63	37	3	22
Oregon	20,482,709	267,136	3,569,409	84.22	1.10	14.68	33	40	7
Pennsylvania	170,376,853	2,717,852	3,255,829	96.61	1.54	1.85	1	34	48
Rhode Island	14,312,647	389,415	348,214	95.10	2.59	2.31	2	20	47
South Carolina	14,557,148	......	3,018,911	82.82	......	17.18	46	......	3
South Dakota	17,249,063	682,585	1,659,255	88.05	3.48	8.47	19	13	36
Tennessee	23,221,197	1,089,398	2,632,265	86.19	4.04	9.77	26	7	26
Texas	54,786,355	1,326,750	7,818,117	85.70	2.07	12.23	29	27	17
Utah	11,397,619	......	1,501,514	88.36	......	11.64	17	......	21
Vermont	4,977,336	246,474	742,429	83.43	4.13	12.44	39	6	15
Virginia	21,467,036	789,708	4,818,673	79.29	2.91	17.80	48	18	1
Washington	28,525,743	1,108,560	4,407,266	83.80	3.26	12.94	35	15	12
West Virginia	25,455,946	1,006,051	2,681,276	87.35	3.45	9.20	22	14	31
Wisconsin	43,828,880	2,656,466	6,066,268	83.40	5.06	11.54	40	2	23
Wyoming	5,932,132	......	809,008	88.00	......	12.00	20	......	19

1 Data furnished through the land grant college survey.

data, are presented in Table 85.   Whether this table presents a picture of
the average situation in the United States is uncertain.   For the fourteen
states on which data are available, elementary school costs per pupil are
slightly more than half of the secondary school costs.   This statement
applies to both current expenses and capital outlays.   In West Virginia, the
current per-pupil costs in secondary schools are nearly four times those for

TABLE 85.—ELEMENTARY AND SECONDARY SCHOOL COSTS IN FOURTEEN STATES [1]

State	Cost per Pupil in Elementary School[2]		Cost per Pupil in Secondary School		Percent Elementary Costs per Pupil Are of Secondary Costs per Pupil	
	For Current Expenses	For Capital Outlay	For Current Expenses	For Capital Outlay	For Current Expenses	For Capital Outlay
1	2	3	4	5	6	7
Fourteen states..	$71.06	$15.86	$139.01	$28.01	51.12	56.62
Arizona.........	$84.20	$4.55	$163.33	$11.90	51.55	38.24
Arkansas.......	26.81	..........:	36.59	....	73.27	....
Connecticut.....	82.61	18.91	168.21	32.88	49.11	57.51
Maryland.......	62.51	6.69	107.35	21.60	58.23	30.97
Montana........	92.79	12.19	130.88	26.00	70.90	46.88
Nebraska.......	71.25	6.22	120.54	20.06	59.11	31.01
Nevada.........	116.98	14.05	159.08	42.20	73.54	33.29
New Hampshire..	74.57	4.14	130.49	28.09	57.15	14.74
New Jersey......	100.48	33.72	174.16	41.24	57.69	81.77
Oregon.........	83.79	16.98	121.84	37.89	68.77	44.81
Utah...........	58.23	6.41	101.41	35.22	57.42	18.20
Washington.....	81.94	....	125.72	....	65.18	....
West Virginia....	49.29	8.86	180.65	15.61	27.28	56.76
Wisconsin[3].....	61.19	10.29	148.36	23.43	41.24	43.92

[1] U. S. Department of the Interior, Office of Education. *Statistics of State School Systems,
1927–1928.*   Bulletin, 1930, No. 5.   Washington, D. C.: Government Printing Office. p. 50.
[2] Includes kindergartens.
[3] Data for reorganized types of high schools not included in this table.

elementary schools; while in Nevada and Arkansas, secondary schools are
only about half as much again as expensive per pupil as elementary schools.[1]

[1] The fact that a larger area is ordinarily needed to support a high school economically has led,
in some states, to the organization of high-school districts which may include within their borders
all or parts of several elementary school districts.   Three types of organization may be noted
in this connection:
     1. States which use a sufficiently large local unit of administration so that secondary
school facilities are economically feasible in every unit without the need of combining elementary districts.   Maryland or any other county-unit state may be taken as an example of
this type.   In such a situation, the schools of each unit are administered very much like the
schools in the typical city system.   The problem of financial articulation becomes merely a
matter of local internal budgeting.
     2. States in which all or parts of several elementary school districts may be included in a
single high-school district, the high-school district and the included elementary districts being each under separate administrative boards.   These larger high-school districts are vari-
ously called union high schools and joint union high schools in California, township high
schools in Illinois, county high schools in Florida, and consolidated high schools in North
Dakota.   This overlapping of jurisdictions creates, as far as the local area is concerned, two
separate school systems—elementary and secondary.   Since both systems draw on the same
tax base, there may arise competition for funds and unnecessary and extravagant expenditures.
     3. States in which overlapping exists between the areas covered by elementary and second-
ary school units but in which the organization of the separate administrative boards facilitates
the financial and educational coordination of the elementary-secondary schools.   Pennsylvania is a good example of the states in this group.   In this state, the controlling board of a
joint high-school district is made up of the members of the boards governing the included
elementary school district.

Trends in costs and enrolments at various levels—Thus far, we have been considering only the existing financial relationships between various units and levels of education. It is of interest also to observe the trends of these relationships over a period of years. Such comparisons of costs and enrolments have been made for 1922, 1924, 1926, and 1928 in Tables 86 and 87. Table 86 shows that the enrolment of each unit has increased steadily since 1922, but that the rate of increase has been very different at different levels. Enrolment in elementary-secondary schools has increased by eight percent since 1922, while enrolment in teacher training and higher education has increased much more rapidly; in fact, by 28 percent and 57 percent respectively. Enrolment in teacher-training institutions has therefore increased three times as rapidly as enrolment in elementary-secondary schools. In higher institutions enrolment has increased over seven times as fast as that in the lower schools.

TABLE 86.—ENROLMENT IN PUBLIC TAX-SUPPORTED SCHOOLS IN THE UNITED STATES [1]

Year	Public School Enrolment				Percent of Enrolment Increase Since 1922 in		
	Kindergarten, Elementary, and Secondary Schools	Teacher-Training Institutions	Higher Institutions	Total	Kindergarten, Elementary, and Secondary Schools	Teacher-Training Institutions	Higher Institutions
1	2	3	4	5	6	7	8
1922	23,239,227	212,164	220,523	23,671,914	....	....	....
1924	24,288,808	236,708	255,630	24,781,146	5	12	16
1926	24,741,468	252,907	290,893	25,285,268	6	19	32
1928	25,179,696	271,990	347,537	25,799,223	8	28	57

[1] Data from *Biennial Surveys of Education*, compiled and published by the U. S. Office of Education.

TABLE 87.—COSTS OF PUBLIC TAX-SUPPORTED SCHOOLS IN THE UNITED STATES [1]

Year	Expenditures for		Receipts for Higher Education	Total School Costs	Percent of Increase in Costs Since 1922 in		
	Kindergarten, Elementary, and Secondary Schools	Teacher Training			Kindergarten, Elementary, and Secondary Schools	Teacher Training	Higher Institutions
1	2	3	4	5	6	7	8
1922	$1,580,671,296	$32,622,411	$128,117,243	$1,741,410,950	....	....	....
1924	1,820,743,936	40,680,022	151,781,079	2,013,205,037	15	24	19
1926	2,026,308,190	44,462,475	174,480,662	2,245,251,327	28	33	36
1928	2,184,336,638	58,522,944	205,773,979	2,448,633,561	38	79	60

[1] Data from *Biennial Surveys of Education*, compiled and published by the U. S. Office of Education.

The actual rates of increase in costs as shown in Table 87 have not, however, followed the ratio of increases in enrolment. While elementary-secondary costs have increased 38 percent, teacher-training and higher education costs have increased 79 percent and 60 percent respectively since 1922. Thus, while teacher-training enrolments have increased thrice as rapidly as elementary-secondary enrolments, teacher-training costs have increased only about twice as much as elementary-secondary school costs. While higher education enrolments have increased more than twice as fast as teacher-training enrolments, higher education costs have increased at a lower rate than have teacher-training costs. Finally, while the rate of increase in enrolments is seven times as fast in higher as in elementary-secondary education, the costs of higher education have increased less than twice as rapidly as the costs for elementary-secondary schools.

However, it need not be concluded that the cost increases at any given level are not justified. Certain reservations are essential. In the first place, enrolment is at best only a crude measure of need even within school units of the same general nature. It is probably a less reliable measure when used for comparing the needs of different units. Second, there is nothing to indicate that the distribution of school income as it existed in the basal year of these tables, 1922, represented an ideal state of affairs, and that subsequent changes have been unjustifiable. Finally, and most important, national statistics such as occur in Tables 86 and 87 tend to cover up most important differences between states. The chief value of these tables, and indeed of all tables in this chapter, resides in the fact that they may suggest more refined procedures which will facilitate the intelligent and objective study of fiscal aspects of articulation by the several state school systems.

Trends in proportionate costs and enrolments—Tables 86 and 87 have dealt with comparisons between the trends of the actual enrolments and amounts spent for education in three units. The analysis can be carried one step further by comparing the trends in the percent of total enrolments and the trends in the percent of total costs accounted for by elementary-secondary schools, teacher training, and other higher education respectively. This analysis has been made in Tables 88 and 89, and has been put in graphic form in Chart VII on page 338. From these tables, the following conclusions are drawn:

1. The proportion of total public school enrolment found in elementary-secondary schools is slowly decreasing (Column 5, Table 88).

2. The proportion of enrolment in higher and teacher-training institutions, although small, is rapidly increasing (Columns 6 and 7, Table 88).

3. The proportion of total enrolment in teacher-training institutions is not increasing as rapidly as proportionate enrolments in other higher educational units (Columns 6 and 7, Table 88).

4. The proportion of total school income devoted to elementary-secondary schools is slowly decreasing (Column 5, Table 89).

5. The proportion of total income devoted to elementary-secondary schools is decreasing more rapidly than proportionate enrolment in this unit of education (Column 5, Tables 88 and 89).

6. The proportion of total school income devoted to higher and teacher-training institutions is rapidly increasing (Columns 6 and 7, Table 89).

7. The proportion of total school income devoted to teacher training is increasing more rapidly than the proportion devoted to other higher education (Columns 6 and 7, Table 89).

8. The proportion of income devoted to higher education is not increasing as rapidly as the proportion of all students enrolled in higher institutions (Column 7, Tables 88 and 89).

9. The proportion of income devoted to teacher training is increasing more rapidly than the proportion of all students enrolled in teacher-training institutions (Column 6, Tables 88 and 89).

TABLE 88.—TRENDS IN RELATIVE ENROLMENTS AND INDICES OF THESE TRENDS, 1922-1928 [1]

Year	Percent of Total Enrolment in			Index of Percent of Enrolment (1922 equals 100)		
	Kindergarten, Elementary, and Secondary Schools	Teacher Training	Higher Education	Kindergarten, Elementary, and Secondary Schools	Teacher Training	Higher Education
1	2	3	4	5	6	7
1922	98.17	.90	.93	100	100	100
1924	98.01	.96	1.03	99.8	106.7	110.8
1926	97.85	1.00	1.15	99.7	111.1	123.7
1928	97.60	1.05	1.35	99.4	116.7	145.2

[1] Calculated from data presented in Table 86.

TABLE 89.—TRENDS IN RELATIVE SCHOOL EXPENDITURES AND INDICES OF THESE TRENDS, 1922-1928 [1]

Year	Percent of Total Expenditures for			Index of Percent of Total Expenditures (1922 equals 100)		
	Kindergarten, Elementary, and Secondary Schools	Teacher Training	Higher Education	Kindergarten, Elementary, and Secondary Schools	Teacher Training	Higher Education
1	2	3	4	5	6	7
1922	90.8	1.8	7.4	100	100	100
1924	90.5	2.0	7.5	99.7	111.1	101.4
1926	90.2	2.0	7.8	99.3	111.1	105.4
1928	89.2	2.4	8.4	98.2	133.3	113.5

[1] Calculated from data presented in Table 87.

CHART VII

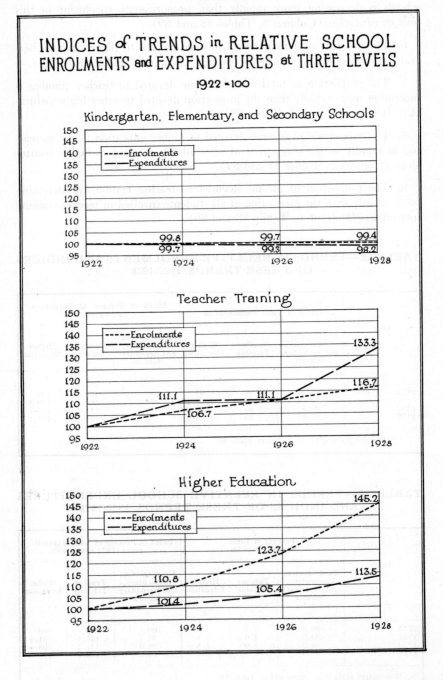

INDICES of TRENDS in RELATIVE SCHOOL ENROLMENTS and EXPENDITURES at THREE LEVELS

1922 - 100

Kindergarten, Elementary, and Secondary Schools

Teacher Training

Higher Education

Summary

The arrays of data which are presented in this chapter should serve three purposes.

First, they serve to call attention to the fact that the coordination of educational agencies to promote the maximum educational progress of children is in several important respects a financial problem. The causes of educational inarticulations may be sought in a variety of conditions. The curriculum, the teachers, the educational leadership, and the organization of school units each plays an important part in coordinating a state or local school system. Finance is one of these articulating features, and it is, in a special sense, a feature basic to all others. The statistical data just presented serve to reveal in a quantitative way certain significant aspects of the financial problem of coordination.

Second, the financial and other statistics presented in the chapter serve to indicate roughly certain important national conditions and trends in the financial articulation of the various school units with other government enterprises and with each other. Such facts raise a number of questions fundamental to policy-forming in public education. Is there any fundamental reason why local sources should be the primary source of support for the lower schools, while higher education derives support chiefly from the state? What is the significance of the fact that when comparative enrolment increases are taken into account, higher education costs are increasing at a much slower rate than elementary-secondary costs? Such questions as these are basic to the coordination of the fiscal aspects of public education. This chapter has not sought to answer these problems; it has merely called attention to their existence.

The third and by far the most important purpose of this chapter lies in the demonstration of the imperative need for local and state investigations of the fiscal aspects of educational articulation. Time after time the divergencies among states have been noted. Repeatedly the necessity for local investigation has been shown. The assembly of national statistics which have a bearing on this problem provides a basis and a starting point for local studies.

CHAPTER XIX

SPECIAL FINANCIAL FACTORS AFFECTING ARTICULATION

THE VITAL relationship of school finance to the development of educational institutions is not always recognized. It is a fact, however, that the character of the machinery set up to pay for the various units which compose our school system will in a large measure determine what these schools will be. It will not only significantly influence the development of the units found at each educational level—elementary, secondary, and higher—but will crucially affect the ability of these units to work together, to build upon the work of the preceding level, and to add the largest possible educational increment before passing the child on to the next level. A few illustrations will emphasize this fact.

Financial policies and educational inarticulations—Let us assume two states, each of which provides a substantial central state school fund to be apportioned among the various local school districts, and each of which apparently assumes the same attitude toward the kindergarten or pre-primary level. These two states have permissive laws granting local communities complete freedom to develop educational facilities for children below six years of age. But in one of these states children below six cannot be included in determining the basis for distributing the central state school fund. All money to pay for the education of such children must come from local school taxes. In the other of these states all children in attendance, even though less than six years of age, share in the apportionment of the state fund.

The development of education on the pre-primary level is likely to be quite different in these states. In the first, educational development on the pre-primary level is likely to be slow and spotted. A few communities which are unusually progressive, wealthy, or both, will probably develop kindergartens, and even nursery schools. But many communities, particularly those with little educational vision or meager financial resources, will do little if anything to develop classes on this level. In the second state, a different situation will exist. Some kind of provision for children below six years of age is likely to be found in all but exceptional communities. The education of children below six years of age will rather generally be accepted as a recognized function and will be developed coordinately with that for children above six. The whole educational policy as it affects the children of the primary and pre-primary levels will differ radically in these two states. And this difference results not from any difference in the fundamental educational desires of the people but rather as an outcome of financial legislation which has failed to envision a unified educational system.

Let us assume another pair of states, both of which are similar in their attitude toward education, but whose provisions for financing education differ. In the first state, elementary and secondary schools draw substantial revenue from the state treasury in a way which guarantees continuity and adequacy of financial support throughout the state, while the support granted higher education is both meager and fortuitous in character. The lower schools in such a state are in a position to do their task well, while the higher educational institutions are likely to suffer. Education on the college level in such a commonwealth may be partly taken care of by private institutions. Some high-school graduates may go to other states for their higher education while others may be denied the opportunity to continue.

In the second state, an opposite situation exists. The available state educational revenue is devoted almost entirely to the higher institutions. The lower schools must depend almost wholly upon local support which, due to the uneven distribution of weath, is sufficient in some communities, but far short of adequacy in others. Education on the lower levels will follow a halting and uneven development.

These two contrasting situations may not be the result of a recent and studied decision of the people in one of these states to exalt the lower schools and to submerge higher education, and of the people in the other state to do the opposite. Rather the contrast may be almost wholly the result of circumstances, which in a remote generation or at the demand of special interests set up the plans which exist in these states for the financing of schools.

The ways in which the forty-eight states use, or fail to use, the financial set-up of their schools to secure a coordinated educational program are sufficiently varied to offer abundant opportunity for study and comparison. The financial program of public education has grown by the process of accretion rather than by integration. When a new educational activity seemed desirable, the states have provided for its separate maintenance, often on a permissive local basis or by means of an allocated tax. With the passage of time the new enterprises gain wider acceptance and become more and more integral parts of the educational system. The separate financing, however, continues as before. Thus, the financial status of public schools often fails to reflect the accepted educational theory, and lags behind as the educational policy develops.

Obviously, a detailed study of the present financial practices of each of the states would be necessary if it were desired to identify every possible example of educational inarticulation which results from an uncoordinated financial policy. Such a list of inarticulations cannot be presented within the limitations of a brief report. Attention will therefore be centered upon certain financial factors affecting the articulation of education which possess special interest or importance. These include the complexity of school support, the use of allocated taxes and appropriations, and special plans for the maintenance of certain educational levels.

Complexity of sources of school revenue—Educational support is now secured through a complex and confused series of sources and funds that have developed in patchwork fashion. To sort out the patches of similar kind from a number of states and group them together as types would be significant only as showing the imitative character of states in adopting devices for educational support. It would not aid in understanding the restraints and limitations placed upon unified educational development by the piecemeal fiscal legislation under which state educational agencies must now be supported. It is proposed, therefore, merely to describe briefly the funds and methods used by three states that are illustrative of the complex character of educational support found in practically all. These examples will be followed by pointing out some of the more significant implications of the policies that are thus embodied in fiscal practice. The states chosen for illustrative purposes have been selected because rather complete information was available. This selection implies neither special adverse comment nor commendation; the practices that they illustrate are general.

J. M. McConnell, Commissioner of Education in Minnesota, has for the purposes of this study prepared the following statement as of January 1, 1930, concerning the contributions of the state to public schools.

The state's contribution consists of the following:

First—The semi-annual apportionment of the Current School (Apportionment) Fund computed by the State Department of Education and distributed by the state through the county treasurer twice a year to all public school districts maintaining school at least seven months during the year. This distribution is based on the number of pupils attending school at least forty days and the amount per pupil for the last year was $7.00; the total amount, $3,584,315.

This money comes from two sources—the income (interest) from invested permanent school and swamp land funds amounting to approximately $60,000,000 on June 30, 1929, and from the one-mill state school tax. The first source brings approximately $2,150,000 a year; the latter, $1,950,000. Of this the amount of $500,000 is transferred to the State Aid Fund.

Second—Special State Aid to Schools, Classes, and Departments amounting to $6,394,793 for the year 1929 and distributed as follows:

1. Regular or Flat Aid—		
High and Graded Elementary.........	$638,614.08	
Ungraded Elementary Districts........	991,063.80	$1,629,677.88*
2. Supplemental Aid		1,495,320.39*
3. Special Department Aid		308,494.21*
4. Aid to Classes for Defectives.............................		394,402.68*
5. Transportation Aid		823,845.26*
6. Building Aid		15,151.50*
7. Association Aid		23,766.21*
8. Tuition for Non-Resident High-School Pupils...............		1,222,381.00
9. Aid to Teacher-Training Departments....................		192,749.00
		$6,105,788.13
Less deductions on account of adjustments in last year's Aid....$		16,496.69
Net..............		$6,089,291.44

*Prorated at 96.2 percent.

```
                (Brought Forward)............... $6,089,291.44
10. Federal Aid under the Smith-Hughes Act...................    147,912.42
11. Aid to Evening Schools for Adults........................     19,372.00
12. Gross Earnings Tax Aid...................................    109,873.00
13. Aid to Public School Libraries...........................     28,344.06**

                              Total........... $6,394,792.92
```

These sums are appropriated by the legislature and payable out of the state's Revenue Funds except the item of Federal Aid for Vocational Education. The money is raised partly from a direct property state tax. By far the greater amount, however, comes from Gross Earnings Taxes on Railroad, Insurance, Telegraph, Telephone, Express, Freight Line, and Sleeping Car Companies; Inheritance Taxes; Occupation and Royalty Tax on Iron Ore, etc. For a more detailed statement of special state aid payments see mimeographed copy of "Listing of Special State Aid to Public Schools in Minnesota for the School Year Ending July 31, 1929." Following is a statement of the Permanent School and Swamp Land Funds as of June 30, 1929:

Permanent School Fund Accumulations

```
Sales of Land, Right-of-Way, Leases, etc.................... $15,421,202.52
Sales of Timber............................................   9,210,935.97
Mineral Permits and Leases.................................     336,650.77
Royalty on Iron Ore........................................  21,633,014.15
Occupation Tax on Iron Ore.................................   7,391,140.58
Profits on Sale of Bonds...................................     365,672.64

                              Total........... $54,358,616.63
```

Swamp Land Fund Accumulations

```
Sales of Land, Right-of-Way, Leases, etc.................... $3,886,955.72
Sales of Timber............................................   5,008,084.29
Mineral Permits and Leases.................................      87,037.00
Royalty on Iron Ore........................................   1,921,908.19

                              Total........... $10,903,985.20
```

The law provides that one-half of the income (interest) from the Swamp Land Fund shall be added to the Current School (Apportionment) Fund. The other half is distributed to the state university, state teachers colleges, and state charitable institutions. It may therefore be taken for granted that one-half of the Swamp Land Fund accumulations, or $5,451,992.60, should be added to the Permanent School Fund accumulations, making this total nearly $60,000,000 as stated above.

G. W. Rosenlof, Director of Secondary Education and Teacher Training in Nebraska, has furnished the following statement of state apportionments to the schools and the sources of the funds as of June 22, 1925, and of December 21, 1925.

**Prorated at 61 percent.
All items of aid not starred are paid in full.

State Apportionment as Reported by State Treasurer
June 22, 1925

Interest on Bonds	$256,391.59
Cold Storage Licenses	600.00
Warehouse Licenses	311.00
Insurance Licenses	44,317.50
Liquor Licenses	528.10
Employment Agency Licenses	850.00
School Land Interest	68,007.22
School Land Lease	199,461.64
Total	$570,467.05

December 21, 1925

Interest on Bonds	$227,464.22
Cold Storage Licenses	30.00
Warehouse Licenses	37.00
Insurance Licenses	12,649.00
Liquor Licenses	312.00
Employment Agency Licenses	400.00
School Land Interest	41,792.34
School Land Lease	174,731.68
Total	$457,416.24
Total Funds from Licenses	$60,034.60
Total from Interest on Bonds, School Land, and School Land Leases	967,848.69
Total	$1,027,883.29

Dr. Howard A. Dawson, Director of the Division of Research and Surveys in the Arkansas State Department of Education, lists the state funds for elementary-secondary school purposes for the year 1929-30 as follows:

3-mill General Property Tax	$1,727,000
Severance Tax	794,000
Cigar and Cigarette Tax	1,300,000
Interest on Permanent School Funds	65,000
Miscellaneous State Sources	8,000
School Supervision Funds	105,000
Vocational Education Fund	120,000
Net Income	750,000
Appropriations for State Department	60,000
	$4,929,000

The complexity of educational support represented by the examples given above would be considerably increased if all the sources for support of the state's higher educational program were also listed for these states. It will be noted that, in addition to current revenues derived from taxation and appropriations, permanent funds, permanent debts, and other forms of endowment constitute one element of support. All of the states except Georgia have permanent funds or debts of which the income or interest is allocated to the public schools. In addition, the state universities and land grant colleges have substantial endowments derived from the sale of lands and from private donations. The state normal schools and teachers colleges, with very few exceptions, have practically no endowments. Endowment funds almost always belong to a single institution and may be used only by it. A notable exception to this general statement is Virginia, where the principal of the literary fund administered by the state board of education may be, and has been, loaned for capital outlay purposes both to the local city and county school boards operating elementary and secondary schools and to the boards operating the public higher institutions. This fund consists of about $6,000,000 made up from fines, escheatments, etc., extending over a period of about one hundred years. The fund is dedicated to the rural schools, but as much as thirty percent of it may be loaned to higher institutions.

These permanent funds for special purposes and for specific units in the state's educational system are in the nature of trust funds. It is, of course, especially difficult to change the terms of trust funds when the conditions or the purposes under which they were created become obsolete or antiquated. Fortunately, except in the case of certain minor trusts for higher institutions, the restrictions upon educational permanent funds are usually not so narrow as to prevent adaptation to changing conditions. Multiplicity of permanent funds and variety of purpose and condition do not, therefore, present serious problems in articulation of educational finance. The problems are primarily those of efficient management of the funds themselves, or of the coordination of other methods of support with the purposes served by such permanent funds.[1]

Allocated[2] *taxes*—Two other aspects of support present special problems with respect to general fiscal policy. These arise frequently from the need for support of specific educational activities that have previously not occupied a prominent place in the state educational program. Such needs often lead either to the imposition and allocation of special taxes for these purposes or to continuing appropriations which are earmarked to be devoted to these objects. Allocated taxes are included in the sources of educational support listed for many states. Florida is an excellent example of a state that uses allocated taxes as the sole method of tax for state support of elementary and secondary education. Thus Florida has:

A one-mill property tax for common schools
A ¾-mill property tax for free textbooks
A 2/3-cent per gallon gasoline tax for county schools
A one-cent per gallon gasoline tax for elementary schools and for buildings for higher institutions
A one-mill property tax for equalization.

Only the appropriations for Smith-Hughes purposes, for the state board of education, and for county high-school teacher-training departments are

---

[1] Income from private sources such as gifts and bequests also constitutes an important supplementary source of school support. See page 323 for a brief discussion of this source.
[2] The term "allocated" or "earmarked" is used to refer to taxes or appropriations which are levied or set aside for designated purposes and which may be used for no other purpose.

made from the general fund of the state, and since these amount to less than one percent of the total state aid, Florida state public school support may be said for all practical purposes to be entirely derived from allocated taxes. At the other extreme is California, which since 1927 has had no allocated school taxes for elementary, secondary, or higher education. With the exception of income from permanent funds and school lands, all state school money is derived from appropriations from the general treasury of the state.

It should be noted that, in addition to allocated state taxes for elementary and secondary schools, many states levy allocated property taxes or other types of taxes for higher education including teacher training. Thus Kentucky levies a graduated inheritance tax for these institutions. Allocated state millage taxes on general property are also widely used. A study of the mill-tax method of support for state teachers colleges and state normal schools in 1924 points out that 27 such institutions in ten states derive from over one-half to nearly all of their support from millages.[1] The opinions of presidents of teachers colleges concerning the merits of the mill-tax method were collected by this study. Reasons for favoring the mill-tax were given as follows:

1. The income is certain.
2. The income is continuous and allows for advance planning.
3. Institutions are freed from political influence.
4. Work for periodical appropriations is unnecessary.

The three principal objections stated to the millage-tax method are:

1. It is necessary to supplement it by special appropriations.
2. Legislative appropriations have been adequate and satisfactory.
3. Millage taxes cannot provide for rapid growth of the institution.

As an illustration of a thorough trial of both the millage and the periodic appropriation methods, the following quotation from the secretary of the Iowa State Board of Education is significant. This state has had experience with both methods of support.

> If the educational institutions of a state have been developed to such an extent that the budget will be practically the same year after year, or for a series of years, a millage tax would be most desirable. If, however, the institutions are growing and, as a result, increased appropriations are necessary, I fail to see wherein such a law is preferable to flat appropriations. Since a General Assembly has the power to reduce or to change a law enacted by a previous legislature, it is just as likely to repeal a millage tax measure as it is to reduce stated appropriations.[2]

However, once a tax is levied and allocated to a specific activity, it becomes extremely difficult to change the amount either up or down. The legislature and the public tend to be convinced by the gross size of the yield for a particular purpose that the state is generously supporting that

[1] Whitney, Frederick L. "The Mill-Tax Method of Support for State Teachers Colleges and State Normal Schools." *Yearbook, 1925,* American Association of Teachers Colleges. p. 54-69.
[2] *Ibid.,* p. 68.

activity, although the sum may in fact be entirely inadequate to an activity that has been developed successfully and become an essential part of the educational program. On the other hand, adjustments of the educational program may be desirable or may in fact have taken place that make the amount yielded by an allocated tax for a specific object disproportionately large. Schoolmen and the interests that are concerned with this special activity fear to consent to reduction of the specific support lest in making a change the reduction be extreme and result in the fiscal starvation of the activity. In fact, the purpose for which a tax is allocated may be entirely outgrown with the passage of time and become obsolete without change in the allocation.

Earmarked appropriations—The same objections apply to appropriations earmarked for a particular small type or unit of education although appropriation acts tend to be more frequently considered and adjusted than are tax methods. Nevertheless, appropriations for specific purposes when provided over a period of years take on something of the hallowed character of permanent obligations which are not subject to change. Support for continued or even larger provision for outgrown purposes can always be found. In addition, a policy of making specific appropriations is also subject to the criticism that it responds readily to propaganda among legislators for promotion of activities that sound educational judgment might reject. Thus, much publicity for aviation backed by commercial interests may lead to legislative enthusiasm for schools of aviation that are not at all needed. Booster organizations may force through the legislature bills for the establishment and support of textile instruction in a state where the manufacturing and employment opportunities in that field are negligible. The live stock industry or some other specialized business may secure legislation for instruction or research in their industry that distorts the educational and research program of the state educational institutions. And these illustrations might be multiplied a hundredfold. Under conditions of excessive dependence upon allocated taxes and detailed appropriations, it is inevitable that inarticulations of educational program will develop out of the fiscal basis of education. Such inarticulations have been clearly recognized in various states, although the fact that they grew out of a chaotic financial policy is not so clearly perceived.

Examples of incoordinated school finance—Allocated taxes and specific appropriations are, however, not the only forms of state fiscal procedure in support of education that tend to distort educational articulation. Another fiscal influence upon the coordination of educational development arises from the failure of state programs of educational finance to respond to changes in educational organization. This failure may be illustrated by both the junior college and the kindergarten. The kindergarten is practically omitted from most state-wide plans for financing education.[1] No

---

[1] A detailed analysis of kindergarten legislation is available in: Vandewalker, Nina C. *Kindergarten Legislation.* U. S. Department of the Interior, Bureau of Education, Bulletin, 1925, No. 7. Washington, D. C.: Government Printing Office.

state maintains a special fund for the benefit of pre-school or kindergarten classes. A few states (Florida, Kansas, Minnesota, Nevada, Pennsylvania) specifically permit the use of state funds for pre-school education. Other states (California, Utah) specifically forbid the use of state funds to maintain schools below grade one. On the other hand, in some states, local school boards use state funds for kindergartens although not directly authorized to do so. In Maryland kindergartens are authorized under the general state school law as interpreted by the Attorney-General. The State Board of Education, under this interpretation, authorizes county commissions of education to appropriate county funds for kindergartens in the county school budget. Also in computing the amount of state aid due to any local unit the attendance in kindergartens of all children six years of age and over is added to the elementary school attendance.

In addition to the lack of state fiscal interest in kindergartens, there are financial handicaps to their establishment and maintenance in local districts. Four states (Arkansas, Georgia, Maryland, Mississippi) do not, by statute, recognize kindergartens as a part of the public school system, although in some of these states the school law has been interpreted so as to apply to schools below the first grade. Fifteen other states, while mentioning kindergartens in the school law, limit the areas in which they may be conducted at public expense, eight permitting the operation of public kindergartens only in cities and towns.

The nature of the problem of financially coordinating the kindergarten with the rest of the public school system is well summarized by the following quotation:

> The special tax plan suggests the attitude of the early years of the kindergarten movement instead of that of the present. At that time the kindergarten was still in the experimental stage so far as its value to the school as a whole was concerned. In consequence, those who framed the laws apparently felt obliged to exercise caution lest public funds for the support of kindergartens be secured too easily. The special tax for their support implies that the kindergarten is not an essential part of the school but is an educational luxury to be allowed such communities as are themselves willing to foot the bills. Not being considered an organic part of the school, the relation between the kindergarten and the school as a whole is a loose one. The fund for their support being separate from the general school fund, kindergartens can be attached to or detached from the school at any time without special disturbances, either to the curriculum or to the school finances. This looseness of relation between the kindergarten and the school as such is a source of weakness. The continuance of the kindergartens established is not assured, since the special tax that makes their continuance possible must be voted separately each year. This uncertainty, in addition to the looseness of the relation between the kindergarten and the remainder of the school, prevents the kindergarten from functioning as it should and does in the modern school.[1]

Another more recent development, the junior college, affords an illustration of the influence that state financial policy may play in the encouragement or retardation of educational organization. It is generally recognized by educational leaders that the junior college belongs to the period of

---

[1] Vandewalker, Nina C. *Kindergarten Legislation.* U. S. Department of the Interior, Bureau of Education, Bulletin, 1925, No. 7. Washington, D. C.: Government Printing Office. p. 11.

secondary education. Shall this unit develop as a part of and in close conjunction with the established secondary school system, or shall it pass through the state of separatism from and incoordination with the high-school system? The answer to this question lies largely with the state and more particularly with the state's fiscal policy with reference to this unit. Unless the junior college is recognized as an element in the state supported system of secondary education, and its status for purposes of public support defined in terms of secondary education, the development is likely to be haphazard and we shall have another unit that is inadequately and inefficiently related either to the high school or the state higher institutional system.

At present, the junior college is financially recognized by law as a part of the public school system in only ten states. In very few states have state funds been made available for junior college purposes. In California alone there is a state junior college fund from which apportionments are made to the local junior college districts. In Tennessee there is an annual recurring appropriation of $75,000 for the Tennessee Junior College, an institution controlled by the trustees of the state university. In Colorado the legislature has appropriated $5,000 for improving the sites donated for two public junior colleges. In Arkansas four state junior colleges are maintained by legislative appropriation. With few exceptions, all money for junior colleges in the United States is derived from local taxes, endowments, gifts, operating income, or tuition fees. The establishment and support of junior colleges by these means may easily result in uncontrolled and unplanned distortion of both the secondary and higher educational programs that the state now fosters. It is true that some states have taken action to minimize these effects by imposing certain restrictions upon the use of local public funds for junior college purposes. The following are typical of action taken for this purpose:

1. Fixing of a minimum assessed valuation before a junior college district can be established ($10,000,000, California; $5,000,000, Arizona).

2. Requiring definite action by citizens of proposed junior college districts (500 electors and majority of high-school board must sign petition, California; majority of electors must favor establishment, Kansas, Iowa; two-thirds vote required except in cities over 50,000 in population, Minnesota).

3. Requiring certain attendance, population, and enrolment conditions. (High-school average daily attendance of at least 400, California; of at least 100, Arizona; junior college average daily attendance of at least 75, California; school district population of 50,000, Minnesota; of 25,000, Michigan.)

But measures of this kind, while valuable, still fall short of adequate financial control which will insure correct adjustment of the three factors, high school, junior college, and university, in an educational articulation adjustable to constant development and changing relationships.

The illustrations of inarticulated school financing afforded by the kindergarten and the junior college might be duplicated many times. Such inarticulations exist to a greater or less degree in every state. Historically, their explanation is simple. The initiation of new types of educational service and new units of administration necessarily involves a departure from established policies, both educational and financial. The newly established institutions need financial support, especially during the experimental period. The institutions and services already well established, however, naturally tend to regard the newcomers conservatively. Consequently, the new services have been established on a try-out basis and the question of their financing has been temporarily settled by allotting to them some special source of public revenue. In time the institutions grow and expand and become accepted phases of the general educational program; the original methods of financing remain substantially unchanged. Hence arises financial and frequently educational inarticulation.

Such has been, in broad outline, the history of the kindergarten, the junior college, vocational education, adult education, and other phases of education which have only recently been accepted generally as legitimate phases of education, or which are now in process of attaining such recognition. Elements which entered the school system on an experimental basis as unimportant details have grown into sturdy maturity. But before they can be fully articulated with the general program the ancient methods of financing them must be replaced with methods more appropriate to their modern status and more closely coordinated with the entire fiscal scheme.

CHAPTER XX

SUMMARY AND RECOMMENDATIONS

THIS DISCUSSION of fiscal articulation of public educational effort has presented in successive chapters these major phases of the problem:

1. In an introductory chapter, the relationship existing between a coordinated school system and a coordinated method of financing the school system was pointed out. Emphasis was laid on the fact that an articulated program of education is not likely to be developed unless the financing of that program also shows the marks of a well-developed and coordinated policy. A number of important factors which retard or advance the development of such a coordinated financial policy were rapidly reviewed.

2. The practice of the states in attempting to secure general and fiscal articulation among the educational units that they support, by means of assigning control over two or more units to a single governing body, was reviewed. It was seen that articulation by this method ranged from entire failure to use it to practical unification of control over all the educational units to which the state contributes support. The units most commonly united under single control are those of the state department of education and the teacher-training institutions.

3. The methods used by the states to budget all state expenditures and thus secure articulation among the educational units and between educational and other state activities were next presented. Special attention was given to the part played by educational activities in state budgeting practices and relationships.

4. A chapter was devoted to the presentation of informal and non-governmental aspects of financial articulation. Various agencies which encourage voluntary cooperation among school authorities and others with respect to the financing of their programs were mentioned and illustrated. The basic necessity for a cooperative point of view among school people with respect to the financing of their enterprises was emphasized. The principle was developed that complete success in fiscal coordination cannot be achieved until this cooperative spirit exists.

5. The distribution of public funds between education and other state activities and among the state's various educational enterprises was given. It was pointed out that statistics of this type are of value chiefly when assembled for specific state and local units and when studied with reference

to the specific educational needs of the geographical unit that is being considered.

6. A few special and important financial factors affecting articulation were noted. These were illustrated by specific facts, and an attempt was made to indicate clearly the effects of piecemeal and fortuitous methods of finance upon the effectiveness and unity of educational effort.

From the preceding chapters it is possible to draw certain general conclusions. These are addressed to educators and to the public interested in the social and economic progress that may be attained through the activities of state government.

1. The development of a coherent program of financing the activities of the state involves considerations of the gravest social and economic importance. What is the proper scope of a public school system fitted to the needs and demands of a great democracy in the twentieth century? Obviously the public school is an institution which in response to insistent demands is rapidly extending its functions and influence. On the whole, the same comment applies to most other governmental services. Obviously, too, the obsolete methods commonly used by American states for securing governmental revenues in general and school revenues in particular are no longer adequate. The pressure of public demands for improved educational facilities makes the problem more acute. Educational leaders must face these and similar socio-economic issues. They need not assume the fields and functions of taxation experts or of professional sociologists, but they should at least have a social viewpoint which recognizes the existence and the importance of these problems. They should particularly possess a general understanding of the theories and principles of public finance and be able to evaluate intelligently the various proposals for the long overdue improvement of the methods for securing public revenues. Such understanding is basic to enlightened leadership in the financial coordination of school and society, school and government.

Although the desirability for coordinating education with other governmental activities is recognized, it must be noted further that there are certain ways in which this coordination can best be secured and certain other procedures and policies which, although they may seem to promise coordination, are more likely to hinder than to help in the development of proper bases of coordination. No ironclad rule can be laid down concerning local practices. A plan of coordination is effective in a given state or city if it results in a well-rounded financial program under which all aspects of governmental service can develop normally and serve the public efficiently. Plans which, although theoretically sound, fail to accomplish real coordination are not desirable. Results are more important than methods. On the whole, however, experience teaches that the financing of public education in cities should be separate from the financing of the activities of municipal government. The principle of fiscal independence of school boards is accepted in the current practice of the majority of city school systems. This means that school boards are responsible only to the people for the proper and economical financing of the schools and are free to determine the school budget and to collect or cause to be collected the funds necessary to operate the schools.

Such fiscal independence is the logical corollary to the separate school board. School boards bear a heavy responsibility; they have been created for the specific purpose of overseeing the management of the schools. They should not be hampered in the exercise of the function for which they are created and for which alone they exist.

The independent management of the schools is a natural corollary to the fact that education is a state and not a municipal function. School districts and municipalities are both creatures of the state, and, although they may be one geographically, they are politically two separate entities. Scores of court decisions might be cited to verify this statement.[1] A few will be cited here to show the general trend of judicial opinion.

A Kentucky decision gives the following clear-cut analysis of the problem:

Prior to the passage of the various acts creating boards of education in the different classes of cities, the schools were under the control of the general councils of those cities. Under that system, it was found that the general councils would expend out of their income large sums for purposes which they deemed the most important, and would turn over to the schools whatever happened to be left. The General Assembly, appreciating the fact that a self-governing people must be enlightened and patriotic in order to be capable of self-government, and that the public school is the most potent means by which to prepare the people to solve the problems of government, decided to place the schools under the management of boards that would be entirely independent of those having charge of the other municipal departments. The Legislature had in view a system of schools where teachers would be employed because of character and merit and which would be free from the polluting hand of partisan politics or of the equally polluting hand of him who would use the schools as a haven of refuge for an unfortunate or incompetent relative or friend, or as a charitable institution to take care of the poor of the community. Having placed the management and control of the schools in the hands of such boards; having given them the power to employ teachers, fix the salaries, provide suitable buildings, etc.; having made it their duty to provide the buildings and teachers sufficient for the education of all the children of the city between the ages of six and twenty years of age, it would certainly be an anomalous condition if the law intended that it should be dependent for its resources to carry out its contracts upon the whims or caprice of the general council, whose duty the law made it to make the necessary levy. Such a condition of affairs was not contemplated by the Legislature. It meant to make the boards of education entirely independent. To that end it made it the duty of the general council to levy a tax sufficient to meet the board's demands, not exceeding, however, the limits prescribed by law.[2]

[1] Schroeder, H. H. *Legal Opinion on the Public School as a State Institution.* Bloomington, Ill.: Public School Publishing Company, 1928. 81 p.
Cubberley, E. P., and Elliott, E. C. *State and County School Administration.* New York: The Macmillan Company, 1915.
[2] *Board of Education of Bowling Green v. Townsend, Mayor, et al.* 140 Kentucky, 248, 251 (1910). Quoted in Schroeder, *op. cit.*, p. 50-51.

More recently a similar case was decided in California, where a tax-collecting body, the Board of Supervisors of the City and County of San Francisco, refused to levy the tax called for by the budget of the City and County Board of Education. The California State Supreme Court held:

It may here be noted that it would have been entirely consistent with our system of government if the power were conferred by the Constitution on the Legislature to vest authority to levy such taxes directly in the board of education. Separate machinery could then be set up for the levy and collection of the same. However, the simpler and more inexpensive method has been followed, namely of vesting the Legislature with power to "provide for" the levy and collection of such taxes by the board of supervisors of the city and county. When this method of raising the tax is prescribed, the responsibility for the amount to be raised for school purposes is with the board of education. . . .

The recent constitutional and statutory provisions referred to were undoubtedly adopted on the theory that boards of education, being constantly in touch with school matters, are more conversant with the needs of such departments and are in better position to judge of the required expenditures for such purposes. Whether placing the responsibility of determining the amount to be raised for school purposes directly on the shoulders of the boards of education and not on the boards of supervisors be the wiser policy may present a subject of legitimate controversy, but with that policy the courts have nothing to do except to see that constitutional bounds are not transcended. It is to be assumed that boards of education will exercise proper regard for the rights of the taxpayers to the end that the burden of taxation be not unduly extended.[1]

It is not the purpose of this report to engage in an extended discussion in justification of the policy of fiscal independence for city school systems. Such statements, based on objective evidence, are available elsewhere.[2] In particular, the argument that fiscal dependence makes for economy has been shown to have no significant basis.[3] In most cases, the fiscal independence of city boards of education, directly responsible to the people of the school district, appears to afford the best basis yet discovered for intelligent coordination between the fiscal aspects of education and other public undertakings.

On the other hand, attempts to subordinate the school board to the city council or other similar bodies may endanger the successful cooperation between the agencies responsible for administering the schools and other governmental bodies. The only workable basis for fiscal cooperation between education and other public services is coordination and not subordination. Just how such coordination is secured is a matter of detail which must be decided in the light of local conditions although, as pointed out above, the method of fiscal independence is well endorsed by both theoretical considerations and practical results. In short, while fiscal independence for school

---

[1] *Esberg v. Badaracco.* 259 Pacific, 730, 733, 734, 735 (1927). Quoted in Schroeder, *op. cit.*, p. 53.

[2] Frasier, George W. *Control of City School Finances.* Milwaukee: Bruce Publishing Company, 1922.

McGaughy, J. R. *Fiscal Administration of City School Systems.* New York: The Macmillan Company, 1924.

[3] For a summary of evidence on this point see: National Education Association, Research Division. "Current Facts on City School Costs." *Research Bulletin*, Vol. II, Nos. 1 and 2; January and March, 1924. Washington, D. C.: the Association.

boards does not guarantee coordination and fiscal dependence does not absolutely prohibit coordinated financing of public enterprises, the best results are usually secured when city boards of education are responsible directly to the people for expenditures and results achieved.[1]

One further reservation must be made to the general principle that educators should view the cost of education as one aspect of the total problem of public finance. Coordinated budgeting, especially as it affects the relationship of higher education to other state activities, is an excellent device provided it is properly administered. However, when state budgeting is allowed to degenerate into domination of the policy-making of the higher educational institutions by the budgeting agency, or when budget control is construed to mean petty or malicious interference with the internal administration of higher education, the state budget is likely to impede rather than to develop the articulation of higher education with the needs of the state as a whole. For this reason the lump-sum appropriation for state educational institutions is preferred over highly itemized and restrictive doles. Furthermore, appropriations in lump-sum form are conducive to greater economy and effectiveness. Morey points out that:

Budgets for legislatures and similar purposes, prepared as an aid to securing the resources necessary to maintain and expand the work and facilities of the institution, can hardly be expected to be in the detailed form necessary for internal administration. . . . Expenditures . . . cannot be forecast in detail with rigid accuracy . . . If an attempt is made to do this, every estimate will quite likely be made ample in order that no chance of embarrassment may result. If appropriations are made in much detail, changing conditions may very likely lead to difficult problems.[2]

The following opinion of the president of a state university coincides with the quotation just given. President Coffman states concerning the University of Minnesota:

Three consecutive Legislatures have granted the University's appropriation for maintenance and operation in a lump sum. This is wise statesmanship; it is good policy; it is good business. That institution which is compelled to operate on a fixed and inflexible budget is hopelessly handicapped. In view of its size and of the varied activities with which the University is concerned, it should be free to shift its funds to correspond with needs and conditions as they arise. . . . The Legislature has wisely recognized this policy and it is hoped that it may be continued in the future.[3]

The budget of a university or other educational institution is fundamental to the realization of its full service to the community which supports it. It is well for the people in every state and city, acting through their legislative representatives, to organize their common schools and public higher institutions so that they can confidently rely on the ability and willingness of their

[1] "Relation of the School Budget to the General Municipal Budget." *Public Management* 12: 551-6; November, 1930. Describes 28 municipal organizations with respect to coordination of school and municipal expenditures.
[2] Morey, Lloyd. *University and College Accounting.* New York: John Wiley & Sons, Inc., 1930. p. 10.
[3] Coffman, L. D. "The University of Minnesota's Needs for the Biennium 1929-1931." Quoted in Morey, *op. cit.,* p. 11. The right of the regents of the University of Minnesota to control the internal financing of the institution has recently been upheld by the State Supreme Court. See: *State of Minnesota on Relation of University of Minnesota and the Board of Regents of the University v. Ray P. Chase, State Auditor.* 220 N. W. Reporter, 951. Also separately printed by the University.

educational leaders to apply public funds to best advantage. Until the legislative basis for such public confidence is provided, the articulation of the school and the society it serves will remain imperfect. When such confidence is secured, appropriations for educational purposes can be made in lump sums without hampering restrictions either as to itemization or purchasing. Such a policy promises most in the direction of economy, educational effectiveness, and smooth cooperation within the school system and between the schools and the public.

2. The financing of education must be thought of as a single problem in a setting of complex social obligations, many of which share with education the right to support by the state. Education should be viewed as a single problem because education itself is a single and continuous process. This does not mean that separate administrative control for the different levels, institutions, and units of a state's educational offering is necessarily undesirable. It does not mean that all education must be under public auspices. It does mean that short-sighted competition for public funds among educators representing different aspects or phases of a school system is thoroughly undesirable. Such competition is not only degrading to the profession and certain eventually to alienate the public's respect and confidence in its educational program, but it is also subversive of the welfare of the students for whom the schools exist. In thus condemning competition for funds, the Committee is not unmindful of the fact that the competitive basis for school support is, in some states, an institution of long standing, hallowed by the strong forces of tradition and sentiment and entrenched behind statutory and even constitutional provisions. But none of these barriers should be allowed permanently to block the realization of some form of coordinated policy in school finance. It is true that in many, perhaps in most, cases the basic cause of such competition is the fact that the revenues available for education are not sufficient to operate all of the aspects of a diversified school system such as is demanded by modern conditions. As a result competition for the funds that are available has developed. Where such is the case, however, the proper and dignified remedy of educators is certainly not to squabble over the partition of a revenue already inadequate to the proper performance of the vitally important services for which they are responsible. On the contrary, the presentation of a unified and coherent program of education which is properly financed at every point should be regarded under these conditions as a primary professional responsibility. Furthermore, the presentation of such a comprehensive program by the solidly unified educational forces of a state is in itself likely to prove an effective method for securing adequate support.

3. In recommending a unified policy of school finance, it is not intended that any particular legislative, administrative, or voluntary device for securing such unification should be universally adopted. The methods which work well in one situation and with a certain personal and historic background may fail utterly in other situations where the history and nature of the problem are very different. The important, the essential thing is that a unified policy be secured. In any particular situation that method is best which best

secures such a unified policy of financing as will make the maximum contribution to the educational effectiveness of the entire school system. This being the case, it will as a rule be undesirable to import bodily and undiscriminatingly any existing plan of unification. While the experience of every state should be levied upon for whatever contribution it can offer to the development of plans for coordinating educational finance, the deciding factor in the last analysis must be whether the plan is adapted to all the elements of the practical situation under consideration.

4. It should be noted as a fourth basic principle that the relation between articulated school finance and articulated educational policies is a reciprocal one. A sound and balanced policy of school finance cannot be created out of thin air. It can only be developed as the aims and principles of education itself become more clearly envisioned. We have already seen (Chapter XIV) how a coherent financial policy may lead to a better coordination of the units of education. But it is important to note that the reverse of this relationship is also true. Not only does articulated school finance lead to articulated schooling, but a well-articulated school system vastly simplifies the problem of financial coordination. In such a school system, the functions and contributions of each unit and institution are clearly understood by that unit and by every other unit. Since, in such a system, each unit knows definitely what it is expected to do, and why, there is less temptation to usurp the functions of other units in order to make a plausible claim for additional support. Instead of such usurpation with its probable duplication of effort and waste of public funds, attention is concentrated on finding ways of doing the assigned job better. A clear definition of functions is an essential phase in financial articulation just as it is in educational articulation. Accidental and unrelated fragments of legislation should not be the determining factors in the evolution of the parts of the school system. Rather the financial machinery for the support of education should reflect a carefully articulated educational program.

5. Finally, it is highly desirable to maintain an attitude of democratic cooperation at every step in the development of a unified financial program for education and the state. A unified financial policy, however excellent in theory, which is dominated by one institution or small group of interests cannot endure. If, in establishing such a policy, the local situation is considered only with respect to certain educational units or institutions, the institutions and units that have been ignored are likely to render the work of the stronger units ineffective. Economic and social vision must certainly be found in the directing agencies of a school system, but it need not be found there exclusively. In fact, as this breadth of vision permeates the entire people, the coordination of the school with society, both financially and otherwise, becomes more certain. So, too, the arbitrary assignment of functions by an educational despotism, however benevolent, is not the surest basis on which to build the financial articulation of a school system. Anarchy is not the only alternative to despotism; but there is no substitute for the

friendly understanding and mutual appreciation which come from sitting around a table for the discussion of common ends. In the long run, an educational system will be best articulated in its financial aspects when all educational interests cooperate under democratic leadership to evolve a unified policy of support which considers the educational needs of the state as a whole, sound economic and social theory, and intelligent allocation of funds and functions.

PART V

PRINCIPLES OF ARTICULATION AND FUNCTIONS OF
UNITS

INTRODUCTION TO PART V

Prepared by

HERBERT S. WEET

Chairman, 1931 Yearbook Commission

The following section of this Yearbook is designed to bring out a point of view concerning the subject of articulation that is not generally accepted by the Commission. It is a section, therefore, that is sponsored by those committee members whose names are attached to the various divisions rather than by the Commission as a whole. On the other hand, the Commission was unanimous in its judgment that the discussion merits a place in this report.

In a word, the underlying theory of this section is that the continuity of growth in the life of the individual should be the controlling principle in all efforts toward improved articulation or coordination. Much present practice, on the other hand, accepts the theory that the major emphasis must be placed upon what are regarded as relatively distinct stages in growth or development. While it cannot be said that the Commission has contented itself with present practice in the preparation of this report, nevertheless it is true that the best in current practice is the foundation upon which the Commission has attempted to build.

It is always difficult to state an issue of this kind without giving the impression that we are forced to choose complete acceptance or complete rejection. Obviously no such choice is presented. None would deny the principle of continuity nor accept the idea of stages of inner life sharply and abruptly marked off. One of the large problems of articulation is the very matter of promoting continuity in individual growth while recognizing the central tendencies and meeting the specific needs of given periods of development. These two principles differ in emphasis rather than in essence.

The references cited below present certain data upon the measurements of rates of physical and mental growth. Results of present experimentation and study are not entirely conclusive with reference either to the continuity principle or the periodicity principle in human development.

BALDWIN, BIRD T., and STECHER, LORLE I. *Mental Growth Curve of Normal and Superior Children.* University of Iowa Studies in Child Welfare, Vol. II, No. 1. Iowa City, Iowa: University of Iowa, 1922. 61 p.

BENEDICT, FRANCIS G., and TALBOT, FRITZ B. *Metabolism and Growth from Birth to Puberty.* Washington, D. C.: Carnegie Institution of Washington, 1921. 213 p.

BROOKS, FOWLER D. *Changes in Mental Traits with Age Determined by Annual Retests.* Contributions to Education, No. 116. New York: Teachers College, Columbia University, 1921. 86 p.

GESELL, ARNOLD L. *Mental Growth of the Pre-School Child.* New York: The Macmillan Company, 1925. p. 15-23.

HARRIS, J. A., and others. *Measurement of Man.* Chapter by Richard E. Scammon. Minnesota Sigma Xi Lectures. Minneapolis: University of Minnesota, 1930.

HOLLINGWORTH, HARRY L. *Mental Growth and Decline.* New York: D. Appleton and Company, 1927. p. 34-48.

CHAPTER XXI

INTRODUCTORY STATEMENT

Prepared by

JESSE H. NEWLON

A CLOSELY articulated system of schools providing an integrated program of education must be organized and administered according to valid guiding principles. A study of varying practices, of promising procedures, of special problems, will always be helpful and suggestive, and may be regarded as indispensable, but will not in itself provide either the basic principles or the overview that must govern in the development of socially effective schools.

In a democracy the two prime considerations underlying educational integration are the nature of the child and the social functions of the school. Every practice of the school must ultimately be determined with reference to these two factors. The curriculum, interpreted to include all the subject-matter and activities employed in the school, must be determined by the requirements of the society in which the individual lives and will live. The theory of the school must be based on social theory. The study of education becomes in large measure a study of society and of contemporary civilization. Unlimited research is needed in these social fields. Through a study of the nature of the child in all its aspects—intellectual, physical, emotional, social—the learning process will be revealed. The method of the school must harmonize with the nature of the child if it is to be efficient and economical. It follows, therefore, that in method the psychological takes precedence over the logical. Research in educational psychology has already very greatly influenced practice, although practice lags far behind tested knowledge. This field of research also seems at the present time to be boundless.

The method of the school as well as its curriculum will be conditioned by its social function. The child is already a member of society, and as an adult he must take his place in a larger society. If he is to live a life of satisfaction to himself and value to society, he must be prepared to engage in socially useful work, be interested in social problems, have social insight, be prepared to contribute to the extent of his endowments to the improvement of the culture in which he lives. Obviously, the methods of the school must harmonize with the best practices and the highest aspirations and ideals of the society of which the school is a part. Fascisti schools are not designed to train for citizenship in a democracy. The schools of pre-war Germany were unsuited in many respects to the democratic era that followed the War. The Russian schools of today are designed to orient youth to a new social order and indoctrinate them with the tenets of Communism. The schools of a democracy should likewise be based on a social theory. Doubtless the American system of education does reflect to a large extent the processes and the ideals of our social order, but in a democracy the school should be concerned with something more than merely maintaining the *status quo*. It should be concerned not only with the preservation of all that is of value in the social heritage, but with the enrichment of that heritage and the improvement of the social order. If the school is to be a constructive social force, it is essential that those who direct education become close students of social problems, in order that they may evolve a social theory upon which a theory of the school may be based. This is especially true in a period of rapid change, such as the dynamic period in which we live. Through rich experience, through his studies and activities, the child should be oriented to the social order, and learn through practice to participate effectively and with satisfaction as a member of society.

Child growth is continuous, and the educative process is likewise a continuous on-going process. The tempo may be somewhat more rapid at one time than at another, but the child is being educated by all his experiences both inside and outside the school. Dewey has described education as a process of "experience remaking experience." Under conditions most favorable to the child's development, one significant experience leads naturally into another. The experience of today represents an enrichment, a broadening, and a reorganization of the experiences that have preceded. It is obvious, therefore, that in education there should be no sharp breaks, but rather a leading on from one experience to another. In harmony with this principle, which is well supported by the findings of psychological research, the studies and activities of the school should proceed in an ascending order of complexity, variety, richness of interest, and difficulty, consistent with the capacity and experience of the learner. One activity should lead naturally into another. Curriculum practice should be based on these principles, and the school units should be organized in harmony with them. Administrative policies and procedures should likewise be governed by these principles. One of the major problems of education today is the discovery and validation of such basic principles and the reconstruction of the school in the light of them—a process that must be continuous.

American schools have arisen in response to the needs of American life. The American system of education has not been to any great degree consciously planned. It has been developed by a process of addition, alteration, and tinkering up here and there. It is not surprising, therefore, that it exhibits many inconsistencies, inarticulations, inefficiencies, and is in many respects poorly adapted to the needs of modern life. At numerous points American schools are encumbered by practices that can be explained only on the basis of tradition and caprice. The need and the importance of educational planning become more obvious every year.

Historically, the American elementary school and the American secondary school had different origins and functions. The secondary school originally served the more favored classes, prepared youth for college, and laid the foundations, at least, of education for the professions. For almost a century that uniquely American institution, the academy, flourished and provided the only opportunities for higher education available to many destined to leadership in American life. The elementary school was called the "common school" and taught the rudiments of learning to the common people. It was designed to place them in possession of the intellectual skills and elementary knowledge regarded as minimum essentials for participation in occupational and civic life.

In the last hundred years these two schools have been brought closer together in spirit, philosophy, aim, and method. In time the high school came to be regarded as essentially a part of the common school. It, too, is rapidly becoming a school for the children of all the people, as is indicated by the fact that today more than half of the youth of high-school age are in attendance on secondary schools, and this enrolment continues to increase by leaps and bounds. The curriculum of the high school was gradually modified, especially by the addition of new subjects of study, in the direction of bringing it more closely into relation with the requirements of modern life.

When the high school became a part of the common school system, the "one educational ladder" was established in America, and educational opportunities were very greatly broadened. The elementary school led to the high school, and the high school, in turn, to the college or professional school. The gaps between the various units of the school system have been gradually narrowed, but the old lines of cleavage in respect to aims and methods still obtain to a large extent, due to different traditions and to different underlying philosophies. The philosophy upon which are based the practices of the secondary school, at least so far as the heart of the curriculum is concerned, is still largely the traditional philosophy of formal discipline, while the new pragmatic philosophy of education to a greater extent characterizes procedures in the elementary school. These differences in philosophy undoubtedly constitute one of the chief sources of the inarticulation between the elementary school and the high school. Preparation for college is still regarded as one of the most important functions of the secondary school. The college is more traditional and conventional in its methods than is the elementary school. It is inevitable, therefore, that the secondary school should be caught between the upper stone of the college and nether stone of the elementary school. The practices of the high school have been determined altogether too much by its relation to the college and by a public and professional opinion altogether too conservative and uninformed regarding the content and method of secondary education. Even the best-educated members of society tend to think of education in terms of the schools they knew. The result is a confused secondary school poorly articulated with either the elementary school or the college, or, what is of greater importance, with society.

In recent years there has been considerable experimentation with new administrative units.   The three-year junior high school has been introduced and has gained a wide vogue.   It arose in response to genuine needs in an attempt to bridge the gap that existed between the elementary school and the high school.   The junior high school has had a liberalizing influence on secondary education.   More recently, the junior college has come into existence, in response both to a genuine social demand that the advantages of education beyond the high school be brought into closer reach of many youths, and as an attempt to bridge the gap between the high school and the college.   This experimentation with new units has been most suggestive, and many beneficial results have accrued.   We are in the incongruous position, however, of having broken the school system into a greater number of units, thus increasing in some respects the problem of articulation and integration.   This is just another evidence of the way in which the American school has grown up without deliberate planning.

The need in this country for a philosophy of administration based on a considered theory of the school, and of administrative practices consistent with the functions of the school, becomes more apparent every year.   Organization into units, supervision of teaching, curriculum, methods of teaching, administrative practices, should be based on educational principles.   Today administrative practices are determined too much by mere tradition or caprice, by the immediate emergencies of a situation, or by the particular educational fashion of the day.   Thus school administrators swallowed at one gulp the testing movement, the vagaries and inconsistencies, the bad along with the good.   Large numbers have, likewise, accepted uncritically the mechanistic psychology.

The report of the Committee on Principles of Articulation is based on the theory that the educative process is an active process.   The learner must assume an active and not a passive attitude.   We learn by experience.   Education is also a social process.   Learning is most effective where the pupil is normally and, therefore, intensely interested in the learning situation.   The measure of his interest is determined by the estimate which he places, whether consciously or otherwise, upon the value to him of the thing which he is doing.   The school should seek to develop a methodology that will provide socially useful studies and activities which will challenge the learner to his best efforts.

It must be obvious to any critical student of the American educational situation that the theory of education which has just been stated is misunderstood by many persons.   This misunderstanding is due in part to the extreme positions that are taken by many ardent advocates of certain principles of method.   In practice some teachers and students of education go to unwarranted extremes in following what they take to be the interests of the child, almost completely losing sight of fundamental social functions of the school.   Schools that go to extremes in the "freedom" which is given to children and in the extent to which teachers abdicate their function of guidance, are in danger of developing an exaggerated individualism on the one hand, while failing to secure a thoroughgoing intellectual development on the other. Only a due regard for the social functions of the school will counteract this tendency. A deeper consideration for social needs and demands, both immediate and future, calls for careful planning of the educational program, but such planning must always be done with reference to the nature and the needs of the individual. To provide for a maximum of pupil growth much latitude must be left to the teacher in the actual selection and utilization of subject-matter, activities, and method. The conventional course of study arranged in logical sequence to be followed in rigidly prescribed fashion defeats to a large extent the purposes of the school.

It may be assumed that one of the chief functions of the school in a democracy is to contribute to the development of critical, inquiring minds. Such a mind is particularly essential in a period of rapid social change such as has been brought about by the industrial revolution. It must be obvious, even to the most cursory student of contemporary American life, that much of present-day confusion in politics, in economics, in morals, is due to the conservative and conventional mind. What is needed is a citizenship that, while highly appreciative of the finest values in its social inheritance, is at the same time critical of the social order and capable of adapting its thinking and its actions to new conditions. Such a mind cannot be developed in a school in which the learner assumes a passive role. It can be developed only in that type of school in which the pupils have daily opportunities to engage in the process of thinking for themselves, under the guidance of skillful teachers who will hold them to account for accurate information and straight thinking. A school conducted on the theories set forth in this report would not be an easy-going institution. It would be a happy place because its pupils would be engaged in socially desirable activities in which they were intensely interested, but such a school would throb with industrious effort. Its pupils would be eager to acquire knowledge in many fields of human endeavor in order that they might apply it to the study of problems in which they were vitally concerned.

If the school is to be a constructive social force, it must strive to release and skillfully direct the creative abilities of the individual. A school such as has been briefly described will provide a maximum opportunity for the pupil to cultivate his special interests and aptitudes, whether they be in the realm of thinking, of artistic appreciation or creation, of executive management, of manual skill, or what not. By discovering and fostering those creative abilities and providing every possible opportunity for their exercise and growth, the school again becomes a constructive social force.

It cannot be too strongly emphasized that American education must be planned with reference to the social functions of the school. At the same time, the methods of the school must be adapted to the nature of the child. In the degree that these two functions are successfully met in school procedure, there will be proper freedom for the individual, and education will be saved from becoming a huge organization for mass production, turning out stereotyped individuals.

This report constitutes a first attempt at a tentative and partial outline, on the basis of our present knowledge of the educative process and the function of the school, of basic principles that must underlie a well articulated and integrated program of education. The report is divided into five parts: the first consisting of this introductory statement; the second, of principles of integration; the third, of principles of administration; the fourth, of an analysis of certain acute inarticulations; and the last section consists of certain recommendations which the Committee desires to make.

CHAPTER XXII

PRINCIPLES OF INTEGRATION

Prepared by

L. Thomas Hopkins and W. D. Armentrout

IT HAS BEEN pointed out previously in the introductory statement to this section that there are two prime considerations in educational integration. These are (1) the nature of the individual, and (2) the social function of the school.

A. From the nature of the individual who attends the school are derived the following principles which underlie effective learning:

> 1. *Learning Takes Place Normally and Most Effectively in Situations Which the Learner Accepts as Being of Intrinsic Significance to Him.*

At each level the school should provide situations which challenge the genuine and socially desirable interests of the learner. It is essential to learning that the activities of the school be such that the learner accept them readily as worth while to him. The application of this principle implies neither the mere indulgence of the whims of the learner, nor the abandonment of education to the caprice of undirected spontaneity. The view implies, however, that the learner's experience and interests constitute the vital point of departure for all properly conceived educational endeavor. Any theory which ignores this principle rests on a mistaken conception of the learning process, and eventually is bound to prove ineffective.

While the ideal end in education should be that the learner accept the experiences of the school as of immediate intrinsic value to him, he may not at the outset reach this ideal condition since he may have no innate or acquired interest for that part of the heritage which society considers of abiding or permanent value. If society demands that all boys and girls include within their experiences certain minimum essentials from the social heritage, (some educators would deny this) then one of the major problems of education, if not the major problem, is to develop technics for teaching these in such a way as to develop in the learner a sympathetic attitude toward and intrinsic interest in them.

> 2. *The Materials of Instruction and the Activities of the School, While Growing Out of the Present Life Experiences of the Learner, Should Progressively Be Identified with Those Aims and Objectives of Education That Are Designed To Serve the Best Interests of a Changing Social Order.*

The immediate intrinsic or felt needs of the learner are basic in determining what is appropriate for education at any stage of the child's development. But in order to be genuinely suitable for present needs, each activity or experience should be such as to lead on to higher and richer experiences. Education is thus a process of providing continuously situations that make for individual growth toward some presumably defined end utilizing the pupil's normal interests progressively. Such integration requires most skilful guidance on the part of the teacher.

While the immediate intrinsic or felt needs of the learner are very valuable in determining what is appropriate for education at any stage in a child's development, the data derived from the analysis of social needs must be utilized to determine what is most likely to be of permanent value and thus correct errors due to the transitory character of immediate interest or to the observation and analysis of it. Unless intrinsic interests of children are in harmony with those activities which are indicated by social analysis and social theory to be desirable, or can be directed toward activities which are socially valuable, they should not be utilized as a basis for a program of formal education.

3. The School Should Recognize the Social Nature of the Individual.

The learner can become the highest type of individual of which he is capable only through development which is based upon active social participation. He grows as an individual by intelligent acceptance or rejection of the modes of behavior with which he is surrounded, in and out of school. It is important that he become aware of the provisions which society makes for his continued growth, because a recognition of these benefits on his part will serve to develop in him a sense of social responsibility. However, this purpose is largely defeated if he feels that he is merely a victim of social pressure. The individual can be genuinely socialized only under conditions that without threat or compulsion enable him to make adjustments normally to social problems and responsibilities.

B. From the function of the school in a democratic society may be derived the following educational principles:

1. The Activities of the School Should at All Times Be Closely Articulated with the Processes and Changing Needs of Society.

In a democracy, one of the important functions of the school is that of giving the individual understanding of the complex, dynamic, industrial civilization in which he lives. This is possible only when the school procedure takes place in a social setting. There is a preponderance of evidence to show that knowledge, skills, and attitudes acquired in isolation from their natural setting not only do not enable the individual to make proper social adjustments, but prove a handicap to him in doing so and all too often actually make him a misfit.

2. The Major Aims of Education Can Be Determined Only by a Study of the Changing Social Order and Its Needs. In the Determination of Aims, Education Must Draw upon All Disciplines.

If the school is to be both a conservative and creative force in society, its procedures must be integrated around aims of education derived in large part from a constant analysis of contemporary life. From such a continuous study should come a social outlook, shared generally by teachers but not imposed on them, that will give direction to education. This process was never more necessary than at the present time of transition from a simple agrarian civilization to a complex industrial order. Much of the ineffectiveness and wasted effort that characterizes American education today arises from the fact that the isolation and definition of aims of education in a constantly changing industrial civilization have been largely ignored by teachers and students of education. Aims of education should be determined from a study of social life as a whole in its most desirable form, not from an analysis of that part of society which appeals to the particular investigator. The genetic philosophies of the past have resulted largely in pushing to the front for a period of years various phases of educational procedure the effectiveness of which has later been seriously questioned. Aims of education should be based upon a telic philosophy which provides standards for the evaluation of present practices and thus gives to all procedures their proper weight in the total process of education.

3. *The School Should through Its Curriculum Aid the Individual in Acquiring That Common Fund of Knowledges, Insights, Meanings, Concepts, Habits, Skills, Appreciations, Attitudes, and Ideals That Will Enable Him To Integrate His Present Experiences and To Participate Effectively in the Changing Social Order.*

For genuinely effective learning, whether in terms of immediate or future use, it is necessary that the school start with the child where he is. Only through an active process of experiencing, of coping with problems real to him can he acquire those knowledges, concepts, habits, skills, appreciations, attitudes, and ideals that will enable him to integrate his experiences and to participate effectively in a changing social order. The school must do more than transmit the social heritage; but insofar as it must care for such transmission, only in this way can it do so effectively. It must provide situations in which the learner may use constantly that which he has learned of the race experience in the solution of his immediate problems. This is one of the best guarantees the school can give society that he will be able to solve his future social problems. Only through a procedure of this kind can education hope to become a force for social reconstruction.

4. *Administratively and with Reference to Its Major Principles of Procedure, Education Must Be Planned in Advance.*

This principle does not imply acceptance of any scheme of curriculum procedures or administrative units as even relatively fixed. The one inherent factor which more than any other must underlie the administrative organization is the actual process of normal individual growth; and there is need for much greater knowledge of that process than is now available.

Attempts to obtain better articulations merely on the basis of tinkering up existing administrative machinery does not go to the heart of the trouble, and so cannot be expected to do more than remove some of the very obvious causes of friction. Readjustment must be effected according to basic educational principles. The educational system must be considered as a whole, and each part of it with respect to what it contributes to the entire process.

In order to serve the best interests of the individual and society, the teacher should prepare in advance a statement of those insights, meanings, skills, and attitudes required for effective participation in contemporary life and for coping with the unpredictable elements in the present civilization. He should designate possible pupil activities, subject-matter learning procedures, methods of organization and direction, and modes of measurement which indicate desirable ways of organizing education so that the interests both of the individual and society will be conserved. Only by such conscious attempts at systematic planning in advance of the entire educational program can the teacher see the relationship of his work to the whole process of education, a highly desirable outcome—indeed an educational necessity.

In a dynamic society goals will be constantly changing. Goals may not be fixed once and for all. Because of this continual shift some educators argue that remote ends be fixed arbitrarily, while others advocate that they be ignored. The former lead education to social impotence, the latter to social chaos.

C. The principle of continuity of growth affords a further criterion for vertical articulation.

1. *Child Growth Is Continuous. This Is True for All Types of Growth.*

It applies equally to all maturing—physical, mental, emotional, social. There can scarcely be any dissent from the statement that individual maturing is a factor of first importance in school articulation, but there has been much difference of opinion with regard to the way personal development actually takes place. Until very recently the view was generally accepted that there were "clear breaks," "violent disturbances," in short, that growth was inherently characterized by "cataclysmic changes." Within comparatively recent years, however, much experimentation and careful study have produced a large body of evidence which seems to disprove this view. Many fields of science, more notably and convincingly biology, physiology, anthropology, and psychology, have thrown much additional light upon the actual process of growth. It would seem to show without any real question that the growth of the individual is a continuous process. Commenting on this, John Dewey says:

> The idea of ripening, maturing, is evidently fundamental in the question of individual growth. Now what needs to be especially borne in mind with reference to maturing is that it is plural, that is, various powers and interests which coexist at the same time mature at different rates. Maturing is a continuous process; . . . the normal maturing as a process goes on all the time; if it does not, there is something the matter with conditions. Arrest of growth, incapacity to cope with subject-matter, and inability to respond to methods employed at a later period are all signs of something wrong. . . .

Since maturing is a continuous process and also a plural one it is not a uniform four-abreast thing. . . . No parent ever makes the mistake of overlooking this plural nature of maturing. When we come to schooling, however, I wonder if there is not too much of a tendency to assume an equal, uniform, four-abreast maturing, and if it does not underlie the conception of "epochs" of growth which correspond to various units of the school system.[1]

It is in consequence easy to assume that changes in personal growth are inherent, when in fact they may be the relatively artificial products of the existing school divisions and insofar abnormal and undesirable.[2]

The point of view set forth here is in essential accord with the conclusions reached by the majority of leading authorities in the various sciences upon the basis of their most recent investigations. The reader should make a clear distinction between the two terms continuity and regularity. Growth may be continuous but not regular. The evidence presented here is in favor of continuity only and does not uphold any doctrine of regularity in the yearly increments of growth in any of the traits discussed.

Further comment will be made briefly under three heads: (a) growth in physical and mental traits; (b) growth in emotional development and control; and (c) growth in social attitudes and practices.

a. *Growth in physical and mental traits*—The evidence available is principally from two sources: (1) repeated measurements of the growth of an individual with respect to certain personal traits, e.g., rate in learning to read, and (2) studies yielding central tendencies in relation to some specific trait as shown by the curve for the eruption of teeth in a large population. These studies of a large number of individuals over a period of years indicate that growth is continuous. According to the curves there is an acceleration at the beginning of the process with a lessening as the adolescent years are approached and a deceleration of rate toward the close. Studies of individual children show that over a period of years growth of any sort whatever when once started goes on continuously, even though at various intervals there may be accelerations and retardations. In mental functions and certain interests there may be apparent waxings and wanings, but the important point is that these are changes in tempo and are not "breaks" in the process of growth.[3]

---

[1] Dewey, John. "General Principles of Educational Articulation." *Proceedings, 1929.* Vol. 67. Washington, D. C.: National Education Association, 1929. p. 677-8.

[2] *Ibid.,* p. 676.

[3] Below are a few selected sources upon which the material of this paragraph is based:

Baldwin, Bird T. *Physical Growth of Children from Birth to Maturity.* University of Iowa Studies in Child Welfare, No. 1. Iowa City: University of Iowa, 1921. 412 p.

Baldwin, Bird T., and Stecher, Lorle I. *Mental Growth Curve of Normal and Superior Children.* University of Iowa Studies in Child Welfare, Vol. 2, No. 1. Iowa City: University of Iowa, 1922. 61 p.

Conklin, Edwin Grant. *Heredity and Environment in the Development of Men.* Princeton, N. J.: Princeton University Press, 1923. 379 p. (Fifth Revised Edition).

Dearborn, Walter Fenno. *Intelligence Tests.* Boston: Houghton Mifflin Company, 1928. 336 p.

Franzen, Raymond. *Physical Measures of Growth and Nutrition.* School Health Research Monographs. No. 2. New York: American Child Health Association, 1929. 138 p.

Gesell, Arnold L. *Infancy and Human Growth.* New York: The Macmillan Company, 1928. 418 p.

Herrick, Charles Judson. *The Thinking Machine.* Chicago: University of Chicago Press, 1929. 386 p.

Hollingworth, Harry Levi. *Mental Growth and Decline.* New York: D. Appleton and Company, 1927. 396 p.

b. *Growth in emotional development and control*—Evidence concerning emotional development is available from three sources: (1) experiments with animals to determine the causes of, nature of, and amount of emotion with particular reference to age and maturity; (2) introspectional, observational, and objective measurements of emotional growth and control in specific traits among school children and adults; (3) analysis and summary of case studies of children and adults who show incipient tendencies or advanced stages of emotional instability. The evidence derived from these sources indicates for large groups that growth in emotional development and control conforms to a continuous curve similar to that for physical and mental traits. While individual differences are pronounced, even in many extreme cases two distant points on the curve indicate a continuous growth, although characterized by intermittent fluctuations.[1]

c. *Growth in social attitudes and practices*—The evidence available concerning growth in social traits is derived from (1) studies of individuals and groups in relation to specific social traits and (2) studies of population growth yielding central tendencies with respect to groups of traits. These studies show the early beginnings of social growth with a tendency toward a continuous increase up through and including the adolescent period at which time social attitudes are somewhat fixed and social consciousness becomes somewhat settled so that increments thereafter are rather gradual due to the process of breaking down old and reconstructing new patterns. Here also there are pronounced individual differences, but over any period of years normal individuals show increased growth in relation to social adjustments.[2]

2. *Social Development Is a Continuous Process.*

The evidence available from the most eminent historians, sociologists, biologists, anthropologists, and social psychologists presents general agreement in the view that social change is a continuous affair. Their studies show that in all ages society has been subject to change, that this condition

---

[1] Some of the sources of the evidence in this paragraph are:
Bigelow, Maurice A. *Adolescence, Educational and Hygienic Problems.* New York: Funk and Wagnalls Company, 1924. 60 p.
Cannon, Walter B. *Bodily Changes in Pain, Hunger, Fear and Rage.* New York: D. Appleton and Company, 1929. 404 p. (Second Revised Edition.)
Hartshorne, Hugh, and May, Mark A. *Studies in Service and Self-Control.* Studies in the Nature of Character, Vol. 2. New York: The Macmillan Company, 1929. 559 p.
Healy, William. *The Individual Delinquent.* Boston: Little, Brown and Company, 1915.
Marston, Leslie R. *The Emotions of Young Children.* University of Iowa Studies in Child Welfare, Vol. 3, No. 3. Iowa City: University of Iowa, 1925. 99 p.
Morgan, John J. B. *The Psychology of the Unadjusted School Child.* New York: The Macmillan Company, 1924. 300 p.

[2] Some of the sources of the evidence in this paragraph are:
Child, Charles M. *Physiological Foundations of Behavior.* New York: Henry Holt and Company, 1924. 330 p.
Hartshorne, Hugh, and May, Mark A. *Studies in the Organization of Character.* Studies in the Nature of Character, Vol. 3. New York: The Macmillan Company, 1930. 503 p.
Strecker, Edward A., and Ebaugh, Franklin G. *Practical Clinical Psychiatry for Students and Practitioners.* Philadelphia: P. Blakiston's Son & Co., 1925.
Watson. John B. *Behaviorism.* New York: W. W. Norton & Company, Inc., 1930. 308 p. (Revised Edition.)
White, William A. *Outlines of Psychiatry.* Nervous and Mental Disease Monograph Series, No. 1. Washington, D. C.: Nervous and Mental Disease Publishing Company, 1926. 408 p. (Eleventh Edition.)

is a constant factor, that the process is still going on, and so is always likely to obtain. This does not mean that progress is inevitable; the point of view emphasizes that change as such is inescapable. At any specific point on a curve there may be depressions or risings; but even with all such periodic fluctuations and differences in rate there is constant and continuous change.[1]

The oft-repeated warning about the dangers in making deduction from data involving central tendencies should be heeded in this connection. "General averages" and curves based on large numbers of individuals are peculiarly susceptible to misinterpretations with reference to any single individual, for he is so lost in the mass that it is not safe to assume that what is true of the group must for that reason and to the same extent be equally true of the individual. Thus in considering the growth of individuals or the development of the social order, one can emphasize similarities by submerging individual variations in group data, or one may emphasize dissimilarities by magnifying the variations in individual growth to the neglect of central tendencies computed for a period of years. Since education is a long-term process and since it involves large numbers of children, it would seem feasible to define policy in terms of the common characteristics of growth in the group to be educated, provided such policy operates through a program which is sufficiently flexible to care for individual variations. It may be remarked that social progress is probably best guaranteed by a refined balance of emphasis upon the development of common attitudes and the recognition and promotion of differentiation.

D. From the facts of continuity, both in individual growth and in the development of the social order, arise important educational implications:

1. Administrative Procedure, Curriculum Practice, and Method Must Harmonize with the Principle of Continuity.

The organization and administration of the school system should provide for continuity of growth. Since the learning process is basically the same at all levels, differing only in the increasing ability to cope with complex situa-

[1] The evidence upon which these statements are based is derived in part from the following sources:

Allport, Floyd H. *Social Psychology.* Boston: Houghton Mifflin Company, 1924.

Boaz, Franz. *Anthropology and Modern Life.* New York: W. W. Norton & Company, Inc., 1928. 246 p.

Jennings, Herbert S. *Biological Basis of Human Nature.* New York: W. W. Norton & Company, Inc., 1930. 384 p.

Lynd, Robert S., and Helen M. *Middletown.* New York: Harcourt, Brace & Company, 1929. 550 p.

Pearl, Raymond. *The Biology of Population Growth.* New York: Alfred A. Knopf, 1925. 260 p.

Randall, John H. *Our Changing Civilization.* New York: Frederick A. Stokes Company, 1929. 562 p.

Storck, John. *Man and Civilization.* New York: Harcourt, Brace & Company, 1927. 449 p. (Third Revised Edition.)

Todd, Arthur J. *Theories of Social Progress.* New York: The Macmillan Company, 1918.

Wissler, Clark. "The Conflict and Survival of Cultures." In: Morgan, Thomas H., and others. *The Foundations of Experimental Psychology.* Worcester, Mass.: Clark University Press, 1929.

NOTE: The classification of sources is for convenience only. No author deals solely with the topic to which his work has been assigned. To obtain an understanding of the amount of evidence supporting any one point, the reader should consult the entire bibliography presented under the four topics.

tions and to utilize accumulated knowledge and experience in the solution of problems, the same general principles and methods should characterize both elementary and secondary education. The work of a grade or an administrative unit should lead naturally into the work of the next grade or unit. Since the principles underlying continuity of administration is the topic around which one part of this section of the report is organized, they will not be discussed here. The reader is referred to that statement for further detail.

2. *There Should Be a Continuous Policy of Education and Guidance for Each Individual Based on a Study of Physical, Social, Emotional, and Mental Traits.*

It must be recognized that at each stage of his development the individual has acquired a body of knowledges, skills, and insights in which he is relatively at home and so is in some respects relatively mature. Personnel problems and all difficulties involving social relationships should be solved by an increasing appeal to meanings, insights, and the critical judgment of the learner; by more and more pupil participation in the control of the school; and by an increase in the practice of adjusting pupil difficulties through self-imposed rules and regulations under teacher direction.

The school should keep an objective record pertaining to all important aspects of the development of the individual. This record should contain data with reference to growth socially, intellectually, physically, in interests, and in achievements, also data pertaining to defects, maladjustments, problems, and their disposition. Such a record is indispensable to a policy of guidance and education based on individual needs.

Since education is properly conceived as a process of continuous growth, it is important that sympathetic and competent counseling be given the individual at all stages of his development. This means providing a type and an amount of guidance that is beyond the possibilities of the classroom teacher. However, such guidance by specially prepared and qualified counselors must not become a thing apart, since it would then tend to introduce more inarticulation, whereas guidance should serve as a very effective agency for better articulation. A basic consideration in all guidance is that it can be effectively done only when it functions through decisions increasingly made by the learner himself.

3. *Studies and Activities of the School Should Be Selected So as To Give a Continuous Series of New Experiences or a More Critical Insight Into Old Experiences.*

This statement implies two very fundamental concepts. One is that there should be no sharp breaks in the introduction of new experiences. The other is that there is no justification for the reintroduction of old experiences except insofar as they are accompanied by a more critical analysis, resulting in new outcomes on a higher level. The sharp breaks in content now found between the elementary school and the junior high school, the junior high school and the senior high school, the senior high school and the college, are a violation of this principle. Furthermore, the enormous amount of overlapping in content within subject fields from one grade to another, or from one division of the school system to another, merely for the sake of repetition and memorization cannot be justified. It is a very undesirable practice to require a pupil entering a new unit to review much of the material of the preceding division. Koos has found that there is an overlapping of thirty-four percent in the curriculum between the high school and the first two years of college. Such a procedure unduly emphasizes the learning of subject-matter as an end in itself apart from felt needs.

4. The Studies and Activities of the School Should Be Arranged in an Ascending Order of Difficulty Consistent with the Interests, Capacities, and Experiences of the Learner.

There must be direction and progress in the school procedure, for it is obvious that interests and capacities normally change with age. The mere engaging in a succession of activities need not necessarily satisfy this criterion, for the individual may obtain experience for too long a time on one level and thus be deprived of the opportunity to measure up to the possibilities of development of which he is capable. Growth in area and level of experiences can best be assured by a critical selection and systematic arrangement of experiences with reference to some desired end. However, this principle should not be interpreted as violating those previously stated to the effect that the materials of instruction should grow out of the present life experiences of the learner, should be of intrinsic interest to him, and should be socially valuable.

5. The School Should Discover and Encourage Desirable Special Interests and Aptitudes When They Appear.

For the greatest possible enrichment of experience it is important that the pupil be encouraged and directed to increase the number, variety, and depth of his interests. This is a first consideration in a democratic social order. Not only does it serve to reveal capacities and open up new opportunities for further growth, but it tends also to increase the range and accuracy of those insights, meanings, and concepts which are fundamental to all critical thinking. The school provides for this discovery of aptitudes and this extension of interests through the type of experiences for which it gives opportunity in its selection of suitable activities. "The teacher," says Sidney Cox, sometime lecturer at Breadloaf Inn, "in one way is like the lookout man in the National Forest Service; the crucial moment in his vocation comes when he sees the smoke from some incipient fire. Only the teacher's duty is wisely feeding, not extinguishing, the flames."

6. The Curriculum in the Later Years of the Secondary School Should Make Provision for Specialization.

In the elementary school there should be that consideration for special interests discussed above. The cultivation of such interests is an essential part of a general education and affords a better basis for the later choosing of a vocation, but the cultivation of these aptitudes and interests is not specialization. To what extent specialization should be a function even of the secondary school is perhaps a moot question. Certainly the beginnings of specialization should not come earlier than in the senior high school. Specialization should be based on a broad general education and should come only with the maturity of the years of later adolescence and in many instances may well be further postponed. A background of general education is essential to a wise choice, under teacher guidance, of special pursuits in the senior high school.

Failure of the school to recognize special interests and adequately to provide for their guidance and care stands in the way of the broad and continuous growth of the individual and results in a serious loss to society. On the other hand specialization at a too early age handicaps the worker for life and narrows greatly the range of occupation in which he may engage. Economically the United States is able to provide education for all through the secondary school period.

7. Under Present Conditions the Secondary School Should Provide Vocational Education for Those Pupils Who Are Forced To Leave School During or at the Close of This Period.

While vocational education should not be deemed a major function of secondary education, it is necessary that provision be made at this stage for a widely-diversified program of studies. It is essential that those youths who must leave school during these years be given sufficient vocational preparation to enable them to engage in some productive work without delay. Such vocational education should be accompanied by a continual pursuit of the liberalizing studies, particularly those that give insight into the conditions, processes, and needs of our urban, industrial civilization.

Not the least important part of that preparation is that youths be made aware of the increasing opportunities for their further growth now being offered through adult education. Society is committed to the policy of providing education at public expense, extending even through the college years, for all who can avail themselves of it. This is as it should be except that it does not go far enough; our scheme of universal education will not be complete until the public school provides adequate opportunities and facilities for further education for all adults and for youths who have been forced to leave school.

8. The Curriculum Should Be Constructed Cooperatively by Representatives of All the Units within the Entire School System Working under the General Direction of a Curriculum Specialist.

To make provision for an ascending order of experiences based upon the present interests of pupils and on social requirements, the responsibility for curriculum construction must be borne by teachers and educators who see the educational process in its entire range from the pre-kindergarten through the university. This cannot be accomplished if the curriculum at one level is made solely by a nursery school group, at another solely by workers in secondary education, and so on through the system. Likewise, it is not possible to provide for continuous growth of the whole child when one part of the curriculum is made independently by academicians and another part by students of education. In order to provide for continuity the curriculum must be made cooperatively by representatives of all divisions of the school system working under a direction that sees the total educational process, and that can contribute to the integration of procedures in the interests of the learner and society.

9. Continuous Revision and Reconstruction of the Curriculum Are Essential.

Since research is constantly furnishing new information concerning child growth, and new insights into changing social values, the school must provide through its curriculum for the growth of the pupil in such a way as progressively to make him an effective member of a changing social order. Unless the curriculum is in process of continuous revision, it is inevitable that the time will come when its offerings are out-of-date, representing interests of the past which no longer obtain. With such a program the school will fail to educate for social responsibility; its work will result in ineffective, inarticulate, and unintegrated experiences. Education will be found trailing social changes, and it will become increasingly an agency making for the retardation of social progress. Under such circumstances society usually bridges the gap by some drastic form of external reorganization.

10. Integration and Articulation Will Be Fundamentally Affected by the Professional Education of Teachers.

An integrated and articulated program of education will always be largely dependent upon the type of professional mind and outlook which the teacher brings to bear on his problems. Teacher training therefore must be designed to lay a basis of understanding of basic principles and technics. It must strive to give the novice an overview of the processes and aims of education. As has been pointed out, the teacher must be concerned not only with the immediate problems of the classroom, but with the deeper issues involved in the relation of the total educative process to the social order.

Integration and articulation are impossible if teachers at one level proceed according to one philosophy of education and one psychology of learning, while those at another level work according to a markedly different philosophy. This condition has been and is to a large extent today characteristic of American education. No one would advocate the imposition of a particular philosophy of education on teachers. Such a program would be fatal. On the other hand, it is essential that all teachers become students of the major problems involved in the processes and aims of education. Through common understandings of basic principles, working agreements relating to philosophic principles can be reached.

It is obvious that a system of teacher training that places chief emphasis on technics and devices or even on scholarship, in chosen fields, as the prime constituent of the teacher's education must fail. Methods, technics, devices, can be used intelligently only by the teacher who has a firm grasp on underlying principles and who has a critical attitude towards the methods which he employs. Teacher training has placed too much emphasis upon technics and relatively too little emphasis on the basic principles. To be more specific, such studies as the history of education, educational psychology, educational sociology, the philosophy of education, the principles of curriculum construction and scientific method as employed in education, should form the foundation of professional training. Study in these fields is of far greater importance than the acquisition of certain skills of teaching or the study of particular methods and devices. The same principles apply to a program of in-service teacher training.

This sharp distinction between the principles of teaching and the skills of teaching is drawn for the purposes of showing the gap which exists between the two, and of raising some important considerations involved in bridging it. No attempt is made to infer that principles are superior to skills or vice versa. The problem is one of defining proper balance between the two. This has best been stated by John Dewey,[1] who says:

> The problem of the relation of theory and practice is a question of how intelligence may inform action and how action may bear the fruit of increased insight into meaning. Theory separated from concrete doing is empty and futile and practice then becomes a mere seizing of opportunities without the direction which theory has power to supply.

[1] Dewey, John. *The Quest for Certainty.* New York: Minton, Balch & Co., 1929. p. 281.

CHAPTER XXIII

PRINCIPLES OF ADMINISTRATION AS THEY ARE INVOLVED IN THE ARTICULATION OF SCHOOL PROGRAMS

Prepared by
A. L. THRELKELD

THE FOLLOWING discussion is an attempt to set forth in a very brief way some of the issues that are involved in the administration of school systems when the integration of education is held to be a fundamental objective. The discussion will be limited to the following questions:

1. Are the principles of learning fundamentally different at the different age levels of the pupils?
2. How may teachers dealing with different age levels of pupils come to have a common integrating understanding of the whole program of education?
3. Should curriculums be organized upon the assumption that each administrative unit of a school system is in a fundamental sense preparatory to the unit next above?
4. Should a school be organized so as to include in its program a cosmopolitan population as opposed to its being limited to a particular, specialized group in the population at large?
5. Are programs of pupil guidance and counseling needed in articulating and integrating the educational program of the individual pupil?
6. Is the status of public opinion a factor in articulating education?

I. Fundamental Principles of Learning Are the Same at All Age Levels

The same principles and methods should characterize teaching on all levels, including the college and university. This is not to deny that there are differences to be observed in types of learning—as learning in terms of information, learning in terms of understanding, learning in terms of emotional reaction—but these differences in types of learning exist at all ages and therefore do not bear on the question of articulating the elementary school with the junior high, the junior high with the senior high, and so on. Further, it may be claimed that such differences in types of learning as those just referred to, while essential, are not fundamental in character. Back of them must operate the same methods of teaching with reference to such factors as "readiness, exercise, and effect." These factors operate through all age levels and back of all types of activities in which real learning occurs. In the kindergarten we begin by organizing a situation calculated to have intrinsic value to the pupil upon the theory that such intrinsic value will cause him to react along lines constructive from the point of view of what we consider proper growth and development for him. We expect him to think and act through a situation successfully and thereby develop his foresight, initiative, ability to organize and carry through, and the like. We expect him to develop a social consciousness in order that he will develop his personality in terms of socialized attitudes, ideals, appreciations, and habits. At this level it is expected that all of these powers or capacities will be given exercise in a very limited way due to the immaturity of the pupil and the necessary simplicity that such immaturity calls for in the educational situation provided for him. In the first grade we attempt to develop these powers further than they were developed in the kindergarten.

A program of activities socially significant to the pupil is carried on from the kindergarten up, making the acquisition of the skills involved in reading, writing, and arithmetic essential but not fundamental in the sense that ends are fundamental. A program of this kind means that the pupil is given a continuous growth experience. The same attitudes, appreciations, ideals, types of insights, and habits desirable even at the very early age represented by the kindergarten are considered desirable at all levels. The only change that occurs is that as a pupil becomes more mature these qualities are developed to a greater extent. A pupil in the high school should be able to see much farther ahead than a pupil in the primary grades. He should be able to evaluate purposes more successfully on account of his greater experience in dealing with the results of his own purposeful activities. Through the continuous program of such activities through which he has come, he should be able to exercise greater initiative, more determination of purpose, greater organizing ability, more skill in habits, and the like. Back of his ever-growing life-purpose, he can use much more of the social inheritance, commonly represented in schools by subject-matter fields, than the elementary school pupil can use. But it is quite clear that no fundamental difference in method of learning as between him and the more immature pupil is here involved.

Such a point of view as the one above indicated assumes a school program adjusted to the natural ways by which people learn. Any arbitrary demands that may be made upon pupils in school systems as they now exist or have existed are not relevant to this discussion. This discussion has to do with how learning occurs when it is genuine.

II. It Is Essential that Teachers at All Levels Have a Common Understanding of the Whole Program of Education

1. One of the most effective ways by which to effect a common understanding of the whole program is to organize the teachers of all levels in a program of continuous curriculum revision. This may be done within a local school system or on a wider basis. If a program of curriculum revision is taken up with the teachers in order to help them meet the teaching difficulties that face them every day, they will welcome the opportunity for assistance which it affords. A proper committee organization, including

provision for working on school time when the best energies are available, leads to a common understanding as to objectives, principles, and methods. Even if one group starts with the idea that it has a highly specialized and isolated field to cover, it will find upon sufficient study into that field that it is related to practically all others. This produces a readiness of mind for cooperation with other groups. Then when groups are thrown together to meet common problems, they come to have a common understanding, without which no teacher's work is of far-reaching importance. Nothing that one observes in our educational situation today can be more disturbing than the all-too-common attitude on the part of a teacher at a given level or in a special field that it is none of his business what is going on at other levels or in other fields and that it is nobody else's business what is going on in his classroom. A person with such a dwarfed vision cannot fit into a program based upon the idea of continuous integrated pupil growth.

2. A supervisory program should be so organized as to contribute to integration through bringing teachers of all grades and departments into close contact. There should be one program for the entire school system with unity of purpose and procedure. From an administrative point of view this calls for one coordinating head for the supervisory system. If supervisors are working by grades, that is, if they are organized horizontally, it will be necessary for someone to be responsible for bringing them together frequently in order that the influence of supervision upon the program will not be in the direction of disintegrating it by grade levels nor by an elementary school level as compared to a junior high, nor by a junior high level as compared to a senior high. If supervision is organized by special subject-matter fields on a vertical basis, the same consideration holds. This coordinating head may be a director of supervision, a director of instruction, an assistant superintendent, or a superintendent, but obviously, if the program is to be one articulated whole, there must be single direction from some source.

No doubt if teachers, principals, supervisors, and the entire educational corps throughout all of the different levels were to become unified in fundamental points of view with regard to how learning best occurs, such unification would do more to integrate education than any specific forms of organization that might be set up for administration and supervision. The fundamental thing is to establish unity upon the basis of points of view from which procedures are worked out.

III. Pupils' Needs Should Determine the Curriculum of Each Administrative Unit

The curriculum of each administrative unit of a school system should be determined and administered in accordance with the needs of pupils, social as well as individual, at that level rather than in accordance with the demands of any succeeding unit or units. This is the only statement on this issue that is consistent with the idea of continuous growth based upon the pupils' purposeful activity. From this point of view, each unit of the school system must take the pupil where he is when he arrives at that unit and carry him forward as far as possible while he is in that unit. It is even misleading to use the word "unit" in this connection if it is to imply separation of growth into mutually exclusive periods. But thinking of a grade as a school year of time, of the elementary school as six or more years of time, and of the junior high school as three years, and so on, perhaps the word "unit" may be used more or less consistently with the idea of continuous pupil growth. In any event, we must think of the work of any grade level as having been determined for it by what was accomplished by the previous levels.

Society has a right to demand that the most possible be done at each level to provide for pupil growth. When a pupil comes to the fifth grade, the obligation resting upon the fifth-grade teacher is to carry him forward as far as possible that year from the point achieved by the fourth-grade teacher. Normal pupil growth each school day and each school year should be our objective. When this is the controlling point of view, there can be no pressing down of requirements from above in terms of formal subject-matter, for such would be external pressure inconsistent with the theories of pupil growth. Such growth must come from activities based upon intrinsic interests.

When we reach the high school with a pupil brought up in this program, the message from the elementary school to the high school is, "Here is a pupil developed thus far, as far as we could develop him in worthy interests, the power of sustaining himself in worthy interests and all implied thereby. Take him and see what you can do with him." Then when he is carried through the high school on that basis, the high school gives him to the college or university with the same sort of message. There will be in it a challenge to the high school to do more for him than the elementary school did and to the college or university to do more for him than the high school did, but actually the demand upon each institution is from the institution below. At the present time, the reverse is the case, and we need to right-about-face.

If we do the most that can be done for pupils at every age level, we need not worry about whether we shall succeed in so transmitting the worth-while elements of our social inheritance as to preserve and promote our civilization. Civilizations are preserved and promoted through the growth of individuals who constitute them. Such growth implies assimilation of the social inheritance. Such assimilation is essential to growth in any worthy use of the term. But our social inheritance is significant only to the extent that individuals grow in making constructive use of it. Except as a brief, transitory phase of growth in some cases, external force cannot be successfully applied in promoting such growth. The individual can be stimulated but he cannot, except in the very minor way just alluded to, be forced to make constructive use of our social inheritance.

By continuous and natural exercise in meeting social situations, the individual becomes an eager student of the social inheritance because of his intrinsic interest in life itself, which interest cannot be satisfied except by the most arduous effort to make a contribution to life. And the making of this contribution depends upon the individual's using wisely those elements of the social inheritance pertinent to his purpose. The social inheritance thus becomes of use to him, but, as a rule, this result cannot be obtained by placing him under a bell jar and pumping the social inheritance about him in the hope of creating so much pressure that he will absorb it. He might absorb some of it under these circumstances, but there would be so much of life repression in this to him that he would not amount to much as a social force.

It is true that a little pressure sometimes breaks down an individual's reserve and transforms him quickly into an active agent on account of his having caught the vision of what it is all about. This was referred to above as a brief, transitory phase in growth in certain cases. When this happens, well and good, but, as a policy, trying to force learning by external pressure is not constructive. Our desire should be to stimulate people at all levels to make the most of their present opportunities and to improve their usefulness in the world.

The number and types of administrative units should, then, be determined by a consideration of the fundamental importance of integration and articulation in education. If we are considering whether a unit should be composed of two grades or six grades, of pupils having a range of two years of age or six years of age, the decision should be determined by what situation offers the best opportunity for growth and development on the part of pupils. It may be that it is not practicable in the early years of education to provide adequately for an experience range running beyond six or seven years. The practicalities of the situation may mean that if a wider range than this is attempted, certain age levels will be neglected. No doubt this consideration has entered into the development of the six-year elementary school based upon one or two years of kindergarten and pre-school education. No doubt this same consideration has been an influence in dividing the secondary school period into the junior and senior high-school groups. Whether this division should be on the basis of two years of junior high school and four years of senior high, or upon a three-three, a four-two, a four-four, or some other basis, remains to be determined, but whatever decision is made should be based upon a consideration of what grouping offers the best opportunity to provide the maximum growth experiences possible for the pupils concerned.

This line of thought implies that within the elementary school, the junior high school, the senior high school, or any other field of education, there should be less emphasis upon arbitrary grade divisions, subject-matter divisions, and the like, and more emphasis upon continuous growth within the group until the time has come for the individual to go to the next group.

IV. As Far as Possible the School Should Be Organized on the Basis of a Cosmopolitan Population Unit

The social setting in which pupils learn is of extreme importance. The mind insofar as we think of it in terms of acquired intelligence is a social product. It is a product of all with which it comes in contact. It therefore is limited in its breadth of view and depth of insight by the extent of its contacts. A narrow range of experience, other things being equal, produces a narrow person, whereas broader contacts stimulate one to greater growth. A school composed of pupils coming exclusively from one social stratum tends to perpetuate a relatively narrow and unsympathetic type of mind with reference to human life in its entirety. This is true whether the school enrolment is made up of the poorest laboring classes or of the wealthiest and most exclusive social group. A single point of view based upon narrow experience whether in economics, politics, religion, or any other aspect of life is insufficient background upon which to promote education in a democracy. Democracy requires breadth of view and the sympathetic understanding of all types of human beings which such breadth of view implies.

It is hardly to be expected that people from different social strata or from groups whose life in the community at large naturally keeps them apart should come together in the everyday workings of life outside the school in such a way as to develop sufficient understanding one of another. Much can be done in community life at large to break down barriers and integrate the human elements that make up our civilization, but who would argue that this should be left until people are grown, to be worked out then as conditions at large may make possible? Except where racial differences make it impracticable, the childhood and youth of the land from practically all types of homes and social groups can be brought together in schools. In such a situation many great lessons in understanding and tolerance are inevitably learned. Such lessons, through proper social engineering on the part of teachers and administrative officials, may be consciously directed.

This broadening and deepening effect of bringing together pupils from different social groups is not limited to just what happens among them in social intercourse as they meet in the classroom, in the hall, on the athletic field, and in other activities of this nature in the schools. The values which we derive from our social inheritance are values which rest upon interpretations of our social inheritance. Merely to know that things have happened in the past without interpreting them in any way could not be called education, as we commonly use the term. We have to interpret the happenings of the past and make applications of them in present living. This is especially true in those phases of our social inheritance which have most to do with our equipment for living together cooperatively in present society.

One can interpret any happening only to the extent that he draws upon his experience background for such interpretation. No one person has more than a limited background upon which to draw for such interpretation under any circumstances. One's background for interpreting and understanding is broadened and deepened if one sees brought to bear, upon any happening that is being considered, many different points of view. One will see this only in that situation in which different backgrounds of experience are present. This type of situation tends to prevail more in that school which draws its enrolment from a variety of social groups rather than in a school which draws its enrolment from a group which tends to possess only one point of view about important social questions. Therefore, other things being equal, a school that is based upon a population district that includes a variety of social groups is more conducive to integration in a democracy than one based upon an exclusive social group.

The practical difficulties in many of our large cities, where population is divided into large geographical areas by social status, of establishing schools based upon districts cosmopolitan in nature are obvious. As pointed out above, exception to this point of view would have to be made in those states committed to racial segregation in the schools. But the contention here is that every practical means should be taken to bring differing points of view in contact in the educative process, so that a broader, more unified understanding of citizenship in a democracy will be developed.

V. Pupil Guidance and Counseling Are Basic to Articulation and Integration

An adequate program of guidance and counseling is basic to a well-integrated system of education. Such a program should be based upon extensive research. This kind of program would help pupils to look ahead and organize their programs in such a way as to avoid the tragic loss of time and life-values involved in following inappropriate objectives when reasonable foresight would have enabled them to see this inappropriateness in the first place. A guidance program based upon adequate research should tend to eliminate the inconsistencies that now exist from one unit to another by influencing all teaching to rest its case upon what is actually needed by the pupil. It is altogether probable that the inarticulation that now exists between high schools and colleges and universities would be obviated by a pupil guidance program running through all these institutions and based upon real scientific research into needs. If each institution does what it most needs to do, surely articulation and integration will result. Technics now available for scientific investigation in education have progressed far enough to make it unnecessary for us to depend merely upon personal opinion as to what ought to be taught in our high schools and colleges and how it should be taught. We here have a way to work out the college entrance problem upon a basis that should be satisfactory to all.

VI. In the Last Analysis We Cannot Integrate Education upon the Basis of a Disintegrated Public Opinion

We are going through a period now in the history of education when it seems that there is much confusion in the public mind with reference to fundamental policies in education. In every community there is the extremely conservative citizen who resists any tendency toward a change to new studies and new methods of teaching in our schools. There are to be found in every community powerful citizens whose education has been of an extremely traditional type. Their philosophy of education goes back to the day of the doctrine of formal discipline and all of its attendant theories.

They insist that this kind of education be maintained in the schools of today, and they tend to support those schools, private or public, which most nearly conform to their point of view. They continually disseminate in the community theories of education which are in conflict with what scientific research has revealed, and thereby hangs a problem before those who would promote education along more progressive lines. There is the extreme radical, on the other hand, who seemingly would overthrow everything that is now being done in the schools and start *de novo* on the whole job. Then, there is perhaps a large middle group which does not claim to know all about it but which has faith in education and wishes to see education promoted under leadership which they believe to be working in the interests of humanity. Many other differences and conflicts in the attitude of the public mind toward education exist. It is merely intended to suggest here that in any effort to unify education in our schools a careful program of interpreting various points of view and promoting general discussion must be carried on with the public to the end of a more general lay understanding.

This suggests more definite attention, on the part of people engaged in education, to plans of cooperation with various civic bodies and organizations in studying the whole problem of education. The Parent-Teacher Association comes in for special consideration at this point. It can be of great service in any community, and through its state and national bodies it can be of great service throughout state and nation in leading public opinion constructively with reference to our schools. It is the one organized school public of national dimensions at this time.

A more intelligent policy of cooperation between the schools and the press should be striven for.

Education cannot today be conceived of as something limited to the schoolroom. That is, not even school education can be so limited. If education is to be a vital force in social development, its policies cannot be divorced from the common intelligence of the people. Not only must there be a vital connection between what is going on in the schoolroom and the thinking of the people, but there must be something of agreement or unity in the general attitude of the public mind toward the major objectives and methods of our schools. By allowing and even inviting the freest criticism of policies we can effect an appreciable degree of unity upon the basis of those policies which are able to survive criticism. Agreement in terms of dynamic policies which if successfully carried out will effect continuous progress is the ideal here suggested.

CHAPTER XXIV

INARTICULATIONS IN AMERICAN EDUCATION

Prepared by

JOHN A. SEXSON

PRELIMINARY studies of the articulation of the units of American education made by the Department of Superintendence showed the existence of certain major inarticulations, and, by presenting the historical development of our public school system, exposed those points at which articulation problems may be expected. These studies suggested the advisability of a nation-wide survey to discover existing inarticulations in American education at all levels.[1] This section presents the results of such a study. In the opinion of the Committee, this report contains most of the available evidences of inarticulation in American education at all points at which inarticulations do or may exist.

In the *Seventh Yearbook* of the Department of Superintendence the problem of articulation was stated as follows:

Articulation means that adequate relation of part to part which makes for continuous forward movement. In terms of education, it implies such adjustments and relationships between and within school units as permit every pupil to make maximum progress at all points in his school life.

Present organization, method, and practice in American education fall far short of this ideal. Many are unaware of the number of places in our schools where inarticulations exist, of the effect of these inarticulations—either upon individual pupil progress or upon the total outcomes of our educational endeavors—of the exact nature or causes of these inarticulations, or of constructive procedures likely to lessen them.

The Committee believes that recommendations calculated to improve articulation in the American school system must be based upon a study of existing inarticulations, that such a study must specifically reveal the inarticulation, its exact location, the kind of impediment it imposes, and the extent to which it prevails throughout the various school systems.

With this in mind, six thousand questionnaires were distributed to teachers in every state, serving at every level, from the kindergarten through the university. To make clear the specific information sought, the Committee stated the problem of articulation somewhat more objectively than

---

[1] See: National Education Association, Department of Superintendence. "The Articulation of the Units of American Education." *Seventh Yearbook*. Washington, D. C.: the Association, 1929. 616 p.

was done in the *Seventh Yearbook*. It emphasized those situations facing the individual pupil in his progress from grade to grade and from one school to another.

The following statement and definition of the problem was submitted with the questionnaire:

> The Committee of the Commission appointed to prepare a chapter of the Year-book on "The Principles of Articulation and Functions of Units" believe it to be essential that recommendations intended to improve articulation and functions of units in the American school system should be based upon the study of existing inarticulations and should be pointed specifically toward the correction of them. To this end they seek from whatever sources are available to them, specific information with respect to existing inarticulations. They have stated the problem as follows:

> Outcomes for the learner are materially affected by the number, kind, and degree of inarticulations which modify his experience.

> An inarticulation is any point within our public school system and the society which it serves at which the continuous and gradual growth, development, progress, or transition of an individual is hindered by reason of the organization, methods, materials, or practices of our schools.

> Such inarticulation may exist between the home and the schools, between units or grades of the school system, between units of subject-matter courses, between courses constituting the school offering at any given level, between the regular school and the special school, between schools offering general education and vocational schools, or between the school and society at large.

> *Examples of such inarticulations:*
> A. Between the High School and the College:
>   1. A system of college entrance requirements lacking a foundation of experimental evidence and sound educational theory.
>   2. The arbitrary prescription of subject-matter requirements for all pupils regardless of abilities, interests, or achievements rather than a program of activities adapted to the individual and based on his needs.
>   3. Course requirements in any field determined by college rather than by the school in which the pupil is studying and tending to compel a continuous acquisition of units of credit after pupil has attained a prescribed standard. (Other examples of inarticulation will be suggested to registrars, teachers and others to whom the inquiry may come. The Committee urges full freedom in reporting all kinds and types of inarticulations, whether they are suggested in the examples herewith submitted or not.)
>
> B. Between the Junior High School and the Senior High School:
>   1. Conflicting methods and aims and lack of common understanding between faculties of these two units.
>   2. A fundamental difference with reference to the philosophy that underlies senior high-school practice and junior high-school practice.
>   3. Lack of sympathy between senior high-school teachers and junior high-school teachers due to a lack of understanding of aims and purposes of the two institutions.
>   4. Lack of understanding of junior high-school teachers of the complexities of the problem of articulating the senior high school with vocations and with institutions of higher learning.
>   5. Other conditions or practices resulting in retardation, elimination, or delay of proper progress and growth should be reported.

C. Inarticulations Due to an Inadequate System of Growth Records Following the Pupil and Accumulating from the Kindergarten to the End of His School Career:
   1. Failure of teacher to understand pupil due to inadequate records.
   2. Necessity of pupil duplicating courses due to inadequate records.
   3. Other impediments to proper progress due to a lack of an adequate practical system of records.

D. Inarticulation Resulting When the Work of One Level Does Not Grow Out of the Work of the Preceding Level:
   1. Arbitrary changes in methods for pupils well advanced in a subject, as for example in arithmetic.
   2. The use of different methods at different levels as the direct method of teaching modern languages in the junior high school followed by the grammar translation method in the senior high school.
   3. Failure to take into consideration at one level the content of a course at preceding levels as in English literature, social studies, commercial studies, etc.

E. Inarticulations Due to the System of Supervision:
   1. Supervision split administratively between the elementary and the secondary schools.
   2. Staffs of supervisors set up and functioning horizontally, largely independent of each other.
   3. Close supervision at one level followed by broad supervision at other levels.

F. Inarticulations Due to the System of Unit Courses and Credits in Secondary Schools:
   1. Over-departmentalization resulting in disjointed and unconnected teaching.
   2. Emphasis on accumulating credits vs. integrated learning.
   3. Teaching corps divided and representing vested subject-matter interests.
   4. The principle of continuous growth violated in the interest of subject-matter emphasis.

G. Inarticulations Due to Over-Departmentalization:
   1. The credit system for measuring school progress.
   2. The traditional concept of subject-matter based on logical categories vs. the new concept of the function of subject-matter as an aid to the learning process.

H. Inarticulations Due to Short Administrative Units:
   1. Present tendency to break the school system into numerous units, necessitating frequent transfer of pupil from one unit to another with the increasing likelihood of inarticulation at points of transfer.
   2. Comparative advantage of the present six grades and kindergarten elementary school as compared to the short three-year junior high school or the shorter junior college unit. Inarticulations due to this condition should be comparatively frequent and easily described.

I. Inarticulations Due to Subject-Matter of the Curriculum Lacking in Social Significance:
   1. Elimination of pupils due to their conviction that the curriculum of the school is not valuable or significant for them.
   2. Same attitude as above on the part of parents.
   3. Difficulties experienced by teachers in presenting subject-matter lacking in significance in an interesting and stimulating manner.

When the results of this preliminary questionnaire had been assembled and tabulated, they showed a list of several hundred inarticulations touching every kind and type of school situation. There were numerous overlappings and repetitions; some statements could be regarded as nothing more than expressions of personal opinion or criticism of local situations. The entire list was analyzed and carefully studied for the purpose of discovering the underlying faults or tendencies to which reference was made. The list of over 400 statements was reduced to 100 descriptive statements of the more basic inarticulations.

These statements were made into a check list and submitted to students of education enrolled in a number of the leading summer schools. The effort was to obtain from as large a number of persons as possible, an expression of opinion as to the importance, prevalence, and comparative effect of the 100 inarticulations contained in the check list which read as follows:

I. Examples of Inarticulation Wherein the School Fails To Meet Individual Needs

1. The school often fails to discover and to measure adequately capacities and abilities as a basis for discovering and meeting individual needs and differences.

2. The school infrequently records the information concerning the individual child by which the teacher may intelligently diagnose his needs, and often fails to provide for the transmission of such record from grade to grade, teacher to teacher, and unit to unit of our public school system.

3. The school fails to govern its procedure with reference to the individual pupil in the light of his capacities and limitations, and fearlessly present the implications thereof to the pupil and to the parents.

4. The school too often fails to proceed to the correction and remedy of physical defects and disabilities revealed by the physical examinations administered by health officers, nurses, and teachers.

5. The school fails to make adequate use of the needs of students as a basis for their classification.

6. The school often fails to provide at every level adequate counseling and guidance service for pupils.

7. The school infrequently correlates and coordinates the agencies for pupil counseling at the various levels and between the various units.

8. The school too often fails to emphasize educational guidance equally with vocational guidance.

9. The school has standardized equipment and curriculum to such an extent that the particular and individual needs of pupils and communities may not be met adequately.

10. The school fails in its kindergarten and first grade to provide a sufficient variety of experiences and procedures out of which its teachers may meet the individual needs of children and adjust their procedures to individual differences arising both from inherent differences of mental and physical capacities and from wide variations of environment outside the school.

11. The school fails to present and to keep before students during training the various types and kinds of opportunities afforded by society in which

the student may render worth-while service and receive adequate remuneration.

12. The school fails to extend its service for the entire period for which it should exercise a proper custodial function with reference to pupils during their period of immaturity, and thus prevent them from entering industry and employment while too young.

13. The school fails to set up in connection with its business, trade, and industrial courses facilities and equipment comparable to those characteristic of the industry for which the pupil is training.

14. The school too often fails to provide vocational training covering a wide variety of occupational possibilities.

15. The school usually fails to impress the tax-paying public with the economic benefits to be derived from the provision of an adequate program in vocational education.

16. The teachers of regular and academic courses fail to understand the character and significance of vocational courses, and assign to them all retarded and maladjusted children, thus hindering the development of adequate courses in vocational education and impeding the progress of worthy and capable students seeking vocational training.

17. Special schools and schools offering special training usually fail to differentiate in their entrance requirements from the prescriptions of institutions offering academic training only, and thus exclude from their courses students with special aptitudes wholly adequate to successful progress therein.

18. Secondary schools in general fail to incorporate in their organization and courses provision for students not planning to enter college or to train for the professions.

19. The college seldom leaves the school in which the pupil is studying free to determine the content and quantity of the courses which the pupil shall study, thus tending to compel students to continue to acquire units of credit after the pupil has already achieved an adequate mastery of content.

20. The school fails to provide for many pupils at upper levels courses which the pupils and their parents regard as valuable or significant for them.

21. School administrators do not hold a unified view of education, and often sanction the setting up of separate agencies for vocational education and general education (a dual system of education).

22. The school often fails to provide adequate placement and follow-up service by which graduates may be placed properly and make proper progress in the positions for which they have received training.

23. The school often fails to organize and administer adequate continuation, part-time, extension, and adult classes.

24. The school seldom sees that teachers render adequate assistance to a pupil who is compelled by reason of change of system, grade, subject, or unit, to adapt himself to new environments and to meet new conditions.

II. Examples of Inarticulation Due to Administrative and Supervisory Practices

25. Administrators, by the imposition of formal and restrictive procedures in the operation and management of schools, impose "red tape" that necessarily impedes the progress of children.

26. Supervisors fail to develop and to apply an adequate and workable policy of supervisory procedure.

27. Principals too often fail to coordinate the various agencies of instruction operating within the building.

28. Teachers too often fail to maintain a receptive attitude toward supervisory agencies.

29. The school too often fails, through carelessness, oversight, or for reasons of expediency, to see that teachers are assigned to the positions for which they have been trained and which they are competent to fill.

30. The school often fails to offer adequate opportunity for teachers to acquire their probationary or practice experience at the level at which they are trained to teach.

III. Examples of Inarticulation Due to the Teacher

31. Too many teachers fail to bring to their profession an adequate knowledge of the developing philosophy of education.

32. Too many teachers fail to bring to their position an adequate knowledge of the laws of child growth and child psychology.

33. Too many teachers fail to apply to the teaching task those professional principles which should determine their practice with reference to the learning situation.

34. Too many teachers fail to exhibit interest in and cooperate with those who provide special services for children, such as counseling, guidance, etc.

35. Too many teachers fail to study, understand, and utilize cumulative records pertaining to the individual child.

36. Too many teachers fail to present subject-matter in an effective manner because of its lack of significance, interest, or value to students.

37. Too many teachers fail to exercise thoroughness and fidelity by requiring their classes to experience in full the prescribed provisions of the curriculum.

IV. Examples of Inarticulation Arising through Faulty or Inadequate Methods

38. The school at all levels fails to use and to apply fundamental, well-organized, and commonly accepted laws and principles of child growth and development.

39. The school too often violates, ignores, or disregards the psychological law of readiness by employing methods, teaching subjects, and requiring pupil responses at times and under conditions which violate fundamental and psychological considerations.

40. The school fails more often than it succeeds in providing learning experiences so integrated as to avoid those gaps, lapses, and long periods of disuse which hinder the development of habits.

41. The school often fails to coordinate those materials of instruction calculated to stimulate mental effort and activity with those materials of instruction designed to stimulate manual activity.

42. Many schools continue to fail to coordinate the methods between units and departments and thus free the children from situations which are contradictory with respect to the necessary satisfactory responses demanded.

43. The school fails to eliminate arbitrary and unnecessary changes in method at different stages with respect to a given subject.

44. The school fails to set up and to maintain a system of discipline which contributes to uniformly satisfactory habits of response.

45. The school fails at all levels to free itself from certain practices and procedures which are wholly traditional as to origin.

V. Examples of Inarticulation Arising from Inadequate Methods for the Measurement of Achievement, and Unscientific Procedures in Promotion

46. The school fails more often than it succeeds in developing and utilizing an adequate technic for measuring and marking the pupil's progress in the academic mastery of subject-matter.

47. The school too often fails to evaluate the success or failure of its methods, practices, and procedures in terms of their effect upon the individual student rather than in terms of their effect upon the group.

48. The school too often fails to set up and to follow a scientific method and procedure with reference to the promotion of pupils.

49. The school, by reason of its frequent changes of pupils from grade to grade, from class to class, and from teacher to teacher, often impairs the growth and progress of children, both by reason of the interruptions incidental thereto, and by reason of the entailed burden of records and reports.

VI. Examples of Inarticulation Arising Out of the Division of Our Public School System into Units

50. The practice of breaking our school system into numerous units fails to provide for a continuous, integrated school experience for the individual pupil.

51. The school fails to reconcile the teaching and practices in one unit with those of the units above and below to the end that the outcomes for the pupils are continuous, cumulative, and progressive.

52. The school fails to eliminate the duplication of subject-matter at different levels, at different grades, and between one field of knowledge and another.

53. The school too often fails at each lower level to give sufficient trial and exploratory experiences out of which the pupil may proceed intelligently toward the requirements of the next higher level.

54. The school too often fails at each higher level to build its procedure upon the trial and exploratory experiences of the pupils at the lower levels.

55. The college fails to build its entrance requirements on the foundation of experimental evidence and sound educational theory.

56. The upper units of the school system usually fail to credit in full all the worth-while accomplishments of pupils at lower levels.

57. The practices in the different units of the public school system are not based upon the same psychological and philosophical principles.

58. The administrative officers in control of the upper units too often fail to contact and cooperate with those in control of the lower units.

59. Supervisors fail to set up similar aims, objectives, methods, and procedures in the different units of the school system, thus making difficult adjustments for pupils going from one unit to another.

60. The school fails to assist the pupil adequately in the necessary adjustment to be made in passing from a unit requiring little or no home study into a unit requiring large amounts of home study.

61. The school fails at each succeeding level to give the pupil adequate training in the use of supplementary books and materials.

VII. Examples of Inarticulation Arising from Defects and Deficiencies in the Curriculum

62. The school fails to select and to arrange the materials of its curriculum upon a psychological rather than a logical basis.

63. The school fails to correlate closely the subject-matter of its curriculum with the experience of the child.

64. Most schools fail to emphasize creative, self-expressive activity more than the mastery of routine, academic material.

65. Most schools fail to reflect in their curriculum important fields of human experience.

66. Most schools fail to base their teaching with reference to fundamental matters, such as health, upon a substantial scientific basis.

67. Most schools fail to maintain a proper balance between curriculum and extra-curriculum activities.

68. The school fails to incorporate in its curriculum experiences calculated to awaken an appreciation in the mind of the pupil of other social institutions.

69. The school fails to integrate the subject-matter in the different fields represented in its curriculum to the end that the student possesses a unified concept.

70. Most schools fail to integrate with, rather than add to, their regular program special departments and subjects.

71. Most schools fail to produce or procure adequate materials of instruction.

72. Most schools fail to use as a criterion for the selection of content for their secondary schools any other than that of value as preparation for college or entrance into professional service.

73. Most schools fail to formulate and offer courses providing training for participation in trades, industries, and business below the professional level.

VIII. Examples of Inarticulation Arising from the Inadequate Financing of Public Education

74. Many communities fail to build school buildings and to provide school facilities adequate in size and suitable in appointment for school activities.

75. Many schools fail to provide adequate funds and adequate equipment for new courses, new subjects, and new activities as they are introduced into the schools.

76. Many schools fail by reason of their meager salaries to attract and hold as teachers persons of adequate ability and training for the proper service of children.

77. Small communities fail to offer a sufficient variety of courses.

78. Small units, local communities, and private agencies fail to confine their educational efforts to actual needs and demands.

79. Many large communities fail, for reasons of economy, to make adequate provision to meet the needs of large numbers of children.

80. Many small communities fail to combine with units large enough to permit the organization of classes of proper size.

IX. Examples of Inarticulation Arising Out of Inadequate Teacher-Training Practices and Lax Regulations of Certification

81. Teacher-training institutions too often fail to articulate their methods and practices closely with those of the public school system for which they are preparing teachers.

82. Teacher-training institutions fail to take into account the conditions of supply and demand within the profession.

83. Teacher-training institutions fail to train teachers with reference to a wide enough range of activities and experiences.

84. Too many standard colleges and other agencies of general education attempting to train teachers fail to adapt their courses to the needs of the profession.

85. By lax regulations concerning uncontrolled agencies for the certification of teachers, the state admits incompetent persons into the teaching profession.

X. Other Examples of Inarticulation

86. Many states fail to set up an adequate central agency of leadership and authority for the exercise of a proper amount of administrative and supervisory control of the state's effort in education.

87. The state, by reason of its attempt through its legislature to prescribe technical and professional procedures, fails to meet the needs of local communities and individual pupils.

88. The nation, through the lack of an adequate national agency for the coordinating of the educational efforts of the various states and agencies, fails to integrate and articulate the national effort in education.

89. The school fails to set up and to maintain proper agencies of contact and conference between itself and the society which it serves.

90. The school fails to know, appreciate, and utilize adequately the out-of-school experience of its pupils.

91. The school fails to create a sustaining interest and enthusiasm in its pupils for the progress, development, and achievement of American civilization.

92. The school too often fails to inculcate in its pupils a proper respect for the whole range of worth-while human activities.

93. Most schools fail to reproduce in their classrooms situations which are comparable to and which offer adequate opportunity for training in life situations.

94. Most schools fail to coordinate their programs and efforts with the efforts of organizations outside the schools to which the pupil will be assigned at the conclusion of his school experience.

95. Most schools fail to assist the pupil consciously to move from under controls based upon autocratic domination toward controls based upon democratic participation.

96. Most schools fail to modify their curriculum in the social studies to conform with rapidly developing concepts of world friendship and peaceful international relations.

97. The state, by reason of its practice of controlling professional procedures within the schools by legal enactment, fails to give the schools sufficient freedom for adjustment and development.

98. Lay control of public education fails to give proper recognition to expert professional service.

99. The democratic control of public education by popular vote fails to provide for a continuous, stable policy with reference to educational practices.

100. The ability of minority groups to impress and control policies of public education in a democratic government fails to insure a stable and balanced educational program.

Each person was requested to select from the foregoing list of 100 inarticulations the 20 which in his opinion were the most significant and which most affect the progress of children through the public school system. It was suggested that one example be selected from each of the 10 major headings indicated in the list and that 10 be selected at random from the entire list of 100. After thus selecting 20 inarticulations, he ranked them in the order of their importance.

The responses were tabulated by using 20 sheets to record the ranking of the 20 most serious inarticulations. Sheet number one recorded all first choices, and sheet number two recorded all second choices. One hundred columns were on each sheet in order to allow any item of the check list to have a place in the ranking. Totals were obtained which indicated which items were most popular in general; which items were least popular in general; which items were favored by particular groups of people, sections of country, types and sizes of schools, or cities.

After these preliminary tabulations and rankings were secured, each of the items was weighted according to rank and frequency. These weighted scores were then totaled and these weighted choices were combined.

A summarized review of the findings follows:

TABLE 90.—RANKING OF THE 20 CHIEF INARTICULATIONS IN AMERICAN EDUCATION

Rank	1	2	3	4	5	6	7	8	9	10	11	12	13	14	15	16	17	18	19	20
Inarticulation Numbers......	76	1	32	45	64	47	63	29	31	18	93	90	81	39	33	48	3	26	5	9

The 20 major inarticulations, listed in order of importance, are these:

1. (76) Many schools fail, by reason of their meager salaries, to attract and hold as teachers, persons of adequate ability and training for the proper service of children.
2. (1) The school often fails to discover and to measure adequately, capacities and abilities as a basis for discovering and meeting individual needs and differences.
3. (32) Too many teachers fail to bring to their position an adequate knowledge of the laws of child growth and child psychology.
4. (45) The school fails at all levels to free itself from practices and procedures which are wholly traditional as to origin.
5. (64) Most schools fail to emphasize creative, self-expressive activity more than the mastery of routine, academic material.
6. (47) The school too often fails to evaluate the success or failure of its methods, practices, and procedures in terms of their effect upon the individual student rather than in terms of their effect upon the group.
7. (63) The school fails to correlate closely the subject-matter of its curriculum with the experience of the child.
8. (29) The school too often fails, through carelessness, oversight, or for reasons of expediency, to see that teachers are assigned to the positions for which they have been trained and which they are competent to fill.
9. (31) Too many teachers fail to bring to their profession an adequate knowledge of the developing philosophy of education.
10. (18) Secondary schools in general fail to incorporate in their organization and courses provision for students not planning to enter college or to train for the professions.
11. (93) Most schools fail to reproduce in their classrooms situations which are comparable to and which offer adequate opportunity for training in life situations.

12. (90) The school fails to know, appreciate, and utilize adequately the out-of-school experience of its pupils.

13. (81) Teacher-training institutions too often fail to articulate closely their methods and practices with those of the public school system for which they are preparing teachers.

14. (39) The school too often violates, ignores, or disregards the psychological law of readiness by employing methods, teaching subjects, and requiring pupil responses at times and under conditions which violate fundamental and psychological considerations.

15. (33) Too many teachers fail to apply to the teaching task those professional principles which should determine their practice with reference to the learning situation.

16. (48) The school too often fails to set up and to follow a scientific method and procedure with reference to the promotion of pupils.

17. (3) The school fails to govern its procedure with reference to the individual pupil in the light of his capacities and limitations, and fearlessly present the implications thereof to the pupil and to the parents.

18. (26) Supervisors fail to develop and to apply an adequate and workable policy of supervisory procedure.

19. (5) The school fails to make adequate use of the needs of students as a basis for their classification.

20. (9) The school has standardized equipment and curriculum to such an extent that the particular and individual needs of pupils and communities may not be met adequately.

The 1599 persons who ranked the list of 100 inarticulations were distributed as to educational positions as follows:

5 College Deans	313 Teachers of High Schools
20 College Professors	59 Principals of Junior High Schools
51 College Teachers	145 Teachers of Junior High Schools
3 College Registrars	153 Principals of Elementary Schools
230 Superintendents of Public School Systems	129 Supervisors
8 Presidents of Junior Colleges	46 Teachers of Elementary Schools
183 Principals of High Schools	254 Miscellaneous Responses (Educational position not designated)

The geographical distribution[1] was as follows: 44 were from the New England States; 213, the Middle Atlantic States; 470, the Southern States; 360, the Middle Western States; and 373 were from the Western States.

Replies from the various levels or units of the school system were widely distributed:

Elementary School	611	Universities	22
Secondary School	805	Rural Schools	139
Teacher-Training Schools	81	Village Schools	299
Standard Colleges	28	City Systems (5000 population and upward)	773

All levels of the public school system, all types of educational position, and all sections of the country were represented in the replies. If any dependence may be placed upon a consensus of professional opinion as to characteristic inarticulations in American education, the judgment expressed in the findings of this study is worthy of careful consideration.

[1] 139 persons answering the check list failed to state their geographical location.

Many educational philosophers and students of American education have expressed an opinion as to the existence of inarticulations in our schools. This study reveals a formidable list of barriers, gaps, and practices that, in the opinion of the profession, impede pupil progress.

Inarticulation number 76 in the check list was selected more often than any other for a place in the list of 20 regarded as most important. Nearly three-fourths of all those ranking the 100 inarticulations in the check list gave it a place in the first 20. It reads: "Many schools fail by reason of their meager salaries to attract and hold as teachers persons of adequate ability and training for the proper service of children." This statement is not a plea by teachers for larger salaries to be used for the more adequate maintenance of themselves and of their dependents, but rather a general agreement by the teaching profession that the greatest barrier confronting the pupil and impeding his school progress is the lack of ability and training on the part of his teacher.

It is significant that out of the 20 inarticulations selected as most significant, eight (1, 3, 8, 9, 13, 14, 15, and 18 in the check list) refer to the ability, training, or practice of the teacher. This ranking by educators, in the light of their own practical experience and intimate knowledge of American schools, would indicate that the ability, training, and practice of the teacher are the most pertinent factors in conditioning child experience in school.

Four of the inarticulations included in the first 20 (7, 10, 11, and 12 in the check list) refer to the imperfect relation of the school to the society it is designed to serve. Seven (4, 5, 10, 11, 12, 14, and 20) refer to the curriculum; one (16) to the routine procedure of the school; one (4) to the influence of tradition; and one (20) to the hampering effects of over-standardization.

The Committee stated as its fundamental proposition that "The two prime considerations underlying educational integration are the nature of the child and the social functions of the schools." The consensus of country-wide opinion in selecting the major inarticulations confirms the Committee's opinion that those inarticulations due to the school's failure to understand adequately child nature and social needs and modify its practices accordingly are its greatest weaknesses.

In general, the chief imperfections of the public school as seen by educators themselves, according to this study, are these:

Meager Salaries Fail To Attract and To Hold Teachers of Adequate Ability, Training, and Personality.

Schools Too Often Fail to Evaluate the Success or Failure of Their Methods, Practices, and Procedures in Terms of Their Effect upon the Individual Student Rather Than in Terms of Their Effect upon the Group.

Too Many Teachers Fail To Bring to Their Position an Adequate Knowledge of the Laws of Child Growth and Child Psychology.

The School Fails at All Levels To Free Itself from Certain Practices
and Procedures Which Are Wholly Traditional as to Origin.
Most Schools Fail To Emphasize Creative, Self-Expressive Activity
More Than the Mastery of Routine, Academic Material.
The School Often Fails To Discover and To Measure Adequately Capacities and Abilities as a Basis for Discovering and Meeting Individual Needs and Differences.

For purposes of analyzing the data more critically, the replies were divided
into three groups. Those coming from university and college teachers were
put in one group; those coming from secondary school teachers in a second
group; and those from elementary teachers in a third group. The replies
from each group were subjected to the same statistical method of weighted
scoring, for the purpose of obtaining the ten inarticulations which, in the
judgment of each group, are the greatest hindrance to pupil progress.

It is obvious that it would not be possible in every case to obtain a clear,
consecutive ranking of a single inarticulation for each rank from each group.
Therefore, where two inarticulations were ranked equally in importance so
far as the smaller groups were concerned, one was listed for the rank for
which they tied, and the other was listed as of the next lower rank. This
procedure is probably not defensible statistically, but since the purpose is to
reveal the consensus of opinion of groups of individuals, it does not seem to
be objectionable to take this much liberty in the placing of inarticulations as
to rank, especially since the list of selected articulations was expanded to include at least ten from each group.

These groups with their selected inarticulations from one to ten inclusive
have been arranged according to the levels of the school systems studied.
Table 91 represents the selections at the college and university level; Table

TABLE 91.—THE TEN MAJOR INARTICULATIONS SELECTED
BY PERSONS WORKING AT THE COLLEGE AND UNIVER-
SITY LEVEL

Groups at College and University Level	Rank									
	1	2	3	4	5	6	7	8	9	10
20 College Professors......................	90	1	61	18	45	29	84	38	55	62
5 College Deans.........................	76	52	32	50	18	1	5	63	....	....
8 Jr. College Presidents..................	76	3	2	85	29	32	5	36	45	46
51 College Teachers......................	76	29	64	18	1	48	45	46	35	47
Accrediting Agencies										
39 Middle States........................	76	31	1	18	39	93	32	63	74	83
134 Southern States......................	1	18	76	45	26	29	27	47	64	81
12 New England States...................	72	1	63	19	9	39	45	53	47	32
22 Northwestern States..................	76	47	84	64	73	90	46	52	50	74
291 North Central States.................	1	76	45	47	26	84	18	35	31	64
81 Teacher-Training Institutions...........	32	45	62	64	76	18	84	1	39	33
28 Colleges..............................	64	18	5	29	1	85	47	92	36	59
22 Universities..........................	45	1	63	76	64	55	9	65	47	93
22 Vocational Training Institutions........	92	6	53	76	31	90	89	16	22	23

Read table thus: In selecting the ten major inarticulations from the check list of 100, 20 college professors rank inarticulation 90 in the check list as 1; inarticulation 1, as 2; inarticulation
61, as 3; etc.

92, the selections at the secondary school level; Table 93, the selections at the elementary school level; and Table 94, the selections by geographical distribution. In the tables are listed the number of replies, the classification of those replying, and the ten major inarticulations selected by each group.

Table 91 lists those inarticulations which college and university teachers deem to be the ten chief hindrances to pupil progress. Three aspects of the problem are reflected in the inarticulations selected by those who are teaching or administering in the public schools at this level.

The first aspect has to do with the general administrative policy and practice of the schools themselves, as shown by the selection of the following inarticulations:

The school fails at all levels to free itself from practices and procedures which are wholly traditional as to origin.

Secondary schools in general fail to incorporate in their organization and courses provision for students not planning to enter college or to train for the professions.

Too many standard colleges and other agencies of general education attempting to train teachers fail to adapt their courses to the needs of the profession.

Many schools fail by reason of their meager salaries to attract and hold as teachers persons of adequate ability and training for the proper service of children.

The school too often fails, through carelessness, oversight, or for reasons of expediency, to see that teachers are assigned to the positions for which they have been trained and which they are competent to fill.

A second aspect of the articulation problem which this group considers important has to do with the manner in which the school deals with the individual pupil. This opinion is reflected by the selection of the following inarticulations:

The school often fails to discover and to measure adequately capacities and abilities as a basis for discovering and meeting individual needs and differences.

The school too often fails to evaluate the success or failure of its methods, practices, and procedures in terms of their effect upon the individual student rather than in terms of their effect upon the group.

The school too often fails to set up and to follow a scientific method and procedure with reference to the promotion of pupils.

The third aspect of the articulation problem which impressed the college and university group has to do with the content of curriculum. This is reflected by the selection of these inarticulations:

The school fails to correlate closely the subject-matter of its curriculum with the experience of the child.

The school fails to know, appreciate, and utilize adequately the out-of-school experience of its pupils.

Most schools fail to emphasize creative, self-expressive activity more than the mastery of routine, academic material.

It is interesting to note that the inarticulation which reads, "Many schools fail by reason of their meager salaries to attract and hold as teachers persons of adequate ability and training for the proper service of children" is selected as the most important by nearly half of all of the group replying at the college and university level. One is interested to know whether those making this selection had in mind the difficulties besètting their own institutions and were replying out of a realization of their own failures in adequately meeting the needs of students entrusted to them, or whether they selected this inarticulation because they attributed many of their difficulties to the inadequate training of students reaching them from the lower levels of the public school system.

While space does not permit a detailed analysis of the ten inarticulations selected by the various groups—collegiate, secondary, and elementary—as the chief hindrances in pupil progress, the following procedure is recommended to those who are interested in such an analysis. Cut the list of 100 inarticulations into slips so that one inarticulation is upon each slip and arrange them in the order in which they have been ranked by the various groups. If this is done, as one reads the selections by groups, one gains an impression of the problems uppermost in the minds of each group as it made its selection.

TABLE 92.—THE TEN MAJOR INARTICULATIONS SELECTED BY PERSONS WORKING AT THE SECONDARY SCHOOL LEVEL

Groups at Secondary School Level	Rank									
	1	2	3	4	5	6	7	8	9	10
230 Superintendents of Public School Systems.	26	46	81	1	18	32	72	25	32	76
183 Principals of Secondary Schools..........	76	32	47	1	64	94	45	81	63	18
313 Teachers of Secondary Schools...........	1	32	47	64	76	81	16	47	45	18
59 Principals of Junior High Schools........	32	63	29	44	47	76	45	63	1	27
145 Teachers of Junior High Schools.........	47	76	1	35	29	32	45	62	54	73
805 Secondary Schools.....................	1	32	45	47	76	63	81	48	82	84

Read table thus: In selecting the ten major inarticulations from the check list of 100, 230 superintendents of public schools rank inarticulation 26 in the check list as 1; inarticulation 46, as 2; inarticulation 81, as 3; etc.

Table 92 gives the responses at the secondary school level. It includes the replies of 230 superintendents of public school systems. While it is obvious that superintendents of schools do not figure more in a class with the secondary schools than in a class with the elementary schools, it seems equally logical to present them with the secondary school group.

An inspection of Table 92 does not give one quite so clear a picture of the problems uppermost in the minds of those working at the secondary school level as did Table 91 of the persons working at the university and college level.

The emphasis in the selections made by the secondary group is distributed between three aspects of the articulation problem. One notes first of all that this group is concerned with the inability of the school to appraise or measure the results which it achieves with its individual pupils. This is reflected by the selection of these inarticulations:

The school often fails to discover and to measure adequately capacities and abilities as a basis for discovering and meeting individual needs and differences.

The school too often fails to evaluate the success or failure of its methods, practices, and procedures in terms of their effect upon the individual student rather than in terms of their effect upon the group.

The secondary school group is evidently thinking more about the curriculum and the problems pertaining to it than are persons working at other levels. This emphasis is indicated by the selection of the following inarticulations:

The school fails at all levels to free itself from practices and procedures which are wholly traditional as to origin.

Secondary schools in general fail to incorporate in their organization and courses provision for students not planning to enter college or to train for the professions.

The school fails to correlate closely the subject-matter of its curriculum with the experience of the child.

Most schools fail to emphasize creative, self-expressive activity more than the mastery of routine, academic material.

This group, too, is impressed by the inarticulation resulting from the lack of adequate training and ability of the classroom teacher. This concern is expressed in the selection of the following inarticulations:

Teacher-training institutions too often fail to articulate closely their methods and practices with those of the public school system for which they are preparing teachers.

Too many teachers fail to bring to their position an adequate knowledge of the laws of child growth and child psychology.

Many schools fail by reason of their meager salaries to attract and hold as teachers persons of adequate ability and training for the proper service of children.

Table 93 summarizes the responses at the elementary school level.

TABLE 93.—THE TEN MAJOR INARTICULATIONS SELECTED BY PERSONS WORKING AT THE ELEMENTARY SCHOOL LEVEL

Persons at Elementary School Level	Rank									
	1	2	3	4	5	6	7	8	9	10
153 Principals of Elementary Schools.........	1	27	32	45	47	32	52	63	76	81
46 Teachers of Elementary Schools..........	39	35	76	93	9	25	33	64	32	40
129 Supervisors.............................	32	64	1	76	47	63	81	29	45	58
254 Miscellaneous Responses................	76	47	32	90	29	1	81	49	62	39
611 Elementary Schools.....................	1	29	32	45	47	76	64	81	99	28
299 in Village Schools......................	1	32	29	45	76	64	63	81	90	28
139 in Rural Schools.......................	45	32	39	76	64	1	47	33	51	48
470 in Cities with Population of 25,000 to 50,000	1	39	45	64	90	25	32	31	47	29
88 in Cities with Population of 50,000 to 100,000	76	1	29	48	32	47	3	11	33	64
329 in Cities with Population over 100,000....	1	32	45	47	64	45	76	81	16	51

Read table thus: In selecting the ten major inarticulations from the check list of 100, 153 principals of elementary schools rank inarticulation 1 in the check list as 1; inarticulation 27, as 2; inarticulation 32, as 3; etc.

In order that the inarticulations selected by people working at the elementary school level may have a vividness and a continuity of meaning, they have been arranged into four groups. The first group has to do with administration and supervision and is indicated by the selection of the following inarticulations:

The school often fails to discover and to measure adequately, capacities and abilities as a basis for discovering and meeting individual needs and differences.

Administrators, by the imposition of formal and restrictive procedures in the operation and management of schools, impose "red tape" that necessarily impedes the progress of children.

Teachers too often fail to maintain a receptive attitude toward supervisory agencies.

The school fails to reconcile the teaching and practices in one unit with those of the units above and below to the end that the outcomes for the pupils are continuous, cumulative, and progressive.

The second group of inarticulations selected by people working at the elementary school level has to do with problems of the curriculum and is reflected by the selection of the following:

The school fails to correlate closely the subject-matter of its curriculum with the experience of the child.

Most schools fail to emphasize creative, self-expressive activity more than the mastery of routine, academic material.

The school fails to know, appreciate, and utilize adequately the out-of-school experience of its pupils.

The school fails at all levels to free itself from certain practices and procedures which are wholly traditional as to origin.

The third group of inarticulations selected by persons working at the elementary school level centers around problems pertaining to the teacher. They are reflected in the selection of the following inarticulations:

Teacher-training institutions too often fail to articulate closely their methods and practices with those of the public school system for which they are preparing teachers.

Many schools fail by reason of their meager salaries to attract and hold as teachers persons of adequate ability and training for the proper service of children.

Too many teachers fail to bring to their position an adequate knowledge of the laws of child growth and child psychology.

The fourth group of inarticulations which commands the attention of the group working at this level has to do with the professional practice of teachers. It is reflected by the selection of the following inarticulation:

Too many teachers fail to apply to the teaching task those professional principles which should determine their practice with reference to the learning situation.

In Table 94 responses are distributed according to the section of the country from which they came.

Table 94 reveals certain interesting reactions. One notes first of all that inarticulation 1, which reads, "The school often fails to discover and to measure adequately the capacities and abilities as a basis for discovering and meeting individual needs and differences" is ranked first by educators in every section of the country, New England excepted, while even here this inarticulation finds a high rank. Such agreement with reference to the ranking of this inarticulation does not exist in any of the other groups or as a result of any of the other comparisons. Is it not of great significance that so many agree that our schools should study more deeply into individual pupil capacities and abilities, and should control procedures more and more in terms of these findings? The need for further study and research in these fields is evident.

The theoretical pronouncements set forth in other sections of this report invite educators everywhere to make practical application of the suggested remedies in particular schools, at specific grade levels, and with reference to individual pupils. When procedures such as those suggested have been tested for some time, data will be available for further guidance.

TABE 94.—RANKING OF TEN MAJOR INARTICULATIONS BY EDUCATORS, DISTRIBUTED ACCORDING TO GEOGRAPHY

Geographical Distribution	Rank									
	1	2	3	4	5	6	7	8	9	10
44 from New England States..............	63	64	45	76	32	1	3	11	14	81
213 from Middle Atlantic States.............	1	29	47	45	76	47	28	64	48	90
470 from Southern States...................	1	18	32	18	47	76	61	45	90	63
360 from Mid-Western States..............	1	29	32	45	48	64	76	81	90	26
373 from Western States...................	1	64	32	45	47	64	47	63	76	26

Read table thus: In selecting the ten major inarticulations from the check list of 100, 44 educators from the New England States rank inarticulation 63 in the check list as 1; inarticulation 64, as 2; inarticulation 45, as 3; etc.

Table 94 reveals significant differences of opinion among educators in different sections of the country as to the major inarticulations in American education. Those representing the New England States emphasize the needs of the individual pupil—their discovery and the adaptations in the curriculum, teaching methods, and pupil guidance which they demand—if one may judge from their selection and ranking of the ten inarticulations which they regard as most serious. While there are included in their ten selected rankings certain inarticulations which have implications other than those pertaining to the individual pupil, there is a preponderance of emphasis upon these phases of the articulation problem.

In the Middle Atlantic States there is this same concern about the individual pupil, but one finds creeping into the selections there inarticulations which refer to such matters as the attitude of teachers toward supervision, curriculum content, method, teacher training, and teacher placement problems.

Teachers from the Southern States show concern about the organization and administration of secondary education, teacher training, and problems relating to the individual pupil and the curriculum.

The respondents from Mid-Western States emphasize problems having to do with teacher training and placement, supervision, method, and promotions.

In the Western States one detects an emphasis on those phases of education which have to do with the introduction into the classroom of methods which have been popularly referred to as the "progressive" type of education, or more generally known perhaps as an "activity program." For example, inarticulation No. 64, which reads "Most schools fail to emphasize creative, self-expressive activity more than the mastery of routine, academic material," is ranked second in importance.

While there is no indication that one particular type of difficulty exists in one section of the country and is entirely non-existent in another, certain phases of the articulation problem are rated as far more important in one section than in another.

It is hoped that as the results of this study are distributed to the various sections of the country, and as they are reviewed by those actively engaged in education, more careful and detailed studies of inarticulations will be conducted in individual school systems. The data which will be forthcoming from these later studies will make plainer the significance of the findings of this present study with reference to the shift of emphasis in different geographical areas.

The grouping of replies according to geographical distribution simply represents another classification of materials which have already been utilized in connection with Tables 90, 91, 92, and 93. In the classification of the replies according to geographical distribution, no effort was made to keep the replies from the collegiate, secondary, and elementary groups segregated, so that this table is a composite of those replying from all of the various grade levels of the school system. It is possible that a preponderance of opinion at certain levels tends to affect materially the results of Table 94. Conclusions, therefore, should not be too hastily drawn without further data.

It is hoped that this check list of inarticulations will be made the basis of careful study and survey by local school systems. To do this it is only necessary that teachers and principals at various grade levels in each school system select and rank the ten or twenty inarticulations which they feel are the major hindrances to their pupils' progress. Then case studies should be collected wherein pupil progress in specific instances has been influenced by these suggested hindrances. When this sort of study has been carefully made, each local school system will be able to decide which local inarticulation actually operates most in slowing up pupil progress. The present study merely points out what the problem is.

The present ranking of inarticulations as to their importance is nothing more than consensus of opinion. It will not be, until the whole check list of 100 items has been made the basis for repeated studies covering large numbers of school systems and checked against the progress of thousands of individual pupils, that more objective information will be available.

It is to be admitted frankly that such a survey as this, conducted under conditions such as have prevailed during this study, will present examples of inarticulations which perhaps exist only in occasional situations or in isolated school systems. It will include examples of inarticulations which have been remedied perhaps for years in some progressive school systems. It may overlook more obscure and less easily recognized faults and defects due entirely to the fact that those reporting are themselves ignorant of the existence as well as the nature of certain inarticulations.

Those actively engaged in teaching will find it interesting to take the theoretical principles set up elsewhere in this report and apply them to one and another of the inarticulations listed, determining by this procedure how far their communities have advanced in their efforts to develop remedies to existing inarticulations. For example, it is reasonable to assume that if judgments were secured from those communities where most progress has been made in curriculum revision, the inarticulations selected as major hindrances to pupil progress there would not relate to the curriculum, but to other problems which have not yet been met successfully in those school systems.

In this study one is somewhat surprised to note that so many of the inarticulations referred to have to do with the evaluation of school procedures with reference to the individual pupil. One would scarcely have expected, after we have given so much emphasis to problems of measurement, that there would still exist such a unanimity of judgment that we are failing seriously in our efforts to measure adequately the capacities and abilities of pupils, and to meet these pupil needs after they have been discovered.

Measurements should be devised that reveal more of the individual pupil's capacities and abilities. Measurements should also be devised that would appraise on a broader basis school achievement and school success in meeting individual needs and differences. Many of our present measuring devices are inadequate means of revealing school success. In other words, studies such as the one reported here are apt to be too negative in their findings. They emphasize the school's failures and bring to light its defects, failing to balance these by revealing the school's successes and bringing to light its notable accomplishments.

Continued study and research are necessary for the solution of the inarticulations in American education.

Summary

The following generalizations are the reactions of the investigator, after a year's study of the problem:

1. Ample evidence is furnished that the teaching profession is keenly conscious of the school's failures and inadequacies, and that it is, therefore, ready to proceed with curative or remedial modifications as soon as adequate professional and lay leadership is available.

2. Teachers need a more adequate knowledge of the laws appertaining to child nature, child growth, and child development in order that they may meet the different needs of individual pupils.

3. Those who administer and teach in our schools need to be more conscious of social objectives, if the schools are to meet the needs of the society they are maintained to serve.

4. Pupil progress through the schools and on into later life would be facilitated by the removal of some of the existing inconsistencies and inarticulations particularly with respect to underlying philosophy, type and kind of school organization, content of curriculum, and unscientific methods.

5. Curriculum materials should have intrinsic significance to pupils as well as possess social value.

6. The school program should provide a sufficient range of activities to give a balanced development to the child intellectually, physically, emotionally, and socially.

7. The types of inarticulations which are the greatest hindrance to pupil progress vary significantly between the elementary, secondary, and college levels.

8. The professional training of teachers is increasingly a problem of preparing teachers to meet scientifically the problems of the classroom.

9. Pupil promotion, grading, marking, and college entrance should not be mechanized, routine procedures.

10. Problems which arise in connection with the individual pupil's progress through the public school system demand continuous study. Their solution depends on extensive and accurate data collected and used by classroom teachers, supervisors, and administrators.

CHAPTER XXV

SUMMARY AND RECOMMENDATIONS

Prepared by
JESSE H. NEWLON and WALTER D. COCKING

THIS SECTION of the report of the Committee on Principles of Articulation and Functions of Units of the school system has been prepared on the assumption that the Committee should make definite constructive suggestions for the elimination of inarticulations.

The study made by Supt. Sexson reveals many of the most acute inarticulations and maladjustments. It becomes increasingly clear, as the results of this inquiry and others made by the Commission are studied, that one of the chief causes of inarticulation is found in the fact that too frequently educational practices are not based on considered theory. The preceding sections of this report attempt to present some of the educational and social principles upon which an integrated system of education must be built. Attention has also been called to the fact that the sources of some of these maladjustments are found in the early history of the American elementary and secondary school. The American system of education has evolved without much deliberate planning. As the schools move into a more complex civilization the need for planning becomes more imperative. Anyone who is responsible for the direction of American education should no longer remain indifferent to a curriculum cluttered up at so many points with useless subject-matter, to methods so often ill-adapted to the nature of the individual and the social function of the school, or to the maladjustment that exists between the secondary school and the college.

In the opinion of the Committee, reconstruction along the following lines is imperative:

I. *American Education Should Be Reconstructed in the Light of a More Adequate Understanding of the Social Functions of the School in an Industrial Democracy.*

The studies conducted by this Commission have only added to the increasing accumulation of evidence to the effect that the American school lags far behind the conditions and the needs of American life. Teachers and principals repeatedly assert that in important respects the subject-matter of the curriculum is lacking in social significance. The curriculum, particularly in the secondary school, still retains a vast amount of subject-matter of little value to the large majority of youth. Great numbers who are pursuing the study of the traditional subject-matter of foreign language, mathematics, and even of science and social studies, find in these studies little of significance to them. At the same time antiquated requirements deprive these youth of opportunities of entering upon studies and experiences intimately connected with the problems of modern life and rich in educational values.

Students of education should devote more attention to the study of American civilization. Unless much larger appropriations are made available for research, much of the intelligence and resources now devoted to the study of the minutiæ of the educative process should be redirected and focused on the study of the school in relation to the problems of contemporary life. We are in danger of getting a lopsided view of education. No one would deny the importance of controlled experimentation or of the application of scientific method to the study of all kinds of problems, but he must be blind who cannot see that we have tended in the past twenty years to emphasize research on certain phases of the educative process to the neglect of others. In the absence of adequate information upon which constantly to readjust the school to social needs, the new instruments for the scientific study of education and of measurement are inevitably used for the refinement of existing procedures, many of which are entirely at variance with the needs of the individual and of society. Of what avail is it to learn how to teach specific subject-matter more effectively to a boy or a girl who should never undertake to learn such subject-matter?

If this need is to be met, the curriculums of schools of education and teacher-training institutions must be reconstructed and broadened to include a more thoroughgoing study of the relation of education to basic social processes and problems. It will mean a reconstruction of the in-service professional study of teachers and of much of the effort being directed by city school systems in the reconstruction of the curriculum. This imperative need for the reconstruction of American education in the light of social needs has been effectively stated by George S. Counts. He says in *Secondary Education and Industrialism:* [1]

> The historian of the future will, I think, find our attack upon the problem of education gravely deficient. He will see us extremely busy with many things, some of which are important; but he will be amazed at the absence of any vigorous and concerted effort to discover the educational implications of the new industrial civilization which is rapidly overwhelming and transforming the traditional social order.[2]
>
> He will see us in this strange, fantastic industrial society repeating formulæ handed down from an agrarian age when we should be searching with tireless effort for formulæ suited to the world as it is; he will see us preoccupied with educational techniques and the minutiæ of school-keeping when we should be wrestling with the basic problems of life; he will see us greatly agitated over the construction of an algebra test or a marking scale, when we should be endeavoring to make the school function in the building of a new civilization.[3]

---

[1] Counts, George S. *Secondary Education and Industrialism.* Cambridge, Mass.: Harvard University Press, 1929. 70 p. (The Inglis Lecture, 1929)

[2] *Ibid.*, p. 3.

[3] *Ibid.*, p. 4.

On its social side secondary educational theory has either clung to the formulæ of a past age or has been guided by a very partial analysis of society. At any rate no one can say that it has grappled courageously with the fundamental problems raised by industrialism.[1]

II. *The Method of the School Should in All Instances Accord with the Nature of the Individual and the Social Function of the School. The Dualism in Method that Characterizes So Much of Present Practice Should Be Resolved by Basing Method on a Considered Theory of Learning.*

In the broadest sense, method must be adapted to the needs of the individual and of society. The school building must be designed to minister to the pupil's physical needs, and its furniture and equipment must likewise be adapted to his comfort and well-being. The building and its equipment should make possible the realization of an educational program based on individual and social needs. The school must plan its educational procedure with reference to the entire child, taking into consideration his physical, mental, emotional, and social nature. The social objectives of education, or lack of them, will always be important factors in determining the method of the school. The fact that American education is to so large an extent drifting, because of the absence of social outlook, is a factor that contributes to the prevailing confusion in method.

In methods of teaching the American school is practising a dualism. Almost without exception there will be found in any school the old memoriter, textbook, cramming method of learning. The learning of subject-matter as an end in itself is still one of the dominant aims of education if we may judge by practices that obtain on every hand in the elementary school, and especially in the secondary school. Objective tests and the new type examination are in themselves instruments that may be used in the correction of these evils, but actually they frequently are used to fasten them more firmly on the schools. College entrance examinations have done much to retard the development of secondary education. President Angell of Yale recently spoke as follows of the evils of the examination system:

If a teacher knows that the success, or failure, of his students in critical examination—especially when set by others—is going to be employed as the principal test of his skill as a tutor, he is bound to be confronted by a dilemma which will gravely tax his intellectual and moral integrity. Shall he conscientiously and uncompromisingly try to give to his men the best education he can, or shall he train them to pass examinations? In theory the two aims and the two results might well be identical; in practice it is very rare that they are. The successful tutor who becomes a mere cram master will enjoy a wide, if ambiguous, popularity and fame. But it is quite certain that he will often be rendering his students a serious disservice.

Some of the earmarks of this type of teaching are the slavish use of textbooks, logically arranged and highly departmentalized courses of study with definite prescriptions of subject-matter set out to be learned, formal re-

[1] *Op. cit.*, p. 50.

views of subject-matter, and the formal use of the examination as a measure of education.

Alongside this traditional method of teaching, based on the old doctrine of formal discipline, American schools are experimenting with newer and more vital methods based on a pragmatic philosophy of education and a new psychology of learning. These methods are founded on the assumption that education is an active process, that the psychological should take precedence over the logical, that there is an intimate relation between purposes, subject-matter, and method. The school is conceived as a social institution and education as a social process. Emphasis is placed on pupil activity in the educative process. Drill has a place, but is subordinated to other processes and is best achieved when the learner has discovered a need for the mastery of certain subject-matter or skills. The socialized recitation, the problem method, the project method, and many other such phrases are only indicative of experimentation to discover ways of teaching more in harmony with the nature of the individual and with the social function of the school.

This newer method of teaching is being carried on alongside the more traditional method. As practiced the two are largely contradictory. The subjection of a pupil daily to both of these methods results in confusion, and tends to produce an ineffective personality. An integrated, articulated system of schools is impossible under such conditions. The more formal method is most widely used in the secondary school, which only increases the inarticulations between this unit and others. This dualism should be recognized and resolved by basing the method of the school on a considered theory of learning consistent with the findings of research and the best thought.

III. *The Curriculum Should Be Reconstructed to Eliminate the Evils of Extreme Departmentalization and of Unnecessary Duplication. A Resynthesis of Subject-Matter Is Needed.*

This criticism applies primarily to the secondary school, but wherever the old rigid teaching by subjects obtains in the elementary school there is much inefficient, disconnected, uncorrelated learning. One of the outstanding characteristics of the American high school is its system of credits based on the study of definite, departmentalized subject-matter units. The extreme to which this practice has been carried has merited almost universal condemnation. It is very difficult to confine learning within the boundaries of an academic subject. While some cogent arguments can be advanced for teaching by subject, especially at the high-school level, where subjects may be broadly conceived and the teacher strives for the maximum number of correlations, it should be remembered that in life subject-matter from numerous fields is drawn upon in the solution of problems, whether in the realm of the sciences or human relationships. To use a favorite illustration of Dewey's, there is, for example, no science of bridge building, but the bridge builder draws upon many sciences.[1] The effect of the system of subjects and

---

[1] Dewey, John. *The Sources of a Science of Education.* New York: Horace Liveright, 1929. p. 34.

credit units is to accentuate disconnected and unintegrated learnings and to increase the difficulties of the teacher. Systematic bodies of knowledge must constitute a part of the professional equipment of the intellectual, of the specialist or professional worker in any field. Teaching should proceed by subjects only when such a procedure is based on a sound pedagogy.

It becomes increasingly apparent that a resynthesis of subject-matter is one of the most imperative needs. Courses of study and methods of teaching should be developed that will in many instances cut across existing subject-matter divisions. Most thorough study should be made of this whole problem with the purpose of eliminating the evils of unintegrated and therefore inefficient learning. To this end the high school should be free to develop its educational procedures without hampering restriction.

IV. *The Administration of Schools Should Be Made To Conform More to a Considered Theory of Education and of the School. Today Administration Is Too Much Characterized by Drift.*

The application of this principle would mean that one philosophy of education should underlie the entire system of education. As has been pointed out, the school is at present confused as to its social function, is attempting to employ simultaneously two psychologies of learning, and is still too much influenced by that traditional philosophy that holds that education above the elementary level is the privilege of an elite class. Method in the high school is still based too largely on the old doctrine of formal discipline. Procedures in the elementary school have to a larger extent been reconstructed in line with the newer pragmatic philosophy of education and the newer psychology of learning. Most school systems have maintained two organizations for the supervision of instruction, one for the secondary school and one for the elementary school. Such a split in supervision only increases the possibilities of inarticulation. Administrative procedures should be reconstructed to eliminate these inconsistencies.

If administration is to serve the purposes of integration and is to strive to make the schools always as socially effective as possible, all the teachers of the school system must be drawn into a cooperative study of the problems of education. In the last analysis theories of education, of administration, and of the curriculum function only through the individual teacher. Teacher participation in the determination of policies is basic to an understanding of policies and, therefore, to a dynamic, integrated, articulated system of education.

In supervision, in the organization of administrative units, in the direction of curriculum reconstruction, in dealing with public opinion, administration must be based on valid educational principles. It must be guided by an educational philosophy. An examination of administrative policy today forces the conclusion that it is based, consciously or otherwise, too much on a philosophy of drift. Supt. Threlkeld has thrown these basic principles of administration into clear relief in his discussion of the problem.

V. *The Professional Education of Teachers Must Be More Broadly
Conceived.*

Again it becomes increasingly evident that drilling the prospective teacher
on the minimum essentials of prescribed and traditional subject-matter, and
on method conceived in terms of technics and devices, will not suffice as a
program of teacher training for the twentieth century. The teacher should
be a student not only of the child and of the learning process in the narrower sense, but of learning in its broad sense, and especially of the function
of education in modern life.

Two years of training above the high school will no longer suffice even
for the elementary school. The movement towards the creation of teachers
colleges offering a four-year curriculum for elementary as well as secondary
teachers is one of the most important contemporary educational developments. The curriculums of teacher-training institutions should be reconstructed with a view to affording prospective teachers an opportunity to
become students of the basic problems of education in an industrial civilization.

Emphasis should be placed on general principles of education, on social
insights, on the study of social trends and the social function of the school,
rather than upon the mere mastery of technics. The history of education,
even in the past thirty years, has been a history of rapid changes in method.
The aim of the teacher-training institution should be to lay a foundation
for method rather than to teach a specific method. The prospective teacher
should be introduced to the scientific study of education and become perme-
ated with the scientific spirit, but should also become conversant with the
larger problems of the school, in the solution of which he must draw upon
many disciplines.

In the last three decades remarkable progress has been made in the
development of a body of professional knowledge in education, in the
development of teacher-training institutions, in elevating the qualifications
required of teachers, and in the improvement of salaries. But notwithstanding this progress, the professional training of teachers still remains one of
our greatest problems. On the whole, American teachers are lacking in the
scholarly attainments that characterize teachers in the best European school
systems. The training of the teacher must be more broadly conceived. The
needs may be briefly summarized.

1. The teacher should bring to his work extensive and thorough scholarship. He should be a scholar not only in his own field but should be equipped
with a broad general education and the finest appreciations that will enable
him to transcend the narrow limits of a subject.

2. The teacher should be equipped with a thorough training in the disciplines basic to his profession such as the principles of education, philosophy
of education, educational psychology, and the use of scientific method in the
study of education. Professional training should provide for a study of the
individual in all his aspects, physical, mental, emotional, social. Broadly

speaking, more emphasis should be laid on general training and less on specific training. The aim should be to give the prospective teacher a thorough training in basic principles rather than in specific methods and devices which will always be meaningless to him unless he understands the principles that underlie them.

3. More attention should be given to the study of the relation of the school to the social order. If this objective is to be achieved, schools of education must make available opportunities for more thoroughgoing study in biology, anthropology, sociology, economics, politics, and in other fields that must contribute to the development of an effective educational policy. Contemporary civilization and its problems must to a far greater extent provide subjects of study in professional schools.

At present our teacher-training institutions are doing their best work with respect to the second need. We are weakest with reference to the first and especially the third.

VI. *College Entrance Requirements Should Be Revised So As To Stimulate and Give the High School Freedom To Adapt Education at That Level to the Needs of Youth.*

The Committee believes that half-way measures with reference to college entrance requirements are no longer justified. The weight of investigation is strongly against present practices. There is no evidence to support the contention that the units prescribed have special values for the preparation of youth to think on the college level. The high school should be left free to develop an educational program to meet the needs of American youth. On the other hand, it is recognized that the school should cooperate with the college in the matter of college entrance. It seems entirely feasible to define a policy that will meet the requirements of the college and at the same time leave the school unhampered. Colleges in recent years have developed new technics of high reliability for the selection of students. The Committee, therefore, recommends that the requirements for entrance to college be constructed along the general line of the following proposals:

1. Admission to college to be based on:

a. An objective report by the school on the work of the pupil, including, where required, a report on his standing in scholarship, habits of industry, attitudes, interest, personality, and character traits.

b. Ability to read English with comprehension. (To be determined insofar as possible by objective measures.)

c. The use of a scholastic aptitude test or an informational test that will afford a measure of the individual's range of information, his intellectual capacity, and his purposes, if such tests can be devised that will not set up a subject-matter examination for which preparation can be made in advance through the study of specific subject-matter units.

d. The use of the personal interview by colleges that deem it necessary.

e. The prescription of special courses for propaedeutic purposes. If a definite knowledge of mathematics is required to enter an engineering school, this should be so stated in the requirements. But such requirements should not be stated in terms of subject-matter units of prescribed content to be pursued over a prescribed number of weeks or months.

2. Secondary schools should be accredited on the following basis:

a. A term of satisfactory length.
b. Adequate buildings and equipment.
c. Adequate budget.
d. Professionally trained leadership.
e. Qualified teachers representing all the fields of the humanities, sciences, and the arts, including all necessary vocational fields.
f. A curriculum that provides offerings in all the great fields of knowledge, the humanities, the arts, the sciences, mathematics, the social sciences, the foreign languages (except in very small schools), and in all necessary vocational fields.
g. A policy of guidance that will provide for pupils the best possible counsel in the selection of studies.

If such policies were put into effect, the result would almost certainly be an improved secondary school. The high school would be free to organize its work according to considered educational principles. Education in citizenship, in the sciences, the arts, mathematics, in all the humanities, may be entrusted to professional leadership in secondary education. There is no reason to suppose that standards would be lowered or the student left with less guidance than at present with reference to his studies if education at this level were left entirely in the hands of workers in this field. As a matter of fact, the prevailing system of units does not prevent a scattering of efforts and lopsided education.

VII. *Every School System Should Provide for Continuous Revision of the Curriculum.*

The curriculum of the schools should be in constant process of revision by the cooperative efforts of all members of the educational staff. The necessity for continuous revision need not be argued further. Only by constant revision can the latest results of educational research be embodied in school practice and the program of education reconstructed in the light of changing social and economic conditions and changing social ideals.

All members of the educational staff should be drawn into this work of revision, but revision must proceed under competent professional guidance. The professional growth and competency of the teacher is dependent upon participation in the development of such important educational policies.

In the process of curriculum revision the contribution of research agencies, experimental schools, educational thinkers and specialists in all pertinent fields must be constantly utilized.

VIII. *Administrative Units Should Be Organized with Reference to Educational Principles.*

It is impossible to lay down a hard and fast pronouncement regarding the organization of administrative units. The type of unit will depend to a large extent on local conditions. It is impossible to say at the present time what is the best organization.

Numerous arguments can be advanced in favor of an administrative unit containing all the grades of a school system. Many problems of inarticulation would disappear if all grades were represented in one school. For many reasons which need not be discussed in detail here, such a program is not feasible. If the school is to be broken into separate administrative units, then it is essential that each unit be composed of a group of pupils physically and socially fairly homogeneous. Consistent with this principle the junior high school was introduced. This reorganization has been accepted widely as a distinct improvement over the old arrangement but it has increased the number of breaks and transitions. The period of a pupil's attendance in one school may be so short as to make it difficult for the school to thoroughly understand him and to render to him the best possible service. Many school systems are now organized into four units—an elementary school consisting of six grades and a kindergarten, a junior high school of three grades, a senior high school of three grades, and a junior college of two grades. There are numerous objections to breaking the school system into four units.

Viewed from many standpoints, the elementary school is the most desirable unit in the school system. Much can be said in favor of the six-year secondary school or the eight-year secondary school. There are also many arguments in favor of the organization of the school system into three units—the elementary school and two four-year secondary schools, the upper school including the junior college grades. This plan was inaugurated by Pasadena, California, and is now being copied by other school systems. Many of the closest students of secondary education believe the Pasadena plan will be widely accepted as the best solution of the problem.

One generalization may be safely made. The administrative unit should include as many grades as is practical, in view of geographical conditions, density of population, and the social and physical homogeneity of the pupils to be accommodated.

IX. *The Public Should Be Informed Regarding the Aims and the Methods of Education. The Development of Socially Effective Schools Should Be Conceived as a Public Responsibility.*

One of the chief difficulties encountered by those who seek to adapt the school to modern needs is the inertia of public opinion. Ordinarily adults tend to think in terms of the schools which they knew. Paradoxical though it may seem, the intellectual is even more hostile to new educational ideas than the man on the street. The adult tends to think of education in terms of his own fancied or vested interests, or of the prejudices which he has absorbed from his environment. The schools cannot get far ahead of the public. The public, therefore, must be enlightened regarding the aims and the purposes of education. In the United States it is especially imperative that leaders of public opinion gain a better understanding of the advance in methods of teaching, of the social significance of education, and of the relation between the curriculum and methods of the school and the problems of American life. In the last analysis, public opinion regarding education will determine the character of the school.

Little study has been made by American educators of the relation of public opinion to education, or of methods of informing the public regarding the processes of education. This is one of the most important problems that confront the schools.

PART VI
OFFICIAL RECORDS

THE CONSTITUTION AND BYLAWS

THE DEPARTMENT OF SUPERINTENDENCE

CONSTITUTION

Article I—Name

The name of this association shall be the Department of Superintendence of the National Education Association.

Article II—Object

The object of this department shall be to promote the general educational welfare in the field of administrative education and supervision, to make constructive studies, to further the effort and increase the efficiency of persons engaged in education, to foster professional zeal, to advance educational aims and standards, to protect and advance the interests of school administration, and to establish and maintain helpful, friendly relationships.

Article III—Membership

SECTION 1. Membership in the Department of Superintendence shall consist of active, associate, life, and honorary.

SECTION 2. All persons shall be eligible to active membership who are members of the National Education Association, and who are engaged in supervisory and administrative positions—namely, state, county, and city superintendents, and associate, assistant, and deputy state, county, and city superintendents, and supervisory and administrative officers in city and county school systems exercising the functions of associate, assistant, or deputy superintendents; all state and national officers of educational administration; the heads of teacher-training institutions, colleges, and universities having departments or colleges of education, the heads of these departments or colleges of education, and professors of school administration or supervision in these institutions.

SECTION 3. All members of the National Education Association, who are actively engaged in any phase of school work, may become associate members of this department by paying the regular membership fee, and shall be entitled to all the privileges of this department except the right to vote and hold office.

SECTION 4. All members of the National Education Association, who have been engaged in supervisory or administrative positions, as defined in Section 2 of this article, and who have retired from such service, may have the privilege of honorary membership in this department upon recommendation of the Executive Committee.

SECTION 5. All members of the National Education Association who are eligible to active membership in the Department of Superintendence shall become life members of the Department upon the payment of a membership fee of $100, which may be made in ten equal annual payments, or upon securing a contribution of $250 to the Permanent Educational Research Fund, which may be paid in five equal annual installments. All such contributions and life membership fees shall become a part of the Permanent Educational Research Fund. Life members shall be exempt from the payment of all other membership fees in the Department of Superintendence, and shall have all the rights and privileges of active members.

SECTION 6. The Executive Committee shall have power to pass upon the credentials of all applicants for membership.

Article IV—Officers

SECTION 1. The officers of this department shall be a president, a first vice-president (who shall be the retiring president), a second vice-president, an executive secretary, and four members of the Executive Committee who, with the other officers of this department, with the exception of the executive secretary, shall constitute the Executive Committee.

SECTION 2. The president and vice-presidents shall hold office for the period of one year from the date of election, including one full year's service in the promotion and operation of one meeting of the department.

SECTION 3. The executive secretary shall be selected by the Executive Committee for an indefinite period.

SECTION 4. Members of the Executive Committee shall hold office for four years, one member retiring each year. At the first election the member receiving the largest number of votes shall serve for a term of four years and the others for three, two, and one years, respectively, according to the number of votes received.

Article V—Election of Officers

SECTION 1. The procedure for the election of officers shall be as follows: Nominations shall be made from the floor on the morning of the second day's session at a time previously agreed upon by the Executive Committee, and announced in the printed program of the meeting.

SECTION 2. *Method of balloting*—The tickets issued by the secretary of the department to the members shall be provided with a detachable stub, to be used as a ballot.

Two places for the balloting shall be provided, one at the secretary's headquarters, the other at the entrance to the auditorium in which the general sessions are held.

The ballot-boxes shall be open for voting from 11 A. M. until 6 P. M. on the third day of the meeting.

Those candidates receiving the highest number of votes for the respective offices shall be considered the choice of the department, and declared elected.

The entire procedure of balloting shall be in charge of the Executive Committee and secretary.

SECTION 3. *Announcement of the results of balloting*—At the last regular business meeting, the president shall call for the report of the secretary, announcing the result of the ballot cast for the several officers of the department. In case of a tie vote, the Executive Committee shall cast lots to determine the successful candidate.

Article VI—Appointive Committees

The appointive committees of this department shall consist of a Resolutions Committee, an Audit Committee, and such other committees as may be authorized by the department from time to time.

Article VII—Annual Meeting

The annual meeting of this department shall be held on the fourth Monday in February, and the three succeeding days.

Article VIII—Amendments

This Constitution may be altered or amended at any annual meeting by two-thirds vote of the active members present, the proposed amendment having been submitted in writing at a previous regular business meeting.

BYLAWS

Article I—Duties of Officers

SECTION 1. It shall be the duty of the president to preside at all meetings and in conjunction with the Executive Committee to prepare programs for the annual meeting of the department; to appoint all committees not otherwise provided for. He shall be chairman and a member of the Executive Committee, and shall call meetings of this committee whenever he deems it necessary, or whenever he is requested so to do by a majority of the members of the committee. He shall perform all other duties appertaining to his office.

SECTION 2. In the absence of the president, the vice-presidents shall preside in turn. In case of vacancy in the office of president, the second vice-president shall at once succeed to the office of president.

SECTION 3. The executive secretary shall keep a complete and accurate record of the proceedings of all meetings of the department and all meetings of the Executive Committee, shall conduct the business of the department, as provided by the Constitution and Bylaws, and in all matters not definitely prescribed therein be under the direction of the Executive Committee, and in the absence of direction by the Executive Committee, shall be under the direction of the president. He shall receive all moneys due the department and transmit them monthly to the secretary of the National Education Association; shall countersign all bills approved for payment by the Executive Committee or by the president in the interval between meetings of the Executive Committee. He shall have his records present at all meetings of the department and Executive Committee. He shall keep a list of members of the department and shall revise said list annually. He shall be secretary of the Executive Committee and custodian of all property of the department. He shall give such bond as may be required by the Executive Committee. He shall submit an annual report to the Executive Committee at each annual meeting. At the expiration of his term of office he shall turn over to his successor in office all money, books, and property of the department. He shall serve during the pleasure of the Executive Committee.

Article II—Duties of Committees

Section 1. The Executive Committee shall assist the president in arranging the annual program, and in arranging for the place of the annual meeting. It shall select an executive secretary and fix his salary. The Executive Committee shall submit an annual report at one of the business sessions of the department, shall recommend to the department the appointment of special committees for investigation and research. It shall recommend the amount of money to be expended in such investigations, but in no case shall it incur debt. It shall decide what sections and departments of the National Education Association may be affiliated with this department.

Section 2. The Resolutions and Audit Committees shall be appointed by the newly elected president immediately upon his election and shall make their report at the next annual meeting succeeding their appointment.

Article III—Dues

The dues of this department shall be $5 per year for both active and associate members, and shall be paid annually to the executive secretary. In lieu of said annual dues, a six-year membership shall be issued by the executive secretary to any active or associate member upon payment of $25 in advance.

Article IV—Vacancies

All vacancies occurring in any office other than that of president shall be filled by the Executive Committee.

Article V—Rules of Order

Roberts' Rules of Order shall govern in all business meetings of this department.

Article VI—Amendments

These Bylaws may be amended at any regular business meeting of this department by a majority vote of the members present, the amendment having been submitted in writing at a previous regular business meeting.

CALENDAR OF MEETINGS

HISTORICAL NOTE—At the meeting of the National Teachers' Association in Harrisburg, Pennsylvania, August, 1865, the state and city superintendents present decided to form an organization, to be composed exclusively of those engaged in supervisory work in the schools.

This group decided to meet in Washington, D. C., in February, 1866, at which time the work of organizing was completed. The new organization was called the National Association of School Superintendents. Nine states and twenty cities were represented.

The National Association of School Superintendents became the Department of School Superintendence of the National Educational Association at a convention held at Cleveland, Ohio, August, 1870.

In 1907 a new act of incorporation which had been passed by Congress and approved by the President of the United States was accepted and adopted by the summer meeting of the parent association at Los Angeles, California. According to one of the provisions of this new act, the name was changed to the Department of Superintendence of the National Education Association.

Following an amendment to the bylaws of the National Education Association at Des Moines, Iowa, in July, 1921, the Department of Superintendence was reorganized under a new constitution of its own, with a full-time executive secretary.

NATIONAL ASSOCIATION OF SCHOOL SUPERINTENDENTS, 1865-1870

1865—HARRISBURG, Pa. (Organization)
August.
  BIRDSEY GRANT NORTHROP, Chairman.
  L. VAN BOKKELEN, Secretary.

1866—WASHINGTON, D. C., February
INDIANAPOLIS, IND., August.
  BIRDSEY GRANT NORTHROP, President.
  CHARLES R. COBURN, Vice-president.
  L. VAN BOKKELEN, Secretary.

1867—No Meeting.

1868—NASHVILLE, TENN., August.
  EMERSON E. WHITE, President.
  DANIEL STEVENSON, Vice-president.
  L. VAN BOKKELEN, Secretary.

1869—TRENTON, N. J., August.
  J. W. BULKLEY, President.
  EMERSON E. WHITE, Vice-president.
  L. VAN BOKKELEN, Secretary.

1870—WASHINGTON, D. C., March.
  JAMES P. WICKERSHAM, President.
  S. S. ASHLEY, Vice-president.
  W. R. CREERY, Secretary.

DEPARTMENT OF SCHOOL SUPERINTENDENCE OF THE NATIONAL EDUCATIONAL ASSOCIATION, 1870-1907

1871—ST. LOUIS, MO., August.
  W. D. HENKLE, President.
  W. M. COLBY, Vice-president.
  WARREN JOHNSON, Secretary.

1872—BOSTON, MASS., August.
  JOHN HANCOCK, President.
  A. P. MARBLE, Secretary.

1873—ELMIRA, N. Y., August.
  WILLIAM T. HARRIS, President.
  JOHN W. PAGE, Vice-president.
  A. P. MARBLE, Secretary.

1874—WASHINGTON, D. C., January.
DETROIT, MICH., August.
  J. H. BINFORD, President.
  ALLEN ARMSTRONG, Secretary.

1875—WASHINGTON, D. C., January.
MINNEAPOLIS, MINN., August.
  J. ORMOND WILSON, President.
  A. ABERNETHY, Vice-president.
  R. W. STEVENSON, Secretary.

1876—BALTIMORE, MD., July.
  CHARLES S. SMART, President.
  A. PICKETT, Vice-president.
  HORACE S. TARBELL, Secretary.

1877—WASHINGTON, D. C., March.
LOUISVILLE, KY., August.
WASHINGTON, D. C., December.
  CHARLES S. SMART, President.
  HORACE S. TARBELL, Secretary.

1878—No Meeting.

1879—WASHINGTON, D. C., February.
PHILADELPHIA, PA., July.
JAMES P. WICKERSHAM, President.
JAMES H. SMART, Vice-president.
R. W. STEVENSON, Secretary.

1880—WASHINGTON, D. C., February.
CHAUTAUQUA, N. Y., July.
M. A. NEWELL, President.
N. A. CALKINS, Vice-president.
S. A. BAER, Secretary.

1881—NEW YORK, N. Y., February.
ATLANTA, GA., July.
A. P. MARBLE, President.
N. A. CALKINS, Vice-president.
SAMUEL FINDLEY, Secretary.

1882—WASHINGTON, D. C., March.
SARATOGA SPRINGS, N. Y., July.
W. H. RUFFNER, President.
N. A. CALKINS, Vice-president.
HENRY S. JONES, Secretary.

1883—WASHINGTON, D. C., February.
SARATOGA SPRINGS, N. Y., July.
N. A. CALKINS, President.
HORACE S. TARBELL, Vice-president.
HENRY S. JONES, Secretary.

1884—WASHINGTON, D. C., February.
MADISON, WIS., July.
B. L. BUTCHER, President.
D. F. DEWOLF, Vice-president.
HENRY R. SANFORD, Secretary.

1885—NEW ORLEANS, LA., February.
SARATOGA SPRINGS, N. Y., July.
LEROY D. BROWN, President.
W. O. ROGERS, Secretary.

1886—WASHINGTON, D. C., February.
TOPEKA, KANS., July.
WARREN EASTON, President.
A. P. STONE, Vice-president.
CHARLES C. DAVIDSON, Secretary.

1887—WASHINGTON, D. C., March.
CHICAGO, ILL., July.
CHARLES S. YOUNG, President.
N. C. DOUGHERTY, Vice-president.
CHARLES C. DAVIDSON, Secretary.

1888—WASHINGTON, D. C., February.
SAN FRANCISCO, CALIF., July.
N. C. DOUGHERTY, President.
HENRY A. WISE, Vice-president.
W. R. THIGPEN, Secretary.

1889—WASHINGTON, D. C., February.
NASHVILLE, TENN., July.
FRED M. CAMPBELL, President.
CHARLES C. DAVIDSON, Vice-president.
W. R. THIGPEN, Secretary.

1890—NEW YORK, N. Y., February.
ANDREW S. DRAPER, President.
J. A. B. LOVETT, Vice-president.
L. W. DAY, Secretary.

1891—PHILADELPHIA, PA., February.
ANDREW S. DRAPER, President.
J. A. B. LOVETT, Vice-president.
L. W. DAY, Secretary.

1892—BROOKLYN, N. Y., February.
HENRY SABIN, President.
VIRGIL G. CURTIS, Vice-president.
L. W. DAY, Secretary.

1893—BOSTON, MASS., February.
EDWARD BROOKS, President.
JOHN E. BRADLEY, Vice-president.
J. H. PHILLIPS, Secretary.

1894—RICHMOND, VA., February.
D. L. KIEHLE, President.
WARREN EASTON, Vice-president.
FREDERICK TREUDLEY, Secretary.

1895—CLEVELAND, OHIO, February.
WILLIAM H. MAXWELL, President.
OSCAR T. CORSON, Vice-president.
JAMES M. CARLISLE, Secretary.

1896—JACKSONVILLE, FLA., February.
LEWIS H. JONES, President.
J. H. PHILLIPS, Vice-president.
ROBERT E. DENFIELD, Secretary.

1897—INDIANAPOLIS, IND., February.
C. B. GILBERT, President.
A. B. BLODGETT, Vice-president.
LAWTON B. EVANS, Secretary.

1898—CHATTANOOGA, TENN., February.
NATHAN C. SCHAEFFER, President.
FRANK B. COOPER, Vice-president.
WILLIAM L. STEELE, Secretary.

1899—COLUMBUS, OHIO, February.
EDGAR H. MARK, President.
GEORGE H. CONLEY, Vice-president.
JAMES H. VAN SICKLE, Secretary.

1900—CHICAGO, ILL., February.
AUGUSTUS S. DOWNING, President.
G. R. GLENN, Vice-president.
CHARLES M. JORDAN, Secretary.

1901—CHICAGO, ILL., February.
LORENZO D. HARVEY, President.
ARTHUR K. WHITCOMB, Vice-president.
FRANK B. COOPER, Secretary.

1902—CHICAGO, ILL., February.
G. R. GLENN, President.
HENRY P. EMERSON, Vice-president.
JOHN W. DIETRICH, Secretary.

1903—CINCINNATI, OHIO, February.
CHARLES M. JORDAN, President.
CLARENCE F. CARROLL, Vice-president.
J. N. WILKINSON, Secretary.

1904—ATLANTA, GA., February.
HENRY P. EMERSON, President.
EDWIN B. COX, Vice-president.
JOHN H. HINEMON, Secretary.

1905—MILWAUKEE, WIS., February.
EDWIN G. COOLEY, President.
LAWTON B. EVANS, Vice-president.
EVANGELINE E. WHITNEY, Secretary.

1906—LOUISVILLE, KY., February.
JOHN W. CARR, President.
J. H. PHILLIPS, Vice-president.
ELLA C. SULLIVAN, Secretary.

1907—CHICAGO, ILL., February.
W. W. STETSON, President.
H. H. SEERLEY, Vice-president.
J. H. HARRIS, Secretary.

DEPARTMENT OF SUPERINTENDENCE OF THE NATIONAL EDUCATION ASSOCIATION, 1907—

1908—WASHINGTON, D. C., February.
FRANK B. COOPER, President.
STRATTON D. BROOKS, Vice-president.
GEORGE B. COOK, Secretary.

1909—CHICAGO, ILL., February.
WILLIAM H. ELSON, President.
DAVID B. JOHNSON, Vice-president.
A. C. NELSON, Secretary.

1910—INDIANAPOLIS, IND., March.
STRATTON D. BROOKS, President.
WALES C. MARTINDALE, Vice-president.
JOHN F. KEATING, Secretary.

1911—MOBILE, ALA., February.
WILLIAM M. DAVIDSON, President.
J. A. SHAWAN, Vice-president.
ARTHUR D. CALL, Secretary.

1912—ST. LOUIS, MO., February.
CHARLES E. CHADSEY, President.
O. J. KERN, Vice-president.
HARLAN UPDEGRAFF, Secretary.

1913—PHILADELPHIA, PA., February.
FRANKLYN B. DYER, President.
SAMUEL HAMILTON, Vice-president.
BURR W. TORREYSON, Secretary.

1914—RICHMOND, VA., February.
BEN BLEWETT, President.
W. E. RANGER, Vice-president.
ANNA E. LOGAN, Secretary.

1915—CINCINNATI, OHIO, February.
HENRY SNYDER, President.
PAUL W. HORN, Vice-president.
MRS. ELLOR C. RIPLEY, Secretary.

1916—DETROIT, MICH., February.
M. P. SHAWKEY, President.
LAWTON B. EVANS, Vice-president.
E. C. WARRINER, Secretary.

1917—KANSAS CITY, MO., February.
JOHN D. SHOOP, President.
FRED L. KEELER, Vice-president.
MARGARET T. MAGUIRE, Secretary.

1918—ATLANTIC CITY, N. J., February.
THOMAS E. FINEGAN, President.
A. A. McDONALD, Vice-president.
LIDA LEE TALL, Secretary.

1919—CHICAGO, ILL., February.
ERNEST C. HARTWELL, President.
DAVID B. CORSON, Vice-president.
MARIE GUGLE, Secretary.

1920—CLEVELAND, OHIO, February.
E. U. GRAFF, President.
D. J. KELLY, Vice-president.
CHARL ORMOND WILLIAMS, Secretary.

1921—ATLANTIC CITY, N. J., February.
CALVIN N. KENDALL, President.
ERNEST A. SMITH, Vice-president.
BELLE M. RYAN, Secretary.

1922—CHICAGO, ILL., February.
ROBINSON G. JONES, President.
WILL C. WOOD, Vice-president.
SHERWOOD D. SHANKLAND, Secretary.

1923—CLEVELAND, OHIO, February.
JOHN H. BEVERIDGE, President.
FRANK W. BALLOU, Vice-president.
SHERWOOD D. SHANKLAND, Secretary.

1924—CHICAGO, ILL., February.
PAYSON SMITH, President.
M. G. CLARK, Vice-president
SHERWOOD D. SHANKLAND, Secretary.

1925—CINCINNATI, OHIO, February.
WILLIAM McANDREW, President.
JOHN J. MADDOX, Vice-president.
SHERWOOD D. SHANKLAND, Secretary.

1926—WASHINGTON, D. C., February.
FRANK W. BALLOU, President.
E. E. LEWIS, Vice-president.
SHERWOOD D. SHANKLAND, Secretary.

1927—DALLAS, TEXAS, February.
RANDALL J. CONDON, President.
DAVID A. WARD, Vice-president.
SHERWOOD D. SHANKLAND, Secretary.

1928—BOSTON, MASS., February.
JOSEPH M. GWINN, President.
FRANK D. BOYNTON, Vice-president.
SHERWOOD D. SHANKLAND, Secretary.

1929—CLEVELAND, OHIO, February.
FRANK D. BOYNTON, President.
FRANK G. PICKELL, Vice-president.
SHERWOOD D. SHANKLAND, Secretary.

1930—ATLANTIC CITY, N. J., February.
FRANK CODY, President.
NORMAN R. CROZIER, Vice-president.
SHERWOOD D. SHANKLAND, Secretary.

1931—DETROIT, MICH., February.
NORMAN R. CROZIER, President.
DANIEL S. KEALEY, Vice-president.
SHERWOOD D. SHANKLAND, Secretary.

REPORT OF AUDITING COMMITTEE

Washington, D. C.
January 16, 1931.

Superintendent Norman R. Crozier
President, Department of Superintendence
Dallas, Texas

Dear Sir:

We, the undersigned committee, appointed to audit the accounts of the Department of Superintendence for the year 1930, report as follows:

1. All financial records of receipts and expenditures as shown by the books of the executive secretary, S. D. Shankland, have been examined and audited. These include the bank deposits, the vouchers for expenditures, and the items in the accounts of the National Education Association which, according to the constitution, acts as the custodian of the funds of the Department of Superintendence. Separate records of the general funds of the Department and of the permanent fund are now being kept. In the general fund we find the total receipts for the year amounted to $56,480.87, which with the balance on hand January 1, 1930 of $12,985.48, makes a total of $69,466.35. The total expenditures from this fund for the year were $56,910.87, leaving a balance on hand December 31, 1930 of $12,555.48. In the permanent fund the balance on hand January 1, 1930 was $7,309.67. The total receipts during the year in this fund amounted to $2,794.67, making a total on December 31, 1930 of $10,104.34. During the year there were no disbursements from this fund which now consists of cash on hand of $625.08, and securities amounting to $9,479.26.

2. This audit covers the transactions of the calendar year 1930, and the receipts of the month of December, 1929, but not those of December, 1930. Under the constitution of the Department, December receipts are not credited on the books of the National Education Association until January.

3. The committee is very much pleased indeed to report that the records as kept are complete and accurate. Permit us to add an expression of our appreciation of the efficiency and courtesy of the executive secretary and of his office force. The committee also acknowledges its indebtedness to Mrs. Helen T. Hixson, director of accounts of the National Education Association. It was necessary on account of the interlocking relations between the Department of Superintendence and the National Education Association, to refer to the accounts of the National Education Association in charge of Mrs. Hixson. Throughout the office we find an atmosphere of courtesy and helpfulness.

Respectfully submitted,
LOUIS NUSBAUM
FRANK M. MARTIN
HARVEY O. HUTCHINSON

ANNUAL REPORT OF THE EXECUTIVE SECRETARY

Detroit Meeting, 1931

To the President, Executive Committee, and Members of the Department of Superintendence:

IN ACCORDANCE with the provisions of the constitution adopted at the Chicago convention in 1922, the ninth annual report of the activities of the Department of Superintendence is presented herewith. It covers the period from January 1, 1930, to December 31, 1930.

The Atlantic City Convention—"Education in the Spirit of Life" was the theme selected by President Frank Cody for the sixtieth anniversary meeting of the Department of Superintendence at Atlantic City and rarely has a theme been so perfectly adjusted to the various convention activities. The following statement in elaboration of this theme appeared on the cover page of the Official Program:

> EDUCATION is life. This statement of the philosopher, which seemed so radical when first uttered, is now generally accepted. American education is engaged in the process of putting the ideal into practise. As we would have life, so must our education be.
>
> Life is idealistic: education must aim high.
> Life is friendly: education must develop a social spirit.
> Life is dynamic: education must move forward aggressively.
> Life is practical: education must be efficient.
> Life is recreative: education must train for leisure.
> Life is progressive: education must adjust itself to new needs.
> Life is cooperative: education must itself cooperate.

A notable feature of the convention was the presentation of a past-president's key to each former president of the Department of Superintendence, nineteen of whom were still living at the time of the Atlantic City convention. Four have died since then: Charles E. Chadsey, Frank D. Boynton, William M. Davidson, and Frank B. Cooper.

The Pageant of Time: an Adventure of Education in the Realm of Leisure, designed to promote interest in training for the worthy use of leisure was the splendid contribution of the schools of Atlantic City and of New Jersey. It was presented on a colossal scale with twenty-five hundred teachers and students of the New Jersey schools participating. A high-school orchestra of 125 pieces and a choral division of over 400 voices provided music for the occasion. It was witnessed by eighteen thousand spectators who overflowed the seating capacity of the world's greatest auditorium leaving hundreds to stand during the performance.

The National High-School Orchestra which made a profound impression at Dallas, added another brilliant musical achievement in its exquisite concert on the final afternoon of the convention. The orchestra was again under the leadership of that splendid conductor and organizer, Joseph E. Maddy, with Walter Damrosch as guest conductor.

The outstanding educational importance of the winter meeting was again emphasized at Atlantic City. Every important educational interest or activity had representation. Two hundred fifty-three firms participated in the exhibit. Eighty-two breakfasts, luncheons, and dinners, and one hundred thirteen other meetings were scheduled in the Official Program. These annual gatherings are periods of inspiration, planning, search for personnel, broad outlooks, and new vision of what American schools are doing. The Boardwalk was unique as a common meeting ground during the balmy days of the Atlantic City convention.

The Executive Committee—Article IV of the constitution provides that the Executive Committee shall consist of seven members. The president and the first and second vice-presidents are members ex-officio and are chosen annually. Four members, chosen by election, hold office for terms of four years, one member retiring each year. Three meetings of the Executive Committee were held during 1930, the first being at the Ambassador Hotel, Atlantic City, New Jersey, February 23. Members present were: Frank Cody, Detroit, Michigan, president; Frank D. Boynton, Ithaca, New York, first vice-president; Norman R. Crozier, Dallas, Texas, second vice-president; E. E. Lewis, Columbus, Ohio; Frank M. Underwood, St. Louis, Missouri; Paul C. Stetson, Dayton, Ohio; and David E. Weglein, Baltimore, Maryland.

Communications were received inviting participation of the Department of Superintendence in the White House Conference. They were referred to a committee consisting of Mr. Stetson and Mr. Weglein.

On motion of Mr. Boynton, the president and executive secretary were authorized to pay all bills of the Department of Superintendence up to the close of the Atlantic City convention, issuing checks against the special account of the Department in the usual manner.

At a dinner preceding this meeting the following past presidents of the Department of Superintendence were present as guests of honor: John W. Carr, 1905-06; Stratton D. Brooks, 1909-10; William M. Davidson, 1910-11; M. P. Shawkey, 1915-16; Ernest C. Hartwell, 1918-19; E. U. Graff, 1919-20; Robinson G. Jones, 1921-22; John H. Beveridge, 1922-23; Payson Smith, 1923-24; Frank W. Ballou, 1925-26; Randall J. Condon, 1926-27; Joseph M. Gwinn, 1927-28; Frank D. Boynton, 1928-29.

The Executive Committee met again at the Atlantic City Auditorium on Thursday morning, February 27. Members present were: Frank Cody, Frank D. Boynton, Norman R. Crozier, Frank M. Underwood, Paul C. Stetson, and David E. Weglein. The second vice-president-elect, Daniel S. Kealey, of Hoboken, New Jersey, and the member-elect of the Executive Committee, Charles B. Glenn, of Birmingham, Alabama, were also in attendance.

Invitations for the 1931 convention were received as follows: Minneapolis, Minnesota; Toronto, Canada; Chicago, Illinois; and San Francisco, California. No action was taken on these invitations. •

Mr. A. H. Skean, Director of the Atlantic City Convention and Publicity Bureau, expressed the pleasure which had come to the citizens of Atlantic City in having the opportunity to entertain the Department of Superintendence.

On motion of Mr. Boynton, it was voted to send flowers and a message of sympathy to Thomas E. Finegan, president of the Department of Superintendence, 1917-18. Mr. Finegan was unable to attend the convention on account of serious illness.

The secretary reported that the annual election had been completed according to the constitution and bylaws and that the Board of Tellers had certified to the election of the following officers: Norman R. Crozier, Superintendent of Schools, Dallas, Texas, president; Daniel S. Kealey, Superintendent of Schools, Hoboken, New Jersey, second vice-president; Charles B. Glenn, Superintendent of Schools, Birmingham, Alabama, member of the Executive Committee for four years.

The annual meeting of the Executive Committee was held at Hotel Pennsylvania, New York City, Friday and Saturday, May 2 and 3. Members present were: Norman R. Crozier, president; Frank Cody, first vice-president; Daniel S. Kealey, second vice-president; Frank M. Underwood, David E. Weglein, and Charles B. Glenn.

C. W. Shirk, Secretary of the Convention Department of the Minneapolis Civic and Commerce Association, and Carl G. Sedan of the Detroit Convention and Tourists Bureau were present and extended invitations for the 1931 convention in behalf of their respective cities. On motion, it was voted to hold the 1931 convention at Detroit, Michigan.

The following resolution, originally adopted in 1929, was reaffirmed and made applicable to the Detroit convention:

Since the members of the Department of Superintendence are properly entitled to preference in assigning reservations of hotel sleeping rooms at their own winter meetings:

Resolved, That the officers of the Department of Superintendence are hereby instructed to include in the contract with the city which proposes to entertain the next convention, a clause providing that for a period of sixty days following the official announcement of the selection of the convention city, no sleeping room reservations shall be honored except for those who hold the official hotel reservation blanks issued by the Department.

On motion of Mr. Cody, it was voted that it is the sense of the Executive Committee of the Department of Superintendence that special efforts should be made to retain the present efficient research workers at headquarters. On motion of Mr. Weglein, seconded by Mr. Glenn, the following resolution was adopted:

Resolved, That it is the unanimous opinion of the Executive Committee of the Department of Superintendence that Mrs. Margaret A. Norton should be retained as a member of the Research Division of the National Education Association and that a letter to this effect, signed by the members of this Executive Committee, be mailed to the president, to the secretary, and to the chairman of the Board of Trustees of the National Education Association.

TABLE 95.—MEMBERSHIP OF THE DEPARTMENT OF SUPERINTENDENCE BY STATES, 1925-1930

State	1925 Cincinnati	1926 Washington	1927 Dallas	1928 Boston	1929 Cleveland	1930 Atlantic City
Alabama	46	61	58	43	53	58
Arizona	19	22	26	21	22	27
Arkansas	23	38	49	33	41	45
California	55	61	92	94	106	116
Colorado	38	35	46	39	41	40
Connecticut	57	84	55	104	81	92
Delaware	10	15	14	12	10	19
District of Columbia	13	30	21	28	29	39
Florida	15	31	34	34	24	25
Georgia	35	61	48	50	48	50
Idaho	5	12	10	10	10	10
Illinois	177	187	194	208	245	238
Indiana	85	100	88	89	122	100
Iowa	66	69	71	73	92	86
Kansas	56	76	77	65	70	68
Kentucky	46	43	34	40	56	59
Louisiana	28	44	49	34	30	29
Maine	20	25	23	75	32	35
Maryland	32	56	33	44	47	65
Massachusetts	115	178	121	318	192	205
Michigan	155	206	152	201	222	201
Minnesota	60	66	65	82	84	81
Mississippi	33	30	53	31	33	39
Missouri	61	69	84	79	91	97
Montana	9	13	13	10	8	9
Nebraska	46	53	44	43	44	48
Nevada	1	7	1	5	3	5
New Hampshire	22	35	19	77	30	37
New Jersey	129	188	133	200	194	277
New Mexico	6	8	13	14	14	18
New York	141	237	178	288	303	364
North Carolina	41	72	48	61	55	64
North Dakota	9	16	13	21	16	14
Ohio	181	178	159	197	300	237
Oklahoma	42	59	86	64	64	71
Oregon	8	9	10	15	18	20
Pennsylvania	173	275	193	288	313	360
Rhode Island	29	32	29	49	36	41
South Carolina	20	23	20	20	20	22
South Dakota	23	21	22	19	21	27
Tennessee	28	35	29	28	36	44
Texas	77	114	334	168	154	176
Utah	23	24	19	30	27	30
Vermont	11	17	11	53	22	28
Virginia	30	51	36	45	44	53
Washington	17	25	20	20	21	20
West Virginia	45	60	43	31	39	52
Wisconsin	77	111	104	98	103	114
Wyoming	15	23	21	19	19	17
Alaska	2	2	1		1	1
Canada	1	1		1	2	2
China			2			1
Cook Islands			1		1	1
England			1			
France						1
Greece	1					
Hawaii	4	5	3	4	4	4
India		1				
Japan	1	1	1			
Mexico					1	1
Newfoundland						1
New Zealand			1	1	1	
Porto Rico	3	3	2	2	16	18
Philippine Islands	4	4	6	6	8	9
Samoa	1	2				
Syria		1	1			
Total	2,470	3,305	3,114	3,684	3,719	4,011

NOTE.—The count for 1930 includes 3992 members who paid dues for the year, 17 six-year members and two honorary members.

The annual report of the executive secretary was presented and approved. The budget for the year 1930 was submitted and adopted. It showed an estimated income of $51,500 and estimated expenditures of $51,247.50.

Attention was called to the fact that among the resolutions adopted at the Atlantic City convention was one directing the Executive Committee to appoint a radio committee which shall be empowered to present to the radio corporations the points of view which should prevail in the development of educational programs. After discussion it was deemed best to have the members of the Executive Committee serve also as the Educational Radio Committee.

The secretary recommended that Katherine V. Allen, an employee of the Educational Research Service of the Department of Superintendence, be transferred from the temporary to the permanent roll of the National Education Association, effective June 1, 1930, and on motion the recommendation was adopted.

President Norman R. Crozier announced the reappointment of State Superintendent Albert S. Cook of Maryland as a member of the Committee on Lay Relations for a term of five years.

On motion of Mr. Weglein, the Executive Committee expressed appreciation to the executive secretary and his staff for the work done during the past year.

President Crozier reported that he had received several communications from public school business officials indicating a desire on their part for closer affiliation with the Department of Superintendence. On motion, the president was authorized to take such steps as seemed best in furtherance of these proposals.

Various topics for the 1933 Yearbook were suggested. On motion of Mr. Cody, it was voted that the 1933 Yearbook be devoted to the subject of Educational Leadership. The president later announced the appointment of Superintendent A. J. Stoddard of Providence, Rhode Island, as chairman of the commission to prepare this yearbook.

Superintendent William A. Smith of Hackensack, New Jersey, was introduced to the meeting and reported gratifying progress made in Bergen County, New Jersey, in promoting the Permanent Educational Research Fund of the Department of Superintendence. Mr. Albert St. Peter of the Equitable Life Assurance Society made an oral report of plans to promote the Permanent Educational Research Fund by bequest insurance, as authorized by the Atlantic City convention. On motion, the following resolution was adopted:

Resolved, That a contributor to the Permanent Educational Research Fund of the Department of Superintendence shall receive the benefits of life membership in the Department of Superintendence when the cash value of his contribution, whether made by endowment insurance policy or otherwise, amounts to $100 or more; provided that, in case of a school or organization, a special membership certificate shall be issued entitling the donor to receive all publications of the Department of Superintendence for a period of twenty-five years.

President Crozier submitted detailed program plans for the 1931 convention and requested suggestions from the members of the Executive Committee. After extended discussion, all matters relating to the 1931 convention were referred to the president with power to act.

The Finances—The Department closed the year 1930 with a balance in the regular fund of $12,555.48. The balance one year ago was $12,985.48, and two years ago it was $13,232.39. The principal source of revenue is the annual membership fee of five dollars. The Department enrolled 1,263 members in 1922; 3,114 in 1927; 3,684 in 1928; 3,719 in 1929; and 4,011 in 1930. The membership distribution by states for the last six years is shown in Table 95 on page 432.

By agreement with the National Education Association, the net income from the exhibits at the winter meetings is divided equally between the Department and the parent Association, each organization thus deriving funds for convention expenses. The active work of organizing and managing the exhibit is done by the Business Division of the National Education Association. The amounts which the Department has derived from this source during recent years are as follows:

1922—Chicago	$3,250.00
1923—Cleveland	4,267.50
1924—Chicago	5,142.81
1925—Cincinnati	8,696.06
1926—Washington	6,830.68
1927—Dallas	8,524.64
1928—Boston	8,883.87
1929—Cleveland	14,687.26
1930—Atlantic City	17,485.71

The statement of receipts and expenditures given below covers the calendar year 1930. It includes expenses of the Atlantic City convention, some preliminary charges for the Detroit convention, and all items of general expense. All bills were paid at the end of the year. A detailed statement regarding the Permanent Educational Research Fund is given elsewhere in this report.

Regular Receipts During Calendar Year 1930

Annual dues, 3,646 members, 1930	$18,230.00
Annual dues, 390 members, 1931	1,950.00
Six-year payments, 2 members	50.00
Yearbooks sold	10,603.43
Atlantic City exhibit	17,485.71
Interest received	49.23
Educational Research Service	8,112.50
Total receipts	$56,480.87
Balance, January 1, 1930	12,985.48
Grand total	$69,466.35

Regular Expenditures During Calendar Year 1930

Atlantic City Convention:

Registration	$681.85
Regular programs	907.63
Pageant programs	1,200.00
Badges	50.63
Publicity	53.93
Stenotype report	222.63
President's expense	333.73
Secretary's expense	303.18
Expense for speakers	555.87
National High School Orchestra	1,514.18
Reception	615.00
Keys for past presidents	200.00

Total Atlantic City Convention $6,638.63

General Expense:

Salary, Executive Secretary	$7,500.00
Printing 11,348 Eighth Yearbook	6,694.61
Reprinting 4M Fourth Yearbook	4,075.00
Printing 5M Atlantic City Official Report	1,476.58
Printing Research Bulletins	904.39
Other printing	5,311.81
Postage, express, and stationery	4,754.07
Special stenographic and clerical service	1,770.87
Telephone and telegraph	270.65
President's expense	499.60
Secretary's expense	592.10
Executive Committee expense	668.54
Audit Committee expense	199.45
1931 Yearbook Commission expense	4,086.26
1932 Yearbook Commission expense	1,220.27
Committee on Lay Relations	399.72
Committee on Financing Educational Research	598.62
Educational Research Service, salaries	5,640.37
Educational Research Service, miscellaneous	1,822.89
Surety bonds	12.50
American Council on Education	100.00
Convention expense, Columbus	26.25
Preliminary expense, Detroit Convention	105.50
Supplies and equipment	129.69
Retirement fund	1,412.50

Total general expense $50,272.24

Total expense for the year $56,910.87
Balance, December 31, 1930 .... 12,555.48

Grand total $69,466.35

Permanent Educational Research Fund—As early as April, 1927, in a communication addressed to the Executive Committee of the Department of Superintendence, the Commission on the Curriculum expressed the opinion that "it would be advantageous for American education at this juncture to secure in a systematic way a sufficiently large educational foundation for purposes of research so that work similar to that which the Commission on the Curriculum has had the opportunity to carry on may be projected in other lines." Accordingly a Committee on Financing Educational Research was appointed with Randall J. Condon, Frank W. Ballou, Frank D. Boynton, Lamont F. Hodge, and Charles H. Judd as its members.

The Boston convention took action directing the Committee to propose a method of creating a fund that should yield an annual income sufficient to enable the Department to carry forward important studies in education on a nation-wide basis, and fixed the sum of one million dollars as the amount necessary for this purpose.

The Atlantic City convention approved the following methods of participation:

1. By life memberships in the Department of Superintendence.
2. By subscriptions from persons and organizations interested in education.
3. By bequests.
4. By endowment insurance policies taken out by members of the Department of Superintendence or others who wish to contribute.

The Atlantic City convention also adopted the following amendment to Article III of the constitution:

All members of the National Education Association who are eligible to active membership in the Department of Superintendence shall become life members of the Department upon the payment of a membership fee of $100, which may be made in ten equal annual payments, or upon securing a contribution of $250 to the Permanent Educational Research Fund, which may be paid in five equal annual installments. All such contributions and life membership fees shall become a part of the Permanent Educational Research Fund. Life members shall be exempt from the payment of all other membership fees in the Department of Superintendence, and shall have all the rights and privileges of active members.

By action of the Executive Committee of the Department of Superintendence, which was approved by the Atlantic City convention, the following plan was adopted for administering the fund:

The Permanent Educational Research Fund of the Department of Superintendence shall be placed in charge of the Board of Trustees of the National Education Association to be invested and conserved in securities that are legal. The Board of Trustees of the National Education Association shall be the Trustees of said Permanent Educational Research Fund.

At each annual meeting of the Department, the Trustees shall report in detail the condition of said Fund.

The income annually shall be credited to the Department of Superintendence, to be expended for such educational research as the Department of Superintendence may direct.

No part of the principal of said Fund shall be spent except after the unanimous written recommendation of the Executive Committee of the Department of Superintendence duly ratified by a two-thirds vote of the members present at a stated annual meeting of the Department.

Pursuant to its instructions, the Committee on Financing Educational Research carried on a vigorous campaign through the fall and early winter in the interest of the Fund. The Committee received effective cooperation from the Equitable Life Assurance Society of the United States. It is not yet possible to determine the results of this campaign since many applications for endowment insurance policies under Plan Four are still in the hands of local agencies, medical examiners, and other insurance officials. The financial depression from which the country has suffered so severely in recent months materially hampered the work of the Committee.

The following statement shows the cash receipts of the Permanent Educational Research Fund:

On hand January 1, 1930	$7,309.67
Interest received	259.67
Thomas E. Finegan, Rochester, N. Y.	250.00
A friend	5.00
Board of Education, Port Washington, N. Y., by Paul D. Schreiber	50.00
Teachers of Port Jervis, N. Y., by Mrs. J. H. Blood	250.00
Yonkers, N. Y., Parent Teacher Associations by L. F. Hodge	50.00
Parkersburg, W. Va., Teachers Association by Wm. F. Cline	50.00
William C. Smith, Albany, N. Y.	25.00
Beta Chapter of Phi Delta Kappa by Max Brunstetter	100.00
Charleston, S. C., Board of School Commissioners by A. B. Rhett	50.00
Board of Education, Hackensack, N. J., by W. A. Smith	25.00
Teachers of Douglas Co., Oregon, by Mrs. Edith S. Ackert	10.00
Southeast Texas School Executives Association	50.00
Hastings-upon-Hudson, N. Y., Parent-Teacher Assn. by John L. Hopkins	50.00
Members of the staff of Supt. Ben G. Graham, Pittsburgh, Pa.	250.00
Mount Vernon, N. Y., Home and School Associations by W. H. Holmes	50.00
Mrs. W. Robinson Brown, Berlin, N. H.	25.00
Faculty of Fairview, N. J., Schools by Z. G. Masten, Jr	25.00
Board of Education, Montclair, N. J., by Frank G. Pickell	250.00
Public Schools of Lyndhurst, N. J., by Reeves D. Batten	250.00
Life Memberships—Cash payments	720.00

Total cash assets as of December 31, 1930................$10,104.34

The Board of Trustees of the National Education Association reports investments for the Permanent Educational Research Fund on December 31, 1930, as follows:

City of New Orleans, $4\frac{1}{2}\%$ bonds, 1931, par value $6,000	$5,984.06
City cf New Orleans, $4\frac{1}{2}\%$ bonds, 1931, par value $1,000	998.23
State of South Carolina, $4\frac{3}{4}\%$ Highways ctfs., par value $2,000	2,077.28
U. S. Fourth Liberty Bonds, par value $400	419.69
Cash on hand	625.08

Total $10,104.34

The Educational Research Service—The Department of Superintendence and the Research Division of the National Education Association work together in conducting the Educational Research Service, with four members of the headquarters staff devoting their entire time to its needs. The $25.00 annual fee entitles subscribers to receive a number of books and bulletins dealing with current topics in school administration, and to get additional help on individual problems. Studies published for the Service during 1930 include a report on 1928-29 city school expenditures, an analysis of school board rules in 95 cities, a report on special education for handicapped pupils, and bimonthly reviews of articles on education in lay magazines. A study now in progress deals with size of class, a topic on which many inquiries are received. Another project under way is the collection of figures on public school salaries for 1930-31, a part of the salary study made biennially by the Research Division. Information is collected regarding questionnaires in circulation, thus providing a clearinghouse of information concerning questionnaire investigations throughout the country.

The Educational Research Service was authorized in 1923 by vote of the Department of Superintendence, and has shown a substantial increase in number of subscribers and income every year. Although the Service is intended more directly to meet the needs of city school systems, it also includes 11 state departments of education and 52 colleges and other higher educational institutions in its list of 323 subscribers. Table 96 gives the facts by years as to number of subscribers and receipts from subscriptions:

TABLE 96.—EDUCATIONAL RESEARCH SERVICE SUBSCRIBERS AND INCOME

Year	Number of Subscribers	Cash Receipts for the Year
1924	40	$525.00
1925	131	2,555.00
1926	177	3,325.00
1927	213	5,790.00
1928	245	6,225.00
1929	271	6,362.00
1930	323	8,112.50

Publications—The Official Report of addresses and proceedings of the Atlantic City convention was published and delivered to members soon after the meeting adjourned. It was a volume of 283 pages. Five issues of the Research Bulletin of the National Education Association were mailed to all members of the Department of Superintendence during the year. These bulletins deal with current, important problems of education and are of especial value to school executives.

The annual yearbook is the principal publication of the Department of Superintendence. The Eighth Yearbook entitled "The Superintendent Surveys Supervision," was distributed to members at the time of the Atlantic

City convention. It dealt with those phases of supervision which are of chief concern to superintendents of schools. Detailed technics and particular methods, which are the concern of specialists, were left to the consideration of those who are actively at work in these fields. The facts regarding the publication and sale of yearbooks are shown in Table 97.

TABLE 97.—YEARBOOKS OF THE DEPARTMENT OF SUPERINTENDENCE

Year	Title	Number copies printed	Cash sales of all yearbooks for the year
1923	Status of the Superintendent............................	3,200	$142.45
1924	The Elementary School Curriculum.......................	4,500	1,364.13
1925	Research in Constructing the Elementary School Curriculum..	11,000	4,707.65
1926	The Nation at Work on the Public School Curriculum.......	12,000	8,467.94
1927	The Junior High School Curriculum.......................	11,000	8,844.57
1928	The Development of the High School Curriculum...........	10,000	9,830.58
1929	The Articulation of the Units of American Education........	11,000	7,842.51
1929	Reprint of Fourth Yearbook..............................	4,000	....
1930	The Superintendent Surveys Supervision..................	11,348	10,603.43

The 1931 Yearbook—The Committee on the Articulation of the Units of American Education was appointed by President Randall J. Condon in 1926. The list of its members is printed in the front of this volume. The field of this research was so great that the Commission voted to publish its report in two yearbooks, the first of which was issued in 1929. The second is presented herewith. The problems referred to this Commission for consideration go to the very heart of American education. The Commission and its sub-committees have held numerous meetings during the five years of its existence. Individual members have given unstintingly of time and effort to the work. Tentative drafts of all chapters of this yearbook were written and mimeographed before the final meeting of the Commission at Lake Placid in September. These drafts were discussed critically during a three-day session and final revisions were then written in the light of these criticisms.

Acknowledgment is due to the hundreds of school systems, higher educational institutions, and individuals through whose cooperation the materials for the report were procured. The Research Division of the National Education Association cordially assisted the Commission in its work. In fact, without the aid of this Division, yearbooks such as the Department has issued in recent years would be impossible.

The 1932 Yearbook—At the annual meeting of the Executive Committee of the Department of Superintendence in May, 1929, President Frank Cody recommended that the 1932 Yearbook be devoted to the subject of character education, which was agreed to. This Commission has held three meetings at which the work was outlined and preliminary reports subjected to critical examination. Much material has been gathered and the cooperation of specialists in this field secured. The members of the Commission are: A. L. Threlkeld, Superintendent of Schools, Denver, Colorado,

Chairman; Bertie Backus, Principal, Powell Junior High School, Washington, D. C.; George S. Counts, Associate Director, International Institute, Teachers College, Columbia University, New York City; Frank N. Freeman, School of Education, University of Chicago, Chicago, Illinois; C. B. Glenn, Superintendent of Schools, Birmingham, Alabama; Paul T. Rankin, Supervising Director of Research and Adjustment, Detroit Public Schools, Detroit, Michigan; Belle M. Ryan, Assistant Superintendent of Schools, Omaha, Nebraska; Goodwin Watson, Associate Professor of Education, Teachers College, Columbia University, New York City; David E. Weglein, Superintendent of Schools, Baltimore, Maryland.

The 1933 Yearbook—"Educational Leadership" is the topic selected by the Executive Committee for the 1933 Yearbook and President Norman R. Crozier announces the appointment of Superintendent A. J. Stoddard of Providence, Rhode Island, as chairman of the commission to prepare this volume. The first yearbook of the Department of Superintendence was issued in 1923 and was entitled "The Status of the Superintendent." The yearbook on "Educational Leadership" to be issued ten years later will report a decade of progress in the field of educational administration.

In Conclusion—The superintendents of schools of America have a heavy burden of responsibility. It is theirs to administer a business which costs $2,184,000,000 annually; to safeguard the interests of 25,000,000 pupils committed to their charge; to lead wisely a teaching force numbering 854,000 women and men, and so to do these things, and many others, as to justify the faith of the founders in the power of education to hold the Great Republic safely on its course.

The task is one for united effort. Superintendents of schools have many resources at their command which can be utilized for the common good through the Department of Superintendence. Our efforts and our vision as well should include a continuing program which shall benefit the profession of teaching in the discharge of its mission, the children in the process of their education, and the Nation in its development of better citizens.

Respectfully submitted,
S. D. SHANKLAND,
Executive Secretary.

List of Members

The Department of Superintendence

of the

National Education Association of the United States

Corrected to January 1, 1931

Abada, Esteban R., A.B.'22, Univ. of Mich.; Div., Supt. of Sch., Iba, Zambales, P. I., since 1927.

Abbett, Merle J., A.B.'07, Franklin Col.; A. M.'18, Tchrs. Col., Columbia Univ.; Supt. of Sch., Bedford, Ind., since 1924.

Abbett, William A., Ph.B.'88, Minnesota Inst. of Pharmacy. Address: 222 W. Superior St., Duluth, Minn.

Abbot, Julia Wade, B.S.'23, Tchrs. Col., Columbia Univ.; Dir., Kdgn. Educ., Grant Bldg., 17th and Pine Sts., Philadelphia, Pa., since 1924.

Abell, J. A., A.B.'10, A.M.'14, Ind. Univ.; Supt. of Sch., 353 N. Main, Nappanee, Ind., since 1923.

Aborn, Caroline D., Dir. of Kdgns., Pub. Sch., 15 Beacon St., Boston, Mass., since 1906.

Ackerman, O. W., Supt. of Sch., 27 N. Fourth St., Bangor, Pa.

Ackerman, William A., State Dept. of Educ., State House, Trenton, N. J.

Ackert, Mrs. Edith S., A.B.'10, Epworth Univ.; Life Diploma '10, Okla. City Univ.; Life Diploma '18, Univ. of Oregon; Co. Supt. of Sch., Court House, Roseburg, Oregon, since 1925.

Ackley, Clarence E., A.B.'10, A.M.'13, Oberlin Col.; Tchr., H. S. English and Latin, Pub. Sch., Pittsburgh, Pa., since 1913.

Ackley, E. L., A.B. and A.M.'05, Pd.B.'08, Syracuse Univ.; Supt. of Sch., H. S. Bldg., Johnstown, N. Y., since 1910.

Adams, Alfred Wallace, Supt. of Sch., 705 Ave. H, N. W., Childress, Texas.

Adams, Edwin W., M.A.'23, Univ. of Pa.; Prin., Philadelphia Normal Sch., 2522 S. Lambert St., Philadelphia, Pa., since 1924.

Adams, Emerson L., A.B.'89, A.M.'92, Bowdoin Col.; Dir. of Voc. Rehabilitation and Adult Educ., State House, Providence R. I.

Adams, Ray H., A.B.'27, M.A.'28, Univ. of Mich.; Supt. of Sch., 483 Nona Ave., Dearborn, Mich., since 1916.

Adams, Waldo L., A.B.'22, Manchester Col.; M.A.'30, Univ. of Chicago; Co. Supt. of Sch., Court House, Goshen, Ind., since 1927.

Adamson, W. H., Prin., Oak Cliff H. S., Dallas, Texas.

Ade, Lester K., A.B.'21, A.M.'24, Bucknell Univ.; Prin., State Normal Sch., New Haven, Conn., since 1928.

Adkins, Alta, Asst. Supt. of Sch., Bd. of Educ., Hammond, Ind.

Adkins, Stanley, A.B.'10, Ohio State Univ.; Dist. Supt. of Sch., Aurora, Minn.

Aery, William Anthony, A.B.'04, Columbia Col.; A.M.'05, Tchrs. Col., Columbia Univ.; Dir., Sch. of Educ., Hampton Inst., Hampton, Va., since 1923.

Ager, G. W., Supt. of Sch., Bend, Oregon, since 1922.

Agnew, Charles E., Dist. Supt. of Sch., Wellsburg, W. Va.

Agnew, Walter D., M.A.'21, Ph.D.'23, Columbia Univ.; Pres., Women's Col. of Ala., Montgomery, Ala., since 1922.

Aguayo, Manuel, Genl. Supt., Dept. of Educ., San Juan, P. R.

Aikin, Wilford M., B.S.'07, Muskingum Col.; M.A.'13, Univ. of Mich.; Dir., John Burroughs Sch., Price Rd., Clayton, Mo., since 1923.

Akers, A. E., B.Ped.'03, Bolecourt Normal Col.; Co. Supt. of Sch., Roanoke Rapids, N. C., since 1915.

Akin, W. P., B.S.'20, Southern Methodist Univ.; M.A.'27, Univ. of Texas; Dean, Texarkana Junior Col., Texarkana, Texas, since 1927.

Alan, John S., A.B.'93, A.M.'00, Thiel Col.; Supt. of Sch., 1612 E. State St., Salem, Ohio, since 1913.

Alberty, Harold B., Ph.D.'26, Ohio State Univ.; Assoc. Prof., Dept. of Prin. of Educ., Ohio State Univ., Columbus, Ohio, since 1926.

Albright, Denton M., A.B.'15, Albright Col.; A.M.'22, Columbia Univ.; Supt. of Sch., Rochester, Pa., since 1926.

Alderfer, C. J., A.B.'17, Swarthmore Col.; A. M.'26, Univ. of Pa.; A.M.'29, Tchrs. Col., Columbia Univ.; Supt. of Sch., Du Bois, Pa., since 1926.

Alderson, James, 888 Yale Ct., Dubuque, Iowa.

Aldrich, McCall, A.B.'13, Northwestern Univ.; A.M.'16, Tchrs. Col., Columbia Univ.; Supt. of Sch., McGill, Nevada, since 1928.

Alexander, Carter, B.S.'05, A.B.'06, A.M.'08, Univ. of Mo.; Ph.D.'10, Columbia Univ.; Prof. of Educ. and Research Assoc., Div. of Field Stud., Tchrs. Col., Columbia Univ., New York, N. Y.

Alexander, Fred Milton, 239 Blair Ave., Newport News, Va.

Alexander, James W., A.B.'02, Princeton Univ.; Supvg. Prin. of Twp. Sch., Hamilton H. S., Trenton, N. J., since 1916.

Alford, H. D., A.B.'25, Hendrix-Henderson Col.; Co. Supt. of Sch., Hamburg, Ark., since 1929.

Alfriend, Kyle Terry, A.B.'95, George Peabody Col. for Tchrs.; A.M.'25, Mercer Univ.; Secy., Ga. Educ. Assn., 400 Vineville Ave., Macon, Ga., since 1923.

Alger, John L., A.B.'90, A.M.'95, Brown Univ.; Ed.D.'21, R. I. State Col.; Pres., R. I. Col. of Educ., Providence, R. I., since 1908.

Allan, Harold A., A.B.'06, Bates Col.; Dir., Business Div., Natl. Educ. Assn., 1201 16th St., N. W., Washington, D. C., since 1923.

Allbaugh, Edgar B., Diploma '01, State Tchrs. Col., Emporia, Kansas; Supt. of Sch., Concordia, Kansas, since 1929.

Allen, A. T., Ph.B.'97, Univ. of N. C.; D.C. L.'24, Elon Col.; LL.D.'27, Univ. of N. C.; State Supt. of Pub. Instr., Raleigh, N. C., since 1923.

Allen, Charles Forrest, Pd.B.'10, State Tchrs. Col., Warrensburg, Mo.; Ph.B.'17, Univ. of Chicago; M.A.'24, Tchrs. Col., Columbia Univ.; Supvr. of Sec. Educ., Eighth and Louisiana Sts., Little Rock, Ark., since 1914.

Allen, Frank E., A.B.'16, A.M.'23, Ind. Univ.; Supt. of Sch., Muncie, Ind., since 1925.

Allen, George A., Jr., B.S. in Ed.'16, State Tchrs. Col., Emporia, Kansas; State Supt. of Pub. Instr., State House, Topeka, Kansas, since 1927.

Allen, Harlan B., B.S.'16, Union Col.; M. A.'19, Union Univ.; Supt. of Sch., Mineola, N. Y., since 1923.

Allen, I. M., A.B.'96, Lawrence Col.; Ph.D. '26, Columbia Univ.; Supt. of Sch., Highland Park, Mich., since 1926.

Allen, J. Edward, B.A.'07, M.A.'08, Wake Forest Col.; Supt. of City and Co. Schools, Warrenton, N. C., since 1919.

Allen, James E., A.B.'98, LL.D.'23, Hampden-Sidney Col.; Pres., Davis and Elkins Col., Elkins, W. Va., since 1910.

Allen, Lyman Richards, B.S.'98, Harvard Univ.; A.M.'20, Columbia Univ.; Union Supt. of Sch., Framingham, Mass.

Allen, Richard D., A.B.'10, A.M.'12, Ph.D. '21, Brown Univ.; Asst. Supt. of Sch., 9 Exchange Ter., Providence, R. I., since 1918.

Allen, Roy R., A.B.'12, Harvard Univ.; A. M.'22, Tchrs. Col., Columbia Univ.; Supt. of Sch., 18 Armstrong Pl., Owego, N. Y., since 1928.

Allen, W. S., A.B.'12, Baylor Univ.; A.M. '15, Ph.D.'23, Columbia Univ.; Dean, Col. of Arts and Sciences and Prof. of Sec. Educ., Baylor Univ., Waco, Texas, since 1924.

Allman, H. B., B.S.'10, Tri-State Col.; Asst. Prof. of Educ., Sch. of Educ., Ind. Univ., Bloomington, Ind., since 1930.

Allman, John I., Supt. of Sch., Dalton, Ga.

Almack, John C., B.A.'18, M.A.'20, Univ. of Oregon; Ph.D.'22, Stanford Univ.; Prof. of Educ., Stanford Univ., 683 Alvarado Row, Stanford University, Calif., since 1921.

Altstetter, M. L., A.B.'09, M.A.'27, Ohio State Univ.; Ph.D.'29, George Peabody Col. for Tchrs.; Dean of Instr. and Registrar, State Tchrs. Col., Fredericksburg, Va., since 1929.

Alverson, S. E., B.S.'17, Univ. of Ga.; A. M.'27, Tchrs. Col., Columbia Univ.; Supt. of Sch., Anniston, Ala., since 1928.

Alves, H. F., B.A.'27, Southwest Texas State Tchrs. Col., San Marcos, Texas; M.A.'28, Univ. of Texas; Dir., Div. of Research

and Service, State Dept. of Educ., Austin, Texas, since 1930.

Amery, Elisabeth, B.S.'13, Univ. of Wis.; A.M.'27, Tchrs. Col., Columbia Univ.; State Supvr. of Home Economic Educ., State Dept. of Educ., Baltimore, Md., since 1927.

Ames, Vernon S., A.B.'04, Colby Col.; Supt. of Sch., Wilton, N. H., since 1923.

Andersen, Erik A., Ed.M.'28, R. I. Col. of Educ.; Deputy Supt. of Sch., 9 Exchange Ter., Providence, R. I., since 1930.

Andersen, Ida M. B., State Normal Sch. Diploma '26, Univ. of Wyoming; Co. Supt. of Sch., Newcastle, Wyo., since 1923.

Andersen, Marvin Verne, Diploma '26, Western State Tchrs. Col., Kalamazoo, Mich. Address: 469 W. Webster Ave., Muskegon, Mich.

Anderson, Adda H., Sr. H. S. Bldg., Hutchinson, Kansas.

Anderson, C. S., Diploma '09, A.B.'19, Phillips Univ.; Supt. of Sch., Broken Arrow, Okla., since 1924.

Anderson, David Allen, B.A.'08, M.A.'10, Ph.D.'12, State Univ. of Iowa; Pres., Northern State Tchrs. Col., Aberdeen, S. Dak., since 1928.

Anderson, Earl William, A.B.'18, Univ. of Ill.; A.M.'25, Ph.D.'26, Tchrs. Col., Columbia Univ.; Assoc. Prof. of Educ., Bureau of Educ. Research, Ohio State Univ., Columbus, Ohio, since 1927.

Anderson, Ernest B., B.A.'09, Gustavus Adolphus Col.; Supt. of Sch., 115 Third St., Cloquet, Minn., since 1923.

Anderson, Homer W., B.A.'10, Des Moines Univ.; M.A.'15, Ph.D.'25, State Univ. of Iowa; Deputy Supt. of Sch., 414 14th St., Denver, Colo., since 1927.

Anderson, J. L., A.B.'21, Mich. State Col.; Supt. of Sch., Trenton, Mich., since 1914.

Anderson, Mrs. L. C., Dist. Supt. of Sch., Gary, W. Va.

Anderson, Raymond L., B.S.'21, N. Y. Univ. Address: 105 E. 22nd St., New York, N. Y.

Anderson, Robert R., Diploma '08, State Normal Sch., Millersville, Pa.; Supvg. Prin. of Sch., Brackenridge, Pa., since 1918.

Anderson, Roy R., A.B.'18, Maryville Col.; M.A.'23, Univ. of N. C.; Supt. of Sch., Lenoir City, Tenn., since 1927.

Anderson, Walter Williams, B.S.'12, Univ. of Nevada; State Supt. of Pub. Instr., State House, Carson City, Nevada, since 1927.

Anderson, Ward, B.A.'23, La. State Univ.; Supt. of Sch., Lake Charles, La., since 1920.

Andrew, William W., Ph.B.'03, Brown Univ.; A.M.'04, Columbia Univ.; Ed.M. '21, Harvard Univ.; Supt. of Sch., Riverview and Lakeview Aves., Rocky River, Ohio, since 1928.

Andrews, Edwin C., A.B.'89, Williams; Supt. of Sch., Greenwich, Conn., since 1910.

Andrews, J. O., B.A.'23, Texas Christian Univ.; Asst. Supt. of Sch., Fort Worth, Texas, since 1923.

Andrews, L. G., '08, Howard Payne Col.; A. B.'18, Univ. of Texas; Supt. of Sch., Navasota, Texas, since 1919.

Andrews, Roy M., A.B.'20, Southwestern Univ., Georgetown, Texas; A.M.'26, Stanford Univ.; Supt. of Sch., Del Rio, Texas, since 1929.

Andrews, Sterling M., B.S.'04, Valparaiso Univ.; Supt. of Sch., Walsenburg, Colo., since 1908.

Andrews, T. Wingate, A.B.'08, Univ. of N. C.; Supt. of Sch., High Point, N. C., since 1924.

Andrews, William A., A.B.'09, Columbia Univ.; Supt. of Sch., Ballston Spa, N. Y., since 1910.

Angel, W. H., A.B.'95, A.M.'99, Ohio Northern Univ.; Supt. of Sch., 823 N. Second St., Dennison, Ohio, since 1905.

Anibal, Earle W., Ph.B.'08, Hamilton Col.; A.M.'23, Tchrs. Col., Columbia Univ.; Supvg. Prin. of Sch., Irvington, N. Y., since 1928.

Ankenbrand, William W., A.B.'20, Marietta Col.; A.M.'24, Ohio State Univ.; Supt. of Sch., Athens, Ohio, since 1930.

Antrim, Eugene M., A.B.'96. Denver Univ.; S.T.B.'00,Boston Univ.; D.D.'04, Denver Univ.; Ph.D.'04, Boston Univ.; LL.D.'27, Kansas Wesleyan Univ.; Pres., Oklahoma City Univ., Oklahoma City, Okla., since 1923.

Antrim, G. Harold, A.B.'25, Washington and Jefferson Col.; M.A.'29, Tchrs. Col., Columbia Univ.; Supvg. Prin. of Sch., 705 Trenton Ave., Point Pleasant Beach, N. J., since 1930.

App, Isaac D., B.S.'05, M.S.'10, Susquehanna Univ.; Co. Supt. of Sch., Harrisburg, Pa., since 1922.

Appel, Frank, A.B.'94, Ohio Wesleyan; Supt. of Sch., 840 Eighth St., Portsmouth, Ohio, since 1908.

Appenzellar, J. L., A.B.'08, Lebanon Valley Col.; A.M.'16, Columbia Univ.; Supvg. Prin. of Sch., Wyomissing, Pa.

Applewhite, W. R., B.A.'09, Millsaps Col.; Supt. of Sch., New Albany, Miss., since 1928.

Archer, C. P., B.A.'20, Iowa State Tchrs. Col.; M.A.'23, Ph.D.'27, State Univ. of Iowa; Head, Educ. Dept., State Tchrs. Col., Moorhead, Minn., since 1923.

Arendshort, William, 118 E. Ninth St., Holland, Mich.

Armstrong, Dallas W., Ph.B.'94, A.M.'05, LL.D.'26, Grove City Col.; Pres., State Tchrs. Col., Lock Haven, Pa., since 1925.

Armstrong, J. Harding, A.B.'07, A.M.'08, Harvard Univ.; Supt. of Sch., 14 Church St., Westborough, Mass., since 1924.

Armstrong, Ray, A.B.'18, M.A.'26, Univ. of N. C.; Supt. of Sch., Goldsboro, N. C., since 1927.

Armstrong, T. H., 532 Genesee Valley Trust Bldg., Rochester, N. Y.

Arnette, W. P., A.B.'22, La. State Univ.; Parish Supt. of Sch., Jennings, La., since 1913.

Arnold, E. J., B.S.'17, Wilmington Col.; M.A.'23, Ohio State Univ.; Supt. of Sch., Bremen, Ohio, since 1927.

Arnold, Joseph M., A.B.'87, A.M.'90, Lafayette Col.; Co. Supt. of Sch., Princeton, N. J., since 1905.

Arnsparger, Mrs. M. M., 1532 Nudringhans Ave., Granite City, Ill.

Arps, George F., A.B.'04, Leland Stanford Jr. Univ.; A.M.'05, Ind. Univ.; Ph.D.'08, Leipzig Univ., Germany; Dean, Col. of Educ. and Prof. of Psych., Ohio State Univ., Education Bldg., Columbus, Ohio, since 1920.

Arrants, John H., A.B.'16, Univ. of Tenn.; Supt. of Sch., South Pittsburg, Tenn., since 1927.

Arrowood, Fred M., M.A.'25, Univ. of N. C.; M.A.'27, Tchrs. Col., Columbia Univ.; Supt. of Sch., Reidsville, N. C., since 1928.

Arthur, Edwin I., A.B. and Pd.B.'13, Hillsdale Col.; A.M.'28, Columbia Univ.; State Supvg. Agt. of Sch., Washington Bldg., Middletown, Conn., since 1922.

Ashbaugh, E. J., A.B.'12, A.M.'13, Ind. Univ.; Ph.D.'19, State Univ. of Iowa; Dean, Sch. of Educ., Miami Univ., Oxford, Ohio, since 1929.

Ashburn, G. L., Prin., Woodrow Wilson H. S., Dallas, Texas.

Ashby, W. S., College St., Bowling Green, Ky.

Atkins, S. G., LL.D.'28, Howard Univ.; Pres., Winston-Salem Tchrs, Col., Winston-Salem, N. C., since 1905.

Attinger, Frank S., A.B.'21, Susquehanna Univ.; Supvg. Prin. of Sch., 338 S. Market St., Selinsgrove, Pa., since 1927.

Atwell, Floyd, Supt. of Sch., Beaver Falls, Pa.

Atwell, Willard Barber, Ph.B.'03, Brown Univ.; Supt. of Sch., H. S. Bldg., Wakefield, Mass., since 1911.

Atwood, Will G., Litt.B.'10, Rutgers Univ.; Co. Supt. of Sch., Court House, Belvidere, N. J., since 1928.

Austin, Everett Lewis, Ph.D.'28, Cornell Univ.; Head, Dept. of Educ., Mich. State Col., East Lansing, Mich., since 1929.

Averill, William A., A.B.'02, Univ. of Chicago. Address: 15 Asburton Pl., Boston, Mass.

Avery, Floyd B., A.B.'03, Syracuse Univ. Address: 88 Lexington Ave., New York, N. Y.

Avery, Lewis B., A.B.'83, A.M.'86, Tabor Col.; Dir. of Tchr. Tr., 1025 Second Ave., Oakland, Calif.

Avery, William J., Supt. of Sch., Alexandria, La., since 1919.

Ayer, Fred C., B.S.'02, Upper Iowa Univ.; M.S.'05, Georgetown Univ.; Ph.D.'15, Univ. of Chicago; Prof. of Educ. Admin., Univ. of Texas, Austin, Texas, since 1927.

Ayer, J. Warren, A.B.'07, Otterbein Col.; M.A.'23, Stanford Univ.; Dist. Supt. and H. S. Prin., Los Gatos Union H. S. Dist., Route 1, Box 215, Los Gatos, Calif., since 1922.

Ayres, Frank M., A.B.'24, M.A.'26, Univ. of Mich.; Supt. of Sch., Dundee, Mich., since 1924.

Ayson, H. F., Resident Commr., Rarotonga, Cook Islands.

Babb, H. A., B.S. in Ed. '11, Univ. of Ky.; Supt. of Sch., Mt. Sterling, Ky,, since 1920.

Babcock, Earl H., Diploma '09, Mich. State Normal; B.A.'22, M.A.'29, Univ. of Mich.; Supt. of Sch., Grand Haven, Mich., since 1923.

Babcock, Ella L., B.S.'12, Tchrs. Col., Columbia Univ.; Dir., Household Arts, Sch. Admin. Bldg., Milwaukee, Wis., since 1913.

Babcock, S. H., Co. Supt. of Sch., Medina, Ohio.

Bachrodt, Walter L., A.B.'20. A.M.'21, Stanford Univ.; Supt. of Sch., San Jose, Calif., since 1921.

Bacon, Francis Leonard, A.B.'12, Southwestern Col.; A.M.'16, Columbia Univ.; Supt., Evanston Twp. H. S., Evanston, Ill., since 1928.

Bacon, Willard H., A.B.'00, Brown Univ.; Supt. of Sch., Westerly, R. I., since 1913.

Badger, Lester B., B.S.'18, Dartmouth Col.; Supt. of Sch., Pittsfield, N. H., since 1923.

Bagby, Richard O., M.A.'22, Tchrs. Col., Columbia Univ. Address: 1003 Auburn Rd., Roanoke, Va.

Baggett, John E., Supt. of Sch., Lake Forest, Ill.

Bailey, Edward Latta, B.S.'92, LL.D.'25, Miss. Col.; Supt. of Sch., Jackson, Miss., since 1900.

Bailey, Norman D., A.B.'25. Boston Univ.; Union Supt. of Sch., North Dighton, Mass., since 1930.

Bain, Harry L., A.B.'15, Union Col.; M.A. '23, Columbia Univ.; Supt. of Sch., West New York, N. J., since 1927.

Bair, Carl M., Ph.B.'09, Grinnell Col.; Supt. of Sch., 650 Fourth Ave., Berlin, N. H., since 1921.

Bair, Frederick H., A.B.'12. Grinnell Col.; M.A.'17, Tchrs. Col., Columbia Univ.; Supt. of Sch., H. S., Shaker Hgts., Ohio, since 1927.

Baird, William J., A.B.'18. Univ. of Ala.; A.M.'21, Tchrs. Col., Columbia Univ.; Prin., Jefferson Co. H. S., Tarrant, Ala., since 1921.

Baisden, Leo B., A.B.'16, A.M.'28, Univ. of Wash.; Asst. Supt. of Sch., Sacramento, Calif., since 1929.

Baker, Asa George, A.B.'88, Amherst Col. Address: 10 Broadway, Springfield, Mass.

Baker, B. B., M.A.'08, Ohio Northern Univ.; Supt. of Sch., Fairfield, Ala., since 1923.

Baker, Chilton Clyde, B.S.'96, A.M.'13, Ohio Northern Univ.; Dist. Supt, of Sch., Grand Rapids, Minn., since 1920.

Baker, Clara Belle, Dir., Children's Sch., Natl. Kdgn. and Elem. Col., Evanston, Ill.

Baker, D. R., B.A.'14, Miami Univ.; M.A. '30, Univ. of Cincinnati; Supt. of Sch., 209 S. Second St., Hamilton, Ohio, since 1929.

Baker, Edna Dean, B.E.'13, Natl. Kdgn. Col.; B.A.'20, M.A.'21, Northwestern Univ.; Pres., Natl. Kdgn. and Elem. Col., Evanston, Ill., since 1920.

Baker, George C., Ph.B.'10, Lafayette Col.; A.M.'13, Univ. of Pa.; Supt. of Sch., 265 W. Main St., Moorestown, N. J., since 1913.

Baker, H. C., A.B.'12, Univ. of Texas; Supt. of Sch., Edinburg, Texas, since 1920.

Baker, Harold V., A.B.'18, Baker Univ.; M. A.'26, Univ. of Colo.; Prin., Osage Sch., 1139 N. Boston Ave., Tulsa, Okla., since 1929.

Baker, Ida Swain, 257 N. Tacoma Ave., Indianapolis, Ind.

Baker, Ira William, A.B. in Ed.'14, Kansas Tchrs. Col.; B.S.'15, Kansas State Agrl. Col.; A.M. in Ed.'20, Univ. of Chicago; Prin., Harding Jr. H. S., 33rd and Shartel, Oklahoma City, Okla., since 1925.

Baker, William Elwood, A.B.'16, A.M.'20, Colo. State Tchrs. Col., Greeley, Colo.; Genl. Secy., Natl. Congress of Parents and Teachers, 1201 16th St., N. W., Washington, D. C., since 1930.

Balcom, Arthur Grant, Asst. Supt. of Sch. in charge of Visual Educ., City Hall Annex, Newark, N. J., since 1918.

Baldwin, Clarence B., Diploma '07, State Tchrs. Col., Buffalo, N. Y.; A.B.'25, Colo. Col.; Dist. Supt. of Elem. Sch., Huntington Beach, Calif., since 1928.

Baldwin, Jay B.. B.L.'99. Univ. of Wis. Address: 325 S. Market St., Chicago, Ill.

Baldwin, Robert Dodge, A.B.'13, Princeton Univ.; A.M.'16, Columbia Univ.; Ph.D.'26, Cornell Univ.; Dir. of Graduate Work in Educ. Admin. and Finance, Col. of Educ., W. Va. Univ., Morgantown, W. Va., since 1930.

Baldwin, William A., B.S.'97. Harvard Univ.; Tch. of Ethics, R. I. Col. of Educ., Providence, R. I., since 1925. Address: 303 Maple St., Springfield, Mass.

Ball, C. C.. B.A.'05, Coe Col.; M.A.'24. State Univ. of Iowa; Dir., Jr. Educ., Bd. of Educ., San Antonio, Texas, since 1926.

Ballentine. Will G., Supt. of Sch., Menomonie, Wis., since 1920.

Balliette, Ralph Ernest, Ph.B.'23, Ph.M.'27 Univ. of Wis.; Supt. of Sch.; Antigo, Wis., since 1928.

Balling, Marie G., M.Pd.'18, State Tchrs. Col., Silver City, N. Mex.; Co. Supt. of Sch., Court House, Albuquerque, N. Mex., since 1927.

Ballintine, O. P., Ph.B.'09, Grove City Col.; Prin., H. S., Brackenridge, Pa., since 1913.

Ballou, Frank Washington, B.S.'04, Tchrs. Col., Columbia Univ.; M.A.'08, Univ. of Cincinnati; Ph.D.'14, Harvard Univ.; Pres., Dept. of Superintendence, 1925-26; Supt. of Sch., 13th and K Sts., N. W., Washington, D. C., since 1930.

Balsbaugh, E. M., B.S.'01, M.S.'05, Lebanon Valley Col.; Supt. of Sch., Lansford, Pa.

Balyeat, F. A., B.A.'11, M.A.'18, Univ. of Okla.; Ph.D.'27, Stanford Univ.; Assoc. Prof. of Educ., Univ. of Okla., Norman, Okla.

Bamberger, Florence E., Prof. of Educ., Johns Hopkins Univ., Baltimore, Md.

Bamesberger, Velda C., Ph.D.'28, Columbia Univ.; Dir. of Elem. Educ., Bd. of Educ., Toledo, Ohio, since 1928.

Bangs, C. W., A.B.'26, Iowa State Tchrs. Col.; M.A.'29, State Univ. of Iowa; Supt. of Sch., 508 N. Franklin St., Manchester, Iowa, since 1921.

Banks, Charles, B.S.'10, Northeast Mo. State Tchrs. Col., Kirksville, Mo.; M.A.'14, Univ. of Wis.; M.A.'25, Columbia Univ.; Supt. of Sch., 6701 Delmar Blvd., University City, Mo., since 1925.

Banks, L. Frazer, A.B.'11, Univ. of Colo.; Officier d'Academie '19, Republic of France; M.A.'28, Peabody Col.; Asst. Supt. of Sch., Birmingham, Ala., since 1921.

Banting, George Orton, Ph.B.'15, Univ. of Chicago; Supt. of Sch., Waukesha, Wis., since 1920.

Barbee, Frederick H., M.S. in Ed.'21, Univ. of Kansas; Supt. of Sch., St. Joseph, Mo., since 1929.

Barber, George A., Diploma '12, State Normal Sch., Geneseo, N. Y.; B.S.'23, Univ. of Rochester; Dist. Supt. of Sch., Genesee Co. Bldg., Batavia, N. Y., since 1930.

Barbour, Albert L., B.A.'92, M.A.'94, Brown Univ.; Supt. of Sch., Whittier Sch. Bldg., Haverhill, Mass., since 1920.

Barbour, Luther H., Co. Supt. of Sch., 915 Darian Ave., Durham, N. C.

Barclay, Edward R., Diploma, State Tchrs. Col., Millersville, Pa.; Supt. of Sch., Huntingdon, Pa., since 1902.

Bardner, H. A., A.B.'96, Ind. Univ.; Supt. of City Sch., P. O. Box 722, Manila, P. I., since 1919.

Bardwell, Richard W., A.B.'10, Univ. of Ill.; M.A.'22, Univ. of Chicago; Supt. of Sch., 22 W. Dayton, Madison, Wis., since 1928.

Barford, George F., B.A.'21, Colgate Univ.; Supt. of Sch., Memorial City Hall, Auburn, N. Y., since 1923.

Barker, Jonathan M., Diploma '02, State Normal School., Buffalo, N. Y.; O.D.'09, Northern Ill. Col. of Ophthalmology and Otology; Union Supt. of Sch., Depew, N. Y., since 1921.

Barkley, Mathew, Ph.B.'29, Marquette Univ.; Supt. of Sch., West Milwaukee, Wis., since 1922.

Barlow, Nathan J., B.S.'24, Univ. of Utah; Co. Supt. of Sch., Cedar City, Utah, since 1924.

Barnard, Anna E., Diploma '20, Central State Tchrs. Col., Stevens Point, Wis.; Co. Supt. of Sch., Chilton, Wis.

Barnes, Harold, A.B.'92, Kansas Univ.; A. M.'11, Tchrs. Col., Columbia Univ.; Supvr. of Elem. Educ., Girard Col., Philadelphia, Pa., since 1911.

Barnes, Percival S., B.S.'17, A.M.'18, Columbia Univ.; Supt. of Sch., East Hartford, Conn., since 1919.

Barnett, D'Arcy C., A.B.'98, A.M.'99, Univ. of Md.; A.M.'11, Columbia Univ.; Supt. of Sch., Academy Rd. and Prospect St., Caldwell, N. J., since 1911.

Barnett, Owen L., M.S. in Ed.'27, Brigham Young Univ.; Dist. Supt. of Sch., Nephi, Utah, since 1927.

Barnum, Walter Lawrence, A.B.'07, Middlebury Col.; Asst. Prin., Evanston Twp. H. S., Evanston, Ill., since 1927.

Barr, Arvil S., A.B. and A.M.'15, Ind. Univ.; Ph.D.'29, Univ. of Wis.; Prof. of Educ., Dept. of Educ., Univ. of Wis., Madison, Wis.

Barr, Oscar O., B.S.'18, Tchrs. Col., Columbia Univ.; Supt. of Sch., South Amboy, N. J., since 1914.

Barr, Ralph R., A.B.'13, Bates Col.; A.M. '15, Harvard Univ.; Supt. of Sch., Town Hall, Amesbury, Mass., since 1924.

Barrett, Harry M., B.A.'90, M.A.'93, Allegheny Col.; Litt.D.'14, Univ. of Denver; Dir., Col. of Educ., Univ. of Colo., Boulder, Colo., since 1920.

Barrett, John Ignatius, Ph.D.'23, Loyola Col.; LL.D.'23, Gonzaga Col.; J.C.L.'12, Catholic Univ. of America; Supt. of Parish Sch., Archdiocese of Baltimore, 415 Cathedral St., Baltimore, Md., since 1922.

Baringer, Benton E., B.S.'15, Cornell Univ.; M.A.'20, Ph.D.'24, Columbia Univ.; Dept. of Educ., State Normal Col., Bowling Green, Ohio, since 1925.

Barthelmeh, Charles, B.S.'22, Kent State Col.; Co. Supt. of Sch., 218 Fifth St., N. W., New Philadelphia, Ohio, since 1914.

Bartholf, William J., B.S.'80, Indiana Normal; B.A.'84, Univ. of Ill.; LL.B.'91, Lake Forest Univ.; Pres., Crane Jr. Col. and Tech. H. S., 453 Roslyn Pl., Chicago, Ill., since 1910.

Bartley, Mary Ellen, Diploma '96, State Normal Sch., Fitchburg, Mass.; B.S.'27, Columbia Univ.; Ed.M.'28, Boston, Univ.; Prin., Jr. High and Elem. Sch., 9 Third St., Fitchburg, Mass., since 1884.

Barton, James Richard, B.A.'13, Hendrix Col.; M.A.'21, Tchrs. Col., Columbia Univ.; LL.D.'29, Hendrix Col.; Supt. of Sch., Oklahoma City, Okla., since 1925.

Bartrug, C. M., B.S.'23, M.S.'27, Iowa State Col.; Supt. of Sch., Iowa Falls, Iowa, since 1928.

Barwis, Bertha M., Primary Supvr. '11, Columbia Univ. Address: 843 W. State St., Trenton, N. J.

Batcheller, Delmer E., Ph.B.'98, Ill. Wesleyan Univ.; Supt. of Sch., North Tonawanda, N. Y., since 1920.

Bate, William G., B.A.'10, M.A.'15, Ripon Col.; Supt. of Sch., 127 N. Tenth St., Richmond, Ind., since 1921.

Bateman, E. Allen, B.A.'17, Univ. of Utah; M.A.'29, Univ. of Chicago; Supt. of Sch., Murray, Utah, since 1928.

Bates, Elizabeth, A.M. in Ed. '28, Univ. of Southern Calif.; Asst. Supt. of Sch., 727 Chamber of Commerce Bldg., Los Angeles, Calif., since 1924.

Bates, Horace Freeman, A.B.'98, Harvard Univ.; Union Supt. of Sch., Somerset, Mass., since 1922.

Bates, Ralph F., A.B.'11, Colgate Univ.; A. M.'14, Columbia Univ.; Supvg. Prin. of Sch., 38 Fairmount Ave., Chatham, N. J., since 1920.

Bathrick, H. A., A.B.'95, Harvard Univ.; Asst. Supt. of Sch., Cleveland, Ohio, since 1927.

Batten, Reeves D., B.S.'05, Pd.M.'08, New York Univ.; Supvg. Prin. of Sch., 264 Oriental Place, Lyndhurst, N. J., since 1905.

Bauer, Nicholas, B.S.'97, M.A.'99, Tulane Univ.; Supt. of Sch., City Hall Annex, New Orleans, La., since 1922.

Baum, R. Al, A.B.'95, Cornell Univ.; Supt. of Sch., 5 Smedley St., Oil City, Pa., since 1926.

Bauman, D. H., Ph.B.'06, Grove City Col.; Supvg. Prin. of Sch., Meyersdale, Pa., since 1920.

Baumgartner, John, M.S.'20, Univ. of Ark.; M.A.'22, Univ. of Chicago; Supt. of Sch., Brinkley, Ark., since 1914.

Bawden, William T., A.B.'96, Denison Univ.; B.S.'10, Ph.D.'14, Tchrs. Col., Columbia Univ.; Editor, Industrial Education Magazine, Manual Arts Press, Peoria, Ill.

Baxter, Kathryn H., Prof. Diploma '10, Damrosch Inst. of Musical Arts, New York, N. Y.; Prof. Diploma for Supvr. of Music and B.S. in Ed. '18, Tchrs. Col., Columbia Univ.; Supvr. of Music Educ., Central H. S., Kalamazoo, Mich., since 1924.

Bay, James Campbell, A.B.'12, Oberlin Col.; A.M.'17, Columbia Univ.; Ph.D.'27, New York Univ.; Supt. of Sch., Easton, Pa., since 1924.

Baylor, Adelaide Steele, Ph.B.'97, Univ. of Chicago; M.A.'18, Columbia Univ.; Sc.D. in Home Economics Educ. '28, Stout Inst.; Chief of Home Economics Educ. Serv., Fed. Bd. for Voc. Educ., 1523 L St., N. W., Washington, D. C., since 1923.

Bayne, Stephen F., B.S.'98, Col. of the City of N. Y.; A.M.'03, Columbia Univ.; Ph.D., Fordham Univ.; Dist. Supt. of Sch., Pub. Sch. No. 1, Ninth St. and Van Alst Ave., Long Island City, N. Y., since 1921.

Beach, Fred F., B.S.'26, M.S.'27, Syracuse Univ.; M.A.'28, Columbia Univ.; Dir. of Research, Pub. Sch., Oyster Bay, N. Y., since 1930.

Beach, M. F., Supt. of Sch., Moberly, Mo.

Beals, R. G., A.B.'07, Earlham Col.; M.A. '08, Ind. Univ.; Supt., Twp. H. S., De Kalb, Ill., since 1922.

Bean, Albert M., A.B.'10, A.M.'14, Dickinson Col.; Co. Supt. of Sch., Court House, Camden, N. J., since 1930.

Bear, George V., B.S.'21, Central Mo. State Tchrs. Col., Warrensburg, Mo.; Supt. of Sch., Donna, Texas, since 1921.

Bear, Harris V., A.B.'03, Otterbein Col.; A. M.'10, Harvard Univ.; Supt. of Sch., 301 S. Fifth St., Miamisburg, Ohio, since 1915.

Beard, R. B., B.S.'18, Bucknell Univ.; A.M. '25, Columbia Univ.; Supvg. Prin. of Sch., Portage, Pa., since 1919.

Beattie, Alfred Wesley, B. S. '22, Allegheny Col.; A.M.'24, Univ. of Pittsburgh; Supvg. Prin., Ben Avon Schools, 271 Center Ave., Emsworth, Pittsburgh, Pa., since 1926.

Beattie, John W., A.B.'07, Denison Univ.; M.A.'22, Tchrs. Col., Columbia Univ.; Prof. of Music Educ., Northwestern Univ., Evanston, Ill., since 1925.

Beatty, Edward, Ph.B.'16, Univ. of Chicago; Supt. of Sch., Warrensburg, Mo., since 1909.

Beatty, Edward C. O., A.B.'16, Univ. of Ill.; M.A.'26, Univ. of Chicago; Supt. of Sch., Woodstock, Ill., since 1927.

Beatty, Willard W., B.S.'13, M.A.'22, Univ. of Calif.; Supt. of Sch., Bronxville H. S., Bronxville, N. Y., since 1926.

Beaty, Ira O., A.B.'26, Randolph-Macon; Prof. of Educ., Md. Col. for Women, Lutherville, Md., since 1928.

Beck, C. E., A.B.'14, State Normal Sch., Muncie, Ind.; A.B.'25, Ind. Univ.; Supt. of Sch., Columbia City, Ind., since 1926.

Beck, Cameron, Personnel Dir., N. Y. Stock Exchange, New York, N. Y.

Bedillion, James C., B.S.'27, A.B.'30, Univ. of Pittsburgh; Supvg. Prin. of Sch., Chartiers Twp., Houston, Pa., since 1928.

Bedwell, Robert L., Ph.B.'10, Miss. Col.; M.A.'17, Univ. of Miss.; Ph.D.'29, George Peabody Col. for Tchrs.; Supt. of Sch., 217 E. Broadway, Yazoo City, Miss., since 1919.

Beebe, Ralph Edwin, B.A.'13, Winona Col.; M.A.'16, Ind. Univ.; Supt. of Sch., Naperville, Ill., since 1927.

Beebe, Robert O., Dir., Essex Co. Voc. Schools, Hall of Records, Newark, N. J., since 1918.

Beede, F. H., B.A.'83, Yale; Supt. of Sch., New Haven, Conn., since 1899.

Beers, John A., A.B.'01, Syracuse Univ.; Supvg. Prin. of Sch., Watkins Glen, N. Y., since 1909.

Beeson, Jasper Luther, A.B.'89, A.M.'90, Univ. of Ala.; Ph.D.'93, Johns Hopkins Univ.; LL.D.'29, Univ. of Ala.; Pres., Ga. State Col. for Women, Milledgeville, Ga., since 1928.

Beggs, V. L., Supt. of Sch., Elmhurst, Ill.

Belisle, Hector Louis, A.B.'96, Harvard Univ.; Supt. of Sch., Fall River, Mass., since 1913.

Bell, Erman W., B.S.'10, Muskingum Col.; M.A.'24, Columbia Univ.; Supt. of Sch., Delphos, Ohio, since 1924.

Bell, H. C., Ph.B.'02, Ottawa Univ.; Supt. of Sch., Luverne, Minn., since 1911.

Bell, L. J., Ph.B.'98, Univ. of N. C.; City and Co. Supt. of Sch., Rockingham, N. C., since 1906.

Bell, Leslie H., B.S. in Ed.'14, A.B.'15, Univ. of Mo.; Supt. of Sch., 1702 Oneida St., Lexington, Mo., since 1919.

Bell, Requa W., A.B.'16, William Jewell Col.; M.A.'26, Univ. of Okla.; Supvg. Prin. of Sch., 12 Weskora Ave., Pleasantville, N. Y., since 1930.

Bell, W. C., A.B., M.A., George Peabody Col. for Tchrs.; State Supt. of Pub. Instr., Frankfort, Ky., since 1928.

Bellows, Russell H., Supt. of Sch., Great Barrington, Mass.

Bemer, C. W., A.B.'12, Albion Col.; A.M. '26, Columbia Univ.; Supt. of Sch., Wakefield, Mich., since 1927.

Bemiller, J. F., B.S. in Ed.'26, M.A.'28, Ohio State Univ.; Supt. of Sch., Galion, Ohio, since 1928.

Benbow, Alice E., Sch. Admin. Bldg., Trenton, N. J.

Bender, John Frederick, Ph.D.'26, Columbia Univ.; Prof. of Educ. Admin., Univ. of Okla., Faculty Exchange, Norman, Okla., since 1926.

Bender, L. L., A.B.'24, Univ. of Wyo.; Supt. of Sch., Cokeville, Wyo., since 1920.

Benedict, Charles A., A.M.'10, Columbia Univ.; Supt. of Sch., North Tarrytown, N. Y., since 1910.

Bénézet, Louis P., A.B.'99, A.M.'03, Dartmouth Col.; Pd.D.'24, Evansville Col.; Supt. of Sch., Manchester, N. H., since 1924.

Benner, Carl O., Ph.B.'07, Dickinson, Col.; LL.B.'09, Dickinson Law Sch.; A.M.'24, Tchrs. Col., Columbia Univ.; Supt. of Sch., Coatesville, Pa., since 1926.

Bennett, Albert Luther, B.A.'16, Washington and Lee Univ.; M.A.'21, M.S.'24, Univ. of Va.; Ed.M.'26, Harvard Univ.; Co. Supt. of Sch., Charlottesville, Va., since 1919 and Asst. Prof. of Educ., Univ. of Va., Charlottesville, Va., since 1928.

Bennett, Earl W., Supt. of Sch., 1025 Crestwood Rd., Woodmere, L. I., N. Y.

Bennett, Henry Garland, B.A.'07, Ouachita Col.; M.A.'24, Univ. of Okla.; Ph.D.'26, Columbia Univ.; Pres., Okla. Agrl. and Mech. Col., Stillwater, Okla., since 1928.

Bennett, J. M., A.B.'10, Western Md. Col.; Co. Supt. of Sch., Salisbury, Md., since 1917.

Bennett, Omer H., B.S.'24, M.A. in Ed.'29, Univ. of Cincinnati; Co. Supt. of Sch., Court House, Cincinnati, Ohio, since 1923.

Bennett, Thomas G., A.B.'09, Western Md. Col.; A.M.'22, Tchrs. Col.; Supt. of Sch., Centreville, Md.

Bennion, Milton, B.S.'97, Univ. of Utah.; M.A.'01, Columbia Univ.; Dean Sch. of Educ., Univ. of Utah, Salt Lake City, Utah.

Benson, W. W., A.B.'90, M.A.'93, Southern Univ.; Supt. of Sch., Decatur, Ala., since 1920.

Benson, Walter S., Box 1077, Austin, Texas.

Bentley, Jerome H., A.B.'03, Wesleyan Univ., Middletown, Conn.; M.A.'16, Columbia Univ.; Y. M. C. A., 420 Lexington Ave., New York, N. Y.

Benton, George W., A.B.'84, A.M.'87, Wabash Col. Address: 88 Lexington Ave., New York, N. Y.

Bentz, Martin S., A.B.'97, A.M.'00, Albright Col.; Ph.D.'23, St. Francis Col.; Co. Supt. of Sch., 207 Julian St., Ebensburg, Pa., since 1911.

Berg, B. Conrad, B.A.'16, Univ. of Ill.; M.A.'24, Columbia Univ.; Supt. of Sch., Newton, Iowa, since 1922.

Berg, Selmer H., B.A.'17, St. Olaf Col.; M.A.'24, Univ. of Minn.; Supt. of Sch., Stoughton, Wis., since 1924.

Berger, Harry S., B.S.'21, State Tchrs. Col., Kirksville, Mo.; M.A.'29, Univ. of Mo.; Supt. of Sch., Deadwood, S. Dak., since 1928.

Bergerson, Carl I., B.S.'18, Hiram Col.; M.A.'27, Columbia Univ.; Supt. of Sch., Albion, N. Y., since 1925.

Bergquist, E. B., A.B.'02, Gustavus Adolphus Col.; M.A.'29, Univ. of Minn.; Supt. of Sch., Rapid City, S. Dak., since 1929.

Berrioz, Eliseo, Supvr. of Sch., Coamo, P. R.

Berry, Frank A., A.B.'07, Wesleyan Univ., Middletown, Conn.; Supt. of Sch., Bethel, Conn., since 1914.

Best, Bessie Kidd, Elem. Cert. '22, Northern Ariz. State Tcrs. Col., Flagstaff, Ariz.; Co. Supt. of Sch., Court House, Flagstaff, Ariz., since 1929.

Best, E. J., A.B.'02, A.M.'07, Union Col.; Supt. of Sch., Monson, Mass., since 1924.

Bettcher, Elizabeth E., Ph.B.'21, Univ. of Chicago; Dir., Elem. Student Teaching, Col. of Educ., Butler Univ., Indianapolis, Ind., since 1924.

Betts, Emmett A., B.S.'25, Des Moines Univ.; M.A.'28, State Univ. of Iowa; Research Asst., State Univ. of Iowa, Iowa City, Iowa, since 1929.

Betts, George H., Dir. of Research, Northwestern Univ., Evanston, Ill.

Beveridge, John H., B.Pd.'97, Ohio Univ.; M.A.'15, Columbia Univ.; M.A.'15, D.Pd. '17, Ohio Univ.; Pres., Dept. of Superintendence, 1922-23; Supt. of Sch., 601 City Hall, Omaha, Nebr., since 1917.

Bickett, William J., Supt. of Sch., 9 S. Stockton, Trenton, N. J., since 1920.

Bickford, Charles W., A.B.'87, Dartmouth Col.; Supt. of Sch., Lewiston, Maine, since 1916.

Biehl, James C., Asst. Supt. of Sch., Court House, Frederick, Md.

Biernacki, Stanley R., Board of Educ., Hamtramck, Mich.

Biester, Fred L., A.B.'14, North Central Col.; Prin., Glenbard H. S., Glen Ellyn, Ill., since 1918.

Bigelow, Edwin Lawrence, A.B.'13, Middlebury Col.; A.M.'26, Columbia Univ.; Dist. Supt. of Sch., Manchester Center, Vt., since 1926.

Bilderback, Willis E., Supvg. Prin. of Sch., 104 Atlantic St., Keyport, N. J.

Billinghurst, Benson Dillon, B.S.'97, Ohio Wesleyan Univ.; LL.B.'08, Univ. of Wash.; LL.D.'24, Univ. of Nevada; Supt. of Sch., Reno, Nevada, since 1908.

Billman, Dale C., M.A.'27, Univ. of Wis.; Supt. of Sch., Sullivan, Ind., since 1928.

Bimson, Oliver H., A.B.'14, Nebr. Wesleyan Univ.; A.M.'25, Univ. of Nebr.; Asst. Supt. of Sch., Lincoln, Nebr., since 1927.

Binford, Jesse H., A.B.'96, Univ. of Richmond; A.M.'15, Univ. of Wis.; Asst. Supt. of Sch., Richmond, Va., since 1916.

Bingham, Milton T., Supt. of Sch., 21 45th St., Sea Isle City, N. J.

Bingman, C. W., M.Pd.'11, Ohio Univ.; M.A.'26, Univ. of Texas; Pres., South Park Jr. Col., Beaumont, Texas, since 1923.

Birchard, C. C., 221 Columbus Ave., Boston, Mass.

Birckhead, Edward Francis, B.A.'05, Col. of William and Mary; M.A.'12, Columbia Univ.; Ed.M.'23, Harvard Univ.; Supt. of Sch., Winchester, Ky., since 1923.

Bird, V. A., Dir. of Educ., Mooseheart Sch., Mooseheart, Ill.

Birdwell, A. W., A.M.'16, George Peabody Col. for Tchrs.; Pres., Stephen F. Austin State Tchrs. Col., Nacogdoches, Texas, since 1922.

Birge, Edward B., A.B.'91, Brown Univ.; Mus.B.'04, Yale Univ.; Prof. of Music, Ind. Univ., 828 E. Third St., Bloomington, Ind., since 1921.

Bisbee, Harlan M., Dept. of Educ., Univ. of N. H., Durham, N. H.

Bishop, Charles C., A.B.'06, M.A.'19, Univ. of Wis.; Supt. of Sch., Oshkosh, Wis., since 1921.

Bishop, Fred G., Diploma '05, State Normal Sch., Oshkosh, Wis.; A.B.'15, Univ. of Wis.; Supt. of Sch., Two Rivers, Wis., since 1920.

Bishop, Martha Violet, Dist. Supt. of Sch., 7208 Bennett Ave., Chicago, Ill., since 1917.

Bishop, Merrill, B.A.'04, Amherst Col.; M. A.'28, Univ. of Texas; Asst. Dir. of Educ., Bd. of Educ., San Antonio, Texas.

Bishop, Mrs. Rose, Diploma '26, Western State Col.; Co. Supt. of Sch., Court House, Grand Junction, Colo., since 1924.

Bittikofer, F. G., B.Ph.'13, Heidelberg Col.; M.A.'29, Ohio State Univ.; Supt. of Sch., 310 E. Fifth St., Marysville, Ohio, since 1924.

Bixby, Herbert D., Dir., Utica Country Day Sch., New Hartford, N. Y.

Bixler, Mrs. Lena M., B.S.'15, Kansas State Tchrs. Col.; M.A.'27, Temple Univ.; Instr., Primary Methods, Temple Univ., Philadelphia, Pa., since 1924.

Black, Ernest H., B.A.'19, Univ. of Okla.; M.A.'29, Tchrs. Col., Columbia Univ.; Supt. of Sch., 306 W. Tenth St., Bristow, Okla., since 1926.

Black, Frank M., 604 Great Southern Bldg., Houston, Texas.

Black, H. B., M.A.'24, Univ. of Ill.; Supt. of Sch., Mattoon, Ill., since 1921.

Black, Lester, B.S.'14, Denison Univ.; A. M.'26, Columbia Univ.; Co. Supt. of Sch., Court House, Newark, Ohio, since 1923.

Black, Walter Ivan, Diploma '17, Nebr. State Tchrs. Col., Wayne, Nebr.; LL.B. '25, Univ. of Nebr.; Secy., Nebr. H. S. Athletic Assn., Lincoln Hotel, Lincoln, Nebr., since 1927.

Blackhurst, Stephen, M.A.'26, Univ. of Mo.; Supt. of Sch., 911 Kingshighway, St. Charles, Mo., since 1926.

Blackman, Albert Morris, B.A.'25, Univ. of Texas; Chief Supvr. of H. S., State Dept. of Pub. Instr., State Capitol Bldg., Austin, Texas, since 1927.

Blackwell, John Chapman, B.S.'16, George Peabody Col. for Tchrs.; Supt., T. C. I. Sch., Birmingham, Ala., since 1917.

Blair, C. M., Haskell Inst., Lawrence, Kansas.

Blair, Francis Grant, B.S., Swarthmore Col.; LL.D.'12, Colgate Univ.; LL.D.'14, Ill. Wesleyan Univ.; Pres., Natl. Educ. Assn. 1926-27; State Supt. of Pub. Instr., Centennial Bldg., Springfield, Ill., since 1906.

Blair, Herbert, B.S.'99, Northwestern Univ.; A.M.'16, Columbia Univ.; Prof. of Sch. Admin., Boston Univ., Boston, Mass., since 1924. Address: 20 Birch Hill Rd., Newtonville, Mass.

Blair, Parr Dalton, M.E.'99, State Normal Sch., Clarion, Pa.; A.B.'05, A.M.'08, Grove City Col.; Co. Supt. of Sch., 580 Walnut Park, Meadville, Pa., since 1911.

Blake, Percy H., A.B.'05, Bates Col.; A.M. '28, Univ. of Vt.; Supt. of Sch., Chester, Vt., since 1908.

Blanchar, Ora A., 560 Astor St., Milwaukee, Wis.

Blankenship, William C., Supt. of Sch., Big Spring, Texas.

Blanton, Annie Webb, Litt.B.'99, M.A.'23, Univ. of Texas; Ph.D.'27, Cornell Univ.; Assoc. Prof. of Educ. Admin., Univ. of Texas, Austin, Texas, since 1923.

Blee, Robert H., B.S.'07, Occidental Col.; Dist. Supt. of Sch., Puente, Calif., since 1926.

Blodgett, Frank D., A.B.'93, A.M.'96, LL.D. '18, Amherst Col.; Pres., Adelphi Col., Garden City, N. Y., since 1915.

Blom, Edward Charles, A.B.'11, Southeast Mo. State Tchrs. Col., Cape Girardeau, Mo.; B.S. in Ed.'15, A.M.'17, Univ. of Mo.; Ph.D.'30, Columbia Univ.; Dir. of Research, Bd. of Educ., Louisville, Ky., since 1929.

Blom, Victor H., B.S.'29, Univ. of Buffalo; Dist. Supt. of Sch., Attica, N. Y., since 1926.

Bloom, Ernest D., B.A.'15, I. S. T. C.; Dist. Supt. of Sch., Kemmerer, Wyo., since 1927.

Blunt, Katharine, A.B.'98, Vassar Col.; Ph. D.'07, Univ. of Chicago; Pres., Conn. Col. for Women, New London, Conn., since 1929.

Bock, Thomas Andrew, A.B.'10, Ursinus Col.; A.M.'28, Univ. of Pa.; Dean of Educ., State Tchrs. Col., Kutztown, Pa., since 1930.

Bocock, Clarence E., A.B.'99, Univ. of Ill.; Pres., State Normal Sch., Admin. Bldg., Albion, Idaho, since 1920.

Bode, William, A.B.'98, Haverford Col.; A.B.'98, A.M.'99, Penn Col.; B.D.'01, Univ. of Chicago; Diploma '02, Calvin Col.; S.T.D.'14, Temple Univ.; Pres., Grundy Col., Grundy Center, Iowa, since 1916.

Bogan, L. E., A.B.'24, Northeastern Tchrs. Col.; Supt. of Sch., Okay, Okla., since 1920.

Bogan, William J., Ph.B.'09, Univ. of Chicago; Supt. of Sch., 460 S. State St., Chicago, Ill., since 1928.

Bogardus, Glen F., B.S.'16, St. Lawrence; Supt. of Sch., Canastota, N. Y., since 1925.

Boggan, T. K., B.Ph.'03, LL.B.'13, Univ. of Miss.; M A.'24, George Peabody Col. for Tchrs.; Supt. of Sch., Picayune, Miss., since 1926.

Boggs, Robert M., Supt. of Sch., 190 Center Ave., Emsworth, Pittsburgh, Pa.

Bole, Lyman W., B.S.'19, Cornell Univ.; Dist. Supt. of Sch., Bradford, Vt., since 1927.

Bole, Rita L., A.B.'20, Middlebury Col.; Prin., State Normal Sch., Lyndon Center, Vt., since 1927.

Bolin, Clarence G., A.B.'25, Hendrix Col.; Co. Supt. of Sch., Murfreesboro, Ark., since 1925.

Bonar, Hugh S., B.Accts.'16, B.A.'18, Mt. Morris Col.; M.A.'24, Univ. of Chicago; Supt. of Sch., Manitowoc, Wis., since 1927.

Bonar, John Stanley, Diploma '13, State Normal Sch., West Liberty, W. Va.; B. S. in Ed.'26, Ohio Univ.; Pres., State Normal Sch., West Liberty, W. Va., since 1926.

Bond, George A., A.B.'99, Univ. of Calif.; Supt. of Sch., Santa Paula, Calif., since 1924.

Bond, Norman James, B.S.'11, Harvard Col.; A.M.'14, Harvard Univ.; Supt. of Sch., Georgetown, Del., since 1929.

Bond, W. F., A.B.'02, Peabody Col.; State Supt. of Educ., Jackson, Miss., since 1916.

Bonner, Joseph M., Court House, Pulaski, N. Y.

Bonnett, Sister Jeanne Marie, A.B.'17, A. M.'19, Univ. of Minn.; Pd.D.'25, Univ. of Louvain; Prof. of Educ., College of St. Catherine, St. Paul, Minn., since 1919.

Bontrager, O. R., Supt. of Sch., Lone Tree, Iowa.

Booker, W. R., A.B.'16, A.M.'26, Ind. Univ.; Supt. of Sch., 724 Peck, Muskegon Hgts., Mich., since 1928.

Boone, D. J., B.S.'98, Mt. Union Col.; Supt. of Sch., H. S., Lorain, Ohio, since 1914.

Boone, Ilsley, B.Ph.'04, Brown Univ.; S.T. M.'09, Newton Theol. Inst.; Board of Educ., Oakland, N. J.

Boothby, Arthur Z., Pd.B.'00, N. Y. State Col. for Tchrs.; B.S.'16, A.M.'20, Tchrs. Col., Columbia Univ.; Supt. of Sch., 60 Delancey Ave., Mamaroneck, N. Y., since 1917.

Borden, Walter W., B.S.'12, Ohio State Univ.; A.M.'25, Columbia Univ.; Supt. of Sch., Admin. Bldg., South Bend, Ind., since 1919.

Boren, Howard G., B.S., Grove City Col.; M.A.'29, Ohio State Univ.; Supt. of Sch., Hubbard, Ohio, since 1926.

Borgeson, F. C., Ph.D.'27, Tchrs. Col., Columbia Univ.; Assoc. Prof. of Educ., New York Univ., New York, N. Y.

Borst, Guernsey J., A.B.'03, Cornell Univ.; Pd.M.'09, Pd.D.'11, Ph.D.'12, New York Univ.; A.M.'21, Columbia Univ.; Prof. of Educ., Skidmore Col., Saratoga Springs, N. Y., since 1921 and Prof. of Educ., Summer Sessions, Rutgers Univ., New Brunswick, N. J., since 1927.

Bortner, Homer, M.A.'25, Univ. of Pa.; Supt. of Sch., Millville, N. J., since 1928.

Bos, Bert P., Diploma '24, State Normal Sch., Upper Montclair, N. J.; B.S. in Ed. '29, New York Univ.; Supvg. Prin. of Sch., Borough of Wanaque, N. J.

Bosley, L. C., A.B.'91, LL.B.'98, Centre Col.; Supt. of Sch., 219 S. Fourth St., Danville, Ky., since 1918.

Bosshart, John H., B.A.'02, Cornell Univ.; Supt. of Sch., South Orange and Maplewood, N. J., since 1927. Address: South Orange, N. J.

Boswell, G. C., B.A.'26, East Texas State Tchrs. Col., Commerce, Texas; Supt. of Sch., H. S. Bldg., McLean, Texas, since 1930.

Bouelle, Frank A., A.B.'12, Univ. of Southern Calif.; Supt. of Sch., 707 Chamber of Commerce Bldg., Los Angeles, Calif., since 1929.

Boughner, Floyd, Supt. of Sch., Marine City, Mich.

Bouvé, Marjorie, The Bouvé Sch., Inc., 725 Boylston St., Boston, Mass.

Bow, Warren Edward, B.S.'14, Univ. of Ill.; M.A.'20, Univ. of Mich.; Asst. Supt. of Sch., 1354 Broadway, Detroit, Mich., since 1930.

Bowden, A. O., A.B.'08, A.M.'10, Univ. of Ky.; A.M.'12, Harvard Univ.; Ph. D.'28, Columbia Univ.; Pres., State Tchrs. Col., Silver City, N. Mex., since 1922.

Bowden, Grover C., P. O. Box 1863, Atlanta, Ga.

Bowdle, C. P., A.B.'21, Ohio Wesleyan Univ.; A.M.'25, Univ. of Akron; Prin., H. S., East Palestine, Ohio, since 1929.

Bowen, Ray L., Ph.B.'17, Univ. of Chicago; Supt. of Sch., St. Louis, Mich., since 1924.

Bower, John F., Prin., H. S., McKeesport, Pa.

Bower, Roland, A.B.'04, Univ. of Ga.; Co. Supt. of Sch., Bainbridge, Ga., since 1921.

Bowers, Roy B., M.A.'11, Carson and Newman Col.; Supt. of Sch., Bristol, Va., since 1919.

Bowlby, Roswell S., B.S.'13, New York Univ.; Supt. of Sch., Dover, N. J., since 1920.

Bowlus, Edgar S., A.B.'11, St. John's Col.; A.B.'12, Univ. of Md.; A.M.'16, St. John's Col.; Supt. of Sch., Brookhaven, Miss., since 1922.

Bowman, Ernest Lavern, B.Sc.'15, Pa. State Col.; A.M.'22, Tchrs. Col., Columbia Univ.; State Dir. of Voc. Educ., 130 Washington St., Hartford, Conn., since 1929.

Bowman, George A., A.B.'17, Western Reserve Univ.; Supt. of Sch., Marion, Ohio, since 1929.

Bowman, Grover C., B.A.'06, Williams; M.A.'12, Yale Univ.; Supt. of Sch., City Hall, North Adams, Mass., since 1922.

Bowton, R. C., A.B.'11, Ind. Univ.; M.A. '15, Univ. of Wis.; Supt. of Sch., Alexandria, Va., since 1923.

Bowyer, Vernon, S.B.'21, A.M.'23, Univ. of Chicago. Address: 1070 W. Jackson Blvd., Chicago, Ill.

Boyce, Ella Ruth, Diploma '98, Pittsburgh and Allegheny Kdgn. Col; Dir. of Kdgns., Admin. Bldg., Forbes St. and Bellefield Ave., Pittsburgh, Pa., since 1912.

Boyd, Anna B., Ph.B.'14, Univ. of Chicago; Prin., Elem. Sch., 5330 Pershing Ave., St. Louis, Mo., since 1914.

Boyd, Sarah L., B.A.'20, Harris Tchrs. Col.; Prin., Elem. Sch., 5330 Pershing Ave., St. Louis, Mo., since 1921.

Boyden, Arthur Clarke, A.M., L.H.D., Ed. D., Amherst Col.; Prin., State Normal Sch., Bridgewater, Mass., since 1906.

Boyden, Wallace C., A.B.'83, A.M.'86, Amherst Col.; Prin. Emeritus, Tchrs. Col. of Boston, Boston, Mass., since 1929. Address: 64 Oakwood Rd., Newtonville, Mass.

Boyer, Charles B., A.B.'26, Howard Univ.; A.M.'27, Rutgers Univ.; Supt. of Sch., Admin. Bldg., Atlantic City, N. J., since 1893.

Boyer, Clarence Edwin, 503 Monroe St., Boonton, N. J.

Boyer, John B., B.S.'08, A.M.'25, Bucknell Univ.; Asst. Co. Supt. of Sch., Herndon, Pa., since 1922.

Boyes, Walter F., M.A.'27, Knox Col.; Co. Supt. of Sch., Court House, Galesburg, Ill., since 1902.

Boyles, Melville P., A B.'13, W. Va. Univ.; Supt. of Sch., Coal Dist., Clarksburg, W. Va., since 1927.

Bozeman, Elsie I., Diploma '02, State Tchrs. Col., San Jose, Calif.; Co. Supt. of Sch., Court House, Hanford, Calif., since 1927.

Bracken, John L., A.M.'22, Univ. of Chicago; Supt. of Sch., Clayton, Mo., since 1923.

Bradley, Esther Frances, Girls Jr. H. S., St. Petersburg, Fla.

Bradner, J. W., B.S.'94, Tri-State Col.; A.B.'08, Ind. Univ.; A.M.'24, Tchrs. Col., Columbia Univ.; Supt. of Sch., Middlesboro, Ky., since 1922.

Bradshaw, Ruth E., Supt. of Sch., 606 W. Pine St., Fairbury, Ill., since 1928.

Brady, William A., A.M.'08, Brown Univ.; Supt. of Sch., Narragansett, R. I., since 1909.

Bragdon, Clifford S., B.A.'00, Bowdoin Col.; M.A.'18, Tchrs. Col., Columbia Univ.; Acting Supt. of Sch., Central Jr. H. S., New Rochelle, N. Y., since 1930.

Bragdon, Frederick E., B.A.'91, Wesleyan Univ., Middletown, Conn.; M.A.'05, Brown Univ.; Supt. of Sch., Sharon, Mass., since 1926.

Bragg, Mabel C., Asst. Prof. of Educ., Sch. of Educ., Boston Univ., Boston, Mass., since 1930.

Bragg, P. N., B.A.'15, Univ. of Ark.; M.A. '28, Columbia Univ.; Supt. of Sch., Texarkana, Ark., since 1925.

Braham, W. J., A.M.'13; Supt. of Sch., North Platte, Nebr., since 1922.

Brainerd, Mrs. Margaret S., A.B.'02, Wilson Col.; Asst. Supt. of Sch., Martins Ferry, Ohio, since 1924.

Brainerd, William H., A.B.'83, Grinnell Col. Address: 89 Franklin St., Boston, Mass.

Brake, Charles, A.B.'20, Kalamazoo Col.; A.M.'30, Univ. of Mich.; Supt. of Sch., Grosse Ile, Mich., since 1924.

Braman, W. J., B.S.'15, Columbia Univ.; Supt. of Sch., Northacres, Dansville, N. Y., since 1919.

Brame, Scott Miller, A.B.'02, La. State Univ.; Prin., Bolton H. S., Alexandria, La., since 1909.

Bramlette, James DeWitt, A.B.'19, Baylor Univ.; M.A.'24, Univ. of Texas; Supt. of Sch., Kingsville, Texas.

Brandenberger, W. S., M.A.'12, Univ. of Texas; Prin., James S. Hogg Jr. H. S., Merrill and Norhill Sts., Houston, Texas, since 1926.

Brandon, C. N., Supt. of Sch., Columbus, Miss.

Brandt, Rose K., A.B.'14, Univ. of Wis.; M.A.'23, Columbia Univ.; Supvr., Elem. Educ. in Indian Serv., Dept. of the Interior, Washington, D. C.

Branigan, John, B.Sc.'15, Univ. of Nebr.; A.M.'26, Stanford Univ.; Supt. of Sch., Needles, Calif., since 1927.

Brannan, B. J., Supt. of Sch., Sanderson, Texas.

Brannan, R. H., B.A.'22, North Texas State Tchrs. Col., Denton, Texas; M.A.'28, Southern Methodist Univ.; Supt. of Sch., 507 S. W. Third St., Mineral Wells, Texas, since 1928.

Brasure, R. E., Ph.B.'13, Ph.M.'30, Univ. of Wis.; Prin., H. S., Hartford, Wis., since 1926.

Braucher, Howard S., A.B.'03, Cornell Univ.; Secy., Natl. Recreation Assn., 315 Fourth Ave., New York, N. Y., since 1909.

Braughton, Garnett, Diploma '20, State Normal Sch., Conway, Ark.; Co. Supt. of Sch., Hot Springs, Ark., since 1919.

Breckenridge, J. L., A.B.'08, Oberlin Col.; Supt. of Sch., Hood River, Oregon, since 1927.

Breckinridge, Elizabeth G., Prin., Louisville Normal Sch., Louisville, Ky

Breckner, Elmer L., A.B. and B.S. in Ed.'13, Univ. of Mo.; Supt. of Sch., H. S. Bldg., Olympia, Wash., since 1920.

Breedlove, Charles B., B.S.'29, Sul Ross State Tchrs. Col., Alpine, Texas; Supt. of Sch., Haskell, Texas, since 1929.

Breitwieser, Joseph Valentine, A.B.'07, A. M.'08, Ind. Univ.; Ph.D.'11, Columbia Univ.; Dean, Sch. of Educ. and Dir., Graduate Division, Univ. of N. Dak., Grand Forks, N. Dak., since 1928.

Brendlinger, Margaret R., A.B.'95, Vassar Col.; Prin., Hillside Sch., Prospect Hill, Norwalk, Conn., since 1908.

Bres, Joseph Hughes, A.B.'06, Tulane Univ.; Parish Supt. of Pub. Educ., Port Allen, La., since 1908.

Breuer, Leo W., Commr. of Educ., Juneau, Alaska, since 1929.

Brewington, Ann, Asst. Prof., Sch. of Commerce and Admin., Univ. of Chicago, Chicago, Ill.

Brewster, R. E., B.S.'26, North Texas State Tchrs. Col., Denton, Texas; Supt. of Sch., Port Neches, Texas.

Bridges, D. W., Supt. of Sch., 52 Woodland, Fort Thomas, Ky.

Bridges, J. G., B.S.'12, Univ. of Miss.; M.A.'28, George Peabody Col. for Tchrs.; Supt. of Sch., Newton, Miss., since 1926.

Briggs, Eugene S., B.S.'12, Central Col., Fayette, Mo.; B.S. in Ed.'17, A.M.'21, Univ. of Mo.; Pres., Southeastern State Tchrs. Col., Durant, Okla., since 1928.

Briggs, Howard L., B.S.'17, Carnegie Inst. of Tech.; M.A.'23, Univ. of Mich.; Dir., Voc. and Practical Arts Educ., Bd. of Educ., Cleveland, Ohio, since 1922.

Bright, Ira J., B.S.'16, State Tchrs. Col., Emporia, Kansas; M.A.'18, Tchrs. Col., Columbia Univ.; Supt. of Sch., Times Bldg., Leavenworth, Kansas, since 1919.

Briner, Francis William, B.S. in Ed.'23, State Tchrs. Col., Emporia, Kansas; Supt. of Sch., Midian, Kansas, since 1926.

Brink, Loren Roy, Asst. Supt. of Sch., Hamtramck, Mich.

Brinkley, Edward S., Asst. Supt. of Sch., 7814 N. Shore Rd., Norfolk, Va.

Brinser, Ira S., A.B.'20, Franklin and Marshall Col.; Ed.M.'21, Harvard Univ.; Supt. of Sch., Newark, Del., since 1926.

Brister, Robert H., B.A.'17, Baylor Univ.; M.A.'28, Univ. of Texas; Supt. of Sch., Taylor, Texas, since 1922.

Bristol, Everett R., B.S.'24, Mich. State Col.; Supt. of Sch., Milford, Mich., since 1929.

Bristow, William H., B.S.'20, Mo. State Tchrs. Col.; A.M.'22, Tchrs. Col., Columbia Univ.; Asst. Dir. of Sec. Educ., State Dept. of Pub. Instr., Harrisburg, Pa.

Britton, O. C., 921 Northwest Blvd., Winston-Salem, N. C.

Broady, Knute Oscar, B.S.'20, Washburn Col.; M.A.'27, Univ. of Chicago; Ph.D.'30, Columbia Univ.; Assoc. Prof. of Sch. Admin., Tchrs. Col., Univ. of Nebr., Lincoln, Nebr., since 1928.

Brock, George William, A.B.'00, Univ. of Ala.; LL.D.'17, Howard Col.; LL.D.'23, Univ. of Ala.; Pres., State Tchrs. Col., Livingston, Ala.

Brock, Mrs. O. H., P. O. Box 1064, Gallup, N. Mex.

Brodhead, John C., Asst. Supt. of Sch., Boston, Mass., since 1918. Address: 38 Montclair Ave., Roslindale, Mass.

Brodshaug, Melvin, B.S.'23, N. Dak. State Col.; M.A.'27, Univ. of Chicago. Address: 416 W. 122nd St., New York, N. Y.

Broening, Angela M., A.B.'19, Goucher Col.; A.M.'23, Ph.D.'28, Johns Hopkins Univ.; Instr. in Educ., Johns Hopkins Univ., Baltimore, Md., since 1926 and Asst. Dir., Bureau of Educ. Research, Pub. Sch., Carrollton and Lafayette Aves., Baltimore, Md., since 1930.

Brogan, Whit, B.S.'24, Kansas State Tchrs. Col., Emporia, Kansas; M.A.'27, Ph.D.'30, Tchrs. Col., Columbia Univ.; Prin., Sch. Dist. No. 6, Scarsdale, N. Y., since 1929.

Brogden, L. C., Ph.B.'95, Univ. of N. C.; M.A.'12, Columbia Univ.; Dir., Div. of Elem. Instr., State Dept. of Pub. Instr., Raleigh, N. C., since 1909.

Brooker, John W., B.S.'22, Georgetown Col.; M.A.'29, Univ. of Mich.; Dir., Div. of Sch. Bldgs. and Grounds, State Dept. of Educ., Frankfort, Ky., since 1930.

Brooks, B. P., A.B.'06, Union Univ.; Supt. of Sch., 214 Pecan St., Belzoni, Miss., since 1919.

Brooks, Ercell W., A.B.'30, West Texas State Tchrs. Col., Canyon, Texas; Co. Supt. of Sch., Vernon, Texas, since 1927.

Brooks, George F., B.L.'02, Hobart Col.; Ph.B.'08, Kansas Wesleyan Univ.; A.M. '25, Univ. of Wis.; Supt. of Sch., H. S. Bldg., Merrill, Wis., since 1927.

Brooks, John D., A.B.'01, Dickinson Col.; A. M.'06, Ph.D.'25, Univ. of Pa.; Prof. of Educ., Wilson Col., Chambersburg, Pa., since 1923.

Brooks, Myron W., Prin., George Washington Elem. and Jr. H. S., Ridgewood, N. J.

Brooks, Roland E., Supt. of Sch., Albany, Ga.

Brooks, T. Latimer, B.A.'06, Dickson Col.; M.A.'15, Columbia Univ.; Supt. of Sch., Somerville, N. J., since 1921.

Brooks, Thomas Dudley, A.B.'03, Baylor Univ.; M.A.'20, Ph.D.'21, Univ. of Chicago; Prof. of Sch. Admin. and Chairman, Sch. of Educ., Baylor Univ., Waco, Texas, since 1921.

Brooks, Wiley G., B.E.'10, State Tchrs. Col., Peru, Nebr.; A.B.'10, York Col.; A.M.'15, Tchrs. Col., Columbia Univ.; Supt. of Sch., Burlington, Iowa, since 1925.

Broome, Edwin C., Ph.B.'97, A.M.'98, Brown Univ.; Ph.D.'02, Columbia Univ.; LL.B. '07, St. Lawrence Univ.; LL.D.'25, Ursinus Col.; Ed. D.'27, Brown Univ.; Supt. of Sch., 19th St. above Chestnut, Philadelphia, Pa., since 1921.

Brophy, Byron J., A.B.'22, Tri-State Col. Address: 822 Arch St., Ann Arbor, Mich.

Brothers, C. A., A.B.'11, Lake Forest Col.; A.M.'24, Tchrs. Col., Columbia Univ.; Supt. of Sch., Prin., H. S., Dwight, Ill.

Brougher, John F., A.B.'26, Columbia Univ.; M.A.'29, Tchrs. Col., Columbia Univ.; Supvr., Sec. Educ., State Dept. of Pub. Instr., Harrisburg, Pa., since 1929.

Brown, B. Frank, Supt. of Sch., Gulfport, Miss.

Brown, Clark W., B.A.'04, S. Dak.; Supt. of Sch., Clinton, Iowa, since 1924.

Brown, E. Barton, B.S.'27, Univ. of Okla.; Supt. of Sch., Hominy, Okla., since 1929.

Brown, Edwin Putnam, Prin., Wayland Academy, Beaver Dam, Wis.

Brown, Emmett, B.A.'96, Univ. of Nashville; Supt. of Sch., Cleburne, Texas, since 1913.

Brown, Ernest E., A.B.'19, A.M.'25, Univ. of Okla.; Pres., Southwestern State Tchrs. Col., Weatherford, Okla., since 1927.

Brown, Francis James, A.B.'18, State Univ. of Iowa; M.A.'23, Tchrs. Col., Columbia Univ.; Asst. Prof. of Educ., Assoc. Dir. of Extension and Summer Session, Univ. of Rochester, Rochester, N. Y., since 1923.

Brown, Frederic N., A.B.'99, Harvard Univ.; Supvg. Prin. of Sch., Verona, N. J., since 1903.

Brown, George Earl, Diploma '06, State Normal Sch., Emporia, Kansas; A.B.'13, State Tchrs. Col., Greeley, Colo.; A.M.'19, Univ. of Denver; A.M.'26, Columbia Univ.; Dist. Supt. of Sch., Bisbee, Ariz., since 1929.

Brown, Glen David, A.B.'16, State Tchrs. Col., Terre Haute, Ind.; Business Dir., Pub. Schools, Central H. S. Bldg., Muncie, Ind., since 1925.

Brown, Harold S., 381 Fourth Ave., New York, N. Y.

Brown, Harry Alvin, A.B.'03, Bates Col.; A.B.'07, A.M.'23, Univ. of Colo.; Ed. D. '25, Bates Col.; Ed. D.'25, Miami Univ.; Pres., Ill. State Normal Univ., 201 N. School St., Normal, Ill., since 1930.

Brown, Howard E., A.B.'10, Syracuse Univ.; A.M.'23, Columbia Univ.; Supt. of Sch., 517 Ohio St., Medina, N. Y., since 1918.

Brown, J. C., B.S.'01, M.A.'13, Columbia Univ.; Supt. of Sch., Pelham, N. Y., since 1929.

Brown, Mrs. Kate B., B.S.'01, La Grange Col.; Co. Supt. of Sch., McDonough, Ga., since 1924.

Brown, M. Ethel, Ph.B.'20, M.A.'25, Univ. of Chicago; Supvr. of Elem. Grades, 1079 Wendell Ave., Schenectady, N. Y., since 1923.

Brown, Paul V., A.B.'20, Muskingum Col.; A.M.'30, Univ. of Chicago; Supt. of Sch., Church St., Barnesville, Ohio, since 1924.

Brown, R. H., B.S. and M.A., Columbia Univ.; Supt. of Sch., St. Cloud, Minn., since 1925.

Brown, Raymond N., B.S.'09, Amherst Col.; Supt. of Sch., Thomaston, Conn., since 1921.

Brown, Samuel Mortimer, B.A.'26, Univ. of Texas; Supt. of Sch., Sugar Land, Texas, since 1930.

Brown, Stella E., B.S.'18, Tchrs. Col., Columbia Univ.; Supvr., Normal Elem. Dept., State Normal Sch., Towson, Md., since 1924. Address: 4213 Belmar Ave., Baltimore, Md.

Brown, T. O., Parish Supt. of Sch., Monroe, La.

Brownell, Samuel M., A.B.'21, Univ. of Nebr.; A.M.'24, Ph.D.'26, Yale Univ.; Supt. of Sch., Grosse Pointe, Mich., since 1927.

Browning, Leo Hagood, A.B.'04, Univ. of S. C.; Pres., Middle Ga. Agrl. and Mech. Jr. Col., Cochran, Ga., since 1928.

Brubacher, A. R., B.A.'97, Ph.D.'02, Yale Univ.; Pres., N. Y. State Col. for Tchrs., Albany, N. Y., since 1915.

Bruce, Frank, A.B.'05, Wisconsin; A.M.'08, Marquette Univ.; Publisher, American School Board Journal, 407 E. Michigan St., Milwaukee, Wis.

Bruce, William C., A.B.'01, Marquette Col.; A.M.'10, Marquette Univ.; Editor, American School Board Journal, 129 E. Michigan St., Milwaukee, Wis.

Brueckner, Leo John, M.A.'15, Ph.D.'19, State Univ. of Iowa; Prof. of Elem. Educ., Univ. of Minn., Minneapolis, Minn., since 1922.

Brugler, V. C., Supvg. Prin. of Sch., 404 Church St., Hackettstown, N. J., since 1922.

Bruner, Charles, A.B.'10, A.M.'13, Ind. Univ.; Supt. of Sch., Kewanee, Ill., since 1920.

Bruner, Herbert Bascom, A.B.'13, Central; A.M.'15, Univ. of Mo.; Ph.D.'25, Columbia Univ.; Prof. of Educ., Tchrs. Col., Columbia Univ., New York, N. Y., since 1929.

Brunstetter, M. R., A.B.'22, Dickinson Col.; M.A.'28, Univ. of Pa. Address: 509 W. 121st St., New York, N. Y.

Brunswick, Frederick Henry, B.S.'23. Tchrs. Col., Columbia Univ.; Supvg. Prin. of Sch., North Haledon, N. J., since 1929. Address: R. F. D. No. 3, Paterson, N. J.

Brust, Huldah, Supvr. of Primary Grades, Board of Educ., Rockville, Md., since 1924.

Bryan, James E., A.B.'90, Johns Hopkins Univ.; Ph.D.'08, Univ. of Pa.; Supt. of Sch., Camden, N. J., since 1899.

Bryan, John Edward, A.B.'15, Hampden-Sidney Col.; Supt. of Sch., Bessemer, Ala., since 1927.

Bryan, William L., Pres., Ind. Univ., Bloomington, Ind.

Bryant, David C., M.A.'12, Ohio State Univ.; Supt. of Sch., Jr. H. S., Bowling Green, Ohio, since 1918.

Bryant, S. J., M.S.'28, Univ. of Okla.; Supt. of Sch., Hobart, Okla., since 1925.

Bryne, May E., B.S. in Ed. '22, Univ. of Minn.; Dir. of Special Educ., 305 Court House, Minneapolis, Minn., since 1921.

Bubeck, Allan F., A.M.'24, Tchrs. Col., Columbia Univ.; Dept. of Educ., State Tchrs. Col., Kutztown, Pa., since 1928.

Buchanan, Elizabeth, Dist. Supt. of Sch., Kansas City, Mo., since 1912.

Buck, Benjamin F., A.B.'93, Univ. of Mich.; Asst. Supt. of Sch., 460 S. State St., Chicago, Ill., since 1928.

Buck, Frank P., A.B.'04, Univ. of Mich.; Supt. of Sch., St. Johns, Mich., since 1910.

Buck, George L., Ph.B.'01, Colgate Univ. Address: 39 Division St., Newark, N. J.

Buck, J. P., A.B.'16, Baylor Univ.; B.S.A.'19, Agrl. and Mech. Col.; M.S.'25, Cornell; Supt. of Sch., Sour Lake, Texas, since 1927.

Buckingham, Burdette R., A.B.'99, A.M.'00, Wesleyan Univ., Middletown, Conn.; Ph.D. '13, Columbia Univ.; Lecturer, Graduate Sch. of Educ., Harvard Univ., Cambridge, Mass., since 1928.

Buckley, Frank M., A.B.'05, Holy Cross Col.; A.M.'06, Yale Univ.; Ed.M.'13, Harvard Univ.; Supt. of Sch., Derby, Conn., since 1928.

Buckley, Horace Mann, A.B.'08, Northwestern Univ.; M.A.'12, Columbia Univ.; Asst. Supt. of Sch., Engineers Bank Bldg., Cleveland, Ohio, since 1925.

Buckner, Chester A., A.B.'09, A.M.'11, State Univ. of Iowa; Ph.D.'18, Columbia Univ.; Prof. of Sec. Educ., Sch. of Educ., Univ. of Pittsburgh, Pittsburgh, Pa., since 1920.

BuDahn, L. A., M.A.'22, Columbia Univ.; Supt. of Sch., 219 W. High St., Fostoria, Ohio, since 1928.

Buehring, E. C., 536 S. Clark St., Chicago, Ill.

Buell, R. A., B.A.'01, Beloit Col.; M.A.'28, Univ. of Wis.; Supt. of Sch., H. S., Watertown, Wis., since 1924.

Buerk, H. A., A.B.'82, Ind. Univ.; A.B.'84, Harvard; Supt. of Sch., New Albany, Ind., since 1908.

Bufkin, William Ernest, Asst. Supt. of Sch., 641 Buena Vista Ave., Jackson, Miss.

Bugbee, Lloyd Harrison, B.S.'12, Dartmouth Col.; M.A.'29, Columbia Univ.; Supt. of Sch., 51 Seyms St., West Hartford, Conn., since 1922.

Buker, William H., A.B.'10, Bates Col.; M. A.'24, Columbia Univ.; Supt. of Sch., Rochester, N. H., since 1923.

Buker, Welthie B., 1530 Eastern Parkway, Schenectady, N. Y.

Bullock, Russell E., A.B.'12, Dickinson Col.; A.M.'23, Columbia Univ.; Supvg. Prin. of Sch., H. S., Scotch Plains, N. J., since 1924.

Bumgardner, Walter L., B.S.'18, Pa. State Col.; Prin., East Aurora H. S., East Aurora, N. Y., since 1927.

Bunce, Edgar F., M.A.'26, Tchrs. Col., Columbia Univ.; Vice-Pres. and Head, Dept. of Educ., Trenton State Tchrs. Col., Trenton, N. J., since 1930.

Burchard, Edward L., Ph.B.'91, Beloit Col.; Secy., Supt. of Sch. Advisory Council, 460 S. State St., Chicago, Ill., since 1928.

Burdge, Howard G., A.B.'00, Allegheny Col.; A.M.'20, Ph.D.'22, Columbia Univ. Address: Box 1133, Washington, D. C.

Burdick, Ernest H., Supt. of Sch., Middletown, N. Y., since 1922.

Burdick, Raymond C., A.B.'14, Alfred Univ.; M.A.'25, Columbia Univ.; Supt. of Sch., City Hall, Watertown, N. Y., since 1925.

Burdick, William, A.B.'93, Brown Univ.; M.D.'07, Univ. of Pa.; M.P.E.'24, Springfield Col.; State Dir. of Physical Educ., 7 E. Mulberry St., Baltimore, Md., since 1918.

Burdine, W. T., B.A.'24, Ark. State Tchrs. Col., Conway, Ark.; Co. Supt. of Sch., Jasper, Ark., since 1929.

Burgess, Thomas O., B.A.'22, St. Olaf Col.; M.S.'23, Univ. of Ill.; Ph.D.'26, State Univ. of Iowa; Head, Dept. of Psych. and Educ., Concordia Col., Moorhead, Minn., since 1926.

Burkard, William E., B.S. in Ed.'17, M.A. '25, Ph.D.'27, Univ. of Pa.; Prin., Tilden Jr. H. S., 66th and Elmwood, Philadelphia, Pa.

Burke, Harry A., M.A.'28, Stanford Univ.; Supt. of Sch., Gothenburg, Nebr., since 1920.

Burke, Jeremiah Edmund, B.A.'90, M.A.'93, D.L.'15, Colby Col.; LL.D.'22, Villa Nova Col.; LL.D.'25, Holy Cross Col.; Supt. of Sch., 15 Beacon St., Boston, Mass., since 1921.

Burke, Vincent P., St. Johns, Newfoundland.

Burneson, L. G., A.B.'21, Oberlin Col.; M. A.'29, Tchrs. Col., Columbia Univ.; Supt. of Sch., Dover Village, Ohio, since 1924. Address: Bay Village, Ohio.

Burnett, H. C., A.B., Univ. of Ky.; Co. and City Supt. of Sch., Nicholasville, Ky.

Burnett, John M., B.S.'11, A.M.'25, Univ. of Ala.; Supt. of Sch., Tuscaloosa, Ala., since 1919.

Burnham, Archer L., A.B.'16, Liberal Arts Col., Univ. of Nebr.; A.M.'27, Tchrs. Col., Univ. of Nebr.; Supt. of Sch., Beatrice, Nebr., since 1927.

Burns, A. Q., A.B. and Th.B.'15, William Jewell Col.; B.D.'16, Newton Theological Seminary; Th.D.'17, Southern Baptist Theological Seminary; Active Vice-Pres., Dodd Col., Shreveport, La., since 1930.

Burns, Harry B., M.D.'95, New York Univ.; Dir. of Hygiene, Sch. Admin. Bldg., Pittsburgh, Pa., since 1914.

Burns, James P., Acting Div. Supt., Bureau of Educ., Cagayan, Misamis, P. I.

Burns, L. W., Diploma '97, Concord State Normal Sch., Athens. W. Va.; A.B.'10, W. Va. Univ.; A.M.'21, Columbia Univ.; Supt. of Sch., Martinsburg, W. Va., since 1923.

Burns, Robert, B.S.'16, Tchrs. Col., Columbia Univ.; A.M.'19, Ph.D.'28, Columbia Univ.; Prin., Cliffside Park H. S., Grantwood, N. J., since 1918.

Buros, Francis C., B.S.'25, Univ. of Minn.; M.A.'29, Tchrs. Col., Columbia Univ.; Research Dir. and Purchasinig Agent, Pub. Sch., Municipal Bldg., White Plains, N. Y., since 1930.

Buros, Oscar K., B.S.'25, Univ. of Minn.; M.A.'28, Tchrs. Col., Columbia Univ.; Prin., Washington Sch., Millburn, N. J., since 1930.

Burr, Samuel Engle, Litt.B.'19, Rutgers Univ.; M.A.'25, Univ. of Wis.; A.M.'27, Tchrs. Col., Columbia Univ.; Supt. of Sch., Glendale, Ohio, since 1930.

Burrill, Elbert Fielding, A.B.'21, Univ. of Calif. Address: 849 S. Holt Ave., Palms, Los Angeles, Calif.

Burrill, Fred W., A.B.'97, Bates Col.: Supt. of Sch., Augusta, Maine, since 1922.

Burt, Richard F., M.A.'25, Univ. of Okla.; Supt. of Sch., Glenpool, Okla., since 1922.

Burton, H. C., B.S.'14, Univ. of Utah; Dist. Supt. of Sch., Kaysville, Utah, since 1908.

Burton, W. H., A.B.'15, Univ. of Oregon; A.M.'17, Tchrs. Col., Columbia Univ.; Ph. D.'24, Univ. of Chicago; Prof. of Educ., Sch. of Educ., Univ. of Chicago, Chicago, Ill., since 1926.

Bush, Ernest Forrest, B.S. in Ed.'10, Univ. of Mo.; A.B.'13, Washington Univ.; M.A. in Ed.'26, Univ. of Chicago; Supt. of Sch., Wellston, St. Louis, Mo., since 1904.

Bush, George C., A.B.'98, A.M.'99, Ind. Univ.; Supt. of Sch., South Pasadena, Calif., since 1907.

Bush, Maybell G., Diploma '00, State Normal Sch., Potsdam, N. Y.; Ph.M.'28, Univ. of Wis.; Supvr. of Elem. Sch., State Dept. of Pub. Instr., 522 N. Pinckney St., Madison, Wis., since 1916.

Bussey, E. D., B.S.'23, Agrl. and Mech. Col.; Supt. of Sch., Garland, Texas, since 1922.

Buster, N. E., A.B.'25, A.M.'29, Colo. State Tchrs. Col.; Prin., William James Jr. H. S., Fort Worth, Texas, since 1918.

Butler, Harriet L., B.S. in Ed.'23, Univ. of Buffalo; Deputy Supt. of Sch., 267 Elmwood Ave., Buffalo, N. Y., since 1919.

Butler, John H. Manning, A.M.'96, Pd.D.'24, Livingstone Col.; Div. Supt. of Sch., Tuguegarao, Cagayan, P. I., since 1927.

Butler, Leslie A., Ph.B.'13, Univ. of Chicago; M.A.'19, Columbia Univ.; M.Ed.'21, Mich. Normal Col.; LL.D.'27, Alma Col.; Supt. of Sch., City Hall, Grand Rapids, Mich.

Butler, Rock L., B.S.'23, Grove City Col.; Supvg. Prin. of Sch., 20 Meade St., Wellsboro, Pa., since 1914.

Butler, S. B., B.A.'13, Yale Univ.; M.A.'28, Tchrs. Col., Columbia Univ.; Dist. Supt. of Sch., Groton, Conn., since 1928.

Butler, S. R., Co. Supt. of Sch., Huntsville, Ala.

Butterfield, E. W., A.B.'97, Dartmouth Col.; LL.D.'21, Univ. of N. H.; Ed.D.'26, R. I. State Col.; LL.D.'30, Bates Col.; State Commr. of Educ., Hartford, Conn., since 1930.

Butterworth, James F., A.B.'90, A.M.'10, Harvard Univ.; Supt. of Sch., City Hall, Bradford, Pa., since 1918.

Butterworth, Julian E., A.B.'07, M.A.'10, Ph. D.'12, State Univ. of Iowa; Prof. of Rural Educ., Cornell Univ., Ithaca, N. Y., since 1919.

Button, F. C., A.M.'08, Bethany Col.; Pres. Emeritus, State Tchrs. Col., Morehead, Ky., since 1929. Address: 454 Rose Lane, Lexington, Ky.

Butts, Louis Andrew, B.S.'16, McKendree Col.; Prin., Jr. H. S., Belleville, Ill., since 1926.

Butz, Franklin J., Supvg. Prin. of Sch., Wallingford, Pa.

Bye, Morris, B.A.'18, Concordia Col.; Supt. of Sch., Lincoln Bldg., Thief River Falls, Minn., since 1926.

Byerly, C. C., A.B.'18, Manchester Col.; Supt. of Sch., 210 Sophia St., West Chicago, Ill., since 1923.

Byers, B. H., B.S. and B.A.'23, M.S.'29, Pa. State Col.; Supvg. Prin. of Sch., Elizabeth, Pa., since 1927.

Bynum, Charles Hudson, II, A.B.'27, Lincoln Univ.; A.M.'29, Univ. of Pa.; Dir., Dept. of Educ., Agrl. and Normal Univ., Langston, Okla., since 1930.

Bynum, L. D., B.S.'17, Univ. of Ala.; Supt. of Sch., Troy, Ala., since 1925.

Byrd, Rawls, A.B.'18, Col. of William and Mary; M.A.'25, Tchrs. Col., Columbia Univ.; Supt. of Sch., Williamsburg, Va., since 1928.

Byrd, V. A., B.S.'28, Southern Methodist Univ.; Supt. of Sch., Fort Stockton, Texas, since 1928.

Byrne, Christopher J., Supt. of Grade Schools 405 Moloney Bldg., Ottawa, Ill., since 1905.

Byrne, Lee, A.B., Univ. of Ill.; A.M., Univ. of Chicago; Ph.D., Univ. of Pa.; Head, Dept. of Urban Educ., Northern State Tchrs. Col., Aberdeen, S. Dak., since 1925.

Cain, H. L., Supt., The American School Foundation, 9a. San Luis Potosi No. 214, Mexico, D. F.

Caldwell, A. J., A.B.'23, A.M.'29, La. State Univ.; Supt., State Sch. for the Blind, Baton Rouge, La., since 1920.

Caldwell, Alma B., M.A.'12, Hanover, Col.; Genl. Supvr., Pub. Sch., Bd. of Educ., Cleveland, Ohio, since 1918.

Caldwell, D. E., Supt. of Sch., Point Place, Toledo, Ohio.

Caldwell, L. C., A.B.'25, Marshall Col.; M.A.'26, George Peabody Col. for Tchrs.; Co. Supt. of Sch., Catlettsburg, Ky., since 1925.

Caldwell, Otis W., B.S.'94, Franklin Col.; Ph.D.'98, Univ. of Chicago; LL.D.'18, Franklin Col.; Dir., Inst. of Sch. Experimentation and Prof. of Educ., Tchrs. Col., Columbia Univ., 433 W. 123rd St., New York, N. Y.

Calhoun, H. V., B.A., McKendree Col.; Supt. of Sch., Belleville, Ill.

Calhoun, J. B., B.S.'20, Vanderbilt Univ.; M.A.'29, George Peabody Col. for Tchrs.; Dir., Sch. Bldg. Construction, Pub. Sch., Nashville, Tenn., since 1931.

Calhoun, Jesse T., A.B.'96, Millsaps Col.; M.A.'25, Tchrs. Col., Columbia Univ.; Elem. Sch. Supvr., State Dept. of Educ., Jackson, Miss., since 1914.

Callahan, John, State Supt. of Sch., State Capitol, Madison, Wis., since 1921.

Cameron, E. T., M.Pd.'26, Mich. State Normal Col.; Exec. Secy., Mich. Educ. Assn., Mich. Educ. Bldg., Lansing, Mich., since 1921.

Cameron, Norman W., A.B.'95, A.M.'00, Washington Col.; Ph.D.'12, Univ. of Pa.; Pres., State Tchrs. Col., West Chester, Pa., since 1928.

Cammack, Ira I., A.B.'84, Earlham Col.; Supt. Emeritus, Pub. Sch., Kansas City. Mo. Address: 1153 S. Beverwil Drive, Los Angeles, Calif.

Cammack, James W., Jr., LL.B.'24, M.A.'29, Univ. of Ky.; Dir. of Research, State Dept. of Educ., State House, Frankfort, Ky., since 1930.

Camp, Frederick Stanley, B.S.'10, New York Univ.; Field Supvr. of Urban Educ., Hartford, Conn., since 1922.

Camp, Harold L., B.A.'14, Grinnell Col.; M.A.'17, Cornell Univ.; Ph.D.'21, State Univ. of Iowa; Prof. of Educ., State Tchrs. Col., Indiana, Pa., since 1930.

Campbell, Arthur, Supt. of Sch., 696 N. Main St., Franklin, Ind.

Campbell, Doak S., B.A.'11, Ouachita Col.; M.A.'28, George Peabody Col. for Tchrs.; Assoc. Dir., Surveys and Field Studies, George Peabody Col. for Tchrs., Nashville, Tenn., since 1929.

Campbell, Ernest W., A.B.'18, LL.B.'22, Univ. of Wash.; Supt. of Sch., Renton, Wash., since 1928.

Campbell, G. W., A.B.'25, Eastern Ky. State Tchrs. Col., Richmond, Ky.; Supt. of Sch., Corbin, Ky., since 1925.

Campbell, J. L., B.S.'15, State Tchrs. Col., Springfield, Mo.; A.M.'30, Univ. of Mo.; Supt. of Sch., H. S. Bldg., Carthage, Mo., since 1929.

Campbell, John H., Supt. of Sch., 130 Wyoming St., Carbondale, Pa.

Campbell, Raymond G., 501 W. 122nd St., New York, N. Y.

Campbell, W. M., Ph.B.'16, Parsons Col.; Supt. of Sch., Roseburg, Oregon, since 1927.

Campton, Charles E., B.A. in Ed.'13, Univ. of Minn.; M.A.'28, Tchrs. Col., Columbia Univ.; Supt. of Sch., Two Harbors, Minn., since 1915.

Canfield, Emma May, Supt. of Sch., Valley Falls, R. I.

Cannon, Arthur M., Ph.B.'98, DePauw Univ.; Dist. Supt. of Sch., Court House, Toledo, Oregon.

Cannon, O. B., A.B.'98, Newberry Col.; Supt. of Sch., Newberry, S. C., since 1917.

Canon, C. T., A.B.'17, Valparaiso Univ.; A.M.'29, Univ. of Ky.; Supt. of Sch., 179 E. Ninth St., Russellville, Ky., since 1920.

Cantrell, Pauline, Co. Supt. of Sch., Court House, Big Spring, Texas, since 1928.

Cantwell, J. W., A.B.'93, Baylor Univ.; A.B.'94, Yale Univ.; A.M.'02, LL.D.'20, Baylor Univ.; Supt. of Sch., Wichita Falls, Texas, since 1923.

Capen, Samuel Paul, A.B.'98, Tufts Col.; A.M.'00, Harvard Univ.; Ph.D.'02, Univ. of Pa.; LL.D.'20, Lafayette Col.; L.H.D. '24, Hobart Col.; Sc.D'27, George Washington Univ.; Chancellor, Univ. of Buffalo, Buffalo, N. Y., since 1922.

Capps, James A., Co. Supt. of Sch., Newton, N. C.

Caradine, Jane, 2601 Barbee St., Houston, Texas.

Carey, Joseph Caldwell, Supvg. Prin. of Sch., 910 Bedford Ave., Collingdale, Pa.

Carkin, Seth B., B.S.'24, Univ. of Rochester; Pres., Packard Commercial Sch., 253 Lexington Ave., New York, N. Y., since 1925.

Carlisle, John C., B.S.'26, Univ. of Utah; Co. Supt. of Sch., Beaver City, Utah. since 1927.

Carlson, J. E., Jr., A.B. and B.Ed.'20, Univ. of Wash.; Supt. of Sch., Douglas, Ariz., since 1927.

Carlson, Paul A., Ph.B.'21, Univ. of Wis.; Head, Accounting Dept., State Tchrs. Col., Whitewater, Wis., since 1917.

Carmichael, A. Maxwell, Ph.D.'27, State Univ. of Iowa; Dept. of Educ., Ball State Tchrs. Col., Muncie, Ind., since 1930.

Carmichael, H. E., A.B.'25, State Normal Sch., Fairmont, W. Va.; Dist, Supvr. of Sch., Beckley, W. Va., since 1928.

Carmichael, Omer, A.B.'14, Univ. of Ala.; A.M.'24, Columbia Univ. Address: 509 W. 121st St., New York, N. Y.

Carney, Mabel, M.A.'19, Tchrs. Col., Columbia Univ.; Assoc. Prof. of Educ., Tchrs. Col., Columbia Univ., 525 W. 120th St., New York, N. Y., since 1917.

Carothers, Milton W., A.B.'19, Univ. of Ala.; A.M.'27, Tchrs. Col., Columbia Univ.; Supvg. Prin. of Sch., Tampa, Fla., since 1930.

Carpenter, David F., B.Sc.'86, M.Sc.'30, Mass. Agrl. Col.; Supt. of Sch., Millers Falls, Mass., since 1923.

Carpenter, Harry A., B.S.'02, M.S.'12, Rochester; M.A.'13, Columbia Univ.; Specialist in Science for Jr. and Sr. H. S., West High Sch., Rochester, N. Y., since 1925.

Carpenter, Meredith G., A.B.'24, Western Ky. State Tchrs. Col., Bowling Green, Ky.; M.A.'29, Columbia Univ.; Supt. of Sch., Barbourville, Ky., since 1928.

Carpenter, William Weston, Ph.D.'26, Columbia Univ.; Prof. of Educ., Univ. of Mo., 124 Edgewood Ave., Columbia, Mo., since 1928.

Carr, Ernest Palmer, A.B.'01, S.M.'05, Brown Univ.; Supt. of Sch., Marlboro, Mass., since 1912.

Carr, John Pinckney, Supt. of Sch., Vicksburg, Miss., since 1906.

Carr, John R., A.B.'00, Butler Col.; Ph.B. '01, Univ. of Chicago. Address: 724 N. Meridian St., Indianapolis, Ind.

Carr, John Wesley, A.B.'85, A.M.'90, Ind. Univ.; Ph.D.'13, New York Univ.; Pres., Dept. of Superintendence, 1905-06; Dean, State Tchrs. Col., Murray, Ky., since 1926.

Carr, Louis D., Diploma '20, N. J. State Tchrs. Col., Upper Montclair, N. J.; Supvg. Prin. of Sch., Lincoln Sch., North Arlington, N. J., since 1925.

Carrick, C. M., A.B.'91, Ohio Univ.; A.M. '15, Columbia Univ.; Supt. of Sch., Bellevue, Ohio, since 1918.

Carrick, Charles H., A.M., Univ. of Mich.; Supt. of Sch., 408 Walnut St., Three Rivers, Mich.

Carrington, J. W., Diploma '16, Ill. State Normal Univ.; B.S.'22, Univ. of Ill.; Supt. of Sch., Clendenen Bldg., Cairo, Ill., since 1926.

Carris, Lewis H., B.L.'98, Hobart Col.; A. M.'13, Columbia Univ. Address: 370 Seventh Ave., New York, N. Y.

Carroll, George C., Supt. of Sch., Terre Haute, Ind.

Carroll, Mary, Diploma '00, Colegio San Jose, Monterey, Mexico; B.A., Sul Ross State Tchrs. Col., Alpine, Texas; Supt. of Sch., Corpus Christi, Texas, since 1922.

Carroon, Frank, A.B.'02, Ind. Univ.; M.A. '13, Univ. of Denver; Pres., N. Mex. Normal Univ., Las Vegas, N. Mex., since 1923.

Carrothers, George E., B.A.'09, Ind. Univ.; M.A.'15, Tchrs. Col., Columbia Univ.; Ph.D.'24, Columbia Univ.; Dir., Div. of Univ. Inspection of H. S. and Prof. of Educ., Univ. of Mich., Ann Arbor, Mich.

Carse, Elizabeth, A.B.'95, Cornell Univ.; Diploma '97, M.A.'12, Tchrs. Col., Columbia Univ.; Honor Cert. in English '14, Oxford Univ., England; Prin., Northrop Collegiate Sch., 511 Kenwood Parkway, Minneapolis, Minn., since 1915.

Carson, C. C., B.S., Marion Col.; A.B., Ind. State Tchrs. Col.; M.A., State Univ. of Iowa; D.Pd., Univ. of Habana, Cuba; Supvg. Prin. of Sch., Miami Beach, Fla., since 1926.

Carson, Olive G., Dir., Elem. Educ., Bd. of Educ., Akron, Ohio.

Carter, Charles Goodwin, Diploma '22, Western State Normal Sch., Kalamazoo, Mich.; Supvg. Prin., Coggeshall-Sheffield Sch. Dist., Newport, R. I., since 1930.

Carter, Ewell M., B.S. in Ed.'05, Univ. of Mo.; Secy., Mo. State Tchrs. Assn., Columbia, Mo., since 1915.

Carter, George Milton, A.B.'18, Univ. of Maine; Supt. of Sch., Caribou, Maine, since 1923.

Carter, Raymond L., B.S.'19, M.A.'22, Univ. of Toledo; Ph.D.'29, Ohio State Univ.; Prof. of Educ., Univ. of Toledo, Toledo, Ohio, since 1923.

Carter, Mrs. Susanne H., Diploma '96, Southern Oregon State Normal Sch.; Co. Supt. of Sch., Medford, Oregon, since 1920.

Cary, Miles E., 2656 Hillside Ave., Honolulu, Hawaii.

Case, Egbert A., A.B.'04, A.M.'08, Bates Col.; A.M.'27, Tchrs. Col., Columbia Univ.; Supt. of Sch., Willimantic, Conn., since 1910.

Case, L. V., Diploma '97, N. Y. State Normal; B.S.'00, New York Univ.; M.A.'29, Columbia Univ.; Supt. of Sch, Tarrytown, N. Y., since 1900.

Case, R. D., M.A.'23, Univ. of Denver; Supt. of Sch., Brush, Colo., since 1924.

Casey, Charles C., A.B.'04, Ark. Conference Col.; A.M.'06, Univ. of Denver; Pres., Western State Col., Gunnison, Colo., since 1930.

Cassady, E. N., Supt. of Sch., Brookfield, Ill., since 1903.

Cassel, Lloyd S., A.B.'13, Ursinus Col.; M.A.'28, Columbia Univ.; Supt. of Sch., Freehold, N. J., since 1929.

Castle, Lynn E., M.A.'29, State Univ. of Iowa; Supt. of Sch., Stuart, Iowa, since 1923.

Castleberry, W. E., Co. Supt. of Sch., Clarendon, Ark.

Caswell, Hollis L., Ph.D.'29, Columbia Univ.; Assoc. Dir., Div. of Surveys and Field Studies, George Peabody Col. for Tchrs., Nashville, Tenn., since 1929.

Caswell, Omar, Diploma '94, Ind. State Normal Sch.; A.B.'97, Ind. Univ.; A.M. '14, Univ. of Ill.; Head, Dept. of Educ., Tarkio Col., 702 College Ave., Tarkio, Mo., since 1921.

Caulkins, Glenn W., B.A.'01, Univ. of Wash.; Supt. of Sch., Mount Vernon, Wash., since 1929.

Cauthorn, E. B., B.S. in C.E.'94, B.S in Ed. '15, Univ. of Mo.; Asst. Supt. of Sch., Bd. of Educ., Dallas Texas, since 1924.

Certain, C. C., B.S.'06, M.S. in E.E.'07, Ala. Poly. Inst.; M.A.'23, Tchrs. Col., Columbia Univ.; Detroit Tchrs. Col., Detroit, Mich., since 1916.

Cesander, P. K., A.B.'11, Gustavus Adolphus Col.; M.A.'25, State Univ. of Iowa; Research Asst., Col. of Educ., State Univ. of Iowa, Iowa City, Iowa, since 1930.

Chace, S. Howard, A.B.'93, A.M.'96, Brown Univ.; Diploma '02, State Normal Sch., Hyannis, Mass.; Ed M.'25, Harvard Univ.; Supt. of Sch., Beverly, Mass., since 1913.

Chadwick, Raymond D., Ph.B.'09, Frank Col.; M.A.'24, Columbia Univ.; Dean, Jr. Col., Duluth, Minn.

Chalmers, Henry C., Supvg. Prin. of Sch., Wildwood, N. J., since 1907.

Chalmers, James A., A.B.'09, Middlebury Col.; Prin., Fitchburg H. S., Fitchburg, Mass., since 1928.

Chamberlain, Arthur H., B.S.'03, A.M.'04, Columbia Univ.; Secy., Calif. Assn. for Educ. in Thrift and Conservation and Editor, Overland Monthly, 1024 Phelan Bldg., San Francisco, Calif., since 1927.

Chambers, W. Max, Life Cert.'14, Central State Tchrs. Col.; B.S.'15, Berea Col.; A.B.'21, Univ. of Okla.; Supt. of Sch., 913 E. Hobson, Sapulpa, Okla.

Chambers, Will Grant, A.B.'94, Lafayette Col.; B.S.'95, Ind. State Normal Sch.; M.A.'97, Litt.D.'17, Lafayette Col.; Dean, Sch. of Educ. and Dir. of Summer Session, Pa. State Col., State College, Pa., since 1921.

Champion, Ella, Ph.B.'27, Univ. of Chicago; Grade Supvr., Central Sch., Niles, Mich., since 1914.

Champlin, Carroll D., A.B.'14, A.M.'15. Haverford Col.; Ph.D.'25, Univ. of Pittsburgh; Prof. of Educ., Pa. State Col., State College, Pa., since 1926.

Chandler, H. E., A.B.'11, Washburn Col.; A.M.'27, Tchrs. Col., Columbia Univ.; Asst. Prof. of Educ. and Dir. of Tchrs. Appointment Bureau, Univ. of Kansas, 1240 Tennessee St., Lawrence, Kansas, since 1928.

Chandler, Julian Alvin Carroll, A.B.'92, A. M.'93, Col. of William and Mary; Ph.D. '97, Johns Hopkins Univ.; Pres., Col. of William and Mary, Williamsburg, Va., since 1919.

Chapelle, Ernest H., A.M.'25, Univ. of Mich.; Supt. of Sch., Charlotte, Mich., since 1924.

Chapman, Ernest T., Diploma '11, Ashland Col.; B.S.'26, Univ. of Pittsburgh; Supt. of Sch., New Kensington, Pa., since 1924.

Chapman, Harold Benjamin, B.A.'11, Yale Univ.; M.A.'24, Tchrs. Col., Columbia Univ.; Ph.D.'26, Ohio State Univ.; Asst. Dir., Bureau of Research and Statistics, Sch. Admin. Bldg. Annex, Carrollton and Lafayette Aves, Baltimore, Md., since 1926.

Chapman, Ira T., A.B.'03, Ohio Wesleyan Univ.; A.M.'05, Harvard Univ.; Supt. of Sch., 417 S. Broad St., Elizabeth, N. J., since 1923.

Chapman, John L., Ph.B.'00, A.M.'01, Brown Univ.; Supt. of Sch., H S. Bldg., Central Village, Conn., since 1905.

Chappelear, Claude S., B.S.'17, Greenville Col.; A.M.'25, Ph.D.'29, Columbia Univ.; Dean, Illinois Col., Jacksonville, Ill., since 1927.

Charles, Oscar H., B.A.'07, Otterbein Col.; Div. Supt. of Sch., Lingayen, Pangasinan. P. I., since 1927.

Charters, W. W., Bureau of Educ. Research, Col. of Educ., Ohio State Univ., Columbus, Ohio.

Chase, Arthur E., B.A.'89, Univ. of Vt.; Supvg. Prin. of Sch., H. S. Bldg., Ft. Lee, N. J., since 1915.

Chase, Willard O., Diploma '14, Aroostook State Normal Sch, Presque Isle, Maine; Supt. of Sch., Oldtown, Maine, since 1918.

Chastain, James G., Jr., Ph.B.'13, Miss. Col.; Supt. of Sch., H. S., Leland, Miss., since 1921.

Chatterton, Roland H., B.S., R. I. State Col.; Supt. of Sch., Portsmouth and Middletown, R. I., since 1927. Address: Portsmouth, R. I.

Chenault, Robert N., Dir., Richard Hardy Memorial Sch., Richard City, Tenn., since 1926.

Cheney, Charles H., Sc.B.'26, A.M.'28, New York Univ.; Dist. Supt. of Sch., White Plains, N. Y., since 1906.

Cheney, R. E., A.B.'20, Central State Tchrs. Col.; M.A.'25, Univ. of Mich.; Supt. of Sch., Escanaba, Mich., since 1925.

Chenoweth, Arthur S., B.A.'06, Univ. of Colo.; Asst. Prin., Atlantic City H. S., 20 E. New Jersey Ave., Somers Point, N. J., since 1922.

Cherry, H. H., LL.D.; Pres., Western Ky. State Tchrs. Col., Bowling Green, Ky., since 1907.

Cherry, Thomas Crittenden, A.B.'89, Southern Normal Sch.; Supt. of Sch., Bowling Green, Ky., since 1905.

Chester, Joseph Elwood, 5706 Pacific Ave., Wildwood Crest, N. J.

Chew, Samuel L., B. S. '05, Temple Univ.; A.M.'16, Univ. of Pa.; Pd.D.'25, Ursinus Col.; Dist. Supt. of Sch., Northwest Sch., 15th and Race Sts., Philadelphia, Pa., since 1906.

Chewning, John O., A.B.'01, Ind. Univ.; Supt. of Sch., Evansville, Ind., since 1924.

Chidester, Albert J., A.B.'05, Syracuse Univ.; A.M.'12, Harvard Univ.; Prof. of Educ., Berea Col., Berea, Ky., since 1922.

Child, George N., B.S.'13, Univ. of Utah; Supt. of Sch., City and County Bldg., Salt Lake City, Utah, since 1920.

Childs, James R., A.B.'03, Amherst Col.; Supt. of Sch., Holden, Mass., since 1916.

Chiles, E. E., A.B.'10, B.S. in Ed.'12, Univ. of Mo.; A.M.'28, Washington Univ.; Prin., Harrison Elem. Sch., 4163 Green Lea Pl., St. Louis, Mo., since 1926.

Chisholm, Nellie B., Life Cert.'93, Mich. State Tchrs. Col.; Co. Commr. of Sch., Court House, Muskegon, Mich., since 1907.

Chittenden, Harold E., A.B.'09, Yale; Supt. of Sch., Naugatuck, Conn., since 1918.

Chittick, Murray A., B.S.'16, Rutgers Univ.; Supvg. Prin., East Brunswick Twp. Sch., Old Bridge, N. J., since 1929.

Chrane, C. E., B.S. in Ed.'19, M.A.'27, Univ. of Mo.; Supt. of Sch., Boonville, Mo., since 1913.

Christensen, W. W., B.S.'23, Agrl. Col. of Utah; Co. Supt. of Sch., Price, Utah, since 1929.

Christenson, Christine A., Diploma '26, State Tchrs. Col., Oshkosh, Wis.; Co. Supt. of Sch., First Natl. Bank Bldg., Marinette, Wis., since 1927.

Chuang, C. H., Inst. for Educ. Research, Sun Yatsen Univ., Canton, China.

Church, Harry Victor, Ph.B.'94, Univ. of Chicago; Supt., Morton Schools, Cicero, Ill.

Claggett, Arthur E., B.Ph., Ohio State Univ.; Supt. of Sch., 24 Spirea Drive, Oakwood, Dayton, Ohio, since 1922.

Clapp, George I., A.B.'95, Harvard Univ.; Supt. of Sch., 10 Davis St., Woburn, Mass., since 1903.

Clark, Harold F., Ph.D.'23, Tchrs. Col., Columbia Univ.; Prof. of Educ., Tchrs. Col., Columbia Univ., New York, N. Y., since 1928.

Clark, James E., Supvg. Prin. of Sch., 531 Roup St., Tarentum, Pa.

Clark, John E., Ph.B.; Supvg. Prin., Middle Twp. Sch., Cape May Court House, N. J.

Clark, John S., Ph.B.'12, Univ. of Wis.; Supt. of Sch., 923 N. County St., Waukegan, Ill., since 1918.

Clark, M. G., A.M., LL.D.; Supt. of Sch., Woodrow Wilson Bldg., Sioux City, Iowa.

Clark, Randolph Lee, Supt. of Sch., 1213 Milwaukee St., Plainview, Texas.

Clark, Ridgley Colfax, B.A.'08, Bowdoin Col.; M.A.'29, Yale Univ.; Supt. of Sch., Seymour, Conn., since 1917.

Clark, Ronald W., B.S.'27, Univ. of Ill.; Prin., Webster Elem. and Jr. H. S., Main and 13th Sts., Quincy, Ill., since 1927.

Clark, Walter S., Pd.B.'98, N. Y. State Col.; Supt. of Sch, Rensselaer, N. Y., since 1917.

Clark, Zenas R., 509 W. 121st St., New York, N. Y.

Clarke, Edward Richards, B.A.'02, Williams Col.; Ed.M.'26, Harvard Univ.; Supt. of Sch., Winthrop, Mass., since 1927.

Clarke, Ernest P., B.S.'83, Mich. State Col.; Supt. of Sch., 1922 Niles Ave., St. Joseph, Mich., since 1899.

Clarke, George B., A.B.'03, Harvard Univ.; Diploma '10, State Normal Sch., Bridgewater, Mass.; Supt. of Sch., East Pepperell, Mass., since 1920.

Clarke, M. J., B S.'16, Univ. of Ky.; M.A. '28, Univ. of Wis.; Supt. of Sch., Ely, Nevada, since 1929.

Clauson, Robert, A.B.'02, Cornell Univ.; Box 17, Highland, Calif.

Claxton, P. P., A.B.'82, A.M.'87, Univ. of Tenn.; Litt.D., Bates Col.; LL.D., Allegheny Col., Univ. of N. C., Univ. of Md., Western Reserve Univ.; Pres., Austin Peay Normal Sch., Clarksville, Tenn., since 1930.

Clay, Thurman M., A.B '24, Mich. State Normal Col.; Supt. of Sch., Vassar, Mich., since 1924.

Clay, William G., B.S.'24, George Peabody Col. for Tchrs.; Supt of Sch., New Boston, Texas, since 1916.

Clement, J. H., A.M.'10, Univ. of Kansas; A.M.'23, Columbia Univ.; Supt. of Sch., Beldorf Bldg., Independence, Kansas, since 1926.

Clevenger, Arthur Wilbur, 911 W. White St., Champaign, Ill.

Clifton, A. R., Ph.B.'08, Univ. of Wis.; M.A.'18, Univ. of Southern Calif.; Supt. of Sch., Monrovia, Calif., since 1918.

Clifton, J. L, B.S.'03, Ohio Univ.; LL.D. '28, Miami Univ.; Ph.D.'29, Ohio State Univ.; Dir. of Educ. for Ohio, State House, Columbus, Ohio, since 1927.

Cline, Earl D., B.S.'16, Drake Univ.; M A. '22, State Univ. of Iowa; Supt. of Sch., Dubuque, Iowa, since 1930.

Clish, Herbert C., Supvr. of Non-Tenure Tchrs., Pub. Sch., 169 Church St., New Haven, Conn.

Close, Frank H., Ph.B.'10, Lebanon Univ.; Supt. of Sch., Wadsworth, Ohio, since 1926.

Cloud, A. J., B.L.'00, Univ. of Calif.; Chief Deputy Supt. of Sch., City Hall, San Francisco, Calif., since 1923.

Cloud, Roy Walter, A.B '05, Stanford Univ.; Exec. Secy., Calif. Tchrs. Assn., 155 Sansome St., San Francisco, Calif., since 1927.

Clough, G. O., B.A. and M.A., Univ. of Texas; Prof. of Educ., Southern Methodist Univ., Dallas, Texas.

Cloyd, Emerson F., A.B.'15, Earlham Col.; Supt. of Sch., 511 E. Main St., Cambridge City, Ind., since 1924.

Cobb, Bruce B., B.A.'10, M.A.'28, Univ. of Texas; Supt. of Sch., Waco, Texas, since 1915.

Cobb, Charles R, A.B.'03, Greenville Col., Greenville, Ill.; A.B.'04, A.M.'05, Univ. of Mich.; Supt. of Sch., Bessemer, Mich., since 1912.

Cobb, Thomas Howell, M.A.'26, Illinois; Supt. of Sch., Urbana, Ill., since 1929.

Coblentz, C. R., Co. Supt. of Sch., Court House, Eaton, Ohio, since 1923.

Coburn, William G., A.B.'90, Univ. of Mich.; LL.D.'23, Olivet Col.; Supt. of Sch., Battle Creek, Mich., since 1895.

Cochran, J. Chester, B.S.'29, Sul Ross State Tchrs. Col., Alpine, Texas; Supt. of Sch., Mexia, Texas, since 1929.

Cocking, Walter D., B.A.'13, Des Moines Col.; M.A.'22, State Univ. of Iowa; Ph. D.'28, Columbia Univ.; Prof. of Sch. Admin., George Peabody Col. for Tchrs., Nashville, Tenn.

Cody, Frank, Pd.M.'12, Mich. State Normal Col.; M.A.'24, Univ. of Mich.; Pres., Dept. of Superintendence, 1929-30; Supt. of Sch., 1354 Broadway, Detroit, Mich., since 1919.

Coffey, Wilford L., A.B.'22, Mich. State Normal Col.; M A.'24, Ph.D.'29, Univ. of Mich.; Dean, Col. of the City of Detroit, 4841 Cass, Detroit, Mich., since 1928.

Coffman, Lotus D., B.A.'06, M.A.'10, Ind. Univ.; Ph.D.'11, Columbia Univ.; LL.D. '22, Ind. Univ.; LL.D.'22, Carleton Col.; LL.D.'29, Columbia Univ.; D.Sc. in Ed. '30, George Washington Univ.; L.H.D.'30, Univ. of Denver; Pres., Univ. of Minn., Minneapolis, Minn.

Cohen, A. Broderick, B.A.'06, Columbia Col.; Ed.B.'06, Ed.M.'09, Tchrs. Col., Columbia Univ.; M.A.'09, Columbia Univ.; Prof. and Dir. of Evening and Extension Sessions and Summer Session. Hunter Col. of the City of New York, Park Ave. and 68th St., New York, N. Y., since 1925.

Colahan, Wayne J., B.A '16, Univ. of Minn.; Supt. of Sch., South St., Woodstock, Ill., since 1930.

Colburn, Jessie B., Prin., Jr. H. S. 96, Manhattan, 1532 York Ave., New York, N. Y., since 1921.

Cole, Albert S., A.B.'96, Colby Col.; Supt. of Sch., Grafton, Mass., since 1921.

Cole, C. E., B.S.'18, Muhlenberg Col.; A.M. '21, Columbia Univ.; Supt., Muhlenberg Twp. Sch., Temple, Pa., since 1925.

Cole, Page E., M.A.'30, St. Lawrence; Supt. of Sch., 121 Main St., Whitehall, N. Y., since 1923.

Cole, Robert D., A.B. and A.M.'12, Bowdoin Col.; Ph.D.'27, Univ. of Pa.; Prof. of Sec. Educ., Univ. of N Dak., University Sta., Grand Forks, N. Dak., since 1926.

Cole, Thomas R.. Ph.B.'02. A.M.'03, Upper Iowa Univ.; Prof. of Educ., Univ. of Wash., Seattle, Wash., since 1930.

Coleman, W. H., A.B.'09, Nebr. Wesleyan Univ.; A.M.'16, Univ. of Nebr. Address: 553 Undercliff Ave., Edgewater, N. J.

Colgan, Edward J., A.M.'20, Harvard Univ.; Head, Dept. of Educ., Colby Col., Waterville, Maine, since 1924.

Colgan, Philip, Malvern Preparatory Sch, Malvern, Pa.

Collett, C. E., A.B.'08, Nebr. Wesleyan Univ.; M.A.'17, Univ. of Nebr.; Supt. of Sch., Lexington, Nebr., since 1922.

Collier, Paul D., M.A.'25. Tchrs. Col., Columbia Univ.; Supt. of Sch., Simsbury, Conn., since 1928.

Collier, Price L.. B.S. in Ed.'17, A.M.'27, Univ. of Mo.; Supt. of Sch., Richmond, Mo., since 1922.

Collins, Orvis K., A.B.'02, Middlebury Col.; Supt. of Sch., Hingham, Mass., since 1916.

Colson, Ephraim P., A.B.'07, Bates Col.; Supt. of Sch., North Scituate, R. I., since 1920.

Colton, Harold J., Diploma '13. State Tchrs. Col., Slippery Rock, Pa.; A.B.'24, Thiel Col.; A.M.'27, Tchrs. Col., Columbia Univ.; Supvg. Prin. of Sch., Bessemer, Pa., since 1924.

Coltrane, E. J., Supt. of Sch., Salisbury, N. C.

Combs, Morgan LaFayette, A.B.'17, Univ. of Richmond; A.M.'22, Univ. of Chicago; Ed.M.'26, Ed.D.'27, Harvard Univ.; Pres., State Tchrs. Col., Fredericksburg, Va., since 1928.

Compton, Charles Vernon, B.A.'09, Emory and Henry Col.; M.A.'27, Columbia Univ.; Supt. of Sch., McCamey, Texas.

Compton, Lillian C., A.B.'16, W. Va. Univ.; Asst. Supt. of Sch., 105 S. Center St., Cumberland, Md., since 1919.

Comstock, E. B., Prin., North Dallas H. S., Dallas, Texas.

Condon, Randall J., A.B.'86, A.M.'89, LL.D. '13, Colby Col.; LL.D.'25, Univ. of Cincinnati; Pres., Dept. of Superintendence, 1926-27. Address: Friendship, Maine.

Condrey, Ralph S., A.B.'13, McKendree Col.; Supt. of Sch., H. S. Bldg., Mt. Carmel, Ill., since 1929.

Congdon, Fayette K., A.B.'94, A.M.'97, Syracuse Univ.; Supt. of Sch., Northampton, Mass., since 1905.

Congdon, Randolph T., B.A.'00, Syracuse Univ.; M A.'08, Harvard Univ.; Pd.D.'23, Albany State Col. for Tchrs.; Prin., State Normal Sch., Potsdam, N. Y., since 1919.

Congdon, Wray H., A.B.'14, M.A. in Eng.'15, Syracuse Univ.; M.A. in Ed.'22, Ph.D.'29, Univ. of Mich.; Asst. Prof. of Educ., Sch. of Educ., Univ. of Mich., Ann Arbor, Mich., since 1928.

Conger, Lester W., Ph.B.'23, Univ. of Wis.; Supt. of Sch., 118 E. Park Lane, Kohler, Wis., since 1922.

Conklin, Arch B., M.A.'30, Columbia Univ.; Supt. of Sch., Jr. H. S. Bldg., Bowling Green, Ohio, since 1930.

Conn, U. S., A.B.'91, A.M.'01, Valparaiso Univ.; LL.D.'21, Nebr. Wesleyan Univ.; Pres., State Tchrs. Col., Wayne, Nebr., since 1910.

Conner, F. E., A.B.'23, Univ. of S. Dak.; Supt. of Sch., Belle Fourche, S. Dak., since 1925.

Conner, O. T., A.B.'25, Ark. Col.; Supt. of Sch., Marianna, Ark., since 1929.

Conner, Thomas B., A.B.'12, Mercer Univ.; Supt. of Sch., Pelham, Ga., since 1927.

Connor, Miles Washington, A.B.'09, Va. Union Univ.; A.M.'12, Howard Univ.; A.M.'26, Tchrs. Col.; Columbia Univ.; Prin., Coppin Normal Sch., Lafayette and McCulloh Sts., Baltimore, Md., since 1926.

Connor, William L., A.B.'14, Ind. Normal; M.A., Columbia Univ.; Dir. of Research, Pub. Sch., 432 E. 109th St., Cleveland, Ohio, since 1923.

Conrad, B. W., Supt., Union Free Sch. Dist. No. 2, Scotia, N. Y., since 1927.

Conrad, R. D., A.B.'14, A.M.'22, Wittenberg Col.; A.M.'26, Columbia Univ.; Supt. of Sch., Delaware, Ohio, since 1928.

Converse, Frank E., B.L.'88, Univ. of Mich.; Supt. of Sch., H. S., Beloit, Wis., since 1897.

Conway, William F., Supt. of Sch., Edgewater, N. J.

Cook, A. F., B.A.'10, Ripon Col.; Supt. of Sch., Hinsdale, Ill., since 1919.

Cook, Albert S., A.B.'95, A.M.'06, Princeton Univ.; Litt.D.'23, Western Md. Col.; Litt. D.'23, St. John's Col., Annapolis, Md.; Litt.D.'24, Univ. of Md.; State Supt. of Sch., Towson, Md., since 1920.

Cook, Anse J., B.A. and B.B.A.'24, Univ. of Texas; M.A.'28, Southern Methodist Univ.; Supt. of Sch., Mesquite, Texas, since 1926.

Cook, Charles E., A.B.'13, A.M.'17, Ind. Univ.; Supt. of Sch., North Manchester, Ind., since 1923.

Cook, Frederic William, B.S.'14, New York Univ.; Supt. of Sch., Plainfield, N. J., since 1926.

Cook, Hugh Oliver, 2436 Montgall Ave., Kansas City, Mo.

Cook, Jason O., A.B.'06, A.M.'07, Brown Univ.; A M.'30, Tchrs. Col., Columbia Univ.; Supt. of Sch., Town Hall, Amherst, Mass., since 1920.

Cook, Lemuel T., A.M.'30, Univ. of Colo.; Supt. of Sch., H. S., Sherman, Texas, since 1929.

Cook, Paul M., A.B.'18, Central Wesleyan Col.; M.A.'27, Univ. of Chicago; Exec. Secy., Phi Delta Kappa, Republic Bldg., State and Adams Sts., Chicago, Ill., since 1928.

Cook, Walter W., B.A.'23, M.A.'26, State Univ. of Iowa; Col. of Educ., State Univ. of Iowa, Iowa City, Iowa.

Cook, William Cassius, Diploma '07 and '22, A.B.'27, Concord State Normal Sch., Athens, W. Va.; State Supt. of Free Sch., Charleston, W. Va., since 1929.

Cookson, Charles W., A.B. and B.Ped.'95, A. M.'07, Ped.D.'17, Ohio Univ.; Supt. of Sch., Urbana, Ohio, since 1924.

Cooley, Emma Pritchard, Dir., Dept. of Voc. Guidance, Pub. Sch., New Orleans, La.

Cooley, J. C., A.B.'21, DePauw Univ.; Prin., Union Twp. Sch., Greentown, Ind., since 1927.

Cooley, Robert L., Diploma '94, State Normal Sch., Oshkosh, Wis.; M.A.'24, Univ. of Wis.; D. Sc.'25, Stout Inst.; Dir., Milwaukee Voc. Sch., Sixth and State Sts., Milwaukee, Wis., since 1912.

Coolidge, Walter Francis, A.B.'99, A.M.'07, Knox Col.; A.M.'14, Univ. of Chicago; Supt., Community H. S., Granite City, Ill., since 1913.

Cooper, Charles D., Dir. of Tr., State Normal Sch., Brockport, N. Y.

Cooper, Charles H., A.B.'77, A.M.'80, Dartmouth Col.; Pres. Emeritus, State Tchrs. Col., Mankato, Minn., since 1930.

Cooper, Clarence G., B.S.'11, Tchrs. Col., Columbia Univ.; Co. Supt. of Sch., Towson, Md., since 1920.

Cooper, Homer E., A.B.'07, W. Va. Univ.; A.M.'16, Ph.D.'24, Columbia Univ.; Dean, Eastern Ky. State Normal Sch. and Tchrs. Col., Richmond, Ky., since 1924.

Cooper, Homer V., B.Sc.'19, Miss. Agrl. and Mech. Col.; Supt. of Sch., Kosciusko, Miss., since 1924.

Cooper, Leigh G., A.B.'04, M.A.'10, Ph.D.'17, Univ. of Mich.; Prin., Edwin Denby H. S., 12800 Kelly Rd., Detroit, Mich.

Cooper, William John, A.B.06, M.A.'17, Univ. of Calif.; LL.D.'27, Whittier Col.; Ed.D.'28, Univ. of Southern Calif.; Litt.D. '30, R. I. State Col.; U. S. Commr. of Educ., Dept. of the Interior, Washington, D. C., since 1929.

Cope, Alfred B., A.B.'04, Campbell Col.; A. M.'06, Univ. of Kansas; Dept. of Educ., Evansville Col., Evansville, Ind., since 1921.

Copeland, Richard Watson, Supt. of Sch., 406 Spruance St., Hopewell, Va.

Copeland, Starrett Dobson, Asst. Supt. of Sch., 246 Greene St., Augusta, Ga.

Copeland, William R., Asst. Supt. of Sch., Bessemer, Ala.

Corbin, Fred E., A.B.'81, A.M.'84, Williams Col.; Supt. of Sch., Southbridge, Mass., since 1902.

Cornell, H. M., 2311 Commonwealth, Chicago, Ill.

Corning, Hobart M., Ph.B.'11, A.M.'12, Dickinson Col.; Supt. of Sch., Colorado Springs, Colo., since 1927.

Cory, Edward W., Diploma '14, State Normal Sch., Ypsilanti, Mich.; A.B.'18, Univ. of Mich.; Supt. of Sch., Richmond, Mich., since 1923.

Cory, Frank Mirl, A.B.'17, Ind. Univ.; A.M. '23, Tchrs. Col.; Supt. of Sch., 599 E. Main St., Hagerstown, Ind.

Cotton, Carl, A.B.'00, Colby Col.; LL.M.'06, Univ. of Maine; Ed.M.'27, Harvard Univ.; Supt. of Sch., Derry, N. H., since 1920.

Cotton, Charles Ed., B.S.'22, Univ. of Idaho; Supvg. Prin. of Sch., Roosevelt Bldg., Birdsboro, Pa., since 1925.

Cotton, M. L., B.A.'16, Univ. of Okla.; Supt. of Sch., 500 E. Elm, Altus, Okla., since 1925.

Cougill, J. R., Supt. of Sch., Chariton, Iowa.

Coulbourn, John, Asst. Supt. of Sch., 6307 Pinehurst Rd., Baltimore, Md.

Coulomb, Charles A., B.S.'05, Temple Univ.; Ph.D.'10, Univ. of Pa.; Supt., Dist. One, Bd. of Educ., Harrington Sch., Thomas and Baltimore Aves., Philadelphia, Pa.

Coulson, Austin R., Pd.B.'99, State Normal Col., Albany, N. Y.; B.S.'23, M.A.'25, N. Y. State Col. for Tchrs.; Deputy Supt. of Sch., Albany, N. Y., since 1927.

Coulter, Bayard L., B.S.'11, Univ. of Miss.; LL.B.'14, Millsaps Col.; M.A.'28, Peabody Col.; Supt., Miss. Indus. and Tr. Sch., Columbia, Miss., since 1928.

Coultrap, Harry M., A.B.'08, Univ. of Colo.; A.M.'14, Ohio Univ.; Supt. of Sch., Geneva, Ill., since 1912.

Coursen, W. Marshall, B.S. in Ed.'20, Ohio Univ.; Supt. of Sch., Campbell, Ohio, since 1916.

Courter, Claude V., B.S.'11, Kalamazoo Col.; M.A.'25, Univ. of Chicago; Supt. of Sch., Dayton, Ohio, since 1930.

Courtis, Stuart A., B.S.'19, M.A.'21, Tchrs. Col., Columbia Univ.; Ph.D.'25, Univ. of Mich.; Educ. Consultant, Detroit and Hamtramck, Mich., Pub. Sch., and Prof. of Educ., Sch. of Educ., Univ. of Mich., Ann Arbor, Mich., since 1924. Address: 9110 Dwight Ave., Detroit, Mich.

Cousins, Robert Bartow, A.B.'82, Univ. of Ga.; LL.D.'26, Southwestern Univ.; Pres., Texas Col. of Arts and Indus., Kingsville, Texas, since 1924.

Covell, Albert H., A.B.'12, Univ. of Rochester; Supt. of Sch., Sr. H. S., Oneida, N. Y., since 1927.

Covey, George H., Dist. Supt. of Sch., Katonah, N. Y., since 1901.

Cowles, John H., B.S.'06, Univ. of Nashville; A.B.'20, George Peabody Col. for Tchrs.; Supt. of Sch., Lexington, N. C., since 1918.

Cox, Larue, B.A.'22, Howard Payne Sch.; M.A.'26, Univ. of Texas; Supt. of Sch., Jacksonville, Texas, since 1927.

Cox, Philip W. L., A.B.'06, Harvard Col.; A.M.'20, Harvard Univ.; Ph.D.'25, Columbia Univ.; Prof. of Sec. Educ., New York Univ., 100 Washington Square, E., New York, N. Y., since 1923.

Coxe, Charles, A.B., Ph.B.'05, Lafayette Univ.; A.M.'12, Harvard Univ.; Supt. of Sch., Lewistown, Pa., since 1923.

Coxe, Warren W., B.Sc.'11, Dakota Wesleyan Univ.; Ph.D.'23, Ohio State Univ.; Dir., Educ. Research Div., State Educ. Dept., Albany, N. Y., since 1929.

Coy, William Stacy, 856 N. High St., Columbus, Ohio.

Crabb, Alfred Leland, B.S.'16, George Peabody Col. for Tchrs.; M.A.'21, Tchrs. Col., Columbia Univ.; Ph.D.'25, George Peabody Col. for Tchrs.; Prof. of Educ., George Peabody Col. for Tchrs., Nashville, Tenn., since 1927.

Craig, George W., Frostburg, Md.

Craig, Gerald S., A.M.'17, Ph.D.'27, Columbia Univ.; Asst. Prof. of Natural Science, Tchrs. Col., Columbia Univ., New York, N. Y., since 1924.

Craig, John Alexander, A.B.'09, A.M.'10, Univ. of Mich.; Supt. of Sch., Muskegon, Mich., since 1929.

Craig, Katherine L., State Supt. of Pub. Instr., 1253 Downing, Denver, Colo.

Cramer, John Francis, B.A.'20, M.A.'21, Willamette Univ.; Supt. of Sch., First Natl. Bank Bldg., Grants Pass, Oregon, since 1929.

Crandall, W. G., B.S.'20, Cornell Univ.; Chief, Div. of Educ., Clemson Agrl. Col., Clemson College, S. C., since 1922.

Crandell, Charles W., A.M.'23, Univ. of Mich.; Supt. of Sch., Monroe, Mich., since 1925.

Crane, Arthur Griswold, B.A., M.A., Carleton Col.; Ph.D., Columbia Univ.; Pres., Univ. of Wyo., Laramie, Wyo., since 1922.

Crane, R. W., Ph.B.'17, Lafayette Col.; Supvg. Prin. of Sch., Whittier Sch., Dunellen, N. J., since 1927.

Cranmer, Clyde William, Ph.B.'10, Bucknell Univ.; Supt. of Sch., Kittanning, Pa., since 1919.

Cranston, John A., B.S.'87, St. Lawrence Univ.; Supt. of Sch., 119 Church St., Santa Ana, Calif., since 1906.

Crawford, Albert Byron, A.B.'17, Univ. of Ky.; M.A.'25, Columbia Univ.; Supt of Sch., Anchorage, Ky., since 1927.

Crawford, Earle E., A.B.'19, Univ. of Mich.; A.M.'27, Stanford Univ.; Prin., Napa Union H. S. since 1924 and Dist. Supt. of Sch., Route 2, Box 943, Napa, Calif., since 1927.

Crawford, Floyd, W., A.B.'08, LL.B.'09, M. A.'19, Univ. of Mich.; Supt. of Sch., 22 S. Fourth St., Niles, Mich., since 1924.

Crawford, M. J., A.B.'23, Central State Tchrs. Col., Mt. Pleasant, Mich.; Supt. of Sch., Caro, Mich., since 1927.

Crawford, Will C., A.B.'13, Pomona Col.; A.M.'15, Columbia Univ.; Supt. of Pub. Instr., Ter. of Hawaii, 2508 Oahu Ave., Honolulu, Hawaii, since 1925.

Cray, D. J., Ph.D.'14, Grove City Col.; Supt. of Sch., Pittston, Pa., since 1918.

Crediford, Eugene E., B.S. in Ed.'29, Bucknell Univ.; Supvg, Prin, of Sch., Athens, Pa., since 1924.

Creel, L. E., B.S.'29, Ala. Polytechnic Inst.; Supt. of Sch., Sheffield, Ala., since 1917.

Cressman, Henry M., A.B.'95, A M.'01, Lehigh Univ.; Pd.D.'16, Muhlenberg Col.; Co. Supt, of Sch., Egg Harbor City, N. J., since 1909.

Creswell, Mrs. Cordelia M., B.Pd.'11, Grand Rapids Kdgn. Tr. Sch.; Supvr., Special Classes, Bd. of Educ., 143 Bostwick Ave., N. E., Grand Rapids, Mich., since 1910.

Criley, Martha B., Co. Supt. of Sch., Tombstone, Ariz.

Crim, Lulu Henrietta, 227 E. Main St., Elkton, Md.

Crocker, Richard F., B.S.'14, Univ. of Maine; Prin., Madawaska Tr. Sch., Fort Kent, Maine, since 1926.

Croman, W. R., Supvg. Prin. of Sch., Troy, Pa.

Cromwell, P. R., Life License '14, A.B.'17, Ind. State Normal Sch.; A.M.'24, Ind. Univ.; Supt. of Sch., Carlisle, Ind, since 1926.

Crow, Orin Faison, A.B.'17, Univ. of S. C.; A.M.'25, George Peabody Col. for Tchrs.; Dean, Sch. of Educ., Univ. of S. C., Columbia, S. C., since 1930.

Crow, Ralph E., Supt. of Sch., Strongsville, Ohio.

Crowell, Harland D., B.S.'18, Ed.M.'26, Harvard Univ.; Asst. Supt. of Sch., 59 Prospect St., Stamford, Conn., since 1926.

Crozier, Norman R., Pres., Dept. of Superintendence, 1930-31; Supt. of Sch., 3408 Cole Ave., Dallas, Texas.

Crumb, Herbert H., A.B.'05, A.M.'09, Hamilton Col.; Supt. of Sch., Endicott, N. Y., since 1913.

Crumbling, C. S., Supvg. Prin. of Sch., 738 N. Second St., Reading, Pa.

Crumpacker, H. C., B.S.D.'04, A.B.'08, Normal Col., McPherson, Kansas; Ph.M.'10, Univ. of Chicago; Supt. of Sch., Jr. H. S. Bldg., Hoquiam, Wash., since 1922.

Crumrine, M. Ella, Prin., Fulton Sch., 917 Chislett St., Pittsburgh, Pa., since 1926.

Cubberley, Ellwood P., A.B.'91, Ind. Univ.; A.M.'02, Ph.D.'05, Columbia Univ.; LL.D. '23, State Univ. of Iowa; Head, Dept. of Educ., Stanford Univ., since 1898; Dean, Sch. of Educ., Stanford Univ., Stanford University, Calif., since 1917.

Cummings, L. O., A.B.'10, A.M.'11, Ed.D. '21, Harvard Univ.; Prof. of Educ. and Head, Dept. of Educ., Univ. of Buffalo, Buffalo, N. Y., since 1930.

Cunningham, E. C., Diploma '14, W. T. C. Chicago; Co. Supt. of Sch., Lawrenceville, Ill., since 1923.

Curfman, Wayne White, A.M.'20, Tchrs. Col., Columbia Univ.; Supt. of Sch., Lawrence, Kansas, since 1927.

Curry, Charles M., A.M.'95, Franklin Col. Address: 88 Lexington Ave., New York, N. Y.

Curtis, Charles La Rue, B.S. in Ped.'27, New York Univ.; Supvg. Prin. of Sch., 55 Hill St., Rockaway, N. J., since 1919.

Curtis, George H., A.B.'99, Albion, Mich.; A.B.'04, A.M.'12, Univ. of Mich.; Supt. of Sch., 141 State Ave., Alpena, Mich., since 1919.

Curtis, Wilbur R., A.B.'08, Ind. Univ.; A. M.'12, Columbia Univ.; Supt. of Sch., Alton, Ill., since 1921.

Curtis, William F., A.B.'98, Franklin and Marshall Col.; Litt.D.'10, Muhlenberg Col.; LL.D.'28, Franklin and Marshall Col.; Pres., Cedar Crest Col., Allentown, Pa., since 1908.

Curtis, William P., Supvg. Prin. of Sch, Wharton, N. J.

Cusack, Alice M., A.B.'16, Univ. of Nebr.; A.M.'19, Columbia Univ.; Dir. of Kdgn.-Prim. Educ., Bd. of Educ., Kansas City, Mo., since 1921.

Cushing, J. Stearns, Supt. of Sch., Town Hall, Middleboro, Mass., since 1927.

Cushman, Laura, A.B.'11, Morningside Col.; Prin., Cushman Private Sch., N. E. 60th St. and Fifth Court, Miami, Fla., since 1924.

Cutler, Henry F., B.A '86, M.A.'04, Amherst Col.; D.C.L.'16, Syracuse Univ.; LL.D.'25, Wesleyan; Headmaster, Mt. Hermon Sch., Mt. Hermon, Mass., since 1890.

Cytacki, Walter, 2380 Wyandotte Ave., Hamtramck, Mich.

Dabney, O. B., A.B.'29, Univ. of Ky.; Supt. of Sch., Midway, Ky., since 1929.

Daley, Hiram C, Ph.B.'99. Univ. of Mich.; B.Pd.'01, Mich. State Normal Col.; Asst. Supt. of Sch., 121 Elmhurst Ave., Highland Park, Mich., since 1918.

Daley, Mary Wood, Dir. of Educ., Sleighton Farm, Darling, Pa.

Dalke, C. L., Co. Supt of Sch., Court House, Enid, Okla.

Dalthorp, Charles J., B.S.'20, S. Dak. State Col.; Supt. of Sch., Aberdeen, S. Dak., since 1929.

Daniel, Frank C., B.S.'01, A.M.'02, Dickinson Col.; Prin., McKinley Tech. H. S, Washington, D. C., since 1911.

Daniel, J. McT., A.B.'17, Wofford Col.; A. M.'29, Univ. of S. C.; State H. S. Supvr., State Dept. of Educ., Columbia, S. C., since 1926.

Daniel, Roland B., A.B.'91, Emory Univ.; LL.D.'29, Univ. of Ga.; Supt of Sch., 1500 Broadway, Columbus, Ga., since 1909.

Daniels, Mrs. Annie E., Co. Supt. of Sch., Tucson, Ariz., since 1925.

Dann, George J., A.B.'96, Union Col.; Pd.D '14, New York Univ.; Supt. of Sch., Oneonta, N. Y., since 1910.

Dann, Hollis, Mus.D.'06, Alfred Univ.; Head, Dept. of Music Educ., New York Univ., Washington Square, New York, N. Y., since 1925.

Dannelly, Clarence Moore, B.Ped.'07, State Tchrs. Col., Troy, Ala.; A.B.'12, Birmingham-Southern Col.; M.A.'26, George Peabody Col. for Tchrs.; Pres, Ky. Wesleyan Col., Winchester, Ky., since 1928.

Danowsky, N. A., A.B.'15, A.M.'25, Susquehanna Univ.; Supvg Prin. of Sch., Northumberland, Pa., since 1922.

Darling, Frederick R., A.B.'03, Univ. of Chicago; Supt. of Sch., Dunkirk, N. Y., since 1916.

Darling, William T., Ph.B.'26, Ph.M.'29, Univ. of Wis.; Supt. of Sch., Wauwatosa, Wis., since 1924.

Darnall, Maynard C., A.B.'16, Ind. Univ.; Supt. of Sch , H. S. Bldg., Crawfordsville, Ind., since 1930.

Darrow, B. H., Dir., Ohio Sch. of the Air, Woodstock, Ohio.

Daugette, C. W., B.Sc.'93, M.Sc.'94, Ala. Polytech. Inst.; LL.D.'16, Univ. of Ala.; Pres., State Tchrs. Col , Jacksonville, Ala., since 1899.

David, Bert B., Ph.B.'21, Muhlenberg Col.; M.A.'26, Columbia Univ.; Supt. of Sch., Lehighton, Pa , since 1928.

Davidson, Clyde O., Mus.B.'10, Col of Emporia; B.S.'25, Kansas State Tchrs. Col.; M.S.'29, Univ. of Kansas; Supt. of Sch., Columbus, Kansas, since 1923.

Davidson, Frank H., A.B.'20, Univ. of Mich.; A.M.'29, Univ. of Colo.; Supt. of Sch., Leadville, Colo., since 1925.

Davie, Ethel M., Diploma '95, State Tchrs. Col., West Chester, Pa.; Supvr. of Grammar Grades, Administration Bldg , Atlantic City, N. J., since 1915.

Davies, John C., B.A.'05, Upper Iowa Univ.; Supt. of Sch., La Grange, Ill., since 1922.

Davies, William R.. A.B.'15, Ripon Col.; M. A.'21, Univ. of Wis.; Supt. of Sch., H. S. Bldg., Beaver Dam, Wis., since 1925.

Davis, Albert S., Supvg Prin. of Sch., 12 W. Union Ave., Bound Brook, N. J.

Davis, Beatrice Jane, Horace Mann Sch., Broadway and 120th St., New York, N. Y.

Davis, Bert Byron, A.B.'19. A.M.'20, Univ. of Calif.; Educ. Supt., W. Mich. Conference of Seventh-Day Adventists, 120 Madison Ave., S. E., Grand Rapids, Mich., since 1926.

Davis, Carl D., 5632 Kimbarck Ave., Chicago, Ill.

Davis, Charles S., Supt. of Sch., 183 S. Second St., Steelton, Pa , since 1919.

Davis, Chester K., A.B.'22, Univ. of Pittsburgh; Supt. of Sch., Miami, Ariz., since 1927.

Davis, Chester P., A.B.'12, Southwestern Col.; M.A.'15, Columbia Univ.; Supt. of Sch., Stillwater, Okla., since 1927.

Davis, Daniel W., Supvg Prin of Sch., Pitman, N. J., since 1905.

Davis, Donald P., A.B.'20, Univ. of Pittsburgh; Supt. of Sch., Victoria Ave. Bldg., Arnold, Pa , since 1926.

Davis, E. D., 70 Fifth Ave., New York, N. Y.

Davis, Frank G., Ph.B.'11, M.A.'17, Bucknell Univ.; M.A.'24, Tchrs. Col., Columbia Univ.; Ph.D.'30, New York Univ.; Prof. of Educ. and Head, Dept. of Educ., Bucknell Univ., 140 S. Front St , Lewisburg, Pa., since 1924.

Davis, Georgia, Ph.B.'19, Univ. of Chicago; M.A.'23, Tchrs. Col., Columbia Univ.; Asst. Supt. of Sch., 127 N. Tenth St., Richmond, Ind., since 1923.

Davis, H. H., A.M.'23, Ph.D.'28, State Univ. of Iowa; Auditor, State Dept. of Educ.; Asst. Prof., Dept. of Sch. Admin., Ohio State Univ., Columbus, Ohio, since 1928.

Davis, Jackson, A.B.'02, Col. of William and Mary; A.M.'08, Columbia Univ.; LL. D.'30, Univ. of Richmond; Asst. Dir , Genl. Educ. Bd., 804 Grace American Bldg., Richmond, Va., since 1929.

Davis, John C., Supt. of Sch., 69 Grant St , Needham, Mass., since 1921.

Davis, Julia E., 1100 Topeka Ave., Topeka, Kansas.

Davis, M. G., A.B.'14, Ind Univ.; A.M.'20, Univ. of Wis.; Supt. of Sch., Ames, Iowa, since 1926.

Davis, Mary Dabney, Ph.D.'25, Tchrs. Col., Columbia Univ.; Specialist in Nursery, Kdgn. and Prim. Educ , U. S. Office of Education., Washington, D. C.

Davis, Myrtle Ramey, Diploma '25, State Normal Sch., Albion, Idaho; State Supt. of Pub. Instr., State House, Boise, Idaho, since 1929.

Davis, R. F., Supt. of Sch., Nacogdoches, Texas.

Davis, Sheldon E., B.S.'07, A.B.'08, A.M.'09, Univ. of Mo.; Ph D.'17, Columbia Univ.; Pres., Mont. State Normal Col., Dillon, Mont., since 1919.

Davis, T. S., Co. Supt. of Sch , Hollidaysburg, Pa., since 1902.

Davis, Walter B., Ped.D.'23, Alfred Univ.; Supvg. Prin. of Sch., Madison, N. J., since 1920.

Davis, William C., A.B.'04, Harvard; Supvg Prin. of Sch., H. S., Haddon Heights, N. J., since 1925.

Dawson, Howard A., B.S. and M.A.'24, Ph.D.'26, George Peabody Col. for Tchrs.; Dir. of Bureau of Educ. Statistics and Information, State Dept. of Educ., Little Rock, Ark., since 1926.

Day, Arthur L., M.A.'95, Natl. Normal Univ.; M.A.'26, Southern Methodist Univ.; Supt. of Sch., Commerce, Texas, since 1900.

Day, F. D., B.S.'20, M.A.'26, Univ. of Md.; Co. Supt. of Sch., Prince Frederick, Md., since 1927.

Day, Grace A., B.S.'11, M.A.'20, Columbia Univ.; Dir. of Elem. Educ., 8818 150th St., Jamaica, New York, N. Y.

Day, Lorey Clifford, B.A.'13, M.A.'16, Clark Univ.; Supt. of Sch., Livermore Falls, Maine, since 1926.

Deahl, J. N., A.B.'93, Harvard Univ.; A.M. '99, Ph.D.'06, Columbia Univ.; Prof. of Educ., W. Va. Univ., 442 Park St., Morgantown, W. Va., since 1901.

Deamer, Arthur, A.B.'09, Ind. Univ.; A.M. '13, Columbia Univ.; Supt. of Sch., Cedar Rapids, Iowa, since 1921.

Dean, A.B.C., A.B.'20, Howard Payne Col.; Supt., French Ind. Sch. Dist., Beaumont, Texas, since 1928.

Dean, Cecil Helen, Sch. Admin. Bldg., Pittsburgh, Pa.

Dean, H. A., Supt. of Sch., Crystal Lake, Ill.

Dean, Renwick G., A.B.'02, A.M.'05, Grove City Col.; A.M.'29, Univ. of Pittsburgh; Fifth Avenue H. S., 1447 Davis Ave., Pittsburgh, N. S., Pa.

Dearborn, Ned H., Ph.D.'25, Columbia Univ. Address: Sch. of Educ., N. Y. Univ., New York, N. Y.

Deaver, Arthur G., B.Ph.'11, Univ. of Chicago; A.M.'13, York Col.; Dist. Supt. of Sch., 7925 Kingston Ave., Chicago, Ill., since 1925.

De Bell, W. H., B.S.'01, Univ. of Calif.; Deputy Supt. of Sch., City Hall, San Francisco, Calif., since 1914.

De Camp, John A., A.B.'00, M.A.'06, Williams; Supt. of Sch., 13 Elizabeth St., Utica, N. Y., since 1917.

Deck, I. J., A.M., Columbia Univ.; Supt. of Sch., Crockett, Texas, since 1929.

Decker, Ralph, Co. Supt. of Sch., Sussex, N. J.

Deering, E. C., B.A.'20, Baylor Univ.; Supt. of Sch., City, Hall, Marshall, Texas, since 1925.

Deering, John F., Supt. of Sch., 67 Providence St., West Warwick, R. I., since 1913.

Deevers, Roland Gilliford, A.B.'02, M.A.'05, Sc.D.'28, Westminster Col.; Prin., Taylor Allderdice Jr.-Sr. H. S., 7620 Waverly St., Pittsburgh, Pa., since 1927.

De Groat, Harry DeW., Prin., State Normal Sch., Cortland, N. Y.

Dehn, A. O., A.B.'25, Univ. of Toledo; Co. Supt. of Sch., Court House, Port Clinton, Ohio.

DeLaney, L. E., B.S.'02, Wesleyan Univ., Middletown, Conn.; Supt. of Sch., 601 W. Lockhart St., Sayre, Pa., since 1907.

Dellicker, Helen Maude, B.S.'18, M.A.'24, Tchrs. Col., Columbia Univ.; Gram. Supvr., 55 Spear St., Quincy, Mass., since 1918.

Del Manzo, Milton C., Ph.D.'24, State Univ. of Iowa; Provost and Prof. of Educ., Tchrs. Col., Columbia Univ., 525 W. 120th St., New York, N. Y.

De Long, Leo R., A.B.'15, Augustana Col.; M.A.'21, Ph.D.'30, Columbia Univ.; Asst. Dir., Tchr. Tr. Ext., Pa. State Col., 400 N. Third St., Harrisburg, Pa., since 1927.

De Meyer, John E., A.B.'05, Bates Col. Address: 74 Park St., Springfield, Mass.

Deming, Leon J., A.B.'22, Phillips Univ.; M.A.'25, Univ. of Okla.; Supt. of Sch., Oyster Bay, N. Y., since 1928.

Dempsey, Clarence H., A.B.'95, A.M.'13, Boston Univ.; Litt. D. '26, Norwich Univ.; State Commr. of Educ., State House, Montpelier, Vt., since 1920.

Dempsey, Harold E., B.S.'20, A.M.'24, Columbia Univ. Address: The Crogswold, Scarsdale, N. Y.

Dempsey, John A., Supt. of Sch., 306 S. Valley Ave., Olyphant, Pa.

DeMunbrun, H. C., B.S.'27, Northwestern State Tchrs. Col., Alva, Okla.; Supt. of Sch., Vinita, Okla., since 1930.

Dengler, C. F., Diploma '14, Keystone State Normal Sch., Kutztown, Pa.; B.S.'25, Muhlenberg Col.; A.M.'30, Columbia Univ.; Supvg. Prin. of Sch., Palmyra, N. J., since 1930.

Denison, Edmund D., A.B.'99, N. W. Univ.; Supt. of Sch., 224 Warren St., Lake Geneva, Wis., since 1922.

Denison, H. S., A.B.'11, Olivet Col.; Supt., L'Anse Twp. Sch., L'Anse, Mich., since 1926.

Denison, S. A., B.A.'22, Ill. State Normal Univ.; M.A.'28, Univ. of Ill.; Supt. of Sch., Glen Ellyn, Ill.

Denison, William Mason, A.B.'00, Colgate Univ.; A.M.'16 Columbia Univ.; Deputy State Supt. of Pub. Instr., Harrisburg, Pa., since 1925.

Dennis, Merrill L., B.S. in Ed.'19, Ohio Univ.; Co. Supt. of Sch., Court House, Steubenville, Ohio, since 1927.

Dennis, S. C., Supt. of Sch., Toronto, Ohio, since 1916.

Denny, Winfield A., A.B.'98, A.M.'99, Ind. Univ.; A.M.'19, Tchrs. Col., Columbia Univ.; Supt. of Sch., 100 W. Eighth St., Anderson, Ind., since 1914.

Densberger, Frank C., A.B.'08, Syracuse Univ.; A.M.'21, Tchrs. Col., Columbia Univ.; Supt. of Sch., Kenmore, N. Y., since 1915.

Dent, Lettie Marshall, A.B.'15, Western Md. Col.; Co. Supt. of Sch., Leonardtown, Md., since 1928.

Denworth, Katharine M., A.B., Swarthmore Col.; A.M. and Ph.D., Columbia Univ.; Pres., Bradford Academy and Jr. Col., Bradford, Mass., since 1927.

Deputy, M. W., A.M.'05, Ind. Univ.; Pres., State Tchrs. Col., Bemidji, Minn., since 1919.

Derbyshire, Grant E., Supt. of Sch., Princeton, Ind.

Derthick, H. J., M.A.'12, Univ. of Mich.; Pres., Milligan Col., Milligan College, Tenn., since 1917.

Desmond, John J., Jr., A.B.'09, A.M.'10, Harvard Univ.; Supt. of Sch., Sch. Dept., Chicopee, Mass.

De Turck, Werner E., B.S.'02, Keystone State Normal Sch., Kutztown, Pa.; A.B. '05, Franklin and Marshall Col.; A.M.'24, Univ. of Pa.; Supvg. Prin. of Twp. Sch., Erlton, N. J., since 1930.

Dewey, Godfrey, A.B.'09, Harvard Col.; Ed.M.'21, Ed.D.'26, Harvard Univ.; Exec. Vice-Pres., Lake Placid Club Educ. Foundation, Lake Placid Club, N. Y., since 1924.

Dewey, H. Evert, A.B.'13, Kalamazoo Col.; M.A.'19, Oberlin Col.; Prin., Univ. of Chicago H. S., 5833 Dorchester Ave., Chicago, Ill., since 1930.

Dewey, Ralph S., M.S.'19, Allegheny Col.; M.A.'27, Tchrs. Col., Columbia Univ.; Supt. of Sch., Corry, Pa., since 1926.

DeWolf, George E., A.B.'12, Univ. of Nebr.; M.A.'20, Harvard Univ.; Supt. of Sch., Sr. H. S., Creston, Iowa, since 1926.

De Young, Chris A., A.B.'20, Hope Col.; A.M.'29, Columbia Univ.; Sch. of Educ., Northwestern Univ., Evanston, Ill.

Diaz Baldorioty, Hatuey, Normal Diploma '12, Univ. of Porto Rico; Pd.B.'16, M.A. in Ed.'24, Tchrs. Professional Col., Washington, D. C.; Supvr. of Sch., Guanica, P. R.

Dickey, Charles E., M.E.'93, State Normal Sch., California, Pa.; B.A.'20, Univ. of Pittsburgh; Co. Supt. of Sch., 595 Union Trust Bldg., Pittsburgh, Pa., since 1922.

Dickson, Agnes B., 18 S. Euclid Ave., Bellevue, Pa.

Dickson, Myrtle C., A.B.'04, Radcliffe Col.; A.M.'26, Boston Univ.; Headmaster, Roxbury Memorial H. S. for Girls, Roxbury, Boston, Mass., since 1926.

Dickson, Virgil E., A.B.'08, Wash. State Col.; M.A.'17, Ph.D.'19, Stanford Univ.; Asst. Supt. of Sch., 2325 Milvia St., Berkeley, Calif., since 1928.

Diehl, George West, A.B.'13, Washington and Lee Univ.; B.D.'16, Union Theo. Sem.; M.A.'17, Univ. of Richmond; Pres., Morris Harvey Col., Barboursville, W. Va., since 1929.

Diehl, John C., A.B.'87, A.M.'03, Yale; Supt. of Sch., Library Bldg., Erie, Pa., since 1922.

Diemer, G. W., Pres., Tchrs. Col. of Kansas City, Eighth and Woodland, Kansas City, Mo.

Diener, U. E., B.S.'17, Miami Univ.; M.A. '30, Ohio State Univ.; Supt. of Sch., 808 Elm St., Van Wert, Ohio.

Dienst, Charles F., B.S. in Ed.'14, Univ. of Mo.; A.M.'16, Tchrs. Col., Columbia Univ.; Supt. of Sch., Boise, Idaho, since 1922.

Dieterich, H. C., A.B.'05, Ohio State Univ.; Supt. of Sch., 2453 Plymouth Rd., Bexley, Columbus, Ohio, since 1924.

Dietrich, E. N., A.B.'12, Ohio Wesleyan; B.S.'16, Ohio Univ.; M.A.'28, Ohio State Univ.; Supt. of Sch., Central Bldg., Bucyrus, Ohio, since 1927.

Dietrich, George C., Ph.B. '98, Ohio State Univ.; Supt. of Sch., 520 W. Ash St., Piqua, Ohio, since 1909.

Dietrich, Harvey Oscar, Supt. of Sch., Norristown, Pa., since 1922.

Diffendafer, Alton P., Diploma '89, State Normal Sch., Lock Haven, Pa.; Dist. Supt. of Sch., Nanticoke, Pa., since 1902.

Dille, George Earl, B.S.'20, State Tchrs. Col., Kirksville, Mo.; M.A., Tchrs. Col., Columbia Univ.; Supt. of Sch., Chillicothe, Mo., since 1925.

Dillehay, Claude H., A.B.'16, Baylor Univ.; M.A.'17, Brown Univ.; Supt. of Sch., Hereford, Texas, since 1923.

Dillingham, Paul, A.B.'13, Tufts; Supt. of Sch., Town Hall, Falmouth, Mass., since 1923.

Dimmett, W. S., Supt. of Sch., Garfield Sch., Forest Park, Ill., since 1930.

Dimmick, Rex W., B.S.'23, A.M.'24, Tchrs. Col., Columbia Univ.; Supt. of Sch., 89 Allen Ave., Donora, Pa., since 1930.

Dinsmore, B.M., B.A.'27, North Texas State Tchrs. Col., Denton, Texas; Supt. of Sch., Electra, Texas, since 1917.

Dittes, William H., B.S.'21, Univ. of Minn.; M.A.'27, Tchrs. Col., Columbia Univ.; Supt. of Sch., Frazee, Minn., since 1925.

Dixon, Charles R., B.S.'10, New York Univ.; Supvg. Prin. of Sch., 558 Morse Ave., Ridgefield, N. J., since 1921.

Dixon, Henry C., B.S.'93, M.S.'97, Franklin Col.; Co. Supt. of Sch., 216 Johnson St., Salem, N. J., since 1913.

Dixon, John C., A.B.'13, Mercer Univ.; M.A.'26. Tchrs. Col., Columbia Univ.; Supvr. of Negro Educ., State Dept. of Educ., State Capitol, Atlanta, Ga.

Dobbs, Ella Victoria, B.S.'09, Columbia Univ.; A.M.'13, Univ. of Mo.; Assoc. Prof. of Industrial Arts, Univ. of Mo., Columbia, Mo., since 1909.

Dockrill, James C., LL.B.'93, Lake Forest. Address: 330 E. 22nd St., Chicago, Ill.

Dodd, H. W., Ph.B.'08, Yale Univ.; A.M. '14, Tchrs. Col., Columbia Univ.; Pd.D. '21, Muhlenberg Col.; Supt. of Sch., Allentown, Pa., since 1916.

Dodd, John W., B.S.'20, A.M.'21, Tchrs. Col., Columbia Univ.; Supt. of Sch., 317 S. Longbeach Ave., Freeport, N. Y., since 1925.

Dodd, Maurice R., B.A.'14, W. Va. Univ.; Supt. of Sch., Florence, Ariz., since 1925.

Dodge, Harrison S., Supt. of Sch., Hornell, N. Y.

Dodge, Willis E., A.B.'13, Bowdoin Col.; A.M.'25. Bates Col.; Supt. of Sch , Great Neck, N. Y., since 1929.

Dodson, Edwin C., A.B.'04, Ind. Univ.; A.M.'14, Columbia Univ.; Supt. of Sch., 19th St. and Grand Ave, Connersville, Ind., since 1921.

Dodson, William C., Co. Supt. of Pub. Instr., Court House, Nashville, Tenn.

Doe, Chester W., Union Supt. of Sch., Northwood, N. H.

Dohner, A. J., A.M.'05, Findlay; Supt. of Sch., 225 Johnson St., Salem, N. J., since 1920.

Dolph, Arthur H., B.S. in Ed.'26, Univ. of Ill.; Supt. of County High Schools, Lander, Wyo., since 1928.

Dolton, Isabella, Ph.B., Univ. of Chicago; Asst. Supt. of Sch., 460 S. State St., Chicago, Ill., since 1928.

Dominick, Leo H., B.A.'20, M.S.'30, Univ. of N. Dak.; Supt. of Sch., Wahpeton, N. Dak., since 1924.

Dondineau, Arthur, A.M.'15, Univ. of Mich.; Supvg. Dir. of Instr., Pub. Sch., 1354 Broadway, Detroit, Mich., since 1924.

Donley, Herman H., Prin., Brewster H. S., Brewster, N. Y.

Donnell, Jane B., Supt of Sch., Hightstown, N. J.

Donovan, H. L., A.B.'14, Univ. of Ky.; M. A.'20, Tchrs. Col., Columbia Univ.; Ph.D. '25, George Peabody Col. for Tchrs.; Pres., Eastern Ky. State Tchrs. Col., Richmond, Ky., since 1928.

Donovan, Michael Charles, Supt. of Sch., 206 Columbia Blvd., Waterbury, Conn.

Doolittle, Howard S., A.B.'15, A.M.'28, Univ. of Mich.; Supt. of Sch., Negaunee, Mich., since 1921.

Doria, Oscar Porrata, Genl. Supt. of Agr., Dept. of Educ., San Juan, P. R., since 1926.

Dorr, John H., Supt. of Sch., 801 Howard St., Monongahela, Pa.

Dorsey, Julius, M.A.'19, George Peabody Col. for Tchrs.; Dist. Supt. of Sch., 1215 Apple St., Dallas, Texas, since 1922.

Dorsey, Mrs. Susan M., A.B.'77, Vassar Col.; Supt. Emeritus, Pub. Sch., Los Angeles, Calif., since 1929. Address: 1506 Arapahoe St., Los Angeles, Calif.

Dossett, Burgin E., B.A.'22, Univ. of Tenn.; Ed.M.'24, Harvard Univ.; Co. Supt. of Pub. Instr., Jacksboro, Tenn., since 1928.

Dotson, H. L., B.S.'21, Colo. Agrl. Col.; Supt. of Sch., Hayden, Colo., since 1927.

Dougall, John Bernard, B.A.'08, Adelphi Col.; M.A.'24, Yale Univ.; Supt. of Sch., 39 Ashland Rd., Summit, N. J., since 1924.

Dougan, James E., Asst. Supt. of Sch., Newark, N. J.

Dougherty, Mary C., 11 Linden St., River Rouge, Mich.

Douglass, A. A., Ph.D.'17, Clark Univ.; Prof. and Head, Dept. of Educ., Claremont Col., Claremont, Calif., since 1926.

Douglass, Bennett C., Ph.B.'08, Univ. of Vt.; M.A.'20, Ph.D.'24, Columbia Univ.; Head, Dept. of Educ. and Dir., Summer Session, Univ. of Vt., Burlington, Vt., since 1921.

Douglass, Carleton E., Ph.B.'99, Univ. of Chicago; A.M.'17, Columbia Univ.; Asst. Supt. of Sch., Madison and Lafayette, Baltimore, Md., since 1921.

Douglass, Harl R., A.M.'21, Univ. of Mo.; Ph.D.'28, Stanford Univ.; Prof. of Sec. Educ., Univ. of Minn., Minneapolis, Minn., since 1929.

Douglass, Wesley H., A.B.'05, Syracuse Univ.; Union Supt. of Sch., Winchester, N. H., since 1925.

Douthett, Walter R., A.B.'12, Ursinus Col.; A.M.'21, Univ. of Pa.; Supt. of Sch., Seventh and Spruce Sts., Darby, Pa., since 1922.

Dow, H. E., B.A.'06, M.A.'26, State Univ. of Iowa; Supt. of Sch., Villisca, Iowa, since 1924.

Dow, Harold F., B.S.'10, Colby; Supt. of Sch., Swampscott, Mass., since 1920.

Dowling, H. G., B.S.'06, A.M.'26, Birmingham-Southern Col.; Co. Supt. of Sch., Tuscaloosa, Ala., since 1929.

Down, Edgar F., Normal Life Cert.'03, State Normal Sch., Cortland, N. Y.; A.B.'17. Univ. of Mich.; J.D.'25, Detroit Col. of Law; Supt. of Sch., Ferndale, Mich., since 1925.

Downey, James E., A.B.'97, A.M.'05, Amherst Col.; A.M.'12, Harvard Univ.; A.M. '13, Ph.D.'30, Boston Col.; Headmaster, H. S. of Commerce, Boston, Mass., since 1910.

Downey, Michael J., A.B.'04, A.M.'14. Boston Col.; Asst. Supt. of Sch., 15 Beacon St., Boston, Mass., since 1924.

Downey, Walter F., A.B.'06, Amherst Col.; Ed.M.'21, Harvard Univ.; Headmaster, The English H. S., Montgomery St., Boston, Mass., since 1922.

Downing, C. E., B.S.'28, Heidelberg Col.; Supt. of Sch., Kelley's Island, Ohio, since 1929.

Downing, D. L., A.B.'20, Ind. State Normal Sch.; A.M.'28, Columbia Univ.; Supt. of Sch., Covington, Ind., since 1929.

Downing, Elliot Rowland. B.S'89, M.S.'94, Albion Col.; Ph.D.'01, Univ. of Chicago; Assoc. Prof., Teaching of Science. Univ. of Chicago, 6031 Kimbark Ave., Chicago, Ill., since 1911.

Downs, Samuel Edgar, Supt. of Sch., 115 Linwood Ave., Ardmore, Pa.

Doyne, John J., Supt. of Sch., 902 Barnes, Lonoke, Ark., since 1917.

Drake, Ellis H., A.B.'04, Ind. Univ.; Supt. of Sch., Sch. Admin. Bldg., 306 E. Lovell St., Kalamazoo, Mich., since 1915.

Draper, Henry W., LL.M.'04, National Univ.; B.A.'09. M.A.'22, George Washington Univ.; Supvg. Prin. of Sch., 1521 35th St., N. W., Washington, D. C., since 1927.

Dressel, Herman, B.L.'90, M.A.'95, Litt.D. '25, Norwich Univ.; Supt. of Sch., Kearny, N. J. Address: 165 Stewart Ave, Arlington, N. J.

Driver, Lee L., A.B.'19, Ind. Univ.; M.A. '19, Earlham Col.; LL.D.'21, Wabash Col.; Dir. Rural Service Bureau, State Dept. of Pub. Instr., 711 N. Second St., Harrisburg, Pa., since 1920.

Drown, Carroll H., A.B.'01, Univ. of Vt.; Supt. of Sch., Hopedale, Mass., since 1919.

Drummond, Glenn, A.B.'09, Ohio Northern Univ.; A.B.'11, Antioch Col.; M.A.'26, Ohio State Univ.; Co. Supt. of Sch., Bellefontaine, Ohio, since 1923.

Duboc, Jessie L., M.A.'22, Univ. of Chicago; Asst. Prof. of Educ., Mont. State Normal Col., Dillon, Mont.

Dudley, L. Leland, S.B.'21, Ed.M. and Ed. D.'27, Harvard Univ.; Asst. Prof. of Educ. Admin., Grad. Sch. of Educ., Harvard Univ., Cambridge, Mass., since 1924.

Duffey, H. S., A.B.'09, Randolph-Macon Col.; Box 459, Winchester, Va.

Duffy, James P. B., Hotel Rochester, Rochester, N. Y.

Dugan, James, B.A.'02, Amherst Col.; Asst. Supt. of Sch., Cambridge, Mass., since 1920.

Duggan, Mell L., Pd.D., Mercer Univ.; State Supt. of Sch., State Capitol, Atlanta, Ga., since 1927.

Dulebohn, Irl H., B.S.'21, State Tchrs. Col., Emporia, Kansas; A.M.'25. Univ. of Chicago; Supt. of Twp. Sch., Ramsay, Mich., since 1925.

Duncan, Earle C., B.S. in Ed.'22, State Tchrs. Col., Maryville. Mo.; M.A.'29, Univ. of Mo.; Supt. of Sch., Clarinda, Iowa, since 1928.

Dunckel, O. E., Life Cert.'17, Western State Tchrs. Col.; B.S.'21. Mich. State Col.; M.A.'26, Univ. of Mich.; Supt. of Sch., Manchester, Mich., since 1926.

Dunfield, I. Burten, B.A.'11, Bates Col.; Supvr. of Rural Educ., State Bd. of Educ., Naugatuck, Conn., since 1918.

Dungan, John U., B.S.'19, Univ. of Ill.; Supt. of Sch., Lockland, Ohio, since 1923.

Dunkle, John L., B.S.'12, W. Va. Univ.; M.A.'17, Tchrs. Col., Columbia Univ.; Prin., State Normal Sch., Frostburg, Md., since 1923.

Dunkley, Everett W., B.S.'22, Lynchburg Col.; M.A.'29, W. Va. Univ.; Dist. Supt. of Sch., Glen Jean, W. Va., since 1930.

Dunn, Fannie W., B.S.'15, A.M.'17, Ph.D. '20, Tchrs. Col., Columbia Univ.; Assoc. Prof. of Educ., Tchrs. Col., Columbia Univ., New York, N. Y.

Dunsmore, Jessie, A.B.'25, Mich. State Tchrs. Col., Ypsilanti, Mich.; M.A.'26, Columbia Univ.; Asst. Field Supvr. of Rural Educ., State Bd. of Educ., 203 Church St., Naugatuck, Conn., since 1930.

Dunton, John A., A.B.'21, Univ. of Maine; Supt. of Sch., Stonington, Maine, since 1924.

Dunwiddie, Walter R., B.S.'16, M.S.'27, Univ. of Wis.; Supt. of Sch., H. S. Bldg., Port Washington, Wis., since 1926.

Dunwoodie, Fannie, Co. Supt. of Sch., Walla Walla, Wash., since 1925.

Durell, Thomas J., A.B.'07, Princeton; A. M.'30, Columbia Univ.; Co. Supt. of Sch., Cape May Court House, N. J., since 1927.

Durham, Harry L., Supt. of Sch., Bryan, Texas.

Dutch, Herbert W., A.B.'96, Harvard Univ.; Supt. of Sch., Glen Ridge, N. J., since 1926.

Dutter, H. W., A.B.'11, Ind. Univ.; A.M. '16, Columbia Univ.; Supt. of Sch., Coleraine, Minn., since 1925.

Duvall, Claude A., B.S.'22, M.S.'26, Syracuse Univ.; Supt. of Sch., Solvay, N. Y., since 1925.

Dye, Claude R., A.B.'06, Allegheny Col.; Supt. of Sch., Fredonia, N. Y., since 1924.

Dyer, John H., Supt. of Sch., 1416 Jackson St., Scranton, Pa.

Dyer, John Ruskin, Univ. of Idaho, Southern Branch, Pocatello, Idaho.

Dyer, W. P., M.A.'20, Univ. of Minn.; Ph. D.'27, Columbia Univ.; Supt. of Tr. Sch., State Normal Sch., New Britain, Conn., since 1926.

Dyke, Charles B., Supt. of Sch., Short Hills, N. J.

Dykema, Peter W., B.L.'95, M.L.'96, Univ. of Mich.; Prof. of Music Educ., Tchrs. Col., Columbia Univ., New York, N. Y., since 1924.

Eagleson, John Oliver, B.S.'09, Muskingum Col.; Supt. of Sch., 317 S. Pickaway St., Circleville, Ohio, since 1920.

Eakeley, Frank S., M.A.'19, Tchrs. Col., Columbia Univ.; Supt. of Los Angeles Hgts. Sch., 829 W. Mistletoe, San Antonio, Texas, since 1929.

Eakens, H. H., Supt. of Sch., 415 Byron St., Mankato, Minn.

Earhart, Will, Mus.D.'20; Dir. of Music, Bd. of Educ., Forbes St. and Bellefield Ave., Pittsburgh, Pa., since 1912.

Early, J. J., A.B.'01, Ind.; A.M.'27, Tchrs. Col., Columbia Univ.; Supt. of Sch., Sheridan, Wyo., since 1908.

Easson, McGregor, Pub. Sch. Insp., 330 Gilmour St., Ottawa, Canada.

Eastman, Nellie W., Diploma, Kansas State Tchrs. Col. Address: 725 Lincoln St., Emporia, Kansas.

Eaton, George A., A.B. and A.M.'92, Harvard; Asst. Supt. of Sch., 484 J St., Salt Lake City, Utah, since 1920.

Eaton, Henry M., M.Sc.'01, Salins Univ.; B.A.'17, Fremont Col.; Supvg. Prin. of Sch., Westfield H. S., Westfield, N. Y.

Eccleston, Howard B., 176 Matthews St., Binghamton, N. Y.

Eckert, Paul Y., A.B.'06, Dickinson Col.; LL.D.'16, Univ. of Oregon; M.A.'18, Dickinson Col.; Supvg. Prin. of Sch., Palmyra, N. J., since 1928.

Eckles, Isabel Lancaster, M.A.'23, State Tchrs. Col., Silver City, N. Mex.; Supt. of Sch., Santa Fe, N. Mex., since 1927.

Eckles, Mary H., Supt. of Sch., Hurley, N. Mex.

Eckles, Port, A.B.'14, Hiram Col.; A.M.'24, Univ. of Pittsburgh; Supt. of Sch., Homestead, Pa., since 1922.

Eckles, William Gilbert, State Dept. of Educ., Jackson, Miss.

Eddy, Theo V., A.B.'15, Hillsdale Col.; M.A.'28, Univ. of Mich.; Supt. of Sch., St. Clair, Mich., since 1930.

Eddy, William Holden, A.B.'92, A.M.'93, Ph.D.'99, Brown Univ.; Deputy Supt. of Sch., 9 Exchange Ter., Providence, R. I., since 1925.

Edminster, Winfred H., A.B.'16, Univ. of Maine; Supt. of Sch., Norway, Maine, since 1922.

Edmond, Sarah, Supvg. Prin. of Sch., Cranford, N. J.

Edmonson, Frank A., Co. Supt. of Sch., Co. Court House, Charlotte, N. C.

Edmonson, James Bartlett, A.B.'06, M.A. '10, Univ. of Mich.; Ph.D.'25, Univ. of Chicago; Dean, Sch. of Educ., Univ. of Mich., Ann Arbor, Mich., since 1929.

Edwards, Arthur U., A.B.'24, Iowa State Tchrs. Col. Address: 20 N. Dodge St., Iowa City, Iowa.

Edwards, Newton, Sch. of Educ., Univ. of Chicago, Chicago, Ill.

Egan, Mrs. Anna H., Elem. Sch. Prin., 4111 Warwick Blvd., Kansas City, Mo., since 1917.

Egan, Louella E., Dist. Supt. of Sch., 3726 Milan St., New Orleans, La.

Egan, Nora L., Diploma'90, Detroit Normal Sch.; Dist. Prin., Goodale Sch., Detroit, Mich., since 1919.

Eikenberry, D. H., A.B.'11, A.M.'15, Ind. Univ.; Ph.D.'26, Tchrs. Col., Columbia Univ.; Prof. of Sch. Admin., Col. of Educ., Ohio State Univ., Columbus, Ohio, since 1927.

Eikenberry, V. L., A.B.'14, Franklin Col., Ind.; A.M.'15, Ind. Univ.; Supt. of Sch., Vincennes, Ind., since 1929.

Eilenberger, R. J., Diploma'06, State Normal Sch., East Stroudsburg, Pa.; Supvg. Prin. of Sch., H. S., Butler, N. J., since 1920.

Eisenberg, J. Linwood, B.E.'95, Juniata Col.; A.B.'06, A.M.'08, Ursinus Col.; Ph. D.'13, Univ. of Pa.; LL.D.'28, Grove City Col.; Prin., Slippery Rock State Normal Sch., Slippery Rock, Pa., since 1917.

Eisenhart, W. W., B.S.'17, M.A.'21, Univ. of Pa.; Supt. of Sch., Tyrone, Pa., since 1921.

Ekstrom, Claus Emanuel, A.B.'16, A.M.'17, Brown Univ.; Asst. Prof. of Educ., Brown Univ., since 1919 and Chmn., Dept. of Educ., Brown Univ., Providence, R. I., since 1927.

Elcan, E. G., A.B.'08, Hampden-Sidney Col.; Supt. of Sch., Bainbridge, Ga., since 1920.

Elder, Harry E., Diploma'13, Ind. State Tchrs. Col., Terre Haute, Ind.; A.B.'20, Ind. Univ.; M.A.'25, Univ. of Chicago; Supt. of Sch., 211 S. Main St., Monticello, Ind., since 1917.

Eldred, Arvie, A.B.'05, A.M.'21, Williams Col.; Pd.D.'25, N. Y. State Col. for Tchrs.; Exec. Secy., N. Y. State Tchrs. Assn., 240 State St., Albany, N. Y., since 1930.

Eldredge, A. C., B.S.'95, Mt. Union Col.; Asst. Supt. of Sch., Engineers Natl. Bank Bldg., Cleveland, Ohio, since 1914.

Ellenberger, Charles W., B.S.'28, Juniata Col.; Supvg. Prin. of Sch., Brookville, Pa., since 1929.

Elliff, Joseph Doliver, A.B.'03, A.M.'05, Univ. of Mo.; Prof. of H. S. Admin., Univ. of Mo., Columbia, Mo., since 1904.

Elliff, Miles A., B.S.'25, State Tchrs. Col., Pittsburg, Kansas; M.A.'27, Univ. of Mo.; Supt. of Sch., Aurora, Mo., since 1927.

Ellingwood, W. H. S., A.B.'01, Bates Col.; Dist. Supt. of Sch., Westbrook, Maine, since 1923.

Elliott, A. W., A.B., Ohio Wesleyan Univ.; A.M., Univ. of Chicago; Supt. of Sch., 704 N. Gay St., Mt. Vernon, Ohio, since 1921.

Elliott, Charles H., Ph.D.'14, Columbia Univ.; State Commr. of Educ., State House, Trenton, N. J., since 1927.

Elliott, E. A., M.A.'25, Univ. of Kansas; Supt. of Sch., Joplin, Mo., since 1930.

Elliott, Lucy C., 911 Locust, St. Louis, Mo.

Elliott, Robert I., B.S.'01, Normal Col., Wayne, Nebr.; A.B.'14, Univ. of Nebr.; M.A.'28, Columbia Univ.; Pres., Nebr. State Normal Col., Chadron, Nebr., since 1915.

Ellis, H. A., A.B.'14, Wash. State Col.; Supt. of Sch., H. S. Bldg., Colfax, Wash., since 1924.

Ellis, Henry G., A.B.'10, Randolph-Macon Col.; Supt. of Sch., Petersburg, Va., since 1923.

Ellis, Radford Terrell, B.A.'15, Texas Christian Univ.; Exec. Secy., Texas State Tchrs. Assn., 410 E. Weatherford St., Fort Worth, Texas, since 1916.

Ellis, William Daniel, A.M.'08, Randolph-Macon Col.; M.A.'22, Tchrs. Col., Columbia Univ.; Prin., Richmond Normal Sch., Richmond, Va., since 1920.

Elmendorf, George M., Ph.B.'05, A.M.'29, Union Col.; Supt. of Sch., Plattsburgh, N. Y., since 1920.

Elsbree, Willard S., Ph.D.'28, Columbia Univ.; Asst. Prof. of Educ., Tchrs. Col., Columbia Univ., New York, N. Y., since 1926.

Emery, E. W., A.B.'15, Ind. Central Col.; A.M.'24, Ind. Univ.; D.D.'28, York Col.; Dept. of Prin. of Educ., Ohio State Univ., Columbus, Ohio, since 1930.

Endsley, Andrew D., Ph.B.'98, Col. of Wooster; Supt. of Sch., Tarentum, Pa., since 1905.

Engelhardt, Fred, Ph.B.'08, Yale Univ.; M.A.'15, Ph.D.'24, Tchrs. Col., Columbia Univ.; Prof. of Educ. Admin., Col. of Educ., Univ. of Minn., Minneapolis, Minn., since 1924.

Engelhardt, J. L., A.B.'22, Southwestern Col., Winfield, Kansas; M.A.'23, Univ. of Kansas; Supt. of Sch., Kingman, Kansas, since 1925.

Engelhardt, N. L., A.B.'03, Yale Univ.; Ph. D.'18, Columbia Univ.; Prof. of Educ., Tchrs. Col., Columbia Univ., New York, N. Y., since 1921 and Assoc. Dir. of Div. of Field Studies, Inst. of Educ. Research, Tchrs. Col., Columbia Univ., New York, N. Y., since 1929.

Engleman, James O., Diploma'01, State Normal Sch., Terre Haute, Ind.; A.B.'05, Ind. Univ.; A.M.'18, Univ. of Chicago; LL.D.'23, James Millikin Univ.; Pres., Kent State Col., Kent, Ohio, since 1928.

English, Fred C., A.B.'16, Colby Col.; Supt. of Sch., Calais, Maine, since 1930.

English, Harry, B.A.'86, Johns Hopkins Univ.; LL.B.'89, LL.M.'90, Columbian Univ.; Chief Examiner, Pub. Sch., Franklin Admin. Bldg., 13th and K Sts., N. W., Washington, D. C., since 1924.

English, Mildred E., B.S.'21, M.A.'26, George Peabody Col. for Tchrs.; Asst. Supt. of Sch., Raleigh, N. C., since 1924.

English, William J., A.B.'13, Dartmouth Col.; Supt. of Sch., Town Hall, Lebanon, N. H., since 1925.

Englund, Walter E., B.A.'11, Gustavus Adolphus Col.; Supt. of Sch., Ely, Minn., since 1922.

Erdly, Calvin V., B.S.'20, Susquehanna Univ.; Supt. of Sch., Hollidaysburg, Pa., since 1925.

Erickson, Arthur G., A.B.'11, A.M.'16, Univ. of Mich.; M.Ed.'22, Mich. State Normal Col.; Supt. of Sch., Ypsilanti, Mich., since 1919.

Erickson, E. J., B.A.'20, Gustavus Adolphus Col.; M.A.'28, Univ. of Minn.; Supt. of Sch., Volga, S. Dak., since 1925.

Erickson, John E., A.B.'09, A.M.'25, Univ. of Mich.; Supt. of Sch., 139 W. Roberts, Hazel Park, Mich., since 1929.

Ernst, Lillie R., Ph.B.'92, A.M.'07, Wash. Univ.; Asst. Supt of Sch., 911 Locust St., St. Louis, Mo., since 1929.

Erwin, Clayton L., A.B.'03, Dartmouth Col.; Deputy State Commr. of Educ., Bellows Falls, Vt., since 1927.

Erwin, Clyde A., Co. Supt. of Sch., Rutherfordton, N. C., since 1925.

Erwin, Eugene Brown, Co. Supt. of Sch., 1605 14th Ave., S., Birmingham, Ala.

Erwin, Robert L., A.B.'92, A.M.'07, Yale Univ.; D.Pd.'18, Ohio Univ.; Supt. of Sch., Steubenville, Ohio, since 1907.

Erwine, Russell Harvey, B.L.'07, Ohio Wesleyan; M.A.'22, Wittenberg Col.; Asst. Supt. of Sch., 863 Bloomfield Ave., Akron, Ohio, since 1925.

Essex, Don L., A.B.'17, A.M.'25, Ind. Univ. Address: 404 Bancroft Hall, 509 W. 121st St., New York, N. Y.

Esten, Richard Stewart, A.B.'14, Middlebury Col.; A.M.'25, Columbia Univ.; Supt. of Sch., Rockland, Mass.

Estenson, Emil, B.A.'11, Luther Col.; M.S. '27, Univ. of N. Dak.; Supt. of Sch., Buhl, Minn., since 1929.

Estill, Harry F., Litt.D.'07, Austin Col.; Pres., Sam Houston State Tchrs. Col., Huntsville, Texas, since 1908.

Eva, Sister, M.A.'16, Columbia Univ.; Prin., St. Joseph's Academy, St. Paul, Minn., since 1925.

Evans, C. E., B.A.'88, Oxford Col.; M.A. '06, Univ. of Texas; LL.D.'23, Southwestern Univ.; Pres., Southwest Texas State Tchrs. Col., San Marcos, Texas, since 1911.

Evans, C. W., Asst. Supt. of Sch., Decatur, Ill.

Evans, Evan E., A.B.'20, Baker Univ.; A. M.'28, Univ. of Chicago; Prin., Jr.-Sr. H. S., Winfield, Kansas, since 1926.

Evans, Floyd L., Diploma'02, State Normal Sch., Geneseo, N. Y.; Supvg. Prin. of Twp. Sch., Dayton, N. J., since 1907.

Evans, Frank, '83, George Peabody Col.; LL.D.'20, Univ. of S. C.; Supt. of Sch., 169 N. Dean, Spartanburg, S. C., since 1895.

Evans, Howard R., A.B.'25, Ind. State Tchrs. Col., Terre Haute, Ind.; M.A.'28, Columbia Univ.; Ph.D.'30, Northwestern Univ. Address: Univ. of Akron, Akron, Ohio.

Evans, Lawton Bryan, A.B.'80, Emory Col.; A.M.'81, Univ. of Ga.; Supt. of Sch., Augusta, Ga., since 1882.

Evans, R. M., Ph.B.'01, Emory Col.; M.A. '26, Emory Univ.; State Supvr. of Elem. Sch., Capitol Bldg., Tallahassee, Fla., since 1925.

Evans, Robert O., B.Pd.'20, State Tchrs. Col., Maryville, Mo.; B.S. in Ed.'22, Univ. of Mo.; M.A.'24, Tchrs. Col., Columbia Univ.; Supt. of Sch., Helena, Mont., since 1929.

Evans, W. W., Co. Supt. of Sch., Barbourville, Ky.

Evelyn, Sister Mary, Ph.D.'28, Univ. of Fribourg, Suisse, Switzerland; Dean, Rosary Col., River Forest, Ill., since 1928.

Evenden, Edward S., Diploma'03, Oregon Normal Sch.; A.B.'10, A.M.'11, Stanford Univ.; Ph.D.'19, Columbia Univ.; Prof. of Educ., Tchrs. Col., Columbia Univ., 525 W. 120th St., New York, N. Y., since 1919.

Everest, C. A., A.M.'16, Univ. of Mich.; Prin., Union H. S., Grand Rapids, Mich., since 1921.

Everett, Marcia A., 319 Market St., Belvidere, N. J.

Eversull, Frank L., Ph.B.'22, A.M.'27, Univ. of Chicago; Prin., Sr. H. S., East St. Louis, Ill., since 1928.

Evingson, Caroline J., Co. Supt. of Sch., Court House, Fargo, N. Dak., since 1923.

Ewart, Joseph A., A.B.'93, Boston Univ.; Ed.M.'21, Harvard Univ.; Supt. of Sch., Stamford, Conn., since 1926.

Ewing, William F., A.B.'06, Stanford Univ.; M.A.'19, Univ. of Calif.; Asst. Supt. of Sch., Oakland, Calif., since 1927.

Eyman, R. Merle, B.Eng.'20, M.A.'29, Ohio State Univ.; Co. Supt. of Sch., Lancaster, Ohio, since 1928.

Fair, Eugene, A.B.'04, A.M.'09, Univ. of Mo.; Ph.D.'23, Columbia Univ.; Pres., Northeast Mo. State Tchrs. Col., Kirksville, Mo., since 1925.

Fair, Linus R., Supt. of Sch., Moro, Ark.

Fairbrothers, S. Ida, Supvr., Primary Industrial and Fine Arts, 43 Ewing St., Trenton, N. J.

Fairchild, Milton, B.A.'90, Oberlin Col.; '93, Andover Theo. Sem.; Independ. Stud. Character Educ., since 1896; Chmn., Character Educ. Inst., 3770 McKinley St., N. W., Washington, D. C., since 1922.

Fairchild, R. W., A.B.'14, M.A.'19, Univ. of Mich.; Dept. of Sch. Admin., Sch. of Educ., Northwestern Univ., Evanston, Ill., since 1930.

Fairchild, W. W., A.B.'13, Syracuse; Supt. of Sch., City Hall, Rutland, Vt., since 1921.

Falco, Marie C., 41 E. 42nd St., New York, N. Y.

Fales, Lewis A., A.B.'98, Harvard; Supt. of Sch., Attleboro, Mass., since 1905.

Falk, Herbert A., B.A. in Ed.'14, Univ. of Minn.; Supt. of Sch., Fourth and Oak Sts., Sauk Center, Minn., since 1922.

Falls, James David, A.B.'20, Ogden Col.; B.S.'22, A.M.'23, Ph.D.'26, George Peabody Col. for Tchrs.; Supt. of Sch., Sr. H. S., Ashland, Ky., since 1928.

Fanning, Albert W., A B.'22, Northwestern State Tchrs. Col., Alva, Okla.; Pres., Panhandle Agrl. and Mech. Col., Goodwell, Okla., since 1922.

Fannon, E. W., Supt. of Sch., Centerville, Iowa.

Farley, Belmont M., Ph.D.'29, Columbia Univ.; Asst. Dir., Div. of Publications, Natl. Educ. Assn., 1201 16th St., N. W., Washington, D. C., since 1929.

Farmer, Fred B., Supt. of Sch., Storm Lake, Iowa.

Farner, E. F., A.B.'09, Southwestern Col.; A.M.'22, Univ. of Kansas; Prin., Sr. H. S. and Dean, Jr. Col., 2730 Clark, Parsons, Kansas, since 1924.

Farrar, Giles L., A.B.'28, Texas Technological Col.; Supt. of Sch., Wellington, Texas, since 1928.

Farrin, Leon M., A.B.'15, Ed.M.'26, Harvard Univ.; Supt. of Sch., Putnam, Conn., since 1928.

Fast, L. W., A.B.'20, A.M.'24, Univ. of Mich.; Supt. of Sch., Mt. Clemens, Mich., since 1919.

Faulkner, Elizabeth, A.B.'85, Univ. of Chicago; Prin., The Faulkner Sch. for Girls, 4746 Dorchester Ave., Chicago, Ill., since 1909.

Fausey, John R., A.B.'18, Syracuse Univ.; Supt. of Sch., Town Hall, West Springfield, Mass., since 1923.

Fausold, Charles D., A.B.'12, Gettysburg Col.; A.M.'22, Syracuse Univ.; Supt. of Sch., Perry, N. Y., since 1923.

Fausold, Samuel, A.B.'10, Gettysburg Col.; M.A.'25, Univ. of Pittsburgh; Supt. of Sch., Sr. H. S. Bldg., Monessen, Pa., since 1930.

Faust, Hugh G., Ph.B.'06, Tusculum Col.; A.B.'14, Carson-Newman Col.; M.A.'27, Univ. of Chicago; Supt. of Sch., Shawnee, Okla., since 1914.

Favrot, Leo Mortimer, 910 Louisiana Natl. Bank, Baton Rouge, La.

Feik, L. W., B.A.'10, Northwestern Col.; M.A.'26, Univ. of Wis.; Prin., East H. S., 3903 Orleans Ave., Sioux City, Iowa, since 1926.

Fell, E. E., A.B.'02, Alma Col.; A.M.'17, Columbia Univ.; Supt. of Sch., H. S. Bldg., Holland, Mich., since 1910.

Fellows, Ernest W., A.B.'94, Grinnell Col.; A.M.'11, State Univ. of Iowa; A.M.'17, Tchrs. Col., Columbia Univ.; Supt. of Sch., 7 Beacon St., Gloucester, Mass., since 1921.

Fels, Maurice, A.B.'83, Johns Hopkins Univ.; LL.B.'85, Univ. of Pa. Address: Garden Court, 47th and Pine Sts., Philadelphia, Pa.

Felton, Allie Lou, B.S.'21, Fla. State Col. for Women; M.A.'26, State Univ. of Iowa; Specialist in Elem. Educ., 424 W. Peachtree St., N. W., Atlanta, Ga.

Fenner, John K., A.B.'98, Brown Univ.; Supt. of Sch., 18 Shirley Blvd., Cranston, R. I., since 1917.

Fenton, F. C., A.B.'17, Aurora Col.; Supt. of Sch., 176 Mason St., Bensenville, Ill., since 1921.

Ferguson, Arthur W., B.S.'12, Univ. of Pa.; A.M.'20, Lafayette Col.; Ph.D.'24, Univ. of Pa.; Supt. of Sch., York, Pa., since 1930.

Ferguson, Chauncey C., A.B.'92, A.M.'95, Bates Col.; Dist. Supt. of Sch., Millbury, Mass., since 1912.

Ferguson, J. C., P. O. Box 777, Wheaton, Ill.

Ferguson, Lamar, A.B.'25, Georgia; Supt. of Sch., Sr. H. S., Decatur, Ga., since 1925.

Ferguson, Malcolm V., Supt. of Sch., 155 Gratiot Ave., East Detroit, Mich.

Ferner, C. M., B.S.'09, Univ. of Chicago; M.A.'25, Mich. State Normal Col.; Supt. of Sch., Sturgis, Mich., since 1908.

Ferrell, Glover B., B.A.'24, Iowa State Tchrs. Col., Cedar Falls, Iowa; M.A.'30, State Univ. of Iowa; Supt. of Sch., Oelwein, Iowa, since 1927.

Ferriss, Emery N., Ph.B.'04, Western Col.; M.A.'06, Ph.D.'08, State Univ. of Iowa; Prof. of Rural Educ., Caldwell Hall, Cornell Univ., Ithaca, N. Y., since 1920.

Fessenden, Zina, Co. Supt. of Sch., Cresco, Iowa, since 1926.

Fetherston, Roy, B.A.'23, Beloit Col.; Supt. of Sch., H. S., Monmouth, Ill., since 1930.

Fetterly, Clarence A., A.B.'97, A.M.'00, Hamilton; Supvg. Prin. of Sch., Rutherford, N. J., since 1911.

Fichter, Joseph W., B.A.'15, Miami Univ.; Co. Supt. of Sch., Court House, Hamilton, Ohio, since 1923.

Fidler, William L., Jr., Supt. of Sch., 185 Carlisle Rd., Audubon, N. J.

Fielder, Edwin W., 381 Fourth Ave., New York, N. Y.

Files, Ralph E., A.B.'95, Bates Col.; Prin., East Orange H. S., 34 N. Walnut St., East Orange, N. J., since 1912.

Filgo, Holland C., A.B.'20, Baylor Univ.; Supt. of Sch., Van Alstyne, Texas, since 1924.

Fillers, Herbert D., S.B.'16, Univ. of Chicago; M.A.'28, Columbia Univ.; Supt. of Sch., Corsicana, Texas, since 1921.

Finch, Howard A., B.A.'07, Univ. of Kansas; M.A.'26, Univ. of Colorado; Supt. of Sch., Dalhart, Texas, since 1926.

Finck, Edgar M., Litt.B.'10, M.A.'12, Princeton Univ.; Ph.D.'30, New York Univ.; Supvg. Prin. of Sch., Toms River, N. J., since 1919.

Findlay, Francis M., Pub. Sch. Music Diploma '16, Trumpet Soloist Diploma '17, New England Conservatory of Music; Head, Dept. of Pub. Sch. Music. New England Conservatory of Music, Boston 17, Mass., since 1924.

Fine, George B., B.A.'08, Columbia Univ.; Supvg. Prin. of Twp. Sch., Merchantville, N. J., since 1911.

Finegan, Thomas E., M.A.'94, Hamilton Col.; Pd.D.'09, N. Y. State Col. for Tchrs.; LL.D.'12, Colgate Univ.; LL.D. '17, Hamilton Col.; LL.D.'18. Univ. of Maine; Litt.D.'20, Univ. of Pa.; LL.D. '21. Temple Univ.; LL.D.'21, Dartmouth Col.; L.H.D.'22. Susquehanna Univ.; Pres., Dept. of Superintendence, 1917-18. Pres., Eastman Teaching Films, Inc., Eastman Kodak Co., Rochester, N. Y.

Finger, Mary H., Prin., Cadwalader Sch., Trenton, N. J.

Fink, A. O., Supt. of Sch., Columbus, Wis.

Finley, David R., A.B.'13, Union Col.; A.M. '30, Columbia Univ.; Supt. of Sch., Hudson Falls, N. Y., since 1925.

Firman, Sidney G., B.S.'04, Pd.M.'05, N. Y. Univ. Address: 76 Osborn St., Glen Ridge, N. J.

Firoved, Charles G., 4521 McCulloch St., Duluth, Minn.

Fisher, Annie, B.S.'04. Wesleyan Univ.; Dist. Supt. of Sch., Henry Barnard Sch., Hartford, Conn., since 1923.

Fisher, Byrt W., A.B.'07, Lebanon Valley Col.; A.M.'12, Franklin and Marshall Col.; Prin., Boys H. S., Lancaster, Pa., since 1908.

Fisher, C. Edward, A.B.'98, St. Lawrence; A.M.'12, Brown; Supt. of Sch., 39 Oak St., Braintree, Mass., since 1921.

Fisher, Charles M., B.S.'08, Univ. of Fla.; Supt. of Pub. Instr., 1244 S. W. 13 Court, Miami, Fla., since 1921.

Fisher, E. C., B.S.'26, Bradley Polytechnic Inst.; Supt. of Sch., 300 N. Monroe St., Peoria, Ill., since 1923.

Fisher, Henry B., A.B.'96, Northwestern Univ.; Supt. of Sch., Streator, Ill., since 1914.

Fisher, J. M., A.B.'13, Ursinus Col.; A.M. '19, Univ. of Pa.; Supvg. Prin. of Sch., Ambler, Pa., since 1913.

Fisher, Oscar A., Supvg. Prin. of Sch., W. End Ave., Somerville, N. J.

Fisher, R. B., A.B.'24, Northwestern State Tchrs. Col., Alva, Okla.; Supt. of Sch., 126 W. Francis, Pampa, Texas, since 1929.

Fishpaugh, Clara B., A.M., W. Va. Wesleyan Col.; Box 42, Falls Sta., Baltimore, Md.

Fisk, Frank E., Ph.B.'01, Syracuse Univ.; A.M.'26, Univ. of Rochester; Supt. of Sch., Union Sch. Bldg., Canandaigua, N. Y., since 1919.

Fisk, H. Clay, Diploma '10, Northwestern State Tchrs. Col., Alva, Okla.; A.B.'16, B.S. in Ed.'17, Univ. of Kansas; Supt. of Sch., Sand Springs, Okla.

Fistler, J. W., A.B.'22, Central Mich. Normal Sch.; Supt. of Sch., St. Clair Shores, Mich., since 1922.

Fitz-Gerald, Mrs. Mary M., Deputy Supt. of Sch., 777 Hotel Whitcomb, 1231 Market St., San Francisco, Calif.

Fitzgerald, R. G., A.B.'15, Univ. of N. C.; Co. Supt. of Sch., Greenville, N. C.

Fitzgerald, W. Stewart, Co. Supt. of Sch., Princess Anne, Md.

Fitzpatrick, Jerome M., B.S.'14, Univ. of Vt.; Supt. of Sch., H. S. Bldg., Westbury, Long Island, N. Y., since 1925.

Fjelsted, Philip L., A.B.'21, St. Olaf Col.; Supt. of Sch., Biwabik, Minn., since 1926.

Flanders, Jesse Knowlton, A.B.'04, Bates Col.; A.M.'17, Stanford Univ.; Ph.D.'25, Columbia Univ.; Head, Dept. of Educ. and Dir. of Practice Teaching, State Normal Sch., Oswego, N. Y., since 1925.

Flanegin, Leland C., 232 N. University, Peoria, Ill.

Fleetwood, Oscar L., Supvg. Prin., Sch. No. 1, West Paterson, N. J.

Fleming, Samuel Edgar, A.B.'07, Wabash Col.; Asst. Supt. of Sch., 843 Central Bldg., Seattle, Wash., since 1922.

Fletcher, Milton J., A.B.'88, Syracuse Univ.; Supt. of Sch., 509 E. Fifth St., Jamestown, N. Y., since 1919.

Flinner, Ira A., A.B.'11, A.M.'19, Ed.M.'25, Ed.D.'26, Harvard Univ.; LL.D.'27, Grove City Col.; Educ. Dir., Lake Placid Club Educ. Foundation and Dir., Northwood Sch., Lake Placid Club, N. Y., since 1925.

Flora, A. C., M.A.'16, Univ. of S. C.; Supt. of Sch., Columbia, S. C., since 1928.

Flower, Lilian E., Life Cert.'05, Univ. of the State of N. Y.; Dist. Supt. of Sch., Court House, Troy, N. Y., since 1926.

Flowers, William R., B.S.'21, M.A.'24, Johns Hopkins Univ.; Asst. Supt. of Sch., Baltimore, Md., since 1924.

Floyd, Milton R., M.A.'21, Colo. State Tchrs. Col.; Pres., Northeastern Okla. Jr. Col., Miami, Okla., since 1923.

Fly, Murry H., B.A.'20, M.A.'29, Univ. of Texas; Supt. of Sch., Odessa, Texas, since 1924.

Foberg, J. A., B.S.'99, Univ. of Ill. Address: State Normal Sch., California, Pa.

Foght, H. W., Pres., Univ. of Wichita, 1822 Fairmount Ave., Wichita, Kansas.

Fogwell, Jerome P., B.S.'10, Colby Col.; Supt. of Sch., Barnstable, Mass. Address: 24 Maple St., Hyannis, Mass.

Foley, James F., Supvg. Prin. of Sch., Woodbine, N. J.

Fontaine, E. Clarke, A.B.'01, M.A.'11, St. Johns Col.; M.A.'25, Tchrs. Col., Columbia Univ.; State Supvr. of H. S., 114 Water St., Chestertown, Md., since 1921.

Foote, John M., M.A.'23, George Peabody Col. for Tchrs.; State Div. of Reference and Service, State Dept. of Educ., Reymond Bldg., Baton Rouge, La., since 1914.

Ford, Charles F., A.B.'96, Knox Col.; M.A. '22, Univ. of Wis.; Supt. of Sch., Jr. H. S. Bldg., Edwardsville, Ill., since 1911.

Ford, Willard S., A.B.'15, Lawrence Col.; M.A.'25, Tchrs. Col., Columbia Univ.; Ph.D.'26, Columbia Univ.; Prof. of Educ., Univ. of Southern Calif., Los Angeles, Calif., since 1926.

Foreman, John W., B.S.'01, De Pauw Univ.; Supt. of Sch., Goshen, Ind., since 1920.

Forester, John J., Prin., Benjamin Franklin Jr. H. S., Ridgewood, N. J.

Foster, C. R., B.A.'11, M.A.'14, LL.D.'26, Univ. of Pittsburgh; Pres., State Tchrs. Col., Indiana, Pa., since 1927.

Foster, Charles Smalley, A.B.'05, A.M.'06, Antioch Col.; A.M.'11, Univ. of Mich.; Asst. Co. Supt. of Sch., Casstown, Ohio, since 1923.

Foster, Henry L., B.S.'26, Southwest Texas State Tchrs. Col., San Marcos, Texas; Supt. of Sch., Longview, Texas, since 1923.

Foster, Isaac Owen, B.S.'21, M.S.'22, Ph.D. '25, Univ. of Ill.; Assoc. Prof. of Educ., Sch. of Educ., Ind. Univ., Bloomington, Ind., since 1926.

Foster, Richard R., B.A.'23, M.A.'26. Ph.D. '28, State Univ. of Iowa; Asst. Dir. of Research. Natl. Educ. Assn., 1201 16th St., N. W., Washington, D. C., since 1930.

Foster. Talmage D.. B.S.'24, M.A.'27, Col. of William and Mary; Co. Supt. of Sch., Waverly, Va., since 1925.

Foulke, Katharine, A.B.'14, A.M.'16, Univ. of Pittsburgh; Asst. to Assoc. Supt. of Sch. in charge of Personnel, Bellefield at Forbes, Pittsburgh, Pa., since 1930.

Foust, John Lee, Ph.B.'17, Univ. of Chicago; M.A.'27, Columbia Univ.; Supt. of Sch., 1230 Locust St., Owensboro, Ky., since 1921.

Fowler, Burton P., A.B.'07. Syracuse Univ.; A.M.'25. Columbia Univ.; Headmaster, Tower Hill Sch., Wilmington, Del., since 1923.

Fowler, Harry E., B.A.'05. Yale Univ.; Supt. of Sch., Hill St., Shelton, Conn., since 1910.

Fowler, Wade C., B.S. in Ed.'21. State Tchrs. Col., Warrensburg, Mo.; Supt. of Sch., H. S., Nevada, Mo., since 1930.

Fowlkes, John Guy. A.B.'16, Ouachita Col.; A.M.'21, Ph.D.'22, Tchrs. Col., Columbia Univ.; Prof. of Educ., Univ. of Wis., Madison, Wis.

Fox, Clement S., A.B.'16, Univ. of Minn.; A.M.'30, Stanford Univ.; Supt. of Sch., Gilbert, Ariz., since 1927.

Fox, E. E., B.S.'22, George Peabody Col. for Tchrs.; Supt. of Sch., Starkville, Miss., since 1926.

Fox, Feramorz Young, A.B.'06, Univ. of Utah; M.L.'12, Univ. of Calif.; Pres., Latter-day Saints Col., 80 N. Main St., Salt Lake City, Utah, since 1926.

Fox, George, B.S.'23, St. Johns Col.; Co. Supt. of Sch., Annapolis, Md., since 1916.

Fox, Ralph Lewis, A.B.'15, Allegheny Col.; A.M.'27, Tchrs. Col., Columbia Univ.; Asst. Co. Supt. of Sch., Jefferson, Ohio, since 1924.

Frampton, S. A., B.S.'09, Ohio Northern Univ.; A.B.'20, Wittenberg Col.; A.M.'28, Ohio State Univ.; Supt. of Sch., H. S. Bldg., Bellefontaine, Ohio, since 1923.

Francis, George C., Special Diploma, Boston Univ.; Diploma'08, State Normal Sch., Bridgewater, Mass.; Supt. of Sch., City Hall, Chelsea, Mass., since 1926.

Francis, Thomas, Co. Supt. of Sch., Court House, Scranton, Pa.

Frankenfield, Clyde S., Ph.B.'17, Muhlenberg Col.; M.A.'21, Columbia Univ.; Supt. of Sch., 309 E. 19th St., Northampton, Pa., since 1922.

Frantz, William C., Supvg. Prin. of Twp. Sch., Rouseville, Pa.

Franzén, Carl Gustave Frederick, A.B.'08, Univ. of Pa.; M.A.'12, Ph.D.'20, State Univ. of Iowa; Prof. of Sec. Educ., Sch. of Educ., Ind. Univ., Bloomington, Ind., since 1923.

Fraser, Walter S., A.B.'18, N. Y. State Tchrs. Col., Albany, N. Y.; M.A.'24, Columbia Univ.; Supt. of Sch., Central Sch. Bldg., Tonawanda, N. Y., since 1929.

Frasher, David R., B.S.'03, Ohio Northern Univ.; M.A.'30, Western Reserve Univ.; Supt. of Sch., 146 Bennett Ct., Geneva, Ohio, since 1927.

Frazee, George B., Jr., B.M.E.'02, Univ. of Ky.; M.A.'08, Univ. of Louisville; Special Art Diploma '08, Yale Univ.; Prin., George A. Davis Tech. H. S., 129 Bostwick Ave., Grand Rapids, Mich., since 1919.

Frazee. Laura, B.S.'19, Tchrs. Col., Columbia Univ.; Asst. Supt. of Sch., Baltimore, Md., since 1921.

Frazier, Maude, Supt. of Sch., Las Vegas, Nevada.

Frederick, Oliver G., A.B.'05, Univ. of Mich.; M.Pd.'15, Mich. State Normal Col.; Asst. Supt. of Sch., 1354 Broadway, Detroit, Mich., since 1914.

Freegard, Ruth, Ph.B.'23, Univ. of Chicago; M.A.'30, Tchrs. Col., Columbia Univ.; State Supvr. of Home Economics Educ., State Dept. of Pub. Instr., Capitol Bldg., Lansing, Mich., since 1921.

Freeman, Eliot N., A.B.'19. A.M.'22, Univ. of Denver; LL.B.'28, Westminster Law Sch.; Supt. of Sch., Wheatridge, Colo., since 1917.

Freeman, Frank N.. B.A.'04, Wesleyan Univ.; M.A.'06, Ph.D.'08, Yale Univ.; Prof. in Dept. of Educ., Univ. of Chicago, Chicago, Ill., since 1909.

Freeman, H. S., B.A.'19, Morningside Col.; Supt. of Sch., Mobridge, S. Dak.

Freeman, Leland N., B.S.'13. St. Lawrence Univ.; A.M.'16, Columbia Univ.; Supt. of Sch., Elmira Heights, N. Y., since 1927.

French, Mrs. Alice M., B.S.'98. Georgetown Col.; Co. Supt. of Sch., Carrizozo, N. Mex., since 1929.

French, John S., A.B.'20, Univ. of Ill.; M. A.'21, Tchrs. Col., Columbia Univ.; Head, Dept. of Educ.. Colgate Univ., Hamilton, N. Y., since 1928.

French, Lloyd C., A.B.'10, Ripon Col.; A. M.'27, Univ. of Pittsburgh; Supvg. Prin. of Sch., 1336 Virginia Ave., Monaca, Pa., since 1921.

French, Minnie, Prin. of Sch., Hohokus, N. J.

French, W. C., A.B.'07, Univ. of Okla.; A. M.'24, Univ. of Chicago; Ph.D.'29, N. Y. Univ.; Prof. of Educ., George Washington Univ., Washington, D. C., since 1929.

French, Will, A.B.'12, B.S.'14, Univ. of Kansas; A.M.'22, Tchrs. Col., Columbia Univ.; Assoc. Supt. of Sch. in charge of Curriculum Admin., Tulsa, Okla., since 1929.

Fries, H. C., A.B.'20, Bucknell Univ.; A.M. '22, Columbia Univ.; Supvg. Prin. of Sch., South Plainfield, N. J., since 1927.

Frisch, Ottilia M., Life Cert.'21, Central Mich. Normal Sch.; Co. Commr. of Sch., Court House, Saginaw, W. S., Mich., since 1919.

Friswold, I. O., B S. in Ed.'24, M.A. in Ed. '25, Univ. of Minn.; Instr. in Educ., Col. of Educ., Univ. of Minn., Minneapolis, Minn., since 1930.

Fritcher, Mrs. Alice I., M.A.'12, Univ. of Chicago; Co. Supt. of Pub. Instr., 452 Main St., Chadron, Nebr., since 1923.

Fritz, F. Herman, A.B.'09, A.M.'12, Bucknell; Ed.M.'28, Harvard; Supt. of Sch., Pottstown, Pa., since 1929.

Frizzell, Bonner, A.B.'09, Texas Christian Univ.; B.S.'11, Columbia Univ.; Supt. of Sch., Palestine, Texas, since 1919.

Froelicher, Francis Mitchell, A.B.'13, Haverford Col.; A.M.'21, Johns Hopkins Univ.; Head Master, The Fountain Valley Sch., Colorado Springs, Colo., since 1930.

Frohardt, L. P., A.B.'81, Central Wesleyan Col.; Supt. of Elem. Sch., Granite City, Ill., since 1894.

Frost, Alvah G., Supt. of Sch., Port Chester, N. Y.

Frost, Lorena M., Prim. Supvr., 2 Greenridge Ave., White Plains, N. Y.

Frostic, Fred Watson, Supt. of Sch., 355 Oak St., Wyandotte, Mich.

Fry, Levi, B.S.'09, John Tarleton Col.; Supt. of Sch., Texas City, Texas, since 1919.

Fuda, Anna M.,B.S. in Ed.'26, M.A.'28, New York Univ.; Prof. of Educ., N. Y. Tr. Sch. for Tchrs., New York, N. Y., since 1927. Address: 65 Park Place, Meriden, Conn.

Fuller, Albert C., Jr., Assoc. Dir., Extension Div., Iowa State Tchrs. Col., Cedar Falls, Iowa.

Fuller, D. O., Ph.B.'20, Brown Univ.; Supvg. Prin. of Sch., Painted Post, N. Y., since 1929.

Fuller, Edward H., A.B.'12, A.M.'16, Bates Col.; Supt. of Sch., Darien, Conn., since 1923.

Fuller, Robert J., A.B.'98, A.M.'15, Brown Univ.; Supt. of Sch., Hanover, N. H., since 1928.

Fullerton, Charles Hayward, B.Ph.'98, M.A. '11, Ohio State Univ.; Asst. Supt. of Sch., 88 18th Ave., Columbus, Ohio, since 1916.

Fulton, L. W., Supt. of Sch., Viroqua, Wis.

Fulwider, L. A., B.A.'95, M.A.'05, Ind. Univ.; Prin., H. S., Freeport, Ill., since 1904.

Furth, F. Willard, Supt. of Sch., Highland Park, N. J.

Futrall, Alma, Co. Supt. of Sch., Marianna, Ark., since 1921.

Gaarder, A. L., B.S.'09, St. Olaf Col.; Supt. of Sch., Albert Lea, Minn., since 1927.

Gable, H. E., B.A.'10, Southwestern Univ.; Supt. of Highland Park Sch., 3617 Harvard St., Dallas, Texas, since 1920.

Gage, Lucy, Hillsboro Manor, Nashville, Tenn.

Gage, Snyder J., A.B.'99, Union Col.; Pd.B. '01, Albany Normal Col. Address: 98 Grand St., Newburgh, N. Y.

Galbraith, Harry B., B.S.'01, LL.B.'14, Ohio Northern Univ.; Supt. of Sch., Uhrichsville, Ohio, since 1918.

Galey, F. Stanton, Supt. of Sch., Fairmount, Ind.

Gallagher, Oscar C., A.B.'96, A.M.'06, Harvard; Supt. of Sch., Town Hall, Brookline, Mass., since 1919.

Galloway, Carl H., Litt. B.'24, Rutgers Univ.; Supvg. Prin. of Sch., Metuchen, N. J., since 1930.

Galloway, T. O., B.S.A.'09, N. Ga. Agrl. Col.; Pres., Georgia Indus. Col., Barnesville, Ga.

Gallup, E. E., Supvr., Agrl. Educ., State Bd. for Voc. Educ., Lansing, Mich.

Gamble, William D., A.B.'96, A.M.'01, Ped. D.'30, Westminster; Supt. of Sch., 198 Cedar Ave., Sharon, Pa., since 1913.

Gammage, Grady, B.A.'16, M.A.'26, LL.D. '27, Univ. of Ariz.; Pres., Ariz. State Tchrs. Col., Flagstaff, Ariz., since 1926.

Gamper, Hedwig Eloise, 106 E. Pacement Rd., Columbus, Ohio.

Ganders, Harry S., A.M.'22, Univ. of Wash.; Ph.D.'26, Tchrs. Col., Columbia Univ.; Dean, Tchrs. Col., Syracuse Univ., Syracuse, N. Y., since 1930.

Gandy, John Manuel, Pres., Va. Normal and Indus. Inst., Ettrick, Va.

Gandy, Roxana Smith, B.S. in Ed.'20, M.A. in Ed.'22, Univ. of Pa.; Supvr. of Rural Sch., Dennisville, N. J., since 1916.

Ganfield, William Arthur, B.A.'98, M.A.'01, Cornell Col.; D.D.'12, Carroll Col.; LL.D. '16, Univ. of Ky.; Pres., Carroll Col., Waukesha, Wis., since 1921.

Ganiard, George E., Supt. of Sch., 318 E. Cherry St., Mt. Pleasant, Mich.

Gannon, John F., A.B.'96, A.M.'02, Holy Cross; LL.B.'12, Northeastern Univ.; LL. D.'23, Holy Cross; Supt. of Sch., City Hall, Pittsfield, Mass., since 1920.

Gantz, Arthur Leroy, Ph.B.'00, Otterbein Col.; Asst. Co. Supt. of Sch., Akron, Ohio, since 1916. Address: Doylestown, Ohio.

Garcelon, A. B., Ph.B.'02, J.D.'04, Univ. of Chicago; Supt. of Sch., Uxbridge, Mass., since 1928.

Gard, W. L., B.S.'21, M.S.'28, Univ. of Ill.; Supt. of Sch., Beardstown, Ill., since 1927.

Gardner, Carl A., B.A.'11, M.A.'15, Univ of Texas; Prin., N. Ft. Worth Sr. H. S. Park and Blvd. Sts., Ft. Worth, Texas, since 1922.

Gardner, George R., A.B.'01, Bowdoin Col.; A.M.'13, Columbia Univ.; Supt. of Sch., City Bldg., Auburn, Maine, since 1924.

Garlin, R. E., B.A.'20, M.A.'21, Ph.D.'27, Univ. of Texas; Prof. of Educ., Texas Technological Col., Lubbock, Texas, since 1927.

Garrett, R. E., Ph. B.'23, Univ. of Chicago; Supt. of Sch., 520 Pearl St., Belvidere, Ill., since 1923.

Garrison, Edward W., Co. Supt. of Sch., Co. Court House, Paterson, N. J.

Garrison, Noble Lee, B.S. in Ed.'09, A.B. and A.M.'12, Univ. of Mo.; Ph.D.'27, Columbia Univ.; Dir., Elem. Educ., Dept. of Educ., Mich. State Normal Col., Ypsilanti, Mich., since 1925.

Garver, H. B., M.E.'95, Pa. State Normal Sch.; A.B.'27, Elizabethtown Col.; Asst. Co. Supt. of Sch., 137 E. Water St., Middletown, Pa., since 1924.

Garver, Harlie, B.S.'14, Hiram Col.; M.A. '26, Columbia Univ.; Supt. of Sch., Union City, Ind., since 1927.

Garver, V. A., Ph.B.'16, Wooster Col.; M. A.'25, Ohio State Univ.; Supt. of Sch., 24 N. Third St., Rittman, Ohio, since 1925.

Garwood, C. H., Supt. of Sch., Bloomsburg, Pa., since 1930.

Gates, Arthur A., B.S.'15, Colgate Univ.; M.A.'24, Tchrs. Col., Columbia Univ.; Supvg. Prin. of Sch., Port Byron, N. Y., since 1922.

Gates, C. Ray, B.E.'11, State Tchrs. Col., Peru, Nebr.; B.A.'16, Univ. of Nebr.; M. A.'20, Columbia Univ.; Supt. of Sch., 504 N. Elm St., Grand Island, Nebr., since 1922.

Gatton, Harper, A.B.'12, Georgetown Col.; A.M.'26, Univ. of Chicago; Supt. of Sch., Madisonville, Ky., since 1914.

Gayman, H. E., B.S.'16, Cornell Univ.; Dir. of Research and Asst. Exec. Secy., Pa. State Educ. Assn., 400 N. Third St., Harrisburg, Pa., since 1929.

Gecks, Mathilde C., A.B.'22, Harris Tchrs. Col., St. Louis, Mo.; A.M.'26, New York Univ.; Asst. Supt. of Sch., St. Louis, Mo., since 1930.

Gee, John A., Supt. of Bldgs., Pub. Sch., 130 W. Genesee St., Syracuse, N. Y.

Gee, Louis Clyde, M.A.'88, Burritt Col., Tenn.; Supt. of Sch., 3531 Lee St., Greenville Texas, since 1907.

Geer, Florence E., Diploma'91, Mich. State Normal Col.; Dist. Prin., Marcy Sch., 6920 Sylvester, Detroit, Mich., since 1918.

Gehman, A. L., A.B.'09, Franklin and Marshall Col.; A.M.'18, Tchrs. Col., Columbia Univ.; Supvg. Prin. of Springfield Twp. Sch., Chestnut Hill, Philadelphia, Pa., since 1922.

Geiger, Franklin Paul, B.C.S. and A.B.'94, A.M.'12, Mt. Union Col.; D.Pd.'18, Ohio Univ.; Supt. of Sch., New Philadelphia, Ohio, since 1925.

Geiger, William F., A.B.'92, A.M.'22, Dartmouth Col.; Supt. of Sch., 608 North J St., Tacoma, Wash., since 1912.

Geiss, Newton W., A.B.'15, Muhlenberg Col.; A.M.'23, Univ. of Pa.; Asst. Co. Supt. of Sch., Oley, Pa., since 1926.

Genheimer, E. T., Ph.B.'96, Ohio State Univ.; Prin., Sr. H. S., Waco, Texas, since 1907.

Gentry, Charles B., A.B.'11, Warrensburg Normal Sch.; S.B.'12, Univ. of Chicago; M.S.'19, Cornell Univ.; Dean, Div. of Tchr. Tr., Conn. Agrl. Col., Storrs, Conn., since 1920.

Gentry, Samuel Walter, B.S.'18, M.A.'20, Peabody Col.; Supt. of Sch., Walnut Ridge, Ark., since 1927.

Gerard, George R., M. in Com'l. Sc.'30, Rider Col.; Supt. of Sch., H. S., Belleville, N. J., since 1905.

Gerberich, G. B., Dist. Supt. of Sch., Greenville, Pa., since 1908.

Gerling, Henry J., A.B., LL.B. and Pe.B.'94, M.A.'96, Univ. of Mo.; Supt. of Pub. Instr., Bd. of Educ., 911 Locust St., St. Louis, Mo., since 1929.

Germane, Charles E., Ph.D.'20, State Univ. of Iowa; Prof. of Educ., Univ. of Mo., Columbia, Mo., since 1925.

Gerson, Armand J., M.A.'09, Ph.D.'10, Univ. of Pa.; Assoc. Supt. of Sch., Keystone Bldg., 19th at Chestnut St., Philadelphia, Pa., since 1920.

Gibbons, Alice N., A.B.'98, Vassar Col.; Head of Social Science Dept., East H S., Alexander St., Rochester, N. Y., since 1904.

Gibbons, Austin J., A.B.'04, Holy Cross Col., Worcester, Mass.; M.A.'08, Seton Hall Col.; Asst. Supt. of Sch., Manchester, N. H., since 1927.

Gibbons, Emma C., Eastman Sch. of Music, 287 Alexander St., Rochester, N. Y.

Gibbons, Thomas F., A.B.'99, Holy Cross Col.; LL.B.'02, Boston Univ.; Supt. of Sch., H. S., Clinton, Mass., since 1915.

Gibbs, Bert F., Supt. of Sch., Grand St, New Milford, N. J.

Gibbs, Charles B., B.S.'22, N. Y. State Col. for Tchrs., Albany, N. Y.; Supt. of Second Supervisory Sch. Dist., Hancock, N. Y., since 1925.

Gibson, A. J., A.B.'16, W. Va. Univ.; M.A. '20, Columbia Univ.; Supt. of Sch., East Fairmont H. S., East Fairmont, W. Va., since 1929.

Gibson, Charles S., B.S.'29, Syracuse Univ.; Prin., Roosevelt Jr. H. S., Syracuse, N. Y., since 1924.

Gibson, John Arthur, A.B.'91, A.M.'15, Allegheny Col.; LL.D.'27, Westminster Col.; Supt. of Sch., Butler, Pa., since 1896.

Gibson, Joseph E., B.A.'13, Univ. of Miss.; M.A.'27, Columbia Univ.; Supt. of Sch., McComb, Miss., since 1920.

Gibson, Simeon B., A.B.'10, Howard Col.; A.M.'11, Baylor Univ.; Co. Supt. of Sch., Court House, Anniston, Ala., since 1920.

Gifford, Willis Briggs, Prin., H. S., South Hadley Falls, Mass.

Gilbert, George D., Supt. of Sch., Gwinn, Mich.

Giles, J. T., A.B.'94, A.M.'02, Ind. Univ.; State H. S. Supvr., 326 W. Washington St., Madison, Wis., since 1920.

Gill, Charles M., A.B.'10, Yale Univ.; Ph.D. '27, New York Univ.; Prof. of Educ., Sch. of Educ., New York Univ., Washington Square, E., New York, N. Y., since 1923.

Gill, John, A.B.'12, Col. of the Pacific; Supt. of Sch., 14 Hyde St., Redwood City, Calif., since 1927.

Gilland, Edwin C., A.B.'07, Lafayette Col.; Supt. of Sch., Red Bank, N. J., since 1920.

Gilland, Thomas M., A.B.'09, Ursinus Col.; A.M.'26, Tchrs. Col., Columbia Univ.; Supt. of Sch., Donora, Pa., since 1918.

Gillenwater, I. E., Diploma '17, East Tenn. State Normal Sch.; Co. Supt. of Sch., Loudon, Tenn., since 1930.

Gillet, Harry O., B.S.'01, Univ. of Chicago; Prin., Elem. Sch., Univ. of Chicago, Chicago, Ill., since 1915.

Gillett, Arthur D. S., B.L.'02, M.A.'07, Univ. of Wis.; Pres., State Tchrs. Col., Superior, Wis., since 1925.

Gilligan, James R., A.B.'12, Pa. State Col.; Supt. of Sch., Dunmore, Pa., since 1926.

Gilligan, Leo Forest, Supt. of Sch., Bellevue, Ky.

Gillis, Nannie, Co. Supt. of Educ., Magnolia, Miss., since 1924.

Gilmer, Ira T., A.B.'05, LL.B.'10, Univ. of Miss.; Supt. of Sch., Graham, Texas, since 1924.

Gilmore, W. Lee, M.E.'04, State Normal Sch., Slippery Rock, Pa.; A.B.'05, Central Univ.; B.S.'18, Univ. of Pittsburgh; Supt. of Sch., Pa. Ave. and Tenth St., Oakmont, Pa., since 1916.

Gilpin, H. H., Supt. of Sch., Rogers City, Mich.

Giltman, C. W., Prin., Central H. S., Oklahoma City, Okla.

Ging, V. B., Central H. S., Duluth, Minn.

Givens, Willard E., A.B.'13, Ind. Univ.; M.A.'15, Columbia Univ.; Diploma '16, Union Theological Seminary; Supt. of Sch., 1025 Second Ave., Oakland, Calif., since 1928.

Glasgow, George Winfield, A.B.'10, Univ. of Mo.; A.M.'26, Tchrs. Col., Columbia Univ.; Prin., Woodrow Wilson Jr. H. S., Youngstown, Ohio, since 1928.

Glass, Edward C., LL.D.'26, Washington and Lee Univ.; LL.D.'26, College of William and Mary; Supt. of Sch., John Wyatt Sch., Lynchburg, Va., since 1879.

Gleason, Charles H., Jr., Asst. Supt. of Sch., Bd. of Educ., Newark, N. J.

Glenn, Charles B., B.S.'91, M.S.'92, Ala. Poly. Inst.; A.B.'96, Harvard Univ.; LL.D. '18, Univ. of Ala.; Supt. of Sch., 2015 Seventh Ave., Birmingham, Ala., since 1921.

Glenn, Earl R., A.B.'13, Ind. Univ.; A.M. '28, Columbia Univ.; Prof. of Physics, N.J. State Tchrs. Col., Upper Montclair, N. J., since 1928.

Godbey, Josiah J., B.A.'10, Ky. Wesleyan Col.; M.A.'27, Univ. of Texas; Supt. of Sch., Ardmore, Okla., since 1925.

Goddard, V. F., B.A.'13, Maryville Col.; M.A.'28, Univ. of Mich.; Supt. of Sch., 413 Ramsey St., Alcoa, Tenn., since 1924.

Godfrey, Ella M., 73 W. Johnson St., Germantown, Philadelphia, Pa.

Goerner, H. L., B.A.'96, Baylor Univ.; Co. Supt. of Sch., Court House, Dallas, Texas, since 1922.

Goetch, Edward William, 115 E. 15th St., Cedar Falls, Iowa.

Gold, Leslie J., B.S.'24, George Peabody Col. for Tchrs.; Co. Supt. of Sch., Carthage, Tenn., since 1926.

Golden, Gertrude A., Dist. Supt. of Sch., 5413 Christian St., Philadelphia, Pa.

Goldsmith, A. F., B.Ed.'24, Eastern Ill. State Tchrs. Col., Charleston, Ill.; Supt. of Sch., Robinson, Ill., since 1929.

Goldthorpe, J. Harold, A.B.'20, Hamline Univ.; M.A.'24, Ph D.'28, Univ. of Minn.; Asst. Prof. of Educ., Univ. of Buffalo, Buffalo, N. Y., since 1928.

Goode, Benjamin Clifford, B.A.'19, Univ. of Richmond; M.A.'25, Univ. of Va.; Div. Supt. of Sch., Municipal Bldg., Martinsville, Va., since 1925.

Goode, George W., A.B.'23, Marshall Col.; A.M.'28, W. Va. Univ.; Dist. Supt. of Sch., 440 Highland Ave., South Charleston, W. Va., since 1929.

Goodell, M. R., Diploma '16, State Normal Sch., River Falls, Wis.; Co. Supt. of Sch., Hammond, Wis., since 1923.

Goodier, Floyd T., A.B.'03, Colgate Univ.; A.M.'09, Tchrs. Col., Columbia Univ.; Supt. of Sch., Chicago Hgts., Ill., since 1918.

Goodrich, C. Lloyd, A.B.'11, A.M. in Ed.'28, Univ. of Mich.; Deputy Supt. of Pub. Instr., State Dept. of Public Instr., Lansing, Mich., since 1926.

Goodrich, Lowell Pierce, Supt. of Sch., Fond du Lac, Wis.

Goodykoontz, Bess, B.A.'20, M.A.'22, State Univ. of Iowa; Asst. U. S. Commr. of Educ., Office of Educ., Washington, D. C., since 1929.

Goold, Howard R., B.S.'08, Northwestern Univ.; M.A.'22, Univ. of Wash.; Supt. of Sch., 108 W. 18th St., Eugene, Oregon, since 1928.

Gorrell, Harry R., B.S.'06, Ohio Wesleyan Univ.; Supt. of Sch., Massillon, Ohio, since 1924.

Gosch, Olga A., 834 Hudson St., Hoboken, N. J.

Goslin, Willard E., B.S. in Ed.'22, State Tchrs. Col., Kirksville, Mo.; A.M.'29, Univ. of Mo.; Supt. of Sch., Webster Groves, Mo., since 1930.

Gosling, Thomas W., B A.'94, M.A.'04, Yale Univ.; Ph.D.'11, Univ. of Cincinnati; Supt. of Sch., Central H. S., Akron, Ohio, since 1928.

Gossard, A. P., A.B '21, Ohio State Univ.; M.A.'26, Univ. of Chicago; Supt. of Sch., 786 Fillebrowne St., Marseilles, Ill., since 1929.

Gotke, G. W., B A.'19, M.A.'23, State Univ. of Iowa; Supt. of Sch. and Pres., Jr. Col., Brownsville, Texas, since 1928.

Gough, Harry B., Ph.B.'14, Hamline Univ.; M.A.'28, Univ. of Minn.; Supt. of Sch., St. Cloud, Minn., since 1930.

Gould, Arthur, A.B.'01, Pomona Col.; A.M. '04, Yale Univ.; Asst. Supt. of Sch., 720 Chamber of Commerce Bldg., Los Angeles, Calif., since 1918.

Gould, Arthur L., A.B.'12, A.M.'13, Boston Col.; Asst. Supt. of Sch., 15 Beacon St., Boston, Mass., since 1920.

Gourley, David, A.B '15, Brigham Young Univ.; Dist. Supt. of Sch., American Fork, Utah, since 1922.

Gowans, J. W., A.B.'03, Univ. of Kansas; A.M.'18, Columbia Univ.; Supt. of Sch., 202 E. 14th St., Hutchinson, Kansas, since 1922.

Grady, G. Otto, B.Sc.'03, Ohio Wesleyan Univ.; M.A.'17, Ohio State Univ.; Dist. Supt. of Sch., Logan, W. Va., since 1928.

Grady, Joseph E., B.A.'20, M.A.'21, Litt.D. '28, St. Bonaventure's Col.; LL.D.'28, Manhattan Col.; Prin , Aquinas Inst., Rochester, N. Y.

Grady, William E., Supt. of Sch., 263 Dover St., Brooklyn, N. Y.

Graff, E. U., A.B.'97, A.M.'15, Lake Forest Col.; Pres., Dept. of Superintendence, 1919-20. Address: 765 Hillside Ave., Glen Ellyn, Ill.

Graham, Ben G., A.B.'04, A.M '08, Sc.D.'23, Westminster Col.; M.A.'25. Univ. of Pittsburgh; Supt. of Sch., Pittsburgh, Pa., since 1930.

Graham, Edward J., A.B.'00, Hamilton Col.; Supt. of Sch., Norwich, Conn., since 1912.

Graham, Seldon B., B.A.'24, North Texas State Tchrs. Col., Denton, Texas; Supt. of Sch., Franklin, Texas, since 1925.

Graham, William A., A.B.'03, Univ. of N. C.; A.M.'20, Columbia Univ.; Supt. of Sch., Kinston, N. C.

Graham, William C., A.B.'97, Tarkio Col.; A.M.'12, Univ. of Pittsburgh; Supt. of Sch., Wilkinsburg, Pa., since 1929.

Grainger, Josephine F., 31 S. Penn St., Allentown, Pa.

Grant, Alfred E., B.S '23, Tufts Col.; Ed.M. '30, Harvard Univ.; Supvr. of Jr. H. S. Grades and Research Worker, William A. Briggs Sch., Cranston, R. I., since 1930.

Grant, Francis V., B.S.'21, Colgate Univ.; Supt. of Sch., Williamstown, Mass., since 1922.

Grant, L. W., Supt. of Sch., Norwood, Mass.

Grassmuck, Erna, Diploma. Philadelphia Normal Sch.; B.S. in Ed., Univ. of Pa. and Univ. of Chicago; Head, Geography Dept., State Tchrs. Col., Indiana, Pa., since 1927.

Graves, Frank P., Ph.D., Litt.D., L.H.D., LL.D.; Pres., Univ. of the State of N. Y. and State Commr. of Educ., Albany, N. Y.

Graves, S. Monroe, A.B.'02, Colgate Univ.; A.M.'12, Ph.D.'13, Harvard Univ.; Supt. of Sch., 31 Elm St., Wellesley Hills, Mass., since 1914.

Gray, A. D., A.B.'22, Columbia Univ.; Supt. of Sch., Eastport, Maine, since 1926.

Gray, Charles H., Co. Supt. of Sch., Court House, Quincy, Fla., since 1914.

Gray, Julius C., Co. Supt. of Sch., Lake Village, Ark.

Gray, Olive, Ph.B. in Ed.'13, M.A.'20, Univ. of Chicago. Address: 6345 University Ave., Chicago, Ill.

Gray, R. M, Supt. of Sch., Statesville, N. C., since 1921.

Gray, Wil Lou, A.B.'03, Columbia Col., Columbia, S. C.; A.M '11, Columbia Univ., New York, N. Y.; Supvr. of Adult Sch., State Dept. of Educ., Columbia, S. C., since 1918.

Gray, William S., S.B.'13, Univ. of Chicago; M.A.'14, Columbia Univ.; Ph.D.'16, Univ. of Chicago; Dean, Sch. of Educ., Univ. of Chicago, since 1917, and Prof. of Educ., Univ. of Chicago, Chicago, Ill., since 1921.

Graybeal, Lymond B., Concord Col., Athens, W. Va.

Grayum, William H., A.B.'13, State Normal Col.; Box. 327, Puyallup, Wash.

Green, Clyde C., Ph.B.'02, A.M.'07, LL.D.'25, Grove City Col.; Supt. of Sch., 116 East St., New Castle, Pa., since 1926.

Green, George M., Supt. of Sch., Woodstown, N. J.

Green, Raymond E., Dist. Supt. of Sch., Fullerton, Calif.

Green, Roland Daniel, Supt. of Sch., Abilene, Texas, since 1917.

Green, Thomas C., B.A.'18, M.A.'29, State Univ. of Iowa; Supt. of Sch., Ackley, Iowa, since 1926.

Greenawalt, E. Guy, B.A.'18, M.A.'19, Franklin and Marshall Col.; M.A.'25, Columbia Univ.; Supvg. Prin. of Sch., 519 Church St., Susquehanna, Pa., since 1929.

Greenawalt, William C., A.B.'07, A.M.'12, Franklin and Marshall Col.; Supt. of Sch., Olean, N. Y., since 1920.

Greene, Charles E., A.B.'10, A.M.'11, Univ. of Denver; A M.'19, Tchrs Col., Columbia Univ.; Dir. of Research, Pub. Sch., 414 14th St., Denver, Colo., since 1923.

Greene, Crawford, A.B. and B.S.'21, Henderson-Brown Col.; M.A.'26, Peabody; Supt. of Sch., Blytheville, Ark., since 1928.

Greene, David Lyman, 652 Chaming Ave., Palo Alto, Calif.

Greene, Mary C., Ed.B.'24, Women's Col., Brown Univ.; Dir. of Spec. Educ., Sch. Dept., 9 Exchange Ter., Providence, R. I., since 1918.

Greene, William A., A.B '12, Kansas Wesleyan Univ.; Supt. of Sch., Guthrie, Okla., since 1926.

Greer, Wilson, B.A.'17, Wesleyan Univ., Middletown, Conn.; M.A.'28, Yale Univ.; Supt. of Sch., Wethersfield, Conn., since 1928.

Gregg, Jasper Horace, Co. Supt. of Sch., Shelby, N. C.

Gregg, Lucile, Diploma '00, State Tchrs. Col, Huntsville, Texas; Prin., Southmore Sch., 4204 Connor, Houston, Texas, since 1920.

Gregory, Arnold C., Prin., Raupp Sch., Lincoln Park, Mich.

Gregory, Chester A., Univ. of Cincinnati, Cincinnati, Ohio.

Gregory, Leslie R., A.B.'17, York Col.; M.A.'26, Tchrs. Col., Columbia Univ.; Supt. of Sch., Bd. of Educ., Louisville, Ky., since 1929.

Gregory, Marshall W., B.S.'23, Central State Tchrs. Col., Edmond, Okla.; M.S.'26, Univ. of Okla.; Dir., Div. of Research and Serv., State Dept. of Pub. Instr., State Capitol, Oklahoma City, Okla., since 1929.

Greig, R. A., A.B.'20, Macalester Col.; M.A. '27, Columbia Univ.; Supt. of Sch., Fairport Harbor, Ohio, since 1927.

Greist, Oliver Howard, Exec. Secy., Ind. State Tchrs. Retirement Fund, State House, Indianapolis, Ind., since 1925.

Grelis, Howard A., A.M.'16, Villa Nova Col.; Dir. of Studies, Villa Nova Col., Villa Nova, Pa.

Gresham. E. B., Co. Supt. of Sch., Waynesboro, Ga., 1904-1917 and since 1925.

Gress, Harry E., B.S '09, A.M.'17, Bucknell Univ.; Supt. of Sch., 936 Virginia Ave., Lancaster, Pa., since 1924.

Grettenberger, R. A., Supt. of Sch., Imlay City, Mich.

Gribble, S. C., B.S.'17, Univ. of Wis.; M.A. '24, Ph.D.'25, State Univ. of Iowa; Asst. Prof. of Educ., Washington Univ., St. Louis, Mo., since 1926.

Grice, George D., B.S '23, Clemson Col.; M. A.'29, Tchrs. Col., Columbia Univ.; Prin., Julian Mitchell Sch., Charleston, S. C., since 1925.

Gridley, Earl G., A.B.'10, Simpson Col.; Secy.-treas., Bay Section, Calif. Tchrs. Assn., 2163 Center St., Berkeley, Calif., since 1929.

Grieder, Theodore G., A.B.'20, Univ. of Dubuque; A M.'28, State Univ. of Iowa; Supt. of Sch., Clemenceau, Ariz., since 1926.

Grier, B. M., A.B.'16, Erskine Col.; Supt. of Sch., Athens, Ga., since 1929.

Grier, William Pressley, A B.'09, Univ. of N. C.; Supt. of Sch., Gastonia, N. C., since 1921.

Griffey, Carl H., A.B.'10, Ind. Univ.; A.M. '16, Univ. of Chicago; Supt. of Sch., Adrian, Mich., since 1915.

Griffin, Edward T., Co. Supt. of Sch., 470 21st Ave., Milwaukee, Wis.

Griffin, Harold D., B.S. in Ed.'19, Tri-State Normal Col.; A.B.'20, Bethany Col.; Ph.D. '29, Univ. of Mo.; Dean, Crescent Col., Eureka Springs, Ark., since 1929.

Griffin, Isaac C., Exec. Secy., Summer Sch, Univ. of N. C., Chapel Hill, N. C., since 1928.

Griffin, L. D., B.A.'23, Ark State Tchrs. Col., Conway, Ark.; Supt. of Sch., H. S., Stuttgart, Ark., since 1927.

Griffin, Lee H., Ph.'16, Univ. of Chicago. Address: 2301 Prairie Ave., Chicago, Ill.

Griffin, Phila M., Ph.B.'22, Univ. of Chicago; Elem. Sch. Agt., State Bd. of Educ., Concord, N. H., since 1925.

Griffiths, Ethel, 1487 Clarence Ave., Lakewood, Ohio.

Griffiths, Nellie L., **A.B.**'25, Olivet Col.; M.A.'27, Univ. of Chicago; Prof. of Educ. and Elem. Supvr., North Texas State Tchrs. Col., 905 W. Sycamore, Denton, Texas, since 1927.

Griggs, William C., A.B.'98, Howard Col.; Supt. of City and Co. Sch., Barton Bldg., Mobile, Ala., since 1927.

Grill, George W., A.B.'11, Dakota Wesleyan Univ.; Asst. Supt. of Sch., Lakewood, Ohio.

Grimes, Byron J., B.A.'04, M.A.'12, Dickinson Col.; Supt. of Sch., Court House, Hagerstown, Md., since 1920.

Grimm, S. R., A.B.'11, Washington and Jefferson Col.; Supt. of Sch., Sidman, Pa.

Grindle, Thomas S., M.Ed.'24, Harvard Univ.; Supt. of Sch., 5 Bloomfield St., Lexington, Mass., since 1924.

Grinstead, Wren Jones, A.B.'99, A.M.'10, Univ. of Ky.; Ph.D.'16, Univ. of Wis.; Asst. Prof. of Educ., 110 Bennett Hall, Univ. of Pa., Philadelphia, Pa., since 1927.

Groff, Gordon E., Dist. Supt. of Sch., Marcus Hook, Pa.

Gronde, Franklin J., B.S.'11, Bucknell Univ.; Supvg. Prin. of Sch., Bradley Beach, N. J., since 1923.

Groner, H. L., B.S.'27, North Texas State Tchrs. Col., Denton, Texas; Supt. of Sch., Lovington, N. Mex., since 1927.

Grose, Walter R., A.B.'16, W. Va. Wesleyan Col.; Supt. of Sch., Buckhannon, W. Va., since 1912.

Gross, Harry W., B.S.'27, New York Univ.; M.A.'29, Tchrs. Col., Columbia Univ.; Prin., Central H. S., Valley Stream, N. Y., since 1924.

Grounds, Frank Oral, Diploma '21, Ill. State Normal Univ., Normal, Ill.; B.S.'24, State Tchrs. Col., Terre Haute, Ind.; A.M.'25, Univ. of Mich. Address: 411 W. 115th St., New York, N. Y.

Grout, Milfred Albert, 53 Hillman St., Springfield, Mass.

Grove, P. F., A.B.'13, A.M.'23, Univ. of Ill.; Supvg. Prin. of Sch., 603 E. Ridge St., Mt. Carroll, Ill., since 1922.

Grover, Elbridge, C., B.S.'15, Harvard Col.; M.A.'20, Tchrs. Col., Columbia Univ.; Ph.D.'25, Sch. of Educ., New York Univ.; Asst. Supt. of Sch., Bd. of Educ., 1749 Lee Rd., Cleveland Hgts., Ohio, since 1923.

Groves, Charles D., A.B.'21, Mt. Union Col.; A.M.'26, Columbia Univ.; Co. Supt. of Sch., Jefferson, Ohio, since 1920.

Gruelle, Orie P., A.B.'11, William Jewell Col.; A.M.'14, Brown Univ.; Co. Supt. of Sch., Independence, Ky., since 1930.

Gruenberg, Benjamin C., B.S.'96, Univ. of Minn.; A.M.'08, Ph.D.'11, Columbia Univ. Address: 18 E. 48th St., New York, N. Y.

Gruver, Harvey S., A.B.'02, Otterbein Col.; A.M.'10, Harvard; Supt. of Sch., Lynn, Mass., since 1923.

Gugle, Marie, A.B.'97, Ohio State Univ.; A.M.'13, Columbia Univ.; Asst. Supt. of Sch., Woodcliff Lodge, R. F. D. 5, Columbus, Ohio, since 1914.

Gumser, W. W., A.B.'17, Hope Col.; A.M. '26, Univ. of Mich.; Supt. of Sch., Lowell, Mich, since 1926.

Gunstream, John W., Supt. of Sch., Carrollton, Texas.

Gurr, Mrs. Helen G., Co. Supt. of Sch., Dawson, Ga., since 1923.

Guy, J. Freeman, Ph.B.'10, Wooster Col.; A.M.'18, Tchrs. Col., Columbia Univ.; Ph.D.'23, Univ. of Pittsburgh; Assoc. Supt. of Sch., Admin. Bldg., Forbes and Bellefield Sts., Pittsburgh, Pa., since 1929.

Gwinn, J. M., A.B.'02, Univ. of Mo.; A.M. '07, Tchrs. Col., Columbia Univ.; LL.D. '26, Univ. of Mo.; Pres., Dept. of Superintendence, 1927-28; Supt. of Sch., City Hall, San Francisco, Calif., since 1923.

Gyger, John T., B.S.'13, M.A.'17, Tchrs. Col., Columbia Univ.; Union Supt. of Sch., R. D. No. 4, Portland, Maine, since 1928.

Haas, Francis B., B.S.'13, Temple Univ.; M.A.'22, Univ. of Pa.; Pd.D.'25, Temple Univ.; Pres., State Tchrs. Col., Bloomsburg, Pa., since 1927.

Hacker, Myra Ruth, 524 Broad Ave., Leonia, N. J.

Hadsell, H. I., B.A.'08, Ohio State Univ. Address: 3076 Woodbury Rd., Cleveland, Ohio.

Hafner, Gertrude Elizabeth, 915 N. Linden, Bethlehem, Pa.

Hagan, J. J., A.B., Ind. Univ.; A.M., Columbia Univ.; Supt. of Sch., Rock Island, Ill.

Hagan, John R., Ph.D.'10, D.D.'14, Urban Col., Rome, Italy; M.A.'27, Catholic Univ. of America; Supt. of Cleveland Catholic Schools, 605 Guarantee Title Bldg., Cleveland, Ohio, since 1921.

Hager, Walter E., B.S.'16, Univ. of Nebr.; A.M.'27, Tchrs. Col., Columbia Univ.; Asst. Secy., Tchrs. Col., Columbia Univ., 102 Russell Hall, New York, N. Y., since 1928.

Haggerty, Melvin E., A.B.'02, A.M.'07, Ind. Univ.; A.M.'09, Ph.D.'10, Harvard Univ.; Dean, Col. of Educ., Univ. of Minn., Minneapolis, Minn., since 1920.

Hahn, J. M., 2161 Shattuck Ave., Berkeley, Calif.

Hahn, Julia Letheld, B.S.'23, Diploma in Kdgn. Prim. Supvn.'23, Tchrs. Col., Columbia Univ.; Dir. of Kdgns. and Prim. Grades, Pub. Sch., City Hall, San Francisco, Calif., since 1923.

Hailey, John R., 719 Fairview Ave., Webster Groves, Mo.

Haisley, Otto W., M.A.'17, Columbia Univ.; Supt. of Sch., Ann Arbor, Mich., since 1924.

Halberg, Anna D., B.S.'22, A.M.'24, Columbia Univ.; Prin., Wilson Tchrs. Col., Washington, D. C., since 1927.

Hale, Arthur W., A.B.'06, Amherst Col.; Ed. M.'24, Harvard Univ.; Supt. of Sch., Franklin, Mass., since 1918.

Hale, Florence M., Agt. for Rural Educ., State Dept. of Educ., Augusta, Maine.

Hale, Monte Jackson, A.B.'17, A M.'18, Drury Col.; Supt. of Sch., McAlester, Okla., since 1924.

Haley, Harvey H., B.S.'18, Peabody Col.; M.A.'22, Columbia Univ.; Supt. of Sch., Hot Springs, Ark., since 1928.

Haley, Nelle, M.A.'28, Tchrs. Col., Columbia Univ.; Asst. Supt. and Dir. Elem. Educ., Pub. Schools, Saginaw, Mich., since 1921.

Hall, A. F., M.A.'24, Univ. of Mich.; Supt. of Sch., Central Bldg., Manistique, Mich., since 1922.

Hall, Elizabeth, Asst. Supt. of Sch., 305 City Hall, Minneapolis, Minn., since 1911.

Hall, George F., B.E.'06, Union Col.; M.A. '23, Columbia Univ.; Supvg. Prin. of Sch., Cliffside Park, N. J., since 1921. Address: H. S. Bldg., Grantwood, N. J.

Hall, Hiram E., B.S. in Ed.'17, M.A.'27, Columbia Univ.; Co. Supt. of Sch., 602 Wallace Ave., Bowling Green, Ohio, since 1914.

Hall, J. O., A.M.'98, Univ. of Kansas; Supt. of Sch., 110 E. 12th St., Pawhuska, Okla., since 1922.

Hall, John Ruskin, A.B.'14, Otterbein Col.; A.M.'22, W. Va. Univ.; Supt. of Sch., 214 Court Ave., Weston, W. Va., since 1928.

Hall, John W., B.S.'01, M.A.'02, Tchrs. Col., Columbia Univ.; Dean, Sch. of Educ., Univ. of Nevada, Reno, Nevada, since 1920.

Hall, R. C., Diploma '85, Univ. of Va.; Supt. of Sch., 800 Louisiana St., Little Rock, Ark., since 1908.

Hall, Sidney B., A.B.'18, Col. of William and Mary; M.A.'24, Univ. of Va.; Ed. M. '25, Ed. D.'26, Harvard Univ.; State Dept. of Pub. Instr., Richmond, Va., since 1931.

Hall, W. F., M.A.'27, Tchrs. Col., Columbia Univ.; Rural Sch. Supvr., State Dept. of Educ., Little Rock, Ark., since 1928.

Hall, Wells A., A.B.'04, Brown; Supt. of Sch., Concord, Mass., since 1906.

Halsey, Henry Rowland, S.B.'08, Univ. of Chicago; M.A.'27, Ph.D.'29, Columbia Univ. Address: Chanin Bldg., 42nd and Lexington, New York, N. Y.

Halsey, Warren W., Supvg. Prin. of Sch., Garwood, N. J.

Ham, Ernest G., A.B.'94, Dartmouth Col.; A.M.'07, Univ. of Chicago; Supt. of Sch., Springfield, Vt., since 1925.

Hamilton, A. C., Ph.B.'12, Syracuse Univ.; Supt. of Sch., 38 Gesner St., Nyack, N. Y., since 1928.

Hamilton, Ella Jean, Supvr., Primary Dept., Sch. Admin. Bldg., Atlantic City, N. J., since 1913.

Hamilton, James T., Supt. of Sch., Newberg, Oregon.

Hamilton, Katharine, B.S.'95, Eureka; M.A. '13, Columbia Univ.; Asst Supt. of Sch., Endicott Bldg., St. Paul, Minn., since 1917.

Hamilton, O. A., A.B.'10, Univ. of N. C.; A.M.'22, Columbia Univ.; Co. Supt. of Sch., Wilmington, N. C., since 1927.

Hamilton, Otto E., A.B. and LL.B.'11, Ind. Univ.; A.M.'18, Ph.D.'26, Tchrs. Col., Columbia Univ. Address: Oaklandon, Ind.

Hamilton, William J., Supt. of Sch., Oak Park, Ill.

Hamm, Daniel W., Prin., Allentown H. S., Allentown, Pa.

Hamm, William G., Supt. of Sch., Huntsville, Ala.

Hammond, Dana King, A.B.'10, Dartmouth Col.; Pres., Santa Ana Jr. Col., Santa Ana, Calif., since 1916.

Hammond, W. J., 62 Baltimore Pl., Atlanta, Ga.

Hamner, H. B., Co. Supt. of Sch., Seale, Ala.

Hamon, Ray L., B.S.'22, Univ. of Fla.; A. M.'25, George Peabody Col. for Tchrs.; Ph.D.'30, Columbia Univ.; Assoc. Prof. of Educ., George Peabody Col. for Tchrs., Nashville, Tenn., since 1930.

Hampton, A. C., A.B.'18, Univ. of Oregon; Supt., Sch. Dist. No. 1, Shively Sch., Astoria, Oregon, since 1925.

Hanawalt, Paul B., A.B.'18, Col. of Puget Sound; M.A.'25, Univ. of Wash.; Supt. of Sch., Puyallup, Wash., since 1930.

Hancox, Herbert French, A.B.'10, A.M.'11, Univ. of Chicago; Dir., Central Y. M. C. A. Schools, 19 S. LaSalle St., Chicago, Ill., since 1923.

Handy, Anson B., B.A.'08, Ed.M.'30, Harvard Univ.; Supt. of Sch., Plymouth, Mass., since 1926.

Handy, Mabel L., Diploma '07, State Normal Sch., Bridgewater, Mass.; Supvr. of Middle Grades, Sch. Dept., City Hall, Brockton, Mass., since 1923.

Haney, C. L., 430 23rd Ave., W., Duluth, Minn.

Hanifan, L. J., Supt. of Sch., Paducah, Ky.

Hanks, N. A., A.B.'22, Central State Tchrs. Col., Mt. Pleasant, Mich.; Supt. of Sch., H. S. Bldg., Marysville, Mich., since 1928.

Hanley, James Lawrence, A.B.'19, Boston Col.; A.M.'20, Brown Univ.; LL.B.'27, Northeastern Univ.; Supt. of Sch., City Hall, Central Falls, R. I., since 1926.

Hanna, Ben M., A.B.'17, Franklin Col.; M. A.'28, Univ. of Chicago; Prin., Jr. H. S., Rockford, Ill., since 1925.

Hanna, George W., M.Di.'99, Highland Park Col.; A.B.'18, Des Moines Univ.; Supt. of Sch., 620 Normal Ave., Valley City, N. Dak., since 1899.

Hanna, John Calvin, A.B.'81, A.M.'84, Col. of Wooster; State Supvr. of H. S., 1004 S. Second St., Springfield, Ill., since 1914.

Hannum, Roy F., B.A.'07, State Univ. of Iowa; Supt. of Sch., Garner Bldg., Ottumwa, Iowa, since 1927.

Hansen, George S., B.Ed.'16, State Normal Sch., Peru, Nebr.; A.B.'20, State Tchrs. Col., Peru, Nebr.; M.A.'28, Univ. of Ariz.; Supt. of Sch., Safford, Ariz., since 1923.

Hanson, Margaret C., Licentiate of Instr.'90, Peabody Normal Col.; Prin., New Orleans Normal Sch., 1532 Calliope St., New Orleans, La., since 1901.

Harden, Mary, B.S.'15, M.A.'29, Tchrs. Col., Columbia Univ.; Head, Dept. of History, Horace Mann H. S. for Girls and Consultant in Social Studies, Dept. of Curriculum Research, Horace Mann Elem. Sch., Tchrs. Col., Columbia Univ., New York, N. Y., since 1930.

Harding, Ernest Arthur, B.S.'22, Tchrs. Col., Columbia Univ.; Supvg. Prin. of Sch., Wallington, N. J., since 1929.

Hardy, David P., B.S.'12, Univ. of Calif.; Deputy Supt. of Sch. in charge of Business Affairs, 125 Claremont Blvd., San Francisco, Calif., since 1924.

Hardy, H. Claude, B.A.'11, Wesleyan Univ.; M.A.'21, Univ. of Rochester; M.A.'23, Syracuse Univ.; Assoc. Supt. of Sch., 48 Park Ave., White Plains, N. Y., since 1927.

Hardy, John Crumpton, A.B.'89, A.M.'90, Miss. Col.; LL.B.'97, Millsaps Col.; LL. D.'17, Baylor Univ.; Pres., Baylor Col. for Women, Belton, Texas, since 1912.

Hardy, Rose Lees, Asst. Supt. of Sch., Washington, D. C.

Harman, Arthur Fort, B.S., Tchrs. Col., Columbia Univ.; LL.D., Univ. of Ala.; State Supt. of Educ., State Dept. of Educ., Montgomery, Ala., since 1929.

Harned, Perry L., State Commr. of Educ., Nashville, Tenn.

Harner, Melvin C., 617 Hampton Ave., Wilkinsburg, Pa.

Harney, Julia C., B.S.'18, M.A.'20, New York Univ.; Genl. Supvr. of Elem. Grades, 302 Pavonia Ave., Jersey City, N. J., since 1925.

Harper, Anna Belle, B.E.'20, Ill. State Normal Univ.; Lower Grade Supvr., Pub. Sch., 1803 Fifth St., Portsmouth, Ohio.

Harper, James Robb, A.B.'00, Cedarville Col.; Supt. of Sch., Wilmette, Ill., since 1908.

Harper, Thomas B., M.A.'27, New York Univ.; Supvg. Prin. of Sch., 500 Sixth Ave., Belmar, N. J., since 1919.

Harper, William J., Ed. M.; Supt. of Sch., 27 Usher Pl., Bristol, R. I., since 1929.

Harrington, Don, A.B.'12, A.M.'22. Univ. of Mich.; Supt. of Sch., Albion, Mich., since 1919.

Harris, Alice Louise, Asst. Supt. of Sch., City Hall, Worcester, Mass., since 1907.

Harris, Clarence M., A.B.'07, A.M.'08, Acadia Univ.; A.M.'24, Columbia Univ.; Supt. of Sch., Auburn, Mass., since 1925.

Harris, F. R., A.B.'02, Ohio Wesleyan Univ.; M.A.'10, Harvard Univ.; Supt. of Sch., Greenfield, Ohio, since 1923.

Harris, James H., A.B.'91, Univ. of Mich.; Supt. of Sch., Pontiac, Mich., since 1921.

Harris, John, B.S.'02, Carleton Col.; Co. Supt. of Sch., Folkston, Ga., since 1924.

Harris, T. H., State Supt. of Educ., Baton Rouge, La., since 1908.

Harris, William, A.B.'14, A.M.'23, Univ. of Ill.; Supt. of Sch., Cor. Franklin and North, Decatur, Ill., since 1926.

Harrison, W. R., B.S.'99, Univ. of Ala.; Supt. of Sch., Montgomery, Ala., since 1917.

Harry, David P., Jr., A.B.'16, Swarthmore Col.; A.M.'22, Ph.D.'28, Tchrs. Col., Columbia Univ.; Assoc. Prof. of Educ., Graduate Sch., Western Reserve Univ., Cleveland, Ohio, since 1928.

Hart, F. W., A.B.'08, Ind. Univ.; Ph.D.'20, Columbia Univ.; Prof. of Educ., Univ. of Calif., Berkeley, Calif., since 1920.

Hartley, B. W., B.A.'12, Univ. of Chicago; M.A.'15, Columbia Univ.; Supt. of Sch., San Antonio, Texas, since 1929.

Hartman, Albert L., Prin., Edgemont and Watchung Sch., Montclair, N. J.

Hartman, Ethel B., Co. Supt. of Sch., Court House, Mound City, Ill., since 1927.

Hartman, R. M., B.S.'24, M.A.'26, Tchrs. Col.. Columbia Univ.; Supvg. Prin. of Sch., 170 Franklin Ave., Midland Park, N. J., since 1924.

Hartsfield, F. S., A.B.'09, Univ. of Chattanooga; Co. Supt. of Pub. Instr., Court House, Tallahassee, Fla., since 1917.

Hartwell, Ernest C., A.B.'05, Albion Col.; A. M.'10, Univ. of Mich.; M.Pd.'12, Mich. State Normal Col.; D.Pd., N. Y. State Col. for Tchrs.; Pres., Dept. of Superintendence, 1918-19; Supt. of Sch., Buffalo, N. Y., since 1918.

Hartwell, Shattuck O., B.A.'88, Amherst Col.; M.Pd.'11, Mich. State Tchrs. Col.; LL.D.'15, Kalamazoo Col.; Supt. of Sch., Endicott Bldg., St. Paul, Minn., since 1918.

Hartz, Robert E., Supvg. Prin. of Sch., 202 E. Cherry St., Palmyra, Pa.

Hartzell, Oliver Reiff, Ph.B.'14, Franklin and Marshall Col.; M.A.'16, Univ. of Pa.; Supt. of Sch., San Rafael, Calif., since 1920.

Harvey, Carl Oliver, A.B.'17, Dakota Wesleyan Univ.; M.A.'30, Univ. of Southern Calif.; Dist. Supt. of Sch., Brea, Calif., since 1928.

Harvey, Elizabeth B., Assoc. Supt. of Sch., 1025 Pearl St., Belvidere, Ill., since 1923.

Harwood, Virginia C., Diploma '13, Virginia-Intermont Jr. Col.; B.S.'22, State Tchrs. Col., East Radford, Va.; M.A.'26, Tchrs. Col., Columbia Univ.; Supvr. of Graded Practice, State Normal Sch., Salisbury, Md., since 1930.

Haskell, Charles O., B.A.'13, Defiance Col.; M.A.'20, Univ. of Chicago; Supt. of Sch., Bartlesville, Okla., since 1926.

Haskins, P. N., A.B.'21, Defiance Col.; Prin., MacDonald Jr. H. S., 955 Francisco St., Cincinnati, Ohio.

Hastings, D. C., B.S.'20, Univ. of Ark.; Supt. of Sch., Crossett, Ark., since 1906.

Hasty, S. G., Co. Supt. of Sch., Lexington, N. C.

Hatcher, W. B., B.A.'17, M.A.'23, La. State Univ.; Supt. of Sch., Baton Rouge, La., since 1916.

Hathorn, Sam B., B.A.'24, Univ. of Miss.; Supvr. of H. S., State Dept. of Educ., Old Capitol Bldg., Jackson, Miss., since 1929.

Haver, Jennie M., B.S.'23, Tchrs. Col., Columbia Univ.; County Helping Tchr., Center St., Clinton, N. J., since 1916.

Haviland, L. W., Diploma '05, State Normal Sch., Fredonia, N. Y.; Supt. of Sch., Onarga, Ill., since 1917.

Haviland, Walter W., A.B.'93, Haverford Col.; Headmaster, Friends' Select Sch., The Parkway and 17th St., Philadelphia, Pa., since 1911.

Hawfield, S. G., A.B.'15, Duke Univ.; A.M. '26, Univ. of N. C.; Co. Supt. of Sch., Concord, N. C., since 1927.

Hawke, Oscar T., A.B.'14, A.M.'17, Wittenberg Col.; Co. Supt. of Sch., County Bldg., Springfield, Ohio, since 1922.

Hawkes, Franklin Powers, A.B.'17, Amherst Col.; A.M.'21, Ph.D.'27, Boston Univ.; Prin., Jr. H. S. West, Fessenden Rd., Arlington, Mass., since 1923.

Hawkes, William, A.B.'12, Univ. of Ill.; Supt. of Sch., Dist. 98, Lincoln Sch., 16th and Elmwood Ave., Berwyn, Ill., since 1924.

Hawkins, Louis L., Asst. Supt. of Sch., 37 Broadway, Ecorse, Mich.

Hawley, Frederick William, A.B.'88, A.M.'92, Carthage Col.; D.D.'11, Center Col.; LL. D.'16, Knox Col.; Pres., Park Col., Parkville, Mo., since 1915.

Haworth, C. V., A.B.'08, A.M.'21, Ind. Univ.; Supt. of Sch., Kokomo, Ind., since 1914.

Haworth, Chester C., A.B.'10, Earlham Col.; Supt. of Sch., Burlington, N. C.

Hawthorne, Lee B., Ph.B.'03, De Pauw Univ.; B.S.'09, Univ. of Mo.; Supt. of Sch., 705 E. Monroe, Mexico, Mo., since 1906.

Hay, George A. F., A.B.'23, A M.'27, Colo. State Tchrs. Col.; Prin., H. S., 100 Selma Ave., Webster Groves, Mo., since 1930.

Hay, H W., Supvg. Prin. of Sch., 536 Ferndale Ave., Johnstown, Pa.

Haycock, Robert L., B.A.'11, M.A.'12, George Washington Univ.; Asst. Supt. of Sch., Washington, D. C., since 1923.

Hayes, John N., B.S.'24, State Col. for Tchrs., Albany, N. Y.; Supvg. Prin. of Sch., Corinth, N. Y., since 1930.

Hayes, Lewis Everett, A.B.'14, Oberlin Col.; A.B.'22, Tchrs. Col., Columbia Univ.; Asst. Co. Supt. of Sch., Old Court House, Cleveland, Ohio, since 1924.

Hayes, Mercy Jane, M.A.'21, Columbia Univ. Address: 1015 Bishop Rd., Grosse Pointe, Mich.

Hayes, William Young, B.A.'21, Maryville Col.; Co. Supt. of Sch., Centerville, Ala., since 1923.

Haynes, Jessie P., B.S.'21, M.A.'25, Columbia Univ.; Asst. Prin., Richmond Normal Sch., Richmond, Va., since 1928.

Hays, William Leland, A B.'18, Waynesburg Col.; A.M.'29, Univ. of Pittsburgh; Supvg. Prin. of Twp. Sch., Avella, Pa., since 1922.

Hazel, Floyd M., B.S '22, Mich. State Col.; M.A.'26, Univ. of Mich.; Supt., Lakeview Consol. Sch., 300 Highland Ave., Battle Creek, Mich., since 1922.

Heald, F. H. B., A.B.'91, Dartmouth Col.; Dist. Supt. of Sch., Scarsborough and Old Orchard, Maine, since 1914. Address: Scarsborough, Maine.

Healy, Katharine L., B.S.'21, M.A.'29, Johns Hopkins Univ.; Supvr. of Intermediate and Advanced Grades, Hagerstown, Md., since 1924. Address: 3709 Nortonia Rd., Walbrook, Baltimore, Md.

Heard, Homer C., B.S.'17, A.B.'23, Northeastern State Tchrs. Col., Tahlequah, Okla.; Supt. of Sch., Claremore, Okla., since 1928.

Heck, Arch Oliver, B.S.'13, Hedding Col.; M.S.'14, Univ. of Ill.; Ph.D.'24, Ohio State Univ.; Assoc. Prof. of Sch. Admin., Col. of Educ., Ohio State Univ., Columbus, Ohio, since 1927.

Heckert, Eli P., A.B.'02, A M.'04, Bucknell Univ.; Supvg. Prin. of Sch., Mauch Chunk, Pa., since 1915.

Hedges, C. F., Ph.B.'12, Univ. of Wis.; Supt. of Sch., Neenah, Wis., since 1917.

Hedrick, E. H., A.B.'16, M.A '29, Univ. of Oregon; Supt. of Sch., Medford, Oregon, since 1925.

Heemstra, Clarence R., A.M., Univ. of Mich ; Supt. of Sch., Croswell, Mich., since 1926.

Heer, Amos L., A.B. and B. Pd.'14, Tri-State Col.; A.M.'21, Tchrs. Col., Columbia Univ.; Ph.D.'26, Ohio State Univ.; Dir. of Tchr. Tr., Kent State Col., Kent, Ohio.

Heffelfinger, John B., Supt. of Sch., 720 E. Seventh, Newton, Kansas.

Heffernan, Helen, B.A.'24, M A.'25, Univ. of Calif.; Chief, Div. of Rural Educ., State of Calif., State Library Bldg., Sacramento, Calif., since 1926.

Hefley, John T., A.B.'01, Univ of Okla.; M. A.'25, Univ. of Chicago; Supt. of Sch., 1311 W. Third Ave., Stillwater, Okla., since 1930.

Heidelberg, H. B , B.A.'03, Millsaps Col.; Supt. of Sch., H. S. Bldg., Clarksdale, Miss., since 1905.

Heightshoe, Agnes E., A.B.'11, State Univ. of Iowa; A.M.'28, Univ. of Chicago; Supt. of Sch., Perry, Iowa, since 1922.

Heilman, Paul L., B.S.'16, B.S. in Ed. '27, Okla. Agrl. and Mech. Col.; Supt. of Sch., Picher, Okla., since 1922.

Heilman, William F., 1230 Walnut St., Allentown, Pa.

Heinmiller, Louis E., B.S.'11, Rochester Univ.; A.M.'18, Columbia Univ.; Ph.D.'25, New York Univ.; Pres., Silliman Col., Clinton, La., since 1927.

Heisser, Della B., Elem. Diploma, Chico State Tchrs. Col.; Dist. Supt. of Sch., Turlock, Calif., since 1919.

Heller, Daniel B., A B.'13, Iowa Wesleyan Col.; M.A.'24, Univ. of S. Dak.; Supt. of Sch., 804 Jones St., Eveleth, Minn., since 1929.

Heller, Regenia R , Supvr. of Kdgn. and Reading, 153 E. Elizabeth St., Detroit, Mich.

Hellyer, Perry Henry, Diploma '07, Ill. State Normal Univ.; Co. Supt. of Sch., 377 W. Euclid Ave., Lewistown, Ill., since 1919.

Helms, Walter T , Ph. B.'99, Univ. of Calif.; Supt. of Sch., Lincoln Sch., Richmond, Calif., since 1909.

Hemenway, H. S., Ph.B.'18, Univ. of Wis.; Supt. of Sch., Shorewood, Milwaukee, Wis.,

Hempel, Edward C., Ph.B.'08, Brown Univ.; Supt. of Sch., Central Sch., Orange, Mass., since 1929.

Henderson, Frank A., A.M.'16, Columbia Univ.; Supt. of Sch., Burbank, Calif., since 1928.

Henderson, T. C., Diploma '98, State Normal Sch., Cullowhee, N. C. Address: R. F. D. 1, Lake Toxaway, N. C.

Hendren, E. S., Co. Supt. of Sch., 215 Franklin St., Mt. Airy, N. C.

Hendricks, Eldo L., B.S.'94, Franklin Col.; A.M.'99, Ind. Univ.; LL.D.'16, Franklin Col.; Pres., State Tchrs. Col., Warrensburg, Mo., since 1915.

Hendricks, Jake J., M.A.'29, Univ. of Texas; Supt. of Sch., Kerens, Texas, since 1920.

Hendrix, H. E., A.B.'01, North Central Col.; A.M.'23, Stanford Univ.; Ph.D.'29, New York Univ.; Supt. of Sch., Mesa, Ariz., since 1920.

Hendry, Frank, A.B.'09, A.M.'14, Univ. of Mich.; Supt. of Sch., 153 Hendrie Blvd., Royal Oak, Mich., since 1915.

Henkel, A. J., Ph.B.'21, Univ. of Wis.; Supt. of Sch., Portage, Wis., since 1921.

Henkel, Celeste, B.S., Davenport Col.; A.B., Salem Col.; Co. Supt. of Sch., Statesville, N. C., since 1925.

Henman, Stanley T., 517 Dorian Ct., Westfield, N. J.

Hennessy, Sister M. Kathleen, A.B.'19, St. Elizabeth Col.; A.M.'25, Columbia Univ.; Head, Dept. of Educ., College of St. Elizabeth, Convent Station, N. J., since 1920.

Hennon, Harvey N., Supvg. Prin. of Sch., 227 Cornell Ave., West View, Pittsburgh, Pa., since 1916.

Henry, Beryl, Supt. of Sch., Hope, Ark.

Henry, Charles, B. of Didactics '93, Iowa Tchrs. Col.; B.A.'11, Wash. State Col.; M.A.'26, Tchrs. Col., Columbia Univ.; Supt. of Sch., Dillon, Mont., since 1926.

Henry, David W., B.A.'11, Normal Col.; M.A.'16, Tchrs. Col., Columbia Univ.; Dean, Col. of Educ., Univ. of Toledo, since 1919 and Acting Dean, Col. of Arts, Univ. of Toledo, Toledo, Ohio, since 1929.

Henry, W. W., Co. Supt. of Sch., Corning, Ark.

Henzlik, F. E., B.S. in Ed.'16, State Tchrs. Col., Warrensburg, Mo.; M.A.'23, Ph.D.'24, Tchrs. Col., Columbia Univ.; Prof. of Sch. Admin., Tchrs. Col., Univ. of Nebr., Lincoln, Nebr., since 1924.

Hepner, Walter Ray, A.B.'13, M.A.'16, Univ. of Southern Calif.; Supt. of Sch., 825 Union St., San Diego, Calif., since 1928.

Herber, Howard T., B.A.'25, Ursinus Col.; A.M.'26, Tchrs. Col., Columbia Univ.; Prin., Hamilton Sch., Weehawken, N. J., since 1928.

Herbert, Anna Josephine, Asst. Supt. of Sch., 88 Broadway, Bayonne, N. J.

Herlinger, H. V., Ph.B.'13, Grove City Col.; Supt. of Sch., Midland, Pa., since 1928.

Hermann, Barbara V., B.S. in Ed.'28, M.A.'30, Fordham Tchrs. Col.; Supvg. Prin. of Sch., 137 Roosevelt Ave., Carteret, N. J., since 1916.

Hernberg, Sara B., Barnegat, N. J.

Herring, John H., A.M.'09, Ohio Univ.; Supt. of Sch., 36 York St., Lambertville, N. J., since 1917.

Herring, John P., A.B.'00, Brown Univ.; Ph.D.'24, Columbia Univ.; Natl. Dir. of Research in Adult Educ., Natl. Council of the Y. M. C. A., 347 Madison Ave., New York, N. Y., since 1929.

Herron, Helen B.A.'11, M.A.'13, Tulane Univ.; Supvr. of Student Teaching, New Orleans Normal Sch., 1933 Elysian Fields Ave., New Orleans, La.

Hershey, Charles Edward, A.B.'21, Gettysburg Col., Supvg. Prin. of Sch., 360 High St., Sharon Hill, Pa., since 1929.

Hertzler, Silas, B.A.'13, Goshen Col.; B.D.'17, Yale Divinity Sch ; M.A.'18, Tchrs. Col., Columbia Univ.; Ph.D.'27, Yale Univ.; Head, Dept. of Educ. and Registrar, Goshen Col., Goshen, Ind., since 1924.

Hess, Frank D., B.S.'25, Univ. of Okla.; M. A.'29, Univ. of Colo.; Supt. of Sch., 133 E. Maple, Drumright, Okla., since 1929.

Hesse, Ernest, B.A.'10, Ohio State Univ.; A.M.'12, Columbia Univ. Address: Yonkers, N. Y.

Heston, F. M., A.B.'08, Ohio State Univ.; M.A.'25, Columbia Univ.; Prof. of Educ., Asbury Col., Wilmore, Ky., since 1925.

Hetherington, Charles George, Supt. of Sch., South Ave., Penn Yan, N. Y.

Hetzel, George, 1680 E. Mountain St., Pasadena, Calif.

Heusner, William S., A.B.'94, Ohio Wesleyan Univ.; Supt. of Sch., City Hall, Salina, Kansas, since 1913.

Hewes, E. D., A.M.'16, Columbia Univ.; Supt. of Sch., Beacon, N. Y., since 1919.

Hewitt, Hulda K., Helping Tch., Pub. Sch., Mt. Holly, N. J.

Heyl, Helen Hay, Asst. in Rural Educ., State Educ. Dept., Albany, N. Y.

Hibschman, John A., Supvg. Prin. of Sch., Wernersville, Pa.

Hibschman, Ralph Otis, Dir., Andrews Inst., Willoughby, Ohio.

Hick, Hugh R., B.S.'03, Denison Univ.; M.A.'23, Tchrs. Col., Columbia Univ.; Supt. of Sch., 808 N. 12th St., Cambridge, Ohio.

Hicks, Frank W., Dept. of Educ., State Tchrs. Col., Minot, N. Dak.

Hicks, Raymond H., A.B.'22, B.S.'23, Northeastern State Tchrs. Col., Tahlequah, Okla.; M.A.'27, Columbia Univ.; Supt. of Sch., Jenks, Okla., since 1923.

Hicks, Robert S., A.B.'21, Occidental Col.; Supt. of Sch., Casper, Wyo., since 1926.

Hicks, Samuel I., A.B.'24, Univ. of Mich.; M.A.'27, Tchrs. Col., Columbia Univ.; Supvg. Prin. of Sch., Central Park, L. I., N. Y., since 1929.

Higbie, Edgar C., A.B.'07, A.M.'09, Univ. of Minn.; Ph.D.'20, Columbia Univ.; Pres., Eastern State Normal Sch., Madison, S. Dak., since 1920.

Higgins, Lothrop D., Prin., State Normal Sch., Danbury, Conn.

Highley, Albert E., B.S.'99, Marion Col.; Diploma '05, Ind. State Normal; A.B.'10, A.M.'11, Ind. Univ.; Supt. of Sch., Lafayette, Ind., since 1923.

Highsmith, E. M., Ph.B.'07, A.M.'14, Univ. of N. C.; A.M '15, Peabody Col.; Ph.D.'23, Univ. of N. C.; Dean, Summer Sch. and Prof. of Educ., Furman Univ., Greenville, S. C., since 1930.

Highsmith, J. Henry, A.B.'00, A.M.'02, Trinity Col.; LL.D.'25, Catawba Col.; Dir., Div. of Sch. Inspection, State Dept. of Pub. Instr., Raleigh, N. C., since 1920.

Hilbish, Charles E., B.S.'09, Bucknell Univ.; A.M.'29, Susquehanna Univ.; Asst. Co. Supt. of Sch., Court House, Sunbury, Pa., since 1927.

Hill, Albert H., B.A.'87, Richmond Col.; M.A.'14, Tchrs. Col., Columbia Univ.; Supt. of Sch., 1622 W. Grace St., Richmond, Va., since 1919.

Hill, Arthur B., A.B.'04, Ouachita Col.; A.M.'22, Columbia Univ. Address: 112 Scott St., Little Rock, Ark.

Hill, E. N., A.B.'05, A.M.'11, Earlham Col.; Supt. of Sch., Olathe, Kansas, since 1915.

Hill, Henry H., A.B. and M.A.'21, Univ. of Va.; Ph.D.'30, Columbia Univ.; Supt. of Sch., Lexington, Ky., since 1930.

Hill, Orville E., B.S.'26, Ohio Univ.; Supt. of Sch., Carroll, Ohio, since 1929.

Hill, Ralph E., A.B.'01, Albion Col.; M. A.'09, Univ. of Louisville; Registrar, Univ. of Louisville, Louisville, Ky., since 1929.

Hill, Walter Henry, B.S.'23, Gettysburg Col.; Supt. of Sch., Svvedesboro, N. J., since 1924.

Hill, William Colver, A.B.'94, A.M.'12, Brown Univ.; A.M.'23, Harvard Univ.; Prin., Central H. S., Springfield, Mass., since 1910.

Hilleboe, Guy L., A.B.'20, Univ. of Minn.; A.M.'28, Ph.D.'30, Tchrs. Col., Columbia Univ.; Prof. of Educ. and Dir. of Child Development and Parent Educ., New York State Col. for Tchrs., Albany, N. Y., since 1930.

Hillegas, Milo B., Ph.B.'97, Rochester; Ph.D.'12, Columbia Univ.; LL.D.'17, Univ. of Vt.; Prof. of Educ., Tchrs. Col., Columbia Univ., 106 Morningside Drive, New York, N. Y., since 1920.

Hillman, James E., B.Pd.'15, Berea Col.; B.S.'19, A.M.'20, Ph.D.'24, George Peabody Col. for Tchrs.; Dir., Tchr. Tr., State Dept. of Pub. Instr., Raleigh, N. C., since 1923.

Hines, Linnaeus N., A.B.'94, M.A.'08, Ind. Univ.; LL.D.'29, Wabash Col.; Pres., Ind. State Tchrs. Col., Terre Haute, Ind., since 1921.

Hinkel, H. E., Ph.B.'28, Univ. of Chicago; Supt. of Sch.,Ardmore Sch., Villa Park, Ill., since 1925.

Hinson, M. R., A.B.E.'24, Univ. of Fla.; M.A.'25, George Peabody Col. for Tchrs.; State Supvr. of H. S., Capitol Bldg., Tallahassee, Fla., since 1927.

Hirst, Claude Marvin, State Supt. of Pub. Instr., 5412 V St., Little Rock, Ark.

Hitchcock, Clarence C., B.S.'14, St. Lawrence Univ.; Supt. of Sch., 146 Hamilton Ave., Hasbrouck Heights, N. J.

Hitchcock, Fred S., Supvg. Prin., Chapman Tech. H. S., New London, Conn., since 1906.

Hixson, A. F., Supt. of Sch., 98 Sunnyside Drive, Athens, Ohio.

Hixson, J. H., B.S. in Ed. and M.A.'22, Ohio State Univ.; Dir., Buildings and Grounds Division, State Educ. Dept., Education Bldg., Albany, N. Y., since 1929.

Hobbs, Edwin G., B.A.'25, N. Mex. State Tchrs. Col., Silver City, N. Mex.; Supt. of Sch., Melrose, N. Mex., since 1930.

Hobbs, James Beecher, Ph.B.'18, Brown Univ.; Ed.M.'22, Harvard Univ. Address: 30 Huntington Ave., Boston, Mass.

Hodge, Lamont F., A.B.'97, A.M.'21, Pd.D. '26, Colgate Univ.; Supt. of Sch., 50 Hamilton Ave., Yonkers, N. Y., since 1922.

Hodges, J. M., B.S.'23, George Peabody Col. for Tchrs.; Supt. of Sch., H. S., Tyler, Texas, since 1925.

Hodgson, Fred J., Supvg. Prin. of Sch., Springfield, N. J.

Hoech, Arthur A., B.S.'11, Central Wesleyan Col.; B.S. in Ed.'18, Univ. of Mo.; Supt., Ritenour Consol. Sch. Dist., Overland, Mo., since 1920.

Hoefer, Carolyn, B.A.'10, Univ. of Wis.; M.A.'18, Univ. of Chicago. Address: 848 N. Dearborn St., Chicago, Ill.

Hoffman, Mrs. A. H., B.A.'09, State Univ. of Iowa; Supt., Yeomen City of Childhood, Elgin, Ill., since 1927.

Hoffman, C. A., A.B.'18, Manchester Col.; Supt. of Sch., Lake Odessa, Mich., since 1927.

Hoffman, Miss M. Gazelle, B A.'11, Elmira; M.A.'26, Columbia Univ.; Supt. of Sch., Third Supervisory Dist., Niagara Co., Lewiston, N. Y., since 1915.

Hogue, O. Wendell, B.S.'18, Syracuse Univ.; A.M.'22, Tchrs. Col., Columbia Univ.; Supt. of Sch., Lyons, N. Y., since 1927.

Hoke, Kremer J., Ph.D.'14, Columbia Univ.; Dean, Sch. of Educ. and Dean, Col. of William and Mary, Williamsburg, Va., since 1920.

Holbert, William R., Supvg. Prin. of Sch., Manasquam, N. J.

Holbrook, C. Ray, B.Ed.'19, M.A.'22, Univ. of Wash.; Supt. of Sch., Sch. Admin. Bldg., Eighth and F Sts., San Bernardino, Calif., since 1923.

Holbrook, Florence, B.A.'79, Univ. of Chicago; Prin., Phillips Jr. H. S., 244 E. Pershing Rd., Chicago, Ill., since 1924.

Holcomb, Winfield A., Diploma '86, State Normal Sch., Fredonia, N. Y.; Pd.D.'24, State Col. for Tchrs., Albany, N. Y.; Prin., State Normal Sch., Geneseo, N. Y., since 1923.

Holden, Ellsworth B., B.S.'23, Mich. State Col.; Supt. of Sch., Greenville, Mich., since 1928.

Holden Miles C., 53 Hillman St., Springfield, Mass.

Holland, N. S., A.B.'17, Southern Methodist Univ.; A.M.'27, Tchrs. Col., Columbia Univ.; Supt. of Sch., Breckenridge, Texas, since 1929.

Holleman, M. B., A.B.'19, Baylor Univ.; M.A.'27, Univ. of Texas; Supt. of Sch., Brenham, Texas, since 1927.

Holley, Charles E., Ph.D.'15, Univ. of Ill.; Prof. of Sec. Educ., Univ. of Idaho, Moscow, Idaho, since 1930.

Holliday, Lewis P., A.B.'10, Hillsdale Col.; M.A.'17, Columbia Univ.; Assoc. in Educ., Hillsdale Col. and Supt. of Sch., Hillsdale, Mich., since 1929.

Hollis, E. V., B.S., M.S., Miss. Agrl. and Mech. Col.; A.M., Tchrs. Col., Columbia Univ.; Head, Dept. of Educ., State Tchrs. Col., Morehead, Ky., since 1927.

Holloway, H. V., A.B.'95, A.M.'98, Washington Col., Chestertown, Md.; Ph.D.'14, Univ. of Pa.; State Supt. of Pub. Instr., Dover, Del., since 1921.

Holloway, R. F., A.B.'92, Texas Christian Univ.; Supt. of Sch., Ranger, Texas, since 1925.

Holloway, W. J., M.A.'29, Univ. of Texas; Supt. of Sch., Port Neches, Texas, since 1930.

Holloway, William James, A.M.'12, Ph.D. '28, Columbia Univ.; Prin., State Normal Sch., Salisbury, Md., since 1925.

Holman, Carl, A.B.'09, Bates Col.; A.M '27, Columbia Univ.; Supvg. Prin. of Sch., Pearl River, N. Y., since 1923.

Holmes, D. O. W., A.B.'01, A.M.'12, Howard Univ.; A.M.'14, Columbia Univ.; Dean, Col. of Educ., Howard Univ., Washington, D. C., since 1920.

Holmes, Harley W., A B.'25, Western State Tchrs. Col., Kalamazoo, Mich.; Supt. of Sch., H. S., Marshall, Mich., since 1929.

Holmes, Henry Wyman, A.B.'03, A.M '04, Harvard Univ.; Litt.D.'24, Tufts Col.; Dean, Grad. Sch of Educ., 5 Lawrence Hall, Harvard Univ., Cambridge, Mass., since 1920.

Holmes, Jay William, A.B.'16, Hiram Col.; M.A.'27, Ohio State Univ.; Prin., Wilbur Wright Jr. H. S., Dayton, Ohio, since 1927.

Holmes, Joseph R., B A.'15, Hendrix Col.; M.A.'25, Tchrs. Col., Columbia Univ.; Supt. of Sch., Okmulgee, Okla., since 1928.

Holmes, Margaret Cook, A.B.'15, Adelphi Col.; M.A.'24, Tchrs. Col., Columbia Univ.; Asst. Dir. of Kdgns., Pub. Sch., New York, N. Y., since 1921. Address: 136 Cambridge Pl., Brooklyn, N. Y.

Holmes, Stanley H., A.B.'87, A.M.'90, Colby Univ.; Supt. of Sch., 41 Buell St., New Britain, Conn., since 1906.

Holmes, William H., A.B.'97, Colby Col.; Ph.D.'10, Clark Univ.; Supt. of Sch., Mount Vernon, N. Y., since 1913.

Holst, John H., M.A.'21, Columbia Univ.; Supvr. of Indian Schools, Indian Office, Washington, D. C.

Holston, Evelyn Turner, B S.'20, A.M.'21, Tchrs. Col., Columbia Univ.; Elem. Sch. Supvr., Administration Bldg., Springfield, Mass., since 1922.

Holt, Frank E., B S.'06, Amherst Col.; Ed. M.'29, Harvard Univ.; Supt. of Sch., Town Hall, Whitman, Mass., since 1922.

Holton, Edwin L., A.B.'04, Ind. Univ.; Ph. D.'27, Columbia Univ.; Head, Dept. of Educ. and Dean, Summer Sch., Kansas State Agrl. Col., Manhattan, Kansas.

Holton, Holland, A.B.'07, Duke Univ.; J.D. '27, Univ. of Chicago; Head, Dept. of Educ., and Dir., Summer Sch., Duke Univ., Durham, N. C., since 1921.

Holtzman, Herbert P., Ph.B.'13, A.M.'16, Dickinson Col; LL.B.'16, Dickinson Law Sch.; A.M.'23, Univ. of Pa.; Supvg. Prin. of Sch., 718 Reading Ave., West Reading, Pa., since 1924.

Holy, Thomas C., A.B.'19, Des Moines Univ.; M.A.'22, Ph.D.'24, State Univ. of Iowa; Prof. of Educ. and Research Assoc. in Bureau of Educ. Research, Ohio State Univ., Columbus, Ohio, since 1927 and Consultant in Sch. Bldg., Ohio State Dept. of Educ., Columbus, Ohio, since 1929.

Homberger, E. H., A.B.'12, A.M.'20, Colo. State Tchrs. Col.; M.A.'26, Tchrs. Col., Columbia Univ.; Supt. of Sch., 1508 Okla. Ave., Woodward, Okla., since 1921.

Honeycutt, Allison W., A.B.'02, Wake Forest Col.; Supt. of Sch., Hendersonville, N. C., since 1919.

Honiss, L. J., B.A.'92, Wesleyan Univ.; Supvg. Prin. of Sch., Dumont H. S., Dumont, N. J., since 1899.

Honn, Edward F., B.A.'21, Univ. of Ariz.; Supt. of Sch., Prescott, Ariz., since 1928.

Hood, Walter D., B.A.'94, Yale Univ.; Prin., Gilbert Sch., Winsted, Conn., since 1908.

Hook, T. E., C.E.'08, Ohio Northern Univ.; A.B.'14, A.M.'18, Univ. of Mich.; Supt. of Sch., 421 Grant St., Troy, Ohio, since 1919.

Hooker, Charles J., Supvg. Prin. of Sch., Goshen, N. Y.

Hooker, Grover C., B.A., B.E.23, M.A.'24, Univ. of Colo.; Acting Asst. Prof. of Educ., Stanford Univ., since 1929. Address: 1120 Parkinson Ave., Palo Alto, Calif.

Hope, John, A.B.'94, A.M.'07, Brown Univ.; LL.D.'20, Howard Univ.; LL.D.'23, Bucknell Univ.; LL.D.'28, McMaster Univ.; Pres., Morehouse Col., Atlanta, Ga., since 1906 and Pres., Atlanta Univ., Atlanta, Ga., since 1929.

Hopkins, John L., A.B.'09, M.A.'12, Hamilton Col.; Supt. of Sch., Hastings-on-Hudson, N. Y., since 1923.

Hopkins, Thomas W., Prin. of Sch., York St., Jersey City, N. J.

Hopkins, W. Karl, A.B.'06, Univ. of Utah; Supt. of Sch., Ogden, Utah, since 1919.

Hopper. Laura A., Diploma '24, Northern Ariz. State Tchrs. Col., Flagstaff, Ariz.; Co. Supt. of Sch., Prescott, Ariz., since 1929.

Horn, Carl M., B.S.'21, Mich. State Col.; M.A.'28, Univ. of Mich.; Supt. of Sch., Dowagiac, Mich., since 1930.

Horn, Ernest, B.S.'07, A.M.'08, Univ. of Mo.; Ph.D.'14, Columbia Univ.; Prof. of Educ., Dir. of the Univ. Elem. Sch., State Univ. of Iowa, Iowa City, Iowa, since 1915.

Horn, Paul Whitfield, M.A.'88, Central Col., Mo.; LL.D.'17, Baylor Univ.; Pres., Texas Technological Col., Lubbock, Texas, since 1924.

Hornby, A. M., B.S.'12, Ohio Wesleyan Univ.; A.M.'25, Columbia Univ.; Supt. of Sch., 312 E. John St., Maumee, Ohio.

Horner, F. G., A.B.'12, Juniata Col.; A.M. '16, Columbia Univ.; Supt. of Sch., Tamaqua, Pa., since 1927.

Horner, Harlan Hoyt, A.B.'01, Univ. of Ill.; A.M.'15, Pd.D.'18, N. Y. State Col. for Tchrs.; Dir., State Col. Educ., State Educ. Dept., Albany, N. Y., since 1930.

Horsch, M. J., A.B.'25, Earlham Col.; Supvg. Prin. of Sch., 509 George St., Scottdale, Pa., since 1921.

Horstick, Simon M., B.S.'10, M.A.'23, Univ. of Pa.; Supt. of Sch., H. S., Pleasantville, N. J., since 1926.

Horton, A. H., Parish Supt. of Sch., Coushatta, La., since 1913.

Horton, Arthur D., A.B.'98, A.M.'00, Allegheny Col.; Supt. of Sch., Ridgefield, Conn., since 1928.

Horton, Deo Wesley, A.B.'09, A.M.'13, Ind.; Supt. of Sch., 3019 E. Broadway, Logansport, Ind.

Horton, Joseph I., Supt. of Sch., Ipswich, Mass., since 1916.

Horton, Lucile Dee, Co. Supt. of Sch., Colorado Springs, Colo., since 1929.

Hosic, James F., Ph.B.'01, Ph.M. '02, Univ. of Chicago; Ph.D.'20, Columbia Univ.; Prof. of Educ., Tchrs. Col., Columbia Univ., 525 W. 120th St., New York, N. Y., since 1921.

Hoskinson, J. H., A.B.'07, A.M.'11, Ind. Univ.; Supt. of Sch., Whiting, Ind., since 1915.

Hosler, Fred William, Supvg. Prin. of Sch., Hatboro, Pa.

Hostetler, Ivan P., B.S. in Ed.'19, State Tchrs. Col., Emporia, Kansas; M.A. in Ed. '26, Stanford Univ.; Supt., Lower Miami Pub. Sch., Miami, Ariz., since 1927.

Houck, Maurice E., A.B.'13, Univ. of Mich.; M.A.'29, Pa. State Col.; Supt. of Sch., 606 W. Front St., Berwick, Pa., since 1920.

Hougham, Robert Bradley, Co. Supt. of Sch., Franklin, Ind.

Houk, Dale W., Supvg. Prin. of Sch., Fifth St., California, Pa.

House, Robert W., B.A.'21, Emory and Henry Col.; Prin., H. S., Salem, Va., since 1929.

Houseman, W. Lynn, B.S.'08, Colgate Univ.; M.A.'21, Tchrs. Col., Columbia Univ.; Supt. of Sch., Geneva, N. Y., since 1926.

Housh, Early T., Ph.B.'04, No. Ill. Col.; A.B.'12, Highland Park Col.; M.A.'16, State Univ. of Iowa. Address: 412 Shops Bldg., Des Moines, Iowa.

Houx, Kate L., B.S.'26, A.M.'29, Tchrs. Col., Columbia Univ.; Dir. of Tr., Eastern Oregon Normal Sch., La Grande, Oregon, since 1929.

Hovater, Dexter Louis, B.S.'18, Univ. of Ala.; M.A.'26, Tchrs. Col., Columbia Univ.; Supt. of Sch., Piedmont, Ala., since 1928.

Howard, C. A., A.B.'07, Baker Univ.; A.M. '23, Univ. of Oregon; State Supt. of Pub. Instr., Supreme Court Bldg., Salem, Oregon, since 1927.

Howard, Daniel, A.M.'98, Brown Univ.; Supt. of Sch., Windsor, Conn., since 1910.

Howard, George, A.B.'12, Davidson Col.; A.M.'22, Ph.D.'24, Columbia Univ.; Co. Supt. of Sch., Salisbury, N. C., since 1925.

Howard, Harriet, M.A.'16, Tchrs. Col., Columbia Univ.; Supvr. of Student-Teaching, Natl. Kdgn. and Elem. Col., 2770 Sheridan Rd., Evanston, Ill., since 1923.

Howard, James Edgar, B.S. in Ed.'21, Southeast Mo. State Tchrs. Col., Cape Girardeau, Mo.; Supt. of Sch., Clarendon, Ark., since 1920.

Howard, Lowry S., Diploma '13, State Tchrs. Col., Cheney, Wash.; A.B.'17, A.M. '20, Stanford Univ.; Headmaster, Menlo Sch. for Boys and Dir., Menlo Jr. Col., Menlo Park, Calif., since 1927.

Howard, Virgie Marie, B.S.E.'27, Univ. of Ark.; M.A.'29, Univ. of Chicago; Supvr. of Grades, 301 Stickney Ave., Wauwatosa, Wis., since 1927.

Howe, Chester L., B.A.S.'09, Harvard Univ.; Supt. of Sch., Jewett City, Conn., since 1929.

Howell, A. H., Diploma '02, State Normal; B.S.'27, N. Y. Univ.; Co. Supt. of Sch., Court House, Honesdale, Pa., since 1921.

Howell, Charles P., A.B.'20, Univ. of Okla. Address: 1419 S. Seventh, Ponca City, Okla.

Howell, Clarence E., B.S.'17, James Millikin Univ.; A.M.'23, Tchrs. Col., Columbia Univ.; Dir. of Jr. H. S., Bd. of Educ., Trenton, N. J., since 1926.

Howell, D. A., B.S.'16, New York Univ.; Supvg. Prin. of Sch., Linden, N. J., since 1907.

Howell, Harry, Ph.B.'95, Univ. of N. C.; Supt. of Sch., Fayetteville, N. C., since 1924.

Howerth, Joseph, A.B.'94, Cornell Univ.; Supt. of Sch., Shamokin, Pa.

Howes, Alfred F., A.B.'87, A.M.'92, Amherst Col.; Supt. of Sch. 39 Hudson St., Manchester, Conn., since 1911.

Howes, Herbert H., Diploma '02, State Normal Sch., Bridgewater, Mass.; Ed.B.'25, R. I. Col. of Educ.; Prin., State Normal Sch., Hyannis, Mass., since 1930.

Hove, Monica M., B.Ed.'22, Brown Univ.; Elem. Sch. Supvr., 9 Exchange Ter., Providence, R. I., since 1926.

Hoyman, W. H., A.B.'09, Iowa State Tchrs. Col., Cedar Falls, Iowa; Supt. of Sch., Indianola, Iowa, since 1926.

Hubbard, Frank W., A.B.'22, M.A.'26, Univ. of Calif.; Asst. Dir. of Research, Natl. Educ. Assn., 1201 16th St., N. W., Washington, D. C., since 1926.

Hubbard, I. O., Ph.M.'15, Univ. of Wis.; Supt. of Sch., H. S., Ashland, Wis., since 1919.

Hubbard, Louis H., B.S.'03, M.A.'18, Univ. of Texas; LL.D.'29, Austin Col.; Ph.D. '30, Univ. of Texas; Pres., Texas State Col. for Women, Denton, Texas, since 1926.

Hubbard, O. S., B.L.'13, Univ. of Calif.; M.A.'17, Leland Stanford Jr. Univ.; Supt. of Sch., Hawthorne Bldg., Fresno, Calif., since 1928.

Hudson, C. A., B.S.'17, Wooster Col.; A.M. '23, Tchrs. Col., Columbia Univ.; Supt. of Sch., H. S. Bldg., Fremont, Ohio, since 1927.

Hudson, Charles A., A.B.'01, Mercer Univ.; Co. Supt. of Sch., Greenville, Ga., since 1927.

Huff, Leo W., State Life Cert.'17, Central State Normal Sch., Mt. Pleasant, Mich.; A.B.'26, M.A.'29, Univ. of Mich.; Supt. of Sch., 1765 Fort St., Lincoln Park, Mich., since 1928.

Huff, Raymond, B.A.'21, Univ. of Texas; M.A.'30, Univ. of Colo.; Supt. of Sch., Clayton, N. Mex., since 1920.

Huff, Z. T., A.B., Baylor Univ.; A.M., Columbia Univ.; Dean, Wayland Col., Plainview, Texas, since 1925.

Hufnagel, Florence M., 1214 Bloomingdale Rd., Baltimore, Md.

Hughes, Charles C., A.B.'95, Stanford Univ.; Supt. of Sch., 21st and L Sts., Sacramento, Calif., since 1912.

Hughes, F. B., B.S.'97, Vanderbilt; Litt.D. '22, A.M.'26, Austin Col.; Supt. of Sch., 823 Gandy St., Denison, Texas.

Hughes, John Francis, A.B.'09, Washburn Col.; Supt. of Sch., Eldorado, Kansas.

Hughes, Rees H., A.B.'13, Washburn Col.; A.M.'30, Tchrs. Col., Columbia Univ.; Supt. of Sch., Parsons, Kansas, since 1922.

Hughes, William Hardin, 1058 N. Mentor Ave., Pasadena, Calif.

Hughey, Allen H., B.A.'03, Vanderbilt; LL. B.'08, George Washington Univ.; Supt. of Sch., El Paso, Texas, since 1919.

Hull, Jerome, Co. Supt. of Sch., Court House, Youngstown, Ohio.

Hull, Osman R., B.S.'13, M.S.'14, Ph.D.'25, Univ. of Calif. Address: 823 Estes, San Antonio, Texas.

Hulten, Charles E., Ph.B. and Ph.M., Univ. of Wis.; Supt. of Sch., Marinette, Wis., since 1924.

Hulton, John G., Supt. of Sch., Latrobe, Pa.

Hummer, John F., B.S.'08, Bucknell Univ.; A.M.'15, Univ. of Wis.; Asst. Supt. of Sch., Bd. of Educ. Bldg., Syracuse, N. Y., since 1928.

Hunkins, R. V., B.A.'14, Univ. of Nebr.; M.A.'21, Univ. of Chicago; Supt. of Sch., Lead, S. Dak., since 1922.

Hunt, Charles W., A.B.'04, Brown Univ.; A.M.'10, Ph.D.'22, Columbia Univ.; Dean, Sch. of Educ., Western Reserve Univ., Stearns Rd. and E. 109th St., Cleveland, Ohio, since 1924.

Hunt, Harry A., A.B.'01, Col. of William and Mary; Supt. of Sch., Armistead Bldg., Portsmouth, Va., since 1909.

Hunt, Heber U., Supt. of Sch., 906 W. Fifth, Sedalia, Mo.

Hunt, Lyman C., A.B.'12, Univ. of Vt.; Supt. of Sch., Burlington, Vt., since 1922.

Hunt, R. L., A.B.'13, William Jewell Col.; A.M.'27, Colo. State Tchrs. Col.; Supt. of Sch., Madison, S. Dak., since 1929.

Hunter, Frederick Maurice, A.B.'05, Univ. of Nebr.; A.M.'19, Tchrs. Col., Columbia Univ.; Ed.D.'24, Univ. of Calif.; LL.D. '30, Colo. Col.; Pres., Natl. Educ. Assn., 1920-21; Chancellor, Univ. of Denver, Denver, Colo., since 1928.

Hunter, Joseph Symmes, B.A.'01, Ohio State Univ.; M.A.'24, Tchrs. Col., Columbia Univ.; Asst. Co. Supt. of Sch., 445 Ross Ave., Hamilton, Ohio, since 1914.

Hurlbut, Floyd, A.B.'03, Princeton; Pd.M. '16, New York Univ.; Supt. of Sch., 101 Fourth Ave., Bay Shore, N. Y., since 1918.

Hurst, Albert S., B.A.'99, Univ. of Toronto; M.A.'04, Ph.D.'05, Yale Univ.; Dean, Tchrs. Col., Syracuse Univ., Syracuse, N. Y., since 1920.

Hurst, James, Co. Supt. of Sch., 148 Granby St., Norfolk, Va.

Husted, Milton Franklin, B.S.'07, M.A.'10, M.Ped.'12, New York Univ.; Supt. of Sch., Municipal Bldg., North Bergen, N. J., since 1906.

Hutchins, A. J., A.B.'12, Wake Forest Col.; M.A.'24, Columbia Univ.; Supt. of Sch., Grand Blanc, Mich.

Hutchinson, Harvey O., Pd.D.'20, Syracuse Univ.; Supt. of Sch., Elmira, N. Y., since 1921.

Hutchinson, J. L., B.S.'15, State Tchrs. Col., Pittsburg, Kansas; Prin., Sr. H. S., Pittsburg, Kansas, since 1911.

Hutchinson, N. F., A.B.'11, Ind. Univ.; Supt. of Sch., Salem, Ind., since 1921.

Hutt, W. Leon, B.A.'14, Syracuse Univ.; M.A.'24, Tchrs. Col., Columbia Univ.; Supt. of Sch., 10 Barton Ave., Hoosick Falls, N. Y., since 1925.

Hutto, Mrs. Elizabeth D., Co. Supt. of Educ., Court House, Darlington, S. C., since 1925.

Hutto, H. H., B.S.'27, Southwest Texas State Tchrs. Col., San Marcos, Texas; Supt. of Harlandale Schools, 106 W. Huff Ave., San Antonio, Texas, since 1925.

Hyer, F. S., A.B.'11, Ripon Col.; Pres., State Tchrs. Col., Whitewater, Wis., since 1919.

Hyndman, R. W., A.B.'15, Ind. State Normal Sch., Terre Haute, Ind.; A.M.'21, Tchrs. Col., Columbia Univ.; Supt. of Sch., 26 W. Elm St., Canton, Ill., since 1923.

Hynes, Edward, Asst. Supt. of Sch., 920 Music St., New Orleans, La.

Ignatius, Mother M., A.M.'15, Col. of New Rochelle; Dean, Col. of New Rochelle, New Rochelle, N. Y., since 1918.

Igo, Henry J., B.S.'21, M.S.'29, Colo. Agrl. Col.; Supt. of Sch., Simla, Colo., since 1929.

Iler, Ernest, B.S.'14, M.A.'27, Univ. of Chicago; Supt. of Sch., Downers Grove, Ill., since 1923.

Ingram, I. S., Prin., Fourth Dist. Agrl. and Mech. Sch., Carrollton, Ga.

Ingram, Katherine P., A.B.'21, Randolph-Macon Woman's Col.; Co. Supt. of Sch., Bolivar, Tenn., since 1922.

Inman, J. R., A.B.'05, Hillsdale Col.; A.M. '14, Columbia Univ.; Supt. of Sch., Red Oak, Iowa, since 1914.

Inscoe, L. S., B.A.'15, Wake Forest Col.; M.A.'28, Tchrs. Col., Columbia Univ.; Co. Supt. of Sch., Nashville, N. C., since 1919.

Ireland, E. Ward, B.S.'08, M.A.'12, Tchrs. Col., Columbia Univ.; Supt. of Sch., 817 Wilcoxson Ave., Stratford, Conn., since 1926.

Ireland, Elizabeth, B.A.'20, Univ. of Mont.; M.A.'27, Columbia Univ.; State Supt. of Pub. Instr., Helena, Mont., since 1929.

Ireland, Everett W., B.S.'11, Tufts Col.; Supt. of Sch., Somerville, Mass., since 1928.

Ireland, J. W., A.B.'02, A.M.'03, Centre Col.; A.M.'28, Tchrs. Col., Columbia Univ.; Supt. of Sch., 204 Steele St., Frankfort, Ky., since 1918.

Irish, Arthur, A.B.'09, Bates Col.; A.M.'29, Columbia Univ.; Union Supt. of Sch., Rangeley, Maine, since 1927.

Irvine, Paul, A.B.'15, Willamette Univ.; M.A.'24, Ph.D.'28, New York Univ.; Prof. of Educ. and Dir. of Tchr. Tr., Ala. Polytechnic Inst., Auburn, Ala., since 1928.

Irving, Helen A., Co. Supt. of Sch., Rawlins, Wyo., since 1921.

Irwin, W.W., M.E.'96, State Normal Sch., Slippery Rock, Pa.; Supt. of Sch., H. S. Bldg., Farrell, Pa., since 1926.

Isanogle, Alvey M., A.B.'98, St. Johns Col.; A.M.'24, Johns Hopkins Univ.; Prof. of Educ., Western Md. Col., since 1920 and Dean, Sch. of Educ., Western Md. Col., Westminster, Md., since 1928.

Isle, Walter W., A.B.'15, Univ. of Okla.; A.M.'19, Tchrs. Col., Columbia Univ.; Box 1446, Ponca City, Okla.

Ivy, Horace M., A.B.'03, A.M.'04, Central Col., Mo.; Ph.D.'22, Peabody Col.; Supt. of Sch., City Hall, Meridian, Miss., since 1923.

Jack, William B., A.B.'00, Colby Col.; Supt. of Sch., 29 Eastern Promenade, Portland, Maine, since 1922.

Jackman, Harold E., Diploma '99, State Normal Sch., Farmington, Maine; Union Supt. of Sch., Hanover, Mass., since 1928.

Jackson, F. S., M.E.P.'98, State Tchrs. Col., Mansfield, Pa.; Ph.B.'11, Grove City Col.; Supt. of Sch., Jefferson St. Bldg., Punxsutawney, Pa., since 1908.

Jackson, F. W., A.B.'07, Bates Col.; Supt. of Sch., Madison, N. H., since 1921.

Jackson, Halliday R., A.B.'04, Swarthmore Col.; Supvg. Prin. of Sch., Ventnor City, N. J., since 1915.

Jackson, J. A., A.B.'07, Mt. Union Col.; Supt. of Sch., Clarksburg, W. Va., since 1916.

Jackson, Lambert L., Ph.D.'06, Columbia Univ.; D.Pd.'06, Tchrs. Col., Columbia Univ.; First Asst. Supt. of Sch., City Hall, Newark, N. J., since 1928.

Jackson, Leander, Supt. of Sch., 36 Center, Windsor Locks, Conn.

Jacob, Peyton, 509 Adams St., Macon, Ga.

Jacob, Samuel Sprigg, Jr., B.S.'95, W. Va. Univ.; Dist. Supt. of Sch., 111 Oak Ave., Oak Park, Wheeling, W. Va., since 1912.

Jacob, Walter, Jr., Prin., Harrison Ave. Elem. Sch., Ridgewood, N. J.

Jacobs, Chauncey D., B.Sc.'21, Bethany Col.; Supt. of Sch., Follansbee, W. Va., since 1927.

Jacobson, Conrad, A.B.'22, A.M.'27, Univ. of Nebr.; Supt. of Sch., York, Nebr., since 1925.

Jaggers, R. E., A.B.'25, A.M.'26, Univ. of Ky.; Ph.D.'30, Cornell Univ.; State Supvr. of Rural Elem. Sch., State Dept. of Educ., Frankfort, Ky.

Jahr, Charles A., Ph.B.'07, Univ. of Wis.; Supt. of Sch., Elkhorn, Wis., since 1916.

James, Haddon W., Ph.D.'23, State Univ. of Iowa; Dir., Sch. of Educ., Ala. Col., Montevallo, Ala., since 1923.

James, William Alonzo, B.S.'94, M.A.'95, Univ. of Texas; Prin., Ball High Sch., Galveston, Texas, since 1905.

Jammer, George F., B.S.'19, Bucknell Univ.; M.A.'26, Columbia Univ.; Supt. of Sch., Wellsville, N. Y., since 1926.

Janes, Marvin E., Diploma '00, State Normal Sch., Geneseo, N. Y.; Union Supt. of Sch., H. S. Bldg., South Deerfield, Mass., since 1927.

Jantzen, Daniel F., A.B.'21, Univ. of Ariz.; Supt. of Sch., Peoria, Ariz., since 1926.

Jarman, A. M., B.S. and M.S.'20, Univ. of Va.; Asst. Prof. of Educ., Univ. of Va., since 1928. Address: 1228 Prospect St., Ann Arbor, Mich.

Jarman, Joseph L., LL.D.'06, Hampden-Sidney Col.; Pres., State Tchrs. Col., Farmville, Va., since 1902.

Jean, Sally Lucas, A.M.'24, Bates Col.; Consultant, Health Educ., 200 Fifth Ave., New York, N. Y., since 1924.

Jeffers, Fred A., Diploma '91, M.Pd.'06, State Normal Col., Ypsilanti, Mich.; M. A.'26, Univ. of Mich.; Supt. of Twp. Sch., Painesdale, Mich., since 1891.

Jeffords, H. Morton, A.B.'14, Syracuse Univ.; Supt. of Sch., Wallingford, Conn., since 1925.

Jenkins, Cecil, B.S. in Ed.'27, Northwest Mo. State Tchrs. Col., Maryville, Mo.; Co. Supt. of Sch., Savannah, Mo., since 1927.

Jenkins, David S., A.B.'29, St. Johns Col.; Asst. Co. Supt. of Sch., State Circle, Annapolis, Md., since 1927.

Jenkins, F. F., B.A.'18, Col. of William and Mary; Div. Supt. of Sch., Franklin, Va., since 1923.

Jenkins, Ira A., A.B.'87, A.M.'90, Bates Col.; Supt. of Sch., Foxboro, Mass., since 1912.

Jenkins, Ralph C., A.B.'14, Dartmouth Col.; A.M.'18, Middlebury Col.; Prin., State Normal Sch., Johnson, Vt., since 1928.

Jenner, G. Levant, M.A.'23, Univ. of Mich.; Supt. of Sch., City Hall, Bay City, Mich., since 1922.

Jennings, Harold M., A.B.'13, A.M.'15, Cornell Univ.; Supt. of Sch., Mount Kisco, N. Y., since 1920.

Jensen, A. S., A.B.'19, A.M.'23, Ph.D.'27, Univ. of Wash.; Head, Dept. of Educ., Oregon State Normal Sch., Monmouth, Oregon, since 1927.

Jensen, D. C., Supt., Jordan Dist. Sch., Sandy, Utah.

Jensen, Frank A., A.B.'06, Mich. State Tchrs. Col.; M.A.'24, Columbia Univ.; Ph.D.'30, Univ. of Mich.; Supt. of Sch., Admin. Bldg., Rockford, Ill., since 1923.

Jensen, George Charles, B.S.'11, M.S.'12, Univ. of Calif.; Asst. Supt. of Sch., Sacramento, Calif., since 1919.

Jessup, Andrew S., A.B.'11, Ind. Univ.; M.A. '26, Univ. of Colo.; Supt. of Sch., Cheyenne, Wyo., since 1918.

Jessup, Walter Albert, A.B.'03, Earlham Col.; M.A.'08, Hanover Col.; Ph.D.'11, Columbia Univ.; LL.D.'22, Univ. of Wis.; LL.D.'28, Univ. of Mo.; LL.D.'28, Ind. Univ.; LL.D.'29, Columbia Univ.; Pres., State Univ. of Iowa, Iowa City, Iowa, since 1916.

Jimerson, John A., A.B.'22, Nebr. State Tchrs. Col., Peru, Nebr.; M.A.'28, Univ. of Nebr.; Supt. of Sch., H. S. Bldg., Auburn, Nebr., since 1926.

Job, Leonard B., M.A.'19, Ind. Univ.; Ph.D. '26, Columbia Univ.; Prof. of Educ., Ohio Univ., Athens, Ohio, since 1926.

Jobe, A. W., Co. Supt. of Sch., Clarksville, Tenn.

Johns, Charles L., A.B.'08, Northwestern Univ.; Supt. of Sch., 2880 E. Irvington, Huntington Park, Calif., since 1928.

Johns, Roe L., Prof. of Educ. Admin., Ala. Polytech. Inst., Auburn, Ala.

Johnson, A. P., Supt. of Sch., 995 S. Myrtle Ave., Kankakee, Ill., since 1921.

Johnson, Alfred H., 156 Bryant St., N. W., Washington, D. C.

Johnson, Arthur L., Co. Supt. of Sch., 20 Holly St., Cranford, N. J.

Johnson, C. W., Co. Supt. of Educ., Dothan, Ala., since 1920.

Johnson, C. W., B.S. in Ed.'18, Univ. of Cincinnati; M.A.'29, Ohio State Univ.; Supt. of Sch., Norwood, Ohio, since 1923.

Johnson, Eleanor M., Ph.B.'25, Univ. of Chicago; Asst. Supt. of Sch., 1456 Warren Rd., Lakewood, Ohio, since 1930.

Johnson, Frank Clinton, A.B.'97, Dartmouth Col.; M.A.'06, Columbia Univ.; Supt. of Sch., 10 High St., Ayer, Mass., since 1909.

Johnson, G. L. H., A.B. and M.A.'08, Col. of William and Mary; Supt. of Sch., Municipal Bldg., Danville, Va., since 1925.

Johnson, George Anderson, Prin., Howard H. S., Wilmington, Del.

Johnson, Horace M., 1703 Summit, Columbus, Ohio.

Johnson, Ira S., B.S.'18, S. Dak. State Col.; M.A.'28, Columbia Univ.; Supvg. Prin. of Sch., Milton, Fla.

Johnson, J. H., B.S.'22, M.A.'25, Univ. of Ala.; Co. Supt. of Educ., Ozark, Ala., since 1927.

Johnson, James G., B.A.'97, Milligan Col.; M.A.'06, Ph.D.'09, Univ. of Va.; Supt. of Sch., Charlottesville, Va., since 1909. Address: Cabell Ave., University, Va.

Johnson, L. W., B.S.'24, North Texas State Tchrs. Col., Denton, Texas; M.A.'29, Univ. of Colo.; Supt. of Sch., Stamford, Texas, since 1928.

Johnson, Laurence C., B.S.'10, Ph.D.'16, Univ. of Mich.; Supvg. Prin. of Consol. Sch., Orchard Park, N. Y., since 1927.

Johnson, M. K., A.B.'13, Univ. of Ga.; Co. Supt. of Educ., Union Springs, Ala., since 1927.

Johnson, Paul H., 205 Washington Ave., Muskegon, Mich.

Johnson, Ralph W., B.S.'11, Franklin Col.; M.A.'18, Columbia Univ.; Prin., Sr. H. S., Dubuque, Iowa, since 1926.

Johnson, S. Taylor, A.B.'88, Stanford Univ.;
Supt. of Sch., Oceanside, N. Y., since
1917.
Johnson, Walter C., P. O. Box 1064, Dallas,
Texas.
Johnston, L. X., B.S.'24, State Normal Sch.,
Kent, Ohio; M.A.'30, Tchrs. Col., Colum-
bia Univ.; Asst. Co. Supt. of Sch., Lisbon,
Ohio, since 1929.
Johnston, Ruth M., A.B.'02, Vassar Col.;
Dist. Supt. of Sch., Port Leyden, N. Y.,
since 1912.
Johnston, T. K., A.B.'06, Grove City Col.;
Supt. of Sch., Hamilton Bldg., McKees
Rocks, Pa., since 1911.
Johnston, W. D., A.B.'12, Adrian Col.;
Supt. of Sch., Weirton, W. Va., since
1917.
Jolly, Thomas C., Jr., B.S.'17, Univ. of
S. C.; Supt. of Sch., Union, S. C., since
1924.
Jones, Aaron E., Diploma '11, Univ. of
Utah Normal Sch.; B.S.'22, Univ. of
Utah; A.M.'26, Utah State Agrl. Col.;
Supt., North Sanpete Sch. Dist., Mt.
Pleasant, Utah, since 1926.
Jones, Arthur J., A.B.'93, Grinnell Col.;
Ph.D.'07, Columbia Univ.; Prof. of Sec-
ondary Educ., Sch. of Educ., Univ. of Pa.,
Philadelphia, Pa., since 1915.
Jones, Burr F., A.B.'07, Colby Col.; A.M.
'12, Harvard Univ.; State Supvr. of Elem.
Educ., State House, Boston, Mass., since
1917.
Jones, Burton Robert, B.S.'18, Drake Univ.;
M.A.'28, State Univ. of Iowa; Supt. of
Sch., H. S. Bldg., Spencer, Iowa, since
1928.
Jones, C. Edward, Pd.B.'04, Pd.M.'05, N. Y.
State Col. for Tchrs.; B.S.'07, M.A.'08,
Ph.D.'11, New York Univ.; Supt. of Sch.,
City Hall, Albany, N. Y., since 1912.
Jones, Donovan S., Supvg. Prin. of Sch.,
North Bennington, Vt.
Jones, Evan E., A.B.'16, Hamilton; M.A.'25,
Tchrs. Col., Columbia Univ.; Supt. of
Sch., Mechanicville, N. Y., since 1922.
Jones, Frank O., A.B.'97, Brown; A.M.'07,
Yale Univ.; Dist. Supt. of Sch., 865 Tower
Ave., Hartford, Conn., since 1908.
Jones, G. B., B.S.'14, Ottawa Univ.; Supt.
of Sch., Clarkdale, Ariz., since 1926.
Jones, H. S., B.A.'06, Bucknell Univ.; Supt.
of Sch., Plymouth, Pa., since 1926.
Jones, H. V., A.B.'12, Park Col.; M.A.'26,
Univ. of Colo.; Dist. Supt. of Sch., Suth-
erland, Nebr., since 1924.
Jones, H. W., B.S.'09, Cornell Col.; M.A.
'22, Univ. of Calif.; Supt. of Sch., 800
Magnolia Ave., Piedmont, Calif., since
1921.
Jones, J. Morris, Managing Editor, School
Executives Magazine, 1126 Q St., Lin-
coln, Nebr.
Jones, M. G., A.B.'11, Univ. of Mich.; A.M.
'29, Tchrs. Col., Columbia Univ.; Prin.,
Union H. S., Huntington Beach, Calif.,
since 1919.
Jones, Olive M., B.S.'28, New York Univ.;
Pres., Natl. Educ. Assn., 1923-24; Dir.,
Calvary House, 61 Gramercy Park, N.,
New York, N. Y.
Jones, Perry A., A.B.'10, Bethany Col.;
Prin., Sharon H. S., Sharon, Pa., 1914-
1918 and since 1922.
Jones, Robinson G., A.B.'94, Ohio Northern
Univ.; A.B., M.A.'12, Columbia Univ.;
D.Ped.'21, Ohio Northern Univ.; LL.D.'30,

Western Reserve Univ.; Pres., Dept. of
Superintendence, 1921-22; Supt. of Sch.,
Engineers Natl. Bank Bldg., Cleveland,
Ohio, since 1919.
Jones, T. J., B.L.'96, Univ. of Wis.; Supt
of Sch., 621 71st Ave., West Allis, Wis.,
since 1907.
Jones, Thomas E., A.B.'12, Earlham Col.;
B.D.'15, Hartford Theological Seminary;
M.A.'17, Ph.D.'26, Columbia Univ.; Pres.,
Fisk Univ., Nashville, Tenn., since 1926.
Jones, Walter P., Supt. of Sch., Court
House, Macon, Ga.
Jordan, Dana S., A.B.'09, Bates Col.; Supt.
of Sch., Lisbon, N. H., since 1924.
Jordan, R. H., B.A.'93, M.A.'13, Yale Univ.;
Ph.D.'19, Univ. of Minn.; Prof. of Educ.
and Dir. of Summer Session, Cornell
Univ., 252 Goldwin Smith Hall, Ithaca,
N. Y., since 1921.
Jordan, Roy Vail, Supt. of Sch., 417 E.
Broadway, Centralia, Ill.
Joslyn, H. L., Music Diploma '10, Maryville
Col.; B.S.'13, M.S.'16, N. C. State Col.;
Supt. of Sch., Morehead City, N. C., since
1922.
Joy, Clarence L., A.B.'99, Dartmouth Col.;
Supvg. Prin. of Sch., Proctor, Vt., since
1926.
Judd, Arthur M., Diploma '24, State Tchrs.
Col., Trenton, N. J.; Supvg. Prin. of Twp.
Sch., Parsons Sch., New Brunswick, N.
J., since 1927.
Judd, Charles Hubbard, A.B.'94, Wesleyan
Univ.; Ph.D.'96, Leipzig Univ.; Dir., Sch.
of Educ., Univ. of Chicago, Chicago, Ill.,
since 1909.
Judd, Zebulon, Ph.B.'03, Univ. of N. C.; A.
M.'14, Tchrs. Col., Columbia Univ.; Dean,
Sch. of Educ. and Dir. of Summer Session,
Ala. Polytechnic Inst., Auburn, Ala., since
1914.
Judkins, Mrs. Eva Austin, Bd. of Educ.,
Glens Falls, N. Y.
Judy, Byron R., B.S.'24, Pa. State Col.;
Supvg. Prin. of Twp. Sch., Cochranville,
Pa., since 1927.
Julian, Norvin Nicholas, Diploma '23, South-
ern Ill. State Normal Univ.; Supt. of
Sch., Lockport, Ill., since 1927.

Kadesch, J. Stevens, A.B.'10, Clark Univ.;
Supt. of Sch., Medford, Mass., since 1930.
Kaemmerlen, John T., A.B.'16, A.M.'17, New
York Univ.; Supt. of Sch., 129 William
St., Catskill, N. Y.
Kaiser, Paul L., Diploma '23, State Tchrs.
Col., Oshkosh, Wis.; Ph.B.'27, Ripon Col.;
Co. Supt. of Sch., Juneau, Wis.
Kalp, William Lawrence, A.B.'03, Bucknell
Univ.; A.M.'26, Columbia Univ.; Prin., Jr.
H. S., Long Branch, N. J., since 1923.
Kantner, John N., A.B.'14, Ursinus Col.;
A.M.'28, Univ. of Mich.; Supt. of Sch.,
East Detroit, Mich., since 1930.
Kaser, Louis J., Co. Supt. of Sch., Mt.
Holly, N. J.
Katterjohn, Henry, M.A.'18, Washington
Univ.; Prof. of Educ., Elmhurst Col., 176
Margaret Pl., Elmhurst, Ill., since 1922.
Kaye, Orin W., A.B.'20, Olivet Col.; M.A.
'30, Columbia Univ.; Supt. of Sch., Paw
Paw, Mich., since 1913.
Kays, V. C., Diploma '02, Northern Ill. State
Tchrs. Col.; B.A.'06, Univ. of Ill.; B.S.A.
'07, M.S.A.'08, N. Mex. Col. of Agr. and
Mech. Arts; Pres., Agrl. and Mech. Col.,
Jonesboro, Ark., since 1910.

Kealey, Daniel S., A.B.'14, LL.B.'17, Fordham Univ.; '18, Stevens Marine Eng. Sch.; LL.D., Gonzaga; Supt. of Sch., Hoboken, N. J., since 1922.

Keating, John Francis, A.B.'92, Ohio Wesleyan Univ.; M.A.'06, D.L.'14, Univ. of Denver; Ed. D.'27, Univ. of Colo.; Supt. of Sch., Pueblo, Colo., since 1896.

Keating, Joseph S., A.B.'10, Univ. of Maine; Supt. of Sch., Davis St., Turners Falls, Mass.

Keboch, F. D., M.Pd.'07, State Normal Sch., Millersville, Pa.; A.B.'14, Lebanon Valley Col.; A.M.'25, Univ. of Pittsburgh; Supt. of Sch., 109 Emerson Ave., Aspinwall (Pittsburgh), Pa., since 1917.

Kee, Edwards W., B.A., Univ. of Texas; Supt., Gonzales Ind. Sch. Dist., Gonzales, Texas, since 1924.

Keefauver, L. C., A.B.'15, A.M.'24, Gettysburg Col.; Supvg. Prin. of Sch., Gettysburg, Pa., since 1926.

Keeler, L. W., Ph.B.'00, A.M.'10, Ph.D.'29, Univ. of Mich.; Asst. Prof. of Educ. Psych. and Asst. Dir., Bureau of Educ. Research, Univ. of Mich., Ann Arbor, Mich., since 1929.

Keene, Charles H., A.B.'98, M.D.'02, Harvard; Prof. of Hygiene, Univ. of Buffalo, Buffalo, N. Y., since 1926.

Kefauver, Grayson N., B.A.'21, Univ. of Ariz.; M.A.'25, Stanford Univ.; Ph.D.'28, Univ. of Minn.; Assoc. Prof. of Educ., Tchrs. Col., Columbia Univ., New York, N. Y., since 1929.

Keister, W. H., Supt. of Sch., Harrisonburg, Va., since 1894.

Keith, Allen P., Diploma '94, State Normal Sch., Bridgewater, Mass.; Ed.M.'29, R. I. Col. of Educ.; Supt. of Sch., New Bedford, Mass., since 1908.

Keith, Edna, Diploma '12, Western Ill. State Tchrs. Col., Macomb, Ill.; Elem. Supvr., Pub. Sch., 1211 Cass St., Joliet, Ill., since 1912.

Keith, John A. H., A.B.'99, A.M.'00, Harvard; D.Pd.'19, Miami Univ.; D.Ed.'28, Temple Univ.; LL.D.'29, Grove City Col.; LL.D.'30, Lebanon Valley Col.; State Supt. of Pub. Instr. State Dept. of Pub. Instr., Harrisburg, Pa., since 1927.

Keith, W. P., A.B.'06, Ouachita Col.; Co. Supt. of Sch., Court House, Pine Bluff, Ark., since 1919.

Kelder, J. W., A.B.'04, Hope Col.; A.M.'14, Columbia Univ.; M.Pd.'14, Tchrs. Col., Columbia Univ.; Supt. of Sch., 313 S. Michigan Ave., Big Rapids, Mich., since 1923.

Keller, Fred, A.B.'14, Univ. of Ark.; B.J.'15, Univ. of Mo.; Pd.D.'19, New York Univ.; Supt. of Sch., Jonesboro, Ark., since 1926.

Keller, Harold E., A.B.'20, M.A.'22, St. Vincent Col.; Supt. of Catholic Schools of South Central Pa., 309 S. George St., York, Pa., since 1926.

Keller, J. A., Co. Supt. of Sch., Andalusia, Ala.

Keller, Paul G. W., B.S.'01, Univ. of Chicago; Supt. of Sch., Eau Claire, Wis., since 1924.

Kelley, D. J., B.A.'17, Monmouth Col.; M.A.'29, State Univ. of Iowa; Supt. of Sch., Tipton, Iowa, since 1930.

Kelley, J. Herbert, B.S.'00, Cornell Col., Iowa; A.M.'08, Harvard Univ.; D. Litt. '16, Univ. of Denver; Exec. Secy., Pa. State Educ. Assn., 400 N. Third St., Harrisburg, Pa., since 1921.

Kelley, Roy B., B.S.'19, Syracuse Univ.; Supt. of Sch., H. S. Bldg., Lockport, N. Y., since 1921.

Kellogg, Albert B., B.A.'09, Wheaton Col.; Supt. of Sch., 16 Union Block, Claremont, N. H., since 1921.

Kellum, Howard Albert, Ph.B.'17, Lebanon Univ.; B.S.'18, Antioch Col.; M.A.'27, Univ. of Cincinnati; Supt. of Sch., 634 Jefferson Ave., Reading, Ohio, since 1922.

Kelly, Daniel James, B.S.'04, Pd.D.'19, Syracuse Univ.; Supt. of Sch., Binghamton, N. Y., since 1912.

Kelly, Fred J., Ph.D.'14, Columbia Univ.; Lecturer in Higher Educ., Univ. of Chicago, Chicago, Ill., since 1930.

Kelly, Glenn K., B.A.'16, Franklin Col.; M.A.'28, Univ. of Chicago; Supt. of Sch., Houghton, Mich., since 1925.

Kelly, William A., A.B.'23, A.M.'25, Seton Hall Col.; LL.B.'26, Fordham Univ.; Ph. D.'29, New York Univ.; Chmn., Dept. of Educ., Creighton Univ., Omaha, Nebr., since 1929.

Kelsay, H. Paul, A.B.'12, Earlham Col.; Supt. of Sch., H. S. Bldg., Hartford City, Ind., since 1929.

Kelso, Charles C., B.S.'96, Geneva Col.; D.Ped.'29, Westminster Col., New Wilmington, Pa.; Supt. of Sch., H. S., Swissvale, Pa., since 1914.

Kemmerer, W. W., B.A.'24, Lehigh Univ.; Ph.D.'30, Columbia Univ.; Dir. of Research, Pub. Sch., 617 Great Southern Life Bldg., Houston, Texas, since 1929.

Kemp, Alvin F., B.S.'00, State Normal Sch., Kutztown, Pa.; B.S.'13, Muhlenberg Col.; A.M.'21, Univ. of Pa.; Co. Supt. of Sch., Mertztown, Pa., since 1926.

Kemp, Fletcher, Co. Supt. of Sch., Rosslyn, Va.

Kemp. J. F., A.B.'96, Texas Christian Univ.; A.M.'23, Univ. of Texas; Supt. of Sch., Seymour, Texas, since 1920.

Kemp, W. W., Ph.D.'12, Tchrs. Col., Columbia Univ.; Dean, Sch. of Educ., Univ. of Calif., Berkeley, Calif., since 1923.

Kennedy, W. F., A.B.'12, M.A.'14, Univ. of Pittsburgh; Assoc. Supt. of Sch., Admin. Bldg., Pittsburgh, Pa., since 1928.

Kennedy, William H. J., A.B.'12, Harvard Univ.; A.M.'22, Ph.D.'25, Boston Col.; Prin., Tchrs. Col. of the City of Boston, Huntington and Longwood Aves., Boston, Mass., since 1929.

Kenney, C. Belle, Prin., Oldfields School, Glencoe, Md.

Kent, Ernest B., A.B.'94, Grinnell Col.; A.M.'01, Ph.D.'03, Columbia; Dir. of Manual and Indus. Tr., Bd. of Educ., 2 Harrison Ave., Jersey City, N. J., since 1907.

Kent, Raymond A., A.B.'03, Cornell Col.; A.M.'10, Ph.D.'17, Columbia Univ.; Pres., Univ. of Louisville, Belknap Campus, Louisville, Ky., since 1929.

Kent, Ronald W., A.B.'13, Ind. Univ.; Asst. Dir. Essex Co. Voc. Schools, Hall of Records, Newark, N. J., since 1925.

Kepner, Lee David, A.B.'16, Allegheny Col.; Supt. of Sch., Lisbon, Ohio, since 1927.

Kerl, Jules J., Supt. of Sch., Forest City, Pa.

Kersey, Vierling, State Supt. of Pub. Instr., Sacramento, Calif.

Kerstetter, Newton, A.B.'13, A.M.'17, Susquehanna; Dir., Training Sch., California, Pa., since 1922.

Kessler, Sue A., Co. Supt. of Sch., Rock Rapids, Iowa, since 1924.

Ketler, Frank C., A.B.'11, Grove City Col.; A.M.'29, Columbia Univ. Address: 509 W. 121st St., New York, N. Y.

Key, David Martin, B.A.'98, Central Col.; M.A.'06, Vanderbilt Univ.; Ph.D.'16, Univ. of Chicago; LL.D.'26, Emory Univ.; Pres., Millsaps Col., Jackson, Miss., since 1924.

Keyes, Charles Edwin, M.A.'91, Marietta Col.; Supvr. of Educ. Guidance, Admin. Bldg., Oakland, Calif., since 1929.

Keyes, Charles H., A.B.'08, Amherst Col.; Ed.M.'24, R. I. Col. of Educ.; Supt. of Sch., Barrington, R. I., since 1919.

Keyes, John J., Supt. of Sch., 914 Meridian St., Nashville, Tenn.

Keyworth, Maurice R., M.A.'23, Univ. of Mich.; Supt. of Sch., Bd. of Educ., Hamtramck, Mich., since 1923.

Kibbe, Delia E., A.M.'21, Univ. of Chicago; State Supvr. of Elem. Sch., State Dept. of Pub. Instr., Madison, Wis., since 1924.

Kidder, Gordon E., Ph.B.'10, Hamline Univ.; M.A.'28, Columbia Univ.; Supt. of Sch., 611 N. Kendrick Ave., Glendive, Mont., since 1925.

Kiefer, Richard John, B.Sc.'94, Ohio Northern Univ.; A.B.'02, Heidelberg Col.; A.M. '09, Univ. of Chicago; Supt. of Sch., Niles, Ohio, since 1923.

Kiely, Margaret, Ph.D., Tchrs. Col., Columbia Univ.; Prin., Bridgeport Normal Sch., Bridgeport, Conn., since 1924.

Kilpatrick, James F., B.S.'16, East Texas Normal Col.; Supt. of Sch., Farmersville, Texas, since 1923.

Kimball, Philip H., A.B.'11, Bowdoin Col.; Ed.M.'27, Harvard Univ.; Prin., Washington State Normal Sch., Machias, Maine, since 1927.

Kimball, Reginald Stevens, A.B.'21, A.M. '22, Brown Univ.; Ed.M.'29, Harvard Univ.; Union Supt. of Sch., 43 Gilbert St., North Brookfield, Mass., since 1930.

Kinard, Knox, Supt. of Sch., Oklaunion, Texas, since 1924.

Kincaid, W. A., Montpelier, Vt.

King, LeRoy Albert, Prof. of Educ., Univ. of Pa., Philadelphia, Pa.

King, Starr M., B.Sc.'21, Mass. Agrl. Col.; Supt. of Sch., Newburyport, Mass., since 1928.

Kinnan, Marjorie, Asst. Supt. of Sch., Muskegon, Mich.

Kirby, David, A.M.'28, W. Va. Univ.; Pres., Morris Harvey Col., Barboursville, W. Va., since 1930.

Kirby, Thomas J., A.B.'06, Ind. Univ.; M.A.'10, Ph.D.'13, Tchrs. Col., Columbia Univ.; Prof. of Educ., State Univ. of Iowa, Iowa City, Iowa, since 1920.

Kircher, H. W., Ph.B.'03, M.Ph.'04, Univ. of Wis.; Supt. of Sch., Sheboygan, Wis., since 1924.

Kirk, H. H., A.B.'13, Ohio Wesleyan; A.M. '26, Columbia Univ.; Supt. of Sch., Faribault, Minn., since 1924.

Kirk, John R., B.S. in Ed., State Tchrs. Col.; A.M., George Peabody Col.; L.L.D.'07, Mo. Wesleyan Col.; L.L.D.'07, Park Col.; Pres. Emeritus and Prof. of Psych., State Tchrs. Col., Kirksville, Mo., since 1925. Address: 603 S. High St., Kirksville, Mo.

Kirk, Raymond V., A.B.'24, Ph.B.'28, Duquesne Univ.; Dean, Sch. of Educ., Duquesne Univ., Pittsburgh, Pa., since 1929.

Kirk, W. H., B.A.'87, M.A.'90, Baldwin-Wallace Col.; Supt. of Sch., East Cleveland, Ohio, since 1891.

Kirkland, D. D., A.B.'28, Northwestern State Tchrs. Col., Alva, Okla.; Supt. of Sch., Burbank, Okla., since 1926.

Kirkpatrick, Lee, A.B.'04, Georgetown Col.; A.M.'21, Columbia Univ.; Supt. of Sch., Paris, Ky., since 1918.

Kitowski, J. E., Diploma '18, State Tchrs. Col., Oshkosh, Wis.; B.A.'26, Ripon Col.; Supt. of Sch., Menasha, Wis., since 1926.

Kittle, Logan Blair, Clay Sch., Wheeling, W. Va.

Kittrell, Charles A., M.A.'20, State Univ. of Iowa; Supt. of Sch., Waterloo, Iowa, since 1926.

Kjerstad, Conrad Lund, B.A.'11, Univ. of S. Dak.; M.A.'16, Ph.D.'17, Univ. of Chicago; Pres., State Normal Sch., Dickinson, N. Dak., since 1929.

Klager, Benjamin, B.Pd.'15, Mich. State Normal; A.B.'19, M.A.'26, Univ. of Mich.; Supt. of Sch., Manistee, Mich., since 1921.

Klapper, Paul, B.A.'04, Col. of the City of New York; Ph.D.'09, New York Univ.; Prof. of Educ., Dean, Sch. of Educ., Col. of the City of New York, New York, N. Y., since 1921.

Klaus, Roland A., B.A.'20, Lawrence Col.; M.A.'27, Univ. of Wis.; Supt. of Sch., Child Memorial H. S. Bldg., Edgerton, Wis., since 1929.

Kline, Charles W., A.B.'04, Univ. of Kansas; M.A.'19, Columbia Univ.; LL.D.'24, Coe Col.; Supt. of Sch., Waterloo, Iowa, since 1911.

Klingaman, William K., A.B.'11, Franklin and Marshall Col.; A.M.'18, Tchrs. Col., Columbia Univ.: State Supvr. of H. S., 912 Hamilton Blvd., Hagerstown, Md., since 1925.

Klonower, Henry, B.S.'15, M.A.'20, Univ. of Pa.; Dir., Tchrs. Bureau, State Dept. of Pub. Instr., Harrisburg, Pa., since 1925.

Klontz, Vernon E., B.A.'17, Univ. of Wis.; A.M.'29, Univ. of Chicago; Prin., H. S., Janesville, Wis., since 1926.

Kluckholm, Harvey N., B.A.'21, Des Moines Univ.; M.A.'28, State Univ. of Iowa; Supt. of Sch., Central Bldg., Le Mars, Iowa, since 1928.

Knapp, Thad. Johnson, Ph.B.'98, A.M.'27, Univ. of Mich. Address: 548 Dunlap St., Northville, Mich.

Knight, F. D., Bd. of Educ., Duluth, Minn.

Knight, Melvin Colby, B.A.'13, Bates Col.; Supt. of Sch., 15 Washburn Square, Leicester, Mass., since 1928.

Knoelk, William C., A.B.'07, M.A.'25, Univ. of Wis.; Asst. Supt. of Sch., 1522 E. Kane Pl., Milwaukee, Wis., since 1923.

Knowles, Robert Reily, B.S.'09, M.A.'27, Univ. of Colo.; Supt. of Sch., 514 S. Third Ave., Sterling, Colo., since 1929.

Knox, Francis S., A.B.'08, Amherst Col.; Supt. of Sch., Glastonbury, Conn., since 1917.

Knox, Herman N., A.B.'95, Bates Col. Address: 386 High St., Newburyport, Mass.

Knox, W. F., B.S.'13, Drury Col.; A.M.'21, Univ. of Mo.; Supt. of Sch., Jefferson City, Mo., since 1926.

Knox, W. J., B.S.'24, Southwest Texas State Tchrs. Col., San Marcos, Texas; M.A.'27, Univ. of Texas; Asst. Supt. of Sch., Bd. of Educ. Bldg., San Antonio, Texas, since 1919.

Knudsen, Charles W., Ph.D.'27, Univ. of Ill.; Prof. of Sec. Educ., George Peabody Col. for Tchrs., Nashville, Tenn., since 1927.

Knudsen, Milton H., A.B.'17, Brigham Young Univ.; M.S.'20, Iowa State Col.; Ph.D.'22; Pres., Snow Col., Ephraim, Utah, since 1924.

Koch, J. Wilbur, A.B.'12, Park Col.; M.A. '30, Ohio State Univ.; Prin., Mantua Twp. Sch., 266 Jefferson St., Ravenna, Ohio, since 1930.

Kocher, Walter L., A.B.'20, Muskingum Col.; Supt. of Sch., Martins Ferry, Ohio, since 1927.

Koepke, William Charles, Ph.B.'13, Univ. of Wis.; M.A.'27, Columbia Univ.; Prin., Siefert Sch., Milwaukee, Wis., since 1929.

Kohl, Elwood, Jr. H. S., Upper Darby, Pa.

Kolb, Philip A., Ph.B.'01, Univ. of Wis.; Prin., Okla. Ave. Sch., Milwaukee, Wis., since 1924.

Koonsman, G. L., M.A.'20, Univ. of Denver; Supt. of Sch., Brighton, Colo., since 1930.

Koontz, James A., M.S.D., Northeast Mo. State Tchrs. Col., Kirksville. Mo.; A.B., Leland Stanford Univ.; A.M.'17, Tchrs. Col., Columbia Univ.; Supt. of Sch., 827 Pearl Ave., Joplin, Mo., since 1926.

Koontz, Norman C., B.A.'11, Yale Univ.; M.A.'26, Columbia Univ.; Supt. of Sch., Indiana, Pa., since 1928.

Koos, Frank H., Ph.D.'27, Columbia Univ.; Asst. Supt. of Sch., 832 Piedmont Ave., Winston-Salem, N. C., since 1922.

Koos, Leonard V., A.B.'07, Oberlin Col.; A.M.'15, Ph.D.'16, Univ. of Chicago; Prof. of Sec. Educ., Univ. of Chicago, Chicago, Ill., since 1929.

Kopp, Charles L., A.B.'09, Gettysburg Col.; A.M.'25, Tchrs. Col., Columbia Univ.; Supt. of Sch., 105 S. Centre St., Cumberland, Md., since 1928.

Korb, O. J., B.S.'18, Kent State Col.; M.A. '27, Tchrs. Col., Columbia Univ.; Supt. of Sch., 1676 Green Rd., South Euclid, Ohio, since 1921.

Kramer, Frank H., A.B.'14, Gettysburg Col.; A.M.'16, Ph.D.'20, Univ. of Pa.; Prof. of Educ., Gettysburg Col., Gettysburg, Pa., since 1921.

Kramer, H. N., M.A.'16, Columbia Univ.; Prin. of Sch., Oxford, Ohio, since 1919.

Kramer, Stephen E., B.S.'06, A.M.'09, George Washington Univ.; First Asst. Supt. of Sch., Washington, D. C., since 1924.

Kratzer, John W., B.A.'01, Temple Univ.; M.A.'25, Yale Univ.; Supvg. Prin. of Sch. and Prin. of H. S., Merchantville, N. J., since 1925.

Kraushaar, R. W., B.A. in Ed.'21, Northern State Tchrs. Col., Aberdeen, S. Dak.; State H. S. Supvr., State Dept. of Pub. Instr., Pierre, S. Dak., since 1929.

Kraybill, A. E., B.Pd.'02, State Normal Sch., Millersville, Pa.; A.B.'04, Franklin and Marshall Col.; A.M.'05, Harvard; Supt. of Sch., 1113 Third Ave., Asbury Park, N. J.

Kraybill, D. B., A.B.'11, Franklin and Marshall Col.; A.M.'16, Columbia Univ.; Ph. D.'27, Pa. State Col.; Supt. of Sch., 2125 Chapline St., Wheeling, W. Va., since 1929.

Krebs, Matilda, Supvg. Prin., Southmont Pub. Sch., Johnstown, Pa.

Kretchman, W. H., A.B.'01, A.M.'05, Franklin and Marshall Col.; Co. Supt. of Sch., Somerset, Pa., since 1920.

Kriesel, C. A., Diploma '82, State Normal Sch., River Falls, Wis.; Ph.D.'94, Gale Col.; Prin., Greenbush St. Sch., Milwaukee, Wis., since 1892.

Kruschke, Walter F., Ph.B.'20, Univ. of Wis.; Supt. of Sch., Rhinelander, Wis., since 1928.

Kruse, Paul J., B.A.'06, State Univ. of Iowa; A.M.'12, Univ. of Wash.; Ph.D.'17, Columbia Univ.; Prof. of Educ. Psych., Cornell Univ., since 1917 and Head, Dept. of Rural Educ., Cornell Univ., Ithaca, N. Y., since 1927.

Kruse, Samuel Andrew, A.B. and B.S. in Ed. '09, Univ. of Mo.; A.M.'15, Univ. of Wis.; Ph.D.'28, George Peabody Col. for Tchrs.; Head, Dept. of Educ., State Tchrs. Col., Cape Girardeau, Mo., since 1915.

Kuhn, Ray, A.B.'16, B.Pd.'17, Tri-State Col.; M.A.'27, Columbia Univ.; Supt. of Sch., Lincoln Sch., Plymouth, Ind., since 1930.

Kulp, A. M., Co. Supt. of Sch., Norristown. Pa.

Kulp, Claude L., B.S.'27, Univ. of Rochester; M.A.'30, Cornell Univ.; Supt. of Sch., 117 E. Buffalo St., Ithaca, N. Y., since 1930.

Kuntz, Elmer E., A.B.'97, A.M.'98, Dickinson Col.; Supvg. Prin. of Sch., East Stroudsburg, Pa., since 1922.

Kurtz, A. R., A.M.'22, Franklin and Marshall Col.; A.M.'28. Columbia Univ.; Supvg. Prin., Tchr. Tr. Sch., 2304 Jenny Lind St., McKeesport, Pa., since 1924.

Laborde, Cliffe E., B.S.'09, Spring Hill Col.; Parish Supt. of Educ., Marksville, La., since 1920.

Lachmund, Mrs. Fannie L., Ph.B.'84, M.A. '05, Washington Univ.; Prof., Dept. of Educ., Harris Tchrs. Col., St. Louis, Mo., since 1904.

Lackey, Ira C., A.B.'17, Allegheny Col.; Supvg. Prin. of Sch., Bentleyville, Pa., since 1926.

Lackey, W. W., Supt. of Sch., Midland, Texas, since 1906.

Lafferty, Annie L., Prin., Friendship Sch., Friendship Ave. and Roup St., Pittsburgh, Pa., since 1925.

Laidlaw, Arthur J., Supt. of Sch., Ogdensburg, N. Y.

Laidlaw, O. W., M.A.'24, Univ. of Mich.; Supt. of Sch., Tecumseh H. S., Tecumseh, Mich., since 1924.

Lake, Charles H., B.A.'09, M.A.'10, Ohio State Univ.; First Asst. Supt. of Sch., Cleveland, Ohio, since 1920.

Lake, George H., B.A.'20, M.A.'27, Univ. of Nebr.; Supt., Hoehne Consol. School, Hoehne, Colo., since 1926.

Lakey, Melvin Dallas, B.A.'23, Cornell Col.; Supt. of Sch., Fabens, Texas, since 1926.

Lamb, Earl M., A.B.'23, Huntington Col.; Supt. of Sch., Eighth and Walnut, Dayton, Ky., since 1925.

Lamb, L. H., B.S.'22, Stout Inst.; M.A.'30, Univ. of Mich.; Supt. of Sch., 920 Kennelworth Ave., Flint, Mich., since 1930.

Lambert, Jesse W., Supt. of Sch., Saugus, Mass.

Lamberton, C. D., Ph.B.'25, Ripon Col.; Supt. of Sch., Berlin, Wis., since 1920.

Lamberton, Horace H., A.M.'15, Columbia Univ.; Supt. of Sch., 45 Second St., Malone, N. Y., since 1920.

Lamkin, Nina B., B.L.'93, Univ. of Ill.; A. M.'25, Tchrs. Col., Columbia Univ.; Supvr. of Health Educ., 325 E. 38th St. and Instr., Tchrs. Col., Columbia Univ., New York, N. Y.

Lamkin, Uel W., Pres., Natl. Educ. Assn., 1928-29; Pres., Northwest Mo. State Tchrs. Col., Maryville, Mo., since 1921.

Lancaster, J. W., B.Ped.'06, M.S.'13, Univ. of Ky.; Supt. of Sch., Georgetown, Ky., since 1923.

Land, John N., A.B.'07, Franklin and Marshall Col.; Supvg. Prin. of Sch., 141 S. Third St., Hamburg, Pa., since 1910.

Landers, E. J., Jacksonville, Ala.

Landers, J. S., B.S.C.E.'87, Valparaiso Univ.; A.B.'17, M.A.'18, Univ. of Colo.; Pres., Oregon Normal Sch., Monmouth, Oregon, since 1921.

Landis, Cloyce Ivan, B.S. in Ed.'16, Kent State Col.; M.A.'28, Ohio State Univ.; Supt. of Sch., 801 Dale Ave., Willard, Ohio, since 1929.

Landis, Ira C., Supt. of Sch., Riverside, Calif., since 1928.

Landis, William D., Diploma '98, State Tchrs. Col., Kutztown, Pa.; Ph.B.'17, Muhlenberg Col.; A.M.'20, Albright Col.; Dir., Tr. Sch., State Tchrs. Col., Kutztown, Pa., since 1922.

Landreth, Austin, B.A.'19, Ind. Univ.; M.A. '29, Stanford Univ.; Supt. of Sch., Pendleton, Oregon, since 1929.

Lane, David Alphonso, Jr., A.B.'17, Bowdoin Col.; A.M.'20, Harvard Univ.; Dean, W. Va. State Col., Institute, W. Va., since 1924.

Lang, Andrew J., Supt. of Sch., 962 Nebraska Ave., Huron, S. Dak.

Lang, Edgar F., Supt. of Sch., Princeton, Wis.

Lange, Edward G. A., Supt. of Sch., 113 S. Fifth St., Delavan, Wis., since 1925.

Langvick, Mina M., B.S.'21, M.A.'25, Tchrs. Col., Columbia Univ.; Sr. Specialist in Elem. Sch. Curriculum, U. S. Office of Educ., Washington, D. C., since 1927.

Langwith, J. E., A.B.'13, Southwestern Univ.; M. A. '29, Southern Methodist Univ.; Supt. of Sch., 902 N. Rockwell Ave., Terrell, Texas, since 1923.

Langworthy, Harry W., Ph.B.'07, Alfred Univ.; M.A.'25, Columbia Univ.; Supt. of Sch., Gloversville, N. Y., since 1925.

Lantman, Edgar G., Diploma '81, State Normal Sch., Cortland, N. Y.; M.Ped.'28, State Col. for Tchrs., Albany, N. Y.; Secy., State Tchrs. Retirement Board, Standard Bldg., 112 State St., Albany, N. Y., since 1913.

Lantz, P. G., A.B.'10, Ind. Univ.; A.M.'13, Univ. of Wis.; Supt. of Tr. Sch., Central State Tchrs. Col., Mt. Pleasant, Mich., since 1923.

Laramy, Robert Edward, B.A.'96, M.A.'99, Lehigh; Supt. of Sch., H. S. Bldg., Altoona, Pa., since 1922.

LaRowe, Eugene, A.B.'96, A.M.'98, Univ. of Mich.; Supt. of Elem. Sch., Maywood, Ill., since 1913.

LaSalle, Jessie, B.S.'18, A.M.'20, Tchrs. Col., Columbia Univ.; Asst. Supt. of Sch., Thomson School Bldg., 12th and L Sts., N. W., Washington, D. C., since 1923.

Lash, Frederick M., B.Pd.'11, Pa. State Tchrs. Col.; A.B.'23, A.M.'26, Univ. of Wash.; Supt. of Sch., 835 Fifth St., Camas, Wash., since 1924.

Lasher, Norman J., A.B.'20, Marion Col.; M.A., Univ. of Wis.; Supt. of Sch., Seymour, Ind., since 1925.

Latham, O. R., A.B.'11, M.A.'19, Ph.D.'28, State Univ. of Iowa; Pres., Iowa State Tchrs. Col., Cedar Falls, Iowa, since 1928.

Latham, Rowland H., B.A. and M.A.'03, Univ. of Va.; Supt. of Sch., West End Sch. Bldg., Winston-Salem, N. C., since 1910.

Latkin, Lena, Asst. Co. Supt. of Sch., Court House, Little Rock, Ark., since 1924.

Lau, John A., LL.B.'06, Univ. of Wis.; Ph. B.'18, Univ. of Chicago. Address: 623 S. Wabash Ave., Chicago, Ill.

Laudenslager, E. B., A.B.'22, Swarthmore Col.; Supt., Hatfield Joint Schools, Dublin, Pa., since 1922.

Laughlin, Butler, Diploma '10, Ind. State Normal Sch., Terre Haute, Ind.; A.B.'14, A.M.'16, Ind. Univ.; Pres., Chicago Normal Col., 6800 Stewart Ave., Chicago, Ill., since 1928.

Lausen, Manette M., Whitehouse Station, N. J.

Law, Bertha V., 1427 Mervin Ave., Pittsburgh, Pa.

Lawes, Estella, A.B.'10, Western Reserve Univ.; Dir., Dept. for Sight Saving, Pub. Schools, Heberle Bldg., Cincinnati, Ohio, since 1915.

Lawing, J. Leslie, A.B.'20, Univ. of Mo.; M.A.'26, Ph.D.'30, Tchrs. Col., Columbia Univ.; Supt. of Sch., 210 W. Seventh, Maryville, Mo., since 1929.

Lawrance, Charles William, S.B.'16, Mass. Inst. of Tech.; Union Supt. of Sch., 11 Evergreen St., Kingston, Mass., since 1930.

Lawrence, B., A.B.'21, Howard Col.; Co. Supt. of Sch., Clanton, Ala., since 1925.

Lawrence, Carl Gustavus, B.L.'94, Univ. of Wis.; M.A.'19, Univ. of S. Dak.; Pres., Southern State Tchrs. Col., Springfield, S. Dak., since 1919.

Laws, Minnie, Co. Supt. of Sch., Estancia, N. Mex.

Lawson, J. M., B.S.'27, Univ. of Ala.; Co. Supt. of Sch., Athens, Ala., since 1930.

Lawson, W. F., Jr., B.A.'26, Col. of William and Mary; Prin., Pub. Sch., Eastville, Va., since 1927.

Lawson, Miss Willie, B.S.'27, M.A.'28, George Peabody Col. for Tchrs.; Co. Supt. of Sch., Court House, Blytheville, Ark., since 1927.

Leamer, Emery W., A.B.'09, Univ. of Nebr.; A.M.'19, Univ. of Chicago; Dir. of Tr., State Tchrs. Col., La Crosse, Wis., since 1925.

Lease, R. A., B.S.'24, M.A.'26, Univ. of Minn.; Supt., Grade and H. S., Sycamore, Ill., since 1928.

Leavenworth, Mrs. Sarah T., B.A.'94, Smith Col.; Supt. of Sch., Castleton-Fair Haven Dist., Fair Haven, Vt., since 1927.

Leavitt, Frank M., Assoc. Supt. of Sch., Sch. Admin. Bldg., Bellefield at Forbes St., Pittsburgh, Pa., since 1917.

Leavitt, Russell Hall, B.S.'16, Dartmouth Col.; H. S. Agent, State Bd. of Educ., Patriot Bldg., Concord, N. H., since 1927.

Lederle, E. J., A.B.'12, Univ. of Mich.; Co. Commr. of Sch., Pontiac, Mich., since 1923.

Lee, Charles A., B.S. in Ed.'17, Univ. of Mo.; State Supt. of Sch., Jefferson City, Mo., since 1922.

Lee, Edgar D., A.B. and B.S. in Ed.'08, A.M. in Ed.'09, Univ. of Mo.; Pres., Christian Col., Columbia, Mo., since 1920.

Lee, J. R. E., A.B.'89, M.A.'03, Bishop Col.; LL.D.'17, Wilberforce Univ.; Pres., Fla. Agrl. and Mech. Col., Tallahassee, Fla., since 1923.

Lee, James Allen, Co. Supt. of Educ., Selma, Ala.

Lee, Robert B., B.A.'21, M.A.'27, State Univ. of Iowa; Supt. of Sch., Rawlins, Wyo., since 1927.

Lee, Will L., Co. Commr. of Sch., Mt. Clemens, Mich.

Leech, Carl G., Co. Supt. of Sch., 317 Trites Ave., Norwood, Pa.

Lefler, Mark R., A.M.'23, Columbia Univ.; Supt. of Sch., Westport, Conn., since 1926.

Lefler, Millard C., B.A.'11, State Tchrs. Col., Peru, Nebr.; M.A.'16, Nebr.; Supt. of Sch., 15th and M Sts., Lincoln, Nebr., since 1920.

Lehman, C. W., A.B.'17, Univ. of Nebr.; M.A.'27, Tchrs. Col., Columbia Univ.; Supt. of Sch., Friend, Nebr., since 1924.

Lehman, Clarence O., B.A.'16, Bluffton Col.; M.A.'25, Ph.D.'29, Ohio State Univ.; Dir. of Tr. and Head, Dept. of Educ., State Normal Sch., Geneseo, N. Y., since 1929.

Lehman, Eugene Heitler, B.A.'02, M.A.'10, Yale Univ.; Pres., Highland Manor Jr. Col., Tarrytown, N. Y.

Lehman, Ezra, Ph.B.'99, Bucknell Univ.; Ph.D.'03, Univ. of Pa.; LL.D.'25, Bucknell Univ.; Pres., State Tchrs. Col., Shippensburg, Pa., since 1913.

Lehn, Homer M. B., A.B.'08, Lebanon Valley Col.; A.M.'22, Grove City Col.; Supt. of Sch., Grove City, Pa., since 1913.

Leighton, Frederick, B.S.'13, Tchrs. Col., Columbia Univ.; Supt. of Sch., City Hall, Oswego, N. Y., since 1910.

Leinbaugh, Howard M., Supt. of Sch., Lewistown, Ill.

Leister, Leroy L., Ph.B.'17, Muhlenberg Col.; Ed.M.'24, Grad. Sch. of Educ., Harvard Univ.; Union Supt. of Sch., New London, Conn., since 1925.

Leiter, Nora C., Diploma '02, State Normal Sch., Geneseo, N. Y.; Helping Tchr., 173 Euclid Ave., Hackensack, N. J., since 1920.

Le Marr, S. E., B.E.'18, Normal Univ.; Supt. of Sch., 509 W. Jackson, Abingdon, Ill., since 1918.

Lemme, Carl W., M.A.'29, Columbia Univ.; Supvg. Prin. of Chestnut, Walnut and Bosse Elem. Sch., Evansville, Ind., since 1927.

Lemmel, W. H., Supt. of Sch., Flat River, Mo.

Leonard, H. C., A.B.'14, Mt. Union Col.; Co. Supt. of Sch., Firestone Bank Bldg., Lisbon, Ohio, since 1923.

Lesh, William S., A.B.'96, A.M.'97, Dickinson Col.; Supt. of Sch., 20 Stephens St., South River, N. J., since 1919.

Lessenberry, David D., 3979 Brandon Rd., Pittsburgh, Pa.

Lester, L. Marvin, A.B.'08, A.M.'12, Emory Univ.; A.M.'20, Columbia Univ.; Supt. of Sch., Griffin, Ga., since 1924.

Lettinger, Leonard Austin, Supvg. Prin. of Twp. Sch., 108 Cedar Ave., Willow Grove, Pa.

Letts, George Leman, B.S.'10, Tri-State Col.; Ph.B.'17, Univ. of Chicago; Prin., York Community H. S., Elmhurst, Ill.

Le Van, Herbert M., Ph.B.'11, Franklin and Marshall Col.; Supvg. Prin. of Sch., North Wales, Pa., since 1924.

Lewis, Charles W., A.B.'02, A.M.'05, Hamilton Col.; Supt. of Sch., Frankfort, N. Y., since 1929.

Lewis, E. E., A.B.'07, A.M.'09, Stanford; Ph.D.'20, Columbia Univ.; Chmn., Dept. of Sch. Admin., Ohio State Univ., Columbus, Ohio, since 1926.

Lewis, Mrs. Inez Johnson, 217 E. Del Norte St., Colorado Springs, Colo.

Lewis, R. F., B.A.'15, M.A.'28, Univ. of Wis.; Supt. of Sch., Marshfield, Wis., since 1928.

Lewis, R. I., Supt. of Sch., 16 Wentz Ave., Shelby, Ohio.

Lewis, W. A., Pres., State Tchrs. Col., Hays, Kansas.

Libbey, Fred S., A.B.'91, Bates Col.; Supt. of Sch., Franklin, N. H., since 1922.

Libby, Herschel S., Supt. of Sch., Southington, Conn.

Libby, Richard J., Agent for Rural Educ., State Dept. of Educ., Augusta, Maine.

Licking, R. H., B.A.'23, M.A.'25, Univ. of Wis.; Supvg. Prin. of Sch., 615 First St., Kewaunee, Wis., since 1928.

Lienbard, John, Dist. Supt. of Sch., S. Beloit Community H. S., Beloit, Wis.

Liggitt, Earle O., B.S.'17, Muskingum Col.; A.M.'27, Univ. of Pittsburgh; Supvg. Prin. of Sch., 87 Union Ave., Crafton, Pa., since 1930.

Light, N. Searle, B.A.'08, Yale; Sr. Supvr. of Rural Educ., State Bd. of Educ., Hartford, Conn., since 1915.

Light, U. L., B.S.'00, Ohio Northern; Ph.B. '12, Univ. of Chicago; Supt. of Sch., 521 N. Fifth St., Barberton, Ohio, since 1913.

Lindeman, Clarence W., R. F. D. No. 4, Waynesboro, Pa.

Lindquist, Everet Franklin, Ph.D.'27, State Univ. of Iowa; Asst. Prof. of Educ., Col. of Educ., State Univ. of Iowa, Iowa City, Iowa, since 1928.

Lindquist, Rudolph D., A.B.'15, M.A.'22, Univ. of Calif.; Asst. Supt. of Sch., Oakland, Calif., since 1925.

Lindsay, E. E., Sch. of Educ., Univ. of Pittsburgh, Pittsburgh, Pa.

Lindsay, Frank B., A.B.'21, Ind. Univ. Address: San Bernardino Valley Union Jr. Col., San Bernardino, Calif.

Lindsey, Frank G., B.S. in Ed.'20, New York Univ.; Supvg. Prin. of Dist. Sch., Montrose, N. Y., since 1907.

Lindsey, John Clark, B.A.'19, Univ. of S. Dak.; M.A.'23, Tchrs. Col., Columbia Univ.; Supt. of Sch., Mitchell, S. Dak., since 1918.

Lindsey, Loa S., Supt. of Sch., St. Clair Shores, Mich.

Lindsey, R. V., B.E.'10, Ill. State Normal Univ.; Ph.M.'26, Univ. of Wis.; Prin., Pekin Community H. S., Pekin, Ill., since 1923.

Lindstol, Carl F., B.S.'15, Tufts Col.; Ed.M. '25, Harvard Univ.; Supt. of Sch., H. S. Bldg., Revere, Mass., since 1928.

Ling, Edward S., B.S.'93, Valparaiso Univ.; Supt., Abington Twp. Sch., Abington, Pa., since 1913.

Linn, Sheridan, A.B.'11, Lafayette Col.; A.M.'16, Columbia Univ.; Supt. of Sch., 225 S. Ocean Ave., Patchogue, N. Y., since 1919.

Linscheid, A., B.S.'12, Fremont Col.; M.A. '20, Univ. of Okla.; Ph.D.'28, Columbia Univ.; Pres., E. Central State Tchrs. Col., Ada, Okla., since 1920.

Linton, Clarence, A.B.'19, State Tchrs. Col., Wayne, Nebr.; A.M.'21, Univ. of Nebr.; Ph.D.'27, Columbia Univ.; Secy., Tchrs. Col., Columbia Univ., 106 Morningside Drive, New York, N. Y., since 1925.

Lippitt, Walter O., B.S.'03, Carleton Col.; M.A.'11, Univ. of Minn.; Supt. of Sch., Westwood, N. J., since 1929.

Liston, V. M., Supt. of Sch., Library Bldg., Fort Scott, Kansas.

Littel, C. L., A.B.'12, Univ. of Nebr.; A.M. '26, Stanford Univ.; Supt. of Sch., Centralia, Wash., since 1923.

Little, Harry A., A.B.'19, Hendrix Col.; M.A.'28, Peabody; Asst. Dir., Div. of Research and Surveys, State Dept. of Educ., Little Rock, Ark., since 1929.

Littlejohn, Elbridge G., L.I.'82, Peabody Normal Col.; M.A.'99, Texas Christian Univ.; Supt. of Sch., Municipal Bldg., Galveston, Texas, since 1924.

Litzner, Herman A., A.B.'26, Mich. State Normal Col., Ypsilanti, Mich.; Supt. of Sch., Van Dyke, Mich., since 1929.

Llewelyn Edgar Julius, A.B.'07, Earlham Col.; A.M.'10, Ind. Univ.; '10, '13, Tchrs. Col., Columbia Univ.; Supt. of Sch., Newcastle, Ind., since 1917.

Lloyd, Frank Howard, Supt. of Twp. Sch., H. S. Bldg., Leonardo, N. J., since 1923.

Lobban, James A., A.B.'98, Middlebury; A.M.'99, Harvard; Supt. of Sch., Webster, Mass., since 1929.

Lobingier, Mrs. Ella H., A.B.'15, Univ. of Pittsburgh; Asst. Dir. of Pittsburgh Teaching Center, Pa. State Col., 424 Duquesne Way, Pittsburgh, Pa., since 1921.

Lock, Mrs. Ethel, A.B.'11, A.M.'29, Univ. of Kansas; Prin., Community H. S., Columbus, Kansas, since 1923.

Locke, David C., B.E.'94, M.E.'96, Slippery Rock State Normal Sch., Slippery Rock, Pa.; B.S.'00, Volant Col.; A.B.'13, Grove City Col.; Co. Supt. of Sch., Court House, Beaver, Pa., since 1908.

Lockhart, Albert V., A.B.'15, Mo. Wesleyan Col.; A.M.'17, Northwestern Univ.; Prin., Thornton Fractional Twp. H. S., Calumet City, Ill.

Lockhart, John C., A.B.'12, Univ. of N. C.; Co. Supt. of Sch., Court House, Raleigh, N. C., since 1918.

Lockwood, Charles M., A.B.'16, Furman Univ.; Supt., Olympia Pub. Sch., Columbia, S. C., since 1923.

Lockwood, Luther A., A.B.'17, Ind. State Tchrs. Col.; Supt. of Sch., Rushville, Ind., since 1930.

Loftus, John J., M.A.'23, Ph.D.'27, New York Univ.; LL.D.'28, St. Francis Col.; Prin., P. S. 80, 2830 W. 17th St., Brooklyn, N. Y., since 1915.

Logan, Anna E., M.A.'06, Miami Univ. Address: 112 N. Campus, Oxford, Ohio.

Logan, John Hubbard, A.B.'00, Mercer Univ.; A.M.'04, Union Theological Seminary; A.M.'04, Columbia Univ.; Supt. of Sch., Newark, N. J., since 1927.

Lohrie, Robert F., Supt. of Sch., Chippewa Falls, Wis., since 1922.

Lomax, Paul S., B.S. in Ed. '17, Univ. of Mo.; Ph.D.'27, New York Univ.; Prof. of Educ. and Head, Dept. of Business Educ., Sch. of Educ., New York Univ., New York, N. Y., since 1924.

Long, Edwin B., A.B.'19, Dickinson Col.; A.M.'25, Tchrs. Col., Columbia Univ.; Supvg. Prin. of Sch., 769 E. Union St., Millersburg, Pa., since 1923.

Long, Glenn S., B.S. in Ed.'23, M.A.'24, Ohio State Univ.; Asst. Supt. of Sch., 833 Rice Ave., Lima, Ohio, since 1924.

Long, J. K., B.S.'27, Tchrs. Col., Columbia Univ.; Supt. of Sch., Ayden, N. C., since 1928.

Long, P. J., Co. Supt. of Sch., Jackson, N. C., since 1897.

Longanecker, F. M., B.A.'99, Hiram Col.; M.A.'04, Univ. of Mich.; Supt. of Sch., Racine, Wis., since 1918.

Longbotham, Gilmore Thomas, Co. Supt. of Sch., Court House, Janesville, Wis., since 1923.

Longfellow, J. T., B.S.'15, State Col. of Wash.; Supt. of Sch., La Grande, Oregon, since 1925.

Longman, Marion W., Diploma '98, Mich. State Normal Col., Ypsilanti, Mich.; A.B. '10, Albion Col.; A.M.'11, Univ. of Mich.; Supt. of Sch., 98 Grand St., Newburgh, N. Y., since 1930.

Longsdorf, A. J. B., Ph.B.'12, Wooster Col.; A.M.'21, Columbia Univ.; Supt. of Sch., 232 S. Lawn Ave., Bluffton, Ohio, since 1925.

Longstreet, R. J., M.A.'16, LL.B.'17, Stetson Univ.; Supvg. Prin. of Sch., Peninsula Sta., Daytona Beach, Fla., since 1920.

Loomis, Arthur K., A. B. '09, Baker Univ.; A.M.'17, Univ. of Kansas; Ph.D.'26, Tchrs. Col., Columbia Univ.; Dir. of Curriculum Dept., Pub. Sch., 511 S. Williams, Denver, Colo., since 1925.

Loomis, G. F., A.B.'96, A.M.'01, Beloit Col.; Supt. of Sch., 6207 Seventh Ave., Kenosha, Wis., since 1921.

Loper, John D., M.A.'15, Univ. of Ariz.; Supt. of Sch., 331 N. First Ave., Phoenix, Ariz., since 1909.

Lopez, Estanislao R., A.B.'17, Univ. of the Philippines; A.B.'20, Univ. of Calif.; Ed.M.'22, Harvard Univ.; Div. Supt. of Sch., Romblon, Romblon, P. I., since 1930.

Lopez, Manuel, Prin. Cert. '23, Univ. of Porto Rico; Supvr. of Sch., Cabo Rojo, P.R., since 1924.

Lord, Arthur B., State Supvr. in Educ., State Dept. of Educ., Boston, Mass., since 1923.

Lord, Carl B., B.S.'15, Colby Col.; Supt. of Sch., North Vassalboro, Maine, since 1924.

Lord, Charles E., A.B.'11, Bates Col.; Supt. of Sch., Camden, Maine, since 1923.

Lord, Livingston C., LL.D.'04, Univ. of Ill.; A.M.'12, Harvard Univ.; Pres., Eastern Ill. State Tchrs. Col., Charleston, Ill., since 1898.

Lorton, Raymond L., A.B.'16, Oberlin Col.; Supt. of Sch., H. S., Archbold, Ohio, since 1921.

Loucks, S. Walter, Normal Diploma '00; Supvr. of Greenwich Twp. Sch., 214 Thomson Ave., Paulsboro, N. J., since 1912.

Love, John H., Ph.D.'01, Ill. Wesleyan; Supvg. Prin. of Sch., 95 Green St., Woodbridge, N. J., since 1895.

Love, William, Supvg. Prin. of Sch., Borough of Middlesex, N. J.; Box 601, Bound Brook, N. J., since 1910.

Lovejoy, Philip C., A.B.'16, M.A.'25, Univ. of Mich.; First Asst. Secy., Rotary International, 211 W. Wacker, Chicago, Ill., since 1930.

Lovett, A. J., A.B.'79, Northwestern; A.M. '80, McKendree Col.; Supt. of Sch., 209 Hayes-Ken. Bldg., Blackwell, Okla., since 1908.

Lowden, Joseph J., 317 W. Sixth Ave., Columbus, Ohio.

Lowe, Harold T., Supt. of Sch., North Providence, R. I., since 1926.

Lowe, Myron J., Co. Supt. of Sch., 190 S. Main, Fond du Lac, Wis.

Lowery, M. L., A.B.'08, Denison Univ.; A.M.'14, Columbia Univ.; Ph.D.'24, Univ. of Pa.; Co. Supt. of Sch., Co. Office Bldg., New Brunswick, N. J., since 1925.

Lowery, W. R., A.B.'09, Muskingum Col.; Supt. of Sch., 611 S. Fifth St., Hoopeston, Ill., since 1916.

Lowrey, Harvey H., M.A.'20, Univ. of Mich.; Supt. of Fordson Sch., Dearborn, Mich.

Lowry, Charles Doak, B.S.'08, A.M.'13, Northwestern Univ.; Dist. Supt. of Sch., Chicago, Ill., since 1928. Address: 628 Foster St., Evanston, Ill.

Lowry, H. D., B.A.'23, M.A.'28, W. Va. Univ.; Supt. of Sch., Philippi, W. Va., since 1924.

Lowry, William J., A.B.'16, Univ. of Okla.; A.M.'28, Univ. of Mont.; Supt. of Sch., Whitehall, Mont., since 1920.

Lucas, Homer C., A.B.'20, Ohio Wesleyan Univ. Address: 340 Fallis Rd., Columbus, Ohio.

Luckey, G. W. A., B.S.'83, N.I.N.S., Valparaiso, Ind.; A.B.'94, Stanford Univ.; M. A.'95, Clark Univ.; Ph.D.'00, Columbia Univ. Address: 1401 Fairmont St., N. W., Washington, D. C.

Luckie, W. V., B.S. in Ed. '22, Univ. of Ala.; A.M.'27, Tchrs. Col., Columbia Univ.; Co. Supt. of Sch., Gadsden, Ala., since 1927.

Ludlow, Alwilda M., 100 Grove St., Haddonfield, N. J.

Lull, Herbert Warren, A.B.'74, Harvard Univ.; Ed. D.'27, R. I. Col. of Educ.; Supt. of Sch., City Hall, Newport, R. I., since 1900.

Lumbard, John W., B.A.'96, Amherst Col.; Supt. of Sch., 8 Lenox Ave., White Plains, N. Y., since 1912.

Lunak, Charles J., Asst. Supt. of Sch., 460 S. State St., Chicago, Ill.

Lund, John, A.B.'13, Clark Univ.; M.A. 14, Columbia Univ.; Supt. of Sch., Norwalk, Conn., since 1925.

Lundgren, Leonard, B.S.C.E.'04, Armour Inst. of Tech.; M.S.'08, State Univ. of Iowa; Ph.D.'23, Columbia Univ.; Dir. of Adult and Voc. Educ., 150 Page St., San Francisco, Calif., since 1923.

Lunn, J. E., A.B.'08, Univ. of Minn.; Supt. of Sch., Nashwauk, Minn., since 1923.

Lutes, O. S., Ph.D.'26, State Univ. of Iowa; Head, Dept. of Educ., Univ. of Maine, Orono, Maine, since 1926.

Luzader, E. A., A.B.'15, Salem Col.; Supt. of Sch., Richwood, W. Va., since 1926.

Lyman, Warren B., Ph.B.'06, Yale; Supt. of Sch., Stoughton, Mass., since 1930.

Lynch, Wilbur H., A.B.'99, Harvard; Supt. of Sch., Amsterdam, N. Y., since 1922.

Lyon, Clyde L., A.B.'05, Eureka Col.; Pres., Eureka Col., Eureka, Ill., since 1930.

Lyon, Gilbert R., B.A.'17, Hamilton Col.; M.A.'28, Tchrs. Col., Columbia Univ.; Supvg. Prin. of Sch., Smithtown Branch, L. I., N. Y., since 1928.

Lyon, Hubert Calloway, B.S.'24, Potomac Univ.; B.A.'29, Simmons Univ.; Supt. of Sch., Ballinger, Texas, since 1925.

Lyons, S. Warren, A.M.'28, Grove City Col.; Supt. of Sch., H. S. Bldg., New Brighton, Pa., since 1917.

McAlister, Royce D., A.B.'17, Univ. of Maine; A.M.'27, Columbia Univ.; Supt. of Sch., Suffield, Conn., since 1927.

McAllister, Cloyd North, B.A.'92, Ph.D.'00, Yale; Dean, Normal Sch., Berea Col., Berea, Ky., since 1913.

McAllister, Elmer A., Diploma '09, State Normal Sch., Cortland, N. Y.; Supvg. Prin. of Sch., 124 W. Hamilton Ave., Sherrill, N. Y., since 1920.

McAndrew, William, A.B.'86, Univ. of Mich.; M.Pd.'12, Mich. State Normal Col.; Pres., Dept. of Superintendence, 1924-25; Editor, Educational Review: School and Society, since 1923. Address: Silvermine Falls Rd., Norwalk, Conn.

McBee, Mary Vardrine, B. A.'06, Smith Col.; M.A.'08, Columbia Univ.; Prin., Ashley Hall, Charleston, S. C., since 1909.

McBride, Guy T., Diploma '07, Southwest Texas State Tchrs. Col., San Marcos, Texas; Supt. of Sch., Boling, Texas, since 1929.

McBride, John H., Jr., B.A.'11, Col. of the City of New York; Div. Supt. of Sch., Sorsogon, Sorsogon, P. I., since 1926.

McCall, H. N., B.S. in Ed.'22, Central Mo. State Tchrs. Col., Warrensburg, Mo.; Supt. of Sch., Greenfield, Mo., since 1928.

McCallum, Arthur N., B.A.'87, Davidson Col.; Supt. of Sch., 101 E. Ninth St., Austin, Texas, since 1903.

McCance, Meredith L., Supt. of Sch., Seneca, Ill.

McCants, E. C., B.S.'86, The Citadel, Charleston, S. C.; Litt.D.'27, Univ. of S. C.; Supt. of Sch., Anderson, S. C., since 1907.

McCarthy, John C., B.A.'08, Yale Col.; Asst. Supt. of Sch., 169 Church St., New Haven, Conn., since 1913.

McCartney, Livingstone, Supt. of Sch., Hannibal, Mo., since 1909.

McCauley, G. Kent, A.B.'21, Univ. of Denver; Supt. of Sch., Las Animas, Colo., since 1929.

McCleary, Thomas Galbraith, A.B.'03, Univ. of Chicago; D.Ped.'30, Westminster Col., New Wilmington, Pa.; Supt. of Sch., 438 Second St., Braddock, Pa., since 1920.

McClelland, Clark R., A.B.'15, Grove City Col.; A.M.'24, Univ. of Pittsburgh. Address: New York Univ., New York, N. Y.

McClelland, Donald W., A.B.'11, A.M. '25, Univ. of Vt.; Supt. of Sch., 109 Elm St., Bennington, Vt., since 1919.

McClintock, R. D., A.B.'08, Geneva Col.; M.A.'28, Colo. State Tchrs. Col.; Supt. of Sch., Julesburg, Colo., since 1923.

McClinton, J. W., A.B.'03, Northwestern Univ.; M.A.'18, Columbia Univ.; Exec. Secy., Natl. Sch. Supply Assn., 176 W. Adams St., Chicago, Ill., since 1929.

McCloskey, James L., Supt. of Sch., 982 Moosic St., Jessup, Pa.

McClun, Blanche I., 415 S. Lincoln, Chanute, Kansas.

McClure, Clarence H., B.S. in Ed.'09, A.M. '13, Univ. of Mo.; Ph.D.'26, George Peabody Col. for Tchrs.; Head, Div. of Social Sciences and Prof. of Political Science, Northeast Mo. State Tchrs. Col., Kirksville, Mo.

McClure, Worth, A.B.'08, Simpson Col.; A.M.'20, Univ. of Wash.; Supt. of Sch., Seattle, Wash., since 1930.

McCombs, Newell D., A.B.'20, Simpson Col.; M.A.'27, State Univ. of Iowa; Supt. of Sch., Cherokee, Iowa, since 1926.

McConnell, James M., A.B.'10, Carleton Col.; State Commr. of Educ., State Capitol, St. Paul, Minn., since 1919.

McConnell, John Preston, B.A.'90, M.A.'96, Milligan Col.; Ph.D.'04, Univ. of Va.; Pres., State Tchrs. Col., East Radford, Va., since 1911.

McConnell, W. W., B.S.'17, State Tchrs. Col., Emporia, Kansas; M.S.'28, Univ. of Kansas; Supt. of Sch., Winfield, Kansas, since 1925.

McCorkle, Charles E., Ph.B.'09, Ped.D.'18, Ohio Univ.; A.M.'14, Clark Univ.; A.M. '17, Harvard Univ.; Supt. of Sch., 46 Jackson Ave., Morgantown, W. Va.

McCormack, Thomas J., A.B.'84, A. M.'87, M.S., Princeton Univ.; LL.D.'30, Northwestern Univ.; Supt., Twp. H. S., since 1903 and Dir., LaSalle-Peru-Oglesby Jr. Col., Fifth and Chartres Sts., La Salle, Ill., since 1924.

McCormick, B. E., A.B.'04, Univ. of Wis.; Secy., Wis. Tchrs. Assn., 716 Beaver Bldg., Madison, Wis., since 1928.

McCormick, F. S., A.B.'19, Tri-State Col.; A.M.'24, Tchrs. Col., Columbia Univ.; Prin., Brownell Jr. H. S., Cleveland, Ohio, since 1929.

McCormick, J. Scott, Bureau of Educ., Manila, P. I.

McCoy, Dwight Wesley, A.B.'12, Univ. of Ill.; A.M.'23, Tchrs. Col., Columbia Univ.; Prin., H. S., Springfield, Ill., since 1923.

McCoy, M. L., Supt. of Sch., Lennox, S. Dak.

McCoy, O. R., A.B.'09, A.M.'11, Brown Univ.; Supt. of Sch., Hope Valley, R. I., since 1926.

McCracken, Charles Chester, A.B.'08, A.M. '11, Monmouth Col.; Ph.D.'16, Harvard Univ.; Pres., Conn. Agrl. Col., Storrs, Conn., since 1930.

McCready, Elmer Thomas, Supt. of Sch., 65 W. Holland, Summit Hill, Pa.

McCuistion, Ed. T., A.B.'17, Hendrix Col.; M.A.'22 Peabody Col.; Supt. of Sch., Wilson, Ark., since 1923.

McCulloch, G. L., B.S.'92, Northern Ind. Normal Sch.; Asst. Supt. of Sch., Jackson, Mich., since 1912.

McCullough, A. M., A.B.'18, Colo. State Tchrs. Col.; M.A.'27, Univ. of Chicago; Supt. of Sch., Wellington, Kansas.

McCullough, J. Clair, M.A.'11, Dickinson Col.; Supt. of Sch., Waynesboro, Pa., since 1918.

McCurdy, Allan M., A.B.'09, Dartmouth Col.; Supt. of Sch., Milan, N. H., since 1925.

McCutcheon, Wilford, B.S.'14, W. Va. Wesleyan Col.; A.B.'14, W. Va. Univ.; A.M. '27, Tchrs. Col., Columbia Univ.; Supt. of Sch., Princeton, W. Va., since 1929.

McDade, James E., A.B.'12, A.M.'13, Lake Forest Col.; Asst. Supt. of Sch., 7959 S. Peoria St., Chicago, Ill., since 1928.

McDaniel, M. R., M.S.'05, Rio Grande Col.; A.M.'09, Univ. of Chicago; Litt.D.'21, Rio Grande Col.; Supt., Oak Park and River Forest Twp. High Sch., Oak Park, Ill., since 1914.

McDermott, Irene E., Dir. of Household Economy, Pub. Sch., Admin. Bldg., Bellefield Ave. at Forbes, Pittsburgh, Pa., since 1912.

McDonald, Alexander M., B.Pd.'08, Mich. State Normal Col.; B.L.'13, Detroit Col. of Law; A.B.'15, M.A.'30, Univ. of Mich.; Supt. of Sch., 1411 Coolidge Highway, River Rouge, Mich., since 1909.

McDonald, Archibald A., A.B.'00, Oberlin Col.; M.A.'16, Columbia Univ.; Supt. of Sch., Sioux Falls, S. Dak., since 1907.

McDonald, C. D., A.B.'24, Muskingum Col.; Supvg. Prin. of Sch., H. S. Bldg., Freedom, Pa., since 1926.

McDonald, Eugene Chester, Prin., H. S., Beaumont, Texas.

McDonald, Leslie C., B.S.'21, Southwest Texas State Tchrs. Col., San Marcos, Texas. Address: 2302 Trinity St., Austin, Texas.

McDonald, W. H., A. B.'20, William Jewell Col.; B.S.'23, Northwest Mo. State Tchrs. Col., Maryville, Mo.; Supt. of Sch., Trenton, Mo., since 1927.

McDowell, Samuel Kline, B.S.'09, Tri-State Col.; Supt. of Sch., Bloomington, Ill., since 1920.

McElfish, R. C., A.B.'14, Dickinson Col.; A.M.'16, Columbia Univ.; Supvg. Prin. of Sch., 213 Lehigh St., Edgewood, Pittsburg, Pa., since 1920.

McElhannon, Joseph Cooper, A.B.'09, Baylor Univ.; M.A.'22, Ph.D.'26, Univ. of Chicago; Dean, Sam Houston State Tchrs. Col., Huntsville, Texas.

McElhinney, C. F., Tchrs. Col., Columbia Univ., New York, N. Y.

McFarland, Adaline, 1313 Castle Court, Houston, Texas.

McGaughy, J. R., A.B.'12, M.A.'15, Park Col.; M.A.'21, Ph.D.'24, Columbia Univ.; Prof. of Educ., Tchrs. Col., Columbia Univ., New York, N. Y.

McGee, R. R., A.B.'11, A.M.'15, Univ. of Nebr.; Supt. of Sch., Columbus, Nebr., since 1922.

McGill, Ruby, B.A.'23, Univ. of Texas; Co. Supt. of Sch., Colorado, Texas, since 1928.

McGinnis, W. C., A.B., Univ. of Vt.; A.M., Ph.D., Columbia Univ.; Supt. of Sch., Perth Amboy, N. J., since 1929.

McGlade, John C., Ph.B.'04, Parsons Col.; M.A.'20, State Univ. of Iowa; Deputy Supt. of Sch. in charge of H. S., City Hall, San Francisco, Calif., since 1927.

McGucken, W. J., B.A.'09, Marquette Univ.; M.A.'17, St. Louis Univ.; Ph.D.'27, Univ. of Chicago; Regent, Sch. of Educ., St. Louis, Univ., Univ. Station, St. Louis, Mo., since 1930.

McHale, Kathryn, B.S.'19, A.M.'20, Ph.D.'26, Columbia Univ.; Prof. of Educ., Goucher Col., Baltimore, Md., and Exec. and Educ. Secy., American Assn. of Univ. Women, 1634 Eye St., N. W., Washington, D. C.

McHale. P. J., Supvg. Prin. of Sch., Locust Gap, Pa.

McHenry, Howard Scott, Sch. of Educ., Univ. of Pa., Philadelphia, Pa.

McHugh, Sister Antonia, A.B. and B.E.'09, M.A.'10, Univ. of Chicago; Pres., Col. of St. Catherine, St. Paul, Minn., since 1914.

McIlhattan, William H., A.B.'22, Univ. of Pittsburgh; A.M.'27, Tchrs. Col., Columbia Univ.; Supvg. Prin. of Sch., Somerset, Pa., since 1929.

McIntosh, William A.,B.S.'11, Ala. Polytech. Inst.; Supt. of Sch., 1220 Polk St., Amarillo, Texas, since 1922.

McIntyre, Annie L., Asst. Supt. of Sch., Glendale, Calif., since 1924.

McKee, Clyde V., B.S.'22, George Peabody Col. for Tchrs.; Supt. of Sch., Pontotoc, Miss., since 1926.

McKee, Margaret G., B.S.'29, Univ.. of Pittsburgh; Supvg. Prin. of Sch., McDonald, Pa., since 1925.

McKee, Paul, A.B.'20, Monmouth Col.; M. A.'21, Ph.D.'24, State Univ. of Iowa; Dir., Div. of Elem. Sch. Experimentation and Prof. of Elem. Educ., Colo. State Tchrs. Col., Greeley, Colo., since 1926.

McKee, William Parker, A.B.'83, Wabash Col.; B.D.'87, Univ. of Chicago; A.M.'97, Univ. of Minn.; Pres., Frances Shimer Sch., Mt. Carroll, Ill., since 1897.

McKenney, H. L., B.S.'07, A.B. in Ed.'22, Valparaiso Univ.; Supt. of Sch., 406 N. Jackson St., Auburn, Ind., since 1923.

McKenny, Charles, A.M.'04, Univ. of Wis.; LL.D.'12, Olivet Col.; D.Ed.'28, Miami Univ.; Pres., Mich. State Normal Col., Ypsilanti, Mich., since 1912.

McKenzie, Jane Elizabeth, B.S.'26, Univ. of Pittsburgh; Prin., Daniel Webster Sch., Scotland and Reedsdale Sts., Pittsburgh, Pa., since 1927.

McKenzie, Ury, A.B.'00, B.S.'20, George Peabody Col. for Tchrs.; Supt. of Sch., Batesville. Ark., since 1929.

McKinney, Charles S., Diploma '17, Concord State Normal Sch., Athens, W. Va.; Co. Supt. of Sch., Court House, Beckley, W. Va., since 1927.

McKinney, H.T., B.S.'04, Valparaiso Univ.; B.A.'13, M.A.'15, Ph.D.'21, Univ. of Ill.; Prof. of Educ., Bethany Col., Bethany, W. Va.

McKnight, Mrs. Mary T., Muskegon, Mich.

McKusick, Leon R., A.B.'11, Bates Col.; Supt. of Sch., Central Sch., Winsted, Conn., since 1928.

McLean, David S., Prin., Kenilworth Elem. Sch., Ridgewood, N. J.

McLean, Jessie A., M.A.'26, Columbia Univ.; Asst. Supt. of Tr. Sch., Central State Tchrs. Col., Mt. Pleasant, Mich., since 1929.

McLeod, Beatrice, B.S.'20, Univ. of Oregon; M.A.'22, Univ. of Wash.; State Dir. of Spec. Educ., State Dept. of Educ., Cheyenne, Wyo., since 1923.

McLure, John R., B.S.'11, Univ. of Ala.; M.A.'14, Ph.D.'25, Columbia Univ.; Prof. of Sch. Admin., since 1924; Dir. of Summer Sch., since 1926; and Dir. of Field Studies, Col. of Educ., Univ. of Ala., University, Ala., since 1928.

McMahan, Corwin L., A.B.'20, Marietta Col.; Supt. of Sch., Wellsburg, W. Va., since 1928.

McMahon, Rolla James, Ph.B.'23, Ripon Col.; Ph.M.'28, Univ. of Wis.; Supt. of Sch., New London, Wis., since 1923.

McManaman, Edward P., A.B.'23, St. Bonaventure Col.; S.T.L.'27, American Col., Rome, Italy. Address: 230 W. Tenth St., Erie, Pa.

McManis, John T., Junior Col. of Flint, Flint, Mich.

McManus, James B., B.S.'95, Normal Sch., Dixon, Ill.; Supt. of Sch., 748 Gooding St., La Salle, Ill., since 1900.

McNally, J. V., A.B.'08, Univ. of Chicago; A.M.'25, Columbia Univ.; Prin., MacKenzie H. S., 9275 Wyoming Ave., Detroit, Mich., since 1928.

McNally, Stephen S., Supt. of Sch., Lancaster, Wis.

McNally, William P., S.T.L.'12, Catholic Univ. of America; Ph.D.'25, St. Joseph's Col., Philadelphia, Pa.; Prin., Roman Catholic H. S., Broad and Vine Sts., Philadelphia, Pa., since 1919.

McNamara, James M., Supt. of Sch., Fitchburg, Mass.

McNown, F. L., B.A.'16, Univ.of Nebr.; Supt. of Sch., Basin, Wyo., since 1918.

McQuilkin, D. E., A.B.'05, A.M.'06, W.Va. Univ.; A.M.'08, Harvard Univ.; Supt. of Sch., Roanoke, Va., since 1918.

McVay, H. R., B.Ph.'90, D.Ped.'15, Ohio Univ.; Co. Supt. of Sch., Athens, Ohio, since 1923.

McWhorter, L. N., Asst. Supt. of Sch., City Hall, Minneapolis, Minn.

McWilliam, Janet, Supvg. Prin., Henry Sch., 2142 K St., N. W., Washington, D. C., since 1924.

Macelwane, Francis J., A.B.'11, M.A.'21, St. John's Col., Toledo, Ohio; Supt. of Sch., Diocese of Toledo, 2572 Cherry St., Toledo, Ohio, since 1922.

MacInnis, Earl C., B.A.'16, Lawrence Col.; M.A.'17, Univ. of Wis.; Supt. of Sch., Jefferson, Wis., since 1920.

MacKay, Donald William, A.B.'25, A.M. '29, Colo. State Tchrs. Col., Greeley, Colo.; Supt. of Sch., 733 S. Sixth, Raton, N. Mex., since 1928.

Mackenzie, Harold, A.B.'09, Wheaton Col.; A.M.'22, Univ. of Chicago; Supt. of Sch., 619 Second St., N.E., Watertown, S. Dak., since 1927.

MacLaughlin, Nellie A., Diploma '97, Columbia Univ. Extension Course; Yale Univ. Extension Course, State Normal Sch., New Britain, Conn.; Supt. of Sch., South Windsor, Conn., since 1924.

MacNeill, Harold J., 176 W. Adams St., Chicago, Ill.

MacQuarrie, Archibald E., LL.B.'16, Univ. of Wis.; Prin., Washburn H. S., Wentworth Ave. and W. 49th St., Minneapolis, Minn., since 1924.

Macy, C. B., A.B., Ind. State Tchrs. Col., Terre Haute, Ind.; A.M., Columbia Univ.; Supt. of Sch., Bremen, Ind., since 1920.

Madden, G. H., L.I.'01, Peabody Col.; A. B.'15, Univ. of Southern Calif.; Supt. of Sch., Winslow, Ariz., since 1925.

Maddocks, Carl W., Supt. of Sch., 69 Gulf St., Milford, Conn.

Maddy, Joseph E., Diploma '20, Chautauqua Summer Schools; Instr., Univ. Sch. of Music, Univ. of Mich., P. O. Box 386, Ann Arbor, Mich., since 1924.

Madison, W. P., A.B.'30, Central State Tchrs. Col., Mt. Pleasant, Mich.; Supt. of Sch., Sheridan, Mich., since 1930.

Magill, Walter H., B.S. in Ed. '20, M.A.'22, Ph.D.'30, Univ. of Pa.; Prof. of Industrial Educ., 117 Bennett Hall, Univ. of Pa., Philadelphia, Pa., since 1930.

Magnusson, Amanda, A.B.'17, Bethany Col.; A.M.'23, Univ. of Kansas; Head, Dept. of Educ., Bethany Col., Lindsborg, Kansas, since 1918.

Mahan, Thomas W., A.B.'21, Holy Cross Col., Worcester, Mass.; Supt. of Sch., Lenox H. S., Lenox, Mass., since 1927.

Mahoney, Lewis A., Supt. of Sch., Moline, Ill., since 1915.

Majewski, Stephen A., 2380 Wyandotte Ave., Hamtramck, Mich.

Malcolm, David J., S.B.'13, Harvard Col.; Union Supt. of Sch., Charlemont, Mass.

Malcolm, Francis M., B.S.'23, Cornell Univ.; Supt. of Sch., Bellows Falls, Vt., since 1927.

Malcolm, George Gordon, A.B.'06, Univ. of Mich.; M.A.'26, Tchrs. Col., Columbia Univ.; Supt. of Sch., Sault Ste. Marie, Mich., since 1916.

Mallett, Wilbert G., Diploma '86, State Normal Sch., Farmington, Maine; A.B.'91, A.M.'21, Bowdoin Col.; Prin., State Normal Sch., Farmington, Maine, since 1909.

Mallory, Clara, Dir., Elem. Grades, Bd. of Educ., Beaumont, Texas, since 1919.

Mann, Annette, B.S.'19, Johns Hopkins Univ.; Supvr. of English in Jr. High Sch., Carrollton and Lafayette Aves., Baltimore, Md., since 1923.

Mann, Carleton H., A.B.'08, DePauw Univ.; M.A.'22, Ph.D.'28. Columbia Univ.; Lecturer in Educ., Univ. of Southern Calif., 2903 S. Hoover St., Los Angeles, Calif., since 1930.

Mann, Charles Riborg, Ph.D.'95, Univ. of Berlin, Germany; Sc.D.'19, Lafayette; Dir., American Council on Educ., 744 Jackson Pl., Washington, D. C., since 1922.

Mann, John P., B.A.'22, Ripon Col.; M.A. '27, Univ. of Wis.; Supt. of Sch., Evansville, Wis., since 1927.

Manning, Ada M., Supt. of Sch., 131 N Main St., Lombard, Ill.

Manning, C. G., A.B.'07, Morningside Col.; Supt. of Sch., Lewiston, Mont., since 1920.

Mansur, Frank L., A.B.'10, Brown Univ.; Supt. of Sch., Walpole, Mass., since 1922.

Manuel, H. T., A.B.'09, De Pauw Univ.; A.M.'14, Univ. of Chicago; Ph.D.'17, Univ. of Ill.; Prof. of Educ. Psych., Univ. of Texas, Austin, Texas.

Manuel, Lulu Preston, B.S.'25, New York Univ.; Grade-Supvr., Bd. of Educ., Uniontown, Pa., since 1926.

Manville, Lela A., A.B.'22, State Tchrs. Col., Silver City, N. Mex.; Supt. of Sch., Washington, Bldg., Silver City, N. Mex., since 1917.

Mapes, Elmer Stephens, Supt. of Sch., Bristol, R. I., since 1930.

Maria, Sister Josefita, B.A.'18, M.A.'22, Ph. D.'25, Univ. of Pa.; Community Supvr., Mt. St. Joseph's Academy, Chestnut Hill, Philadelphia, Pa., since 1926.

Markman, Frank H., A.B.'11, McKendree Col.; M.A.'28, Univ. of Colo.; Prin., Jersey Twp. H. S., Jerseyville, Ill., since 1921.

Marks, Sallie B., A.B.'23, Southwestern State Tchrs. Col., Weatherford, Okla.; M.A.'25, Tchrs. Col., Columbia Univ.; Assoc. Prof. of Elem. Educ., Univ. of N. C., Chapel Hill, N. C., since 1927.

Marquis, Robert Lincoln, A.B.'01, Texas Christian Univ.; B.S.'02, Univ. of Texas; M.S.'03, Univ. of Chicago; LL.D.'25, Austin Col.; Pres., North Texas State Tchrs. Col., Denton, Texas, since 1923.

Marrs, S. M. N., B.S.'84, Natl. Normal Univ.; State Supt. of Pub. Instr., Capitol Sta., Austin, Texas, since 1923.

Marsden, Carl A., Supt. of Sch., Central Blvd., Palisades Park, N. J.

Marshall, Farnsworth G., A.B.'03, Bowdoin Col.; Supt. of Sch., Malden, Mass., since 1913.

Marshall, George H., M.A.'29, Univ. of Kansas; Supt. of Sch., 614 Osage St., Augusta, Kansas, since 1917.

Marshall, Paul M., B.S. in Ed.'23, Central Mo. State Tchrs. Col., Warrensburg, Mo.; M.A.'28, Tchrs. Col., Columbia Univ.; Prin., Jarrett Jr. H. S., Springfield, Mo., since 1929.

Marshall, Thomas Franklin, A.B.'94, Lake Forest Col.; A.M.'08, Columbia Univ.; B.D.'08, Union Theological Seminary; Ph.D.'14, Campbell Univ.; Pres., Crescent Col., Eureka Springs, Ark., since 1930.

Martin, A. S., Diploma, State Normal Sch., Millersville, Pa.; B.S.'05, A.M.'10, Univ. of Pa.; Supt. of Sch., 300 Chews Landing Rd., Haddonfield, N. J., since 1923.

Martin, Archie O., B.S.'19, Okla. Agrl. and Mech. Col.; M.A.'28, Tchrs. Col., Columbia Univ.; Supt. of Sch., Vinita, Okla., since 1924.

Martin, B. W., Supt. of Sch., Kirbyville, Texas.

Martin, C. F., A.B.'89, Ky. Wesleyan Col.; Supt. of Sch., Owingsville, Ky., since 1905.

Martin, Cora M., B.S.'19, M.A.'22, Tchrs. Col., Columbia Univ.; Adjunct Prof. of Elem. Educ., Univ. of Texas, Austin, Texas, since 1927.

Martin, E. W., Supt. of Sch., Berwyn, Ill.

Martin, Frank M., A.B.'05, Washington and Lee Univ.; Supt. of Sch., Durham, N. C., since 1923.

Martin, Frederick F., Diploma '07, Central State Tchrs. Col., Edmond, Okla.; B. Pd.'08, Southwest State Tchrs. Col., Springfield, Mo.; B.S.'08, Drury Col., Springfield, Mo.; M.A.'11, Yale Univ.; Supt. of Sch., 1333 Sixth St., Santa Monica, Calif., since 1924.

Martin, George E., A.B.'14, Univ. of Nebr.; A.M.'19, Columbia Univ.; Pres., Nebr. State Normal Sch. and Tchrs. Col., Kearney, Nebr., since 1919.

Martin, H. G., B.S.'08, Univ. of Mo.; Dir., Isaac Delgado Central Trades Sch., City Park Ave., New Orleans, La., since 1920.

Martin, Horace F., B.A.'95, Midland Col., Fremont, Nebr.; M.A.'14, Ph.D.'18, Univ. of Iowa; Pres., Midland Col., Fremont, Nebr.

Martin, John Eppes, A.B.'11, M.A.14, Washington and Lee Univ.; Supt. of Sch., Suffolk, Va., since 1917.

Martin, Joseph Oscar, State Sch. Supvr., 103 State Capitol, Atlanta, Ga.

Martin, L. C., A.M.'25, Tchrs. Col., Columbia Univ.; Supt. of Sch., Millersburg, Ohio, since 1927.

Martin, Melrowe M., B.L.'09, Univ. of Calif.; Dist. Supt. of Sch., Union H. S., Salinas, Calif., since 1930.

Martin, N. J., Life Cert. '17, A.B.'23, Northern State Tchrs. Col., Marquette, Mich.; Supt. of Sch., Baraga, Mich., since 1925.

Martin, Robert W., Diploma '98, State Normal Sch., Farmington, Maine; Diploma '25, State Normal Sch., Hyannis, Mass.; Union Supt. of Sch., Greenwood Ave., Vineyard Haven, Mass., since 1917.

Martin, W. H., A.B.'04, Mo. Valley Col.; A.M.'25, Columbia Univ.; Diploma '25, Tchrs. Col., Columbia Univ.; Dist. Supt. of Sch., Pub. Library Bldg., Kansas City, Mo., since 1920.

Martin, W. P., A.B.'98, Mercer Univ.; Supt. of Sch., Gainesville, Ga., since 1924.

Marvin, William B., Litt.B.'18, Princeton Univ.; Supvg. Prin. of Sch., Barnegat, N. J., since 1926.

Mason, C. W., Supt. of Sch., Bank and Charlotte Sts., Norfolk, Va.

Mason, H. C., Supt. of Sch., River Falls, Wis.

Mason, Jesse H., B.A.'15, Ohio Wesleyan; Supt. of Sch., Canton, Ohio.

Mason, Josephine Dwight, A.B.'15, George Washington Univ.; Dir., Dept. of Evening Schools and Immigrant Educ., City Hall, Springfield, Mass., since 1920.

Mason, M. Phyllis, Ph.B.'15, Dickinson Col.; M.A.'26, Tchrs. Col., Columbia Univ.; Rural Sch. Supvr., County Bldg., Wilmington, Del., since 1923.

Mason, Noah M., B.Ed., Dixon Col.; Supt. of Sch., Oglesby, Ill., since 1908.

Masson, J. S., S.B.'16, Univ. of Chicago; Asst. Supt. of Sch., Lorain, Ohio, since 1922.

Masten, Zach G., Jr., Supvg. Prin. of Sch., Fairview, N. J.

Maston, R. C., Ph.B.'15, Col. of Wooster; Supt. of Sch., Elyria, Ohio, since 1924.

Matheison, C. L., A.B.; Supt. of Sch., Memphis, Mich.

Matheson, Kenneth G., A.M.'97, Leland Stanford Univ.; LL.D.'06, Washington and Lee Univ.; LL.D.'15, Univ. of Ga.; Sc.D. '23, Univ. of Pa.; Pres., Drexel Institute, Philadelphia, Pa., since 1922.

Mathews, C. B., A.B.'04, Univ. of Chicago; Supt. of Sch., Newnan, Ga., since 1929.

Matters, W. J., B.S.'20, Wash. State Col.; Asst. State Supt. of Pub. Instr., 1712 Capitol Way, Olympia, Wash., since 1929.

Matteson, I. F., Supt. of Sch., Findlay, Ohio, since 1917.

Matthews, Arthur J., LL.D.'17, Syracuse Univ.; Pres. Emeritus, Ariz. State Tchrs. Col., Tempe, Ariz., since 1930.

Matthews, Henry V., Diploma '06, State Normal Sch., Mansfield, Pa.; Supt. of Sch., Lodi, N. J., since 1921.

Matzen, John M., M.A.'28, Univ. of Nebr. Address: Hooper, Nebr.

Maue, August, Diploma '85, Adrian Normal Sch.; B.L.'91, Univ. of Ill.; Co. Supt. of Sch., Court House, Joliet, Ill., since 1919

Maul, Ray C., 901 Merchant St., Emporia, Kansas.

Maurer, George C., Ph.B.'90, Ph.M.'93, Univ. of Wooster; Supt. of Sch., 323 N. Market St., Wooster, Ohio, since 1912.

Maurer, Irving, B.A.'04, Beloit Col.; M.A., B.D.'09, Yale; D.D.'24, Carleton Col.; LL.D.'24, Wooster Col.; D.D.'25, Oberlin Col.; Pres., Beloit Col., Beloit, Wis., since 1924.

Maxwell, C. R., Dean, Col. of Educ., Univ. of Wyo., Laramie, Wyo.

Maxwell, Charles F., Asst. Co. Supt. of Sch., Greensburg, Pa.

May, Albert L., B.S.'23, George Peabody Col. for Tchrs.; Supt. of Sch., Biloxi, Miss., since 1923.

May, E. O., B.S.'11, Valparaiso Univ.; M.A. '27, Univ. of Chicago; Prin., Twp. H. S., 708 N. Cross St., Robinson, Ill., since 1921.

May, Walter M., A.B.'05, A.M.'24, Dartmouth Col.; Deputy State Commr. of Educ., Patriot Bldg., Concord, N. H., since 1919.

Mayberry, Lawrence W., A.B.'01, Univ. of Kansas; A.B. and A.M.'18, Columbia Univ.; D.Ed.'28, Wichita Univ.; Supt. of Sch., 1548 Park Pl., Wichita, Kansas, since 1912.

Mayhew, Herman, Prin., Morgan Park Military Academy, Morgan Park, Chicago, Ill., since 1918.

Maynard, Milton M., A.B.'08, Univ. of Okla.; M.A.'20, Univ. of Ill.; Prof. of Educ., Monmouth Col., 734 E. Boston Ave., Monmouth, Ill., since 1909.

Mayo, Talmadge D., B.A.'14, East Texas State Normal Sch., Commerce, Texas; B. A.'22, East Texas State Tchrs. Col., Commerce, Texas; M.A.'27, Southern Methodist Univ.; Supt. of Sch., Lancaster, Texas, since 1927.

Mays, Jesse Thomas, Supt., Knox Co. H. S., Barbourville, Ky.

Mead, H. W., A.B.'01, Harvard; Supt. of Sch., East Aurora, N. Y., since 1906.

Meader, James Laurence, A.B.'15, Bates Col.; M.A.'23, Ph.D.'28, Columbia Univ.; Pres., Russell Sage Col., Troy, N. Y., since 1928.

Meadows, John C., M.A.'21, Ph.D.'26, Peabody Col.; Prof. of Educ., Col. of Educ., Univ. of Ga., Athens, Ga., since 1930.

Means, Herbert G., M.E.'02, State Tchrs. Col., Slippery Rock, Pa.; Ph.B.'13, Grove City Col.; M.A.'26, Univ. of Pittsburgh; Supt. of Sch., 316 W. Sixth St., East Liverpool, Ohio, since 1929.

Meating, A. G., A.B.'02, Lawrence Col.; Co. Supt. of Sch., Court House, Appleton, Wis., since 1903.

Medsker, Frank Olan, Supt. of Sch., 401 Walnut St., Alexandria, Ind.

Meek, Charles S., A.B.'91, Ind. Univ.; A.M. '08, Columbia Univ.; Supt. of Sch., Bd. of Educ., Toledo, Ohio, since 1921.

Meek, Lois Hayden, Ph.D.'24, Columbia Univ.; Dir. Child Development Inst. and Prof. of Educ., Tchrs. Col., Columbia Univ., 514 W. 126th St., New York, N. Y., since 1930.

Meisberger, D. T., Supt., Coal Twp. Sch. Dist., Shamokin, Pa., since 1924.

Melady, Thomas Sylvester, B.A.'21, Univ. of Toronto; Inspector of Separate Schools., 314 Campbell Ave., Windsor, Ontario, Canada, since 1922.

Melcher, George, B.S.'89, M.S.'92, Odessa Col.; A.B.'98, Drury Col.; A.M.'19, Tchrs. Col., Columbia Univ.; LL.D.'23, Mo. Valley Col.; LL.D.'25, Drury Col.; Supt. of Sch., Library Bldg., Kansas City, Mo., since 1928.

Melchior, William T., Ph.D.'23, Columbia Univ.; Dir. of Educ. Extension, Syracuse Univ., Syracuse, N. Y., since 1926.

Mellor, William J., A.B.'27, Northwestern State Tchrs. Col., Alva, Okla.; Supt. of Sch., Three Sands, Okla., since 1928.

Mellyn, Mary C., Ed.M.'24, Boston Univ.; Ed.D.'25, Boston Col.; Asst. Supt. of Sch., 15 Beacon St., Boston, Mass., since 1916.

Melton, Monroe, A.B.'15, Ind. State Normal Sch., Terre Haute, Ind.; Supt. of Sch., 504 Normal Ave., Normal, Ill., since 1925.

Mendenhall, Raymond E., A.B.'12, Penn Col.; A.M.'16, Des Moines Univ.; Ph.D. '25, New York Univ.; Dir. of Tchr. Tr., Otterbein Col., Westerville, Ohio, since 1928.

Mensch, Harry R., M.S. in Ed.'30, Rutgers Univ.; Supvg. Prin. of Sch., Milltown, N. J., since 1921.

Menschel, M. R., A.B.'17, Oberlin Col.; A.M. '24, Columbia Univ.; Supt. of Sch., 804 W. Anglaize St., Wapakoneta, Ohio, since 1927.

Merchant, Claude J., B.S. in Ed.'22, M.A.'22, Syracuse Univ.; M.A.'23, Tchrs. Col., Columbia Univ.; Dir. of Educ., N. J. State Home for Boys, Jamesburg, N. J., since 1924.

Meredith, Albert B., A.B.'95, M.A.'16, Wesleyan Univ.; Pd.D.'18, Muhlenberg Col.; L.H.D.'19, Upsala Col.; LL.D.'21, Wesleyan Univ.; LL.D.'30, Boston Univ.; Prof. of Educ. and Head, Dept. of Admin. and Supvn., Sch. of Educ., New York Univ., New York, N. Y., since 1930.

Merideth, G. H., B.S.'24, Central Mo. State Tchrs. Col., Warrensburg, Mo.; M.A.'25, Tchrs. Col., Columbia Univ.; Asst. Supt. of Sch., Bd. of Educ. Bldg., 320 E. Walnut St., Pasadena, Calif., since 1928.

Merrell, Amos N., 279 N. Fourth St., Provo, Utah.

Merrell, George Bewley, 917 Arlington Ave., St. Petersburg, Fla.

Merriam, Burr J., Diploma '98, State Normal Sch., Oneonta, N. Y.; B.S.'16, Columbia Univ.; Ed.M.'27, Harvard Univ.; Supt. of Sch., Framingham, Mass., since 1922.

Merrill, Joseph F., B.S.'93, Univ. of Mich.; Ph.D.'99, Johns Hopkins Univ.; D.Sc.'20, Univ. of Utah; Commr. of Educ., L. D. S. Church, 47 E. South Temple St., Salt Lake City, Utah, since 1928.

Merrill, Sanford E., Supt. of Sch., 910 Garden St., Park Ridge, Ill.

Merritt, Mrs. Lillian H., Elem. Supvr. of Sch., 321 Turin St., Rome, N. Y., since 1920.

Mertching, R. A., B.S.'15, M.A.'18, New York Univ.; Supvg. Prin. of Sch., Oradell Ave., Oradell, N. J., since 1910.

Messler, William Allen, B.S.'98, M.Sc.'01, Rutgers Col.; M.Pd.'11, Pd.D.'15, New York Univ.; Prin., State Normal Sch., Jersey City, N. J., since 1929.

Messner, J. C., Supt. of Sch., Harrington, Del.

Mets, William Forder, M.A.'02, Rutgers Col.; Supvg. Prin. of Sch., 469 Prospect Ave., New Market, N. J., since 1905.

Metts, Albert C., A.B.'16, M.A.'23, Col. of Wooster; M.A., Tchrs. Col., Columbia Univ. Address: 1237 Browning Blvd., Los Angeles, Calif.

Metzner, Alice B., Diploma '02, B.S.'24, Detroit Tchrs. Col.; Dir. of Special Educ., Pub. Sch., 2915 Hogarth Ave., Detroit, Mich., since 1928.

Meyer, Ivan I., A.B.'15, Ellsworth Col.; A.M.'23, State Univ. of Iowa; Supt. of Sch., 122 Fifth St., Savanna, Ill., since 1927.

Meyer, J. W., Prin., Washington Jr. H. S., Duluth, Minn.

Meyer, William W., Ph.B.'24, Univ. of Chicago; Supt. of Sch., Harvard, Ill., since 1926.

Meytrott, Mrs. Cornelia B., A.B.'99, Western Reserve Univ.; Asst. Dir., Dept. of Instr. and Agencies of N. J., State House, Trenton, N. J., since 1919.

Michael, Mrs. Elias, Member of Bd. of Educ., 4383 Westminster Pl., St. Louis, Mo., since 1922.

Michael, H. E., A.B.'19, Otterbein Col.; M.A.'26, Ohio State Univ.; Supt. of Sch., Chagrin Falls, Ohio, since 1926.

Micheals, William H., A.B.'07, Dickinson Col.; A.M.'24, Univ. of Pa.; Supt. of Sch., Media, Pa., since 1920.

Midkiff, Frank E., A.B.'12, Colgate Univ.; Pres., Kamehameha Schools, Honolulu, Hawaii, since 1923.

Milam, Mrs. Lena, 593 Penn Ave., Beaumont, Texas.

Miles, Homer U., B.S.'23, Texas Agrl. and Mech. Col.; M.A.'27, Tchrs. Col., Columbia Univ. Address: Edinburg Col., Edinburg, Texas.

Miller, Alexander W., A.B.'12, Harvard Univ.; A.M.'22, Columbia Univ.; Supt. of Sch., Glens Falls, N. Y., since 1927.

Miller, Benjamin H., B.L.'09, A.B.'11, East Texas State Normal Col., Commerce, Texas; B.A.'24, M.A.'27, Univ. of Texas; Supt. of Sch., Eagle Pass, Texas, since 1924.

Miller, Bertha May, A.B.'01, Allegheny Col.; Prin., Jr. H. S., 120 E. Fulton St., Butler, Pa., since 1919.

Miller, Charles A., A.B.'23, Franklin and Marshall Col.; Ed.M.'24, Harvard Univ.; Dist. Supt. of Sch., Lee, Mass., since 1926.

Miller, Charles A., B.S.'11, Susquehanna Univ.; Supt. of Sch., South Brownsville, Pa., since 1921.

Miller, Charles F., Ph.B.'96, DePauw Univ. Address: 5766 Central Ave., Indianapolis, Ind.

Miller, Charles S., A.B.'13, Allegheny Col.; A.M.'15, Univ. of Pittsburgh; Supt. of Sch., Lansdowne, Pa., since 1929.

Miller, Chester F., A.B.'07, A.M.'09, McKendree Col.; A.M.'19, Tchrs. Col., Columbia Univ.; Litt.D.'28, McKendree Col.; Supt. of Sch., Saginaw, Mich., since 1928.

Miller, Claude J., B.Pd.'13, Central State Normal Sch.; Supt. of Sch., Ecorse, Mich., since 1914.

Miller, Clyde R., A.B.'11, Ohio State Univ.; Dir., Bureau of Educ. Serv., Tchrs. Col., Columbia Univ., New York, N. Y., since 1928.

Miller, Edwin L., A.B.'90, A.M.'91, Univ. of Mich.; M.Pd.'24, Mich. State Tchrs. Col.; Asst. Supt. of Sch., 1354 Broadway, Detroit, Mich.

Miller, Elmer G., 1129 S. Negley Ave., Pittsburgh, Pa.

Miller, Frank L., B.A.'82, M.A.'85, Ohio Wesleyan Univ.; Supt. of Sch., 15410 Lexington Ave., Harvey, Ill., since 1892.

Miller, Fred B., B.S.'27, Central Mo. State Tchrs. Col., Warrensburg, Mo.; Supt. of Sch., Normandy Consol. Sch. Dist. of St. Louis Co., 6701 Easton Ave., St. Louis, Mo., since 1912.

Miller, Harry W., B.S.'25, Mich. State Normal Col., Ypsilanti, Mich.; Supt. of Sch., Center Line, Mich., since 1926.

Miller, Mrs. Ida Zener, Bennett Hall, Univ. of Pa., Philadelphia, Pa.

Miller, J. A., Asst. Co. Supt. of Sch., College Park, Md.

Miller, J. E. Wesley, Diploma '94, Western Normal Col. and Business Inst., Bushnell, Ill.; Co. Supt. of Sch., Court House, Edwardsville, Ill., since 1927.

Miller, James Collins, B.S.'07, Throop Col. of Tech.; M.A.'10, Ph.D.'13, Tchrs. Col., Columbia Univ.; Prof. of Educ. Admin., Bennett Hall, Univ. of Pa., Philadelphia, Pa., since 1925.

Miller, Joseph Warren, A.B.'22, Midland Col.; A.M.'30, Univ. of Nebr.; Co. Supt. of Sch., Court House, Beatrice, Nebr., since 1927.

Miller, M. B., Supt. of Sch., Calvin, Okla.

Miller, W. L., A.B.'16, Muskingum Col.; Supt. of Sch., Chillicothe, Ohio, since 1928.

Miller, Ward I., A.B.'14, A.M.'15, Univ. of Denver; Supt. of Sch., Delta, Colo., since 1924.

Millikan, Ben S., A.B.'10, M.A.'12, Baker Univ.; Dist. Supt. of Sch., Covina, Calif., since 1918.

Milliken, William H., Jr., 41 E. 42nd St., New York, N. Y.

Millmann, Anna, Diploma '07, State Normal Sch., Milwaukee, Wis.; LL.B.'23, Ph.B. '27, Marquette Univ.; Prin., Johnson Woods Sch., Milwaukee, Wis., since 1929.

Mills, H. L., Diploma '11, Sam Houston State Tchrs. Col., Huntsville, Texas; LL. B.'15, Houston Law Sch.; Business Manager, Independent Sch. Dist., Houston, Texas, since 1922.

Mills, Lewis Sprague, B.S.'08, A.M.'13, Columbia Univ.; Field Supvr., State Bd. of Educ., 55 Walnut St., Winsted, Conn.

Mills, W. R., Supt. of Sch., Louisburg, N. C.

Milne, John, B.S., Univ. of N. Mex.; Supt. of Sch., 804 Park Ave., Albuquerque, N. Mex., since 1911.

Minard, George C., B.S., A.M.; Dir., Hgts. Division, Sch. of Educ., and Asst. Prof. of Educ., New York Univ., Washington Square, New York, N. Y.

Miner, W. F., A.B.'96, Brown Univ.; Supt. of Sch., Farmington, Maine, since 1923.

Minnich, Robert E., A.B.'19, Dickinson Col.; A.M.'25, Columbia Univ.; Supt. of Sch., Tupper Lake, N. Y., since 1926.

Miracle, J. T., A.B.'23, Univ. of Ky.; M.A. '28, Columbia Univ.; Supt. of Sch., Catlettsburg, Ky., since 1923.

Mitchell, Claude, A.B.'12, Susquehanna Univ.; A.M.'25, Univ. Pittsburgh; Supt. of Sch., West Newton, Pa., since 1918.

Mitchell, Clovis W., B.S.'08, R. I. State Col.; Supt. of Sch., Putnam Ave., Greenville, R. I., since 1918.

Mitchell, Irving C., B.S.'13, R. I. State Col.; A.M.'20, Brown Univ.; Dir., Surveys and Research, State Dept. of Educ., State House, Providence, R. I., since 1929.

Mitchell, J. C., Supt. of Sch., Murfreesboro, Tenn.

Mitchell, John G., M.A.'19, Univ. of Okla.; Pres., Central State Tchrs. Col., Edmond, Okla., since 1919.

Mitchell, M. S., A.B.'07, Ohio Wesleyan Univ.; A.M.'18, Tchrs. Col., Columbia Univ.; Supt. of Sch., Ashtabula, Ohio, since 1924.

Mitchell, O. M., Supt., Winthrop Tr. Sch., Rock Hill, S. C.

Mitchell, S. C., Supt. of Sch., Benton Harbor, Mich.

Mitchell, William Roy, A.B.'09, Lawrence Col.; Ph.M.'26, Univ. of Wis.; Head, Dept. of Educ., Mo. Valley Col., 304 E. Gordon St., Marshall, Mo., since 1928.

Mniece, Leonard A., A.B.'20, A.M., Univ. of Mich.; Supt. of Sch., Hancock, Mich., since 1924.

Moehlman, Arthur B., A.B.'12, A.M.'21, Ph. D.'23, Univ. of Mich.; Prof. of Admin. and Supvr., Sch. of Educ., Univ. of Mich., Ann Arbor, Mich., since 1923.

Moffitt, Frederick James, A.B.'18, Hobart Col.; Supt. of Sch., Hamburg, N. Y., since 1927.

Mohr, Dean, B.S. and Ph.C.'17, Ohio State Univ.; Pres., Paul Quinn Col., Waco, Texas, since 1928.

Mohr, Lloyd C., B.S.'16, Adrian Col.; M.A. '22, Tchrs. Col., Columbia Univ.; Supt. of Sch., South Haven, Mich., since 1920.

Moll, Richard M., Diploma '05, State Normal Sch., Kutztown, Pa.; A.B.'15, Lebanon Valley Col.; A.M.'25, Univ. of Pa.; Asst. Co. Supt. of Sch., 313 W. Penn Ave., Robesonia, Pa., since 1928.

Molloy, Hugh J., Supt. of Sch., 16 Rutland St., Lowell, Mass.

Monahan, Catherine E., Diploma '11, R. I. Normal Sch.; Supvr., Elem. Schools, 9 Exchange Ter., Providence, R. I., since 1927.

Monroe, Edwin S., A.M.; Dean of Faculty, Oakland City Col., Oakland City, Ind., since 1923.

Montgomery, A. D., A.B.'16, Ind. State Tchrs. Col.; A.M.'25, Columbia Univ. Address: 109 N. Grant Ave., Crawfordsville, Ind.

Montgomery, E. W., A.B.'09, A.M.'13, Ind. Univ.; Supt. of Union High Schools and Jr. Col., Union H. S., Phoenix, Ariz., since 1924.

Montgomery, T. T., Supt. of Sch., Chicasha, Okla.

Montoya, Atanasio, State Supt. of Pub. Instr., Santa Fe, N. Mex.

Moody, A. E., A.B.'07, Ohio State Univ.; A.M.'24, Tchrs. Col., Columbia Univ.; Supt. of Sch., Bedford, Ohio, since 1918.

Moody, Van Buren, A.B.'12, A.M.'15, Harvard Univ.; Supt. of Sch., Middletown, Conn., since 1925.

Moody, Von Willis, B.S. in Ed.'29, Central Univ.; Dist. Supt. of Sch., Anawalt, W. Va., since 1930.

Moon, Ward Clinton, Diploma, State Normal Sch., Cortland, N. Y.; A.B.'05, Amherst Col.; Pd.M.'13, New York Univ.; Supt. of Sch., Poughkeepsie, N. Y., since 1919.

Mooney, Mary F., Dir., Texts and Libraries Dept., Pub. Sch., 360 Hyde St., San Francisco, Calif., since 1924.

Moore, C. H., A.M.'17, George Peabody Col. for Tchrs.; Supt. of Sch., H. S. Bldg., Clarksville, Tenn., since 1927.

Moore, C. O., B.S.'25, Univ. of Okla.; M.A. '29, Columbia Univ.; Supt. of Sch., Prague, Okla., since 1927.

Moore, Clyde B., A.B.'12, Nebr. Wesleyan Univ.; B.Ed.'13, Nebr. Tchrs. Col.; A.M.'16, Clark Univ.; Ph. D.'24, Columbia Univ.; Prof. of Educ., Caldwell Hall, Cornell Univ., Ithaca, N. Y., since 1925.

Moore, D. H., Co. Supt. of Sch., Tavares, Fla.

Moore, George O., A.B.'04, A.M.'09, Syracuse Univ.; Asst. Supt. of Sch., Library Bldg., Erie, Pa., since 1922.

Moore, Harry L., A.B.'01, Bates Col.; Supt. of Sch., City Hall, Portsmouth, N. H., since 1925.

Moore, Harry W., Ph.B.'13, Lafayette Col.; Co. Supt. of Sch., Flemington, N. J., since 1928.

Moore, J. Layton, Supvg. Prin. of Sch., 417 Free St., Ridley Park, Pa.

Moore, James Alexander, B.Pd.'94, Southern Univ.; LL. D.'24, Univ. of Ala.; Co. Supt. of Sch., Jasper, Ala., since 1920.

Moore, James G., Supt. of Sch., Fargo, N. Dak.

Moore, John R., Diploma '22, State Tchrs. Col., Shippensburg, Pa.; B.S.'27, Ursinus Col.; Supvg. Prin. of Sch., 47 Centre Ave., Norristown, Pa., since 1927.

Moore, John W., B.S.'00, The Citadel; A.M. '13, Col. of Charleston; Supt. of Sch., H. S., Florence, S. C., since 1923.

Moore, M. E., A.M.'14, Univ. of Kansas; Supt. of Sch., Beaumont, Texas, since 1919.

Moore, Millard C., A.B.'07, Colby Col.; Ed. M.'27, Harvard Univ.; Supt. of Sch., College Highway, Southwick, Mass., since 1930.

Moore, Milton H., A.B.'21, M.A.'30, Texas Christian Univ.; Supt. of Sch., 409 E. Weatherford St., Fort Worth, Texas, since 1915.

Moore, R. L., A.B.'92, Ed.D.'27, Wake Forest Col.; Pres., Mars Hill Col., Mars Hill, N. C., since 1897.

Morales, Stella Marquez, Diploma '12, Univ. of Porto Rico; Supvr. of Sch., Salinas, P. R., since 1918.

Morehart, Grover C., Ph.D.'27, Columbia Univ.; Assoc. Prof. of Educ., Syracuse Univ., Syracuse, N. Y., since 1923.

Morelock, Oliver J., A.B.'92, Franklin and Marshall Col.; A.M.'20, Columbia Univ.; Co. Supt. of Sch., Newark, N. J., since 1913.

Morgan, Frederic Evan, A.B.'19, Washington Univ.; Dir., The Principia, St. Louis, Mo., since 1919.

Morgan, Lewis V., A.B.'13, Wheaton Col.; Co. Supt. of Sch., Court House, Wheaton, Ill., since 1921.

Morgan, Walter E., A.B.'19, M.A.'22, Univ. of Calif.; Chief, Division of Research and Statistics, State Dept. of Educ., Sacramento, Calif., since 1926.

Morgan, Walter P., Diploma '95, Ind. State Normal; A.B.'00, Ind. Univ.; Ph.M.'09, Univ. of Chicago; D.Ed.'26, Miami Univ.; Pres., Western Ill. State Tchrs. Col., Macomb, Ill., since 1912.

Morrill, T. C., A.B.'07, Bates Col.; A.M.'19, Tchrs. Col., Columbia Univ.; Supt. of Sch., Park Ridge, N. J., since 1930.

Morris, Charles A., B.S.'05, Rutgers Col.; Co. Supt. of Sch., Toms River, N. J., since 1906.

Morris, Frank A., B.A.'14, M.A.'20, Univ. of Maine; Supt. of Sch., Newport, N. H., since 1930.

Morris, Lyle L., B.S.'20, Drake Univ.; A.M. '26, Ph.D.'30, Tchrs. Col., Columbia Univ.; Supt. of Sch., Northport, N. Y., since 1930.

Morris, M. G., Ph.B.'09, Grove City Col.; Supt. of Sch., Natrona, Pa., since 1918.

Morris, W. B., Co. Supt. of Sch., Hartwell, Ga.

Morrisett, L. N., Prin., Roosevelt Jr. High Sch., Ninth and Klein, Oklahoma City, Okla.

Morrison, J. Cayce, A.B.'12, Valparaiso Univ.; M.A.'16, Ph.D.'22, Columbia Univ.; Asst. Commr. for Elem. Educ., State Educ. Dept., Albany, N. Y., since 1926.

Morse, Charles Kennedy, Diploma '09, Nebr. State Normal Sch., Peru, Nebr.; A.B.'14, Univ. of Nebr.; A.M.'30, Columbia Univ.; Supt., Nebr. Sch. of Agr., Curtis, Nebr., since 1919.

Morse, Frank P., A.B.'90, Bowdoin Col.; A. M.'01, Harvard Univ.; State Supvr. of Sec. Educ., State House, Boston, Mass., since 1923.

Mort, Paul R., Ph.D.'24, Columbia Univ.; Prof. of Educ. and Dir., Sch. of Educ., Tchrs. Col., Columbia Univ., New York, N. Y., since 1929.

Morton, Clifford A., A.B.'98, A.M.'02, Princeton Univ.; M.Pd.'19, New York Univ.; Asst. Supt. of Sch., Union City, N. J., since 1926.

Morton, H. D., A.B.'15, Ouachita Col.; Th. M.'18, Southwestern Baptist Theological Seminary, Ft. Worth, Texas; M.A.'30, George Peabody Col. for Tchrs.; Co. Supt. of Sch., Warren, Ark., since 1930.

Morton, Katharine A., State Supt. of Pub. Instr., Capitol Bldg., Cheyenne, Wyo.

Morton, Orion A., Diploma '00, State Normal Sch., Farmington, Maine; Union Supt. of Sch., 19 Bates St., Northampton, Mass., since 1923.

Morton, William Henry, A.B.'09, York Col.; A.M.'12, Univ. of Nebr.; A.M.'23, Columbia Univ.; Ph.D.'28, Univ. of Nebr.; Dir. of Tchr. Tr., Tchrs. Col., Univ. of Nebr., Lincoln, Nebr., since 1927.

Morton, William Morris, 330 E. 22nd St., Chicago, Ill.

Moseley, Clark C., Diploma '07, State Normal Col., Jacksonville, Ala.; A.B.'11, A. M.'29, Univ. of Ala.; Supt. of Sch., Dothan Ala., since 1922.

Moses, Kathryn T., Supt. of Sch., Santa Rita, N. Mex.

Mosher, Charles L., Ph.B.'99, Ph.M.'02, Hamilton Col.; Dir., Attendance Division, State Educ. Dept., Albany, N. Y., since 1927.

Mosiman, S. K., A.B.'97, Wittenberg Col.; B.D.'05, McCormick Theological Sem., Chicago, Ill.; Ph.D.'07, Univ. of Halle, Germany; Litt.D.'20, Wittenberg Col.; Pres., Bluffton Col., Bluffton, Ohio, since 1908.

Moss, John R., B.S.'21, Univ. of Ill.; Supt. of Sch., H. S., Paris, Ill., since 1922.

Mossman, Frank Earnest, Ph.B.'03, A.M.'05, Morningside Col.; D.D.'09, Upper Iowa Univ.; LL.D.'29, Southwestern Col.; Pres., Morningside Col., Sioux City, Iowa, since 1917.

Mossman, Mrs. Lois Coffey, B.S.'11, M.A.'20, Ph.D.'24, Tchrs. Col., Columbia Univ.; Asst. Prof. of Educ., Tchrs. Col., Columbia Univ., New York, N. Y., 1911 to 1913 and since 1917.

Mott, Hubert, B.S.'19, Wesley Univ.; Supt. of Sch., Seneca Falls, N. Y., since 1928.

Moulton, Onsville Joshua, B.A.'14, Bates Col.; Supvg. Prin. Twp. Sch., Neptune, N. J., since 1928.

Mowls, John Nelson, B.S. in Ed.'24, Kent State Col.; M.A.'28, Univ. of Pittsburgh; Supt. of Sch., Bellevue, Pa., since 1926.

Mowry, Wendell A., A.B.'93, A.M.'94, Brown Univ.; Supt. of Sch., Cohannet Sch. Bldg., Taunton, Mass., since 1922.

Moyer, Harry C., B.S.'21, Columbia Univ.; Co. Supt. of Sch., Lebanon, Pa., since 1926.

Moyers, Edison, A.B.'12, Tabor Col.; M.S. '22, Iowa State Col.; Supt. of Sch., Sidney, Iowa.

Moyse, George U., A.B.'97, Univ. of Calif.; Dist. Supt. of Sch. and Prin., Glendale Jr. Col. and H. S., 1440 E. Broadway, Glendale, Calif., since 1902.

Mueller, Rudolph C., B.A.'13, Fargo Col. Address: 7449 Warren Ave., Forest Park, Ill.

Muerman, J. C., A.B.'10, Washington State Col.; A.M.'16, Ph.D.'22, George Washington Univ.; Prof. of Rural Educ., Agrl. and Mech. Col., Stillwater, Okla., since 1930.

Mugan, Mary A. S., Ed.M.'27, Boston Univ.; Lecturer, Boston Univ., since 1923 and Asst. Supt. of Sch., Fall River, Mass., since 1913.

Muir, James N., B.S.'04, Univ. of Pa.; Supt. of Sch., Quincy, Mass., since 1926.

Mulford, Charles W., 366 Fifth Ave., New York, N. Y.

Mullen, J. O., A.B.'28, Univ. of Ariz.; Supt. of Sch., Jerome, Ariz., since 1918.

Mulrine, Clifford L., 2588 Richards St., Milwaukee, Wis.

Mummert, Ira C., Supvg. Prin. of Sch., Valley Stream, N. Y.

Munich, Austin Francis, Diocesan Sch. Supvr., St. Thomas Seminary, Bloomfield, Conn., since 1929.

Munn, J. B., B.S.'12, A.B.'16, Tri-State Col.; A.M.'24, Columbia Univ.; Supt. of Sch., Waterloo, Ind., since 1928.

Munroe, Frank D., A.B.'18, Lafayette Col.; Supt. of Sch., Phillipsburg, N. J., since 1930.

Munson, Irving, A.B.'13, Augustana Col.; A.M.'29, Univ. of Ill.; Supt. of Sch., Momence, Ill., since 1920.

Munson, J. M., Ph.B.'11, Univ. of Chicago; M.Pd.'13, Mich. State Normal Col., Ypsilanti, Mich.; Pres., Northern State Tchrs. Col., Marquette, Mich., since 1923.

Murphy, David R., A.B.'92, A.M.'95, Bethel Col.; Pres., State Normal Sch., Daphne, Ala., since 1924.

Murphy, J. W., A.B.'03, Univ. of Kansas; A.M.'26, Columbia Univ.; Supt. of Sch., Great Bend, Kansas, since 1926.

Murphy, Joseph E., A.B.'04, Univ. of Mich.; Supt. of Sch., Hurley, Wis., since 1904.

Murphy, Mary E., Ph.B.'05, Univ. of Chicago; Dir., Elizabeth McCormick Memorial Fund, 848 N. Dearborn St., Chicago, Ill., since 1925.

Murray, Donald A., A.B.'23, Olivet Col.; Supt. of Sch., H. S., Mason, Mich., since 1927.

Murray, Milo Clifton, A.B.'02, A.M.'09, Olivet Col.; Supt. of Sch., Michigan City, Ind., since 1926.

Musselman, Fren, A.B.'10, Ind. Univ.; A.M. '16, Columbia Univ.; Dept of Educ. and Psych., Kent State Col., Kent, Ohio, since 1924.

Myers, John C., B.A.'00, M.A.'03, Bridgewater Col.; Co. Supt. of Sch., Harrisonburg, Va., since 1917.

Myers, Orvil F., A.B.'18, Ohio Wesleyan Univ.; A.M.'22, Ph.D.'26, Univ. of Chicago; Los Angeles Jr. Col., 855 N. Vermont Ave., Los Angeles, Calif.

Mylin, Arthur P., Ph.B.'12, Franklin and Marshall Col.; Co. Supt. of Sch., 353 N. W. End Ave., Lancaster, Pa., since 1922.

Nanninga, Simon P., B.S.'16, State Tchrs. Col., Emporia, Kansas; M.A.'22. Leland Stanford Jr. Univ.; Ph.D.'25, Univ. of Calif.; Dean, Col. of Educ., Univ. of N. Mex., Albuquerque, N. Mex., since 1925.

Nash, G. W., B.S.'91, M.S.'95, LL.D.'11, Yankton Col.; LL.D.'23, Colo. Col.; LL. D.'24, Drury Col.; Pres., Yankton Col., Yankton, S. Dak., since 1925.

Nash, M. A., B.A.'10, M.A.'27, Univ. of Okla.; LL.D., Okla. Baptist Univ.; Pres., Okla. Col. for Women, Chickasha, Okla., since 1927.

Nash, Raymond W., B.S.'21, Colgate Univ.; M.A., Columbia Univ.; Supt. of Sch., 6 Battery St., Ticonderoga, N. Y., since 1925.

Naylor, Arthur H., A.B.'02, Hamilton Col.; Supt. of Sch., Port Jervis, N. Y., since 1913.

Neal, Elma A., B.A.'23, M.A.'26, Columbia Univ.; Asst. Supt. of Sch., San Antonio, Texas, since 1930.

Neale, Mervin Gordon, B.S. in Ed.'11, Univ. of Mo.; A.M.'17, Ph.D.'20, Tchrs. Col., Columbia Univ.; Pres., Univ. of Idaho, Moscow, Idaho, since 1930.

Neer, Mary L., B.S.'09, Tchrs. Col., Columbia Univ.; Supvr. of Primary Grades, 1401 Kaighn Ave., Camden, N. J.

Nefflen, Myra M., A.B.'16, W. Va. Univ.; M.A.'23, Columbia Univ.; Asst. State Supvr. of Rural Sch., State Dept. of Educ., Charleston, W. Va., since 1926.

Negron, Julio Fiol, Normal Sch. Diploma '14, Univ. of Porto Rico. Address: 2 Padre Isern St., Stop 43, Santurce, P. R.

Neidig, Joseph Shine, Supvg. Prin. of Sch., 310 Franklin St., Quakertown, Pa.

Neighbours, Owen J., A.B.'05, Western Md. Col.; Ph.M.'10, Univ. of Chicago; Supt. of Sch., Wabash, Ind., since 1916.

Neil, Jane A., Dist. Supt. of Sch., 550 Surf St., Chicago, Ill.

Nelson, Burton E., B.S.'91, M.S.'95, Western Normal Col.; Pres., The Stout Inst., Menomonie, Wis., since 1923.

Nelson, Edwin J., Supt. of Sch., 214 Monmouth Ave., Lakewood, N. J.

Nelson, George O., B.A.'25, Luther Col., Decorah, Iowa; Supt. of Sch., Bigelow, Minn., since 1929.

Nelson, Gertrude M., Co. Supt. of Sch., Sidney, Nebr., since 1927.

Nelson, H. G., 525 S. Ross, Santa Ana, Calif.

Nelson, John V., M.S.'09, Ohio Northern Univ.; Supt. of Sch., 4490 Noble St., Bellaire, Ohio, since 1918.

Nelson, Thomas Hawley, A.B.'13, Otterbein Col.; Sr. Secy., Educational Serv., Natl. Council, Y. M. C. A., 347 Madison Ave., New York, N. Y., since 1928.

Nelson, William E., A.B.'10, Baker Univ.; A.M.'23, Univ. of Chicago; Prin., H. S., 341 S. 12th St., Quincy, Ill., since 1924.

Nelson, William J., B.S.'11, Trinity Col., Hartford, Conn.; Union Supt. of Sch., Plaistow, N. H., since 1927.

Nera, Venancio, 1559 Highland, Columbus, Ohio.

Neulen, Leon Nelson, A.B.'16, St. Olaf Col.; M.A.'21, Columbia Univ.; Supt. of Sch., Champaign, Ill., since 1928.

Neulen, Lester N., B.A.'16, St. Olaf Col.; M.A.'23, Ph.D.'28, Columbia Univ.; Supvg. Prin. of Twp. Schools, Teaneck, N. J., since 1928. Address: 452 Ogden Ave., West Englewood, N. J.

Neveln, Edward W., Supt of Sch., Ankeny, Iowa.

Neveln, S. T., A.B.'16, Iowa State Tchrs. Col.; Dist. Supt. of Sch., Austin, Minn., since 1921.

Neverth, Albert A., A.B.'23, A.M.'27, Univ. of Mich.; Supt. of Sch., Roseville, Mich., since 1922.

Neville, E. L., Supt. of Sch., 217 Hudson Ave., Monroe, La.

Newbury, Maud C., B.S.'12, A.M.'21, Columbia Univ.; Co. Supt. of Sch., Currituck, N. C., since 1924.

Newell, J. E., A.B.'97, A.M.'04, Otterbein Col.; M.A.'23, Ohio State Univ.; Prin., Barrett Jr. H. S., 274 N. Hague Ave., Columbus, Ohio, since 1924.

Newell, William Atwood, Ed.M.'28, R. I. Col. of Educ.; Supt. of Sch., 1093 Central Ave., Pawtucket, R. I., since 1922.

Newlon, Jesse H., A.B.'07, Ind. Univ.; A. M.'14, Columbia Univ.; LL.D.'22, Univ. of Denver; Pres., Natl. Educ. Assn., 1924-25; Prof. of Educ. and Dir. of Lincoln Sch., Tchrs. Col., Columbia Univ., 425 W. 123rd St., New York, N. Y., since 1927.

Newman, Ross B., A.B.'06, Univ. of Wis.; Supt. of Sch., Oskaloosa, Iowa, since 1923.

Newton, Arthur E., A.B.'04, A.M.'07, Hamilton Col.; Supt. of Sch., H. S., Baldwin, L. I., N. Y., since 1922.

Newton, Ralph, A.B.'97, Mercer Univ.; Supt. of Sch., Waycross, Ga., since 1928.

Newton, Robert M., L.I.'15, B.S.'16, Col. of William and Mary; Div. Supt. of Sch., Court House, Hampton, Va., since 1923.

Nichols, Claude Andrew, B.A.'98, Southwestern Univ.; Ph.D.'05, Univ. of Havana, Cuba; Head, Dept. of Educ., Southern Methodist Univ., since 1919 and Dir., Sch. of Educ., Southern Methodist Univ., Dallas, Texas, since 1928.

Nichols, Harold E., B.S. in Ed.'27, Ohio Univ.; M.A.'30, Tchrs. Col., Columbia Univ.; Supt. of Sch., H. S. Bldg., Frankfort, Ohio, since 1930.

Nichols, Raymond A., B.S.'28, Central State Tchrs. Col., Edmond, Okla.; Supt. of Sch., Hominy, Okla., since 1928.

Nicholson, Jane H., Diploma '07, B.S.'08, M.A.'09, Tchrs. Col., Columbia Univ.; Asst. Dir. of Kdgns., P. S. No. 76, 921 Lexington Ave., New York, N. Y., since 1914.

Nickerson, Frederick M., Diploma '05, East Maine State Normal Sch.; Supt. of Sch., Newport, Maine.

Nickerson, William A., Diploma '06, State Normal Sch., Hyannis, Mass.; B.S. in Ed. '23, Boston Univ.; Supt. of Sch., Washington St., Holliston, Mass., since 1928.

Nicklas, Victor C., A.B.'17, Univ. of Pittsburgh; M.A.'23, Columbia Univ.; Supt. of Sch., Memorial H. S., Millville, N. J., since 1930.

Nielsen, P. M., Co. Supt. of Sch., Tooele, Utah.

Nilsson, R. F., A.B.'17, Brigham Young Univ.; Supt., Wasatch Co. Sch. Dist., Heber, Utah, since 1923.

Nisbet, S. S., A.B.'19, Alma Col.; M.A.'30, Univ. of Mich.; Supt. of Sch., Fremont, Mich., since 1923.

Nissen, Harry, B.S.'14, Mass. Agrl. Col.; Diploma '23, Posse Normal Sch. of Gymnastics; Pres., Posse-Nissen Sch. of Physical Educ., 779 Beacon St., Boston, Mass., since 1924.

Noble, Edward Martin, Co. Supt. of Sch., Denton, Md., since 1905.

Noble, James B., A.B.'98, A.M.'12, St. John's Col., Annapolis, Md.; Co. Supt. of Sch., Cambridge, Md., since 1916.

Noetling, Franklin S., Ph.B.'13, Heidelberg Col.; A.M.'29, Columbia Univ.; Supvg. Prin. of Sch., Trevorton, Pa., since 1929.

Nolan, Walter C., B.S.'12, Univ. of Calif.; Deputy Supt. of Sch. in charge of Personnel, Certification, and Retirement, City Hall, San Francisco, Calif., since 1926.

Nolcox, Matthias, 2866 Highland Pl., Indianapolis, Ind.

Nolte, K. F., B.A.'12, Iowa State Tchrs. Col.; Supt. of Hudson Consol. Sch. and Assoc. Prof. of Rural Educ., Iowa State Tchrs. Col., Hudson, Iowa, since 1926.

Noonan, Joseph F., Pd.B.'09, Pd.M.'14, State Tchrs. Col., Millersville, Pa.; Ph.B. '23, Muhlenberg Col.; A.M.'25, Ph.D.'26, New York Univ.; Supt. of Sch., 125 W. Centre St., Mahanoy City, Pa., since 1914.

North, Samuel Maith, B.S.'12, A.M.'13, Tchrs. Col., Columbia Univ.; Litt.D.'25, Western Md. Col.; State Supvr. of High Schools for Md., 2014 Lexington Bldg., Baltimore, Md., since 1916.

North, Ward T., B.S.'15, Drake Univ.; Supt. of Sch., Corydon, Iowa, since 1925.

Norton, John K., A.B.'16, A.M.'17, Stanford Univ.; Ph.D.'26, Tchrs. Col., Columbia Univ.; Visiting Prof., Tchrs. Col., Columbia Univ., New York, N. Y., 1930-31; Dir. of Research, Natl. Educ. Assn., 1201 16th St., N. W., Washington, D. C., since 1922.

Norton, Margaret Alltucker (Mrs. John K.) B.L.'14, M.A.'19, Ph.D.'22, Univ. of Calif.; Assoc. Dir., Research Div., Natl. Educ. Assn., 1201 16th St., N. W., Washington, D. C., since 1923.

Norton, Warren P., A.B.'15, Brown Univ.; A.M.'23, Tchrs. Col., Columbia Univ.; Supt. of Sch., Meadville, Pa.

Norvell, George W., M.A., Oxford Univ., Englald; State Supvr. of English, State Educ. Bldg., Albany, N. Y., since 1928.

Nourse, Laurence G., A.B.'17, Dartmouth Col.; A.M.'20, Harvard Univ.; Supt. of Sch., Norton and Plainville, Mass., since 1924. Address: Norton, Mass.

Noyes, Charles H., B.L.'92, Dartmouth Col.; Supt. of Sch., 25 Auburn St., Nashua, N. H., since 1920.

Noyes, Ernest C., A.B.'98, Yale; A.M.'00, Harvard; Asst. Co. Supt. of Sch., 610 Shady Drive, E., S. Hills Sta., Pittsburgh, Pa., since 1917.

Noyes, William B., A.B.'95, Harvard; Supt. of Sch., East Haven, Conn., since 1923.

Noyes, William E., B.A.'11, Macalester Col.; Dist. Supt. of Sch., Tower, Minn., since 1922.

Nugent, James A., A.B.'98, A.M.'99, St. Peter's Col.; LL.D.24, Seton Hall Col.; Ph.D.'26, Fordham Univ.; Supt. of Sch., Admin. Bldg., 2 Harrison Ave., Jersey City, N. J., since 1924.

Nugent, M. E., B.A.'10, Carleton Col.; M.A. '26, Ed.D.'30, Univ. of N. Dak.; Supt. Univ. H. S., Univ. of N. Dak., Grand Forks, N. Dak.

Nunn, W. N., A.B.'27, Oglethorpe Univ.; Supt. of Sch., Buford, Ga., since 1909.

Nurnberger, T. S., A.B.'26, M.A.'29, Univ. of Mich.; Supt. of Sch., Oscoda, Mich., since 1930.

Nusbaum, Louis, B.S.'08, Ped.D.'30, Temple Univ.; Assoc. Supt. of Sch., Keystone Bldg., 19th and Ludlow Sts., Philadelphia, Pa., since 1915.

Nuttall, James A., B.S.'26, Brigham Young Univ.; Co. Supt. of Sch., Huntington, Utah, since 1926.

Nuttall, L. John, Jr., B.S.'11, A.M.'12, Columbia Univ.; Dean. Col. of Educ., Brigham Young Univ., Provo, Utah, since 1923.

Nygaard, E. L., Supt. of Sch., Kenilworth, Ill., since 1923.

Nystrom, Wendell C., A.B.'14, Bethany Col.; Supt., Community H. S., Norton, Kansas, since 1921.

Oakes, Ralph G., B.Pd.'18, M.A. in Ed.'28, Univ. of Maine; Union Supt. of Sch., Freeport, Maine, since 1925.

O'Bannon, Maurice N., A.B.'17, Ind. Univ.; A.M.'25, Columbia Univ.; Supt. of Sch., 217 E. Sixth St., Mt. Vernon, Ind., since 1925.

Oberholtzer, Edison Ellsworth, Ph.B.'10, M.A.'15, Univ. of Chicago; LL.D.'21, Univ. of Tulsa; Supt. of Sch., Houston, Texas, since 1924.

Oberholtzer, K. E., B.S.'24, Univ. of Ill.; M.S.'28, Agrl. and Mech. Col. of Texas; Supt. of Sch., El Campo, Texas, since 1928.

O'Brien, Ida, B.S. in Sch. Supvn. '27, State Univ. of Iowa; Southern Oregon Normal Sch., Ashland, Oregon.

Obuch, W. A., Supt. of Sch., Lamont, Okla., since 1922.

O'Connor, Mary Elizabeth, B.S. in Ed. and M.E.'25, Boston Univ.; Supvr. of Elem. Sch., Sch. Dept., Natick, Mass., since 1926.

Oday, H. A., Ph.B.'99, Syracuse Univ.; Supt. of Sch., Mahanoy City, Pa., since 1916.

O'Dell, Clyde H., B.S.'22, State Tchrs. Col., Pittsburg, Kansas; A. B. '28, Univ. of Mo.; Supt. of Sch., Miami, Okla., since 1928.

Odgers, Harry Elliott, A.B.'02, Dickinson Col.; Supt. of Sch., Parkersburg, W. Va., since 1918.

O'Donnell, William F., A.B.'12, Transylvania Col.; Supt. of Sch., Richmond, Ky., since 1926.

Offenhauer, R. E., B.S.'03, Marion Normal Col.; A.B.'05, Otterbein Col.; A.M.'17, Columbia Univ.; Supt. of Sch., Lima, Ohio, since 1924.

Offerman, Elizabeth J., B.S. in Ed.'20, State Normal Sch., Bowling Green, Ohio; Asst. Co. Supt. of Sch., Oak Harbor, Ohio, since 1923.

Offerman, Kate M., B.S.'20, State Normal Sch., Bowling Green, Ohio; Asst. Co. Supt. of Sch., Bowling Green, Ohio, since 1929.

Ogan, R. W., 158 Harper St., New Concord, Ohio.

Ogden, Benjamin E., A.B.'13, Cotner Col.; Head, Dept. of Educ., Prof. of Educ., and Dir. of Summer Sch., Cotner Col., Lincoln, Nebr., since 1927.

Ogle, Fletcher A., A.B.'06, Ind. Univ.; A.M. '27, Colo. State Tchrs. Col.; Co. Supt. of Sch., 1940 Tenth Ave., Greeley, Colo., since 1925.

Oglee, Frank J., Diploma '12, New York Univ.; Supvg. Prin. of Sch., East Rutherford, N. J., since 1896.

O'Hara, Donald, Supt. of Sch., East Lansing, Mich.

O'Hern, Francis J., A.B.'14, A.M.'16, St. Louis Univ.; Pres., St. Mary's Col., St. Marys, Kansas, since 1928.

O'Hern, Joseph P., A.B.'92, A.M.'94, Univ. of Rochester; Pd.D.'30, State Col. for Tchrs., Albany, N. Y.; Deputy Supt. of Sch., 300 Educ. Bldg., Rochester, N. Y., since 1929.

Ohlson, Henry C., B.S.'23, Ohio State Univ.; Dir., Health and Physical Educ., Lincoln Jr. H. S., Huntington, W. Va., since 1924.

Ohrt, Alta S., Diploma '08, State Tchrs. Col., Chico, Calif.; Co. Supt. of Sch., 421 Lincoln St., Red Bluff, Calif., since 1929.

Ojemann, Ralph H., B.S.'23, M.S.'24, Univ. of Ill.; Ph.D.'29, Univ. of Chicago; Research Assoc. in Parent Educ., Iowa Child Welfare Research Sta., State Univ. of Iowa, Iowa City, Iowa, since 1929.

Oldham, James R. D., A.B.'97, Brown Univ.; Supt. of Sch., 184 Taunton Ave., East Providence, R. I., since 1911.

O'Leary, John, A.B.'10, Antioch Col.; Supt. of Sch., Eaton, Ohio, since 1910.

O'Leary, Wesley A., B.S.'95, Dartmouth Col.; Asst. State Commr. of Educ., Trenton, N. J., since 1918.

Oliver, George J., Div. Supt. of Sch., Cape Charles, Va., since 1927.

Oliver, Stanley C., B.S.'19, M.S.'26, Pa. State Col.; Prof. of Rural Educ., Southwestern Mo. State Tchrs. Col., Springfield, Mo., since 1929.

Oliver, W. W., A.B.'23, Muskingum Col.; A.M.'27, Columbia Univ.; Supt. of Sch., Caldwell, Ohio, since 1924.

Oliver, William I., B.S. in Ed.'16, A.M. '26, Univ. of Mo.; Supt. of Sch., 910 Rogers St., Columbia, Mo., since 1920.

Olson, Oscar A., Bd. of Educ., Keewatin, Minn.

O'Malley, Margaret, B.S.'27, Univ. of Buffalo; Prin., Elem. Sch. No. 66, Tacoma and Parkside Aves., Buffalo, N. Y., since 1909.

Oman, C. H., A.B.'27, Univ. of Colo.; Supt. of Sch., 122 E. Second, Garnett, Kansas, since 1901.

Omo, Charles Howard, A.B.'15, Juniata Col.; M.A.'28, Pa. State Col.; Supt. of Sch., Vandergrift, Pa., since 1917.

Oppelt, J. L., A.B.'20, Otterbein Col.; Supt. of Sch., Avon Lake, Ohio, since 1925.

Opstad, Iver A., B.A.'11, Luther Col.; M.A. '19, State Univ. of Iowa; Supt. of Sch., 530 E. Jefferson St., Iowa City, Iowa, since 1920.

Orem, Nicholas, A.B.'98, A.M.'10, St. Johns Col., Annapolis, Md.; A.M.'10, Tchrs. Col., Columbia Univ.; Co. Supt. of Sch., Upper Marlboro, Md., since 1921.

Orner, Lawrence T., M.A.'28, Columbia Univ.; Supvg. Prin. of Sch., Orangeville, Pa., since 1930.

Orr, Estelle B., B.Sc.'30, Western Reserve Univ.; Prin., Lafayette Sch., 12415 Abell Ave., Cleveland, Ohio, since 1916.

Ortiz, J. Vasquez, Supvr. of Sch., P. O. Box 338, 82 Muñoz Rivera St., Fajardo, P. R., since 1918.

Osborn, G. Henry, Supvg. Prin. of Twp. Sch., Livingston, N. J., since 1913.

Osborne, Raymond W., B.A.'06, Yale Col.; M.A.'08, Yale Univ.; Asst. Prin., Francis W. Parker Sch., 330 Webster Ave., Chicago, Ill., since 1922.

Osburn, W. J., A.B.'03, Central Col.; A.M. '04, Vanderbilt Univ.; B.S. in Ed.'11, Univ. of Mo.; Ph.D.'21, Columbia Univ.; State Dir. of Educ. Research and Prof. of Sch. Admin., Ohio State Univ., Columbus, Ohio, since 1928.

O'Shea, William J., B.A., Col. of the City of New York; B.S., M.S., Manhattan Col.; LL.D., Fordham Univ.; Supt. of Sch., 500 Park Ave., New York, N. Y., since 1924.

Osuna, J. J., A.B.'12, Pa. State Col.; A.M. '20, Ph.D.'23, Columbia Univ.; Dean, Col. of Educ., Univ. of Porto Rico, Rio Piedras, P. R., since 1928.

Otero-Warren, Mrs. Adelina, Co. Supt. of Sch., Santa Fe, N. Mex., since 1927.

Otis, Arthur S., A.B.'10, A.M.'15, Ph.D.'20, Stanford Univ. Address: 313 Park Hill Ave., Yonkers, N. Y.

Otis, E. M., Ph.B.'03, Adelbert Col., Western Reserve Univ.; A.M.'20, Tchrs. Col., Columbia Univ.; Supt. of Sch., Willoughby, Ohio, since 1909.

Ott, Emory D., A.B.'12, Gettsyburg Col.; M.A.'25, Columbia Univ.; Supvg. Prin. of Sch., Barnesboro, Pa., since 1920.

Ott, Hal Lee, Supvr., **Primary Grades,** 19 Rosemont Ave., Frederick, Md.

Ottermann, Charles, B.A.'06, M.A.'08, Univ. of Cincinnati; M.A.'15, Columbia Univ.; Asst. Supt. of Sch., 216 E. Ninth St., Cincinnati, Ohio, since 1922.

Otto, Henry J., M.A.'27, Univ. of Minn.; Asst. Prof., Sch. of Educ., Northwestern Univ., Evanston, Ill., since 1930.

Overberger, Edwin W., A.B.'28, Univ. of Pittsburgh; Supvg. Prin. of Sch., Keystone Ave., Cresson, Pa., since 1923.

Overmyer, J. F., M.A.'24, Ohio Northern Univ.; Supt. of Sch., Algona, Iowa, since 1904.

Overn, A. V., B.A.'15, M.S.'26, Ph.D.'30, Univ. of Minn.; Prof. of Educ.. Univ. of N. Dak., Univ. Sta., Grand Forks, N. Dak., since 1930.

Overturf, Jesse R., B.A.'20, Univ. of Nebr.; M.A.'23, Stanford Univ.; Deputy Supt. of Sch., 1524 36th St., Sacramento, Calif.

Owen, Helen Mildred, B.S.'18, Tchrs. Col., Columbia Univ.; Managing Editor, Normal Instructor and Primary Plans, 514-516 Cutler Bldg., Rochester, N. Y.

Owen, Mary E., A.B.'17, Smith Col.; A. M.'20, Univ. of Chicago; Assoc. Editor, Normal Instructor and Primary Plans, 514-516 Cutler Bldg., Rochester, N. Y.

Owens, Anderson D., A.B.'18, M.A.'26, Transylvania Col.; Supt. of Sch., Newport, Ky., since 1925.

Owens, Morgan R., A.B.'14, Ouachita Col.; M.A.'24, George Peabody Col. for Tchrs.; State H. S. Supvr., State Dept. of Educ., Little Rock, Ark., since 1925.

Oxnam, G. Bromley, A.B.'13, Univ. of Southern Calif.; S.T.B.'15, Boston Univ.; D.D.'25. Col. of the Pacific; LL.D.'29, Ohio Wesleyan Univ.; LL.D.'29, Wabash Col.; Litt.D.'30, Boston Univ.; Pres., De-Pauw Univ., Admin. Bldg., Greencastle, Ind., since 1928.

Packard, Bertram E., A.B.'00, Bates Col.; LL.B.'10, Univ. of Maine; State Commr. of Educ., State House, Augusta, Maine, since 1929.

Packer, P. C., A.B.'18, State Univ. of Iowa; M.A.'21, Univ of Mich.; Ph.D.'23, Tchrs. Col., Columbia Univ.; Dean, Col. of Educ., State Univ. of Iowa, Iowa City, Iowa, since 1923.

Paden, William Guy, B.A.'08, Univ. of Calif.; J.D.'16, Kent; Supt. of Sch., City Hall, Alameda, Calif., since 1925.

Page, A. R., B.A.'15. Washburn Col.; Supt. of Sch., H.S., Whitewater, Wis., since 1920.

Page, Fred J., L.I.'82, M.A.'00. Peabody Col.; Co. Supt. of Sch., Franklin, Tenn., since 1898.

Page, John Caleb, B.S.'08, Univ. of N. H.; Ed.M.'24. Ed.D.'28 Harvard Univ.; Union Supt. of Sch., West Newbury, Mass., since 1928.

Page, John S., A.B.'22, M.A.'24. Univ. of Mich.; Supt. of Sch., 402 E. Clinton St. Howell, Mich., since 1922.

Painter, J. E., Supvr. of Indus. Arts, Bd. of Educ., Minneapolis, Minn., since 1893.

Painter, Walter S., A.M.'14, Columbia; Supt. of Sch., Garrett, Ind., since 1925.

Palmer, A. Ray, Diploma'11, State Normal Sch., Cortland, N. Y.; Supvg. Prin. of Sch., Ridgefield Park, N. J., since 1918.

Palmer, Bertha R., Diploma'03, State Tchrs. Col., Mayville, N. Dak.; State Supt. of Pub. Instr., State Capitol, Bismarck, N. Dak., since 1927.

Palmer, C. E., B.S. in Ed.'20, Ohio Northern Univ.; A.M.'27, Columbia Univ.; Supt. of Sch., 48 W. North Ave., East Palestine, Ohio, since 1928.

Palmer, G. Lloyd, B.S.'25, Johns Hopkins Univ.; Co. Supt. of Sch., Frederick, Md., since 1914.

Palmer, Luella A., B.S.'06, M.A.'15, Columbia Univ.; Dir. of Kdgn., 424 E. 57th St., New York, N. Y., since 1921.

Palmer, Rufus H., A.B.'09, A.M.'12, Univ. of Denver; A.M.'24, Tchrs. Col., Columbia Univ.; Asst. Supt. of Sch. in charge of Elem. Educ., Denver, Colo.

Palmore, R. A., A.B.'24. Ky. State Tchrs. Col., Bowling Green, Ky.; Supt. of Sch., Glasgow, Ky., since 1924.

Pape, Nina Anderson, Prin., The Pape Sch., Savannah, Ga., since 1900.

Park, James Holt, Supvg. Prin of Sch., Orlando, Fla.

Park, James Williams, A.B.'03, Amherst Col.; A.M.'15, Harvard Univ.; Chmn., Dept. of Educ., Adelphi Col., Garden City, N. Y., since 1916.

Parke, Newcomb Gilbert, Supt. of Sch., 664 E. Greene St., Waynesburg, Pa.

Parker, A. Courtney, Supt. of Sch., Chelsea, Vt.

Parker, C. A., B.A.'16, Hendrix Col.; M.A. '28, Univ. of Okla.; Supt. of Sch., 821 Flynn St., Alva, Okla., since 1925.

Parker, Ernest, A.B.'87, Ky. Military Inst.; Prin., Jr. H. S., 3123 Travis Ave., Ft. Worth, Texas, since 1918.

Parker, Robert C. B., Supvg. Prin. of Sch., Mt. Holly, N. J.

Parker, W. E., A.B.'14, Univ. of Mich.; Supt. of Sch., Rochester, Mich., since 1919.

Parker, Walter W., A.B.'12, Hendrix Col.; A.M.'15, Columbia Univ.; Pres., Northwestern State Tchrs. Col., Alva, Okla., since 1928.

Parker, William E., B.S.'99, Wesleyan Univ., Middletown, Conn.; Supt. of Sch., Danielson, Conn., since 1924.

Parker, Wylie A., B.S.'07, Baylor Univ.; Prin., Forest Ave. H. S., Dallas, Texas, since 1920.

Parkinson, Burney Lynch, B.S.'09, Erskine Col.; A.M.'20, Ph.D.'26, George Peabody Col. for Tchrs.; Dir. of Tchr. Tr., State Dept. of Educ., Montgomery, Ala.

Parkinson, William D., A.B.'78, Dartmouth Col.; LL.B.'81, Natl. Univ.; Lecturer, Boston Univ., Boston, Mass. Address: 321 Highland Ave., Fitchburg, Mass.

Parkman, Edgar H., B.A.'89, Amherst Col.; Supt. of Sch., Enfield, Conn., since 1926. Address: 35 Franklin St., Thompsonville, Conn.

Parmer, Wayne Rutter, B.S.'19, Franklin and Marshall Col.; M.A.'23, Univ. of Pa.; Supt. of Sch., 311 West Ave., Jenkintown, Pa., since 1926.

Partch, Clarence E., B.S. in M.E.'09, Univ. of Mich.; Ed.M.'25, Ed.D.'26, Harvard Univ.; Dean, Sch. of Educ. and Dir. of Summer Session, Rutgers Univ., New Brunswick, N. J., since 1927.

Partridge, H. R., A.B.'13, Nebr. Wesleyan Univ.; Supt. of Sch., Alliance, Nebr., since 1923.

Pate, W. R., A.B.'17, Univ of Nebr.; A.M. '29, Columbia Univ.; Pres., State Tchrs. Col., Peru, Nebr., since 1923.

Pate, Wylie G., Supvg. Prin. of Sch., 17 Stokes Ave., Westmont, N. J.

Patrick, W. Burton, Supt. of Sch., Orange, N. J.

Patterson, Herbert, B.A.'08, M.A.'11, Wesleyan Univ., Middletown, Conn.; M.A.'11, Ph.D.'13, Yale Univ.; Dean, Sch. of Educ. and Dir. of Summer Sch., Okla. Agrl. and Mech. Col., Stillwater, Okla., since 1919.

Patterson, James Howard, A.B.'14, W. Va. Univ.; A.M.'20, Columbia Univ.; Dist. Supt. of Sch., Thomas, W. Va., since 1921.

Patterson, John R., Ph.B.'14, Wooster Col.; M.A.'26, Columbia Univ.; Supvg. Prin. of Sch., Roselle, N. J.

Patterson, Walter B., A.B.'83, Dartmouth Col.; LL.B.'85, LL.M.'86, George Washington Univ.; A.M.'88, Dartmouth Col.; Supvr. of Special Sch. and Activities, Franklin School Bldg., 13th and K Sts., N. W., Washington, D. C., since 1906.

Patterson, Weldon M., Supt. of Sch., Chickamauga, Ga.

Patty, Willard Walter, A.B.'14, Iowa State Tchrs. Col.; M.A.'20, Ph.D.'25, Univ. of Calif.; Prof. of H. S. Admin. and Sec. Educ., Ind. Univ., Bloomington, Ind., since 1927.

Paul, Arthur G., A.B.'09, Occidental Col.; Dir., Jr. Col., Riverside, Calif., since 1920.

Pauley, James J., B.S.'15, Waynesburg Col.; Supvg. Prin. of Sch., Luzerne Twp., Fayette Co., South Brownsville, Pa., since 1924.

Paulin, Eugene A., B.S.'09, Univ. of Dayton; M.S.'12, Univ. of Fribourg, Switzerland; Ph.D.'29, Univ. of Texas; Insp. of Sch., Maryhurst Normal, Kirkwood, Mo., since 1929.

Pauly, Frank R., Diploma '14, Central Tchrs. Col.; B.A.'17, Univ. of Okla.; M.A. '25, Columbia Univ.; Dir. of Research, Bd. of Educ., 410 S. Cincinnati, Tulsa, Okla., since 1929.

Paxton, W. A., B.S.'23, Brigham Young Univ.; Co. Supt. of Sch., Duchesne, Utah, since 1925.

Payne, Bruce R., Pres., George Peabody Col. for Tchrs., Nashville, Tenn.

Peacock, Joseph Leishman, A.B.'00, Brown Univ.; A.M.'02, Harvard; D.D.'21, Colby Col.; D.D.'25, Brown Univ.; Pres., Shaw Univ., Raleigh, N. C., since 1920.

Peairs, Hervey B., Supt., Haskell Inst., Lawrence, Kansas, since 1930.

Pearce, Webster H., A.B.'04, Albion Col.; A.M.'12, Univ. of Mich.; LL.D.'28, Albion Col.; State Supt. of Pub. Instr., 608 Seymour Ave., Lansing, Mich., since 1927.

Pearsall, Carl C., B.S.'24, M.A.'26, Univ. of Pittsburgh; Supvg. Prin of Sch., 573 Fourth St., Pitcairn, Pa., since 1928.

Pearse, Carroll Gardner, LL.D.'14, N. H. State Col.; Pres., Natl. Educ. Assn., 1911-12. Address: 315 Ludington Ave., Milwaukee, Wis.

Pearson, Irving F., B.S.'22, Univ. of Ill.; Co. Supt. of Sch., Court House, Rockford, Ill., since 1927.

Pearson, M. E., B.D.'85, Univ. of Kansas; A.M., Baker Univ.; Supt. of Sch., Kansas City, Kansas, since 1902.

Pearson, Parker T., A.B.'99, Colby Col.; Supt. of Sch., Weymouth H. S., East Weymouth, Mass., since 1909.

Pease, J. E., A.B.'29, Central State Tchrs. Col., Mt. Pleasant, Mich.; Supt. of Sch., North Muskegon, Mich., since 1930.

Pease, T. H., A.B.'18, Nebr. State Tchrs. Col., Kearney, Nebr.; Supt. of Sch., Summit, Ill., since 1929.

Pebly, Harry E., A.B.'17, Thiel Col.; Supvg. Prin of Sch., Sharpsville, Pa., since 1928.

Peck, Lora B., Diploma '04, Peabody Col.; A.B.'28, Sam Houston State Tchrs. Col., Huntsville, Texas; Dir. of Elem. Grades, Great Southern Life Bldg., Houston, Texas, since 1925.

Peck, William R., B.A.'16, M.A.'20, Holy Cross Col.; Supt. of Sch., 98 Suffolk St., Holyoke, Mass., since 1920.

Peebles, James Fernald, A.B.'16, Boston Univ.; Supt. of Sch., Bourne and Sandwich, Mass., since 1927. Address: Bourne, Mass.

Peet, John Herbert, A.B.'16, Cornell Col.; M.A.'28, Univ. of Chicago; Supt. of Sch., H. S. Bldg., Washington, Iowa, since 1925.

Peirce, W. M., Ph.B.'99, Ill. Wesleyan Univ.; Ph.D.'13, Grove City Col.; Supt. of Sch., Ridgway, Pa., since 1897.

Peixotto, Bridget Caulfield, Diploma '95, Hunter Col. of the City of New York; Prin., Pub. Sch. No. 108, Queens, New York, N. Y., since 1918.

Pence, A. C., B.A.'08, Ohio Wesleyan Univ.; Supt. of Sch., 514 S. Seventh St., Coshocton, Ohio, since 1925.

Pence, W. G., A.B.'12, B.S.'21, State Tchrs. Col., Kirksville, Mo.; M.S.'22, Univ. of Chicago; Supt. of Sch., Fairfield, Iowa, since 1927.

Penley, F. J., B.S.'18, Univ. of Maine; M.A. '26, Columbia Univ. Address: Unionville, Conn.

Pennell, Mary E., B.S.'11, A.M.'18, Tchrs. Col., Columbia Univ. Address: Butler Hall, 119th St. and Morningside Dr., New York, N. Y.

Peregoy, C. G., A.B.'23, Wash. Col.; Dist. Supt. of Sch., Glen Hedrick, W. Va., since 1930.

Perham, Mrs. Grace S., Asst. Co. Supt. of Sch., Gravity, Pa., since 1919.

Perkins, John W., 1534 N. Charles St., Decatur, Ill.

Perley, S. Todd, Supt of Sch., 911 Malvern Rd., Avalon, Pittsburgh, Pa.

Perrin, Ethel, 370 Seventh Ave., New York, N. Y.

Perrin, H. Ambrose, Diploma '03, Ill. State Normal Univ., Normal, Ill; Ph.B.'12, Univ. of Chicago; M.S.'16, James Milliken Univ.; M.A.'22, Univ. of Chicago; Supt. of Sch., Library Bldg., Joliet, Ill., since 1922.

Perry, Arthur C., Ph.D.'92, New York Univ.; Dist. Supt. of Sch., New York, N. Y., since 1913. Address: 226 Halsey St., Brooklyn, N. Y.

Perry, Charles F., B.S.'94, Worcester Polytech. Inst.; M.E.'04, Cornell Univ.; Asst. Supt. of Sch. in charge or Indus. Educ., Milwaukee, Wis., since 1906.

Perry, Nellie A., Supvr. of Americanization, since 1920; Supvr. of Practical Arts, since 1925. Address: School Dept., Quincy, Mass.

Perry, William H., A.B.93, A.M.'96, Syracuse Univ.; Pd.B.'96, State Normal Col., Albany, N. Y.: Pd.M.'08, Ph.D.'09, New York Univ.; Supt. of Sch., City Hall, Leominster, Mass., since 1914.

Pesta, Rose A., B.L.'02, M.L.'03, Univ. of Wis.; Asst. Supt. of Sch., 460 S. State St., Chicago, Ill., since 1928.

Peters, E. C., B.A. and B.S.A.'16, Univ. of Tenn.; M.A.'25, Univ. of Chicago; Pres., Paine Col., 1235 15th St., Augusta, Ga., since 1929.

Peters, Martin L., B.S.'13, Gettysburg Col.; A.M.'24, Univ. of Pa.; Supt. of Sch., Phoenixville, Pa., since 1924.

Peters, Stacy Eugene, B.A.'08, M.A.'11, Gettysburg Col.; M.A.'25, Univ. of Pa.; Prin., Senior High Schools, Lancaster, Pa., since 1930.

Petersen, Louis A., A.B.'12, Univ. of Utah; Supt. of Sch., 170 N. Church Ave., Logan, Utah, since 1926.

Peterson, Amos T., Supt. of Sch., Billings, Mont., since 1929.

Peterson, Charles A., B.S.'93, Natl. Normal Univ., Lebanon, Ohio; Supt. of Sch., Brady, Texas, since 1925.

Peterson, Elmer T., Col. of Educ., State Univ. of Iowa, Iowa City, Iowa.

Peterson, M. V., B.S.'98, Natl. Normal Univ., Lebanon, Ohio; Supt. of Sch., Rosenberg, Texas, since 1928.

Petit, L. H., A.B.'10, Campbell Col.; Supt. of Sch., 410 S. Highland, Chanute, Kansas, since 1923.

Petty, A. F., Intermediate Supvr. of Sch., Belleville, Ill.

Pfaff, Caroline S., B. O.'14, New Orleans Col. of Oratory; B.A.'16, M.A.'18, Tulane Univ.; Dist. Supt. of Sch., 4868 Constance St., New Orleans, La., since 1922.

Pfeiffer, Carl A., A.B.'14, Univ. of Wis.; Supt. of Sch., Iron River, Mich., since 1927.

Phelan, Anette M., Diploma '10, State Normal Sch., Oshkosh, Wis.; B.S.'26, M.A.'28, Tchrs. Col., Columbia Univ.;

Instr. in Health Educ., Columbia Univ., 525 W. 120th St., New York, N. Y., since 1926.

Phelps, B. J., A.B.'02, Yale Univ.; A.M. '13, Tchrs. Col., Columbia Univ.; Supt. of Sch., Agawam, Mass., since 1921.

Phelps, C. L., A.B.'01, A.M.'03, Dartmouth; Supt. of Sch., Ishpeming, Mich., since 1915.

Philhower, Charles Alpaugh, B.S.'09, A.M. '12, Dickinson Col.; A.M.'15, Columbia Univ.; Supt. of Sch., 303 Mountain Ave., Westfield, N. J., since 1917.

Phillips, Claude A., A.M., Univ. of Chicago; Ph.D., George Peabody Col.; Prof. of Educ., Dir., Elem. Sch., Univ. of Mo., Columbia, Mo., since 1924.

Phillips, Clyde U., B.S.'18, Kansas State Tchrs. Col., Pittsburg, Kansas; A.M.'26, Univ. of Chicago; Supt. of Sch., 313 N. Mulberry, Eureka, Kansas, since 1921.

Phillips, Eugene M., 2284 Otto Ave., St. Paul, Minn.

Phillips, F. R., B.S.'14, Alma Col.; M.A. '29, Univ. of Mich.; Supt. of Sch., Alma, Mich., since 1926.

Phillips, Frank W., A.B.'11, Ill. Col.; Supt. of Sch., DeKalb, Ill., since 1929.

Phillips, Guy B., A.B.'13, Univ. of N. C.; Supt. of Sch., Greensboro, N. C., since 1929.

Phillips, J. J., B.S.'06, Ohio Wesleyan Univ.; Supt of Sch., Lancaster, Ohio, since 1921.

Phinney, R. V., B.S. in Ed.'21, State Tchrs. Col., Emporia, Kansas; Supt. of Sch., 218 W. 13th St., Larned, Kansas, since 1908.

Phipps, Harrie J., B.S.'03, Ed.M.'21, Harvard; Supt. of Northbridge, Mass. Sch., since 1922. Address: Grammar Sch. Bldg., Whitinsville, Mass.

Phipps, Paul E., B.S. in Ed.'17, Univ. of Mo.; A.M.'27, Tchrs. Col., Columbia Univ.; Supt. of Sch., Harlingen, Texas, since 1920.

Phipps, W. E., B.A.'09, Westminster Col., Tehuacana, Texas; M.A.'25, George Peabody Col. for Tchrs.; Supt. of Sch., 22nd and Main, North Little Rock, Ark., since 1925.

Phipps, William Rodgers, Supvr. of Elem. Sch., Bd. of Educ., Easton, Md., since 1929.

Pickell, Frank G., A.B.'09, Ind. Univ.; A.M.'17, Tchrs. Col., Columbia Univ.; Supt. of Sch., 22 Valley Rd., Montclair, N. J., since 1923.

Pickett, Lulu Leigh, B.S.'21, Columbia Univ.; M.A.'26, Univ. of Chicago; Supt. of Sch., Superior, Wis., since 1927.

Pieper, Charles J., Sch. of Educ., New York Univ., Washington Square, E., New York, N. Y.

Pierce, Anne E., B.A.'27, State Univ. of Iowa; M.Mus.'28, American Conservatory of Music; M.A.'30, Columbia Univ.; Assoc. in Music, Head, Dept. of Music, Univ. Experimental Schools, State Univ. of Iowa, Iowa City, Iowa, since 1926.

Pierce, Franklin E., Diploma '01, State Normal Sch., Cortland, N. Y.; A.B.'05, Amherst Col.; A.M.'17, Tchrs. Col., Columbia Univ.; State Supvr. of Sec. Educ., State Capitol, Hartford, Conn.

Pierce, Mary D., M.A.'17, Tchrs. Col., Columbia Univ.; Assoc. Prof. of Educ., State Tchrs. Col., Farmville, Va.

Pierson, Harry, B.A.'00, Lebanon Univ.; M.A.'12, Columbia Univ.; Supvg. Prin. of Sch., 626 Oxford St., Belvidere, N. J., since 1928.

Pietzsch, Louis Robert, B.A. and E.E.'07, Univ. of Texas; Supt. of Sch., Nederland, Texas, since 1927.

Pillsbury, W. Howard, A.B.'06, Carleton Col.; Supt. of Sch., Schenectady, N. Y., since 1929.

Pinkham, Raymond Edward, Supt. of Sch., 1 Liberty Pl., Weehawken, N. J.

Pipkin, John G., B.A.'09, Vanderbilt Univ.; LL.B.'13, Univ. of Ark.; M.A.'23, Univ. of Chicago; Asst. Supt. of Sch., Bd. of Educ., Little Rock, Ark., since 1930.

Pitkin, Fred E., A.B.'16, Wesleyan Univ.; M.A.'26, Columbia Univ.; Supt. of Sch., North Andover, Mass., since 1927.

Pitkin, Royce S., B.S. in Agr.'23, Univ. of Vt.; M.A.'28, Columbia Univ.; Supvg. Prin. of Sch., Wallingford, Vt., since 1927.

Pitman, Joseph Asbury, Ed.D.'29, R. I. Col. of Educ.; Prin., State Normal Sch., Salem, Mass., since 1906.

Pitt, Felix Newton, A.B.'16, A.M.'17, St. Mary's Univ., Baltimore, Md.; Supt. of Catholic Sch., 443 S. Fifth St., Louisville, Ky., since 1925.

Pittenger, Benjamin Floyd, B.A.'08, State Normal Sch., Ypsilanti, Mich.; M.A.'12, Univ. of Texas; Ph.D.'16, Univ. of Chicago; Prof. of Educ. Admin. and Dean, Sch. of Educ., Univ. of Texas, Austin, Texas, since 1916.

Pittenger, Lemuel Arthur, A.B.'07, A.M. '08, Ind. Univ.; Pres., Ball State Tchrs. Col., Muncie, Ind., since 1927.

Place, George A., Supt. of Sch., Salamanca, N. Y.

Planck, Carl G., B.S. in M.E.'29, Rose Polytech. Inst.; Supt. of Sch., Haines City, Fla., since 1930.

Plenzke, O. H., A.B.'14, Lawrence Col.; A.M.'24, Univ. of Wis.; First Asst. State Supt., State Dept. of Pub. Instr., Madison, Wis., since 1926.

Plummer, Louis E., B.S.'09, B.C.S.'09, Ohio Northern Univ.; Prin., Fullerton Union H. S. and Jr. Col., Fullerton, Calif., since 1918.

Poley, Irvin C., A.B.'12, Haverford Col.; Ed.M.'27, Harvard Univ.; Vice Prin. and Dir. of Studies, Germantown Friends Sch., Philadelphia, Pa., since 1927.

Polk, Clara M., Diploma '95, R. I. Col. of Educ.; Asst. Supt. of Sch., 193 Washington Ave., Providence, R. I., since 1914.

Pollock, Thomas L., B.S., Univ. of Pittsburgh; Supt. of Sch., Mapleview, Charleroi, Pa., since 1912.

Poole, Henry H., Diploma '97, State Normal Sch.; Supvg. Prin. of Sch., 127 Broad St., Leetsdale, Pa., since 1906.

Poor, Charles L., Life Cert. '10, Western State Tchrs. Col., Kalamazoo, Mich.; A. B.'20, M.A.'25, Univ. of Mich.; Supt. of Sch., 407 Fifth St., Traverse City, Mich., since 1920.

Poor, Lillian B., Asst. Dir. of Kdgn., 15 Beacon St., Boston, Mass., since 1915.

Pope, Alvin E., B.A.'98, Univ. of Nebr.; M.A.'99, Gallaudet Col.; Supt., N. J. Sch. for the Deaf, Trenton Junction, N. J., since 1917.

Pope, Arthur Stanley, A.B.'08, Univ. of Wash.; Co. Supt. of Sch., Court House, Santa Barbara, Calif., since 1920.

Pope, Delmer Neal, A.B.'03, Roanoke Col.; M.Acct.'08, Boulder Business Col.; Supt. of Sch., 101 S. Washington Ave., Roswell, N. Mex., since 1917.

Pore, Orin Eugene, A.B.'06, Col. of Wooster; A.M.'16, Tchrs. Col., Columbia Univ.; Supt. of Sch., 241 S. Freedom, Ravenna, Ohio, since 1925.

Porrata, Oscar E., LL.B.'23, Univ. of Porto Rico; A.B.'29 Polytech. Inst. of Porto Rico; Supvr. of Sch., San German, P. R., since 1925.

Porter, Frederick W., B.S.'14, Tufts Col.; Ed.M.'27, Harvard Univ.; Supt. of Sch., Greenfield, Mass., since 1929.

Portwood, Thomas B., B.S.'19, Kansas State Tchrs. Col., Emporia, Kansas; A. M.'22, Columbia Univ.; Asst. Supt. of Sch., Bd. of Educ., San Antonio, Texas.

Postell, Mary W., Asst. Supt. in charge of Elem. Sch., Bd. of Educ., Atlanta, Ga.

Poteet, Ernest H., B.A.'21, Baylor Univ.; Supt. of Sch., Mercedes, Texas, since 1926.

Pottenger, Mary O., Elem. Supvr. of Sch., Springfield, Mass.

Potter, I. B., A.B.'11, Ill. Col.; Supt. of Sch., H. S., Dixon, Ill., since 1921.

Potter, J. W., Ph.B.'13, Dickinson Col.; A.M.'23, Columbia Univ.; Supt. of Sch., Lamberton Bldg., Carlisle, Pa., since 1927.

Potts, D. Walter, Supt. of Sch., Sixth and St. Louis Aves., East St. Louis, Ill., since 1911.

Potwin, R. W., A.B.'10, Univ. of Kansas; A.M.'27, Univ. of Chicago; Supt. of Sch., McPherson, Kansas, since 1915.

Pound, Jere M., LL.D.'16, Univ. of Ga.; Pres., Ga. State Tchrs. Col., Athens, Ga., since 1912.

Powell, Harley J., M.A.'30, Univ. of Wis.; Supt. of Sch., Mt. Horeb, Wis., since 1930.

Powell, John Rush, B.A.'97, Yale Col.; M. A.'99, Yale Univ.; Dist. Supt. of Sch., St. Louis, Mo., since 1929.

Power, Leonard, B.S. in Ed.'16, Central Mo. State Tchrs. Col., Warrensburg, Mo.; M.A.'27, Univ. of Chicago; Asst Supt. in charge of Elem. Sch., Bd. of Educ. Bldg., Tulsa, Okla., since 1929.

Power, Thomas F., A.B.'08, Amherst Col.; Asst. Supt. of Sch., City Hall, Worcester, Mass., since 1920.

Powers, Elmer Walter, Ph.B.'25, Univ. of Chicago; Supt. of Sch. and Prin., Community H. S., Watseka, Ill., since 1925.

Powers, F. R., A.B.'13, Oberlin Col.; A.M. '20, Tchrs. Col., Columbia Univ.; Supt. of Sch., Amherst, Ohio, since 1918.

Powers, Guy W., B.S.,'11, Univ. of Vt.; Supt. of Sch., Windham Central Dist., R. F. D., Cambridgeport, Vt., since 1922.

Powers, Sue M., B.S.'20, George Peabody Col. for Tchrs.; Co. Supt. of Sch., Court House, Memphis, Tenn., since 1922.

Poynter, J. W., A.B.'25, State Tchrs. Col., Peru, Nebr.; Supt. of Sch., Winner, S. Dak., since 1927.

P'Pool, Mrs. Ethie Lee, Diploma '04, Southwest Texas State Normal Sch., San Marcos, Texas; Co. Supt. of Sch., Benjamin, Texas, since 1927.

Prater, Mrs. Lulu O., Co. Supt. of Educ., Marks, Miss., since 1928.

Prather, A. P., A.B.'24, Univ. of Ky.; M. A.'28, Columbia Univ.; Supt. of Sch., 306 Farren Ave., Earlington, Ky., since 1924.

Pratt, C. H., A.B.'08, Bates Col.; A.M.'27, Columbia Univ.; Union Supt. of Sch., Harwich, Mass., since 1930.

Pratt, Orville C., Ph.B.'95, DePauw Univ.; Supt. of Sch., Admin. Bldg., Spokane, Wash., since 1916.

Preston, Everett C., B.S.'21, Mass. Agrl. Col.; Ed.M.'26, Harvard Univ. Address: Tchrs. Col., Columbia Univ., New York, N. Y.

Preston, Mrs. Josephine Corliss, M.A.'14, Whitman Col.; L.H.D.'25, Carleton Col.; Pres., Natl. Educ. Assn. 1919-20. Address: Burton, Vashon Island, King Co., Wash.

Price, Clyde S., Life Cert.'11, Western State Normal Sch., Kalamazoo, Mich.; B.S.'21, M.S.'22, Kalamazoo Col.; Supt. of Sch., 412 Evergreen Ave., Flat Rock, Mich., since 1925.

Price, E. D., B.A.'12, Phillips Univ.; M.A. '20, Univ. of Mo.; Supt. of Sch., Enid, Okla., since 1915.

Price, Joseph St. Clair, A.B.'12, Lincoln Univ.; A.B.'17, Univ. of Mich.; Ed.M.'27, Harvard Univ.; Head, Dept. of Educ., W. Va. State Col., Institute, W. Va. since 1920.

Price, Wilfred H., Supt. of Sch., 92 Marshall St., Watertown, Mass.

Price, William Raleigh, A.B.'98, Cornell Univ.; Ph.D.'11, Columbia Univ.; State Supvr. of Modern Languages, State Educ. Bldg., Albany, N. Y., since 1911.

Pride, R. H., A.B.'24, Col. of William and Mary; Supt. of Sch., South Norfolk, Va., since 1928.

Prince, Frank C., B.Sc.'16, Hastings Col.; Supt. of Sch., Bayard, Nebr., since 1925.

Prince, Percy S., B.S.'23, La. Polytech Inst.; State Dir., Physical and Health Educ., 548 S. State St., Dover, Del., since 1925.

Pringle, James N., B.A.'97, Dartmouth Col.; State Commr. of Educ., State House, Concord, N. H., since 1930.

Pringle, Lewis A., A.B.'02, Univ. of Chicago; Supt. of Sch., 53 W. 150th St., Harvey, Ill., since 1906.

Prior, Charles F., Supt. of Sch., Town Hall, Fairhaven, Mass., since 1912.

Proctor, Arthur Marcus, A.B.'10, Duke Univ.; A.M.'22, Ph.D.'30, Tchrs. Col., Columbia Univ.; Prof. of Sec. Educ., Duke Univ., Durham, N. C., since 1923.

Proctor, L. C., M.A.'08, Texas Christian Univ.; Supt. of Sch., Temple, Texas, since 1920 and Pres., Jr. Col., Temple, Texas, since 1928.

Proctor, Milton D., B.S.'08, Colgate Col.; Supt. of Sch., Ella Peach Sch. Bldg., Uniontown, Pa., since 1926.

Prodoehl, A. L., B.A.'14, Univ. of Minn.; Supt. of Sch., H. S., Cudahy, Wis., since 1928.

Prose, Charles T., B.S.'07, Denison Univ.; Supt. of Sch., Market Bldg., Zanesville, Ohio, since 1926.

Prout, F. J., B.L.'06, Ohio Wesleyan Col.; D.Ped.'16, Ohio Univ.; Supt. of Sch., H. S. Bldg., Sandusky, Ohio, since 1921.

Pruitt, Eugent Watts, M.A.'26, Tchrs. Col., Columbia Univ.; Co. Supt. of Sch., Easton, Md., since 1929.

Prunty, Merle, A.B.'09, Univ. of Kansas; A.M.'27, Univ. of Chicago; LL.D.'28, Univ. of Tulsa; Supt. of Sch., Tulsa, Okla., since 1929.

Prutzman, Stuart E., B.A.'23, Pa. State Col.; Co. Supt. of Sch., Court House, Mauch Chunk, Pa., since 1928.

Pucey, Michael H., 317 E. 67th St., New York, N. Y.

Puderbaugh, J. F., A.B.'16, Dickinson Col.; M.A.'28, Tchrs. Col., Columbia Univ.; Supt. of Sch., Lock Haven, Pa., since 1929.

Pugh, L. R., B.S. in Ed.'26, State Normal Col., Bowling Green, Ohio; Supt. of Sch., Portage, Ohio, since 1928.

Pugliese, Anthony J., Dist. Supt. of Sch., 182nd St. and Bathgate Ave., New York, N. Y.

Purcell, Thomas M., A.B.'03, Birmingham-Southern Col.; Supt. of Sch., Cochran, Ga., since 1929.

Purdom, J. Leslie, A.B.'06, Centre Col.; A.M.'11, Ph.D.'18, Harvard Univ.; Pres., Harris and Stowe Tchrs. Colleges, St. Louis, Mo., since 1930.

Purks, J. E., Supt. of Sch., Cedartown, Ga.

Quickstad, N. J., B.A.'14, Univ. of Minn.; Supt. of Sch., Mountain Iron, Minn., since 1926.

Quigg, B. F., A.B.'09, Davidson Col.; Supt. of Sch., 307 Third Ave., Rome, Ga., since 1920.

Quigley, Samuel, A.B.'05, State Univ. of Iowa; M.A.'11, Univ. of Chicago; D.Litt. '19, Univ. of Denver; Assoc. Prof. of Educ. and Dir., Bureau of Sch. Inquiries, Univ. of Texas, 4932 Walker Ave., Houston, Texas, since 1927.

Quinn James Joseph, A.B.'12, Amherst Col.; A.M.'14, Harvard Univ.; Supt. of Sch., Winchester, Mass., since 1923.

Rabb, S. W., A.B.'06, Erskine Col.; Supt. of Sch., Greer, S. C., since 1928.

Race, Stuart R., A.B.'11, Lafayette Col.; A.M.'27, New York Univ.; Supvg. Prin. of Sch., Central Sch., Glen Rock, N. J., since 1930.

Radcliffe, Paul Rodney, A.B.'99, Maryville Col.; Supt. of Sch., Nutley, N. J., since 1920.

Radcliffe, Ralph, A.B.'21, M.A.'28, Univ. of Pittsburgh; Supt. of Sch., Dormont, South Hills Branch, Pittsburgh, Pa., since 1920.

Ragland, Fannie J., Diploma '06. B.A.'08, Miami Univ.; M.A.'14, Columbia Univ.; Supvr., Pub. Schools, 216 E. Ninth St., Cincinnati, Ohio, since 1929.

Ragsdale, J. G., A.B.'15, Col. of Idaho; A.M. '22, Columbia Univ.; Supt. of Sch., Admin. Bldg., Butte, Mont., since 1930.

Rahn, G. O. G., A.B.'13, Luther Col. Address: 4008 Morris Blvd., Shorewood, Milwaukee, Wis.

Ramsey, Floyd Archer, AB.'15, Austin Col.; M.S. in Ed.'28, Univ. of Okla.; Supt. of Sch., 508 N. Walnut St., Pauls Valley, Okla., since 1924.

Ramsey, James William, A.B.'13, Ouachita Col.; M.A.'21, George Peabody Col. for Tchrs.; Supt. of Sch., Fort Smith, Ark.

Randall, John A., Ph.B.'05, Wesleyan; Pres., Rochester Athenæum and Mechanics Institute, 55 S. Plymouth Ave., Rochester, N. Y., since 1922.

Randall, Mrs. Margaret T., Diploma '96, Col. Parker's Sch.; Co. Supt. of Sch., Florence, Ariz., since 1926.

Randolph, Corliss F., A.B.'88, L.H.D.'03, Alfred Univ.: LL.D.'13, Salem Col.; Prin., Fifteenth Ave. Sch., Newark, N. J., since 1899. Address: 83 Jefferson Ave., Maplewood, N. J.

Ranger, Walter E., A.B.'79, A.M.'83, Bates Col.; A.M.'02, Univ. of Vt.; LL.D.'07, Bates Col.; Ed.D.'22, R. I. State Col.; State Commr. of Educ., State House, Providence, R. I., since 1905.

Ranheim, Glen A., B.A.'27, St. Olaf Col.; Supt. of Sch., Lafayette, Minn., since 1928.

Rankin, Paul T., A.B.'15, Mich. State Normal Col.; M.A.'21, Ph.D.'26, Univ. of Mich.; Supvg. Dir. of Research and Adjustment, Detroit Public Schools, 1354 Broadway, Detroit, Mich., since 1928.

Rasely, Hiram N., A.B.'12, Clark Univ.; Vice-Pres., Burdett Col., 156 Stuart St., Boston, Mass., since 1922.

Ratchford, A. J., A.B.'25, Susquehanna Univ.; Supt. of Sch., 30 N. White St., Shenandoah, Pa., since 1927.

Rathbun, Franklin E., Co. Supt. of Sch., Court House, Oakland, Md.

Rathbun, Mrs. Roy E., A.B.'10, Syracuse Univ.; Dist. Supt. of Sch., Cincinnatus, N. Y., since 1926.

Rather, Arthur A., A.B.'16, M.A.'24, Univ. of Mich.; Supt. of Sch., 442 Pleasant, Ionia, Mich., since 1917.

Rathke, Mary, A.B.'09, Univ. of Nebr.; Co. Supt. of Sch., Glenwood, Iowa, since 1924.

Rauch, M. B., Life Cert.'14, State Normal Sch.; Supt., Riverview Schools, Wyandotte, Mich., since 1923.

Rawdon, Howard L., A.B.'04, A.M.'14, Oberlin Col.; Supt. of Sch., Oberlin, Ohio, since 1908.

Rawlins, Robert E., B.S.'16, Huron Col.; M.A.'29, State Univ. of Iowa; Supt. of Sch., Pierre H. S., Pierre, S. Dak., since 1918.

Ray, Annie, Western Carolina Tchrs. Col., Cullowhee, N. C.

Ray, Mrs. Willie C., Supt. of Sch., Shelbyville, Ky., since 1930.

Rea, A. A., Acting Supt. of Sch., Montgomery, Ill.

Reace, Homer, Bd. of Educ., Marenisco, Mich.

Read, M. H., A.B.'19, Univ. of Kansas; A.M.'22, Tchrs. Col., Columbia Univ.;

Head, Dept. of Sec. Educ., Tchrs. Col. of the City of Boston, 625 Huntington Ave., Boston, Mass., since 1922.

Reagan, Chester L., B.S.'12, M.A.'25, Earlham Col.; Prin., Moorestown Friends' Sch., Moorestown, N. J., since 1925.

Reagan, G. H., Acting Prin., Dallas Tech. H. S., Dallas Texas.

Reagle, Fred P., Asst. Supt. of Sch., 22 Valley Rd., Montclair, N. J.

Reavis, William C., Ph.B.'08, A.M.'11, Ph. D.'25, Univ. of Chicago; Prof. of Educ., Univ. of Chicago, 5819 Blackstone Ave., Chicago, Ill.

Record, Louis De Witt, A.B.'87, Amherst Col.; Union Supt. of Sch., 16 Summer St., Nashua, N. H., since 1919.

Redick, Charles B., Supt. of Sch., 307 E. Aztec Ave., Gallup, N. Mex.

Redifer, Frederick L., Asst. Supt. of Sch., Glencoe, Ill.

Reed, Carroll R., B.A.'06, M.A.'14, Harvard Univ.; Supt. of Sch., City Hall, Minneapolis, Minn., since 1929.

Reed, Lula A., B.S.'17, M.A.'24, Tchrs. Col., Columbia Univ.; Supvr., Early Elem. Sch., 338 W. Washington Ave., Jackson, Mich., since 1913.

Reetz, O. A., Supt. of Sch., H. S., Shawano, Wis., since 1929.

Reeves, Charles E., A.B.'15, Huron Col.; A.M.'20, Univ. of Chicago; Ph.D.'25, Columbia Univ.; Prof. of Educ., Elmira Col., Elmira, N. Y., since 1925.

Reeves, Floyd W., Ph.D.'25, Univ. of Chicago; Prof. of Educ., Univ. of Chicago, Chicago, Ill., since 1929.

Regan, Teresa A., 625 Huntington Ave., Boston, Mass.

Rego, Guy P., Supt. of Sch., 45 S. Main, Spring Valley, N. Y.

Reiche, Karl A., B.L.'09, Trinity Col., Hartford, Conn.; Supt. of Sch., Bristol H. S., Bristol, Conn., since 1913.

Reid, Charles F., A.B.'23, Colgate Univ.; A.M.'29, Columbia Univ. Address: 1237 John Jay Hall, Columbia Univ., New York, N. Y.

Reid, E. M., A.B.'16, M.A.'18, Univ. of Utah; Co. Supt. of Sch., Kamas, Utah.

Reid, E. T., Dist. Supt. of Sch., Manti, Utah.

Reid, Henry J., Co. Supt. of Sch., Monticello, Ind.

Reid, O. L., A.B.'98, Ind. Univ.; LL.B.'05, Univ. of Louisville; M.A.'22, New York Univ.; Supt. of Yale Sch., Youngstown, Ohio, since 1926.

Reid, Robert Lee, M.D.'97, A.B.'02, Univ. of Mo.; Supt. of Sch., Keokuk, Iowa, since 1921.

Reiff, Cecil K., A.B.'15, A.M.'17, Ind. Univ.; Supt. of Sch., 201 N. 15th St., Muskogee, Okla., since 1925.

Rein, Marion Batchelder, Supt. of Sch., 2 Morton St., Riverside, N. J., since 1923.

Reiner, Joseph, A.M.'14, St. Louis Univ.; Dean, Col. of Arts and Sciences, Loyola Univ., Chicago, Ill., since 1923.

Reinertsen, S. G., B.A.'11, St. Olaf Col.; M.A.'21, Univ. of Colo.; Supt of Sch., Moorehead, Minn., since 1926.

Reinoehl, C. M., A.B.'09, A.M.'10, Ind. Univ.; Ph.D.'20, Univ. of Chicago; Prof. of Sch. Admin., Univ. of Ark., Fayetteville, Ark., since 1921.

Remaley, Frank H., A.B.'01, A.M.'09, Otterbein Col.; Asst. Co. Supt. of Sch., 333 Carnegie Pl., Pittsburgh, Pa., since 1920.

Remington, Mrs. Pearl M. T., Diploma '94, R. I. Col. of Educ.; Asst. Supt. of Sch., Grove Ave. Sch., East Providence, R. I., since 1927.

Remy, Ballard D., Ph.B.'02, Franklin Col.; Franklin, Ind.; A.M.'18, Tchrs. Col., Columbia Univ.; Supt. of Sch., Jr. H. S., Longmeadow, Mass., since 1928.

Reynolds, F. E., B.A.'89, Natl. Normal Univ.; B.A.'08. Defiance Col.; Secy.-Treas., Ohio Educ. Assn., Chamber of Commerce, Columbus, Ohio.

Reynolds, Fordyce Thomas, Ph.B.'00, Brown Univ.; A.M.'20, Columbia Univ.; Supt. of Sch., City Hall, Gardner, Mass., since 1913.

Reynolds, James J., B.S.'93. Col. of the City of New York; LL.B.'00. New York Univ.; M.A.'01, Columbia Univ.; Dist. Supt. of Sch., Brooklyn, N. Y., since 1916.

Reynolds, O. Edgar, Diploma '14, Ill. State Normal Univ.; A.B.'16, Univ. of Ill.; M.A.'17, Ph.D.'27, Columbia Univ.; Head, Dept. of Educ. and Psych., Lebanon Valley Col., Annville, Pa., since 1924.

Rhett, A. Burnet, M.A. and B.A.'99, Univ. of Va.; Supt. of Sch., Charleston, S. C., since 1912.

Rice, DuFay R., Pd.B.'07, Mo. State Normal; A.B.'11, Univ. of Colo.; A.M.'17, Tchrs. Col., Columbia Univ.; Supt. of Sch., Ironwood, Mich., since 1920.

Rice, H. A., A.B.'20, A.M.'26, W. Va. Univ.; Supt. of Sch., Grafton, W. Va., since 1923.

Rice, Louis A., B.C.S.'21, B.S. in Ed.'27, M.A.'30, New York Univ.; Asst. in Sec. Educ., State Dept. of Pub. Instr., Trenton, N. J., since 1927.

Rice, W. H., A.B.'01, Ohio Wesleyan; Supt. of Sch., London, Ohio, since 1909.

Richards, W. M., B.S.'19, State Tchrs. Col., Emporia, Kansas; M.S.'27, Univ. of Kansas; Supt. of Sch., Dodge City, Kansas, since 1928.

Richardson, Charles C., A.B.'87, A.M.'91, Colby Col.; Union Supt. of Sch., North Adams, Mass., since 1923.

Richardson, E. S., Parish Supt. of Sch., Minden, La.

Richardson, James W., B.S.'06, Iowa Wesleyan Univ.; M.A.'13, State Univ. of Iowa; Supt. of Sch., H. S., Hibbing, Minn., since 1923.

Richardson, W. H., A.M.'04, Defiance Col.; Supt. of Sch., 844 Chestnut Blvd., Cuyahoga Falls, Ohio, since 1908.

Richardson, William Leeds, A.B.'01, Univ. of Toronto; Ph.D.'19, Univ. of Chicago; Dean, Col. of Educ., Butler Univ., Indianapolis, Ind., since 1930.

Richeson, John J., B.S.'10, Ohio Univ.; Ped.D.'17, Miami Univ.; A.M.'21, Tchrs. Col., Columbia Univ.; Supt. of Sch., Youngstown, Ohio, since 1926.

Richey, Warren L., B.S. in Ed.'18, Miami Univ.; Supvg. Prin. of Sch., Scienceville, Ohio, since 1918.

Richison, Willard E., Co. Supt. of Sch., 108 E. Locust, Watseka, Ill., since 1923.

Richmond, Dean S., A.B.'19, M.A.'20, Univ. of Southern Calif.; Dist. Supt. of Sch., Brawley, Calif., since 1922.

Richmond, J., Supt. of Sch., Maplewood, Mo.

Rickards, James S., A.B.'08, DePauw Univ.; Exec. Secy., Fla. Educ. Assn., 33 Centennial Bldg., Tallahassee, Fla., since 1929.

Riddering, Albert A., A.B.'18, M.A.'30, Univ. of Mich.; Supt. of Twp. Sch., Bd. of Educ., Melvindale, Mich.

Riddle, Walter, A.B.'17, A.M.'27, W. Va. Univ.; Supt. of Sch., Elkins, W. Va., since 1926.

Ridgley, Douglas Clay, A.B.'93, Ind. Univ.; M.S.'22, Univ. of Chicago; Ph.D.'25, Clark Univ.; Prof. of Geography in Educ., Clark Univ., Worcester, Mass., since 1922.

Riefling, B. Jeannette, B.S.'11, A.B.'13, Univ. of Mo.; A.M.'20, Columbia Univ. Address: 3171 Portis Ave., St. Louis, Mo.

Riemer, G. C. L., A.B.'95, A.M.'96, Bucknell Univ.; A.M.'00, Harvard Univ.; Ph.D.'05, Leipzig Univ.; LL.D.'26, Bucknell Univ.; Pres., State Tchrs. Col., Clarion, Pa., since 1928.

Riffle, I. N., Dist. Supt. of Sch., Masontown, Pa.

Riggs, James G., A.B.'88, A.M.'91, Amherst Col.; Ped.D.'12, State Col. for Tchrs., Albany, N. Y.; Prin., State Normal Sch., Oswego, N. Y., since 1913.

Riggs, Ora M., B.S.'17, Univ. of Chicago; Prin., Knickerbocker Sch., 2301 N. Clifton Ave., Chicago, Ill., since 1922.

Ringle, Mrs. Lillian Newton, A.B.'98, Ottawa Univ.; A.M.'25, Columbia Univ.; Prin., Andrew Drumm Inst., Independence, Mo., since 1929.

Rising, Charles S., B.S.'19, M.A.'28, Univ. of Vt.; Supvg. Prin., Orleans High and Graded Sch., Orleans, Vt., since 1923.

Risley, James H., A.B.'07, Ind. Univ.; Ph.M.'10, Univ. of Chicago; Supt. of Sch. Dist. No. 1, Pueblo, Colo., since 1921.

Ritchie, R. R., B.S. in E.E.'08, M.A. in E.E.'19, Purdue Univ.; A.M. in Ed.'25, Columbia Univ.; Asst. Supt. of Sch., Atlanta, Ga., since 1925.

Ritter, E. L., A.B.'14, Ind. Univ.; M.A.'16, Ph.D.'20, State Univ. of Iowa; Prof. of Elem. Educ., Iowa State Tchrs. Col., Cedar Falls, Iowa, since 1922.

Ritter, John B., A.B.'10, Gettysburg Col.; A.M.'18, Univ. of Pa.; Supvg. Prin. of Sch., 633 Stokes Ave., Collingswood, N. J., since 1924.

Robbins, Chester, A.B.'13, Ursinus Col.; A.M.'22, Univ. of Pa.; Supt. of Sch., H. S. Bldg., Bridgeton, N. J., since 1927.

Robe, T. S., A.B.'22, Muskingum Col.; Supt. of Sch., Frazeysburg, Ohio, since 1922.

Roberts, Alexander Crippin, A.B.'06, Univ. of Wis.; M.A.'17, Ph.D.'22, Univ. of Wash.; Pres., State Tchrs. Col., San Francisco, Calif., since 1927.

Roberts, Bertha E., Life Sec. Admin. Credential '26, State Tchrs. Col., San Francisco, Calif.; Deputy Supt. of Elem. Sch., City Hall, San Francisco, Calif., since 1919.

Roberts, Clarence R., B.A.'20, Univ. of Okla.; M.A.'28, Univ. of Colo.; Supt., Fairview Independent Sch. Dist., Thrift, Texas.

Roberts, Edward D., B.A.'99, M.A.'07, Univ. of Cincinnati; M.A.'08, Tchrs. Col., Columbia Univ.; Supt. of Sch., 216 E. Ninth St., Cincinnati, Ohio, since 1929.

Roberts, Ezra C., Tuskegee Inst., Tuskegee, Ala.

Roberts, L. A., B.S.'27, North Texas State Tchrs. Col., Denton, Texas; M.A.'29, Southern Methodist Univ.; Supt. of Sch., Wortham, Texas, since 1929.

Roberts, Thomas R., Ph.B.'05, Upper Iowa Univ.; Supt. of Sch., Independence, Iowa, since 1918.

Robertson, Arthur H., A.B.'09, Univ. of Wis.; Ph.M.'10, Univ. of Chicago. Address: 104 Spruce St., Dowagiac, Mich.

Robertson, C. L., B.A.'11. Univ. of N. Dak.; Supt. of Sch., 215 Fourth Ave., S., Jamestown, N. Dak., since 1924.

Robertson, Martin Brown, B.S.'18, Trinity Col.; M.A.'20, Pa. State Col.; M.A.'21, Columbia Univ.; Field Supvr. of Rural Educ., State Bd. of Educ., Willimantic, Conn., since 1929.

Robinson, Berton W., A.B.'24, Western State Tchrs. Col., Kalamazoo, Mich.; A. M., Univ. of Mich.; Supt. of Sch., Springfield Sch., Battle Creek, Mich., since 1927.

Robinson, Edward Kilburn, B.S.'04, Dartmouth Col. Address: 15 Ashburton Pl., Boston, Mass.

Robinson, Ernest W., Supt. of Sch., West Bridgewater, Mass., since 1929.

Robinson, J. R., A.B.'09, M.A.'12, Univ. of Ky.; Ph.D.'27, George Peabody Col. for Tchrs.; Registrar, George Peabody Col. for Tchrs., Nashville, Tenn., since 1927.

Robinson, Louis C., A.B.'05, Washington Col., Chestertown, Md.; Co. Supt. of Sch., Chestertown, Md.; since 1922.

Robinson, Raymond W., Supt. of Twp. Sch., 433 Center Ave., Greensburg, Pa.

Robinson, Ross N., A.B.'15, Carson-Newman Col.; A.B.'19, Univ. of Tenn.; A.M. '21, Columbia Univ.; Supt. of Sch., Kingsport, Tenn., since 1924.

Robinson, William Theodore, B.A.'03, Univ. of Tenn.; M.A.'17, George Peabody Col. for Tchrs.; Supt. of Sch., City Hall, Chattanooga, Tenn., since 1927.

Rock, B. J., A.B.'14, Ripon Col.; M.A.'22, Columbia Univ.; Supt. of Sch., 116 Thorn St., Ripon, Wis., since 1923.

Rockett, James F., A.B.'08, A.M.'22, Holy Cross Col.; Supt. of Sch., Park Pl., Woonsocket, R. I., since 1925.

Roderick, Edward E., A.B.'12, A.M.'13, Oskaloosa; Deputy State Commr. of Educ., 37 Bangor St., Augusta, Maine.

Rodes, Lester A., A.M.'17, Univ. of Pa.; Supt. of Sch., 921 Queen St., Cape May, N. J., since 1921.

Rodewald, John W., Supt. of Sch., 310 Third St., Oconomowoc, Wis.

Rodgers, J. Harvey, Ed.M.'21, Harvard Univ.; Supvg. Prin. of Sch., Glassboro, N. J., since 1921.

Rodman, Benedict J., A.B.'06, A.M.'11, St. Louis Univ.; Pres., John Carroll Univ., Cleveland, Ohio, since 1928.

Roeder, J. N., A.B.'17, Franklin and Marshall Col.; A.M.'23, Tchrs. Col., Columbia Univ.; Supt. of Sch., 308 Columbia Ave., Palmerton, Pa., since 1926.

Rogers, C. E., A.B.'05, LL.B.'07, Univ. of Chattanooga; A.M.'15, Columbia Univ.; Supt. of Sch., Johnson City, Tenn., since 1924.

Rogers, George Calvin, Asst. Supt. of Sch., 190 Tradd St., Charleston, S. C.

Rogers, James Edward, M.S. in Ed.'08, Univ. of Calif.; Dir., Natl. Physical Educ. Serv. of the Natl. Recreation Assn., 315 Fourth Ave., New York, N. Y., since 1925.

Rogers, Lester Burton, Ph.D.'15, Tchrs. Col., Columbia Univ.; Dean, Sch. of Educ. and Dean, Summer Session, Univ. of Southern Calif., Los Angeles, Calif., since 1919.

Rogers, Virgil M., A.B.'21, Wofford Col.; M.A.'24, Western State Col.; Supt. of Sch., Gunnison, Colo., since 1926.

Rogers, V. Z., A.B.'14, Trinity Univ.; Supt. of Sch., Lamesa, Texas, since 1925.

Rohan, Ben. J., B.A.'16, Lawrence Col.; Supt. of Sch., Appleton, Wis., since 1925.

Rohde, Carl G., B.Sc.'14, Univ. of Nebr.; M.Sc.'28, Colo. Agrl. Col.; Supt. of Sch., Ogallala, Nebr., since 1929.

Rohn, Ross W., Prin., Jr. H. S., Owensboro, Ky.

Rohn, W. L., M.E.'85, Normal; Supvg. Prin. of Sch., 201 Central Ave., North Wildwood, N. J., since 1918.

Rohrabaugh, J. H., Supt. of Sch., Clarksburg, W. Va.

Rohrbach, Quincy A. W., A.B.'22, Franklin and Marshall Col.; A.M.'23, Ph.D.'25, Univ. of Pa.; Prof. of Educ., Sch. of Educ., Univ. of Pittsburgh, Pittsburgh, Pa., since 1925.

Rohrbough, E. G., A.B.00, Allegheny Col.; A.M.'06, Harvard Univ.; Pres., State Normal Sch., Glenville, W. Va., since 1908.

Roland, H. M., A.B.'20, Wake Forest Col.; Supt. of Sch., Washington, N. C., since 1926.

Rolfe, Stanley H., Asst. Supt. of Sch., Newark, N. J.

Ronnei, Herman L., B.A.'16, Luther Col.; M.A.'30, Tchrs. Col., Columbia Univ.; Supvg. Prin., Union Free Sch. No. 1, Valhalla, N. Y., since 1930.

Root, Benjamin H., B.A.'13, Univ. of Rochester; M.A.'29, Columbia Univ.; Supt. of Sch., East Rochester, N. Y., since 1930.

Root, Frank S., B.Di.'92, Des Moines Univ.; Supt. of Sch., Fayetteville, Ark., since 1906.

Rorem, S. O., A.B.'09, Morningside Col.; M.A.'26, Univ. of Chicago; Supt. of Sch., 323 Chestnut St., Lebanon, Pa., since 1926.

Rose, Clinton E., A.B.'99, Kansas; A.M.'13, Columbia; Supt. of Sch., Tucson, Ariz., since 1920.

Rose, Junius H., A.B.'13, Duke Univ.; A.M. '26, Columbia Univ.; Supt. of Sch., Greenville, N. C., since 1920 and Dir., Experimental Sch., East Carolina Tchrs. Col., Greenville, N. C.

Rose, Marion M., B.S.'19, State Tchrs. Col., Pittsburg, Kansas; M.S.'28, Univ. of Kansas; Supt. of Sch., Pittsburg, Kansas, since 1924.

Roselle, Ernest N., Supt., Natl. Sch. of the Royal Order of Moose, Mooseheart, Ill., since 1927.

Rosier, Joseph, A.M.'15, Salem Col.; Pres., State Normal Sch., Fairmont, W. Va., since 1915.

Ross, Carmon, Ph.B.'05, Lafayette Col.; A.M.'16, Ph.D.'22, Univ. of Pa.; Supvg. Prin. of Sch., Doylestown, Pa., since 1906 and Dir., Summer Demonstration Sch., State College, Pa.

Ross, Meta, 5440 Cass, Detroit, Mich.

Ross, Paul S., B.S.'27, New York Univ.; Supvg. Prin. of Sch., Mountain Lakes, N. J., since 1929.

Ross, William Robert, B.S.'21, M.S.'24, Colo. Agrl. Col.; Supt. of Sch., Delta, Colo., since 1930.

Rossman, John G., A.B.'08, A.M.'11, Franklin and Marshall Col.; A.M.'17, Tchrs. Col., Columbia Univ.; Supt. of Sch., 4819 Magoun Ave., East Chicago, Ind., since 1929.

Roudabush, Charles E., A.B.'03, Lebanon Valley Col.; A.M.'24, Columbia Univ.; Supt. of Sch., 320 N. Fifth St., Minersville, Pa., since 1915.

Roudebush, Charles M., A.B.'14, Ohio Wesleyan Univ.; A.M., Ohio State Univ.; Dir., Y. M. C. A. Sch., Columbus, Ohio, since 1916.

Roudebush, G. E., B. S. in Ed.'18, Ohio State Univ.; M.A.'23, Tchrs. Col., Columbia Univ.; Asst. Supt. of Sch., Columbus, Ohio, since 1927.

Roudebush, Roy R., A.B.'14, A.M.'27, Ind. Univ.; Asst. State Supt. of Pub. Instr., State House, Indianapolis, Ind., since 1928.

Rounds, Charles R., 536 S. Clark St., Chicago, Ill.

Routt, Forrest V., B.L.'06, Univ. of Calif.; Supt. of Sch., Alhambra, Calif., since 1925.

Rowe, F. F., Supt. of Sch., LaGrange, Ga.

Rowe, Frank D., A.M.'20, Columbia Univ.; Supt. of Sch., Warren, Maine, since 1918.

Rowe, John R., A.B.'19, Beloit Col.; M.A.'22, Univ. of Chicago; Supt. of Sch., Western Springs, Ill., since 1924.

Rowell, Arthur B., A.B.'95, Yankton Col.; Supt. of Sch., Glencoe, Ill., since 1903.

Rowland, Albert Lindsay, A.B.'08, Temple Univ.; M.A.'11, Ph. D.'14, Univ. of Pa.; Supt., Cheltenham Township Schools, Elkins Park, Pa.

Rowland, Sydney V., B.S.'14, Temple Univ.; M.A.'21, Univ. of Pa.; Supt. of Twp. Sch., Wayne, Pa., since 1920.

Roy, Calista, Diploma '02, State Normal Sch., Fitchburg, Mass.; Asst. Supt. of Sch., Newton, Mass., since 1930.

Roy, William Milton, B.A., Pa. State Col.; Asst. Co. Supt. of Sch., 614 Second St., Towanda, Pa., since 1922.

Royce, Asa M., Pd. B.'04, Univ. of Wis.; Pres., State Normal Sch., Platteville, Wis., since 1916.

Rubins, Ralph B., B.A.'03, Ohio Wesleyan; M.A.'19, Univ. of Chicago; Supt. of Sch., 606 Alabama St., Bristol, Tenn., since 1914.

Ruch, Giles Murrel, A.B.'14, Univ. of Oregon; Ph. D.'22, Stanford Univ.; Prof. of Educ., Univ. of Calif., Haviland Hall, Berkeley, Calif., since 1926.

Ruediger, William C., Ph. B.'99, Ph. M.'03, Univ. of Wis.; Ph. D.'07, Columbia Univ.; Prof. of Educ., since 1907 and Dean, Sch. of Educ., George Washington Univ., Washington, D. C., since 1912.

Rufi, John, B.S.'18, Kansas State Tchrs. Col., Emporia, Kansas; M.A.'19, Ph. D.'26, Tchrs. Col., Columbia Univ.; Prof. of Educ., Univ. of Mo., Columbia, Mo., since 1928.

Rugg, Earle U., A.B.'15, A.M.'17, Univ. of Ill.; Ph. D.'23, Columbia Univ.; Head, Dept. of Educ., Colo. State Tchrs. Col., Greeley, Colo., since 1923.

Rugg, Harold, B.S.'08, Dartmouth Col.; C. E.'09, Thayer Sch. of Eng.; Ph. D.'15, Univ. of Ill.; Prof. of Educ., Tchrs. Col., Columbia Univ., New York, N. Y., since 1919.

Rugg, L. S., B.S.'19, A.M.'25, Peabody; Prin., West End Elem. Sch., 2023 Polk St., Alexandria, La., since 1920.

Rugh, C. E., A.B.'03, Stanford; M.L.'07, Univ. of Calif.; Prof. of Educ., Univ. of Calif., Haviland Hall, Berkeley, Calif., since 1908.

Ruhl, Howard T., A.B.'07, St. John's Col.; A.M.'17, Columbia Univ.; Co. Supt. of Sch., Elkton, Md.

Rule, James N., B.S.'98, M.S.'01, Sc. D.'27, Washington and Jefferson Col.; Deputy State Supt. of Pub. Instr., Harrisburg, Pa., since 1921.

Rundle, John, B.S.'96, Normal Sch., Lebanon, Ohio; L.I.'98, Peabody Col.; Supt. of Sch., Grenada, Miss., since 1920.

Rundlett, Louis John, A.B.'81, A.M.'87, Dartmouth Col.; Supt. of Sch., Concord, N. H., since 1885.

Runk, Jeshua Paul, B.S.'29, Univ. of Pittsburgh; Supt. of Sch., East McKeesport, Pa., since 1918.

Runyon, Charles, Supvg. Prin. of Sch., 246 Grant Ave., New Brunswick, N. J.

Rupert, W. Earle, Supvg. Prin. of Sch., Kennett Square, Pa.

Rush, Harry E., B.S.'26, Mich. State Col.; Supt. of Sch., Mancelona, Mich., since 1928.

Russ, C. C., Co. Supt. of Sch., Whiteville, N. C.

Russell, Charles, B.S.A.'15, McGill; Ph. D. '22, Columbia Univ.; Prin., State Normal Sch., Westfield, Mass., since 1925.

Russell, Claude C., Asst. Supt. of Sch., New Haven, Conn.

Russell, I. Howard, Co. Supt. of Sch., 84 S. Lake, North East, Pa.

Russell, John Dale, A.B.'17, A.M.'24, Ind. Univ.; Asst. Dir. of the Survey of Educ. Institutions, M. E. Church, 740 Rush St., Chicago, Ill.

Russell, Mrs. Lawrence M., Pd. B. and Pd. M.'97, N. Y. State Col.; A.B.'10, Univ. of Chattanooga; M.A.'14, Columbia Univ.; Supvr. of Intermediate Grades, Pollyanna Apts., Chattanooga, Tenn., since 1919.

Russell, Melvin E., A.B.'17, Univ. of Fla.; Co. Supt. of Pub. Instr., Key West, Fla., since 1925.

Russell, Ralph, Supt. of Sch., Superior, Wyo.

Russell, Ralph D., Ph. D.'23, State Univ. of Iowa; State Dept. of Educ., Boise, Idaho, since 1930.

Russell, Walter B., S.B.'97, Mass. Inst. of Technology; Dir. of Franklin Union, 41 Berkeley St., Boston, Mass., since 1908.

Russell, Walter Earle, A.B.'93, Wesleyan Univ.; Prin., State Normal Sch., Gorham, Maine, since 1905.

Russell, William F., A.B.'10, Cornell Univ.; Ph. D.'14, Columbia Univ.; LL. D.'28, George Washington Univ.; LL. D.'28, Univ. of Pittsburgh; LL. D.'29, Colby Col.; Dean, Tchrs. Col., Columbia Univ., New York, N. Y., since 1927.

Rutan, Olen, Co. Supt. of Sch., Wellsburg, W. Va.

Rutherford, Kenneth L., A.B.'16, Hobart Col.; M.A.'24, Tchrs. Col., Columbia Univ.; Supvg. Prin. of Sch., Monticello, N. Y., since 1928.

Ryan, Belle M., Asst. Supt. of Sch., City Hall, Omaha, Nebr.

Ryan, Jack R., Supt. of Sch., 701 N. Maddell St., McKinney, Texas.

Ryan, W. Carson, Jr., A.B.'07, Harvard; Ph. D.'18, George Washington Univ.; Dir. of Educ., Office of Indian Affairs, Dept. of the Interior, Washington, D. C., since 1930.

Ryan, W. J., B.S.'15, Univ. of Minn.; Supt. of Sch., Gilbert, Minn., since 1928.

Ryder, H. E., B.S.'20, M.S.'21, Ohio Northern Univ.; M.A.'24, Ohio State Univ.; Co. Supt. of Sch., Fremont, Ohio, since 1925.

Saam, Theodore, B.S.'98, Lennox Col.; A.M. '03, State Univ. of Iowa; Supt. of Sch., Elgin, Ill., since 1930.

Sabold, Harvey C., Supvg. Prin. of Sch., Springfield, Pa.

Safford, Adelbert Leon, A.B.'89, A.M.'92, Bates Col.; Dist. Supt. of Sch., Reading, Mass., since 1913.

Sahm, Edgar Arthur, A.B.'26, Univ. of Texas; Supt. of Sch., 145 N. Academy Ave., New Braunfels, Texas, since 1927.

St. Clair, L. W., B.A.'26, North Texas State Tchrs. Col., Denton, Texas; Supt. of Sch., Bremond, Texas, since 1926.

St. John, Claude E., Diploma '03. Kansas State Normal Col.; Supt. of Sch., Arkansas City, Kansas, since 1918.

Saler, Bayard W., A.B.'26, Bethany Col., Bethany, W. Va.; Supvg. Prin. of Sch., Blawnox, Pa., since 1930.

Salgado, S. Morales, Supvr. of Sch., Isabela, P. R., since 1921.

Salley, Nathaniel Moss, A.B.'97, Wofford Col.; Dean, Sch. of Educ., Fla. State Col. for Women, Tallahassee, Fla., since 1910. Address: 553 W. Jefferson St., Tallahassee, Fla.

Sampson, William C., Ph. B.'02, Dickinson Col.; Supt. of Twp. Sch., Upper Darby, Pa., since 1926.

Samuelson, Agnes, M.A.'28, State Univ. of Iowa; State Supt. of Pub. Instr., State House, Des Moines, Iowa, since 1927.

Sanberg, George H., B.A.'19, Univ. of N. Dak.; Supt. of Sch., Rochester, Minn., since 1925.

Sanborn, Channing T., A.B.'00, Dartmouth Col.; Supt. of Sch., Tilton, N. H., since 1915.

Sanborn, Fred C., A.B.'26, Mich. State Normal Col., Ypsilanti, Mich. Address: Public Schools, East Detroit, Mich.

Sanborn, Henry C., A.B.'95, Dartmouth Col.; Supt. of Sch., Andover, Mass., since 1916.

Sanders, Bertha Cook, Co. Supt. of Educ., 728 Pecan, Helena, Ark.

Sanders, Ira G., Diploma '00, State Tchrs. Col.; Co. Supt. of Sch., Middleburg, Pa., since 1930.

Sanders, Joel L., Diploma '21, State Normal Sch., Troy, Ala.; Co. Supt. of Educ., Troy, Ala., since 1923.

Sanders, Walter F., A.B.'09, A.M.'17, Univ. of Chicago. Address: Education Bldg., Ohio State Univ., Columbus, Ohio.

Sandin, Andrés, Supvr. of Sch., Comerio, Porto Rico, since 1921.

Sandwick, Richard L., Supt., Deerfield-Shields Twp. H. S., Highland Park, Ill.

Sanford, Robert G., A.B.'05, Yale Univ.; M.A.'24, Tchrs. Col., Columbia Univ.; Co. Supt. of Sch., Court House, Somerville, N. J., since 1928.

Santee, A. M., Prin., Central H. S., Duluth, Minn.

Sarver, Clifford L., B.A.'15, Hanover Col.; A.M.'27, Tchrs. Col., Columbia Univ.; Supt. of Sch., Spring Valley, Ill., since 1920.

Saunders, C. E., B.S.'87, Miss. Agrl. and Mech. Col.; Supt., Aberdeen Separate Sch. Dist., Aberdeen, Miss., since 1923.

Saunders, Joseph H., A.B., Col. of William and Mary; A.M.'24, Univ. of Chicago; Supt. of Sch., Newport News, Va., since 1921.

Saunders, Robert L., Supt. of Sch., Irvington, N. J.

Sauvain, Nelson, Supt. of Sch., Devils Lake, N. Dak.

Sauvain, Walter Howard, Prin. of Sch., West Winfield, N. Y.

Savides, Antonios P., A.B.'00, Robert Col., Constantinople; A.M.'11, Ph. D.'17, Harvard Univ.; Prof. of Psych. and Educ., Russell Sage Col., Troy, N. Y., since 1927.

Savitz, J. J., Prin., State Normal Sch., Glassboro, N. J.

Sawdon, Jonas, A.B.'18, Univ. of Mich.; Supt. of Sch., Grand Ledge, Mich., since 1910.

Saxe, Henry W., Diploma '93, State Normal and Tr. Sch., Oswego, N. Y.; Supt. of Sch., 50 Church St., New Canaan, Conn., since 1908.

Saxer, A. H., B.S.'10, Utah Agrl. Col.; M. S.'12, Ph. D.'15, Univ. of Calif.; Dean, Sch. of Educ., Utah Agrl. Col., Logan, Utah, since 1927.

Saxvik, H. O., B.A.'05, Luther Col.; Supt. of Sch., 622 Eighth St., Bismarck, N. Dak., since 1922.

Scarborough, William Acree, A.B.'19, Randolph-Macon Col.; M.A.'21, Univ. of Pa.; Co. Supt. of Sch., Dinwiddie, Va., since 1923.

Schafer, J. J., A.B.'20, M.A.'24, Univ. of Mich.; Supt. of Sch., 1521 W. Carpenter St., Midland, Mich., since 1919.

Schatz, Clarence R., B.A., State Tchrs. Col., Fresno, Calif.; Prin., Washington Sch., Dinuba, Calif., since 1925. Address: Route 10, Box 93, Fresno, Calif.

Schinnerer, Mark C., A.M.'23, Tchrs. Col., Columbia Univ.; Prin., Kennard Jr. H. S., 2610 E. 46th St., Cleveland, Ohio, since 1928.

Schlagle, F. L., B.S.'16, State Tchrs. Col., Emporia, Kansas; M.A.'23, Tchrs. Col., Columbia Univ.; Asst. Supt. of Sch., Library Bldg., Kansas City, Kansas, since 1924.

Schlaifer, Osher, A.B.'03, Univ. of Nebr.; Supt. of Sch., Dundee, Ill., since 1916.

Schlegel, Albert G. W., A.B.'20, Moravian Col.; A.M.'27, Pa. State Col.; Supvg. Prin. of Sch., 328 N. Main St., Red Lion, Pa., since 1927.

Schliebner, R. V., 465 Washington St., Buffalo, N. Y.

Schmidt, A. W., A.B.'19, Cornell Col., Iowa; M.A.'26, Tchrs. Col., Columbia Univ.; Asst. in Educ. Finance, State Educ. Dept., Albany, N. Y., since 1928.

Schmidt, Carl J., A.B.'27, Central Normal Col.; Asst. Prin., Union Twp. H. S., Greentown, Ind., since 1929.

Schmidt, H. W., A.B.'08, Univ. of Minn.; Supvr. of H. S. and Bldg., State Dept. of Pub. Instr., 2117 Rowley Ave., Madison, Wis.

Schmitt, Irvin H., B.A.'16, Coe Col.; Supt. of Sch., Grade Bldg., Sac City, Iowa, since 1928.

Schniepp, A. E., Supt., Sch. Dist. No. 182, Twp. H. S., Girard, Ill.

Schoch, Parke, A.B.'88, A.M.'91, Lafayette Col.; Assoc. Supt. of Sch., 19th St. above Chestnut, Philadelphia, Pa., since 1930.

Schrader, Carl L., M.P.E.'28, Springfield Col.; State Supvr. of Physical Educ., State House, Boston, Mass., since 1922.

Schreiber, Paul D., B.S.'12, Bucknell Univ.; Supt. of Sch., Port Washington, N. Y., since 1920.

Schroeder, H. H., Ill. State Normal Sch., 1004 Broadway, Normal, Ill.

Schroedermeier, Alvin G., B.A.'18, Northwestern Univ.; Supt. of Sch., Hiawatha, Kansas, since 1929.

Schultz, Frederick, Ph. B.'22, Univ. of Chicago; A.M.'24, Columbia Univ.; Prin., Sch. No. 24, Buffalo, N. Y., since 1929.

Schumacher, Matthew, A.B.'99, Univ. of Notre Dame; S.T.B.'03, Ph.D.'05, Catholic Univ. of America; Pres., Col. of St. Thomas, St. Paul, Minn., since 1928.

Schumpert, Bailey T., A.B.'02, Peabody Col.; Supt. of Sch., West Point, Miss., since 1918.

Schuyler, Paul M., A.B.'28, Univ. of Mich.; Co. Sch. Commr., Menominee, Mich., since 1923.

Schwall, H. E., A.B.'17, M.A.'29, Ohio State Univ.; Supt. of Sch., H. S., Wauseon, Ohio, since 1927.

Schwartz, Harwood Muzzy, B.S.'07, M.S.'10, Hamilton Col.; Ph. D.'27, Tchrs. Col., Columbia Univ.; Head, Dept. of Educ., St. Lawrence Univ., 17 Goodrich St., Canton, N. Y., since 1926.

Schwebel, George A., LL.B.'17, LL.M.'20, Chicago-Kent Col. of Law; Supt. of Sch., 2324 S. 49th Ave., Cicero, Ill., since 1926.

Schwegler, Raymond A., A.B.'99, Brown; M.A.'06, Ottawa; Ph. D.'29, Columbia Univ.; Dean, Sch. of Educ. and Dir., Summer Session, Univ. of Kansas, Lawrence, Kansas, since 1927.

Schwerin, Emma Mary, Diploma '99 and '08; Co. Supt. of Sch., Hartington, Nebr., since 1915.

Scofield, Belle C., Diploma '13, Pratt Inst.; B.Ph.'21, Univ. of Chicago; Asst. Supvr. of Art, Pub. Schools, 1644 N. Talbott Ave., Indianapolis, Ind., since 1921.

Scolley, Jennie E., Asst. Supt. of Sch., Holyoke, Mass., since 1917.

Scott, Clifford John, Supt. of Sch., East Orange, N. J.

Scott, Frank A., A.B.'03, Harvard; A.M.'13, Dartmouth; Ed.M.'23, Harvard; Supt. of Sch., 31 Blake St., Belmont 78, Mass., since 1921.

Scott, Ira Oscar, B.S.'15, State Tchrs. Col., Emporia, Kansas; A.M.'24, Tchrs. Col., Columbia Univ.; Dean of Jr. Col. and Supt. of Sch., H. S. Bldg., Garden City, Kansas, since 1927.

Scott, Julius E., Ph.D.'30, Columbia Univ.; Prin., Jr. H. S., Peekskill, N. Y., since 1930.

Scott, Walter E., Supt. of Sch., Fairbury, Nebr.

Scott, Zenos E., B.S.'10, Evansville Col.; A.M.'13, Tchrs. Col., Columbia Univ.; Supt. of Sch., Springfield, Mass., since 1923.

Scudder, Jesse Melvin, Supt. of Sch., 958 Salamonia Ave., Huntington, Ind.

Scully, John F., M.Pd.'18, Dartmouth Col.; Supt. of Sch., City Hall, Brockton, Mass., since 1916.

Seagers, Paul W., A.B.'27, Cornell; Dir. of Guidance, Pub. Sch., 18 W. Morris St., Bath, N. Y., since 1927.

Sealock, W. E., A.B.'05, Ohio State Univ.; Ph.D.'16, Columbia Univ.; Dean, Tchrs. Col., Univ. of Nebr., Lincoln, Nebr., since 1922.

Seaman, William H., A.B.'24, Oberlin Col.; A.M.'27, Tchrs. Col., Columbia Univ.; Dir. of Admissions, Oberlin Col., Men's Bldg., Oberlin, Ohio, since 1928.

Searl, Mabel, Co. Supt. of Sch., Court House, Clarinda, Iowa, since 1926.

See, Otis A., B.S.'17, Northeast Mo. State Tchrs. Col., Kirksville, Mo.; M.A.'22, Tchrs. Col., Columbia Univ.; Supt. of Sch., Jennings, Mo., since 1925. Address: 8741 Jennys Rd., St. Louis, Mo.

Seeley, Hutchison A., Supvg. Prin. of Sch., Mendham, N. J.

Segarra, R. A., Diploma '14, Univ. of Porto Rico; Supvr. of Sch., Guayanilla, P. R., since 1917.

Selecman, Charles C., D.D.'16, Central Col.; D.D., Univ. of Southern Calif.; D.D., Ky. Wesleyan; LL.D.'23, Centenary Col.; LL. D.'24. Austin Col.; Pres., Southern Methodist Univ., Dallas, Texas, since 1923.

Selke, George A., B.A.'16, Univ. of Minn.; M.A.'26, Columbia Univ.; Pres., State Tchrs. Col., St. Cloud, Minn., since 1927.

Selleck, Eugene R., Ph.B.'29, Univ. of Wis.; Supt. of Sch., 930 Woodlawn Ave., Des Plaines, Ill., since 1929.

Selover, Jesse, Supvg. Prin. of Sch., South River, N. J., since 1901.

Senter, Andrew Franklin, B.S. in Science '94, Salina Normal Univ.; B.S. in Ed.'16, State Tchrs. Col., Emporia, Kansas; Supt. of Sch., 941 S. Main, Ottawa, Kansas, since 1916.

Senty, Walter B., B.S.'16, North Central Col.; M.A.'26, Univ. of Wis.; Supt. of Sch., H. S., Plymouth, Wis., since 1930.

Serena, Joseph A., A.B.'04, LL.D.'22, Eureka Col.; Pres., Southeast Mo. State Tchrs. Col., Cape Girardeau, Mo., since 1921.

Sessions, Herbert Alanson, Asst. Supt. and Rural Supvr. of Sch., Kings Co., Hanford, Calif., since 1926.

Severn, William E., B.S.'22, Allegheny Col.; Supt. of Sch., Corning Free Academy, Corning, N. Y., since 1929.

Sewell, L. P., B.S.'14, Iowa State Col.; Supt. of Sch., Denison, Iowa, since 1928.

Sexson, John A., B.A.'12, Colo. State Tchrs. Col.; M.A.'19, Univ. of Denver; Supt. of Sch., 320 E. Walnut St., Pasadena, Calif.

Sexton, Jay Wesley, A.B.'02, Albion Col.; M.A.'12, Univ. of Mich.; Supt. of Sch., Bd. of Educ., Lansing, Mich., since 1916.

Shackelford, B. G., A.M.'84. Central Col.; Asst. Supt. of Sch., 911 Locust St., St. Louis, Mo., since 1922.

Shackelford, Edward W., A.B.'85, A.M.'88, LL.D.'13, Univ. of Ala.; Pres., State Normal Sch., Troy, Ala., since 1899.

Shafer, B. F., M.A.'23, Univ. of Chicago; Supt. of Sch., Freeport, Ill., since 1929.

Shafer, Harry M., B.S.'87, M.S.'90, Eureka; A.B.'99, A.M.'00, Harvard; Asst. Supt. of Sch., 1268 Fifth Ave., Los Angeles, Calif., since 1918.

Shaffer, Roy Lee, Ph.B.'09, Dickinson Col.; A.M.'17, Columbia Univ.; Prin., State Normal Sch., Paterson, N. J.

Shambaugh, J. B., B.S.'19, Franklin and Marshall Col.; Supvg. Prin. of Sch., Succasunna, N. J., since 1927.

Shangle, C. Paine, B.A.'10, Univ. of Oregon; M.A.'11, Univ. of Wis.; Supt. of Sch., 402 Ferry, Sedro-Woolley, Wash., since 1922.

Shank, Theodore, 1709 Washington Ave., St. Louis, Mo.

Shank, W. Raymond, Co. Supt. of Sch., Gettysburg, Pa.

Shankland, B. C., A.B.'16, Valparaiso Univ.; A.M.'26, Tchrs. Col., Columbia Univ.; Supt. of Sch., Cadillac, Mich., since 1925.

Shankland, Sherwood D., A.B.'94, Western Reserve Univ.; A.M.'18, Columbia Univ.; Exec. Secy., Dept. of Superintendence, Natl. Educ. Assn., 1201 16th St., N. W., Washington, D. C., since 1922.

Shanley, Miss M. V., Asst. Supt. of Sch., 2 Harrison Ave., Jersey City, N. J., since 1923.

Sharpe, E. Alma, A.B.'13, Univ. of Mich.; Co. Supt. of Sch., Court House, Howell, Mich., since 1920.

Sharrard, Kate, B.S.'14, M.A.'22, Tchrs. Col., Columbia Univ.; Supvr. of Elem. Instr., Pub. Sch., Grand Island, Nebr., since 1928.

Shaw, Edwin Adams, B.S.'98, Tufts Col.; A.M.'16, Ph.D.'18, Harvard Univ.; Head, Dept. of Educ., Tufts Col., Tufts College, 57, Mass., since 1927.

Shaw, Edwin O., A.B.'02, Ph.B.'12, Grayson Col.; LL.B.'21, Univ., of Chicago; M.S. in Ed.'27, Univ. of Okla.; Supt. of Sch., Henryetta, Okla., since 1926.

Shaw, John, A.B.'14, Transylvania Col.; A.M. '25, Columbia Univ.; Supt. of Sch., Maysville, Ky., since 1929.

Shaw, Lloyd, A.B.'13, LL.D.'28, Colo. Col.; Dist. Supt. of Sch., 1527 Winfield Ave., Broadmoor Park, Colorado Springs, Colo., since 1916.

Shawkey, Morris P., A.B.'94, M.A.'09, Pd.D. '16, Ohio Wesleyan Univ.; LL.D.'28, W. Va. Wesleyan Col.; Pres., Dept. of Superintendence, 1915-16; Pres., Marshall Col., Huntington, W. Va., since 1923.

Shea, James T., B.A.'15, M.A.'24, Univ. of Detroit; Asst. Dir. of Educ., Bd. of Educ. Bldg., San Antonio, Texas, since 1925.

Sheffer, William E., A.B.'12, Allegheny Col.; Supt. of Sch., 1731 Leavenworth St., Manhattan, Kansas, since 1926.

Sheffield, John P., B.S.'21, State Tchrs. Col., Pittsburg, Kansas: M.A.'27, Columbia Univ.; Supt. of Sch., 413 E. Fifth St., Cherryvale, Kansas, since 1924.

Shelburne, L. F., M.A.'14, Univ. of Va.; Supt. of Sch., Staunton, Va., since 1925.

Shelby, Thomas Hall, B.A.'07, Univ. of Texas; M.A.'21, Univ. of Chicago; Dean of Extension, Univ. of Texas, Austin, Texas, since 1920.

Shelters, Ronald R., A.B. in Ed. and A.M. '27, Univ. of Mich.; Supt. of Sch., Watervliet, Mich., since 1927.

Shelton, Frank M., B.S.'99, Mt. Union Col.; M.A.'11, Columbia Univ.; Supt. of Sch., 2117 Elmwood Ave., Springfield, Ohio, since 1924.

Shepard, Alvin W., B.S.'91, Cornell Univ.; Deputy Supt. of Sch., Genesee Bldg., Buffalo, N. Y., since 1926.

Shepard, Edwin LeRoy, A.B.'10, Hillsdale Col.; M.A.'28, Univ. of Pittsburgh; Supvg. Prin. of Twp. Schools, Bridgeville, Pa., since 1924.

Shepherd, Fred S., A.B.'84, Beloit Col.; Ph.D. '97, Univ. of Pa.; Supt. of Sch., 18 Belmont Pl., Passaic, N. J., since 1914.

Shepherd, Grace M., 803 N. Mulberry, Maryville, Mo.

Shepherd, Homer P., Supt. of Sch., Knoxville, Tenn.

Shepherd, James William, B.A.'04, Mo. Valley Col.; M.A.'17, Univ. of Texas; B.S. '20, Univ. of Wis.; Head, Dept. of Educ. Cooperation, Extension Div., Univ. of Okla., Norman, Okla., since 1920.

Sherburne, James Wilson, A.B.'27, Greenville Col.; A.M.'28, Univ. of Mich.; Supt. of Sch., Lane, S. Dak., since 1929.

Sheridan, Bernard M., A.B.'87, A.M.'03, Boston Col.; Supt. of Sch., Lawrence, Mass., since 1904.

Sherman, Warren A., A.B.'11, A.M.'16, Brown Univ.; Supt. of Sch., Warwick, R. I., since 1930.

Sherrard, R. M., A.B.'91, A.M.'94, Washington and Jefferson Col.; Pd.D.'25, Duquesne Univ.; Assoc. Supt. of Sch., Bellefield at Forbes St., Pittsburgh, Pa., since 1912.

Sherrod, Charles C., Ph.D.'24, George Peabody Col. for Tchrs.; Pres., East Tenn. State Tchrs. Col., Johnson City, Tenn., since 1925.

Shetlock, William, Ph.B.'17, Muhlenberg Col.; M.A.'22, Columbia Univ.; Supvg. Prin. of Sch., Coplay, Pa., since 1916.

Shield, George W. H., A.B.'00, Northwestern Col.; Supvr. of Modern Languages, 1240 S. Main St., Los Angeles, Calif., since 1924.

Shields, Arthur W., A.B.'13, Grove City Col.; Supt. of Sch., H. S. Bldg., Wellington, Ohio, since 1924.

Shiels, Albert, A.B.'86, Col. of the City of New York; Pd.M.'96, A.M.'99, New York Univ.; L.H.D.'11, Muhlenberg Col.; Prof. of Educ., Tchrs. Col., Columbia Univ., New York, N. Y., since 1922.

Shilling, John, Ph.B.'08, A.M.'10, Dickinson Col.; A.M.'25, Columbia Univ.; Asst. State Supt. of Sch., Dover, Del., since 1919.

Shilling, Robert Edward, Dist. Supt. of Sch., Milford, Del.

Shingle, Francis R., Diploma '01, State Normal Sch., West Chester, Pa.; Asst. Supt. of Sch., 130 W. Genesee St., Syracuse, N. Y., since 1928.

Shinn, Anna Lois, Supt. of Sch., 923 N. Forest Ave., River Forest, Ill., since 1920.

Shipherd, H. Robinson, A.B.'08, A.M.'12, Ph. D.'14, Harvard Univ.; Pres., Lincoln Memorial Univ., Harrogate, Tenn., since 1930.

Shipp, J. H., Supt. of Sch., 221 N. East Ninth, Washington, Ind.

Shirley, William F., B.A.'07, Wabash Col.; M.A.'21, Columbia Univ.; Supt. of Sch., Marshalltown, Iowa, since 1920.

Sholty, Myrtle, Ph.B. in Ed.'12, Univ. of Chicago; M.A.'24, Tchrs. Col., Columbia Univ.; Dir., Tchr. Tr.; Humboldt State Tchrs. Col., Arcata, Calif., since 1927.

Shott, John A., B.Ph. and B.Ped.'93, M.Ph. '95, Ohio Univ.; A.M.'01, Harvard Univ.; Prof. of Educ. and Dir., Tchr. Tr., Westminster Col., New Wilmington, Pa., since 1911.

Shotwell, Fred C., Ph.B.'16, Lafayette Col.; A.M.'21, Tchrs. Col., Columbia Univ.; Supvg. Prin. of Sch., Franklin, N. J., since 1923.

Shouse, John L., A.B.'95, A.M.'96, William Jewell Col.; A.M.'28, Univ. of Chicago; Asst. Supt. in charge of High Schools, Pub. Library Bldg., Kansas City, Mo., since 1929.

Showalter, Benjamin R., A.B.'17, Oberlin Col.; M.A.'21, Ph.D.'25, Tchrs. Col., Columbia Univ.; Dir. of Extension Teaching and Prof. of Educ., Ala. Polytechnic Inst., Auburn, Ala., since 1925.

Shows, S. M., A.B.'26, La. State Normal Col.; Supt. of Parish Sch., Mansfield, La., since 1926.

Shuck, Albert C., A.B.'11, A.M.'12, Dickinson Col.; Supt. of Sch., Ocean City, N. J., since 1929.

Shue, J. Milton, Co. Supt. of Sch., Henrico Court House, Richmond, Va.

Shulkey, B. C., A.B.'16, Baylor Univ.; Supt. of Sch., 607 W. Second St., Olney, Texas, since 1925.

Shull, S. E., A.M.'98, Lafayette. Address: 184 Kearny Ave., Perth Amboy, N. J.

Shultz, Birl E., Educ. Dir., New York Stock Exchange, New York, N. Y.

Shuman, W. L., A.B.'21, M.A.'29, Ohio State Univ.; Supt. of Sch., Mayfield Hgts., Ohio, since 1922.

Sias, Azariah Boody, Ph.B.'03, M.A.'22, Univ. of Rochester; Ph.D.'26, Stanford Univ.; Prof. of Educ., Ohio Univ., Athens, Ohio, since 1926.

Sickles, Frederick James, A.B.'08, Syracuse Univ.; A.M.'18, Tchrs. Col., Columbia Univ.; Supt. of Sch., Roosevelt Jr. H. S., New Brunswick, N. J., since 1923.

Siders, Walter R., B.S.'91, Fremont Col.; D. Paed.'27, Univ. of Idaho; Field Agent, World Fed. of Educ. Assns., 1201 16th St., N. W., Washington, D. C., since 1927.

Siepert, Albert F., B.S.'13, Tchrs. Col., Columbia Univ.; A.M.'24, Univ. of Chicago; Head, Dept. of Educ., Bradley Polytech. Inst., since 1913; Fellow in Educ., Univ. of Chicago, 1926-27; Dir. of Freshmen Personnel, Bradley Polytech. Inst., Peoria, Ill., since 1927.

Sies, Mrs. Alice Corbin, B.S.'09, Columbia Univ.; A.M.'25, Tchrs. Col., Columbia Univ. Address: Indianapolis,. Ind.

Sifert, E. R., A.B.'13, Des Moines Univ.; M. A.'26, State Univ. of Iowa; Prin., Central H. S., Oklahoma City, Okla., since 1930.

Silke, Lucy S., Supvr. of Art, Elem. Sch., since 1914; Dir. of Art, Elem. and Jr. H. S., Chicago, Ill., since 1924. Address: 830 Oakwood Blvd., Chicago, Ill.

Silver, Ernest L., B.L.'99, Pd.D.'24, Dartmouth Col.; Pres., State Normal Sch., Plymouth, N. H., since 1911.

Silvernale, John L., Ph.B.'00, Hamline Univ.; Ed.M.'22, Mich. State Normal Col.; Supt. of Sch., 408 Michigan Ave., Menominee, Mich., since 1914.

Silverwood, Olney J., A.B.'00, Ohio Wesleyan Col.; Supt. of Sch., Ellsworth, Kansas, since 1909.

Simley, Irvin T., A.B.'11, Luther Col.; M. A.'27, Columbia Univ.; Supt. of Sch., South St. Paul, Minn., since 1926.

Simmons, Ernest Pitkin, A.B.'13, Creighton Univ.; M.A.'25, State Univ. of Iowa; Supt. of Sch., Elliott, Iowa, since 1918.

Simon, H. B., B.S.'11, A.M.'26, Columbia Univ.; Supt. of Sch., Norfolk, Nebr., since 1920.

Simpson, Alfred Dexter, A.B.'13, Syracuse Univ.; M.A.'23, Yale Univ.; Ph.D.'27, Columbia Univ.; Asst. Commr. for Finance, State Educ. Dept., Albany, N. Y., since 1928.

Simpson, I. Jewell, A.B.'99, **Western Md.** Col.; A.M.'24, Columbia Univ.; Asst. State Supt. of Sch., Baltimore, Md., since 1925.

Sims, G. M., B.A.'04, Baylor Univ.; Supt. of Sch., Webster Bldg., Port Arthur, Texas, since 1914.

Singer, Wildy V., State Normal Sch., Newark, N. J.

Singleton, Gordon G., B.S.'19, Univ. of Ga.; M.A.'24, Ph.D.'25, Tchrs. Col., Columbia Univ.; Dir., Div. of Information and Statistics, State Dept. of Educ., Atlanta, Ga., since 1925.

Sipple, E. M., B.P.'07, Mo. State Normal; B.S.'14, Univ. of Mo.; M.A.'24, Tchrs. Col., Columbia Univ.; Dir., Park Sch., Baltimore, Md., since 1925.

Sisk, H. C., A.B.'15, Univ. of N. C.; Supt. of Sch., Belmont, N. C., since 1918.

Sisk, Horace, A.B.'13, Univ. of N. C.; A.M. '25, Columbia Univ.; Supt. of Sch., North Wilkesboro, N. C., since 1922.

Skaggs, Mrs. Buena C. D., A.B.'20, Ouachita Col.; A.M.'24, Univ. of Mo.; Co. Supt. of Sch., 737 W. Emerson St., Paragould, Ark., since 1928.

Skeeles, Arthur G., Supvr. of Writing, Pub. Sch., 270 E. State St., Columbus, Ohio, since 1923.

Skidmore, Charles H., M.A.'01, Brigham Young Col.; Supt. of Box Elder Sch. Dist., Court House, Brigham City, Utah.

Skiles, James Roy, Supt. of Sch., 2309 Sherman Ave., Evanston, Ill.

Skillen, Mary, B.S.'25, Tchrs. Col., Columbia Univ.; Dir. of Elem. Educ., Lancaster, Pa., since 1925.

Skinkle, James, Supt. of Sch., 520 Egan St., Chadron, Nebr.

Skinner, Avery W., A.B.'92, Syracuse Univ.; Ph.D.'24, State Col. for Tchrs., Albany, N. Y.; Dir., Exam. and Insp. Div., Univ. of the State of New York, State Educ. Dept., Albany, N. Y., since 1919.

Skinner, Clyde T., 1036 Book Bldg., Detroit, Mich.

Skinner, John J., Sc.B.'06, Upper Iowa Univ.; M.A.'25, Univ. of Minn.; Supt. of Sch., Owatonna, Minn., since 1919.

Slade, A. A., A.B.'11, State Univ. of Iowa; Supt. of Sch., Laramie, Wyo., since 1927.

Slade, William, Jr., B.S.'17, Middlebury Col.; M.A.'20, Tchrs. Col., Columbia Univ.; Dir. of Research, Shaker Hgts. Village Sch. Dist., Cleveland, Ohio, since 1928.

Slager, Fred C., B.Sc. in Ed. '20, Ohio Northern Univ.; M.A.'22, Ohio State Univ.; Prin., Mound Jr. H. S., Columbus, Ohio, since 1926. Address: 157 E. 12th Ave., Columbus, Ohio.

Slayton, William H., A.B.'04, Dartmouth Col.; Supt. of Sch., H. S., Waltham, Mass.

Sliffe, Helene, Ph.B., Mo. Valley Col.; Ph.B. in Ed.'18, Univ. of Chicago; M.A.'29, Columbia Univ.; Asst. Elem. State Supvr., State Dept. of Educ., Baton Rouge, La., since 1926.

Sloop, Arthur H., A.B.'02, A.M.'09, Dickinson Col.; Supt. of Sch., 138 E. Curtin St., Bellefonte, Pa., since 1918.

Slothower, Harry W., B.S.'15, Albright Col.; M.A.'27, Columbia Univ.; Prin., H. S., Mt. Union, Pa., since 1921.

Small, Ernest W., A.B.'93, Bates Col.; Supt. of Sch., Meredith, N. H., since 1923.

Small, Irving W., Diploma '06, State Normal Sch., Farmington, Maine; Supt. of Sch., H. S. Bldg., Bangor, Maine, since 1927.

Smart, Frank L., A.B.'96, Harvard; Supt. of Sch., 1001 Harrison, Davenport, Iowa, since 1906.

Smiley, William H., A.B.'77, Harvard; A.M. '06, Univ. of Denver; Litt.D.'13, Colo. Col.; LL.D.'13, Univ. of Colo.; LL.D.'14, Univ. of Denver; Supt. Emeritus, Sch. Admin. Bldg., 414 14th St., Denver, Colo., since 1924.

Smith, A. H., A.B.'22, Baylor Univ.; Supt. of Sch., 624 N. Main St., Winters, Texas, since 1923.

Smith, A. Haven, A.B.'04, Dickinson Col.; Supt. of Sch., 270 N. Pine St., Orange, Calif., since 1928.

Smith, Arthur J., Prin., Rural Normal Sch., Union Grove, Wis.

Smith, Arthur O., B.S.'11, M.A.'14, New York Univ.; Supt. of Sch., Hudson Trust Bldg., Union City, N. J., since 1926.

Smith, B. O., B.S. in Ed.'25, Univ. of Fla. Address: Col. of Educ., Univ. of Fla., Gainesville, Fla.

Smith, Bela B., B.A.'07, Lafayette Col.; Supt. of Sch., Connellsville, Pa., since 1920.

Smith, Benjamin L., A.B.'16, Duke Univ.; Supt. of Sch., Shelby, N. C., since 1929.

Smith, C. C., A.B.'12, Lebanon Valley Col.; A.M.'19, Columbia Univ.; Supt. of Sch., Mt. Union, Pa., since 1920.

Smith, C. O., Diploma '16, State Tchrs. Col.; Emporia, Kansas; Supt. of Sch., H. S. Bldg., Beloit, Kansas, since 1924.

Smith, Carleton Blose, A.B.'19, Oskaloosa, Iowa; Supt. of Sch., 807 S. Ninth St., Pekin, Ill., since 1923.

Smith, Charles A., B.S.'21, Univ. of Utah; M.A.'26, Ph.D.'30, Tchrs. Col., Columbia Univ.; Supt. of Sch., 267 N. First, E., Provo, Utah, since 1927.

Smith, Charles C., Diploma '05, State Normal Sch., Florence, Ala.; Co. Supt. of Sch., Chatom, Ala., since 1917.

Smith, Mrs. Dorothy Johnston, A.B.'18, Univ. of Mich.; Co. Supt. of Sch., Court House, Globe, Ariz., since 1929.

Smith, E. L., B.S.'23, North Texas State Tchrs. Col., Denton, Texas; Supt. of Sch., Healdton, Okla., since 1929.

Smith, Elmer Francis, B.S.'09, R. I. State Col.; M.A.'21, New York Univ.; Supt. of Sch., Grant Ave. and Locust St., Roselle Park, N. J., since 1919.

Smith, Erman S., Supt. of Sch., Barrington, Ill.

Smith, Ethel L., B.S.'14, M.A.'25, Tchrs. Col., Columbia Univ.; Asst. Dir., Elem. Educ., Admin. Bldg., 9 S. Stockton St., Trenton, N. J., since 1928.

Smith, Felix E., M.S.'00, Univ. of Texas; Supt. of Sch., San Angelo, Texas, since 1905.

Smith, Ferdinand E., A.B.'87, A.M.'90, Hamilton Col.; Supt. of Sch., 15 Lincoln St., Cortland, N. Y., since 1896.

Smith, Frank L., B.S.'10, Syracuse Univ.; Supt. of Sch., 118 E. Main St., Lancaster, N. Y., since 1921.

Smith, G. D., 648 Arlington St., Westfield, N. J.

Smith, George A., Diploma '18, Ill. State Normal Univ.; Supt. of Elem. Schools, 830 Madison Ave., Wood River, Ill., since 1916.

Smith, George A., B.Pd.'15, A.B.'19, Mich. State Normal Col.; A.M.'24, Univ. of Mich.; Supt. of Sch., Plymouth, Mich., since 1918.

Smith, George E., M.D.'07, Univ. of Buffalo; Deputy Supt. of Sch., Genesee Bldg., Buffalo, N. Y., since 1912.

Smith, George J., Supt. of Sch., Clifton, N. J.

Smith, George Owen, B.S.'01, Valparaiso Univ.; Supt. of Sch., Princeton, Ill., since 1923.

Smith, Guy D., A.B.'98, Kalamazoo Col.; A. B.'00, Univ. of Chicago; Supt. of City Sch. and of Educ. at State Prison, H. S., Stillwater, Minn., since 1924.

Smith, H. B., Supt. of Sch., New Bern, N. C.

Smith, H. L., B.S.'25, George Peabody Col. for Tchrs.; Supt. of Sch., 500 Walnut St., Paris, Tenn., since 1924.

Smith, Harold W., A.B.'16, East Texas State Normal Sch., Commerce, Texas; M.A.'30, Univ. of Calif.; Supt., Grammar Sch., Glendale, Ariz., since 1925.

Smith, Harry Pearse, A.B.'09, A.M.'15, State Univ. of Iowa; Ph.D.'25, Columbia Univ.; Prof. of Educ., Syracuse Univ., Syracuse, N. Y., since 1927.

Smith, Harvey A., A.B.'14, Franklin and Marshall Col.; A.M.'21, Univ. of Pa.; Ph. D.'30, Columbia Univ.; Prin., Central H. S., Washington, D. C., since 1929.

Smith, Henry E., Ph.B.'20, Ph.M.'28, Univ. of Wis.; Supt. of Sch., 1017 N. Chicago Ave., South Milwaukee, Wis., since 1928.

Smith, Henry Lester, A.B.'98, A.M.'99, Ind. Univ.; A.M.'10, Ph.D.'16, Columbia Univ.; Dean, Sch. of Educ., Ind. Univ., Bloomington, Ind.

Smith, Hubert H., B.A.'15, Wabash Col.; M. A.'26, Tchrs. Col., Columbia Univ.; Supvg. Prin. of Sch., Hammonton, N. J., since 1926.

Smith, Ira M., LL.B.'09, Ind. Univ.; Registrar, Univ. of Mich., Ann Arbor, Mich., since 1925.

Smith, Ivan G., A.B.'09, Harvard Univ.; A. M.'21, Columbia Univ.; Supt. of Sch., Danvers, Mass., since 1928.

Smith, J. W., Supt. of Sch., 413 Closson Ct., Ludlow, Ky.

Smith, James M., A.B.'21, McMaster Univ.; A.M.'22, Univ. of Chicago; Supt. of Sch., Lockport, Ill., since 1925.

Smith, James M., Pd.B.'13, Valparaiso Univ.; B.A.'21, La. State Univ.; M.A.'25, Ph.D. '27, Columbia Univ.; Pres., La. State Univ., Baton Rouge, La., since 1930.

Smith, James W., M.A.'27, Univ. of Chicago; Supt. of Sch., Bemidji, Minn., since 1929.

Smith, Jesse Lowe, Supt. of Sch. Dist. 107, 334 Vine Ave., Highland Park, Ill., since 1902.

Smith, John E., B.A.'20, Univ. of Dubuque; M.A.'27, State Univ. of Iowa; Supt. of Sch., 926 Elm St., Webster City, Iowa, since 1925.

Smith, Leon O., B.A.'10, M.A.'18, State Univ. of Iowa; Asst. Supt. of Sch., City Hall, Omaha, Nebr., since 1919.

Smith, Lewis Wilbur, A.B.'02, Denison Univ.; A.M.'13, Ph.D.'19, Univ. of Chicago; LL.D.'28, Denison Univ.; Supt. of Sch., Berkeley, Calif., since 1928.

Smith, Montgomery C., A.B.'00, Syracuse Univ.; Supt. of Sch., Hudson, N. Y., since 1922.

Smith, Nelson C., B.L.'01, Boston Univ.; M. L.'10, Univ. of Calif.; Supvg. Prin. of Sch., Leonia, N. J., since 1921.

Smith, Payson, A.M.'03, Tufts Col.; LL.D. '08, Univ. of Maine; Litt.D.'09, Bates Col.; Litt.D.'11, Bowdoin Col.; D.Ed., R. I. Col. of Educ.; L.L.D., Norwich Col.; Pres., Dept. of Superintendence, 1923-24; State Commr. of Educ., Boston, Mass., since 1916.

Smith, Preston H., Ph.B.'93, Colgate; Supt. of Sch., 93 W. 34th St., Bayonne, N. J., since 1917.

Smith, R. K., M.E.'97, Central Pa. Normal Sch.; Supt., Dunbar Twp. Sch., Dawson, Pa., since 1919.

Smith, R. O., A.B.'16, Maryville Col.; Supt. of Sch., Maryville, Tenn., since 1923.

Smith, Ralph R., Diploma, '15, State Normal Sch., Millersville, Pa.; B.S. in Ed.'24, M. A.'27, Univ. of Pa.; Supt. of Sch., Lansdale, Pa., since 1926.

Smith, Raymond A., A.B.'00, A.M.'04, Butler Col.; B.D.'05, Yale; Dir., Sch. of Educ., Texas Christian Univ., Ft. Worth, Texas, since 1920.

Smith, Sim Joe, A.B.'15, Trinity Univ.; LL.B.'21, Univ. of Texas; M.A.'27, Tchrs. Col., Columbia Univ.; Asst. Supt. of Sch., New Rochelle, N. Y., since 1930.

Smith, Van H., B.S.'16, M.A., N. Y. Univ.; Supvg. Prin. of Sch., Burlington, N. J., since 1920.

Smith, W. E., B.S.'27, Southwest Texas State Tchrs. Col., San Marcos, Texas; Supt. of Sch., Moulton, Texas, since 1925.

Smith, W. Ray., B.S.'19, M.A.'29, Univ. of Pittsburgh; Supt. of Sch., Lincoln H. S., Ellwood City, Pa., since 1924.

Smith, W. S., B.S. in Ed.'16, Univ. of Mo.; Supt. of Sch., H. S. Bldg., Excelsior Springs, Mo., since 1921.

Smith, William Alexander, A.B.'90, Williams; A.M.'12, Columbia; Supt. of Sch., Hackensack, N. J., since 1923.

Smith, William C., B.S.'24, Columbia Univ.; Chief, Adult Educ. Bureau, State Educ. Dept., Albany, N. Y., since 1917.

Smith, William E., Supt. of Sch., Boston, Post Rd., Fairfield, Conn.

Smith, William F., A.B.'06, Ind. Univ.; A. M.'26, Columbia Univ.; Supt. of Sch., Elwood, Ind., since 1923.

Smith, William H., 114 S. Arlington Ave., East Orange, N. J.

Smith, William M., A.B.'12, Dickinson; Co. Supt. of Sch., Court House, Freehold, N. J.

Smith, Z. Mayo, A.B.'01, A.M.'05, De Pauw Univ.; B.S.A.'19, Purdue Univ.; Ph.D.'29, Ind. Univ.; State Dir. of Voc. Educ. and State Supvr. of Agrl. Educ., 202 Sylvia St., West Lafayette, Ind., since 1913.

Smith, Z. Merrill, Supt. of Sch., Greenfield, Ind.

Smyth, James Marvin, A.B.'18, Westminster Col.; Supt. of Sch., Canton, Miss., since 1925.

Snavely, Henry E., Supt. of Sch., New Castle, Del.

Snead, Judson, B. Voc. Ed., B.S. in Ed. and M.A.'24, Univ. of Ala.; Supt. of Sch., Talladega, Ala., since 1925.

Snedden, David, Ph.D.'07, Columbia Univ.; Prof. of Educ., Tchrs. Col., Columbia Univ., 525 W. 120th St., New York, N. Y., since 1916.

Sneed, Jeter Dewey, B.S.'28, East Central State Tchrs. Col., Ada, Okla.; Supt. of Sch., Ft. Cobb, Okla., since 1928.

Snider, E. Q., A.B.'06, M.A.'21, Univ. of Ill.; Supt., Union H. S., Yuma, Ariz., since 1924.

Snively, Carrie A., Diploma '07, Am. Normal Sch. of Physical Educ.; Supvr. Physical Educ., Pub. Sch., 714 Union St., Ft. Wayne, Ind., since 1907.

Snodgrass, George M., Ph.B.'00, Hamline Univ.; Pres., State Tchrs. Col., La Crosse, Wis., since 1927.

Snow, William Brackett, A.B.'85, Boston Univ.; Asst. Supt. of Sch., 15 Beacon St., Boston, Mass., since 1921.

Snowden, Foster B., Ph.B.'15, Lafayette Col.; M.A.'29, Univ. of Pittsburgh; Dist. Supt. of Sch., First St., Conemaugh, Pa., since 1924.

Snyder, J. W., Diploma '14, State Tchrs. Col., Bowling Green, Ky.; A.B.'23, Univ. of Ky.; Co. Supt. of Sch., Owensboro, Ky., since 1926.

Snyder, Lewis N., A.B.'16, Gettysburg Col.; A.M.'24, Univ. of Pa.; Supvg. Prin. of Sch., Sellersville, Pa.

Snyder, R. H., A.B.'12, Ind. Univ.; M.A.'19, Univ. of Chicago; Supt. of Sch., Idaho Falls, Idaho, since 1919.

Snyder, Ray Perkins, Chief, Rural Educ. Bureau, State Educ. Dept., 28 Menand Rd., Albany, N. Y., since 1923.

Snyder, William R., Supt. of Sch., Norwich, Conn.

Solomon, R. W., Ph.B. in Ed.'15, Univ. of Chicago; Supt. of Sch., 2201 Linden Ave., Middletown, Ohio, since 1917.

Somers, Florence A., Diploma '08, Sargent Sch. of Physical Educ.; B.S.E.'23, Boston Univ.; M.A.'29, N. Y. Univ.; Dir., Health and Physical Educ., 79 Washington St., East Orange, N. J.

Somers, Wilson Edward, Diploma and B.A. '15, Col. of William and Mary; M.A.'23, Tchrs. Col., Columbia Univ. Address: North Emporia, Va.

Somerville, Irwin B., Prin., Ridgewood H. S., Ridgewood, N. J.

Somerville, Leslie G., M.A.'29, Univ. of Mo.; Co. Supt. of Sch., Maryville, Mo., since 1921.

Sooy, Wendell, A.B.'16, A.M.'25, Univ. of Pa. Address: Public Schools, Gloucester City, N. J.

Sorensen, R. R., B.S.'15, Carleton Col.; A.M. '24, Columbia Univ.; Supt. of Sch., Tracy, Minn., since 1921.

Sorum, Marie, B.A.'17; Co. Supt. of Sch., Court House, Estherville, Iowa, since 1918.

Souder, Alan W., Supvg. Prin. of Sch., Williamstown, N. J.

Southerland, R. H., B.S.'21, M.A.'22, George Peabody Col. for Tchrs.; Co. Supt. of Sch., Livingston, Ala., since 1928.

Spain, Charles L., A.B.'93, M.A.'20, Ph.D.'23, Univ. of Mich.; Deputy Supt. of Sch., 1354 Broadway, Detroit, Mich., since 1914.

Spalsbury, Ross L., Dist. Supt., U. S. Indian Service, 309 E. 19th St., Lawrence, Kansas, since 1921.

Spargo, John A., Asst. State Commr. of Educ., State House, Trenton, N. J.

Sparks, Robert Burdette, A.B.'19, Southwestern Univ.; A.M.'26, Univ. of Chicago; Prin., H. S., Marshall, Texas, since 1926.

Sparling, E. A., B.S. in Ed.'16, State Tchrs. Col., Kirksville, Mo.; Supt. of Sch., Muscatine, Iowa, since 1926.

Spaulding, C. E., A.B.'97, Ind. Univ.; Supt. of Sch., Plymouth, Ind., since 1924.

Spaulding, Frank E., A.B.'89, Amherst; A. M., Ph.D.'94, Leipzig; LL.D.'20, Amherst; A.M., Hon.'20, Yale; Prof. of Educ., Yale Univ., 68 Cold Spring St., New Haven, Conn., since 1920.

Speare, Guy Edwin, A.B.'03, Dartmouth Col.; Ed.M.'26, Harvard Univ.; Supt. of Sch., Supvr. of Tr., State Normal Sch., 20 High St., Plymouth, N. H., since 1921.

Speer, Owen D., A.B.'16, Univ. of Mont.; Supt. of Sch., Deer Lodge, Mont., since 1914.

Speerbrecher, Henry George, B.S.'22, Univ. of Chicago; M.A.'28, Univ. of Wis.; Prin., Roosevelt Jr. H. S., Milwaukee, Wis., since 1926.

Speltz, Arthur F., Dist. Supt. of Sch., Pontiac, Ill.

Spencer, John O., Ph.D.'95, Ill. Wesleyan Univ.; A.M.'02, Columbia Univ.; LL.D.'26, Wash. Col.; Pres., Morgan Col., Baltimore, Md., since 1902.

Spencer, Robert R., A.B.'23, Univ. of Hawaii; Prin., Washington Jr. H. S., Punahou and King Sts., Honolulu, Hawaii, since 1926.

Spencer, Thomas E., 911 Locust, St. Louis, Mo.

Spencer, William L., B.A.'02, Williams Col.; M.A.'15, Tchrs. Col., Columbia Univ.; Dir. of Sec. Educ., State Dept. of Educ., Montgomery, Ala., since 1920.

Spiess, G. Adolph, Prin., Livermore Union H. S. Livermore, Calif.

Spigelmyer, William W., Supt. of Twp. Sch., 720 S. Brady St., Du Bois, Pa.

Spitznas, James E., Ph.B.'15, Dickinson Col.; M.A.'28, Tchrs. Col., Columbia Univ.; Co. Supvr. of H. S., Center St., Cumberland, Md., since 1929.

Spofford, Judson G., 28 James, Hillside, N. J.

Sprague, Harry A., B.S.'15, M.A.'17, Tchrs. Col., Columbia Univ.; Pres., N. J. State Tchrs. Col., Upper Montclair, N. J., since 1927.

Sprenkle, William Howard, M.S.'01, Gettysburg Col.; Prin., Carrick H. S., 112 Birmingham Ave., Mt. Oliver Branch, Pittsburgh, Pa., since 1926.

Springsteed, Clara B., B.A.'08, Mt. Holyoke Col.; Pd.B.'10, New York State Col. for Tchrs., Albany, N. Y.; M.A.'17, Univ. of Wis.; Asst. Supt. of Sch., Amsterdam, N. Y., since 1921.

Spry, Edward W., A.M.'22, Univ. of Rochester; Supt. of Sch., LeRoy, N. Y.

Srygley, Hubbard F., B.S.'16, George Peabody Col. for Tchrs.; Supt. of Sch., Hume-Fogg H. S., Eighth and Broad Sts., Nashville, Tenn., since 1930.

Stacy, Chester R., Diploma '00, Mass. State Normal Sch.; Union Supt. of Sch., South Yarmouth, Mass., since 1929.

Staffelbach, Elmer H., 115 S. 12th St., San Jose, Calif.

Staffelbach, Ralph E., A.B.'17, Univ. of Wichita; A.M.'25, Univ. of Okla.; Supt. of Sch., 126 S. Pecan, Nowata, Okla., since 1929.

Stahl, H. E., A.B.'14, Ind. Univ.; A.M.'18, Columbia Univ.; Supt. of Claymont Special Sch. Dist., Claymont, Del., since 1922.

Staley, A. H., Supt. of Sch., Hastings, Nebr.

Staley, George R., B.S.'00. Syracuse Univ.; Supt. of Sch., 106 N. George St., Rome, N. Y., since 1912.

Staley, Raymond E., A.B.'12, St. John's Col.; A.M.'24, Tchrs. Col., Columbia Univ.; Asst. Supt. and Prin., Haskell Inst., Lawrence, Kansas, since 1929.

Stambaugh, J. Lee, B.A.'20, M.A.'24, Univ. of Texas; Supt. of Pharr-San Juan Pub. Sch., San Juan, Texas, since 1920.

Stanforth, A. T., Ph.D.'28, New York Univ. Address: 1050 Tenth Court, Boulder, Colo.

Stansbury, V. E., A.B.'19, S.W.; A.M.'20, Univ. of Chicago. Address: 3615 Garretson, Sioux City, Iowa.

Stanton, Benjamin F., B.A.'96, Oberlin Col.; M.A.'00, Harvard Univ.; Supt. of Sch., Alliance, Ohio, since 1913.

Stanton, George J., Supt. of Sch., Highland, N. Y.

Stanwood, Mrs. Edward B., B.L.'98, Univ. of Calif.; Prin., Sarah Dix Hamlin Sch., 2120 Broadway, San Francisco, Calif., since 1927.

Staples, Leon C., A.B.'03, Colby Col.; Supt. of Sch., Plainville, Conn.

Staples, Le Roy G., A.B.'00, Bates Col.; Supt. of Sch., City Hall, Warren, R. I., since 1910.

Starbuck, Edwin Diller, Prof. of Philosophy, Univ. of Southern Calif., Los Angeles, Calif., since 1930.

Stark, Leonard J., B.S.'21, Kansas State Tchrs. Col., Emporia, Kansas; Supt. of Sch., Lincoln, Kansas, since 1924.

Stark, M. F., B.S. in Ed.'22, State Tchrs. Col., Emporia, Kansas; Supt. of Sch., Greensburg, Kansas, since 1925.

Stark, William E., A.B.'95, A.M.'01, Harvard Univ.; Dean of the Col., Hampton Inst., Hampton, Va.

Starkweather, James A., A.B.'01, Shurtleff Col.; A.M.'16, Tchrs. Col., Columbia Univ.; Asst. Supt. of Sch., 226 N. First Ave., E., Duluth, Minn., since 1919.

Starr, Fred M., A.B.'01, De Pauw Univ.; A. M.'15, Tri-State Col.; Supt. of Sch., Noblesville, Ind., since 1927.

Stauffer, Harry F., 92 S. Tenth St., Newark, N. J.

Stayman, Joseph W., Ph.B.'94, A.M.'97, Dickinson Col.; Pres., Potomac State Sch., Keyser, W. Va., since 1912.

Steegar, William H., Supvg. Prin. of Sch., Garfield, N. J.

Steele, E. J., A.B.'22, Ohio Univ.; Prin., H. S., Frankfort, Ohio, since 1925.

Steele, Harold, B.S.'02, Albion Col.; M.A.'08, Univ. of Wis.; Supt. of Sch., 114 W. Wesley St., Jackson, Mich., since 1930.

Steele, N. E., M.A.'27, State Univ. of Iowa; Secy., S. Dak. Educ. Assn., Perry Bldg., Sioux Falls, S. Dak., since 1924.

Steele, Robert McCurdy, Pres., State Tchrs. Col., California, Pa.

Steere, William S., Ed.M.'28, R. I. Col. of Educ.; Asst. Supt. of Sch., 9 Exchange Ter., Providence, R. I., since 1926.

Steffey, A. J., A.B.'14, Northwestern Univ.; M.A.'28, State Univ. of Iowa; Supt. of Sch., Knoxville, Iowa, since 1925.

Steiner, John H., Supt. of Sch., 2225 Hampshire St., Quincy, Ill.

Steiner, Melvin A., B.A.'09, Col. of Wooster; M.A.'13, Ph.D.'30, Univ. of Pittsburgh; Supvg. Prin. of Sch., Ingram, Pittsburgh, Pa., since 1918.

Stengle, F. E., A.M.'30, Lebanon Valley Col.; Supvg. Prin. of Sch., Hummelstown, Pa., since 1929.

Stephens, Edwin L., A.B.'92, La. State Univ.; Pd.M.'97, Pd.D.'99, New York Univ.; Pres., Southwestern La. Inst., Lafayette, La., since 1900.

Stephens, Ernest, A.B.'10, Dartmouth Col.; Ed.M.'27, Harvard Univ.; Deputy Supt. of Sch., 40 Franklin St., Lynn, Mass., since 1927.

Stephens, W. R., Jr., A.B.'15, Hendrix Col.; Co. Supt. of Sch., Star City, Ark., since 1921.

Stephens, William Logan, A.B.'89, Univ. of Nebr.; Supt. of Sch., 715 Locust Ave., Long Beach, Calif., since 1912.

Stern, Bessie C., A.B.'09, Cornell Univ.; M. Ed.'21, Harvard Univ.; Statistician, Md. State Dept. of Educ., Lexington Bldg., Baltimore, Md., since 1921.

Stetson, G. Arthur, B.S.'19, Allegheny Col.; M.A.'27, Tchrs. Col., Columbia Univ.; Supt. of Sch., Titusville, Pa., since 1928.

Stetson, Paul C., A.B.'07, Kalamazoo Col.; A.B.'07, A.M.'17, Univ. of Chicago; Supt. of Sch., 150 N. Meridian St., Indianapolis, Ind., since 1930.

Stevens, Benjamin A., Assoc. Prof. of Educ. Admin., Univ. of N. C., Chapel Hill, N. C.

Stevens, E. R., M.S.'25, Univ. of Kansas; Prin., Jr. Col. and High Schools, Independence, Kansas, since 1926.

Stevenson, Dwight H., Ph.D.'26, Ohio State Univ.; Head, Dept. of Educ., State Normal Sch., Potsdam, N. Y., since 1924.

Stevenson, Fred G., A.B.'08, Univ. of Mich.; A.M.'29, Univ. of Chicago; Supt. of Sch., Central Bldg., Dubuque, Iowa, since 1926.

Stevenson, Idabelle, A.B.'16, Smith Col.; Exec. Secy., Natl. Safety Council, 1 Park Ave., New York, N. Y., since 1926.

Stewart, David H., B.S.'15, Pa. State Col.; A.M.'25, Columbia Univ.; Supvg. Prin. of Sch., Beaver Sr. H. S., Beaver, Pa., since 1923.

Stewart. E. L., Life Cert. '11, Ind. State Normal Sch.; A.B.'22, Ind. Univ.; Supt. of Sch., 115 Kimmel St., Berrien Springs, Mich., since 1925.

Stewart, Paul E., L.I.'03, Peabody Col.; A. B.'11, Stanford Univ.; Supt. of Sch., Santa Barbara, Calif., since 1919.

Stiers, J. C., Supt. of Sch., Washington Trust Bldg., Washington, Pa.

Stiles, Chester D., A.B.'00, A.M.'09, Williams; Sc.Pd.'17, Clark Univ.; Supt. of Sch., 186 Main St., Westfield, Mass., since 1918.

Stillwell, Roy P., Supvg. Prin. of Twp. Sch., 7 Fairview Pl., Morristown, N. J.

Stilwell, H. W., B.A.'09, M.A.'19, Univ. of Texas; Supt. of Sch., Texarkana, Texas, since 1920.

Stilwell, William Earle, A.B.'01, A.M.'03, Harvard; Headmaster, Univ. Sch., Blair and Hartford Aves., Cincinnati, Ohio, since 1903.

Stinebaugh, Virgil, A.M.'27, Columbia Univ.; Dir. of Sch. Inspection, State Dept. of Educ., Indianapolis, Ind., since 1928.

Stockard, L. V., A.B.'11, A.M.'19, Univ. of Texas; Dist. Supt. of High Schools, 5315 Tremont St., Dallas, Texas, since 1924.

Stockton, K. L., B.S.M.E.'12, Purdue Univ.; Dist. Supt. of Sch., 6020 Miles Ave., Huntington Park, Calif., since 1925.

Stoddard, A. J., B.S.'21, Univ. of Nebr.; M. A.'22, Tchrs. Col., Columbia Univ.; Supt. of Sch., 9 Exchange Ter., Providence, R. I., since 1929.

Stoddard, George D., B.A.'21, Pa. State Col.; Diplôme '23, Univ. of Paris; Ph.D.'25, State Univ. of Iowa; Dir., Iowa Child Welfare Research Sta., State Univ. of Iowa, Iowa City, Iowa, since 1929.

Stoddard, J. A., A.B.'02, Univ. of S. C.; M. A.'24, George Peabody Col. for Tchrs.; LL.D.'30, Presbyterian Col. of S. C.; Prof. of Sec. Educ. and Dir. of Summer Sch., Univ. of S. C., Columbia, S. C., since 1918.

Stokes, Ella Harrison, B.S.'99, M.A.'01, Ohio Wesleyan Univ.; Ph.D.'10, Univ. of Chicago; Head, Dept. of Educ. and Philosophy, Penn Col., Oskaloosa, Iowa, 1901-1908 and since 1911.

Stokes, Joel R., Diploma '21, Eastern Ill. State Normal Sch., Charleston, Ill.; Ph.B. '26, Univ. of Chicago; Dist. Supt. of Sch., Roosevelt School, Bellwood, Ill., since 1929.

Stolen, Alvin T., B.A.'18, St. Olaf Col.; Supt. of Sch., Fergus Falls, Minn., since 1929.

Stone, Charles T., B.A.'96, Bowdoin Col.; Supt. of Sch., 90 Washington St., Long Branch, N. J., since 1921.

Stone, Elton E., A.B.'16, Univ. of Nebr.; A. M.'24, Tchrs. Col., Columbia Univ.; Prin., Sr. H. S., 227 Bushkill St., Easton, Pa., since 1924.

Stoops, R. O., A.B.'97, Lake Forest Col.; A. M.'06, Ill. Col.; Ph.D.'22, Columbia Univ. Address: York, Pa.

Storm, Howard Charles, Supt. of Sch., 194 Main St., Batavia, Ill.

Stott, James W., A.B.'03, A.M.'07, Ind. Univ.; Supt. of Sch., Frankfort, Ind., since 1922.

Stouffer, Samuel M., B.Sc.'17, Susquehanna Univ.; M.A.'27, New York Univ.; Supt. of Sch., Wilmington, Del., since 1929.

Stout, A. J., B.S.'19, Tchrs. Col., Columbia Univ.; Supt. of Sch., Topeka, Kansas, since 1918.

Stout, John E., A.B.'04, Cornell Col., Mt. Vernon, Iowa; Ph.M.'08, Ph.D.'18, Univ. of Chicago; Dean, Sch. of Educ., Northwestern Univ., Evanston, Ill., since 1926.

Stover, Edgar S., B.S.'03, Oskaloosa; A.M. '27, Columbia Univ.; Supt. of Sch., H. S., Bloomfield, N. J., since 1928.

Stover, James D., B.A.'12, M.A.'13, Princeton Univ.; Asst. Supt. of Sch., 216 E. Ninth St., Cincinnati, Ohio, since 1929.

Stover, John H., Box 243, Oklahoma City, Okla.

Stowe, A. Monroe, A.M.'04, N. W. Univ.; A.M.'05, Harvard Univ.; Ph.D.'09, Columbia Univ.; Prof. of Educ., Randolph-Macon Woman's Col., Lynchburg, Va., since 1926.

Strahan, Charles J., Deputy State Commr. of Educ., State Office Bldg., Trenton, N. J., since 1922.

Strang, Annie M., 348 Central St., Auburndale, Mass.

Straub, J. Harold, Prin., Willard Elem. Sch., Ridgewood, N. J.

Strayer, George D., A.B.'03, Johns Hopkins Univ.; Ph.D.'05, Columbia Univ.; LL.D. '25 Col. of William and Mary; Litt.D.'29, Columbia Univ.; Pres., Natl. Educ. Assn., 1918-19; Prof. of Educ. Admin., Tchrs. Col., Columbia Univ., New York, N. Y.

Strayer, George D., Jr., B.S.'27, Princeton Univ.; M.A.'28, Tchrs. Col., Columbia Univ.; Statistician, Pub. Sch., Franklin Admin. Bldg., Washington, D. C., since 1929.

Streitz, Ruth, Ph.B.'21, A.M.'22, Univ. of Chicago; Ph.D.'26, Columbia Univ.; Prof. of Educ. and Chmn., Dept. of Elem. Educ., Col. of Educ., Univ. of Cincinnati, Cincinnati, Ohio, since 1926.

Strickland, Charles P., Supt. of Sch., Alvin, Texas.

Stringer, Simeon Lafayette, B.S.'00, Southern Normal Univ.; B.A.'02, Western Ky. State Normal Sch., Bowling Green, Ky.; M.A.'28, Univ. of Miss.; Pres., Pearl River Col., Poplarville, Miss., since 1925.

Strohm, G. E., Secy., Bd. of Educ., Trenton, Mich., since 1911.

Stromstad, Emily, Diploma '13, State Tchrs. Col., La Crosse, Wis.; Co. Supt. of Sch., La Crosse, Wis., since 1926.

Strong, Solomon C., Diploma '02, State Normal Sch., East Stroudsburg, Pa.; B.S.'16, New York Univ.; Supt. of Sch., West Orange, N. J., since 1918.

Strong, William M., B.S.'13, Tufts Col.; Ed. M.'29, Harvard Univ.; Field Supvr. of Rural Educ., Westbrook, Conn., since 1919.

Stroup, F. Neff, Ph.B.'13, Dickinson Col.; M.A.'18, Columbia Univ.; Supt. of Sch., Newark, N. Y., since 1921.

Stuart, Herman H., Supt. of Sch., Melrose, Mass.

Stuart, Josephine B., 549 County St., New Bedford, Mass.

Stubblefield, Garland A., Supt. of Sch., Springdale, Ark.

Stubbs, G. T., A.B.'26, Southeastern State Tchrs. Col., Durant, Okla.; Supt. of Sch., Durant, Okla., since 1929.

Stube, John H., B.S.'85, North Central Col.; Dist. Supt. of Sch., 2041 Morse Ave., Chicago, Ill., since 1917.

Studebaker, John W., B.S.'10, Leander Clark Col.; A.M.'17, Columbia Univ.; Supt. of Sch., Des Moines, Iowa, since 1920.

Study, H. P., A.B.'03, Baker Univ.; M.A. '11, Boston Univ.; A.M.'28, Columbia Univ.; Supt. of Sch., Springfield, Mo., since 1924.

Stull, Arthur Maurer, B.S.'27, M.A.'29, Univ. of Pittsburgh; Supvg. Prin. of Dale Public Sch., 30 Akers St., Johnstown, Pa., since 1926.

Stumberg, Charles H., A.B., L.B.'89, A.M. '92, Univ. of Mo.; Prof. of German, La. State Univ., since 1895; Dir. of Univ. Ext. Division, La. State Univ., since 1924. Address: Univ. Sta., Baton Rouge, La.

Sturtevant, Arthur L., B.S.'12, B.A.'25, Univ. of Maine; Supvg. Prin. of Sch., Franklin, Vt., since 1926.

Sturtevant, Merle Alton, B.S.'08, Univ. of Maine; Supt. of Sch., Shrewsbury, Mass., since 1923.

Stutsman, Isaac Edward, A.B.'09, State Univ. of Iowa; Supt. of Sch., 1622 13th Ave., Greeley, Colo., since 1929.

Stutzman, G. C., B.A.'17, Knox Col.; M.A. '23, State Univ. of Iowa; Supt. of Sch., Hanover, Ill., since 1923.

Suhrie, Ambrose L., Ph.B.'06, John B. Stetson Univ.; A.M.'11, Ph.D.'12, Univ. of Pa.; LL.D.'19, John B. Stetson Univ.; Prof. of Normal Sch. and Tchrs. Col. Educ., Sch. of Educ., New York Univ., Washington Square, East, New York, N. Y., since 1924.

Sullivan, Ella C., Edgewater Beach Hotel, Chicago, Ill.

Sullivan, Katharine C. V., Prin., James Madison Morton Jr. H. S., Fall River, Mass., since 1926.

Sullivan, Nora T., 55 Glenwood Ave., Jersey City, N. J.

Sunday, Angeline M., N. Market St., Frederick, Md.

Sutherland, Ora Clyde, B.A.'29, State Univ. of Iowa; Supt. of Sch., Bellevue, Iowa, since 1929.

Sutton, Henry F., Ph.B.'20, Univ. of Wis.; Supt. of Sch., 523 Howe St., Green Bay, Wis., since 1929.

Sutton, Willis A., Ph.B.'03, B.LL.'04, Emory Col.; Pres., Natl. Educ. Assn., 1930-31; Supt. of Sch., Atlanta, Ga.

Swaim, Laura Grey, Permanent State Supvg. Prin. Cert. '21; Supvg. Prin. of Sch., Maple Shade, N. J., since 1922.

Swan, Grace G., Dir. of Primary Instr. and Elem. Practice, Admin. Bldg., Bellefield Ave. at Forbes St., Pittsburgh, Pa., since 1923.

Swank, George L., A.B.'01, Grove City Col.; A.B.'04, Harvard Univ.; A.M.'17, Susquehanna Univ.; Co. Supt. of Sch., 205 Fairmount Ave., Sunbury, Pa., since 1921.

Sweeney, Ella L., Asst. Supt. of Sch., 9 Exchange Ter., Providence, R. I., since 1902.

Sweet, Walter Prescott, B. S. '17, Tufts Col.; Ed.M.'30, Harvard Univ.; Asst. Supt. of Sch., City Hall, Somerville, Mass., since 1928.

Swetman, Ralph Waldo, Ph.B.'07, Hamilton Col.; A.M.'17, Columbia Univ.; Ph.D. '28, Stanford Univ.; Pres., Humboldt State Tchrs. Col., Arcata, Calif., since 1924.

Swicker, Harold B., B.A. in Ed.'21, Univ. of Maine; M.A. in Ed.'27, Columbia Univ.; Supt. of Sch., Bennington S. W. Dist., 306 Silver St., Bennington, Vt., since 1926.

Swigart, Forrest Damon, B.S.'21, Denison Univ.; M.A.'29, Ohio State Univ.; Supt. of Sch., 562 E. Livingston, Celina, Ohio, since 1928.

Swing, Glenn O., B.A.'16, M.A.'17, Ohio State Univ.; Supt. of Sch., City Bldg., Covington, Ky., since 1927.

Symons, John T., Life Cert. '12, Mich. State Normal Col.; Supt. of Sch., Central Bldg., Coldwater, Mich., since 1928.

Symons, Wilfred L., B—305 Monterey, 43rd and Chester Ave., Philadelphia, Pa.

Tall, Lida Lee, B.S.'14, Columbia Univ.; Litt.D.'26, Univ. of Md.; Prin., State Normal Sch., Towson, Md., since 1920.

Tallman, Pearle, A.B.'20, Iowa State Tchrs. Col., Cedar Falls, Iowa; M.A.'28, Columbia Univ.; Asst. Dir. of H. S., 603 Great Southern Life Bldg., Houston, Texas, since 1926.

Tanger, Landis, Ph.B.'05, Franklin and Marshall Col.; A.M.'13, Univ. of Pa.; Pd.D. '25, Muhlenberg Col.; Sc.D.'30, Franklin and Marshall Col.; Pres., State Tchrs. Col., Millersville, Pa., since 1929.

Tannahill, Sallie B., B.S.'15, A.M.'26, Columbia Univ.; Asst. Prof. of Fine Arts, Tchrs. Col., Columbia Univ., New York, N. Y., since 1906.

Taylor, E. B., A.B.'12, A.M.'13, Univ. of Rochester; Prof. of Educ., Univ. of Rochester, 389 Rockingham St., Rochester, N. Y.

Taylor, E. W., A.B.'25, Marshall Col.; Supt. of Sch., Hinton, W. Va., since 1927.

Taylor, George D., Diploma '01, State Normal Sch., Oswego, N. Y.; B.S.'13, M.A. '22, Univ. of Rochester; Prin., Susan B. Anthony Sch. No. 27, Central Park and First St., Rochester, N. Y., since 1922.

Taylor, Hilles M., A.B.'13, State Univ. of Iowa; A.M.'15, Des Moines Col.; Supt. of Sch., 309 Scott Ct., Shenandoah, Iowa, since 1924.

Taylor, Rachel W., M.A.'28, Tchrs. Col., Columbia Univ.; State Dir. of Art Educ., Commercial Law Bldg., Dover, Del., since 1929.

Taylor, V. E., Supvr. of Sch., San Juan, P. R., since 1926.

Taylor, William Hall, B.S.'23, Mich. State Col., East Lansing, Mich.; Ed.M.'28, Harvard Univ.; Supt. of Sch., Okemos, Mich., since 1927.

Taylor, William S., B.S.'12, Univ. of Ky.; M.S.'13, Univ. of Wis.; Ph.D.'24, Columbia Univ.; Dean, Col. of Educ., Univ. of Ky., Lexington, Ky., since 1923.

Teach, Charles Elden, A.B.'03, A.M.'14, Univ. of Nebr.; Supt. of Sch., San Luis Obispo, Calif., since 1928.

Teal, Fred L., Diploma '18, B.S. in Ed.'19, Ohio Northern Univ.; M.A.'23, Ohio State Univ.; Supt. of Sch., Charleston, W. Va., since 1929.

Teal, Harvey D., A.B.'18, Defiance Col.; M.A.'27, Ohio State Univ.; Dist. Supt. of Sch., Clairton, Pa., since 1929.

Tebow, Eric T., B.S.'26, Kansas State; Supt. of Sch., Glasco, Kansas, since 1929.

Telfer, Vera M., B.S., Tchrs. Col., Columbia Univ.; Helping Tchr., Rural Schools, Court House, Belvidere, N. J.

Temple, Alice, Ph.B.'08, Univ. of Chicago; Assoc. Prof., Sch. of Educ., Univ. of Chicago, Chicago, Ill., since 1909.

Templin, R. J. W., Sc.B.'16, A.M.'19, Bucknell Univ.; Supt. of Sch., Montgomery and Wyoming Aves., West Pittston, Pa., since 1923.

Terhune, Beekman R., A.B.'01, Princeton; A.M.'02, Columbia; Supt. of Sch., Somerset Sch., North Plainfield, N. J., since 1923.

Tew, Derwood J., A.B.'06, Colgate Univ.; Genl. Supvr., Elem. and Jr. High Schools, Haddon and Newton Aves., Camden, N. J., since 1918.

Tews, Arthur C., Diploma '12, State Normal Sch., Platteville, Wis.; Diploma '16, Stout Inst.; Co. Supt. of Sch., Court House, Waukesha, Wis., since 1925.

Thackston, A. J., Supt. of Sch., Whitman St., Orangeburg, S. C.

Thackston, John A., Ph.D., New York Univ.; Dean, Col. of Educ. and Dir. of Summer Quarter, Univ. of Tenn., Knoxville, Tenn.

Thalman, J. L., A.B.'00, Ohio Wesleyan Col.; A.M.'10, Univ. of Mich.; A.M.'29, Tchrs. Col., Columbia Univ. Address: 1217 Victory Court, Anderson, Ind.

Thalman, John W., A.B.'00, Ohio Wesleyan Univ.; M.A.'23, Tchrs. Col., Columbia Univ.; Supt. of Sec. Sch., Waukegan, Ill.

Thames, W. I., A.B.'87, Natl. Normal Univ.; Supt. of Sch., Hattiesburg, Miss., since 1922.

Theisen, W. W., B.Sc.'07, Univ. of Nebr.; A.M.'15, Ph.D.'16, Columbia Univ.; Asst. Supt. of Sch., 1111 N. Tenth St., Milwaukee, Wis., since 1922.

Thomas, Alfred D., A.B.'05, Lafayette Col.; M.A.'18, Tchrs. Col., Columbia Univ.; Supt. of Sch., Hazleton, Pa., since 1922.

Thomas, Augustus O., B.Ed.'94, State Normal Sch., Peru, Nebr.; Ph.B. and Ph.D. '96, Amity Col.; LL.D.'25, Bates Col.; Fellow '25, Educational Institute of Scotland. Address: 177 State St., Augusta, Maine.

Thomas, Frank W., A.B.'05, Ind. Univ.; A.M.'10, Univ. of Ill.; Ph.D.'26, Stanford Univ.; Pres., State Tchrs. Col., Fresno, Calif., since 1927.

Thomas, H. W., A.B.'15, Univ. of Rochester; A.M.'26, Univ. of Vt.; Supt. of Sch., Johnson, Vt., since 1921.

Thomas, John Q., Ph.B.'20, Univ. of Chicago; A.M.'21, Stanford Univ.; Supt. of Sch., Flagstaff, Ariz., since 1921.

Thomas, L. Ralston, B.S.'13, Haverford Col.; Ed.M.'25, Harvard Univ.; Headmaster, Moses Brown Sch., 257 Hope St., Providence, R. I., since 1924.

Thomas, M. H., A.M.'22, Gettysburg Col.; M.C.S.'26, Rider Business Col.; B.S. in Ed. '28, Lebanon Valley Col.; Supt. of Sch., 121 Chestnut St., Harrisburg, Pa., since 1930.

Thomas, Malcolm G., A.B.'98, A.M.'02, Union; Supvg. Prin. of Sch. and Prin. of H. S., Woodbury, N. J., since 1914.

Thomas, Oren R., 810 Hubbell Bldg., Des Moines, Iowa.

Thompson, A. G., A.B.'19, Hendrix Col.; Supt. of Sch., Carlisle, Ark., since 1926.

Thompson, Alfred C., B.A.'92, Yale; Ph.D. '13, New York State Col. for Tchrs., Albany, N. Y.; Prin., State Normal Sch., Brockport, N. Y., since 1910.

Thompson, C. C., B.S.'16, State Tchrs. Col., Emporia, Kansas; M.A.'17, Tchrs. Col., Columbia Univ.; Supt. of Sch., City Hall, Meriden, Conn., since 1926.

Thompson, Clem O., A.B.'13, Ind. State Tchrs. Col., Terre Haute, Ind.; A.M.'20, Univ. of Chicago; Instr., Sch. of Educ., Univ. of Chicago, Chicago, Ill., since 1930.

Thompson, E. M., A.B.'12, Nebr. Wesleyan Univ.; A.M.'29, Colo. State Tchrs. Col.; Supt. of Sch., Rock Springs, Wyo., since 1925.

Thompson, Fred, B.S.'10, A.M.'12, New York Univ.; Dir., Special Activities, Bd. of Educ., City Hall, Paterson, N. J., since 1923.

Thompson, French W., A.B.'97, Ark. Col.; B.D.'02, Chicago Theological Seminary; D.D.'20, Daniel Baker Col.; Pres., Greenbrier Col., Lewisburg, W. Va., since 1925.

Thompson, G. E., A. B.'15 Defiance Col.; Supt. of Sch., St. Charles, Ill., since 1919.

Thompson, J. B., B.S.'12, Colby Col.; M.A. '27, Tchrs. Col., Columbia Univ.; Asst. Supvg. Prin. of Sch., 1616 Parker Ave., Fort Lee, N. J., since 1927.

Thompson, Joseph W., 301 S. Spring St., Springfield, Ill.

Thompson, Kenneth H., A.B.'30, Nebr. State Tchrs. Col., Chadron, Nebr.; Supt. of Sch., H. S., Northport, Nebr., since 1930.

Thompson, Mary A., A.B.'18, Harris Tchrs. Col.; A.M.'22, Tchrs. Col., Columbia Univ.; Prin., George Dewey Sch., 1111 McCausland Ave., St. Louis, Mo., since 1912.

Thompson, Mrs. May F., Life Diploma '01, Mich. State Normal Col.; Co. Commr. of Sch., Court House, Lapeer, Mich., since 1923.

Thompson, O. S., Dist. Supt. of Sch., 601 S. Acacia St., Compton, Calif.

Thompson, Roger M., A.B.'17, Ind. State Normal Sch., Terre Haute, Ind.; A.M.'23, Tchrs. Col., Columbia Univ.; Dir. of Research and Surveys, State Bd. of Ed., Hartford, Conn., since 1927.

Thompson, William O., A.B.'78, Muskingum Col.; Pres., Ohio State Univ., Columbus, Ohio, 1899-1925; Pres. Emeritus since 1925. Address: 55 Woodland Ave., Columbus, Ohio.

Thoms, F. H., Supt. of Sch., 14 Buena Vista Ave., Hawthorne, N. J.

Thomson, Willis, A.B.'18, Univ. of Minn.; M.A.'27, Columbia Univ.; Prin., Isaac E. Young Jr. H. S., New Rochelle, N. Y., since 1928.

Thornburgh, W. B., Supt. of Sch., Seaford, Del.

Thorne, Norman C., B.A.'02, M.A.'04, Yale; Second Asst. Supt. of Sch., Portland, Oregon, since 1925.

Thoroman, A. M., A.B.'09, Univ. of Kansas; Supt. of Sch., Iola, Kansas, since 1921.

Thorsberg, W. E., A.B.'20, Univ. of Mich.; Supt. of Sch., Crystal Falls, Mich., since 1929.

Threlkeld, A. L., B.Pd.'11, State Normal Sch., Kirksville, Mo.; B.S.'19, Univ. of Mo.; A.M.'23, Tchrs. Col., Columbia Univ.; LL.D.'30, Univ. of Denver; Supt. of Sch., Admin. Bldg., Denver, Colo., since 1927.

Threlkeld, C. H., Prin., Columbia H. S., 17 Parker Ave., South Orange, N. J.

Tibbetts, Keim Kendall, A.B.'10, Oberlin Col.; Supt. of Sch., H. S. Bldg., Wheaton, Ill., since 1928.

Tibbetts, Vinal H., A.B.'14, Colby Col.; Supt. of Sch., Manhasset, N. Y., since 1930.

Tidwell, Clyde J., A.B.'10, Ouachita Col.; M.A.'26, Ph.D.'28, Columbia Univ.; Dir., Bureau of Publications, Tchrs. Col., Columbia Univ., New York, N. Y., since 1922.

Tidwell, Robert E., B.S.'05, Univ. of Ala.; LL.D.'23, Birmingham-Southern Col.; M. A.'25, Columbia Univ.; LL.D.'27, Univ. of Ala.; Dir. of Extension, Univ. of Ala., University, Ala., since 1930.

Tigert, John James, A.B.'04, Vanderbilt; B.A.'07, M.A. (Oxon) '15, Oxford; M.A. '16, Univ. of Minn.; LL.D.'21, Univ. of Ky.; Ed.D.'23, R. I.; LL.D.'24, Bates Col.; LL.D.'24, Univ. of N. Mex.; LL.D. '28, Dickinson Col.; D.C.L.'28, Hillsdale Col.; L.H.D.'28, Muhlenberg Col.; Pres., Univ. of Fla., Gainesville, Fla., since 1928.

Tiley, Pearl M., Ph.B.'26, Univ. of Chicago; Prim. Supvr. of Sch., 3105 W. Main St., Belleville, Ill., since 1911.

Tillman, Frank P., A.B.'13, B.S. in Ed. '16, Univ. of Mo.; Supt. of Sch., John Pitman Bldg., Kirkwood, Mo., since 1924.

Tink, Edmund L., A.B.'23, Lawrence Col.; A.M.'27, Ph.D.'29, Columbia Univ.; Dir. of Research, Pub. Sch., Montclair, N. J., and Instr., Inst. of Educ., New York Univ. Address: 120 Union St., Cedar Grove, N. J.

Tinsley, G. J., B.S.'25, M.S.'26, La. State Univ. Address: Box 2164, Stanford Univ., Calif.

Tippett, James S., Univ. of Pittsburgh, Pittsburgh, Pa.

Tirey, Ralph Noble, A.B.'18, A.M.'28, Ind. Univ.; Supt. of Sch., Bloomington, Ind., since 1922.

Tiss, A. I., A.B.'10, Drake Univ.; M.A.'19, State Univ. of Iowa; Supt. of Sch., Ft. Madison, Iowa, since 1920.

Titsworth, Paul Emerson, Ph.B.'04, Alfred Univ.; Ph.D.'11, Univ. of Wis.; LL.D.'27, Alfred Univ.; Pres., Washington Col., 400 Washington Ave., Chestertown, Md., since 1923.

Toaz, Robert K., A.B.'93, Rochester; A.M. '12, Tchrs. Col., Columbia Univ.; Supt. of Sch., H. S. Bldg., Huntington, N. Y., since 1906.

Tobey, S. B., Supt. of Sch., Wausau, Wis., since 1905.

Tobie, H. E., M.A.'27, Univ. of Oregon; Supt. of Sch., Stayton, Oregon, since 1927.

Todd, Glenn Wentworth, B.S. in Ed. '16, State Tchrs. Col., Pittsburg, Kansas; M. A.'26, Univ. of Colo.; Supt. of Sch., Lewiston, Idaho, since 1929.

Todd, Lindsey O., B.S.'25, Peabody; M.A. '28, Tchrs. Col., Columbia Univ.; Supt. of Sch., Philadelphia, Miss., since 1927.

Todd, William Hall, A.B.'23, Mo. Valley Col.; M.A.'25, Univ. of Alberta; A.M.'26, Ph.D.'27, Columbia Univ.; Prin., Pub. Sch., 2606 Louisiana Ave., St. Louis, Mo., since 1930.

Tompkins, Jonas M., Supt., North-East Sch. Dist., 64 Greenfield St., Hartford, Conn., since 1913.

Tompkins, Roy R., A.B.'14, Ouachita Col.; A.M.'28, Univ. of Okla. Address: 1329 N. Fifth Ave., Durant, Okla.

Toole, Clarence E., A.B.'08, Ursinus Col.; A.M.'24, Columbia Univ.; Supt. of Sch., Garfield Bldg., Pottsville, Pa., since 1928.

Toole, James D., Ph.B.'15, Lafayette Col.; Asst. Co. Supt. of Sch., 422 Sunbury St., Minersville, Pa., since 1929.

Torres, Luis, Normal Diploma '18, Univ. of Porto Rico; Supvr. of Sch., Box 2, Guayanilla, P. R., since 1924.

Torres Reyes, C., B.S. in E.E.'07, Pa. State Col.; Supvr. of Sch., Lares, P. R., since 1909.

Touchstone, Thompson Nolan, Supt. of Sch., Marks, Miss.

Tower, Willis E., B.S.'94, M.S.'08, Univ. of Ill.; Dist. Supt. in charge of Sr. H. S., 460 S. State St., Chicago, Ill., since 1925.

Towle, Clifton A., A.B.'99, Bowdoin Col.; Union Supt. of Sch., Exeter, N. H., since 1919.

Towle, L. U., B.Di.'05, Iowa State Tchrs. Col.; Ph.B.'07, Univ. of Wis.; Supt. of Sch., Detroit Lakes, Minn., since 1921.

Towne, Charles Franklin, A.B.'00, Colby Col.; A.M.'16, Brown Univ.; Asst. Supt. in charge of Sec. Educ., 9 Exchange Ter., Providence, R. I., since 1926.

Towne, R. H., B.S.'09, Carleton Col.; M.A., Columbia Univ.; Supt. of Sch., 402 E. Second St., Fairmont, Minn., since 1925.

Townsend, Howell, Supvg. Prin. of Sch., Walton, N. Y.

Townsend, M. Ernest, A.B.'12, A.M.'22, Colgate Univ.; A.M.'27, Tchrs. Col., Columbia Univ.; Prin., State Normal Sch., Newark, N. J., since 1929.

Trabue, M. R., B.A.'11, Northwestern Univ.; M.A.'14, Ph.D.'15, Columbia Univ.; Prof. of Educ. Admin., Univ. of N. C., Chapel Hill, N. C., since 1922.

Tracey, Earle Thurman, A.B.'12, Middlebury Col.; Asst. Supt. of Sch., Nashua, N. H., since 1927.

Tracy, Aaron W., A.B.'19, Brigham Young Univ.; Pres., Weber Col., Ogden, Utah, since 1922.

Tracy, Bettie M., B.S.'21, M.A.'25, Tchrs. Col., Columbia Univ.; Dir. of Research, Wheeling Independent Sch. Dist., H. S., Wheeling, W. Va., since 1925.

Trainor, Harry J., A.B.,'26, Central State Tchrs. Col., Mt. Pleasant, Mich.; Supt. of Sch., Lake Linden, Mich., since 1927.

Travell, Ira Winthrop, B.A.'90, Williams; Supt. of Sch., Ridgewood, N. J., since 1912.

Travis, Martin B., A.B.'09, A.M.'10, Univ. of Mich.; Supt. of Sch., Iron Mountain, Mich., since 1917.

Tremain, Eloise R., B.A.'04, Bryn Mawr Col.; M.A.'27, Lake Forest Col.; Prin., Ferry Hall, Lake Forest, Ill., since 1918.

Tremaine, Charles M., Dir., Natl. Bureau For the Advancement of Music, 45 W. 45th St., New York, N. Y., since 1916.

Tremper, George Nelson, A.B.'01, Univ. of Mich.; M.A.'28, Univ. of Ill.; Prin., Sr. H. S., 6611 Fifth Ave., Kenosha, Wis., since 1911.

Trescott, E. O., Ph.B.'91, Hiram Col.; Supt. of Sch., 413 Broadway, Girard, Ohio.

Tressler, S. M., Supvg. Prin. of Sch., Washington, N. J., since 1904.

Tritt, Jessie A., B.A.'13, M.A.'15, Univ. of Southern Calif.; Asst. Supt. of Sch., Chamber of Commerce Bldg., Los Angeles, Calif., since 1924.

Tritt, William Winters, Asst. Supt. of Sch., 135 N. Normandie Ave., Los Angeles, Calif.

Trostle, L. S., Supvg. Prin. of Sch., 522 Cooper St., Beverly, N. J., since 1928.

Troxel, Oliver L., B.S.'14, North Central Col.; A.M.'22, Ph.D.'26, Univ. of Minn.; Prof. of Educ. Admin., Colo. State Tchrs. Col., Greeley, Colo., since 1929.

Truax, Mrs. Grace Greves, Educational Lecturer, 711 W. 12th St., Sioux Falls, S. Dak.

True, J. A., A.B.'18, Univ. of Nebr.; A.M. '23, Univ. of Chicago; Supt. of Sch., Council Bluffs, Iowa, since 1930.

Trumper, May, B.S.'17, M.A.'29, Columbia Univ.; Head, Dept. of Rural Educ., State Normal Sch., Geneseo, N. Y., since 1929.

Truscott, Raymond W., A.B.'05, Simpson Col.; Supt. of Sch., Loveland, Colo., since 1905.

Tucker, E. B., A.B.'05, Vanderbilt Univ.; LL.D.'25, Ark. Col.; Pres., Ark. Col., Batesville, Ark., since 1923.

Tucker, Isabel, A.B.'24, Harris Tchrs. Col., St. Louis, Mo.; A.M.'27, Tchrs. Col.; Columbia Univ.; Prin., Shenandoah Sch., St. Louis, Mo., since 1926.

Tucker, Walter J., Supt., Mystic Oral Sch., Mystic, Conn.

Turner, H. B., A.B.'03, Hiram Col.; Supt. of Sch., Bd. of Educ. Bldg., Warren, Ohio, since 1916.

Turner, Horace F., A.B.'11, Bates Col.; Supt. of Sch., Milton, Mass., since 1926.

Turner, John E., A.B.'04, A.M.'05, LL.D.'25, Lincoln Univ.; Pres., State Normal Sch., Lewiston, Idaho, since 1925.

Turner, R. R., Supt. of Sch., Dallas, Oregon, since 1921.

Turpin, Lacy Telford, Ph.B.'06, Franklin, Col., Franklin, Ind.; M.A.'27, Tchrs. Col., Columbia Univ.; Prin., Alton Community Consol. H. S., College Ave., Alton, Ill., since 1926.

Tweedy, Ira, B.S.'11, Univ., of Idaho; Supt. of Sch., Rupert, Idaho, since 1919.

Twente, John W., A.M.'16, Univ. of Kansas; A.M.'22, Ph.D.'23, Columbia Univ.; Prof. of Educ., Univ. of Kansas, 934 Indiana, Lawrence, Kansas, since 1925.

Tyler, Bertha M., B.A.'12, Simpson Col.; M.A.'27, State Univ. of Iowa; Supt. of Consol. Sch., Orient, Iowa, since 1918.

Tyler, Leon Lewis, LL.B.'00, Univ. of Mich.; A.B.'06, Earlham Col.; A.M.'25, Univ. of Mich.; Prof. of Educ., Alma Col., Alma, Mich., since 1928.

Tyler, Ralph W., A.B.'21, Doane Col.; A.M.'23, Univ. of Nebr.; Ph.D.'27, Univ. of Chicago; Assoc. Prof. of Educ. and Research Assoc. in Bureau of Educ. Research, Ohio State Univ., Columbus, Ohio, since 1929.

Tyler, Tracy F., A.B.'16, Doane Col.; A.M.'23, Univ. of Nebr. Address: 509 W. 121st St., New York, N. Y.

Tyler, William, Co. Supt. of Sch., Pensacola, Fla.

Ueland, Elsa, B.A.'09, Univ. of Minn.; M.A.'11, Columbia Univ.; Diploma '11, New York Sch. of Social Work; Pres., Carson Col. for Orphan Girls, Flourtown, Pa., since 1916.

Umstattd, James G., B.S. in Ed.'18, M.A. '24, Univ. of Mo.; Ph.D.'30, Univ. of Minn.; Asst. Prof. of Educ., Col. of Educ., Univ. of Minn., Minneapolis, Minn.

Underhill, Ralph I., B.A.'06, Harvard Univ.; M.A.'25, Columbia Univ.; Supt. of Sch., 5 Church Lane, Scarsdale, N. Y., since 1921.

Underwood, Clarence C., Ph.B.'07, M.A.'10, Kenyon Col.; Asst. Supt. of Sch., 150 N. Meridian, Indianapolis, Ind.

Underwood, Frank M., A.B.'02, Univ. of Mo.; A.M.'25, Tchrs. Col., Columbia Univ.; Asst. Supt. of Sch., St. Louis, Mo., since 1930.

Unger, Jacob J., A.B. '06, Lebanon Valley Col.; Co. Supt. of Sch., Court House, Bridgeton, N. J., since 1913.

Unger, Maurice S. H., A.B.'94, Franklin and Marshall Col.; A.M.'18, Columbia Univ.; Litt.D.'25, Western Md. Col.; Co. Supt. of Sch., Court House, Westminster, Md., since 1916.

Unnewehr, C. A., A.B.'02, A.M.'11, Ind. Univ.; Prin., Continuation H. S., 655 W. 14th St., Chicago, Ill., since 1928.

Updegraff, Harlan, Ph.B.'94, Cornell Col.; M.A.'98, Ph.D.'08, Columbia Univ.; LL.D. '26, Syracuse Univ.; Research Consultant, Natl. Advisory Com. on Educ., 744 Jackson Pl., Washington, D. C., since 1930.

Updyke, Austin H., B.S.'08, M.Pd.'11, New York Univ.; Co. Supt. of Sch., Court House, Jersey City, N. J., since 1917.

Uphill, Jared L. M., B.S., Rochester; Diploma, State Normal School, Geneseo, N. Y.; Dist. Supt. of Sch., 8 Fairmont Ave., Batavia, N. Y., since 1916.

Upjohn, Hubert S., Ph.B.'03, Univ. of Chicago; Co. Supt. of Sch., 132 N. Broadway, Los Angeles, Calif., since 1928.

Uthoff, Mary L., Co. Supt. of Sch., Princeton, Ill., since 1923.

Utz, Leonard M., B.S.'19, Muhlenberg Col.; Supvg. Prin. of Sch., Waverly, Pa., since 1927.

Vail, Guy W., A.B.'11, Colby Col.; Supt. of Sch., Winchendon, Mass., since 1922.

Valentine, Byron W., A.B.'01, Colgate Univ.; Hebrew and Greek Diploma '06, Hamilton Theol. Seminary; A.M.'15, Colgate Univ.; LL.D.'22; B.D.'25, Colgate Univ.; Head, Dept. of Educ., Otterbein Col., Westerville, Ohio, since 1922.

Van Buskirk, D.A., Diploma '12, Western State Tchrs. Col., Kalamazoo, Mich.; A. B.'16, A.M.'23, Univ. of Mich.; Supt. of Sch., Hastings, Mich., since 1923.

Van Camp, H. L., A.B.'28, Concord State Normal Sch., Athens, W. Va.; Dist. Supt. of Sch., Glen Jean, W. Va., since 1922.

Vance, C. E., Supt. of Sch., 141 Woodlawn Ave., Danville, Ill.

Van Cott, Harrison H., B.S.'06, Tchrs. Col., Columbia Univ.; A.B.'15, State Col. for Tchrs., Albany, N. Y.; Supvr. of Jr. H. S., State Education Bldg., Albany, N. Y., since 1926.

van den Berg, Lawrence H., A.B.'98, Univ. of Mich.; M.A.'13, Tchrs. Col., Columbia Univ.; Pd.D.'26, State Col. for Tchrs., Albany, N. Y.; Prin., State Normal Sch., New Paltz, N. Y., since 1923.

Vandenbergh, Ora H., 234 E. Palmer Ave., Detroit, Mich.

Vander Beke, George E., A.B.'23, Columbia Col., Dubuque, Iowa; M.A.'25, Ph.D. '26, State Univ. of Iowa; Prof. of Educ., Marquette Univ., Milwaukee, Wis., since 1928.

Vanderbilt, Mabel Tilden, A.B.'01, Vassar Col.; Supvg. Prin. of Sch., Princeton, N. J., since 1914.

Vanderhoef, W. Howard, B.S.'16, Colgate Univ.; M.A.'29, Columbia Univ.; Supt. of Sch., Bath, N. Y., since 1925.

Vanderslice, Harvey R., A.B.'15, Ursinus Col.; A.M.'25, Univ. of Pa.; Supt. of Sch., Harding H. S., Aliquippa, Pa., since 1926.

Van Dusen, Earl C., A.B.'15, Lawrence Col.; M.A.'25, Univ. of Minn.; Supt. of Sch., H. S. Bldg., Little Falls, Minn., since 1926.

Van Horn, F. C., Supvg. Prin. of Sch., Morris Plains, N. J.

Van Kleeck, E. R., Supt. of Sch., Walden, N. Y.

Vannatta, Harry E., B.S. in Ed. '22, M.A. '24, Univ. of Pittsburgh; Asst. Prof. of Educ., Tchrs. Col., Syracuse Univ., Syracuse, N. Y., since 1926.

Van Ness, Carl Condit, A.B.'16, Columbia Univ. Address: 35 W. 32nd St., New York, N. Y.

Van Slyke, E. A., Supt. of Sch., Hicksville, N. Y.

Van Voorhis, Samuel, A.B.'09, Huron Col.; M.A.'25, Columbia Univ.; Supt. of Sch., Redfield, S. Dak., since 1922.

Varney, Charles E., Diploma, State Normal Sch., Farmington, Maine; B.S. in Ed., Boston Univ.; Supt. of Sch., H. S. Bldg., Stoneham, Mass., since 1929.

Vasey, Frank T., A.B.'04, Univ. of Nebr.; A.M.'18, State Univ. of Iowa; Supt. of Sch., Springfield, Ill., since 1930.

Vaughan, John S., State Supt. of Pub. Instr., Oklahoma City, Okla.

Vaughan, William H., A.B.'23, Georgetown Col.; A.M.'27, George Peabody Col. for Tchrs.; Dean, Morehead State Normal Sch. and Tchrs. Col., Morehead, Ky., since 1928.

Vedder, Almon V., A.B.'21, Mich. State Normal Sch.; M.A.'25, Univ. of Mich.; Supt. of Sch., Rockford, Mich., since 1928.

Velte, Charles Henry, A.B.'14, Hastings Col.; M.A.'29, Univ. of Nebr.; Supt. of Sch., Crete, Nebr., since 1919.

Vermillion, Kenneth R., B. S. in Ed. '24, Ohio Univ.; Prin., Chambers Elem. Sch., East Cleveland, Ohio, since 1929.

Verplanck, Fred A., B.A.'88, Yale; Supt. of Sch., South Manchester, Conn., since 1893.

Vevle, Mendus R., B.A.'14, St. Olaf Col.; Supt., Minn. Sch. for the Blind, Faribault, Minn., since 1930.

Vigor, Charles F., Asst. Supt. of Sch., Mobile, Ala., since 1909.

Viles, N. E., M.A.'29, Univ. of Mo.; Supt. of Sch., Neosho, Mo., since 1926.

Vincent, E. P., 188 Biltmore Ave., Wheeling, W. Va.

Vincent, P. M., Supt. of Sch., 622 Church St., Stevens Point, Wis.

Vincent, Quincy G., Supt. of Sch., 1205 Fourth Ave., Ford City, Pa.

Vincent, W. D., State Commr. of Educ., 1009 Harrison, Boise, Idaho.

Vinson, Thomas W., B.L.'17, Transylvania Univ. Address: Brown Hotel, Louisville, Ky.

Vivion, King, B.A.'16, Drury Col.; M.A. and B.D. '19, Southern Methodist Univ.; Pres., Southwestern Univ., Georgetown, Texas, since 1928.

Vliet, Clarence, A.B.'15, Univ. of Mich.; Supt. of Sch., Birmingham, Mich., since 1915.

Vogel, George J., A.B.'91, Cornell Univ.; Supt. of Sch., 68 Church St., Torrington, Conn., since 1914.

Von Borgersrode, Fred, Ph.D.'27, Univ. of Minn.; Prof. of Educ., Univ. of Mo., Columbia, Mo., since 1929.

Vorhies, F. W., B.A.'11, Iowa State Tchrs. Col.; M.S.'14, State Univ. of Iowa; Supt. of Sch., Colfax, Iowa, since 1927.

Vosburgh, C. D., Supt. of Sch., Lynbrook, N. Y.

Voss, Edwin F., B.S.'17, S. Dak. State Col.; M.A.'26, Tchrs. Col., Columbia Univ.; Supt. of Sch., Clark, S. Dak., since 1923.

Wade, Edwin C., A.B.'07, Hampden-Sidney Col.; A.M.'11, Columbia Univ.; Supt. of Sch., Bluefield, W. Va., since 1923.

Wade, John E., B.S.'97, Col. of the City of New York; A.M.'02, Columbia Univ.; Assoc. Supt. of Sch., 2267 Andrews Ave., New York, N. Y., since 1927.

Wager, Warren William, A.M.'99, Tri-State Col., Angola, Ind.; A.B.'00, A.M. '04, Hiram Col. Address: Worthington, Ohio.

Wagner, H. Ray, B.S.'23, M.A.'28, Ohio State Univ.; Supt. of Twp. Sch., West Alexandria, Ohio.

Wagner, Jonas E., B.S.'02, M.S.'05, Pa. State Col.; Dir., Statistics, Research, and Reports, State Dept. of Pub. Instr., Harrisburg, Pa.

Wagner, M. Channing, B.A.'13, Wittenberg Col.; A.M.'23, Columbia Univ.; Asst. Supt. in charge of Sec. Educ., H. S. Bldg., Wilmington, Del., since 1929.

Wagner, Thomas J., A.B.'10, Franklin and Marshall Col.; A.M.'13, Tchrs. Col., Columbia Univ.; Pd.D.'23, New York Univ.; Prin., Croton Harmon H. S., Croton-on-Hudson, N. Y.

Wahl, James Frank, B.A.'20, Hendrix Col.; M.A.'26, George Peabody Col. for Tchrs.; Supt. of Sch., H. S. Bldg., Helena, Ark., since 1928.

Wahlert, Jennie, M.A.'27, Tchrs. Col., Columbia Univ.; Primary Supvr., Pub. Sch., 2918 Harper, St. Louis, Mo., since 1923.

Waits, H. E., Diploma '98, Ill. State Normal Univ.; A.M.'12, Univ. of Ill.; Supt. of Sch., 712 Brother St., Ludington, Mich., since 1918.

Wakeley, John Everett, Prin., H. S., Danville, Ill., since 1930.

Waldo, Dwight Bryant, Ph.B.'87, A.M.'90, Albion Col.; LL.D.'10, Kalamazoo Col.; Pres., Western State Tchrs. Col., Kalamazoo, Mich.

Waldo, Karl D., A.B.'06, Univ. of Ill.; A.M.'14, Univ. of Chicago; Supt. of Sch., East Side, Aurora, Ill., since 1928.

Waldron, Edward F., Ph.B.'17, Brown Univ.; Supvg. Prin. of Twp. Sch., Union, N. J., since 1928.

Walk, George E., A.B.'99, Ohio Wesleyan Univ.; A.M.'11, Columbia Univ.; Ph.D. '14, New York Univ.; Dean, Tchrs. Col., Temple Univ., Philadelphia, Pa., since 1919.

Walker, A. L., Ph.B.'13, Col. of Wooster; Supt. of Sch., Hudson, Ohio, since 1928.

Walker, C. H., A.B.'05, Bates Col.; Supt. of Sch., Maynard, Mass., since 1928.

Walker, Charles W., A.B.'13, A.M.'14, Brown Univ.; Asst. Supt. of Sch., Parker Sch., Concord, N. H., since 1923.

Walker, David E., Asst. Supt. of Sch., Evanston, Ill.

Walker, Deane E., A.B.'22, Tri-State Col.; A.M.'28, Tchrs. Col., Columbia Univ.; Co. Supt. of Sch., Plymouth, Ind., since 1926.

Walker, Mrs. Grace M., Life Diploma '14, Mich. State Tchrs. Col.; Co. Commr. of Sch., Hart, Mich., since 1927.

Walker, Helen M., Ph.B.'12, Iowa Wesleyan Col.; M.A.'22, Ph.D.'29, Columbia Univ.; Asst. Prof. of Educ., Tchrs. Col., Columbia Univ., New York, N. Y., since 1929.

Walker, James E., LL.B.'07, Chattanooga Col. of Law; A.B.'12, Univ. of Chattanooga; A.M.'22, Columbia Univ.; Co. Supt. of Sch., 804 Lewis St., Chattanooga, Tenn., since 1925.

Walker, J. Henry, A.B.'87, Univ. of Ga.; Pres., Ga. Voc. and Trades Sch., Walker Park, Ga., since 1929.

Walker, Knox, A.B.'15, Mercer Univ.; Supt. of Sch., Dublin, Ga.

Wallace, Frederick W., A.B.'04, Bates Col.; Supt. of Sch., College St., Poultney, Vt., since 1923.

Wallace, S. C., Asst. Co. Supt. of Sch., 428 Oakland Ave., Greensburg, Pa., since 1915.

Wallack, Walter M., B.S.'24, Kansas State Tchrs. Col., Pittsburg, Kansas; M.A.'29, Columbia Univ.; Dir. of Industrial Schools of Haiti, Serv. Technique, Port au Prince, Haiti, since 1929.

Waller, DeWitt L., A.B.'11, Epworth Univ.; A.M.'28, Univ. of Mo.; Prin., H. S., Enid, Okla., since 1915.

Waller, J. Flint, B.A.'16, Univ. of Va.; M.A.'28, Columbia Univ. Address: John Jay Hall, Columbia Univ., New York, N. Y.

Walling, W. Levern, A.B.'07, Mich. State Normal Col.; A.B.'14, Univ. of Mich.; Dist. Supt. of Sch., 20935 Yale Blvd., St. Clair Shores, Mich., since 1927.

Walls, William Alfred, A.B.'07, Mt. Union Col.; A.M.'13, Columbia Univ.; Supt. of Sch., 10 Green Ter., Kent, Ohio, since 1920.

Walpole, Branson Alva, B.S. in Ed.'15, Ohio Univ.; M.S.'25, Mich. State Col.; Assoc. Prof. in Agrl. Educ. and Supvr. of Tchr. Tr., Mich. State Col. of Agr. and Applied Science, East Lansing, Mich., since 1921.

Walshe, Minnie E., Asst. Supt. of Sch., 705 Post Rd., Fairfield, Conn.

Walter, Z. M., B. Sc. in Ed. '21, M.A.'23, Ohio State Univ.; Supt. of Sch., Hillsboro, Ohio, since 1927

Walters, Rolland J., A.B.'04, Tri-State Col.; A.M.'14, Tchrs. Col., Columbia Univ.; D. Litt. '20, Univ. of Denver; Dir., Tchr. Tr., Univ. of Denver, 2045 S. Clarkson St., Denver, Colo., since 1924.

Walton, C. E. A., B.S.'16, New York Univ.; Supvg. Prin. of Sch., Little Falls, N. J., since 1912.

Wannamaker, George W., A.B.'15, A.M.'17, Wofford Col.; Supt. of Sch., St. Matthews, S. C., since 1924.

Ward, David A., B.S.'04, Rio Grande Col.; A.M.'11, Univ. of Chicago; Ed.D.'28, Rio Grande Col.; Supt. of Sch., Larkin Sch., Chester, Pa., since 1929.

Ward, L. C., A.B.'03, Ind. Univ.; Supt. of Sch., Montgomery and Clinton Sts., Ft. Wayne, Ind., since 1920.

Ward, W. H., A.B.'14, Furman Univ.; Supt. of Sch., Walterboro, S. C., since 1924.

Ward, W. Scott, A.B.'83, Tufts Col.; Supt. of Sch., 73 Green St., Athol, Mass., since 1897.

Wardlaw, Patterson, A.B.'80, LL.D.'06, Erskine; Litt.D.'24, Presbyterian Col. of S. C.; Prof. of Educ., Univ. of S. C., Columbia, S. C., since 1894.

Ware, Charles Milton, Diploma '04, Kansas State Tchrs. Col.; A.B.'15, Fairmount Col.; M.A.'24, Univ. of Colo.; Prin., State Preparatory Sch., 980 Lincoln Pl., Boulder, Colo., since 1924.

Warner, Rodney J., Supt. of Sch., Osborn, Ohio.

Warner, William E., B.S.'23, M.S.'24, Univ. of Wis.; Ph.D.'28, Columbia Univ.; Assoc. Prof. of Practical Arts and Voc. Educ., Ohio State Univ., Columbus, Ohio, since 1925.

Warrek, George R., B.S.'25, Conn. Agrl. Col. Address: Univ. of Porto Rico, Rio Piedras, P. R.

Warren, Benjamin O., B.A.'11, Univ. of Maine. Address: 381 Fourth Ave., New York, N. Y.

Warren, James T., B.S.'21, M.A.'26, George Peabody Col. for Tchrs.; LL.D.'29, Georgetown Col.; Pres., Carson-Newman Col., Jefferson City, Tenn., since 1927.

Warren, Jule B., A.B.'08, Duke Univ.; Secy., N. C. Educ. Assn., Box 274, Raleigh, N. C., since 1922.

Warren, Julius E., A.B.'10, Dartmouth Col.; M.A.'23, Tchrs. Col., Columbia Univ.; Supt. of Sch., Bd. of Educ., Warren Rd., Lakewood, Ohio, since 1927.

Warren, Milton Charles, B. Sc. in Ed. '10, Ohio State Univ.; Co. Supt. of Sch., Circleville, Ohio, since 1916.

Warren, Worcester, A.B.'12, Knox Col.; A.M.'21, State Univ. of Iowa; Supt. of Sch., Bridgeport, Conn., since 1929.

Washburn, Justin, Diploma '16, Western Ill. State Tchrs. Col., McComb, Ill.; Co. Supt. of Sch., Court House, Rock Island, Ill., since 1920.

Washburne, C. W., Ed. D. '22, Univ. of Calif.; Supt. of Sch., Skokie Sch., Winnetka, Ill., since 1919.

Wassung, Frank R., Ph.B.'13, Ph.M.'17, Hamilton Col.; Supt. of Sch., Norwich, N. Y., since 1919.

Waterhouse, A. H., A.M.'08, Univ. of Nebr.; Supt. of Sch., Fremont, Nebr., since 1908.

Waterhouse, R. H., B.S.'30, Ohio State Univ.; Asst. Supt. of Sch., Central H. S. Bldg., Akron, Ohio, since 1925.

Waterpool, W. F., B. A.'20, Lawrence Col.; Ph.M.'26, Univ. of Wis.; Supt. of Sch., Richland Center, Wis., since 1927.

Watkin, Earl P., Ph.B.'12, Ph.M.'17, Hamilton Col.; M.A.'30, Columbia Univ.; Supt. of Sch., Municipal Bldg., Ilion, N. Y., since 1923.

Watkins, Catharine R., Dir. of Kdgns., Pub. Schools, 2120 P St., N. W., Washington, D. C., since 1899.

Watkins, Richard Henry, B.A.'95, Hampden-Sidney Col.; Supt. of Sch., Laurel, Miss., since 1907.

Watson, F. B., Graduate '97, Col. of William and Mary; Div. Supt. of Pittsylvania Co. Sch., Chatham, Va., since 1921.

Watson, Frank K., A.M.'99, Princeton; Supt. of Sch., 20 West St., Danbury, Conn., since 1920.

Watson, G. E., B.A.'21, Lawrence Col.; Supt. of Sch., H. S. Bldg., Waupaca, Wis., since 1924.

Watson, Norman E., A.B.'21, Wabash Col.; A.M.'29, Univ. of Chicago; Supt. of Sch., Northbrook, Ill.

Watson, Vesta, 322 Normal Ave., Denton, Texas.

Watts, Charles H., A.B.'96, Ohio Northern Univ.; Co. Supt. of Sch., Court House, Urbana, Ill., since 1902.

Watts, George Benjamin, B.A.'23, Millsaps Col.; M.A.'26, Columbia Univ.; Supt. of Consol. Sch., Lambert, Miss., since 1929.

Weagly, William E., B.S.'25, Capital Univ.; Supt. of Sch., Huron, Ohio, since 1928.

Weaver, David Andrew, A.B.'27, Mercer Univ.; M.A.'29, Tchrs. Col., Columbia Univ.; Instr., Sch. of Educ., New York Univ., New York, N. Y., since 1929.

Weaver, Ernest L., A.B.'05, Nebr. Wesleyan Univ.; M.A.'21, Univ. of Nebr.; Supt. of Sch., 1510 Fourth Ave., Scottsbluff, Nebr., since 1928.

Weaver, Lawrence S., A.B.'26, Asbury Col.; Supt. of Sch., Indian Rd., Ottawa Hills, Toledo, Ohio, since 1929.

Weaver, Paul H., A.B.'21, Heidelberg Col.; M.A.'27, Ohio State Univ.; Supt. of Sch., Shiloh, Ohio, since 1929.

Webb, A. S., A.B.'96, Duke Univ.; Supt. of Sch., 42 Bell Ave., Concord, N. C., since 1910.

Webb, F. E., B.A.'11, Bellevue Col.; Supt. of Sch., Globe, Ariz., since 1923.

Webb, Henry P., Supt. of Sch., Olton, Texas, since 1921.

Webb, J. O., B.A.'14, Southwestern Univ.; M.A.'24, Univ. of Texas; Asst. Dir. of High Schools, Houston, Texas, since 1928.

Webb, James T., B.A.'10, Miss. Col.; M. A.'24, Univ. of Chicago; Supt. of Sch., Union City, Tenn., since 1929.

Webb, Jesse Clement, A.B.'98, M.A. '01, Franklin Col., Franklin, Ind.; M.A.'19, Columbia Univ.; Supt. of Sch., Portland, Ind., since 1922.

Webb, W. H., B. S. in Ed. '25, Ohio Univ.; Co. Supt. of Sch., Marietta, Ohio, since 1924.

Webber, Elmer Harrison, Diploma '07, State Normal Sch., Farmington, Maine; B. Pd. '15, Univ. of Maine; A.M.'23, Bates Col.; Supt. of Sch., Mapleton, Maine, since 1918.

Weber, Ernest, A.B.'23, Western State Normal Sch., Kalamazoo, Mich.; M.A. '28, Tchrs. Col., Columbia Univ.; Prin., Tr. Sch., Richland, Mich., since 1923.

Weber, S. E., Ph. D. '05, Univ. of Pa.; Assoc. Supt. of Sch. in charge of Personnel, Pittsburgh, Pa., since 1929.

Webster, George E., M.Pd.'06, State Normal Sch., Millersville, Pa.; M.S.'09, Bucknell; M.A.'10, Columbia Univ.; Ph.D.'13, Kansas City Univ.; Supvg. Prin. of Sch., 11 Elm Pl., Rye, N. Y., since 1913.

Weed, Clarence M., B.Sc.'83, M. Sc. '84, Mich. Agrl. Col.; D.Sc.'91, Ohio State Univ.; Prin., State Normal Sch., Lowell, Mass., since 1921.

Weeden, Ethel R., Diploma '95, New Haven Normal Sch. of Gymnastics; B.A.'20, Harris Tchrs. Col.; M.A.'24, New York Univ.; Prof. of Educ., Harris Tchrs. Col., 1517 S. Theresa Ave., St. Louis, Mo.

Weersing, Frederick J., A.B. in Ed.'15, Univ. of Minn.; M.A.'22, Tchrs. Col., Columbia Univ.; Ph.D.'27, Univ. of Minn.; Prof. of Educ., Univ. of Southern Calif., Los Angeles, Calif., since 1927.

Weet, Herbert S., B.A.'99, M.A.'01, Univ. of Rochester; Pd.D.'18, New York State Col.; Supt. of Sch., Education Bldg., Rochester, N. Y., since 1911.

Weglein, David E., A.B.'97, Johns Hopkins Univ.; A.M.'12, Columbia Univ.; Ph.D.'16, Johns Hopkins Univ.; Supt. of Sch., Madison and Lafayette Aves., Baltimore, Md., since 1925.

Wegner, F. R., A.B.'21, Cornell Univ.; M.A.'28, N. Y. State Col. for Tchrs.; Supt. of Sch., Little Falls, N. Y., since 1930.

Wegner, H. C., Ph.B.'21, Ph.M.'24, Univ. of Wis.; Supt. of Sch., 215 E. Jefferson St., Waupun, Wis., since 1926.

Weidner, Herman W., B.A.'98, M.A.'02, Franklin and Marshall Col.; Supvg. Prin., Vineland and Landis Twp. Sch., Vineland, N. J., since 1926.

Weigl, August W., A.B.'15, Kingfisher Col.; A.B.'28, Univ. of Okla.; M. A. '30, Univ. of Mo.; Supt. of Consol. Sch., Ramona, Okla., since 1924.

Weir, Daniel T., A.B.'91, A.M.'93, Ind. Univ.; Asst. Supt. of Sch., 150 N. Meridian St., Indianapolis, Ind.

Weir, Samuel, B.D.'87, Garrett Biblical Inst.; A.B.'89, Northwestern Univ.; Ph. D.'95, Univ. of Jena; Head, Dept. of Educ., Col. of Puget Sound, Tacoma, Wash., since 1922.

Weirick, Joseph C., Prin., H. S., Abington, Pa.

Weisel, Willard F., Supvg. Prin. of Sch., Hampton, N. J.

Welch, Ray DeForest, B.A.'24, Univ. of Pittsburgh; Supt. of Sch., H. S. Bldg., Kane, Pa., since 1928.

Weld, Frank A., 601 E. 14th St., Minneapolis, Minn.

Welles, James B., A.B.'09, Union Col.; A. M.'13, Columbia Univ.; Supt. of Sch., Roslyn, N. Y., since 1920.

Wellman, Justin Owen, A.B.'98, A.M.'22, Colby Col.; Ed. M. '24, Harvard Univ.; Head, Dept. of Educ., Univ. of N. H., Durham, N. H., since 1924.

Wells, Agnes E., A.B.'03, Univ. of Mich.; A.M.'16, Carleton Col.; Ph.D.'24, Univ. of Mich.; Dean of Women and Prof. of Mathematics, Ind. Univ., Bloomington, Ind., since 1918.

Wells, Clyde P., Ph.B.'08, Syracuse Univ.; Supt. of Sch., Batavia, N. Y., since 1923.

Wells, George N., Co. Supt. of Sch., 13 Elmwood Parkway, Elmwood Park, Ill.

Wells, Guy H., A.B.'15, Mercer Univ.; A.M.'25, Columbia Univ.; Pres., Ga. Normal Sch., Statesboro, Ga., since 1926. Address: Collegeboro, Ga.

Wells, Jere A., B.S.C.'24, Ga. Tech.; Co. Supt. of Sch., Court House, Atlanta, Ga., since 1925.

Wells, Mrs. Olivia M., Co. Supt. of Sch., Lordsburg, N. Mex., since 1928.

Welshimer, A. G., A.B.'14, Ohio State Univ.; Co. Supt. of Sch., Court House, Urbana, Ohio, since 1921.

Wenner, William E., A.B.'97, Westminster; Supt. of Sch., 1 Lake St., Ashtabula Harbor, Ohio, since 1909.

Werner, J. C., Supvg. Prin. of Sch., 1045 Vance Ave., Coraopolis, Pa.

Werner, Oscar H., A.B.'10, Central Wesleyan Col.; A.M.'12. Northwestern Univ.; Ph.D.'17, Columbia Univ.; Prof. of Educ., Univ. of Nebr., 1835 Lake, Lincoln, Nebr., since 1924.

Wesley, Marian J., B.S.'17, M.A.'22, Tchrs. Col., Columbia Univ.; Supvr. of Elem. Grades, Pub. Sch., Waltham, Mass., since 1930.

West, Henry S., A.B.'93, Ph.D.'99, Johns Hopkins Univ.; Dean, Col. of Liberal Arts and Prof. of Educ. and Dir. of Tchr. Tr., Univ. of Miami, Miami, Fla., since 1926.

West, John C., B.A.'15, Fargo Col.; M.S.'25, Univ. of N. Dak.; Supt. of Sch., Central H. S., Grand Forks, N. Dak., since 1929.

West, John Franklin, Supt. of Sch., 602 Pomona Ave., Albany, Calif.

West, Nathaniel G., A.B.'07, A.M.'20, Rochester; Diploma '24, Tchrs. Col., Columbia Univ.; Prin., Andrews Sch. No. 9, Rochester, N. Y.

West, Parl, A.B.'21, Univ. of Nebr.; A.M. '28, Tchrs. Col., Columbia Univ.; Prin., Washington Irving Sch., Tarrytown, N. Y. since 1928.

West, Roscoe L., A.B.'14, Ed.M.'23, Harvard Univ.; Prin., State Tchrs. Col., Trenton, N. J., since 1930.

Westerfield, Butler, B.A.'28, Univ. of Texas; Supt. of Sch., Burkburnett, Texas, since 1927.

Westover, Raymond Miller, 6725 Benson St., Huntington Park, Calif.

Wetherow, E. B., Supt. of Sch., La Porte, Ind., since 1922.

Wetzel, William A., A.B.'91, A.M.'93, Lafayette Col.; Ph.D.'95, Johns Hopkins Univ.; Prin., Sr. H. S., 12 Belmont Circle, Trenton, N. J., since 1901.

Wheable, Goeffrey Alfred, B.A.'21, Queen's Univ., Kingston, Ont.; Sr. Insp. and Administrator of Sch., Bd. of Educ., London, Ontario, Canada, since 1925.

Wheeler, Frederic A., A.B.'93, Univ. of Vt.; Supt. of Sch., East Longmeadow, Mass., since 1919.

Wheeler, George R., A.B.'12, Mercer Univ.; Co. Supt. of Sch., Sanford, N. C., since 1930.

Wheeler, Ulysses G., A.B.'87, A.M.'00. Bates Col.; Supt. of Sch., Newton, Mass., since 1914.

Wheelock, Lucy, Litt. D.'25, Univ. of Vt.; Head, Wheelock Sch., 100 Riverway, Boston, Mass., since 1888.

Whistler, E. M., B.S.'24, Lebanon Valley Col.; Supvg. Prin. of Sch., H. S. Bldg., East Mauch Chunk, Pa., since 1929.

Whitcomb, Emeline S., B.S.'10, M.A.'18, Columbia Univ.; Specialist in Home Economics, U. S. Office of Educ., Dept. of the Interior, Washington, D. C., since 1923.

White, B. F., A.B.'17, Southwestern; A.M. '26, Univ. of Kansas; Supt. of Sch., Lyons, Kansas, since 1929.

White, Carroll H., B.S.'96, Dartmouth Col.; Supt. of Sch., Barre, Vt., since 1914.

White, Edna N., A.B.'06, Univ. of Ill.; LL.D.'28, Mich. State Col.; D.Ped.'30, N. Y. State Col. for Tchrs, Albany, N. Y.; Dir., Merrill Palmer Sch., 71 E. Ferry Ave., Detroit, Mich., since 1920.

White, George G., Supvg. Prin. of Sch., Hillsdale, N. J.

White, Heath E., B.A.'08, Amherst Col.; Supvg. Prin. of Sch., Fonda, N. Y., since 1924.

White, Howard Dare, A.B.'97, Franklin and Marshall Col.; A.M.'13, Columbia Univ.; Asst. State Commr. of Educ., Trenton, N. J., since 1928.

White, Leslie Arthur, A.B.'10, Upper Iowa Univ.; M. A. '20, Tchrs. Col., Columbia Univ.; Supt. of Sch., 116 Ninth St., S. E., Minot, N. Dak., since 1918.

White, Neil K., Supt. of Sch., H. S., Lansingburgh, N. Y.

White, Richardson D., A.B.'93, Hampden-Sidney Col.; LL.B.'00, Wash. Univ.; Supt. of Sch., Glendale, Calif., since 1913.

White, Robert P., Supt. of Sch., Vance, Miss.

White, Warren Travis, B.A.'26, Univ. of Texas; Supt. of Sch., Bonham, Texas, since 1927.

White, Winton John, A.B.'04, A.M.'05, Univ. of Pa.; Supt. of Sch., Englewood, N. J., since 1918.

Whiteside, Frederick W., A.B.'12, Univ. of Chicago; Supt. of Sch., Camden, Ark., since 1926.

Whiteside, Harold C., B.S.'24, M.A.'26, Univ. of Pa. Address: 525 N. 22nd St., Philadelphia, Pa.

Whiting, Edward T., A.B.'27, Univ. of Nebr.; Supt. of Sch., 810 Oak St., Gordon, Nebr., since 1928.

Whitley, Samuel H., B.L.'01, Trinity Univ.; Litt.D.'25, Austin Col.; M.A.'26, Southern Methodist Univ.; LL.D.'29, Trinity Univ.; Pres., East Texas State Tchrs. Col., Commerce, Texas, since 1924.

Whitman, Willard M., A.B.'09, Harvard Univ.; Supt. of Sch., 602 Spruce, Marquette, Mich., since 1920.

Whitmer, J. W., Ph.B.'15, Wooster Col.; Co. Supt. of Sch., 411 Michigan St., Toledo, Ohio, since 1915.

Whitney, Albert W., Vice-Pres., Natl. Safety Council, 1 Park Ave., New York, N. Y.

Whitney, Anne L., A.B.'09, Bryn Mawr Col.; Dir., Div. of Health Educ., American Child Health Assn., 370 Seventh Ave., New York, N. Y.

Whitney, Fairfield, A.M.'92, Bates Col.; Supt. of Sch., 548 Broadway, Everett, Mass., since 1910.

Whitt, J. P., Registrar, State Tchrs. Col., East Radford, Va.

Whitten, Charles W., Diploma '00, Ill. State Normal Univ.; A.B.'06, Univ. of Ill.; Mgr., Natl. Fed. of State H. S. Athletic Assns., 411 S. Kenilworth Ave., Elmhurst, Ill., since 1922.

Whittier, Amy Rachel, Diploma '92, Mass. Sch. of Art; Head, Tchr. Tr. Dept., Mass. Sch. of Art, 98 Chestnut St., Boston, Mass., since 1918.

Whittier, John D., Union Supt. of Sch., South Hamilton, Mass., since 1923.

Whittinghill, Roscoe T., B.Ped.'03, Univ. of Ky.; A.M.'28, Univ. of Chicago; Supt. of Sch., Hazard, Ky., since 1926.

Wichman, J. H., Diploma '12, Nebr. State Tchrs. Col., Wayne, Nebr.; B.A.'14, North Central Col.; M.A.'28, Univ. of Chicago; Supt. of Sch., Redwood Falls, Minn., since 1926.

Wickenden, William Elgin, B.S.'04, Denison Univ.; D.Eng.'26, Lafayette Univ.; D.Eng.'27, Worcester Polytech. Inst.; D. Sc.'28, Denison Univ.; D.Eng.'29, Case Sch. of Applied Science; LL.D.'30, Oberlin Col.; D.Sc.'30, Bucknell Univ.; Pres., Case Sch. of Applied Science, Cleveland, Ohio, since 1929.

Wickersham, E. B., 620 Santa Fe Bldg., 1033 Young St., Dallas, Texas.

Wickey, H. J., Ph. B. '02, Taylor Univ.; A.B.'24, Elizabethtown Col.; Supt. of Sch., 172 Nisley St., Middletown, Pa., since 1899.

Wickey, Rose S., A.B.'21, A.M.'22, Univ. of Denver; A.M.'25, Columbia Univ.; Dir., Curriculum Dept., Library Bldg., Kansas City, Mo., since 1926.

Wickham, William Terry, A.B.'20, Heidelberg Col.; M.A.'27, Ohio State Univ.; Supt., Orange Village Schools, S. Kinsman Rd., Chagrin Falls, Ohio, since 1924.

Wiedefeld, M. Theresa, B.S.'25, Johns Hopkins Univ.; Supvr. of Elem. Sch., State Dept. of Educ., 2014 Lexington Bldg., Baltimore, Md.

Wiedman, D. E., A.B.'14, Colo. Tchrs. Col.; Supt. of Sch., Bellingham, Wash., since 1920.

Wight, Glen D., B.S.'12, Univ. of Calif.; Supt. of Sch., H. S., Corona, Calif., since 1919.

Wightman, Clair S., A.B.'20, Syracuse Univ.; M.A.'23, Columbia Univ.; Prin., Park Ridge Sch., Park Ridge, N. J., since 1927.

Wilber, Flora, B.S.'10, M.A.'11, Tchrs. Col., Columbia Univ.; Dir., Bureau of Tests and Measurements, Pub. Sch., Fort Wayne, Ind., since 1922.

Wilber, H. Z., A.B.'08, Mich. State Normal Col.; A.B.'10, A.M.'11, Univ. of Mich.; Prof. of Educ., State Normal Col., Ypsilanti, Mich., since 1921.

Wilcox, Erroll K., B.S.'13, R. I. State Col.; Supt. of Sch., Wakefield, R. I.

Wilcox, George M., A.B.'11, Cornell Col.; A.M.'18, State Univ. of Iowa; Head, Dept. of Educ., Huron Col., Huron, S. Dak., since 1928.

Wilde, Anna A., Prin., Union St. Elem. Sch., Ridgewood, N. J.

Wilde, Arthur Herbert, Ph.D.'01, Harvard; Dean, Sch. of Educ., Boston Univ., 125 Fair Oaks Park, Needham, Mass., since 1918.

Wiley, Alice D., Prin., Monument Demonstration Sch., 41 Prospect St., Trenton, N. J., since 1923.

Wiley, F. L., A.B.,B.S.'05, Univ. of Mo.; A.M.'09, Tchrs. Col., Columbia Univ.; Supt. of Sch., Cleveland Hgts., Ohio, since 1923.

Wiley, George M., Jr., A.B.'99, A.M.'03, Union Col.; Pd.D.'20, New York State Col. for Tchrs.; LL.D.'20, Syracuse Univ.; Asst. Commr. of Educ., State Educ. Dept., Albany, N. Y., since 1920.

Wiley, Guilford M., B.A.'06, De Pauw Univ.; Supt. of Sch., 117 S. 13th St., La Crosse, Wis., since 1926.

Wiley, J. Burton, A.B.'05, Lafayette Col.; Supt. of Sch., Morristown, N. J., since 1912.

Wiley, J. F., Ph.B.'02, De Pauw Univ.; A.M. '14, Univ. of Ill.; Supt. of Sch., H. S., Elkhart, Ind., since 1921.

Wiley, Virgil Brooks, A.B.'22, George Washington Univ.; A.M.'28, Columbia Univ.; Supt. of Sch., H. S., Dover, Del., since 1928.

Wiley, Will E., Dist. Supt. of Sch., Lodi, Calif.

Wilkes, L. L., B.A.'12, M.A.'30, Univ. of Texas; Supt. of Sch., Hubbard, Texas, since 1927.

Wilkinson, Garnet Crummel, A.B.'02, Oberlin Col.; LL.B.'09, Howard Univ.; First Asst. Supt. of Sch., Washington, D. C., since 1924.

Wilkinson, Thomas G., Supt. of Sch., Eufaula, Ala.

Willard, F. E., Diploma '89, Grinnell Col.; Asst. Supt. of Sch., Central Bldg., Seattle, Wash., since 1907.

Willard, W. A. L., B.S.'23, Mich. State Col.; M.A.'26, Univ. of Mich.; Supt. of Sch., Marenisco, Mich., since 1926.

Willett, G. W., A.B.'08, Des Moines Univ.; A.M.'14, Univ. of Iowa; Ph.D.'23, Univ. of Chicago; Supt., Lyons Twp. H. S. and Jr. Col., La Grange, Ill., since 1923.

Willey, Gilbert S., B.S.'20, Univ. of Ill.; Ph.D.'26, Univ. of Wis.; Supt. of Sch., Trinidad, Colo., since 1927.

Williams, Charles O., A.B.'04, Valparaiso Univ.; LL.B.'08, Indianapolis; Secy., Ind. State Tchrs. Assn., Indianapolis, Ind., since 1917.

Williams, Clifton H., A.M.'27, Columbia Univ.; Co. Supt. of Sch., Hillsboro, Ohio, since 1928.

Williams, Daniel S., Diploma '01, State Normal Sch., Whitewater, Wis.; Supt. of Sch., Bozeman, Mont., since 1924.

Williams, E. I. F., Ph.B.'14, Heidelberg Col.; A.M.'20, Tchrs. Col., Columbia Univ.; Prof. of Educ., Heidelberg Col., Tiffin, Ohio, since 1915.

Williams, Harrison E., A.B.'12, Syracuse Univ.; A.M.'26, Columbia Univ.; Prin., Oakfield H. S., Oakfield, N. Y., since 1922.

Williams, Leroy Everett, B.A.'01, M.A.'26, Bates Col.; Supt. of Sch., Municipal Bldg., Rumford, Maine, since 1916.

Williams, Mercer L., A.B.'16, Roanoke Col.; Supt. of Sch., 304 Tenth St., Point Pleasant, W. Va., since 1927.

Williams, R. C., M.A.'29, State Univ. of Iowa; Dir. of Research, State Dept. of Pub. Instr., Des Moines, Iowa, since 1930.

Williams, R. Moore, B.S.'23, Col. of William and Mary; Co. Supt. of Sch., Suffolk, Va., since 1920.

Williams, T. E., Diploma '07, Ind. State Normal Sch.; Ph.B.'21, Univ. of Chicago; A.M.'26, Tchrs. Col., Columbia Univ.; Supvg. Prin. of Twp. Sch., Lawrenceville, N. J., since 1927.

Williams, Thomas C., B.S.'15, Va. Military Inst.; Co. Supt. of Sch., Chester, Va., since 1921.

Williams, W. C., B.A.'96; Supt. of Sch., Greenwood, Miss., since 1923.

Williamson, Edith E., Elem. Sch. Prin., 22 Arbor St., Pittsburgh, Pa., since 1909.

Williamson, Pauline Brooks, B.S.'18, Columbia Univ.; Chief, Sch. Health Bureau, Welfare Division, Metropolitan Life Insurance Co., 1 Madison Ave., New York, N. Y.

Willingham, Henry J., A.B.'91, A.M.'94, LL. D.'11, Howard Col.; LL.D.'28, Univ. of Ala.; Pres., State Tchrs. Col., Florence, Ala., since 1913.

Willingham, W. O., B.S.'97, East Texas Normal Col., Commerce, Texas; Supt. of Sch., Albany, Texas, since 1919.

Willis, Benjamin C., A.B.'22, George Washington Univ.; M.A.'26, Univ. of Md.; Prin., Caroline H. S., Denton, Md., since 1927.

Williston, Arthur L., S.B.'89, Mass. Inst. of Technology. Address: 986 High St., Dedham, Mass.

Willman, Edward J., A.B.'18, A.M.'24, Univ. of Mich.; Supt. of Sch., Owosso, Mich., since 1921.

Wills, Mrs. Minnie B., 458 Columbia Ave., Palmerton, Pa.

Willsey, Elsie Mae, Ph.B.'13, Univ. of Chicago; Asst. Prof. of Educ. and Head, Home Economics Dept., Univ. of Porto Rico, Rio Piedras, Porto Rico, since 1926.

Wilson, Clinton D., A.B.'13, Bates Col.; Supt. of Sch., 72 Front St., Bath, Maine, since 1923.

Wilson, E. A., M.Pd.'99, State Normal Col., Ypsilanti, Mich.; A.M.'06, Univ. of Chicago. Address: 1206 Washtenaw, Ann Arbor, Mich.

Wilson, Harry Bruce, A.B.'05, Ind. Univ.; M.A.'10, Columbia Univ.; LL.D.'17, Washburn Col.; Natl. Dir., American Jr. Red Cross, Washington, D. C., since 1928.

Wilson, Harry G., 330 E. 22nd St., Chicago, Ill.

Wilson, J. A., Prin., Sunset H. S., Dallas, Texas.

Wilson, James H., A.B.'13, Sterling Col.; A.M.'28, Univ. of Chicago; Supt. of Sch., Rocky Ford, Colo., since 1924.

Wilson, John R., B.S.'13, Columbia Univ.; Supt. of Sch., Paterson, N. J., since 1906.

Wilson, Lloyd C., Co. Supt. of Sch., Brownsville, Tenn.

Wilson, Mrs. Lucy L. W., Ph.D.'97, Univ. of Pa.; Prin., S. Phila. H. S., Philadelphia, Pa., since 1916.

Wilson, Melvin, B.S.'14, M.S.'24, Univ. of Utah; Supt. of Nebo Sch. Dist., Payson, Utah, since 1924.

Wilson, Otis G., A.B.'07, A.M.'11, W. Va. Univ.; Supt. of Sch., Fairmont, W. Va., since 1915.

Wilson, Paul S., B.A.'21, Carleton Col.; Supt. of Sch., Glencoe, Minn., since 1928.

Wilson, Zeal Z., B.A.'22, Ind. Univ.; M.A. '26, Univ. of Wis.; Supvr. of Later Elem. Grades, Bd. of Educ. Bldg., Jackson, Mich., since 1926.

Wiltse, Earle W., A.B.'22, Nebr. Wesleyan Univ.; A.M.'26, Columbia Univ.; Supt. of Sch., Franklin, Nebr., since 1927.

Winchell, Lawrence Romie, B.S.'25, Col. of the City of New York; Supvg. Prin. of Sch., 11 Morehouse Pl., New Providence, N. J., since 1923.

Winden, Julius, Ph.B.'00, Ph.M.'28, Univ. of Wis.; Supt. of Sch., 1001 Elm St., Wisconsin Rapids, Wis., since 1923.

Windrow, J. E., B.S.'24, M.A.'25, George Peabody Col. for Tchrs.; Alumni Secy., George Peabody Col. for Tchrs., Nashville, Tenn., since 1925.

Wing, Francis H., Deputy Supt. of Sch. in charge of Voc. Educ., Genesee Bldg., Buffalo, N. Y., since 1926.

Wingate, Harold C., B.A.'05, Clark; Supt. of Sch., Scituate and Marshfield, Mass., since 1926. Address: Egypt, Mass.

Wingate, James, B.S.'97, M.A.'27, Union Col., Schenectady, N. Y.; Pd.D.'29, State Col. for Tchrs., Albany, N. Y.; Dir., Motion Picture Div., State Educ. Dept., 220 W. 42nd St., New York, N. Y.

Winship, A. E., Litt.D.'98, Univ. of Nashville; LL.D.'11, Univ. of Vt.; Editor, Journal of Education. 6 Beacon St., Boston, Mass., since 1886.

Winslow, Harry D., A.B.'27, Pa. State Col.; A.M.'28, Tchrs. Col., Columbia Univ.; Asst. Supt. of Sch., Park Ridge, Ill., since 1929.

Winslow, Howard L., B.S.'05, Wesleyan Univ.; Union Supt. of Sch., Somersworth, N. H., since 1928.

Winstrom, J. Harry, A.B.'16, Univ. of Nebr.; M.A.'23, State Univ. of Iowa. Address: 1729 Noble Ave., Springfield, Ill.

Winter, Olice, 3210 W. 66th, Chicago, Ill.

Winters, Thomas Howard, A.B.'96, Ohio Wesleyan Univ.; A.M.'24, Ph.D.'30, Ohio State Univ.; Asst. Dir. of Educ., State Dept. of Educ., Columbus, Ohio, since 1928.

Wippermann, Edgar G., Ph.B.'22, Ph.M.'30, Univ. of Wis.; Supt. of Sch., Sheboygan Falls, Wis., since 1922.

Wirsig, O. A., A.B.'14, Univ. of Nebr.; A.M. '24, Columbia Univ.; Supt. of Sch., Kearney, Nebr., since 1921.

Wisdom, Tom, State Auditor, Atlanta, Ga.

Wisehart, Roy Parker, A.B.'10, Ind. Univ.; A.M.'26, Columbia Univ.; State Supt. of Pub. Instr., State House, Indianapolis, Ind., since 1927.

Wiseltier, Joseph, B.S.'13, A.M.'29, Columbia Univ.; Dir. of Art Educ., State Bd. of Educ., Hartford, Conn., since 1923.

Wish, Fred D., Jr., A.B.'13, Bowdoin Col.; Supt. of Sch., Municipal Bldg., Hartford, Conn., since 1923.

Witham, Ernest C., B.S.'04, Tufts Col.; Assoc. Prof. of Educ., Rutgers Univ., New Brunswick, N. J.

Withers, John W., B.S.'90, B.A.'91, Pd.D.'96, Natl. Normal Univ.; M.A.'02, Ph.D.'04, Yale Univ.; LL.D.'17, Washington Univ.; LL.D.'18, Univ. of Mo.; Dean, Sch. of Educ., New York Univ., 32 Waverly Pl., New York, N. Y., since 1921.

Witmeyer, Paul E., A.B.'16, Lebanon Valley Col.; A.M.'23, Columbia Univ.; Supt. of Sch., H. S. Bldg., Columbia, Pa., since 1923.

Witter, Fred L., A.B.'07, Beloit Col.; Supt. of Sch., Burlington, Wis., since 1912.

Wivel, Claude Burns, Supt. of Sch., 33 E. Eighth St., Tempe, Ariz.

Wofford, Kate V., A.B.'16, Winthrop Normal and Industrial Col.; Co. Supt. of Sch., Court House, Laurens, S. C., since 1923.

Woglom, Russell S., Ph.B.'15, Lafayette Col.; M.A.'28, New York Univ.; Supvg. Prin. of Sch., High Bridge, N. J., since 1928.

Wolfe, J. M., Bureau of Educ., Archdiocese of Dubuque, Dubuque, Iowa.

Wolfe, William D., A.B.'17, Col. of Emporia; M.A.'30, Univ. of Kansas; Supt. of Sch., Ingalls H. S., Atchison, Kansas, since 1929.

Wolford, C. H., Supt. of Sch., Duquesne, Pa.

Womack, Albert L., B.S.'26, Central Mo. State Tchrs. Col., Warrensburg, Mo.; Supt. of Sch., Choteau, Okla., since 1926.

Womack, J. P., B.A.'03, Univ. of Ark.; M.A. '19, George Peabody Col. for Tchrs.; Pres., Henderson State Tchrs. Col., Arkadelphia, Ark., since 1929.

Wood, Claude Rodolphus, B.S.'12, M.S.'14, Ala. Polytech. Inst.; Ph.D.'28, George Peabody Col. for Tchrs.; Chmn., Classification Com.; State Tchrs. Col., Jacksonville, Ala., since 1920.

Wood, Francis Marion, Dir., Coppin Normal Sch., McCulloh and Lafayette Sts., Baltimore, Md.

Wood, H. A., A.B.'23, Mich. State Normal Col.; M.A.'27, Tchrs. Col., Columbia Univ.; Supt. of Sch., Munising, Mich., since 1925.

Wood, James M., Ph.B.'01, State Normal Sch., Warrensburg, Mo.; A.B. and B.S. in Ed.'07, Univ. of Mo.; A.M.'11, Columbia Univ.; LL.D.'30, Hiram Col.; Pres., Stephens Col., Columbia, Mo., since 1912.

Wood, Stella Louise, Prin., Miss Wood's Kdgn.-Prim. Tr. Sch., 2017 Bryant Ave. S., Minneapolis, Minn., since 1896.

Wood, Thomas D., A.B.'88, A.M.'91, Oberlin Col.; M.D.'91, Col. of Physicians and Surgeons, Columbia Univ.; Prof. of Health Educ., Tchrs. Col., Columbia Univ., New York, N. Y., since 1901.

Wood, W. A., B.S.'15, Kansas State Tchrs. Col., Emporia, Kansas; Supt. of Sch., Pratt, Kansas, since 1919.

Woodburn, Ethelbert Cooke, A.B.'04, Ind. Univ.; LL.D.'25, Yankton Col.; A.M.'28, Univ. of Chicago; Pres., Spearfish Normal Sch., Spearfish, S. Dak., since 1919.

Woodfield, Arthur G., B.A.'97, Western Md. Col.; Supvg. Prin. of Sch., Hillside, N. J., since 1906.

Woodley, Helen Jane, Bd. of Educ., Academy Bldg., Frederick, Md.

Woodruff, Caroline S., M.A.'25, Middlebury Col.; Prin., State Normal Sch., Castleton, Vt., since 1921.

Woods, Elizabeth L., A.B.'09, A.M.'10, Univ. of Oregon; Ph.D.'13, Clark Univ.; Dir., Dept. of Psych. and Educ. Research, Pub. Sch., Los Angeles, Calif.

Woods, L. A., M.A.'25, Baylor Univ.; Co. Supt. of Sch., Court House, Waco, Texas, since 1926.

Woodson, H. N., A.B.'14, Univ. of Ky.; Supt. of Consol. Sch., Shelby, Iowa, since 1930.

Woofter, Thomas Jackson, A.M.'93, Univ. of Nashville, Peabody Col.; Ph.D.'00, American Univ.; LL.D.'09, Ill. Col. of Law; Dean, Sch. of Educ., Univ. of Ga., Athens, Ga., since 1903.

Wooster, B. C., B.S.'05, Columbia Univ.; Co. Supt. of Sch., 126 Main St., Hackensack, N. J., since 1905.

Workman, J. H., A.B.'13, Univ. of N. C.; Co. Supt. of Educ., Beaufort, N. C., since 1924.

Workman, John Hunter, 1217 E. Mallory St., Pensacola, Fla.

Wosinski, Max A., 2380 Wyandotte Ave., Hamtramck, Mich.

Wozniak, Stanley L., 2380 Wyandotte Ave., Hamtramck, Mich.

Wray, C. F., Commr. of Educ., 256 State St., Rochester, N. Y.

Wright, Arkley, A.B.'11, Georgetown Col.; Supt. of Sch., 1610 S. Walnut St., Hopkinsville, Ky., since 1927.

Wright, Arthur Davis, A.B., A.M.'04, Col. of William and Mary; Ed. M.'22, Harvard; Birmingham-Southern Col., Birmingham, Ala., since 1930.

Wright, C. C., Co. Supt. of Sch., Hunting Creek, N. C., since 1899.

Wright, C. Milton, A.B.'06, Western Md. Col.; Co. Supt. of Sch., Bel Air, Md., since 1915.

Wright, Charles S., Supt. of Sch., H. S., Lawrence, N. Y., since 1923.

Wright, Clark G., Supt. of Elem. Sch. Dist. 108, 542 S. Linden Ave., Highland Park, Ill., since 1914.

Wright, Frank Lee, A.M.'15, Univ. of Wis.; Ed.D.'25, Harvard; Head, Dept. of Educ., Washington Univ., St. Louis, Mo., since 1924.

Wright, Frank W., A.B.'07, Harvard; Deputy State Commr. of Educ., State House, Boston, Mass., since 1917.

Wright, Isaac Miles, B.S.'04, Alfred Univ.; Pd.M.'14, Pd.D.'16, New York Univ.; Dir., Sch. of Educ., Muhlenberg Col., Allentown, Pa., since 1917.

Wright, Jasper H., B.S.'05, Univ. of Rochester; Supvg. Prin. of Sch., Enosburg Falls, Vt., since 1925.

Wright John Clarence, B.A.'06, Oberlin Col.; Pres., Bricks Jr. Col., Bricks, N. C., since 1929.

Wright, P. A., A.B. in Ed.'26, Univ. of Wash.; Supt of Sch., Snohomish, Wash., since 1924.

Wright, Robert H., B.S.'97, Univ. of N. C.; Ed.D.'28, Wake Forest Col.; Pres., East Carolina Tchrs. Col., Greenville, N. C., since 1909.

Wright, Wendell W., A.B.'16, Ind. State Normal Sch.; A.M.'25, Ph.D.'29, Tchrs. Col., Columbia Univ.; Prof. of Educ., Sch. of Educ., Ind. Univ., Bloomington, Ind., since 1924.

Wright, William W., Prin., Syracuse City Normal Sch., Syracuse, N. Y.

Wrinkle, H. E., B.A.'22, Univ. of Okla.; Supt. of Sch., El Reno, Okla., since 1930.

Wriston, Henry Merritt, A.B.'11, A.M.'12, Wesleyan Univ.; Ph.D.'22, Harvard Univ.; LL.D.'26, Ripon Col.; Pres., Lawrence Col., Appleton, Wis., since 1925.

Wyandt, J. W., Supt. of Sch., Bryan, Ohio, since 1903.

Yaden, J. L., A.B.'21, Lincoln Memorial Univ.; Supt. of Sch., Moultrie, Ga., since 1924.

Yager, W. D., Supt. of Sch., Colmar, Iowa.

Yakel, Ralph, LL.B.'12, A.B.'13, Ill. Wesleyan Univ.; A.M.'24, Ph.D.'29, Tchrs. Col., Columbia Univ.; Supt. of Sch., H. S. Bldg., Jacksonville, Ill., since 1929.

Yape, D. S., B.A.'16, Mich. State Normal Col.; M.A.'18, Northwestern Univ.; Supt. of Sch., 124 E. Ash St., Wayne, Mich., since 1925.

Yarbrough, T. W., A.B.'90, Emory Col.; Co. Supt. of Pub. Instr., Sarasota, Fla., since 1921.

Yates, Mrs. Dorothy Hazeltine, A.B.'10, Wellesley Col.; M.A.'19, Ph.D.'21, Univ. of Calif.; Assoc. Prof. of Psych. and Asst. Dir. of Research, State Tchrs. Col., San Jose, Calif., since 1922.

Yawberg, A. G., Ph.B.'07, A.M.'11, Univ. of Wooster; Supt. of Sch., Berea, Ohio, since 1929.

Yeager, Tressa C., B.S.'28, Univ. of Pittsburgh; Supvg. Prin. of Twp. Schools, Washington Sch., Mt. Lebanon, Pittsburgh, Pa., since 1923.

Yeager, William A., A.B.'14, Ursinus Col.; A.M.'18, Ph.D.'29, Univ. of Pa.; Asst. Dir., Tchr. Bureau, State Dept. of Pub. Instr., Harrisburg, Pa., since 1930.

Yeingst, Wilbur M., Ph.B.'97, M.A.'11, Dickinson Col.; Pd.D.'24, Susquehanna Univ.; Supt. of Sch., H. S., Mt. Carmel, Pa., since 1918.

Yeomans, C. A., A.B.'06, Col. of Emporia; M.A.'14, Univ. of Kansas; Prin., Chase Co. H. S., Cottonwood Falls, Kansas.

Yerger, Warren K., A.M.'14, Univ. of Pa.; Prin., A. I. du Pont Sch., 717 N. Rodney St., Wilmington, Del., since 1909.

Yoakam, G. A., B.A.'10, M.A.'18, Ph.D.'22, State Univ. of Iowa; Head, Dept. of Elem. Educ., Univ. of Pittsburgh, Pittsburgh, Pa., since 1923.

Yoder, C. M., Dir., Commercial Educ., State Tchrs. Col., Whitewater, Wis.

Yoder, J. J., A.B.'21, A.M.'28, Univ. of Denver; Supt. of Sch., 606 N. 11th St., Marysville, Kansas, since 1924.

York, Ada, Co. Supt. of Sch., Court House, San Diego, Calif., since 1921.

Yost, E. W., Co. Sch. Commr., 1001 Lawyers Bldg., Detroit, Mich.

Young, Arthur L., A.B.'04, Brown Univ.; A.M.'30, Yale Univ.; Field Supvr. in Rural Educ., State Bd. of Educ., Maple St., Ellington, Conn.

Young, Dale S., B.S.'16, Hedding Col.; M.S. '17, Univ. of Ill.; M.A.'26, Ph.D.'28, Columbia Univ.; Dir. of Research and Information, State Dept. of Educ., Montgomery, Ala., since 1927.

Young, G. P., A.B.'11, Colo. State Tchrs. Col.; A.M'23, Univ. of Colo.; Supt. of Sch. and Dir. of Tr., Adams State Tchrs. Col., Alamosa, Colo., since 1926.

Young, John Adams, Ph.B.'03, A.M.'12, Bucknell Univ.; Asst. Supt. of Sch., Bridgeport, Conn., since 1922.

Young, L. P., B.S.'22, State Tchrs. Col., Emporia, Kansas; A.M.'29, Tchrs Col., Columbia Univ. Address: 501 W. 120th St., New York, N. Y.

Young, Leonard, A.B.'98, Ind. Univ.; Supt. of Sch., 226 N. First Ave., E., Duluth, Minn., since 1923.

Young, Mary H., Laurelton, N. J.

Young, Oliver O., A.B.'04, Bethany Col.; M.A.'14, Univ. of S. Dak.; Supt. of Sch., Library Bldg., Galesburg, Ill., since 1928.

Young, W. Rankin, Diploma '16, B.S.'22, State Tchrs. Col., Pittsburg, Kansas; M.A. '25, Tchrs. Col., Columbia Univ.; Supt. of Sch., Anthony, Kansas, since 1926.

Young, Walter S., B.S.'01, Dartmouth Col.; Supt. of Sch., City Hall, Worcester, Mass., since 1923.

Young, Wilbur S., B.S.'15, Vanderbilt Univ.; M.A.'28, Peabody Col.; Supt. of Sch., 740 Fifth Ave., Springfield, Tenn., since 1923.

Youngblood, Genia W., Diploma '10, Ind. State Normal Sch., Terre Haute, Ind.; A.B.'14, Ind. Univ.; A.M.'21, Columbia Univ.; Supt. of Sch., H. S., Peru, Ind., since 1923.

Youngblood, Joe A., A.B.'07, Hendrix Col.; M.A.'13, Vanderbilt Univ.; Co. Supt. of Pub. Instr., West Palm Beach, Fla., since 1925.

Yount, Warren J., A.B.'12, Franklin Col.; Supt. of Sch., Greencastle, Ind., since 1927.

Zeiser, Harry H., M.A.'00, Lafayette Col.; Supt. of Sch., 81 N. Washington St., Wilkes-Barre, Pa., since 1916.

Zellner, Harrison C., A.B.'17, Heidelberg Col.; M.A.'27, Ohio State Univ.; Supt. of Sch., Castalia, Ohio, since 1925.

Zellner, O. D., B.A.'20, Univ. of N. Dak.; Supt. of Sch., Graceville, Minn., since 1926.

Zener, Virgil C., A.B.'10, Univ. of Mich.; M.A.'18, Albright Col.; Prof. of Educ., Albright Col., 19 Behney Ave., Myerstown, Pa., since 1916.

Ziegler, Samuel H., A.B.'10, A.M.'12, Ursinus Col.; Ph.D.'23, Univ. of Pa.; Head, Dept. of Educ., Cedar Crest Col., Allentown, Pa., since 1926.

Zimmerman, Harold C., Diploma, State Tchrs. Col., Whitewater, Wis.; Ph.B.'29, Univ. of Wis.; Supt. of Sch. and Prin., H. S., Pardeeville, Wis., since 1923.

Zinn, W. R., Supt. of Sch., Oxford, Mich.

Zirbes, Laura, Ph.D.'27, Tchrs. Col., Columbia Univ.; Assoc. Prof. of Educ., Ohio State Univ., and State Consultant in Elem. Educ., State Dept. of Educ., Columbus, Ohio, since 1928.

Ziskie, Albert, 2380 Wyandotte Ave., Hamtramck, Mich.

Zoe, Sister Mary, A.M.'27, Univ. of Dayton; Dean, Col. of Mt. St. Joseph, Seton Hall, Mt. St. Joseph, Ohio, since 1927.

Zoll, O. R., Diploma '99, Ill. State Normal Univ.; Dist. Supvr. of Sch., Matoaka, W. Va., since 1922.

Zook, D. E., M.A. in Ed. '23, Ph.D. in Ed. '30, Univ. of Chicago; Asst. Statistician, U. S. Office of Educ., since 1930. Address: 6048 Kenwood Ave., Chicago, Ill.

Zuber, H. E., B.S. in Ed. '24, Miami Univ.; M.A.'28, Columbia Univ.; Supt. of Sch., Nelsonville, Ohio, since 1928.

Zuerner, Frank DeWitt, Supt. of Sch., 825 Bell Ave., Braddock, Pa.

LIBRARIES, COLLEGES, AND SCHOOLS

E. P. Murphy Memorial Library for Etowah County, Gadsden, Ala.

College of Education, University of Arkansas, Fayetteville, Ark.

Lange Library of Education, University of California, Berkeley, Calif.

Library, University of California, Berkeley, Calif.

Teachers Library, Board of Education, 715 Locust Ave., Long Beach, Calif.

City School Library, F. W. Braun Bldg., Los Angeles, Calif.

Golden Gate College, Y. M. C. A., 220 Golden Gate Ave., San Francisco, Calif.

Dominican College, San Rafael, Calif.

State Board of Education, Hartford, Conn.

Library, Yale University, New Haven, Conn.

State Normal School, Willimantic, Conn.

Douglass School, First and Pierce Sts., N. W., Washington, D. C.

Library, University of Florida, Gainesville, Fla.

Library, University of Georgia, Athens, Ga.

Library, Eastern Illinois State Teachers College, Charleston, Ill.

Chrisman Township High School, Chrisman. Ill.

Western Illinois State Teachers College. Macomb, Ill.

Lincoln Library, Springfield, Ill.

Normal College of the American Gymnastic Union, Indianapolis, Ind.

Public Library, Indianapolis, Ind.

Library, Purdue University, Lafayette, Ind.

Library, Indiana State Teachers College, Terre Haute, Ind.

Administration Library, Independent School District, Garfield Bldg., Des Moines. Iowa.

Administration Club, Woodrow Wilson School, Sioux City, Iowa.

Kellogg Library, Kansas State Teachers College, Emporia, Kansas.

Porter Library, Kansas State Teachers College, Pittsburg, Kansas.

Library, Louisville Normal School, Louisville, Ky.

Library Department, State Normal College, Natchitoches, La.

College of Education, University of Maryland, College Park, Md.

Library, State Normal School, Salem, Mass.

St. Mary's Academy, Monroe, Mich.

Library, University of Minnesota, Minneapolis, Minn.

State Teachers College, Winona, Minn.

Progressive Series Teachers College, Bonhomme and Bemiston Ave., Clayton, St. Louis, Mo.

Public Library, St. Louis, Mo.

Teachers Library, Board of Education, 911 Locust St., St. Louis, Mo.

State Normal School, Keene, N. H.

Teachers Organization of Boonton, 302 Lathrop Ave., Boonton, N. J.

Bergen County Schoolmen's Club, Hackensack, N. J.

Board of Education, 355 State St., Hackensack, N. J.

Broadway School, Hackensack, N. J.

Fairmount School, Hackensack, N. J.

Jackson Avenue School, Hackensack, N. J.

State Street School, Hackensack, N. J.

Leonia Teachers Club, Leonia, N. J.

Public Schools, Lyndhurst, N. J.

Edgemont School, Montclair, N. J.

Watchung School, Montclair, N. J.

Public Library, Newark, N. J.

Benjamin Franklin Junior High School, Ridgewood, N. J.

Harrison Avenue Elementary School, Ridgewood, N. J.

Kenilworth Elementary School, Ridgewood, N. J.

Ridgewood High School, Ridgewood, N. J.

Union Street Elementary School, Ridgewood, N. J.

George Washington Elementary and Junior High School, Ridgewood, N. J.

Willard Elementary School, Ridgewood, N. J.

Public Schools, Westwood, N. J.

New York State Library, University of the State of New York, Albany, N. Y.

Richmond Library, Batavia, N. Y.

State Normal School, Fredonia, N. Y.

Hornell Teachers Association, 107 Maple St., Hornell, N. Y.

Lincoln School of Teachers College, Columbia University, 425 W. 123rd St., New York, N. Y.

Niagara Falls Teachers Association, Niagara Falls, N. Y.

Port Jervis Public School Teachers, Port Jervis, N. Y.

School No. 16, North Broadway, Yonkers, N. Y.

Bierce Library, University of Akron, Akron, Ohio.

Carnegie Library, Ohio University, Athens, Ohio.

Library, Bluffton College, Bluffton, Ohio.

Library, Ohio State University, Columbus, Ohio.

Department of Education, College of Wooster, Wooster, Ohio.

Oklahoma College for Women, Chickasha, Okla.

Library, University of Oregon, Eugene, Oregon.

Oregon Normal School, Monmouth, Oregon.

State Department of Public Instruction, Harrisburg, Pa.

Free Library of Philadelphia, Logan Square, Philadelphia, Pa.

Pedagogical Library, Board of Education, School District of Philadelphia, Keystone Annex, 19th above Chestnut, Philadelphia, Pa.

Temple University, Philadelphia, Pa.

Academic Division Library, Bureau of Education, Manila, P. I.

College of Education, University of Tennessee, Knoxville, Tenn.

Library, George Peabody College for Teachers, Nashville, Tenn.

Library, Simmons University, Abilene, Texas.

Library, West Texas State Teachers College, Canyon, Texas.

East Texas State Teachers College, Commerce, Texas.

Stephen F. Austin School, Dallas, Texas.

John Henry Brown School, Dallas, Texas.

Cumberland School, Dallas, Texas.

Dallas Technical High School, Dallas, Texas.

Forest Avenue High School, Dallas, Texas.

Lida Hooe School, Dallas, Texas.

Sam Houston School, Dallas, Texas.

Obadiah Knight School, Dallas, Texas.

Sidney Lanier School, Dallas, Texas.

William Lipscomb School, Dallas, Texas.

Maple Lawn School, Dallas, Texas.

North Dallas High School, Dallas, Texas.

Oak Cliff High School, Dallas, Texas.

Ascher Silberstein School, Dallas, Texas.

Sunset High School, Dallas, Texas.

Trinity Heights School, Dallas, Texas.

Woodrow Wilson High School, Dallas, Texas.

Agricultural College of Utah, Logan, Utah.

Washington State Normal School, Ellensburg, Wash.

State College of Washington, Pullman, Wash.

Public Library, Racine, Wis.

LIST OF TABLES

LIST OF CHARTS

INDEX OF NAMES

SUBJECT INDEX

Subject Index (Cont.)

Subject Index (Cont.)

YEARBOOKS

Third Yearbook, 1925—
Research in Constructing the Elementary School Curriculum. 408 pp. -------------------------- $2.00

Fourth Yearbook, 1926—
The Nation At Work on the Public School Curriculum; together with a reprint of Research Bulletin, Vol. III, Nos. 4 and 5, *Keeping Pace with the Advancing Curriculum.* Reprinted under one cover, November, 1929. 560 pp. ------------------------- 2.00

Fifth Yearbook, 1927—
The Junior High School Curriculum. 562 pp. -------- 2.00

Sixth Yearbook, 1928—
The Development of the High School Curriculum. 584 pp. --- 2.00

Seventh Yearbook, 1929—
The Articulation of the Units of American Education. 616 pp. -------------------------------------- 2.00

Eighth Yearbook, 1930—
The Superintendent Surveys Supervision. 472 pp.--- 2.00

Ninth Yearbook, 1931—
Five Unifying Factors in American Education. 544 pp. -------------------------------- ------------- 2.00

Department of Superintendence
of the
NATIONAL EDUCATION ASSOCIATION
1201 Sixteenth Street Northwest
WASHINGTON, D. C.